MW00426868

To Die in Cuba

To Die

Louis A. Pérez Jr.

The University of North Carolina Press   Chapel Hill & London

in Cuba

Suicide
and
Society

© 2005

The University of North Carolina Press

All rights reserved

Set in Scala types by Tseng Information Systems, Inc.

Manufactured in the United States of America

The paper in this book meets the guidelines for permanence
and durability of the Committee on Production Guidelines for
Book Longevity of the Council on Library Resources.

This book was published with the assistance of the H. Eugene
and Lillian Youngs Lehman Fund of the University of North
Carolina Press. A complete list of books published with the
assistance of the Lehman Fund appears at the end of the book.

Library of Congress Cataloging-in-Publication Data

Pérez, Louis A., 1943–

To die in Cuba : suicide and society / Louis A. Pérez Jr.

p. cm.

Includes bibliographical references and index.

ISBN 0-8078-2937-4 (alk. paper)

1. Suicide—Cuba. 2. Suicide—Political aspects—Cuba. I. Title.

HV6548.c88p47 2005

306.9—dc22   2004019097

09 08 07 06 05   5 4 3 2 1

To
Jordan M. Young,
Mario Rodríguez,
and the Memory of
Edwin Lieuwen

CONTENTS

TABLES AND FIGURES

ILLUSTRATIONS

ACKNOWLEDGMENTS

It is in the approach to the completion of this book, in retrospective moments given to reflections on the past ten years of research and writing, that the importance of the contribution of others becomes apparent. This is not to suggest, of course, that the generosity to which one has been beneficiary was not apparent at the time. It is, rather, to observe that only as one contemplates the end does it become possible to appreciate fully the part played by so many people and institutions whose support and assistance have made this book possible. This includes archivists, librarians, bibliographers, and the staffs of the many research institutions that have provided indispensable assistance in the identification, location, and use of vital research materials. In Cuba, I am most appreciative of the generosity extended at the Archivo Nacional de Cuba by Berarda Salabarría, Director, and members of the Archivo staff. At the Biblioteca Nacional José Martí I received the unflagging assistance of Eliades Acosta Matos, Director, as well as the reference staff. In this regard, I cannot adequately express my gratitude to Director Nuria Gregori Torada at the Instituto de Literatura y Lingüística for graciously facilitating consultation of the Instituto's magnificent research collections. I am similarly grateful to the staff at the Archivo Histórico Provincial de Pinar del Río for making available important records bearing on nineteenth-century suicide on the estates of the province. At the Archivo Provincial Histórico de Matanzas, Director Graciela Milián provided both a warm welcome and indispensable knowledge of the record and manuscript collections housed in the archive. It is necessary also to acknowledge with appreciation the years of sponsorship of the research associated with this book, specifically the support of Pablo Pacheco López, Director of the Centro de Investigación y Desarrollo de la Cultura Cubana Juan Marinello, and Francisco López of Unión de Escritores y Artistas de Cuba (UNEAC).

In the United States, I am most appreciative of the assistance received from the staffs of the Library of Congress, the National Archives in Washington, D.C., the History of Medicine Division of the National Library of Medicine in Bethesda, the New York Public Library, and the New-York Historical Society. At the Davis Library at the University of North Carolina at

Chapel Hill, the reference personnel and especially the staff of the Inter-Library Loan Department provided indispensable assistance. In this regard, I owe a particular debt of gratitude to Teresa Chapa for her assistance in locating important research materials.

A project so long in the making could not but have benefited from the knowledge and expertise of others. Out of countless discussions both formal and casual, in conversations and correspondence, emerged new possibilities of inquiry. These exchanges with friends and colleagues were a source of valuable information, of thoughtful suggestions, of anecdotes and details, at times in the form of observations drawn from firsthand involvement, often as painful personal experiences, other times as bibliographical recommendations, sometimes as suggestion of a relevant poem or song—precisely the kind of stuff that makes possible a highly textured and nuanced treatment of the circumstances under which people decide to end their lives. Francisco Pérez Guzmán gave unstintingly of his time and his vast knowledge of the Cuban nineteenth century and was especially generous in obtaining important research materials, for which I will long remain in his debt. I am also especially grateful to Gabino La Rosa Corzo, whose research assistance in gathering early-twentieth-century press accounts of suicide in Cuba was of inestimable value. In this regard, gratitude must be acknowledged to Ana Cairo, Rey Mauricio Figueredo, Ambrosio Fornet, Rafael Hernández, Jorge Ibarra, Milagros Martínez, Olga Portuondo Zúñiga, Alfredo Prieto, Pedro M. Pruna Goodgall, Marel Suzarte García, and Oscar Zanetti, all of whom in ways large and small contributed to the development of many aspects of this book. I am most appreciative of the suggestions made by Jean Stubbs, from whose early reading of the prospectus of this book came a number of helpful recommendations. Rebecca J. Scott read early drafts of several chapters and provided thoughtful comments on some of the central formulations around which this book is organized. Lars Schoultz gave close attention to some of the key arguments advanced early in the book, providing clearer focus to the themes of nation and nationality. I also appreciate the thoughtfulness of Rosalba Díaz Quintana, Mariola Espinosa, Amy Ferlazzo, Susan Fernández, Robert P. Ingalls, Lisi Lotz, Luis Martínez-Fernández, Tom Miller, Gary Mormino, David Sartorius, and William Van Norman, who in the course of their own research were generous to identify materials having to do with suicide in Cuba. Pamela Fesmire and Linda Howe provided assistance at various points in the writing of the manuscript that allowed me to continue toward its completion. As so often in the past, Mayra Alonso helped me get to where I needed to be.

The material and moral support received from Gladys Marel García and Fidel Requeijo have been vital to the completion of this book. Their unflagging generosity contributed to the indispensable conditions that made the completion of the research and writing of the book possible.

I am particularly grateful for the support I have received over the years that has provided the time to complete the research and writing of the book. In this regard, I am most appreciative to the John Simon Guggenheim Memorial Foundation, whose generous support was indispensable to the completion of this project. A National Endowment for the Humanities fellowship allowed me to complete the research in Cuba and Washington, D.C., and turn my attention fully to finishing the writing. I am also very grateful for the sustained support I have received from the University of North Carolina at Chapel Hill during the years that the research and writing of this book was in process. An appointment to the Arts and Humanities Institute at the University of North Carolina with colleagues from across the university was especially useful in providing me with the opportunity to undertake early exploration of some of the key issues subsequently developed in this book. Leave time was generously provided by the Kenan-Pogue program at the University of North Carolina at Chapel Hill and the Research and Study leave program from the Department of History. Additional support was provided in the form of a Latané Stipend from the Odum Institute for Research in Social Science at the University of North Carolina and a publication grant from the University of North Carolina Research Council.

The support and assistance from Elaine Maisner at the University of North Carolina Press have been unflagging all through the research and writing of this book. Her thoughtful and critical reading of chapters in various draft stages, suggestions regarding the illustrations, and recommendations for the format of the book have been invaluable and very much appreciated. A particular note of gratitude to the Manuscript Editing and Production staffs at the Press for the creative thoughtfulness and expert attention they have given to this book. Their efforts on behalf of the book have been most gratifying.

Deborah M. Weissman was an essential part of the process in which the ideas that follow developed, the way they assumed initial form then reformulated, over and over again, through all the years that this book was in the making, and for which I am enormously grateful. There is much in this book that emerged from conversations on the long stretches of Bolin Creek Trail.

And for Amara and Maya—"kids," they are still called—our discussions of many of the themes examined on the pages that follow have been a source of gratification. So too with Lisa and Alanna, who have interested themselves in the circumstances of the human condition. These issues are not without implications for the kinds of things to which they have all dedicated their lives.

Chapel Hill, North Carolina
June 2004

To Die in Cuba

The long island that is washed by the restless

waters of the Atlantic and by the blue waves of the

Caribbean Sea and by the warm currents of the Gulf

Stream, was known to all the Indians of the Lucayas

and of the Antilles. They called it Cuba, the Beautiful

Country of the Dead.

Florence Jackson Stoddard,

As Old as the Moon. Cuban Legends:

Folklore of the Antilles *(1909)*

Introduction

SUICIDE IN CUBA

Being Cuban isn't about being a member of some elite group or community. It is about dealing with the life you were dealt.

   Virgil Suárez, Going Under *(1996)*

In Cuba the Apocalypse comes as no surprise: it has always been an everyday occurrence.

   Abilio Estévez, Tuyo es el reino *(1997)*

In Cuba things are what they must not be.

   Ricardo Pau-Llosa, Cuba *(1993)*

There are things that never get to be what they're supposed to be.

   Manuel Pereiras García, Santiago *(1993)*

In Cuba the past never passes.

   Eliseo Alberto, Informe contra mí mismo *(1997)*

The indigenous people of the New World perished in many ways in their encounter with Europeans. Some were killed in battle. Others died of abuse and exploitation. Many succumbed to disease and illness.

The experience of the Native American people in Cuba was no different. They too died of all these things. But they also died by their own hands, many thousands of men and women who chose to commit suicide rather than submit to subjugation by the Spanish. Demographer Juan Pérez de la Riva has estimated that perhaps as many as 30,000 Indians—almost one-third of the total pre-Columbian population of Cuba—perished as a result of suicide during the early decades of European conquest and colo-

Indian suicides. From Girolamo Benzoni, *History of the New World*, trans. W. H. Smith (London, 1857).

nization.[1] They chose death by way of hanging. They ingested poison. They ate dirt in order to die.[2] "The exploited Indians," Fr. Bartolomé de las Casas wrote in 1527, "seeing themselves die daily, began to flee from the mines and other workplaces where they were killed through starvation and continual and excessive work." Las Casas wrote of Indians hanging themselves, "sometimes as entire households together, fathers and sons, the old and the young, adults and children, and some villagers urged others to hang themselves as a way out of the endless torment and calamity that had befallen them."[3] Fifteen years later, Girolamo Benzoni visited the Caribbean and learned that "the natives, finding themselves intolerably oppressed and worked on every side, with no chance of regaining their liberty, with sighs and tears longed for death." Benzoni continued:

Wherefore many went to the woods and there hung themselves, after having killed their children, saying it was far better to die than to live so miserably, serving such and so many ferocious tyrants and wicked thieves. The women, with the juice of a certain herb, dissipated their pregnancy, in order not to produce children, and then following the example of their husbands, hung themselves. Some threw themselves from high cliffs down precipices; others jumped into the sea; others again into rivers; and others starved themselves to death. Sometimes they killed themselves with their flint knives; others pierced their bosoms or their sides with pointed stakes.[4]

Local lore recounts the story of a band of Indians in flight from a Spanish slave-hunting expedition reaching the precipice of the promontory overlooking the Yumurí Valley, with no further place to go. Rather than surrender to their pursuers, hundreds of Indians, including scores of families, chose to leap to their deaths.[5] It was a "proper thing," one local resident explained to ethnographer José Barreiro in 1989. "The conquistadors treated them so badly in the mines and the fields. After they had lost in combat, this was their only way left to defeat the Spanish, by killing themselves. That way they could not be humiliated. And they died with their dignity."[6]

The legend of Yumurí has endured for centuries, principally as moral and metaphor in the service of the discursive hierarchies around which the cosmology of Cuban has been assembled. Not for the last time would resistance in Cuba be registered as an act of self-destruction. The recorded history of Cuba begins with suicide.

✝ This is a study of the Cuban way of death, specifically an examination of the circumstances under which Cubans from the colonial period through the present have embraced the efficacy of suicide as a plausible response to life. For more than 150 years, the rate of suicide in Cuba has ranked consistently among the highest in the world. It has long been the highest in all of Latin America. From the late colonial period into the early republic, under capitalism as well as socialism, men and women in Cuba have killed themselves at a higher rate than people in almost all other countries.

Suicide has loomed large in the Cuban imagination. Perhaps the most noteworthy and indeed the most celebrated form of voluntary death in Cuba was registered as a gesture of collective purpose, that is, an injunction to sacrifice one's life on behalf of one or another nationalist formulation associated with *patria* (homeland). The theme of self-sacrifice reached deeply into the narratives of nation, those deliberations that speak to the nature of nationality and embody the content of collective self-representation. The popular discourse on the nation, transacted always within the most public of spaces, early conflated sacrifice of self with salvation of nation. The lyric of the Cuban national anthem, "La Bayemesa" (1868) — "To die for the patria is to live" (*Morir por la Patria es vivir*) — consecrated exemplary death as an attribute of nationality at the very outset of the liberation project.

Sacrifice of self early assumed a place of prominence in the canons of Cuban. It is indeed possible to speak of a discourse of death as the dominant narrative device through which patria entered the realms of nineteenth-century popular awareness, principally as an ethos inscribed into the norms that shaped the terms of nationality into recognizable form.

The duty to die was arranged as a formulation in response to the needs of a historic moment, imagined by men and women who were themselves deeply engaged in the process of liberation. They sought to understand the world they aspired to change, if only to make that understanding accessible to all and thereby hasten the change. This was a meditation that spanned much of the nineteenth century, as Cubans searched for vernacular forms through which to represent their condition, a way to give narrative structure and political coherence to the circumstances of their time and, simultaneously, to fashion the ethic to sustain the project of liberation. Successive generations were implicated in a complex covenant with the past, whereby the discharge of the duty to die was transacted as an attribute of being Cuban. That death was included in the evocation of patria acknowledged that the pursuit of nation would cost dearly. The connection between the summons *morir por la Patria* in the independence struggles of the nineteenth century and the exhortation *Patria o muerte* of the Cuban revolution in the twentieth century is straight and direct.

The idea of voluntary death in Cuba also insinuated itself into less heroic realms and certainly into far more private spheres. The motives that impelled Cubans to kill themselves were generally no different from the range of reasons that people everywhere chose to end their lives. Every year a significant number of men and women in Cuba arrived at the conclusion that suicide was an appropriate response to circumstances with which they no longer wished to cope. Death by suicide was deemed a readily admissible response to prospects in which the material resources or the moral resolve — or both — seemed inadequate to sustain life. Precipitating factors ranged from individual acts of protest and rebellion to anguished responses to inconsolable hurts, the point at which people refused to continue to bear up under the burdens of life. Suicide promised remedy for physical disability, economic distress, and existential despair. Cubans, especially women who suffered from neglect, infidelity, and violence, killed themselves as a result of unhappy marriages. The young—mostly women—took their own lives as a response to unhappy personal relationships, thwarted romance, and interpersonal conflict. The old—mostly men—tended to kill themselves out of loneliness, sometimes out of despair associated with feelings of isolation and uselessness. Cubans of all ages often chose to die as a way to end chronic pain associated with illness and disease that seem insurmountable or interminable. Many Cubans deemed suicide a proper method to preserve self-esteem, or a way to expiate pusillanimity. Many chose to end their lives out of a sense of dignity, preferring to die with decorum rather than live in disgrace, electing death with honor in preference to life in ignominy, or illness, or helplessness. The impoverished and indigent, men and women without means of subsistence, often gave themselves readily to death, defeated by crushing poverty and worn down by a lifetime of effort to bear up under the burdens of living. Some determined to die as a result of their inability to get out from under the unbearable weight of grief. The death of key family members, especially when it involved the homemaker or wage earner, could shatter the psychological and physical security of a household, often with devastating consequences. Family disputes also took their toll, and not a few Cubans chose suicide in the face of household tensions, particularly those that arose from volatile family conflicts, as in domestic violence or when children rebelled against the authority of parents.

The rate at which Cubans committed suicide changed over the course of the nineteenth and twentieth centuries. So did the choice of methods. So too did patterns of motives. Gender differentiation was striking. Men and women tended to kill themselves in very different ways and usually for very different reasons. The young and the old also arrived at the decision to end their lives for different reasons and by way of different methods as each stage of the life cycle presented its own unique set of prospects and problems. The different regions of the island, distinguished by different types of local economies as well as different local traditions, also saw differences in the motives and methods by which Cubans chose to end their lives. Class differences further shaped the nature of suicide. Race too appears to have had an impact on the act of suicide.

It was not, hence, that men and women in Cuba necessarily have had motives different from people in other countries for killing themselves. Rather, what has made Cuba different are the circumstances of dispositions, the frame of reference that appears to have lent general endorsement to the efficacy of suicide as an appropriate solution and that has served to lower the threshold at which this solution enters the realm of the admissible.

✣ The disposition to suicide must be understood within the larger context of Cuban, but without losing sight of the specific significance associated with individual decisions to choose death over life. The act of suicide is the result of complex and cumulative processes, possessed of specific meanings, and the extent to which the decision to die was exercised as a matter of choice could not but implicate the larger normative systems that permitted some behaviors and proscribed others. It thus becomes necessary to examine the cultural sources of emotional susceptibilities and social sentiments as a way to understand the setting in which men and women in Cuba contemplated ending their lives. It suggests too the need to appreciate the ways that cultural knowledge served to render the act of suicide both imaginable and reasonable, within domains of shared beliefs and common practices. To decide to die was not simply or even principally to respond to a lack of alternatives but rather to choose one alternative among others. It was a choice made for complex personal reasons, but always in a social context as an enactment of cultural models.

Suicidal behavior acquired specific social meaning, rendered as a comprehensible deed conditioned by and indeed contingent on normative ratification. It developed within specific cultural domains, under particular historical circumstances, in the form of behavior authorized as proper and appropriate. The degree to which the choice of death by suicide resulted from internal prompting or external cues—or a combination of both—was not always clear, of course, but neither is it possible to separate the psychology of self-destruction from the sociology of suicide.

The practice of suicide in Cuba thus came to assume an internal logic of its own, one that was then and is now both accessible and intelligible. It suggests a pattern of responses to specific social circumstances and changing historical conditions, a pattern deeply embedded in the normative assumptions by which vast numbers of people routinely ordered their daily lives. Suicide is an act from which to infer multiple—often simultaneous—meanings that often changed with circumstances and with the passage of time. What may have been on one occasion condemned as a senseless act of self-destruction was at another moment celebrated as a noble gesture of self-sacrifice. At any given time suicide may have simultaneously evoked approval as a sacrifice, or martyrdom, or heroic deed and disapproval as a sin, or crime, or mental illness. These are matters of layered complexity, to be approached with an appreciation for ambiguity and acceptance of uncertainty, often dwelling in those murky spaces between the most concrete and the most abstract, between the real and the ideal, between knowledge and the unknowable.

The deed of self-destruction was at times the final act in a process of self-construction, an act that derived meaning principally in realms of popular conventions and received wisdom, transacted within those spheres of cultural exchange in which human conduct obtains recognition. Philosopher David Wood pondered the "special range of consequences brought about by the fact that the suicide takes his own life," noting that under these circumstances "the meaning of one's act has an effect."[7] To choose to die was to proclaim purpose, in the form of revenge, for example, or self-punishment, or as a way of atonement, or in pursuit of an afterlife reunion. The demands of life were deeply implicated in popular meditations on death and dying, always with the possibility that in the end one's best efforts were insufficient to meet the demands of life. "The battle of life . . . ," affirmed essayist Víctor Zamora, "ends in victory for those who know how to deploy valor and strategy." Zamora continued:

A man without valor and without bravery is one thing: he who fears death can never perform the acts of a man. Do not fear even death and death retreats in the face of your confidence. Man does not die, he kills himself. Outside of violent death that we cannot foresee, any other kind of death is truly a suicide, or better said: a crime that the soul inflicts upon the body as a result of imprudence or ignorance. Man almost always dies from the affliction that he fears most. Foresight consists of knowing how to anticipate possible developments before they take place and prevent beforehand the undesirable consequences.[8]

That life could assume purpose through the act of self-destruction implies a normative hierarchy in which the values assigned to life and death were often tenuously drawn and easily transgressed. The deed of suicide was loaded with social meanings, some more privileged than others, to be sure, as in sacrifice in defense of commonly shared ideals, when collective well-being seemed to call for individual sacrifice in the form of self-destruction. But the decision to die was also a way to register dramatic communication, to respond to unhappiness, pain, betrayal, or disappointment, to proclaim honor and dignity, to affirm self-esteem, to act out of duty and decorum. It was deeply implicated as a reflection of the condition of Cuban, for the decision to die was to make a value judgment on life itself.

It is thus to the cultural environment that attention must be directed for an understanding of the circumstances whereby suicide passed from the unthinkable to the unremarkable. The phenomenon of suicide represented socially patterned behavior, something akin to the enactment of a personal revelation in relation to cultural conventions. To examine suicide is to gain access to the codes and conventions that played so large a part in shaping the terms of social relationships, moral carriage, and economic being. It bears emphasis at the outset that the pages that follow attend to the Cuban condition as experienced by the living. This study is concerned far more with life than with death, sustained by the conviction that the circumstances in which people chose to end their lives deeply implicate everyone else who chose to carry on.

This book seeks to situate the phenomenon of suicide in Cuba less in the realm of national identity than in domains of national sensibility. The distinction provides a far more inclusive and less reified framework in which to explore the disposition to die as a culturally fashioned response to life. This is to evoke the condition of Cuban as possessing content that transcends form, in a context of coherence and consensus, but mostly to approach suicidal propensity as much as a facet of a moral order as a mode of engagement.

The idea here is to suggest the capacity to experience multiple affinities at one time, or in sequence, and act accordingly. It implies a range of susceptibilities spanning—and connecting—cognitive spheres and conative domains through which behavior obtained coherence and bound a people together and from which values and meanings were derived. The notion of sensibility thus allows for the examination of death by suicide within the realms of social relations as transacted into modes of self-expression, as a function of both rational thought and emotions, out of an awareness of being and knowledge of choice. Sensibility is meant to convey those conditions through which individuals responded to experience, which implies, literary critic Stephen Cox has suggested, a process that enables people "to internalize social expectation and incorporate them into consciousness."[9]

Many decades ago writer Lino Novás Calvo pondered the larger meaning and lasting influence of suicide among the Indians of Cuba. "There is no such thing as a people totally and definitively subdued," Novás Calvo reflected. "The vanquished live on within the victor, and if we are attentive to the psychic elements that insinuate themselves into character, [traits] at times survive more in the victor than the vanquished. But if the vanquished perish, as occurred with the primitive population of Cuba, that permeation is a vengeful inheritance: it is a legacy of the dead, similar to a secret Talmudic prophecy, that to this day afflicts the present residents of the island."[10]

Novás Calvo's musing speaks to the phenomenon of suicide as a facet of national conduct and, more specifically, as an attribute of those cultural patterns by which men and women in Cuba arranged their view of the world and thereupon proceeded to make a place for themselves within that version of reality. It is not necessary to agree with him about the sources of the propensity to suicide to share his view of the condition of Cuban. To contemplate suicide as a facet of Cuban suggests the need to examine the sensibility of lo cubano, of what it means to be Cuban in a historical context, of the multiple ways that sentience and susceptibility passed into cognitive realms, there to be enacted into conventions and carriage. The degree to which Cubans looked upon death as an efficacious response to life must be situated within the repertoire of behaviors that can reasonably be included among the attributes of being Cuban.

Under certain circumstances, the deed of suicide was itself a revelatory enactment of the Cuban condition, as a mode of being and a code of comportment converging in a larger cultural environment that informed motive and assigned significance to the gesture of self-destruction. Suicide moved across thresholds of public spheres and private spaces and was loaded with meaning, even if the meaning was not always apparent, and almost always within a context of culturally structured patterns of conduct and approved actions and practices. Some suicides were conceived as public display, a burning on the street, a leaping from a building, or a shooting at a table in a restaurant. On other occasions, the act of self-destruction was completed in solitary isolation, in the privacy of a home or a hotel room.

❧ Life has weighed heavily on Cubans, generation after generation, in the individual pursuit of well-being and the collective stirrings of national fulfillment. Aspirations of freedom, dignity, and happiness have often encountered obstacles of daunting proportions, surmountable only at great cost, sometimes as popular mobilizations, other times simply as endurance, where collective survival was rendered possible only through individual sacrifice. Discernible traces of pathos dwell over the Cuban past, which is filled with heroic struggle against overwhelming odds, with aspirations gone awry and hopes unmet, with things not quite turning out the way they were supposed to—again, and again, and again. To make a living and get by, simply to dedicate oneself to the task of livelihood, often consumed energies well out of proportion to outcomes. The history of Cuba is a chronicle of striving and setbacks, continuous struggle and sacrifice, moments of heroic achievement alternating with occasions of relentless suffering. "To live is very difficult," broods Esteban in Abelardo Estorino's play *La casa vieja*.[11]

The demands of daily life took their toll on vast numbers of people engaged in the ordinary and commonplace tasks of making a living, caring for loved ones, and seeking a better life for themselves and their children. In almost every sense, there was nothing dramatic or unusual about these endeavors. They engage the moral energies of the better part of humanity. Cubans all through their history have persisted in these pursuits, through good times and bad, during times of political tumult and especially through periods of economic dislocation. All through the years of the heroic mobilizations in the name of liberty and liberation, in the throes of insurrection and revolution, during those moments of drama that have so riveted the attention of the historian, vast numbers of people strove to lead their lives as normally as possible.

Cuba seemed to be in a constant state of transition during much of the nineteenth and twentieth centuries. The pace of change varied, to be sure, but transition seemed to be a permanent condition. Many of these changes were apparent at the time, often discerned in those realms of partial recognition and intuitive cognizance, although it is also true that the implications of change were not always apparent immediately, and certainly the consequences almost never were. Dominant value systems increasingly revealed themselves incapable of keeping up, and for vast numbers of people daily life filled with uncertainty, with a sense of bewilderment and foreboding.

Cultural formation in Cuba was driven in response to change, out of changing material settings and moral circumstances from which conventions of collective sensibilities emerged. It developed out of the need to normalize change, which means too that the stability and the staying power associated with tradition, in both private doings and public dealings, was often hardly more than fleeting. It is in this context that suicide provides insight into complex processes of adaptation.

These cultural disjunctions often played havoc with the terms of daily life, as conduct and conventions shaped within the normative domains of one historical moment were subsequently revealed to be of diminishing utility under different historical conditions. The character of suicide in Cuba responded to changing circumstances of life as lived, subject always to the intrusion of national and international forces that often reached deeply into domains of personal and private transactions, in the experience of childhood and the expectations of adulthood, in family structures and household economies, often clashing with received formulations by which individual self-worth and collective self-esteem were measured. The extent to which these meanings and perceived realities entered realms of popular consciousness, thereupon to shape dispositions so vital to the determination to live and the decision to die, is central to this inquiry.

Not to take cognizance of the moral dislocation to which successive generations of Cubans were subject is to ignore the tensions that insinuated themselves as a permanent condition in the daily lives of vast numbers of men and women. Indeed, this dislocation may emerge as the salient and enduring circumstance of the Cuban experience. Certainly the great watershed transitions of the last century, between the colony and the republic, for example, or from capitalism to socialism, stand in sharp relief. But it is also true that these transitions set in motion the adaptations by which one generation to the next defined itself as distinct and different from its predecessors.

Daily life required the deployment of moral energies and allocation of material resources in the pursuit of fulfillment in the multiple domains of private responsibilities and public representations. This implicated Cubans of all classes in the discharge of gender-determined roles, those ways that men and women across generations learned to engage reality and into which were invested the pursuit of livelihood, the development of self-esteem, and the maintenance of social relationships. Patterns of suicide serve to reveal how life failed to meet expectations and fulfill hopes, which means too that attention must be drawn to the circumstances and context from which expectations originated and hopes were formed. What precisely encouraged people to believe their goals were within their reach — and why were they not?

This implies the need to examine the larger emotional logic by which men and women across the island learned to imagine their prospects in life and by what means they contemplated meeting these expectations no less than to reflect on the range of responses available to cope with disappointment and dashed hopes. That suicidal behavior was included among those responses raises questions about the ways that the normative determinants of everyday life acted to validate self-destruction as an appropriate remedy to unmet expectations.

The ways that people deciphered the meaning of their times had much to do with the nature of the expectations to which they could reasonably aspire and from which they proceeded to develop usable categories of social knowledge. Nineteenth- and twentienth-century men and women lived continuously with and within the conventions of their time, for better and for worse. That it was both for the better and the worse meant that Cubans were in a constant state of deliberative engagement with received norms, seeking to make them respond to changing needs of life as lived, over the span of a lifetime, often under historic circumstances very different from those in which received wisdom had originated. This necessarily calls attention to the ways that social forces and cultural canons combined to influence decisions that otherwise appeared as wholly individual and idiosyncratic choices.

It also sets in relief the need to situate people within the identities that mattered most, in those roles that acted relentlessly to shape the purpose of daily life, so very much governed by imperatives of class, race, gender, age, and religion. To discern a disposition to suicide as a condition of Cuban is to locate its sources within historically determined patterns of daily life. Such a disposition was shaped within those habit-forming and action-guiding cultural realms where people learn the cues and codes that govern socially sanctioned behavior.

Aspirations developed largely within the parameters of existing class hierarchies. What people could plausibly aspire to was very much a function of socially construed norms of status and success, of values derived from class-based standards of well-being, of time-honored arrangements and well-considered achievements associated with fulfillment and happiness. Norms of well-being in this instance could not but correspond to the material reality in which men and women experienced daily life. They were transmitted through those cultural models by which social classes reproduced normative coherence, each informed by very different modes of social knowledge, each propounding very different notions of well-being. Success in life for an industrial worker, for example, was registered as something very different than success for an industrialist, but both people could feel "successful" upon having achieved class-determined ideals of well-being. Most people lived most of the time contentedly within the

moral order of their class, finding purpose in life in the pursuit of fulfillment within the possibilities of their social origins. Therein lay the source
of social stability in a system otherwise rife with social inequality.

❊❊ Men and women lived much of their lives with an eye to an imagined
future, toward which they advanced more or less purposefully. But it is
also true that the idea of the future was at once historically contingent and
possessed of a proper history. The future that people anticipated most was
fashioned by normative notions of probability, in which considerations
of social class, intersected by factors of class, gender, race, age, and religion, acted together to give decisive form and function to the aspirations
by which daily life was experienced. It was when class-based ideals of well-
being revealed themselves to be unattainable, when achievement failed
to meet aspirations, when cultural models of reality no longer seemed to
work, that the purpose and plans with which the future was charted were
threatened, and often with devastating consequences. It thus becomes
necessary to examine the history of the future, that is, to acquire appreciation of changing perceptions of the idea of the future as an essential facet
of the moral order that sustained purpose in life.

Changing circumstances affected the ways that Cubans imagined the
time that lay before them, and indeed determined what people understood
they could reasonably expect from life: from one day to the next, from one
year to the next, from one generation to the next. Poet José Jorrín Bramosio reflected at length on the idea of the future as a condition of life, noting
in the poem "El suicida":

> Bitter is the life of the hardworking man
> Who in casting his vision toward the future
> Beholds the dreams of his innermost mind
> and his love and his hopes dead.[12]

Sociologist Diego Tamayo gave poignant expression to the future prospects as motive to persist in life. "Painful pessimism is not what sustains
the energy to live," he suggested in 1893. "To live contemplating the past
without possibility of improvement in the future is to lose the present and
perish overwhelmed by the misfortune of the moment. It is necessary to
enter the struggle for life with hope."[13]

The assumptions that sustained faith in the idea of the future were
themselves products of historical circumstances, always in flux, so that
what may have been vain hopes at one time were plausible expectations at

another. But it was also true that the notion of future was developing into a deepening preoccupation in the Cuban imagination. The future often entered Cuban calculations as the past repeating itself, as an eventuality contemplated with a mixture of anticipation and apprehension. There was more than passing significance to Manuel Márquez Sterling's observation in 1906 that "we [Cubans] never look to the future, for we are always preoccupied with the problems of day to day life." Historian Evelio Rodríguez Lendián brooded in 1919: "What fills us with doubts, what fills our lives with shadows, what we all wish to know when we contemplate the future of Cuba . . . is if Cuba can overcome all the hardships [and] all the obstacles that may appear in its path." Essayist Enrique Gay Calbó similarly despaired about the ways that unrelieved hardship could lead to the forfeiture of the future and wrote in 1938: "Over the course of several generations, a people lose their character, their valor, and their capacity to resist. The struggle becomes increasingly difficult, because the spirit of solidarity, the sentiment of cohesion, and the very consciousness that they make up a nation . . . and have a heritage and a future slowly dies within them."[14]

Prospects for the future were a source of deepening Cuban preoccupation, for they were never presumed to be either self-evident or self-fulfilling. The future was something that people worked at. The idea of the future developed around the belief that the circumstances under which life was lived offered sufficient markers to presume predictability. It was based on the expectation of having some control over those forces that seemed to govern the course of daily life. It implied too presumption of some measure of longevity. As the character of Adela in the play *Donde está la luz*, by Ramón Ferreira, remarks: "What good is the future if you die before it arrives."[15]

But most of all the idea of the future implied faith in the possibility of betterment, in the capacity to summon a vision of what lay ahead with reasonable confidence that things would be better—certainly not worse—than they were before. The power of the future was in its possibility. "It is necessary to have faith in the future," exhorted essayist Miguel Garrido. "It is necessary to believe in the capacity of the future to redeem."[16]

All through the twentieth century, through recurring cycles of economic depression and years of political repression, through good times and bad, Cubans struggled to protect the future as the last chance for a better life. The loss of confidence in the prospects of time yet to come often had devastating effects and transformed the future into an eventuality to dread. The degree to which people could reasonably sustain expectations of fulfillment had much to do with the desire to live. In Eduardo González Velez's short story "Soledad," the protagonist of the title "contemplates the future as one who anticipates an impending disaster. Her heart filled with disquiet and despair, and with the desire to die young."[17] Those whose lives were filled with adversity could be sustained by hopes of better times in the future, by viewing their suffering as a temporary condition, a passing circumstance. Without hope for a better future, however, suffering was deprived of instrumental purpose, with no way up and no way out, giving particular salience to novelist Marguerite Yourcenar's observation that "fear of the future lessens the fear of death."[18]

Vast numbers of men and women of successive generations dedicated lifetimes in preparation to receive the future, living with expectations of what the future would bring, only to find that when the future arrived there was nothing, and worse still: there was no more future. Héctor Quintero's play *Contigo pan y cebolla* (1962), set in Havana during the late 1950s, captured the tenor of the times with poignance. "All my life waiting, waiting, waiting," Lala despairs, "filled with hopes, with ambitions, making plans for the future, and now at 38 years of age, only 38 years, I am tired. . . . And what have I achieved? Nothing. Only hopes. Hopes for the future. And when will that future arrive? When will it arrive?"[19]

❧ Patterns of suicide offer insight into meanings associated with the rhythm and routine of everyday life. The power of the routine resided in the sense of continuity it conveyed, and once it took hold provided a useful measure by which to corroborate that all was well, predictable, and orderly, moving more or less toward some knowable end. Vast numbers of Cubans carried out the tasks of daily existence as a matter of course, living in conformity with the dictates of received wisdom, doing what they had to, the best way they could, to make do and get by. Habit and repetition sustained normality. Routine as an explanatory mode can serve to confirm life as proceeding more or less as expected. The disruption of routine could have far-reaching implications, for to upset the rhythm of life was to disrupt purpose in living. "People are very emotional," Rachel comments perceptively in Miguel Barnet's *Canción de Rachel* (1969), "and they cry and shout and stamp their feet if something happens that is not part of the daily routine."[20]

There is something so utterly inexorable about the character of daily life, so mundane, so matter of fact, as to allow the unremarkable to pass easily enough for the insignificant. But there is much to infer from the ordinary. The reasons that drove people to end their lives tend to reflect the expectations with which they lived their lives. Men and women continued to love, and, when thwarted, some killed themselves. They assembled households, established families, and dedicated their lives to caring for both. They continued to work to make a living, in order to guarantee their security and pursue their well-being, and when security and well-being no longer seemed possible, many gave up on life. They were preoccupied with illnesses and afflictions of all types, often to the point of self-destruction.

Suicidal behavior offers insight into the circumstances under which people took stock of their lives in ordinary times, of course, but especially during extraordinary times, at those points at which powerful forces of history insinuated themselves into private domains of daily life. It is in this context—and indeed in the most personal of ways—that suicide suggests the larger meaning of what passes for the historic, increasing or decreasing in response to the intrusion of the world at large. During the eighteen months of stunning sugar prosperity during 1919–20, for example, suicide rates in Cuba declined markedly. On the other hand, suicide soared during the years of the depression. One of the lowest suicide rates in twentieth-century Cuba was recorded during the 1960s, a time of revolutionary mobilization and exalted collective purpose.

The phenomenon of suicide suggests close-up the workings of a larger framework of power relationships, one in which the option of self-destruction functions as a mode of negotiation in the domains populated by the powerless and the powerful. Simply put, some people, by virtue of class, or skin color, or gender, or age—or some combination thereof—had more power than other people. Most people acted within these categories of power inflections in multiple ways, often at one and the same time, as a function of the multifaceted roles they were called upon to play in the ordinary course of their lives. Such action spans the entire historical panorama of Cuba, and includes relationships between slave-owners and slaves, metropolitan authority and colonial subjects, the state and its citizens, whites and blacks, men and women, parents and children, the old and the young.

But powerlessness was not a condition to which everyone was reconciled. When one's aspirations and expectations were thwarted by the will of others, when longings and yearnings and hopes and dreams were obstructed by others, people were often able to deploy those creative energies by which to affirm agency and assert humanity. Clearly, intent matters, for the deed of suicide was loaded with recognizable purpose and possessed of the capacity to serve as a means of social communication. The gesture of suicide, both as an unsuccessful attempt and a completed deed, offers access to a social environment where the modalities of power relationships are often otherwise impossible for the historian to discern, for they are so thoroughly understood by all implicated in shared cultural domains that they need never be acknowledged. The strategies that people developed as a means to deal with and respond to the demands of day-to-day life and the conditions of their times assumed many forms. Suicide happened to be one.

These are the circumstances into which the disposition to suicide must be placed. The factors that contributed to the decision to die were at least as complex as those that sustained the determination to live. Both were conditioned within the social environment in which people sought to sort out deeply personal matters of love and livelihood, self-respect and well-being, hope and happiness, in pursuit of mostly plausible aspirations within those normative boundaries in which virtually all facets of daily life obtained meaning.

🌿 Some caveats are in order that bear on the character of data and methodology used in the pages that follow. This study was undertaken with an awareness of the limitations of the official published data relating to suicide. The utility of the vast body of vital statistics assembled by public health agencies during the course of the nineteenth and twentieth centuries is often problematical. The collection of data on this scale, prepared and disseminated principally by government agencies over a period of time spanning from the late-colonial period into the republic, through successive changes of governments, often employing different methods of statistical analysis, frequently in very different political environments, must inevitably result in a host of shortcomings, including recurring inconsistencies and inaccuracies. Official statistics were products of complex bureaucratic procedures, many of which were devised to meet objectives of administrative efficiency, often designed to reflect favorably on the policies of public agencies. Budgetary constraints similarly affected the quality of data-gathering procedures, and often what was gathered and preserved was at least as great as what was discarded and disregarded.

The probability of bureaucratic error is further increased by the social circumstances in which suicide entered the public record. The evidence suggests, in fact, that official statistics underestimated the actual number of suicides in Cuba. Death by suicide was not difficult to conceal. Families of means, especially, possessed the resources to protect their privacy, control publicity, and affect the outcome of autopsies and coroners' inquests. A private family physician, for example, could readily participate in the preparation of a death certificate that more than adequately concealed suicidal death.

That statistics on suicide published by government agencies tended to underreport the number and types of deaths is only one problem. Public health statisticians typically recorded only successful suicides, deaths presumed to have been the result of willed intent. No less important to the understanding of suicide in Cuba, however, were the vast numbers of unsuccessful suicides, attempts thwarted before death occurred but for which complete records do not exist. Whether unsuccessful suicide attempts were, in the end, intended to produce fatal outcomes cannot always be determined with precision. In fact, the evidence indicates that in many instances they were not, which suggests another level of social function embedded within the suicidal gesture.

Official characterizations of suicide must also be looked on cautiously. There were undoubtedly occasions when suicides were recorded as accidents or accidents as suicides. And, of course, it was always possible that homicides were made to appear as suicide.[21] Occasionally attempts were made to disguise suicide as death by natural causes as a way to allow beneficiaries to collect on insurance policies.[22] The capacity to make determinations between accidents and suicide, on the one hand, and homicide and suicide, on the other, required skills and resources often beyond the means of local forensic and law enforcement authorities. Suicides reported as the cause of death of prisoners often occurred under suspicious circumstances and raised many questions.[23] On the other hand, it is also true that prisoners subjected to ill-treatment, abuse, and torture did indeed commit suicide.

Forensic procedures used in provincial towns and cities often varied, and inevitably produced different findings. Varying degrees of professional training and differing administrative practices also made for deviations in coroners' findings. In the absence of suicide notes, the distinctions between accident and suicide in cases of death involving an overdose of medicine, for example, or kitchen gas range, were often virtually impossible to make.

Occasionally the plausibility of official classifications cannot be sustained. It may strain credulity to read the verdict of "suicide" rendered as the cause of death for a boy in the age category of five to nine years old who died by way of a firearm, or to read that the drowning of a girl and the poisoning of a boy between the ages of one and four were classified as "suicide."[24]

It must be presumed also that errors contained within official statistics were both basis and by-product of the gender determinants around which the data was compiled. Suicide by hanging and firearms, for example, methods employed principally by men, was difficult to conceal (although, it should be noted, occasionally deaths resulting from a self-inflicted gunshot wound were reported as accidents). In contrast, death by poison and gas, among the preferred methods of suicide used by women, was far easier to attribute as accident or conceal altogether. Although reasons exist to suggest that deaths produced in motor vehicle accidents were occasionally suicides, there does not appear to exist a single officially recorded instance of a motor vehicle fatality recorded as suicide.

No less problematic were racial categories employed by public health officials. The principal categories of *blancos* and *de color* often alternated with classifications of *blancos*, *negros*, *mestizos*, and *amarillos*. Official racial categorizations must be approached warily, for they were subject always to arbitrary personal and idiosyncratic bureaucratic determinations.

Official records are nonetheless valuable. Public health records survive as the most complete—and the only—registry of what must be considered as one of the salient facets of the Cuban condition in the late nineteenth and twentieth centuries. For all their flaws and faults, official statistics do provide a detailed and continuous flow of information unobtainable from any other source. The public record can serve as a useful sample of a larger phenomenon. In the aggregate, the data offers a compilation from which to discern patterns and a way to configure trends of suicide. It may well be that the actual number of people who died by suicide is not known, but what is known suggests much about the way men and women lived. The body of statistics serves as a means by which to obtain an approximation of the phenomenon of suicide in Cuba and to arrive at a general sense of the practice and process men and women used to end their lives. It is instructive, moreover, to look upon public health statistics themselves as an indication of the degree to which the proposition of suicide entered Cuban imaginative spaces, as a representation of how the decision to die derived social meaning and cultural resonance. Insofar as the statistics were themselves gathered and arranged in a fashion congruent with the values that informed them, they also served to reflect and reinforce the social meaning ascribed to self-destruction.

Effort has been made to preserve the consistency of the data. The main body of statistical information utilized in this study has been derived from the serial publications of public health agencies of Cuba during the twentieth century: the Secretaría de Sanidad y Beneficencia (1909–41), the Ministerio de Salubridad y Asistencia Social (1942–59), and the Ministerio de Salud Pública (1959–present). Use has also been made of the Comisión Nacional de Estadística y Reformas Económicas, which published important data between the mid-1920s and the mid-1930s. The statistical information assembled by the Comisión Nacional de Estadística y Reformas Económicas was based on a review of local autopsy reports completed across the island every year. For the period in which the Comisión Nacional de Estadística y Reformas Económicas functioned, it examined an estimated 3,000 autopsy reports annually.

It should be noted that the Comisión Nacional de Estadística y Reformas Económicas recorded far higher rates of suicide than the Secretaría de Sanidad y Beneficencia. The Secretaría de Sanidad y Beneficencia, for example, recorded a total of 2,289 suicides between the years 1926 and 1929, while the Comisión Nacional de Estadística y Reformas Económicas recorded 3,638 suicides for the same period.[25] Much of the discrepancy has to do with the categories used by each agency no less than the determination of what constituted the deed of suicide. Further, the reorganization of the Secretaría de Sanidad y Beneficencia into the Ministerio de Salubridad y Asistencia Pública in 1942 introduced changes in the categories employed to tabulate age, sex, and method of suicide and resulted in a number of discontinuities with the system previously used by the predecessor agency.

For all the information that public health records reveal, much remains elusive. Almost no information was recorded relating to occupational status, leaving many questions about the relationship between class and suicide unanswerable. Similarly, the public health record is all but silent on marital status. Data on mortality rates within specific neighborhoods in Havana and the larger provincial cities, for example, would have provided insight into the patterns of the ecological distribution of suicide in urban centers. Neighborhood data would have yielded highly textured information on suicide with insight into social class, occupations, and family histories. Similarly, data on the relationship between internal migration, principally from the countryside to the city, and suicide would have offered useful information relating to the costs and consequences of uprootedness.

An understanding of the larger meaning of suicide in Cuba necessarily implies an appreciation of the social reality to which statistics pointed. It is a way to explore the encounters with the demands of living everyday life, to give attention to death by suicide not as an occasional occurrence but as a tendency situated within the realm of probability, as behavior likely to be contemplated under a certain set of circumstances. The significance of suicide cannot be limited simply to statistical enumeration, of course. The organization of the pages that follow seeks to give narrative order to the phenomenon of suicide as a facet of the Cuban condition, as an outcome of historical circumstances, to be sure, but also as a means to engage life. It is important to stress, again, that suicide was not necessarily a deed of hopelessness. On the contrary, under certain circumstances, it was undertaken as an affirmation of hope. It could suggest agency, a willingness to act, to take one last measure in the expectations that the act of suicide as symbol or as solution offered a response to the problem of living. The possibility of suicide could be an enabling option, very much a product of life as experienced day to day, further corroborated in life as imagined, and as reflected in literary production, music, and film.

The practice of suicide was deeply embedded within normative purposes and moral imperatives. To choose to die was to act out a version of reality. Behind the statistics and headlines are stories of disappointment and despair, of shattered families and disrupted lives, but also of exalted spirits and high hopes, of selfless love and self-sacrificing valor. The recourse to suicide was registered at virtually every point on the spectrum between triumph and tragedy. The study of suicide in Cuba lends itself to multiple interpretations, at the time of the deed and long after; it offers insight into the assumptions that informed the strategies with which vast numbers of people made their way through life, if only at some point to choose to end it.

Dying to Be Free

SUICIDE ON THE PLANTATION

1

*The plantation is an archetypical world and
materially structured by death.*

    Agnes Lugo-Ortiz, Identidades imaginadas *(1999)*

*He learned herbs, and medicines, and poisons, especially
those. They killed animals in the fields with it, and of
course they killed each other, and themselves sometimes.
Macandal knew what we all do. Any death can hurt a
whiteman somewhere. If it is only a slave or a cow, he is
less rich.*

    Madison Smartt Bell, All Souls' Rising *(1995)*

*In dying one gets the opportunity for a better life. . . . To
die is to leave the visible world for the invisible; it is to say
no to hunger, misery, disease, and worry.*

    Simon Bockie, Death and the Invisible Powers:
    The World of Kongo Belief *(1993)*

*There is no pity. His destiny is to suffer, always to suffer.
And his only consolation is to turn his gaze upward to
heaven and remind himself that one day he will die.*

    Carlos Rafael, "El esclavo" *(1877)*

*Cayetano was the family servant. . . . He was thin,
with muscles of steel, a handsome face with symmetrical
vertical scars on each cheek that revealed that he was
Lucumí. He was of good intelligence, who knew how to*

read and write, with a valor that approaches heroism.
He possessed a character different from those of his
people, for he had not committed suicide, like so many
of the Lucumí who had been brought to Cuba, for the
simple reason that Frasquito had given him timely
freedom so that he could come and go wherever he
wanted.

José Armas y Céspedes, Frasquito *(1894)*

Chinese labourers . . . have to endure hunger and chains,
hardships and wrongs of every class, and are driven to
suicide to the extent that no count can be made of the
number of those who have thrown themselves into wells,
cut their throats, [and] hanged themselves.

Ch'en Ming-yüan *(1872)*

❧ The specter of death loomed large over the planta-
tions of nineteenth-century Cuba. It could not have been otherwise. Commercial agricultural production implied a vast capital outlay, from which
profits were obtained principally through the relentless exploitation of human labor. Workers were readily expendable because they were easily re-
placeable, or perhaps it was the other way around. But it probably did not
much matter, for property holders rarely gave more than fleeting thought
to the rationale of human exploitation as long as labor needs were met.

The possibilities of prosperity seized the Cuban imagination late in the
eighteenth century, in the aftermath of the collapse of plantation production in St. Domingue, revealing a potential for profits on a scale hitherto
unimaginable. Cuban producers did not hesitate. Coffee cultivation expanded rapidly across the island, stimulated by increasing demand and
rising prices. The number of *cafetales* (coffee plantations) increased from
2 in 1774, to 108 in 1802, to 586 in 1804; more than doubled to 1,315 by
1806; and almost doubled again to 2,067 by 1827. More than half of the
total number of coffee plantations (1,207) were located in the Western Department (*Occidente*), principally in Pinar del Río, Havana, and Matanzas,
and accounted for more than 75 percent of total Cuban production in 1827.

Between 1792 and 1804, Cuban coffee exports increased more than seven-fold, from 7,101 arrobas to 50,000 arrobas (1 arroba equals 25 pounds), doubling thereafter every several years. Between the years 1825–30 and 1836–40 production increased annually from an average 2 million arrobas to 3.4 million arrobas.[1]

But it was sugar production that registered some of the most spectacular advances. The scope and speed with which land passed under sugar cultivation was stunning. Forests and woodlands disappeared almost overnight, to be reborn as vast expanses of sugarcane fields. The total amount of new land to pass under sugar cultivation nearly doubled from 510,000 acres in 1831 to almost 1 million acres in 1842, and increased again to nearly 1.5 million acres by 1852. The number of sugar mills (ingenios) increased threefold from 484 in 1778 to 1,442 by 1846. Exports increased in spectacular fashion, doubling from 28,400 tons in 1800 to 58,000 tons in 1809, nearly tripling to 162,000 tons by 1841. By midcentury, good times were buoyed by a record harvest of nearly 264,000 tons.[2]

Cuban prosperity was achieved through unimaginable human suffering, derived from the coerced labor of hundreds of thousands of enslaved Africans. They arrived in vast numbers, many tens of thousands of young men and women, in seemingly endless waves of human cargoes. During the intercensus years between 1792 and 1817 the population of enslaved Africans more than doubled from 85,000 to 199,000. But this was only the beginning. In the five-year period 1816–20 alone, an additional 85,000 slaves entered Cuba through Havana. Between 1830 and 1840, another 125,000 Africans arrived on the island. Between the two census years of 1817 and 1841, the total number of enslaved Africans had again more than doubled, from 199,0000 to 437,000.[3] An estimated 184,000 of 437,000 slaves, that is, more than 40 percent of the enslaved population, had arrived on the island within the previous ten years. By midcentury, three-quarters of all slaves were located in the fields of rural Cuba, on coffee fincas and tobacco vegas, but mostly on the sugar ingenios. Fully one-half of the total number of enslaved people in rural Cuba were engaged in sugar production.

🐚 Africans consigned to sugar production toiled under execrable circumstances. Tens of thousands of men and women were worked remorselessly: six days a week, eighteen hours a day, often for five and six months at a time. Visiting one sugar estate in Güines during the expansion cycle of the 1830s, Richard Madden learned from a local overseer that the daily time allowed to slaves for sleep during the harvest "was about four hours, a little more or less. Those who worked at night in the boiling-house worked also the next day in the field. . . . The treatment of the slaves was inhuman, the sole object of the *administrador* being, to get the utmost amount of labor in a given time out of the great number of slaves that could be worked day and night."[4]

This was a labor regimen from which there were few prospects of relief and even fewer possibilities of release, predicated on the proposition of optimum efficiency in pursuit of maximum profit. The practice of overwork—often literally working slaves to death—was not uncommon, almost always in the expectation that slaves thus lost could be replaced by others, on demand, at low cost and in limitless supply. "The idea of making the slave population supply itself is the last thing that seems to enter a Cuban's mind," observed traveler Robert Baird. Alexander von Humboldt made the observation succinctly during his visit to Cuba: "I have heard discussed with the greatest coolness the question whether it was better for the proprietor not to overwork his slaves, and consequently have to replace them with less frequency, or whether he should get all he could out of them in a few years, and thus have to purchase newly imported Africans more frequently." Joseph John Gurney observed a similar disposition among planters several decades later: "Natural increase is disregarded. The Cubans import the stronger animals, like bullocks, work them up, and then seek a fresh supply." The death of slaves was passed off as depreciation of capital stock—all in all, an acceptable cost of doing business. "There are in Cuba plantations where the slaves work twenty-one out of the four-and-twenty hours," Fredrika Bremer commented while visiting Cuba at mid-century, "plantations where there are only men who are driven like oxen to work, but with less mercy than oxen. The planter calculates that he is a gainer by so driving his slaves, that they may die within seven years, within which time he again supplies his plantation with fresh slaves, which are brought hither from Africa, and which he can purchase for two hundred dollars a head."[5]

The logic of the plantation regimen did not readily admit the reproduction of the slave population through natural growth, demanding instead new purchases as the principal means through which to replenish the labor force (*dotación*). In the buyers' market that prevailed during the early decades of the nineteenth century, the cost of reproduction exceeded the price of replacement. "[Planters] know that it is much cheaper to import slaves than to breed them," Robert Baird observed tersely during his travels to Cuba.[6] Former slave Juan Francisco Manzano gave poetic lament to these conditions:

> What does it matter here, how many lives
> Are lost in labour, while the planter thrives,
> The Bozal market happily is nigh,
> And there the planter finds a fresh supply:
> 'Tis cheaper far to buy new strength, we're told,
> Than spare the spent, or husband out the old;
> 'Tis not a plan by which a planter saves,
> To purchase females, or to rear up slaves.
> . . .
> But where, you ask me, are the poor old slaves?
> Where should they be, of course, but in their graves!
> We do not send them there before their time,
> But let them die, when they are past their prime.
> Men who are worked by night as well as day,
> Some how or other, live not to be grey
> Sink from exhaustion—sicken—droop and die,
> And leave the Count another batch to buy.[7]

"It is a rare thing to see a very old negro," Mary Gardner Lowell confided to her travel journal in 1832.[8]

The discipline of the dotación was sustained through the application of corporal punishment and physical abuse, principally in the form of floggings, beatings, and mutilation. There was method to the means. Corporal punishment assumed fully the character of a system, with an internal logic of its own: cruelty applied purposefully with the intent of social control, to coerce compliance and enforce acquiescence, to give daily salience to the meaning of power and powerlessness by which the rhythm and rationale of the plantation system was sustained. Sanctioned cruelty and systematic violence as an acceptable and, indeed, within the logic of the colonial political economy, a necessary means of social control could not easily contemplate an alternative to the application of terror as a means to obtain both a disciplined labor force and an acquiescent mass of enslaved people. Punishment remained etched vividly in the memory of Juan Francisco Manzano:

> For the slightest crime of boyhood, it was the custom to shut me up in a place for charcoal, for four-and-twenty hours at a time. I was timid in

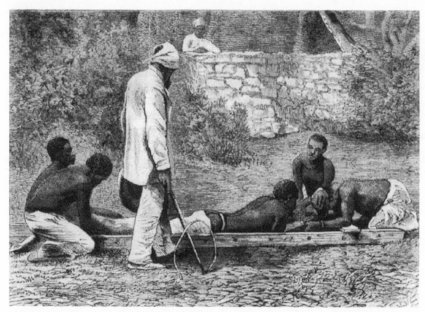

Punishing slaves. From *Harper's Weekly*, November 28, 1869.

the extreme, and my prison . . . was so obscure, that at mid-day no object could be distinguished in it without a candle. Here after being flogged I was placed, with orders to the slaves, under threats of the greatest punishment, to abstain from giving me a drop of water. What I suffered from hunger and thirst, tormented with fear, in a place so dismal and distant from the house, and almost suffocated with the vapours arising from the common sink, that was close my dungeon, and constantly terrified by the rats that passed over me and about me, may be easily imagined. My head was filled with frightful fancies. . . . I would imagine I was surrounded by evil spirits, and I would roar aloud and pray for mercy; and then I would be taken out and almost flayed alive [and] again shut up.[9]

Punishment was also what runaway slave Esteban Montejo recalled vividly many years later. "I saw many horrors of punishment under slavery . . . ," Montejo remembered. "The stocks in the boiler-house were the most cruel. There were stocks for lying down and others for standing up. They were made of thick planks with holes through which slaves were forced to place their head, hands, and feet. They would keep slaves locked up like this for two or three months for the slightest offense. . . . The most common punishment was flogging. This was inflicted by the overseer with a rawhide lash which seared the skin. They also had whips made of the plant fibers which stung like the devil and peeled the skin off in strips. . . . Life was hard and bodies wore out."[10]

Disease and illness claimed easy victims among the weak and weary. Smallpox, yellow fever, and tuberculosis were at once cause and effect of the appalling health conditions that prevailed among the dotaciones of hundreds of plantations. Deficient diets took their toll. Beriberi in particular became known as an illness associated with the sugar estates and often assumed epidemic proportions at the end of the harvest.[11] Those fortunate enough to gain admittance to crude plantation infirmaries rarely obtained adequate medicine or competent care. In any case, illness was not sufficient reason to miss work. "When some black is seen to arrive at the infirmary without having a verifiable reason, as often happens," counseled one plantation administrator, "faking illnesses with something like aches in his bones or somewhere in the body generally, lock him up in a room alone, subject him to an austere diet under lock and key . . . until hunger weakens him. Then without providing any food whatsoever and applying several lashes, return him to the overseer, so that he can be taken back to work. This way he will lose all interest in the infirmary."[12]

Outbreaks of epidemics were common, and almost always resulted in devastating loss of life. Smallpox and typhoid fever periodically swept across the island. A cholera epidemic during the 1830s claimed the lives of thousands of enslaved men and women. Between March and April 1833, an estimated 2,100 slaves perished in Havana. In three jurisdictions of Madruga, Pipián, and Nueva Paz in Havana province, nearly 3,200 slaves perished between January and September 1833. In June 1833, an estimated 700 slaves on 18 sugar estates in the jurisdictions of San Andrés and Sabanillas in Matanzas province succumbed to cholera.[13]

❧❧ Slave mortality rates reached staggering levels as the combination of ill-treatment and illness claimed the lives of many thousands of men and women. Death rates between 10 and 12 percent annually were not uncommon. On some ingenios annual mortality rates reached 15 to 18 percent. Mortality was especially high among newly arrived Africans, among whom Ramón de la Sagra calculated life expectancy on the sugar plantations to average less than seven years. This is also what traveler Robert Baird learned during his visit to Cuba during the late 1840s, when he recorded the conventional wisdom of the time: "It has been said, and it is generally credited by intelligent parties resident in Cuba, that the average duration of the life of a Cuban slave, after his arrival in the island, does not exceed seven or eight years."[14]

The magnitude of mortality among enslaved men and women raises a number of complex issues, central to which was the manner in which African cultural systems intervened to mitigate or otherwise mediate the violation of person so central to the maintenance of the regimen of plantation labor. African responses to New World slavery were expressed through a variety of collective forms and individual acts, mediated further by a combination of factors including age, gender, and cultural norms, and employed daily to negotiate the reciprocities by which the terms of bondage were transacted. African cultural forms that persisted in Cuba served vital instrumental functions, principally as elements of adaptive systems deployed in fashioning the survival strategies necessary to cope with the circumstances of slavery.

Mortality rates suggest a range of complex cognitive processes that gave form and function to death on the plantation. This implied a combination of indeterminate—perhaps indeterminable—instances of, on one hand, death as the result of physical abuse and, on the other, death as a means of resistance to physical abuse. It was at the ambiguous conjuncture where the will to live intersected with the despair for deliverance—where death was received as an acceptable and indeed preferable alternative to life—that slave strategies for engagement with the plantation regimen assumed their most compelling forms.

Many Africans succumbed in body, others succumbed in spirit. A substantial portion of the staggering rate of mortality on the plantation was associated with overwork, corporal punishment, inadequate diet, and disease and illness. That is, a large but unknown number of men and women perished as a result of the decline of physical health and stamina. It is important to stress, too, however, that death under these circumstances did not preclude the presence of agency. Mortality was often at least as much the consequence of the exhaustion of moral resolve as it was the result of the depletion of physical stamina, expressed as acquiescence to unbearable pain and unrelieved suffering in which death was received as a welcomed if not willed release. Death came most readily to those who lost the will to live, to the men and women who chose to let go of life in preference to holding on to it.

The degree to which slaves were implicated in their own deaths thus raises the possibility of a different significance of slave mortality, whereby it becomes possible to construe death as an act of agency, invested with reason and resolve, possessed of a larger logic and a deeper purpose.[15] Suicide assumed a variety of meanings and was exercised at virtually every point at which Africans confronted the circumstances of their enslavement—sometimes as an act of passive resignation, at other times as a deed of active resistance. Suicide implied choice over chance, a common and compelling exercise of will, the deployment of life as a means by which to register protest and transcend circumstances of powerlessness. This is to view the deed of suicide invested with symbolic value and instrumental function. Suicide as an act of willed death passed into the realm of agency as a means through which to affirm control over one's life—even if it meant ending it.

✣ The larger social meanings of suicide among enslaved Africans are not always readily deciphered. Much had to do with nostalgia, a condition to which many Africans succumbed upon arriving to Cuba. The yearning to return to familiar people and places was often a force of irresistible power. In these circumstances, suicide was associated with melancholia that emanated from loss and longing. Expressed as a diminished desire to live, it was a passive way of dying that conveyed indifference to living, driven by the determination to die. Observers at the time frequently characterized melancholia as a disease and mental disorder, and specifically identified nostalgia as an affliction characterized as a "moral sickness," a condition that drove many Africans to induce their own deaths as an act of will.[16]

This response was recorded as early as the middle passage. Physician George Howe, responsible for the health of human cargoes during the trans-Atlantic voyage, was baffled by the death of three or four Africans daily, "notwithstanding their apparent good health. . . . Of what did they die?" Howe described one African who "would mope, squat down with his chin on his knees and arms clasped about his legs, and in a very short time died." Isaac Wilson, also a physician aboard a slave vessel, concluded that melancholia was a disorder that accounted for two-thirds of African deaths aboard his ship. "No one who had it was ever cured . . . ," Wilson observed. "The symptoms are a lowness of spirits and despondency. Hence they refused food." Slave trader Alexander Falconbridge attributed the suicide of slaves to a diseased mind, the principal manifestation of which was the refusal to take food and medical aid, "giving as reason that they wanted to die" as a result of "their strong attachment to their native country, together with a just sense of the value of liberty." On those occasions when slaves sang, Falconbridge recalled, "their songs are generally, as may naturally be expected, melancholy lamentations of their exile from the native country." Nineteenth-century historian W. O. Blake recounted one instance of a woman who "was dejected from the moment she came on board, and refused both food and medicine: being asked by the interpreter what she wanted, she replied, nothing but to die—and she did die. Many other slaves expressed the same wish."[17]

Africans newly arrived in Cuba (*bozales*) often withdrew into themselves, overcome with inconsolable sorrow, refused all food and drink, displayed only the most tenuous interest in living, and soon languished dying. Physician Francisco Barrera y Domingo published a medical treatise on slavery in Cuba and commented extensively on the phenomenon of melancholia, where Africans "became so sad that they die." He offered a diagnostic guide to "the symptoms that announce the onset of this illness," including a "profound sadness that seizes their mind," followed by a "furious passion of wishing to return to their land, to something loved left behind: a mother, or father, or child." The behavior of Africans thus affected included a desire for solicitude and for sleep, a loss of appetite, and "when awake, they move as if in a daze, acting as if they do not hear, and if they are forced to pay attention, they become irate and haughty."[18] A visit to slave quarters (*barracón*) outside Havana housing forty newly arrived Africans made a deep impression on Joseph John Gurney. "They looked emaciated and melancholy," he wrote. "A child lying on a dresser, wrapped in a blanket, was in the article of death. The whole scene . . . was one of mute sorrow and suffering—heart-rendering to ourselves." Richard Madden observed the conditions of slaves on one estate in Güines: "The appearance of the negroes on this estate was wretched in the extreme; they looked jaded to death, listless, stupefied, haggard, and emaciated." One visitor to Havana in 1838 witnessed a slave auction and wrote: "A newly imported cargo of 220 human beings was here exposed for sale. . . . [We] saw some . . . whose appearance told that they, at least, would be liberated from bondage by death. They were those who had suffered most during the voyage,—their situation was most melancholy."[19] In plantation ledgers itemizing the causes of death among slaves often appeared the entry "suicide through mental disorder."[20]

Suicide as a deed of deliverance, contemplated as an act of redemption from inconsolable grief and unbearable physical pain, was often less passive and pursued with the intent of immediate death. The most common form of suicide on the plantation was through hanging, either as an

individual act or, just as often, in collective form as an act of group solidarity.[21] Joseph Goodwin, the administrator of a coffee estate in Matanzas,
recorded the suicide loss of two new slaves in his diary entry of September 28, 1821: "Found the two bozals this morning suspended by a rope in
the woods, not far distant from the house. They were the two best bozals
on the plantation. I have not yet learned the cause of the unfortunate circumstance, for the present suffice it to say they are no more."[22] Slaves often
leaped to their deaths off mountain sides, from bridges into river ravines,
or into well shafts.[23] José María Congo of the coffee estate Amistad died
after leaping into a well. On the coffee estate Petit Versalles in Guanajay
in 1845, the slave Bonifacio plunged to his death into the estate well. The
U.S. consul in Santiago de Cuba reported one instance in which a slave
who "was being flogged in Cobre, tied to a post, asked to be allowed a respite, for a moment for a purpose readily to be convinced, and in passing
the cistern in the yard, jumped down and drowned himself."[24]

Newly arrived Africans in Cuba were especially prone to take their own
lives. One midcentury estimate calculated that as many as 20 percent of
all Africans committed suicide within the first year on the island.[25] The
process of adaptation to the plantation regimen, commonly known as "seasoning," was often hurried and almost always traumatic and inevitably resulted in the deaths of many newly arrived Africans. A "large . . . proportion of these miserable beings die in the seasoning," Joseph John Gurney
observed in 1840. "During the first years," Fredrika Bremer reported learning during her midcentury travels through Cuba, "when they are brought
here free and wild from Africa, it is very hard to them, and many seek to
free themselves from slavery by suicide." The judicial tribunal (*audiencia*)
of Havana concluded that the frequency of suicide was related principally
to seasoning, noting that "few are the number of slaves who commit suicide after having become acclimated on the rural estates."[26]

The propensity toward suicide among slaves appears associated most
prominently with specific African ethnic groups (*naciones*). The principal
African naciones in Cuba included the Macau, Mandinga, Gangá, Mina,
Congo, Carabalí, and Lucumí. Cuban planters early developed cultural
profiles of the African naciones, associating dispositions and behaviors
with specific ethnic groups as a means by which to make informed purchases of new slaves. "In the understanding acquired in the administration
of slavery . . . ," explained the intendant of Cuba, "I have demonstrated the
proposition that among the different naciones or tribes to which the slaves
imported into the Island correspond, there are some that have greater ten-

dencies to despair, anxiety, mental disorganization, and other ordinary causes of suicide." Concluded the intendant: "The frequency and increase of suicide are due directly to those tribes with the greatest propensity to commit the crime."[27] Traveling in western Cuba during the 1830s, Charles Murray recorded the conventional wisdom among local planters concerning the diverse characteristics of the African naciones. The Macau were seen as "generally quiet, docile, and lazy," while the Mandinga were esteemed as "quiet, obedient, and honest"; the Gangá were viewed as "very mild and docile, but lazy," the Mina as "lazy, stupid, and of no marked character," and the Congo as "lazy, mischievous, and apt to run away." It was among the Carabalí and the especially the Lucumí, of Yoruban kingdoms, that the propensity toward suicide was most conspicuously associated. The Carabalí were described as "very industrious and avaricious; also choleric and hasty in temper." The Lucumí were seen as "very proud and haughty; they are brave, and are often known to commit suicide, under the irritation of punishment or disgrace." The Lucumí, wrote José María de la Torre, "are imported from the Slave Coast . . . [and] constitute the majority of slaves [in Cuba]. They are distinguished by the markings on their cheeks; their strength is ideal for work but they are indomitable and possess propensities to suicide by hanging."[28]

The character and composition of the population of enslaved Africans in Cuba responded in large measure to shifting historical circumstances, outcomes related to European rivalries as well as West African conflicts. It happened that the expansion of Cuban plantation agriculture and the heightened demand for African slave labor during the early decades of the nineteenth century coincided with the disintegration of the Yoruban kingdoms of West Africa. Political upheaval and civil war after the 1810s plunged the Yoruba into years of strife and upheaval, producing social disruption and economic dislocation in countless numbers of towns and villages. The wars served to augment the supply of African slaves, and specifically the expansion of enslavement among the Yoruban people, as the warring Yoruban armies sold their captives to slave traders.[29] "Captives from the wars," wrote military historian Robert Smith, "provided the bulk of the slaves exported via the markets of Dahomey and the Lagos lagoon. . . . The supply of slaves was greatly increased and . . . the appetite for taking captives who could be profitably disposed of in this way probably prolonged particular campaigns and may also have prolonged the general state of warfare."[30] Previously one of the principal procurers of slaves for the Atlantic trade, vast numbers of Yoruba themselves passed into the mar-

ket of the enslaved at the precise moment of greatest need among producers in Cuba. "In the beginning of the nineteenth century," historian
F. Amaury Talbot wrote in his study of southern Nigeria, "the Yoruba perhaps suffered more from slavery than any other West African people."[31]
Thus it was that the Lucumí constituted one of the principal ethnic groups
to arrive in Cuba during the early nineteenth century, eclipsing in numbers previous human cargoes of Mandinga and Congo peoples, and estab-
lishing a preponderant cultural influence in the plantations of western
Cuba.

Suicide among Africans responded to a combination of complex but
interrelated adaptive strategies. Comments by contemporary observers
concerning the ritual practices attending suicide alluded to religious beliefs related to the idea of death as a means of resurrection and return to
Africa, and hence freedom. The proposition of suicide suggested the possibility of a new mode of being, no less than the emancipation of the soul
and its transmigration to Africa, and often implied the power of physical transport.[32] "Some nations (pueblos) are more prone to suicide than
others," observed Cuban philosopher José de la Luz y Caballero in 1847.
"The British for being gloomy. The Lucumís for their bravery and love of
their freedom." Fredrika Bremer commented on slave suicide during her
travel in Cuba: "This is frequently the case among the Luccomées, who
appear to be among the noblest tribes of Africa, and it is not long since
eleven Luccomées were found hanging from a guasima-tree—a tree which
has long, horizontal branches. They had each one bound his breakfast in a
girdle around him; for the African believes that such as die here immediately arise again to a new life in their native land." Abiel Abbot learned
during his visit to Cuba in the late 1820s of the widespread practice of suicide among slaves, based on "the expectation of returning by death to their
native country." Abbot noted that "this principle is so strong in the Carro-
baleés that suicide is frequent among them. On one estate eight of these
misguided men were found hanging in company, in one night."[33] Charles
Murray was visiting a sugar estate when a messenger informed the owner
that a slave had hanged himself. Murray recorded the incident:

> On inquiry, he proved to be a young man of the Lucumi tribe. He had
> not been in the island above nine or ten months. . . . He committed
> this suicide under circumstances which . . . usually accompany such an
> action among the negroes: he asked for new suit of clothes, which hap-

pened to be due to him at this time, and put them on; he then took his pig, his 'machete' . . . and whatever moveable property he possessed, and gathering it all into a heap under a tree, hung himself over it. This is doubtless owing to a superstition prevalent in his tribe, that in the world to which he was going, such articles would be useful to him.[34]

"Many African slaves commit suicide," observed José Antonio Saco, "not for the purpose of killing themselves, but rather to live, for they believe that in committing suicide . . . they return to their land to enjoy life once again."[35] In the novel *Francisco* (1875), Anselmo Suárez y Romero depicts the suicide of the slave Francisco, who longs to return to Africa: "In the afternoon Ricardo and Don Antonio, . . . looking out toward the wooded portion of the estate, noticed a flock of vultures circling over a guásima tree, a sure sign of the presence of a dead animal. They approached the tree to investigate, and at first found nothing on the ground, nothing under the guásima and nothing in the vicinity of the tree, until they raised their heads and saw a slave hanging from one of the highest branches, already swollen and picked at by the vultures. The slave was Francisco. At nightfall four of Francisco's friends, slaves of the nación Minas, lowered him from the guásima, and carrying him on their shoulders sang according to the tradition of their land."[36]

The longing to return home insinuated itself into complex religious beliefs that contemplated suicide as a means of release and relief from bondage. "'Tis their belief that when they die they return home to their own country and friends again," observed Captain Thomas Phillips during one middle passage voyage. Another slaver recounted a conversation with a women who was being flogged for not eating: "She had said, the night before she died, 'She was going to see her friends.'"[37] Nineteenth-century anthropologist Henri Dumont, who studied slavery in Cuba while resident on sugar estates, wrote extensively on suicide among the Lucumí. "The frequency of suicide among the Lucumí," commented Dumont, "the ease with which they abandon life, is due to their religious beliefs. They are always found dressed in their best clothing, and gather at the foot of a tree a substantial ration of victuals. All these preparations indicate their belief in making body and soul a long trip to their native land. In the early times of slavery the desire to undertake this eternal trip expanded like an epidemic and suicide inflicted serious losses among many dotaciones."[38] Richard Kimball commented during his travels in Cuba on "the poor African, condemned to a toil not less incessant than severe . . . encouraged to suicide, by the superstition which he believes, of the immediate return of his body to Africa after death." Observed Maturin Ballou in 1854: "Another tribe, known as the Carrobalees, are highly esteemed by the planters, but yet they are avoided when first imported, from the fact that they have a belief and hope, very powerful among them, that after death they will return to their native land, and therefore, actuated by a love of home, these poor exiles are prone to suicide."[39]

The act of hanging often conformed to prescriptive modes. These typically included the selection of the guásima tree, believed to have magical powers, preceded by careful preparations that involved gathering at the site of death foodstuff and tools deemed necessary for the journey into the next life.[40] Investigating the suicide of Nepomoceno Lucumí in Matanzas in 1844, the local government attorney (*fiscal*) concluded that "Nepomoceno was affected by the same ideas that so many of his nación so readily believe, that after their death they again return to their land." The intendant in Cuba described the circumstances of slave suicides during the 1840s: "To commit suicide [slaves] never adopt any means other than hanging themselves from the trees or in their huts. In preparing to do so, they dressed themselves with all their clothes, gather their uneaten food in their hats, and even take with them to the site where they are to die the animals they own, the better to return to their native land well provisioned, where they believe they go body and soul."[41]

Historian Michael Gomez studied Igbo folklore in which reference to flying Africans, associated principally with African-born slaves, appeared as a metaphor for suicide and one of the preferred ways by which to escape from bondage and return to Africa. Runaway slave Esteban Montejo vigorously denied that slaves in Cuba ever committed suicide. Rather, he insisted, "they escaped by flying," and added: "They flew through the sky and left to return to their own lands. The Musundi Congos were the ones who flew the most; they disappeared by way of witchcraft. . . . I know this inside out, and it is absolutely true."[42] In the region around Trinidad, Mandinga slaves were said to have "flown in groups, returning to their native land." On the Corojal sugar estate, twenty Mandingas from one ingenio successively hanged themselves from trees in a small forest adjoining the estate. In response, planter Miguel Cantero ordered the entire forest leveled.[43]

Suicide also served to set in relief complex formulations of honor and self-esteem. The Lucumí and Carabalí were known to kill themselves in response to humiliation associated with public floggings and mutilations.[44] "Their pride is such that they will rarely endure punishment," observed

William Henry Hurlbert. A report of the suicide of the Lucumí Teofilo on the Encarnación coffee estate in 1848 indicated the "the overseer had to reprimand [Teofilo] for carelessness, and this he did with a scolding and preparing to mete out some lashes, the black immediately fled to avoid the whipping." Teofilo was subsequently found hanging from a mango tree on the estate. Commented overseer Elías Rodríguez: "It is very common that [slaves] from the Lucumí nación hanged themselves." In another instance, a slave was punished for having slept late, whereupon he made straight for the engine house and proceeded to kill himself by placing his head into the gears of the iron rollers.[45] Luciano Lucumí attempted to cut his throat with a primitive knife fashioned during his incarceration in solitary confinement. An investigation into the suicide of Nicolás Carabalí of the coffee estate Sivanacán reported finding ten recent whip lacerations on his back. Damián Lucumí hanged himself after having received twenty-five lashes.[46] One traveler to Cuba recounted an instance when a planter singled out one of eight newly arrived Africans for punishment: "The punishment of the whip is applied to the delinquent lying on his face, and when he was ordered to place himself in that position, the other seven lay down with him, and insisted on being also punished. Their request, however, was not granted, but they were told that if at any time they required it, punishment would be inflicted." The planter recounted what happened next:

> The boy was punished before breakfast, when the contra-mayoral . . . came to the door, and advised me to go to the negroes, for they were greatly excited. . . . I immediately seized my pistols, and getting on my horse rode with him to the spot. The eight negroes, each one with a rope tied around his neck, on seeing us, scattered in different directions in search of trees on which to hang themselves. Assisted by the other slaves we made all haste to secure them, but two succeeded in killing themselves; the rest, having been cut down before life was extinct, recovered.[47]

Runaway slaves (*cimarrones*) frequently killed themselves rather than be captured alive, for it was commonly known that slaveholders reserved the severest punishments for captured runaways. Historian José Luciano Franco wrote of cimarrón Vicente "Coba" Sánchez, who "rather than surrender preferred to kill himself, plunging to his death from the heights overlooking the Quiviján river."[48] One slave who fled the Vista Hermosa plantation was found dead two months later in the *platanal* (banana plantation) of the same estate. An autopsy revealed that he had starved to death, which led authorities to conclude that he had committed suicide: "The fertile fields of Cuba are filled always with means of subsistence and this fact makes the Public Ministry believe that [he] killed himself voluntarily."[49]

Suicide was not uncommon among slaves who participated in unsuccessful rebellions, who upon capture could expect certain death by torture as an example to deter others. During one period of slave insurrections in the 1830s and 1840s, scores of slaves committed suicide as an alternative preferable to being captured alive. After an unsuccessful rebellion in Aguacate in 1835, ten slaves hanged themselves. Eight years later, in Alcancía, another forty slaves committed suicide. "Fear of being punished or implicated in the conspiracies discovered in Matanzas in 1843 and 1844," reported the intendant of Cuba, "induced a large number of free people of color and slaves to commit suicide."[50]

For reasons not entirely clear, the overwhelming majority of the suicides reported on the plantations were committed by male slaves. This is not to suggest that women did not kill themselves. On the contrary, archival records preserve occasional accounts of female suicide. One report gave account of Basilia, on the sugar estate San José Beytias in Puerto Príncipe, who in 1838 ended her life by plunging into a well. The Lucumí Carmen of the San Sebastián sugar estate in the area of Mariel hanged herself from a cedar tree in 1844. She had apparently run away from the plantation and chose suicide rather than return to the estate. Another 1884 report gave account of the Conga Eustaquia, of the coffee estate Numancia in Matanzas, who committed suicide by cutting her throat.[51] In fact, however, reports of women committing suicide seem to be the exception, and would suggest that the numbers of enslaved women who died at their own hands were comparatively few.

❧ The statistics of slave suicide in Cuba are available mostly in fragmentary form, but the fragments serve to suggest larger patterns of mortality on the plantation, specifically those circumstances under which slaves determined to end their own lives. Suicide rates appeared to have approached epidemic proportions during the early decades of the nineteenth century. Over the course of the seven years from 1839 to 1845, the audiencia recorded a total of 1,337 suicides in the jurisdiction of the Western Department of the island. This tabulation included 115 suicides among whites, 51 within the population of free people of color, and 1,171 suicides among slaves. Between 1839–40 and 1841–42, the number of suicides among slaves increased from 285 deaths to 449. During 1843–44, the number of slave suicides declined slightly to 403. The "crime [of sui-cide] has risen in an astonishing manner," reported the audiencia in 1846, calculating the rate at 6.1 per every 10,000 slaves. On the basis of the total slave population in the Western Department, it appears that the annual suicide rate approached 104 per 100,000 slaves.[52]

These statistics do not include data for the entire island. Omitted from the report was information on mortality rates in the Eastern Department, in those zones beyond the jurisdictional authority of the audiencia of Ha-vana. Records available for the East suggest that suicide among slaves on local estates was not as prevalent as in the Western Department. There may be a number of explanations for this difference, but certainly the ethnic composition of the dotaciones must be considered as a factor of im-portance. Comparatively fewer Lucumí slaves reached the eastern planta-tions, which were worked principally by the Congo and Carabalí.[53]

It must be presumed, too, that incidents of slave suicide were under-reported. Both the data-collecting capacity of the colonial government and the data-providing propensity of slaveholders contributed to less than complete accounts, particularly from distant and outlying estates. Even within the Western Department, audiencia authorities suspected, the rate of suicide among slaves was far greater than official reports indicated. Be-tween 1839 and 1844, for example, the audiencia identified an additional 238 deaths among slaves believed to be the result of suicide. "No one doubts," the fiscal of the audiencia acknowledged, "that owners and ad-ministrators of the estates to which the dotaciones belong hide this infor-mation to avoid investigation by the authorities." Bishop of Havana Fran-cisco Fleix y Solans similarly informed Captain General José Gutiérrez de la Concha that "the plague of suicide . . . is far more grave than appears [to civil authorities]. The information that reaches me from parishes across the island indicates that many cases of those unfortunate deeds pass un-reported and do not come to the attention of the audiencia or the Superior Government of Your Excellency."[54]

🙚🙘 Planters devised a variety of strategies to dissuade, discourage, or otherwise deter slaves from resorting to suicide, with varying degrees of success. Corpses were often burned in full view of the dotación, to dem-onstrate to the living that the bodies of the dead would not be "flying" back to Africa. Commenting on the frequency of suicide among slaves of sugar estates, one plantation physician noted: "[They] believe that by hanging themselves they are going to be reborn in the land of their birth. Thus, many blacks have been found hanging from trees, with their bundle of clothes and provisions for their journey at their feet. This practice has been well discouraged by burning the cadavers in the presence of their companions, with the objective of dissuading them from similar ideas."[55] Traveler Abiel Abbot described one planter who "collected the negroes on the plantation [and] reduced the corpse to ashes, and dispersed it to the winds, in terror to the survivors, and in discouragement to future suicide." Mary Gardner Lowell made frequent notations of slave suicides in her travel journal while visiting plantations in Havana and Matanzas. An entry written March 6, 1831, in Camarioca read: "Within a very short time one has hung & another scalded himself to death. It is the custom to burn the bodies of those who commit suicide to deter the rest from a similar act for the blacks have an expectation of meeting their friends in the next world and they imagine if the body is burnt that it is dispersed to the winds & cannot unite again & get to heaven."[56]

Authorities also contemplated ways to counter African religious beliefs with Catholic religious instruction, to replace one belief system that imagined suicide as a means of releasing the soul to return to Africa with another that viewed suicide as condemnation of the soul to everlasting perdition. "It is very common that some blacks hang themselves," observed intendant Juan Agustín Ferré as early as 1826, "particularly the Carabalí, with the preposterous idea that they return to their native land. It is very important to adopt measures to destroy this fatal belief, using religion to convince them of their error." The audiencia of Havana attributed suicide to "Africans preoccupied with erroneous beliefs difficult to dispel." Local authorities attributed the suicide of Salvador Gangá "to the consequences of the ignorance that is so common among his people." The "most powerful deterrent to the tendency toward suicide," fiscal José Giralt predicted in 1858, "cannot be found in anywhere other than in the beneficial influence of religion and morality. The proper instillment of religious sentiment will fully guarantee an end to the frightful practice of suicide, prohibited in the Ten Commandments and so thoroughly repudiated in canonical law."[57] Bishop of Havana Francisco Fleix y Solans similarly advocated the expansion of religious instruction as the most efficacious method of reducing suicide among the dotaciones of the island. "The number of suicides is frightful," Fleix y Solans wrote, insisting that "this crime, or obsession, or madness, or fatalism, disappears entirely from those people as soon as they receive the principles of our religion, to whose salutary influence the world owes the incalculable advantages of civilization." The bishop insisted that "the measure deemed most propitious is religious education of slaves in order that their customs can be reformed to the benefit of the State and their owners (*dueños*)," concluding: "Rare are the occasions, and almost never verified, that a black slave is known to commit suicide when sufficiently instructed in the truths and mysteries of our Divine Religion." The dearth of priests on the island together with planter opposition had made evangelization among Africans all but impossible, Fleix y Solans complained. He urged the deployment of Franciscan missionaries—known for their "severe discipline and religious austerity"—among the sugar estates as remedy to suicide, noting:

> The frightful suicide for which the black race is known did not exist when our clergy had responsibility to indoctrinate the slaves in the principles of our Holy Faith, when plantation owners (*dueños de ingenios*) were prohibited from having a determined number of slaves without priest to attend to their customs and their catechism. . . . It is necessary for the Church and if necessary the State to attend to the religious instruction of slaves, for it is an indisputable truth that from the moment that man is persuaded that his life and death are in the hands of God as sole arbitrator, to whom it corresponds exclusively the right to extend or end his days, and that it is the disposition of the Supreme Being that determines his fate, he will abstain from this crime and will live in resignation with his tribulations, even under the most horrible and calamitous of circumstances.[58]

Catholicism also promised to reduce suicide by providing the men and women suffering under the yoke of slavery a source of comfort and consolation. Fiscal Ignacio García Olivares recognized the usefulness of Catholicism as a means to combat suicide among slaves. "[We] deduce from these developments," García Olivares concluded, "that *something* in our slavery leads to suicide, and that *something* . . . is the lack of religious education. . . . It is not necessary to have spent much time in our countryside to learn that with few exceptions . . . slaves do not have any more religion than the stupid idiolatry they brought from the land of their birth. . . . There is no need to look for other causes." The savage people of the New World at the time of the Spanish conquest were "pacified less by armies than by missionaries." It was necessary to end the practice of idolatry among slaves, "to inculcate in half-savage Africans, of ignorant and of ferocious character, . . . the civilizing principles of the religion of Jesus (*la religión del cruci-*

ficado), which will result in lessening the inclination to criminal acts, with great advantages to their owners." He continued:

> Without religion to regulate their lives, they will neither adequately discharge the work to which they are assigned nor develop the loyalty to their master; without religion that instructs and guides them, that teaches them that beyond this world—where one is tested (*lugar de pruebas*)—exists another world of magnificent and eternal glory for those who suffered their misfortune on earth with resignation and who with perfection met their duty to suffer. [Without religion] it is materially impossible that they serve well or preserve a life that is for them an unbearable weight. Finding themselves between the whip and work they abhor, on one hand, and an immediate death, on the other, [slaves] frequently choose the latter, because they are without the Divine Religion that allows those who suffer privation and servitude to persist not only with resignation but with complacency. The spread of Christianity in Rome gained the largest number of converts among slaves, for it revealed itself as the religion of those who suffer and it was soon realized that Christians were the most submissive, the most industrious, and the most loyal slaves. . . . Religious instruction is the most efficacious remedy of the hardships that accompany slavery, through which we seek the alleviation—unable to obtain complete cessation—of the ills that we deplore.[59]

❧ The option of suicide offered enslaved Africans an alternative to bondage, a means through which to negotiate amelioration of conditions of daily life, even if the medium of exchange implicated the forfeiture of their own lives—especially because it implicated the forfeiture of their lives.[60] The deed of self-destruction, in the end, as a recourse impossible to deny a slave determined to commit suicide, came to represent that final act through which the reach of oppression was negated. "[My] purpose," explained one slave who unsuccessfully attempted to commit suicide, "was to end [my] life and obtain respite from the punishment of the slave master."[61]

Suicide thus made possible a mode of resistance, a response registered as deliverance from slavery, to be sure, but at the same time possessed of the capacity to modify the reciprocal bonds through which slave and slaveholder were inexorably linked. That the terms of these bonds were mostly fixed does not mean they were entirely unnegotiable. What appears stable from the distance of time was, in fact, an ongoing negotiated stability, always in the process of adaptation and accommodation. It was not necessary to contemplate suicide as an instrumental act with any objective beyond individual release; that is, the deed was not necessarily undertaken with a purpose to modify either existing circumstances or the larger condition of chattel bondage. To contemplate suicide was to detect in death the potential for freedom unavailable in life. But slaves also understood that the act of suicide signified the diminution of planter wealth and power, and in this sense awareness of the possibility offered by suicide implied a source of consciousness of agency. At least as important a consequence if not intent, hence, was the knowledge that such a diminution of planter control could be obtained through the exercise of slave volition.

Nor did planters fail to understand the larger implications of suicide among slaves. Indeed, it was within this realm of shared understandings that slave and slaveholder arrived at something approximating common interests, where the premise of power was subverted and subject to the overriding larger logic of mutual benefits and the structural conditions of everyday life modified.

The act of self-destruction offered a slave a means to deny a planter the service of labor, and indeed in so doing struck at the very raison d'être of the slave system. This was resistance with a vengeance, a way to settle a score and exact a toll. Suicide offered a slave an immediate and direct way by which to strike back at a slaveholder, a practice that sociologist Mervyn Jeffreys has identified as "Samsonic suicide," by which the determination to die signified an act of revenge.[62] Estate physician Francisco Barrera y Domingo described one instance in which anger was channeled into the deed of self-destruction. Africans "are so offended that when they are called dogs they will kill themselves when it is least expected," Barrera y Domingo observed, and added: "Ordered by the master or overseer to kneel at his feet, the slave often refuses, insisting that only to God does the act of kneeling belong and not to the white man, who is a man just like him, and perhaps even more vicious and evil. In those instances that slaves are punished, since they can not strike back against the person who does them harm, they take revenge on themselves in response to the rage they have against the white man."[63]

Slave suicide challenged the power of the slaveholder, always as a protest, as an act of resistance and rebellion no less than a strike against the economic interests of the slaveholder. The decision to die was transformed as the exercise of the option of freedom. It was through the enactment of suicide, as an act of last recourse, that the enslaved person gained agency and the possibility of advantage in the otherwise unequal struggle against power. The deed of suicide was an act of defiance, a challenge to the authority of the planter, contesting and canceling the premise of power over the life of the slave. The possibility of suicide could thus serve as a means of deterrence, a way to contain or otherwise counter the excesses of slavery. In the end, suicide signaled escape from bondage, the one outcome to which the entire logic of the slave system was dedicated to preventing. Slaves held final power over their lives; they could choose whether or not to exercise that power with complete and uncontested finality.[64]

The larger implications of suicide resided in the capacity of the deed to challenge the premise by which slaveholders presumed to exercise power, and as a consequence modify or otherwise mediate the conditions of slavery. Suicide was a means of agency of last resort, available to the powerless without prospects, to be sure, but a means of agency nonetheless, with the capacity to fashion the reciprocities by which slave and slaveholder were inexorably bound to each other. It could create the opportunity to negotiate the exercise of power, contained in the knowledge that while the slaveholder had power over property, the slave had power over labor. In circumstances where the will to live was itself contingent upon the condition of daily life, the slaveholder was increasingly obliged to negotiate the moral terms and material conditions of slave life. Indeed, the very efficacy of the labor system upon which the plantation depended was increasingly derived from circumstances that more fully accommodated the needs of the dotación. The degree to which the balance of power ebbed at all in favor of slaves was in the end partly a function of the capacity of suicide to overturn the assumptions upon which slavery existed. Slaveholders did not fail to infer correctly the larger meaning of suicide. The challenge was in the act, in the exemplary function of the deed through which others of the dotación could contemplate similar choices as a response to similar circumstances.

The extent to which suicide—the act accomplished or merely attempted—served to mitigate the harshness of everyday slave life is not always clear. The evidence is fragmentary but suggestive. W. O. Blake's nineteenth-century account of slavery documented how the determination of one African slave to die through starvation during the middle passage created the conditions of improved treatment: "Mild means were then used to divert him from his resolution, as well as promises that he should have anything he wished for: but still he refused to eat." This was the counsel offered by Francisco Barrera y Domingo, who urged that when "a black succumbs to grief and becomes melancholic, if one does not want him inevitably to die, there is no alternative but to display kindness and provide him with some affectionate satisfaction so that the offended black comes to understand that the injuring party is repentant for having treated him thusly."[65]

❖ The willingness of Africans to take their own lives assumed new urgency at midcentury. Strategies of sugar production had long been shaped by assumptions of an inexhaustible supply of slaves at low prices. Planters could exact remorselessly the labor of Africans for immediate gain, confident that slaves thus worked to death could be replaced by more slaves easily and cheaply. "The worst of this," notes Isabel, a protagonist in Cirilo Villaverde's novel, *Ceclia Valdés* (1839), "was the strange apathy, the passivity, the inhuman indifference with which the slaveholders . . . looked upon the suffering, the illnesses, and even the death of slaves. As if their lives mattered to nobody under any circumstance. . . . Was not the preservation or the prolongation of the life of the slave in the interest of the slaveholder [as] working capital (*capital vivente*)?"[66]

And it was indeed the matter of *capital vivente* that developed into a concern of abiding preoccupation among producers during the middle decades of the nineteenth century. The issue of treatment of slaves had mattered less to planters earlier in the century during a time of expanding sugar production and rising profits, when the supply of slaves was plentiful and the prices were low, than later, when the suppression of the legal slave trade drove planters from the open market to clandestine negotiations, where risks were commensurately higher and demands on diminishing supply correspondingly greater, when the replenishment of slaves was more difficult, more haphazard, and, of course, more expensive. It is likely too that the toll of cholera epidemics on the plantations during the 1830s had further depleted the labor force precisely at a time of diminishing supply of slaves.

The impact of slave suicide in this environment cannot be minimized. "The void that [slave suicide] leaves cannot be filled," warned Governor General Leopoldo O'Donnell in 1847. "This is a matter of the greatest importance, for the future of the Island depends on it." The *Boletín de Colonización* was explicit: "The lack of workers (*falta de brazos*) that is every year felt with greater adversity in our agriculture and industry suggests the need to put into effect every possible means to attract to the Island sufficient numbers of workers to meet our necessities."[67]

The decline of slave imports after the 1840s had immediate effects, and almost everywhere in Cuba placed the very solvency of the plantations in jeopardy. The inexorable logic of the law of supply and demand was carried to its inescapable end. Slaves valued at 300 pesos in the 1820s were sold for as much as 900 pesos in the 1840s. Slaves possessing specialized skills, including carpenters, masons, boilermakers, and machinists—classified as *los negros de primera clase*—were often sold for more than 1,000 pesos each. Traveler Joseph Dimock reported even higher prices during his travels in Cuba during the 1850s. "An able bodied male slave is now valued at an average of $1200 to $1500," he recorded in his diary, "and some good house servants are held at over $2000." David Turnbull learned during his visit to the Alejandra estate in Güines that sugar production was in a state of crisis due to a condition he ascribed "to a deficiency of labour." Turnbull drew the obvious inference: "The dilapidation had arisen in the ordinary course of nature, no fresh Bozals having been purchased to supply the place of those who had been carried off by that stern law of mortality which so rapidly and ruthlessly cuts down the gangs of negro labourers on the sugar estates of this country."[68]

As the supply of slaves declined and the price of new slaves rose, the value of old slaves increased. So too did concern over mortality rates, and almost immediately attention focused on suicide. The lives of slaves now mattered. In the calculus that was slavery, the death of plantation workers signified a diminution of capital stock and depletion of the labor force; it increased the cost of doing business and lowered the margin of profit. "The health of the black slaves," counseled one administrator, "is for their owners as useful as it is necessary, upon which the subsistence and all their wealth depends."[69] This was to understand slaves as an item in the budgetary outlay in the operation of the plantation, their value set by the larger circumstances of supply and demand and measured against shifting commodity values, production overhead, and replacement costs. At some point in the mid-nineteenth century, it made eminently good economic sense to prolong the working life of the slave.

Exhortations from colonial officials also called for the improvement of the treatment of slaves, and specifically for the amelioration of living conditions of the dotación. "Without the labor of Africans on the island of Cuba . . . ," warned plantation physician Honorato Bernard de Chateusalins, "agriculture, the foundation of the prosperous state of this beautiful land, would quickly be reduced to the final state of decadence."[70] Authorities understood that the sources of suicide were contained within the very circumstances of slavery. Attention was repeatedly drawn to the relationship between the physical treatment of slaves and the maintenance of the labor force upon which the prosperity of the colony depended. "The principal cause of the frequency of suicide with which we are concerned," warned the intendant, "is the very state of servitude. However mild (*suave*) the condition of slavery may be, and even though the fate of the slave imported from Africa may seem materially superior to the scarcity and uncertainty in which the majority of day workers in Europe live, freedom is and always will be the preferable state for these laborers."[71]

The implications of slave suicide in a context of diminishing supplies of slaves at midcentury was apparent to colonial authorities. Most immediately, suicide acted to induce officials to consider ways to ameliorate the circumstances of slavery. As early as 1845, Governor General Leopoldo O'Donnell made a number of suggestions designed to reduce slave mortality on the sugar estates. "It is most important," O'Donnell exhorted, "to reduce the number of work hours on the sugar plantations to rational proportions to bring about the conservation of the robustness and life of the slaves for a longer time. These hours, which presently are distributed in a way that hardly leaves the worker the time necessary for food and for rest, should be arranged in a way that would allow prudent rest capable of avoiding his precipitous ruin."[72] Six years later, the new governor general, José Gutiérrez de la Concha, reiterated the importance of ameliorating the harsh conditions of plantation labor. "It would be convenient . . . ," de la Concha counseled, "to reduce as much as possible the natural tendency of slaves to seek their liberty, and this will be achieved if their owners paid more attention to religious instruction, if they promoted marriage among slaves, and if during certain times of the year they did not demand of slaves excessive work." He continued:

> The well-defined interests of the owners are to be served in the conduct of this class, for the reproduction [of slaves] thus obtained, with the reduction of the large number of frequent suicides, and with the prolongation of the useful life of the slaves, they will not see themselves with the necessity—as they do now—to replace every year the losses that their dotaciones experience. To the Government simply pertains the task to make the owners understand these truths so important for them and not to increase the misery of the poor slaves with undue exactions.[73]

An examination of the conditions of slavery, affirmed fiscal Ignacio González Olivares, revealed "an alarming rate of suicide." Suicide was "not a propensity inherent in the colored race," González Olivares insisted, and thereupon concluded: "It is necessary to seek in slavery the cause of the suicide of blacks." But authorities also recognized the importance of slavery to the well-being of the colonial political economy, and that the remedy for suicide could not come at the expense of slavery. "Slavery is a necessary condition," González Olivares affirmed, "indispensable for the social existence of this Island, at least for the time being. It is thus necessary to investigate ways to halt or reduce suicide without altering the order of existing Society."[74] The audiencia of Havana urged slaveholders to avoid excessive corporal punishment: "Good treatment, a reasonable work load, the assistance of the older slaves of the estate, and the constant vigilance of those responsible for the estate are principal remedies to discourage Africans from the idea of committing suicide." Indeed, the audiencia urged the imposition of sanctions on slaveholders as a way to regulate the treatment of slaves: "This office would be gratified to see enacted measures to determine if slave masters or the overseers of the estates to whom the dotación belongs meted out excessive punishment that cause a slave to commit suicide and thereupon impose a penalty upon the responsible person."[75]

Historian Manuel Moreno Fraginals identified the period of "good treatment" (*buen tratamiento*) to have commenced during the decade of the 1840s, a period in which increasing attention was given to the well-being of slaves with the specific purpose of reducing mortality rates. The objective, Moreno Fraginals suggested, was "to extend the useful life of the slave, modifying those factors that produced his premature death." This included the lessening of the severity of the work regimen, the improvement of nutrition and medical care, and the allocation of more time and land to permit slaves to cultivate small crops for their own subsistence and sale.[76] "An able-bodied slave is worth fifteen hundred dollars, and is becoming dearer every day," James O'Kelly learned from one plantation administrator during his travels in Cuba, "[and] besides, it is almost impossible to replace him, as the demand surpasses, by ever so much, the supply. Knowing this, it did not much surprise me when the director asserted that, except in extreme cases, it was not the custom on the estate to resort to severe corporal punishment." New regulatory constraints also affected the treatment of slaves. One planter, responding to the insubordination of several slaves who refused to work, turned to the local *capitán de partido*: "I asked the captain if I punished them, and they then committed suicide, would I be chargeable with the result; he answered that I certainly would be, if he found the smallest sign of injury on their bodies."[77]

These changing conditions are undoubtedly what prompted Joseph Dimock's observation during his travels in Cuba in 1859. "The slaves have more privileges than in the States," Dimock recorded in his diary, adding:

> A parcel of land is allotted to each negro every year, the products of which belong to him, and it is devoted to the cultivation of yuca, rice, okra, peanuts, sweet potations, corn, etc., etc., during his leisure hours. . . . Slaves are allowed to raise a pig, poultry, and sometimes a mare, and they can always find a market for their stock at the nearest tavern, or sell to their masters. . . . When work is pressing, a bargain is sometimes made with the slaves to labor on Feast days at about fifty cents a day. This price is allowed them also for a cord of wood cut during their own time.[78]

The reported incidents of suicide among the dotaciones diminished during the final decades of slavery in Cuba. The increase in the number of creole slaves was no doubt one factor, as the number of enslaved people socialized within the plantation system increased as a percentage of the total. By the 1880s, local observers could speak of the advances in the "moral and intellectual character" of creole slaves, who were said to have displayed "great aptitude for all types of work" and were more inclined "to imitate whites in everything that refers to the advances of civilized life. . . . In every kind of work, inability and aptitude, the creole blacks are superior to the Africans."[79] The power of melancholia and nostalgia, of memory of places and people lost, as a source of suicide diminished among the increasing numbers of slaves born and raised on the sugar estates. Striking, too, however, and no doubt related, was that as the number of suicides declined, the reported occurrence of acts of insubordination and disobedience increased, and the recorded incidents of direct confrontation between slaves and slaveholders assumed near commonplace frequency. No longer did suicide serve as a common means through which to contest the authority of planters. Increasingly the institution of slavery in colonial Cuba was challenged from within. After the 1860s, reports of instances of "improper conduct" (*conducta incorrecta*), "disobedience" (*resistencia a la obediencia*), and "insubordination and threats to the overseer" (*insubordinación y amenazas al mayoral*) increased in number and frequency.[80] African-born men and women who survived the early years of their enslavement, as well as creole slaves, became increasingly disinclined to take their own lives as a means of release from chattel bondage. "It is reported here in Havana," a *New York Times* correspondent wrote from Cuba in April 1866, "that the negroes on the estates of Zulueta, Aldama, and some other large slave owners in the jurisdiction of Matanzas had struck within the last few days, demanding to be paid for their labor. They are said to have offered no violence but to have refused to work any longer as slaves, saying they were now free."[81]

Developments such as these raise vital questions about the process of empowerment. They speak also to the changing circumstances by which the character of agency was itself transformed, and the ways in which forms of resistance changed from behaviors of self-destruction to acts of self-determination.

✴ Still one other response to the diminishing supply and rising cost of African slaves was the search for alternative sources of cheap agricultural labor. As disquiet deepened within the Cuban planter class over the future supply of Africans, sugar producers located a new source of field labor in the teeming port cities of Canton and Macao in south China. Through a complex network of intermediaries linking local contractors with foreign commission agents, Chinese laborers were contracted at a wage of 4 pesos monthly on the basis of a twelve-hour day for a service period of eight years. By terms of standard labor contract, employers were to subsidize the cost of transportation and provide food as well as lodging, medical care, and two changes of clothing annually for the full length of service. Upon the completion of the service period, employers were to defray the cost of return transportation to China.[82]

It was in the nature of market forces and modalities of sugar production to derive profits principally through the relentless exaction of human labor, on terms designed wholly to meet the needs of capital, made all the more possible by the coercive constraints that obtained—sometimes more, sometimes less—tacit political acquiescence to norms of exploitation as an acceptable means of economic development. These needs found expression in a convergence of interests between colonial producers and the colonial exchequer, where profits for the former signified revenues for the latter and where prosperity validated the efficacy of colonialism for all its beneficiaries.

The outstanding virtue of Chinese contract workers was discerned in what appeared to be an unlimited supply of labor, at costs actually lower

Chinese Quarters, Soledad Estate, ca. 1884.
From Edwin F. Atkins, *Sixty Years in Cuba* (Cambridge, Mass., 1926).

than the purchase of African slaves. Planters did not hesitate. Ramón de la Sagra dates the arrival of the first 600 Chinese contract workers to Cuba in 1847. Over the course of the next thirty years, an estimated total 125,000 Chinese workers arrived in Cuba, most of whom were distributed among the sugar estates of the western jurisdictions.[83] "The Coolie is gradually taking the place of the African negro," observed one commentator in 1865, "and his merits as a laborer are recognized even by the prejudiced and ignorant. . . . [Planters] are just beginning to realize that the Coolies are cheaper and more valuable than the negroes."[84]

At least as important as their abundant supply and low cost as contract laborers, Chinese workers also had a reputation for diligence, docility, and submissiveness. "An experience of four years," planter Francisco Diago commented in 1851, "acquired in my own home and those of my family, as well as of the opinion of neighbors, . . . has confirmed the favorable judgment I first formed at the time of the introduction of Chinese workers about their aptitude for all types of work. When a rational and humane system of work is employed, one that is harmonious with their condition and intelligence, they are controlled with the greatest of ease and without the necessity of physical violence, unlike our African slaves." Planter Urbano Feijóo Sotomayor spoke for many hacendados in Cuba: "We need men to work side by side with the slaves, and for this only the sons of a country governed with the rod will serve. This quality is found in the Chinese. . . . They are generally intelligent, pacific, obedient, and humble; they are not inclined to associate with the [blacks], and if all the planters thought as I do and maintained on their farms a line of separation between the races, I believe it would be possible to make one race a defense against the other."[85]

Death came swiftly to the Chinese in Cuba. The number of workers who perished on the plantations was at least as great as the number who survived. An imperial commission organized in 1872 by the Chinese government to investigate the conditions of laborers on the plantations estimated that a total 114,000 Chinese workers had arrived in Cuba since midcentury, out of which 53,500 had perished: that is, a mortality rate of nearly 50 percent. One survey among ten sugar estates in the jurisdiction of Havana corroborated these estimates, reporting that half the 470 Chinese workers on local plantations had perished since their arrival. But many suspected even higher mortality rates, perhaps as great as 75 percent. "Within the time of contract," New York Herald correspondent James O'Kelly reported during his travels in Cuba in 1874, "seventy-five per cent of the immigrants perish, though, for the most part, they come into the country in the prime of manhood."[86]

Death arrived from many sources. Large numbers of Chinese workers succumbed to overwork and malnutrition. Many died from an assortment of tropical diseases and illness associated with climate. But it was suicide that accounted for the largest single cause of death. The 1862 census registered a total population of 34,050 asiáticos, by which time too the rate of suicide among Chinese workers appears to have overtaken suicide among black slaves. The 1862 census data reported a total of 346 suicides, of which 173 were committed by asiáticos, 130 by slaves, and the balance by whites. The suicide of 173 asiáticos placed the Chinese suicide rate at a staggering 500 per 100,000.[87]

The high rate of suicide was acknowledged early by authorities and was typically attributed to Chinese cultural idiosyncrasies. "The rise of [mortality rates]," explained the regent of the audiencia of Havana, "is due to suicide, and the masters should make efforts to prevent it." He added: "The individuals of this race have such little attachment to life and such addiction to opium that their propensity for suicide should not cause us any surprise. Recently arrived to a strange country, subject to constant work, ignorant of our language, and finding it impossible as a result of understanding and making themselves understood, they seek in suicide through regular use of opium the end of the ills that are exaggerated in their imagination."[88]

The circumstances of suicide among Chinese laborers suggest a pattern of official inattention if not indifference to the conditions on the sugar estates. An investigation into the suicide of one worker on the ingenio San Laureano in Matanzas concluded that "he did not have any reason to kill himself and thus it can be inferred that he has committed the deed in a moment of mental derangement, for he had no conflict or dispute with anyone." In another investigation into the death of a Chinese worker on the Santo Domingo estate in Sabanilla, authorities pleaded ignorance as to the reason for the suicide, "for he has always been well treated on the estate, and it can only be attributed that said Asian suffered periodically from mental derangement, for which reason he was often confined to the infirmary."[89]

But it was more complicated. Even as producers adopted the strategies of *buen tratamiento* of slaves, they practiced remorseless exploitation of Chinese workers. Like enslaved Africans earlier in the nineteenth century, Chinese laborers were treated as disposable means to indispensable profits. The overwhelming sense of powerlessness, the relentless pattern of coercion and abuse, of violence and violation, of labor exacted through floggings, beatings, and mutilations, daily and for months at a time, combined to crush the spirit and stamina of Chinese field workers. It was all the normal facets of everyday life on the sugar plantation.

The imperial commission formed to investigate the conditions of Chinese workers in Cuba completed a detailed report of daily life on the sugar plantations in 1876. Based upon depositions and interviews of hundreds of Chinese workers, the imperial commission report preserved scores of detailed first-person narratives recounting the grim relentlessness of plantation labor. A petition prepared by laborer Li Chao-ch'un was representative:

> [Ninety] percent [of the Chinese workers] are disposed of to the sugar plantations. There the owners rely upon the administrator for the production of a large crop of sugar, and the administrator looks to the overseers for the exaction of the greatest possible amount of labour. They all think only of the profit to be gained and are indifferent as to our

lives. It matters not whether the workmen are miserable or contented, whether they starve or have enough to eat, whether they live or die. . . . The administrator who forces the Chinese to work 20 hours out of the 24 is a man of capacity, if he extorts 21 hours his qualities are of a still higher order, but he may strike, or flog, or chain us, as his fancy suggests to him. If we complain of sickness we are beaten and starved; if we work slowly dogs are urged after us to bite us.[90]

These conditions were corroborated by accounts received from other workers. Ch'en Yü-shu affirmed that "we are dealt with as dogs, horses or oxen, badly fed, and deprived of rest, so that a single day becomes a year." Chao K'un and ninety-five others petitioned that "we suffer from insufficient nourishment, excessive labour enforced night and day, flogging and chaining in the day, and imprisonment and confinement in the stocks at night, so that many have died directly of their sufferings or have tried to escape and met death outside." Hsieh Shuang-chiu described overseers as "more cruel than tigers or wolves. They have no pity in their hearts. They are as terrible as the thunder and beat us constantly with their whips or rods, or throw bricks at us, or kick us, always inflicting an injury from which sometimes death ensues."[91]

🌿 The plantation served as the site of suicide for Chinese workers in much the same fashion as it had for African slaves earlier in the nineteenth century. "No Cuban going . . . to contract for the services of a Chinese coolie ever talks about 'hiring,'" observed Antonio Gallenga in 1873; "he bluntly says he is *buying* a Chino. And the poor Chinaman, here the most unhappy of beings, seems indeed to bear the brand of slavery on his dejected brow." Added Gallenga: "There has been an incredible amount of ill treatment of these poor Asiatics; and the Government has acted with equally shameful dishonesty towards the labourers and their employers. The Chinese have been over-reached in their contracts; they have been reduced to a condition identical with that of the negroes; they have resented the indignity of the lash; they have sought revenge in fire and bloodshed."[92]

The similarities of Chinese contract labor with African slavery were striking. Plantation life was especially difficult for newly arrived Chinese workers, many of whom, like Africans before them, succumbed to a state of severe melancholia. One observer commented on the "suicidal epidemic" that erupted upon their arrival to Cuba, concluding: "We are inclined to believe that it arises from home-sickness." Eliza McHatton Riply observed close up the condition of Chinese workers employed on her sugar estate Desengaño, and commented: "Nostalgia was frequent among the newly imported. Like all diseases of a purely mental and emotional nature, its symptoms varied, usually tending to distressing melancholia, though sometimes to the desperation of suicide. . . . We heard of some shocking instances of suicide by hanging and plunging into wells." Esteban Montejo remembered: "The Chinese did not fly nor did they want to return to their own country. But they did commit suicide. They did it silently. After the passage of several days they would turn up hanging from a tree or dead on the ground. Everything they did was in silence."[93]

With the supply of labor plentiful, life was cheap. Hsieh A-ssu explained in his deposition that "the owner has urged the administrator and the overseers to flog us. He has said that it matters not if one is beaten to death as he is rich enough to buy ten others." And from another estate, Liu A-jui told a similar story, that "the owner continually urges upon the overseer that a large crop of sugar is the only matter of importance, and that no consideration should be shown to the labourers, as if one be beaten to death ten others can be purchased."[94]

Conditions led to frightful desperation, whereby suicide could enter into the realm of the reasonable and rationale, an eminently sensible response to the unbearable hardships of daily life. Unrelieved exploitation on the plantations drove vast numbers to despair and self-destruction. Traveler R. W. Gibbes commented in 1860 on the debilitating impact of the climate and the hard times the Chinese experienced during acclimatization. "They are docile," Gibbes observed, "but many of them become discontented; and if so, or if whipped, they often commit suicide, having no regard for life," adding: "The number who commit suicide is very large."[95]

Estimates vary, but perhaps as much as one-third of all deaths among Chinese workers was the result of suicide. Anecdotal first-person accounts tend to corroborate this data. Ssu T'u-hsing indicated to the imperial commission that of the 43 workers in his crew, 29 committed suicide; of the 100 men in the crew of Ch'en A-fu, 50 hanged themselves. "With me were 20 men," Lin A-i recounted, "of whom, finding the ill usage unendurable, two poisoned themselves, five hanged themselves, and four cut their throats." Wu A-ch'ing reported that "of 50 men who were with me, only 25 survive. There were suicides by drowning, hanging and cutting of the throat."[96] Complained planter José Luis Alfonso to José Antonio Saco in 1866:

Things for me (as well as for everyone else) have gone very badly with the Chinese [workers] contracted a year and a half ago. Due to suicide, runaways, and the death of some and the incapacitation of others, I have lost more than 20 percent of the labor force. They are clearly more intelligent than the blacks, but at the same time they are inferior to them in the matters of agricultural work. They have enormous difficulty learning our language. They bond to no one and nothing, including their very own lives, for they kill themselves with extraordinary ease and with the most horrific indifference. Their use of opium, when it does not kill them, renders them incapacitated.[97]

Chinese field laborers wilted from the effects of hunger and overwork. They were subjected to unspeakable cruelty, until they could endure no more. They hanged themselves by the hundreds; they drowned themselves in rivers, threw themselves into well shafts, and leaped into the boiling cauldrons and furnaces of the sugar mill; they slashed their throats and swallowed massive quantities of opium.[98] On occasions suicide was registered as an individual act; many more times workers ended their lives as collective acts. Reported instances of six or eight workers discovered dead suspended from a branch of a guásima tree were not uncommon. In 1879, 14 workers on the Dos Marías sugar estate hanged themselves in the same evening. "Suicide has been of frequent occurrence among the coolies in Cuba," commented R. J. Levis during his travels across the island in the early 1870s, "and the practice has been often followed by imitation of their associates."[99] The report of the imperial commission is filled with first-person accounts of witnesses to suicide. Li A-wu reported that he saw "three men drown themselves and five hang themselves on account of the cruelties to which they were being subjected." Li A-fu saw "four men hang themselves on account of being flogged with severity," while Feng A-hsiu reported seeing five men hang themselves.[100] "I saw a man jump into a sugar cauldron, two men hang themselves, and another wearing chains throw himself into a well," recounted Ho A-ch'eng. Li Shun saw 11 men commit suicide while Li Yu reported having witnessed 20 men kill themselves. "I saw two men hang themselves, three men throw themselves into wells, and another three poison themselves with opium," reported Li Wen-ts'ai. Li A-wu saw "three men drown themselves, and five hang themselves, on account of the cruelties to which they were being subjected." Ch'ien Yu reported seeing 28 men "hang themselves through [the] inability to endure the cruelty." The deposition of Mai A-an gave an account of two men who had hanged themselves on the plantation: "Their terms of service had expired and they were not permitted to leave."[101]

The testimony collected by the imperial commission gave grim first-person voice to the suffering of Chinese workers and acts of suicide as ordinary facets of daily life. Indeed, there were few themes in the commission report as salient as the subject of suicide. Chang Luan addressed the commissioners, explaining that "in Cuba, within its length . . . are to be found thousands of prisons, tens of thousands of fetters, and a number which cannot be counted of human beings, ever crying out under wrong and in their pain with torn and lacerated bodies, and seeking death by hanging, drowning, or poison, or the knife." Hsien Tso-pang described similar conditions: "We are fed worse than dogs, and are called upon to perform labour for which an ox or a horse would not possess sufficient strength. Everywhere cells exist, and whips and rods are in constant use, and maimed and lacerated limbs are daily to be seen. Almost daily, also, we hear of suicides of our countrymen who have hanged themselves, jumped into wells, cut their throats or swallowed opium." Yang Yüng and others recounted to the commission that "suicides by hanging on trees, by drowning, by swallowing opium, and by leaping into the sugar caldron are the results of wrongs and sufferings which cannot be described."[102]

The larger meanings associated with suicide among Chinese workers suggest recourse to self-destruction as a means of relief from unbearable conditions of life. For many, suicide was the most readily available alternative to unrelieved suffering. "The race of Coolies," observed Julia Ward Howe during her travels in Cuba, "hired at small wages for eight years, and exploitered [*sic*] for that time with murderous severity, have found a suicidal remedy that nearly touches their selfish masters. . . . Self-assassination is, surely, the most available alleviation of despotism. When Death is no longer terrible to the Enslaved, then let the Enslaver look to it."[103] In 1856, the audiencia of Havana urged hacendados to take appropriate measures to reduce the rate of suicide among Chinese workers, including religious instruction, minimum work during the period of acclimation, strict observance of the terms of the contract, the use of prizes to good behavior, and the application of strict justice to those who fail to meet their responsibilities.[104]

Suicide offered a culturally sanctioned means by which to escape from the hardships presented by plantation life. "On the plantations and farms," explained Lin Chin, "we seek refuge in death by every form of suicide." The crushing relentlessness of plantation labor, unrelieved and unremitting, sustained by cruelty and punishment, drove vast numbers to end their lives as a way to end their suffering. First-person accounts by survivors of failed suicide attempts provide insight into the desire to die. "I found the chaining and flogging so unendurable, during the first six months of my service, that I attempted suicide by cutting my throat, and a month elapsed before the wound was healed," recounted Wang Chin. The deposition of Huang Hsing reported that "on the plantation we are constantly chained and beaten, but dare not complain to the officials through fear of being subjected to even greater cruelties. I myself made an attempt to cut my throat."[105]

But this was also suicide as a mode of resistence and means of revenge, specifically to choose to die as a way to retaliate against the planter and avenge past wrongs. Contemporary observers often attributed vindictive tendencies to Chinese workers and pointed to suicide as one of the more prominent manifestations of vengeful behavior. "Sometimes [suicide] seems to have been accomplished in a spirit of vindictiveness towards their employers," observed R. J. Levis of Chinese suicides in Cuba, and added: "The Chinese laborers are of mild and tractable temperament, seem to be contented with their humble duties, and are submissive to the abuse to which they are on some plantations subjected; but when once their revengeful nature is aroused, they mutually combine with each other and have proved dangerous in their rage." James O'Kelly described the Chinese as "revengeful," and said they "are looked on as dangerous. This is due to their superior intelligence, and their keener sense of the wrong done to them." In an 1876 study of Chinese contract workers in Cuba, Manuel Villanueva took note of "a will power infinitely superior to that of the black," with "a fatalism of a good Oriental that disposes him to carry his rancor to the ultimate extreme, with extraordinary cold bloodedness and to sacrifice everything for the purpose of satisfying the most trifling desire for revenge."[106] Reflecting on the suicide of 173 Chinese workers in 1862, José Antonio Saco concluded that the Chinese were "such a corrupt and perverse race that [suicide] was not unusual." Saco continued: "Suicide is very frequent among them. But it is not the frequency of suicide that is noteworthy. Rather, it is the motive that often drives them to suicide, for they kill themselves for the pure purpose of vengeance."[107]

Revenge through suicide, moreover, seems to have been undertaken in the belief that the spirit of the person thus driven to take his own life would return, possessed of the power to avenge in death all the wrongs endured in life, a way of taking revenge upon a tormentor who was otherwise out of reach. The act of dying was a method of transformation, empowering a person weak in life with strength in death to take revenge.[108]

Chinese cultural practices and all that gave them value were transported to Cuba. That colonial authorities, planters, and overseers appeared to have been neither susceptible to nor influenced by the purport of self-destruction does not make the meaning of suicide any less comprehensible. "In China," observed missionary M. Huc in 1860, "it is often the weak who make the strong and powerful tremble, by holding suspended over their heads the threat of suicide, and forcing them by that means to do them justice, spare them, and help them. The poor have recourse sometimes to this terrible extremity, to avenge themselves for the hardheartedness of the rich, and it is by no means unusual to repel an insult by killing yourself." There is, of course, no evidence that "the strong and powerful" in Cuba trembled. On the contrary, as demographer Juan Pérez de la Riva observed in his study of the Chinese in Cuba, "unfortunately, the coolies cost little and were easy—very easy—to replace, as a result of which neither the planters nor the government paid much attention to their death."[109]

Suicide was also intended to shame employers who, by implication, were complicit in the deed of self-destruction, serving as a way to expose employers for having failed to discharge responsibilities commensurate with their status and obligations. Commented Huc:

The extreme readiness with which the Chinese are induced to kill themselves, is almost inconceivable; some mere trifle, a word almost, is sufficient to cause them to hang themselves, or throw themselves to the bottom of the well; the two favourite modes of suicide. In other countries, if a man wishes to wreak his vengeance on an enemy, he tries to kill him; in China, on the contrary, he kills himself. This anomaly depends upon various causes, of which are the principal:—In the first place, Chinese law throws the responsibility of a suicide on those who may be supposed to be the cause or occasion it. It follows, therefore, that if you wish to be revenged on an enemy, you have only to kill yourself to be sure of getting him into horrible trouble; for he falls immediately into the hand of *justice*, and will certainly be tortured and ruined, if not deprived of life. . . . It is to be remarked also, that public opinion, so far from disapproving of suicide, honours and glorifies it. The conduct of a man who destroys his own life, to avenge himself on an enemy whom he has not other way of reaching, is regarded as heroic and magnanimous.[110]

Chinese workers arrived to Cuba imbued with a legal tradition whereby one who incited another to suicide, like one who committed manslaughter, was subject to punishment and thereby possessed of a means with which an aggrieved party, through the act of self-destruction, could exact revenge against his tormentors. By terms of the criminal code of the Ch'ing dynasty (1644–1911), persons determined guilty of having provoked or otherwise induced the act of suicide were subject to criminal prosecution. Under these circumstances, an individual who by word, or deed, or conduct instigated a suicide, whether by design or not, was held legally responsible for the crime of suicide. José Antonio Saco took note of the larger meaning of "vindictive suicide" among the Chinese in Cuba: "The Chinese worker has a quarrel with another person in his country, and he believes that by killing himself judicial authorities will hold his adversary responsible for his death. Hence, he does not hesitate in killing himself as a means to entangle his antagonist in a judicial proceeding and thereby seeking to cause him as much harm as possible."[111]

The Chinese criminal code contemplated the proximate causes of suicide as well as the immediate ones, particularly in instances in which a person, by failing to discharge those duties commensurate with positions of status and authority, induced another to commit suicide. Driving a subordinate to suicide through abusive treatment or other affronts to personal dignity was a punishable offense.[112] While traveling in China during the 1880s, C. F. Gordon Cumming took note of the "terribly numerous" incidents of suicide, observing: "It is rare for a week to pass without one such case, and sometimes there are several within the week; and all for absurdly trivial causes—such as small domestic quarrels, or a wish to spite some one else by getting him into trouble, as being by Chinese law accountable for the death of the person thus aggravated beyond endurance."[113]

That this purpose may have had little cultural relevance to the circumstances of power in nineteenth-century Cuba should not, of course, obscure intent. The reflexive function of suicide contemplated the gesture as a rational act intended as a deed of retribution. Under different circumstances, and at a later time, this purpose would indeed acquire relevance to the Cuban condition.

✨ Decisions of life and death on the nineteenth-century plantations were acted out as a complex drama, daily, where often the circumstances of either one or both were shaped by forces originating in faraway places. The degree to which cruelty, including the use of violence and the systematic infliction of pain, the application of physical punishment to obtain submission and acquiescence, served as the modus operandi of the labor regimen of the plantation more than adequately set in place the social relations upon which much of the colonial economy depended. The use of force as the ordinary and commonplace method of discipline and control achieved the desired results, of course—at least most of the time.

But the resort to violence as a means of social control had other, long-lasting effects. It also acted to reduce the space of autonomy and limit the range of agency, both of which enhanced the efficacy of suicide as a means by which to affirm control of one's life. That suicide was practiced on such a scale and, more, that the deed of suicide gained currency as an option preferable to the endurance of continued exploitation and oppression entered the larger discursive formulations of the sensibility of Cubans. An act denounced by the planter class and colonial government as barbaric, associated with idolatry, insanity, and economic loss, was subsequently appropriated by opponents to slavery and advocates of independence as a deed of exemplary value, a model of dignity and self-esteem worthy of emulation. The deed of suicide as representation of protest against injustice and affirmation of liberty insinuated itself deeply into the narrative of a people, loaded with meanings of self-definition and self-determination, of individual valor and collective virtue.

To Die for the *Patria*

THE LOGIC OF EXEMPLARY DEATH AND THE FORMATION OF NATION

2

Run to combat, men of Bayamo
May the Patria be proud of you.
Do not fear a glorious death,
For to die for the Patria is to live
    "La Bayamesa" (national anthem of Cuba) (1868)

The patria! How great is the feeling that one has for it! It
supercedes everything, it changes all of us, it sweeps all of
us along, without ever looking back upon the path that
our course has taken; inconsolable mothers, grieving
wives, abandoned children—all draped by the black and
red shawl that is bequeathed to them by the war as an
indelible memory.
    Colonel Avelino Sanjenís, Mis cartas: Memorias de
    la revolución de 1895 por la independencia de
    Cuba (1900)

The patria is in mourning and weeps for the death of so
many of its valiant sons. My poor brother Pedro sealed
his vow to return to Cuba with his blood. His patriotism
cost him his life; he has died on the field of honor. Blessed
is he who has earned that immortal honor. His everlast-
ing glory consoles me in his death.
    Carlos Manuel de Céspedes to Ana de Quesada
    (November 21, 1873)

The moment has arrived for us to let the world know that the Cuban knows how to die for the redemption of his patria.

General Antonio Maceo, "Proclama"
(September 5, 1879)

The Patria is blood and a community of pain.
María Luisa Toledo, ¡A la manigua! *(n.d.)*

❦ The proposition of patria entered the Cuban imagination in multiple forms, charged with diverse functions and imbued with divergent meanings. It drew upon many sources, some possessed of sentimental value as ends unto themselves, others invested with instrumental purpose as means to other ends. The boundaries among these categories were neither inalterable nor always discernible. They shifted often; sometimes they collapsed altogether, whereupon the affirmation of patria conveyed many things all at once. These elements coexisted in close proximity to one another, not always in congruent juxtaposition, to be sure, but rather as an amalgam of shifting representations by which to contemplate a frame of reference for affinity and affiliation.

Much had to do with emerging notions of nationality, specifically with the ways that the concept of Cuban (*cubano*) suggested the possibility of a community of shared sensibilities. It is not clear exactly how or precisely when the premise of cubano insinuated itself into the realms of popular awareness. Until late in the eighteenth century, the most common term of usage describing Cubans was *criollo*, denoting native-born residents of the island, as distinct from *peninsular*, Spanish-born inhabitants. By the early nineteenth century, however, the term *cubano* had acquired currency as the means of self-identification of choice, at once product and portent of significant changes by which distinctions between the needs of the island and the interests of the peninsula settled into ever-sharper relief.[1]

Claims that Cuba had concerns distinct from Spain and, more, that these concerns were proper to pursue, were themselves intimations of sovereignty of far-reaching implications. They were expressed principally as a deepening sense of Cuba as a place where the presence of *peninsulares* was unwelcome and their pretension to rule untenable. Old allegiances faltered and new attachments were formed; loyalties were reordered and relocated around new categories of self-definition and self-interest.

✱✤ Long before the proposition of patria acquired political meaning, it had inspired deep sentimental attachments, those most powerful of susceptibilities by which cognitive categories of nation and nationality were charged with purpose and passion. Patria as a place-bound source of self-identification entered the realms of Cuban awareness as a series of cultural revelations, principally by way of artistic expression—both highbrow and low—and folk forms, as a means through which to contemplate the circumstance of place as source of consciousness of self, and vice versa.

It was through the medium of creole aesthetics that patria was first transformed from a source of self-knowledge to a means of self-actualization. The ideal drew upon local fauna and flora in lyric poetry and landscape painting, in the elegies of folkloric writers (*costumbristas*), in the sentimentalized melodic renderings of patria—what historian Jorge Ibarra has aptly described as "the new music of a national popular tendency"—in the verse of the *décimas* and the choreographies of popular dance, all as new expressive genres engaged in a heightened subjectivity by which to construct *lo cubano*.[2] Medium and message together acted to deepen appreciation for things properly Cuban and in the process fashioned usable motifs from which sensibilities of nationality were derived.[3]

The meaning of patria revealed itself in the circumstances of daily life, given visual form and narrative order around stylized renderings of the commonplace, the familiar represented as revelation, as source of vernacular forms by which Cubans arrived at mutual recognition and registered nationhood. Romantic landscape artists (*los paisajistas románticos*) idealized the countryside, achieving atmosphere through the use of the brilliant light patterns of the tropics to render unabashedly sentimental paintings of pastoral tranquility. The landscape art depicted wide plains of royal palms, set against breathtaking vistas of valley landscapes and sweeping mountain elevations.[4]

Poets evoked patria as a sensory experience: sights, scents, and sounds of the land summoned with sentimentality and solemnity. They drew freely upon nature (*la naturaleza cubana*) as source for renderings of patria: the rivers; the seasons of the year; the products of the land; fruits, flowers, and plants; and always—and especially—the palm tree.[5] Francisco Iturrondo (1800–1868) began his poem "Rasgos descriptivos de la naturaleza cubana" with the lines "The profound sighs of the palm tree / The solemn rustling of the swaying bamboo"; while Juan Cristóbal Nápoles Fajardo ("El Cucalamabé") (1829–62) celebrated patria as a real place —not imagined but experienced—as site and source from which criollo attachments were derived. "My Cuba, I adore you!" he proclaimed in "Amor a Cuba" and alluded specifically to "the land that I behold." In "Galas de Cuba," Nápoles Fajardo again affirmed: "Cuba, my beloved land (*mi querido suelo*) / Which from childhood I adore / For you I will long always."[6] Carlota Robreño (d. 1869) gave deeply personal meaning to patria through imagery to which increasing numbers of Cubans were susceptible:

> My loving eyes see you again,
> Oh, my sweet patria!
> My happy heart enjoys again
> Your sky, your countryside, your joy.
> My face turns to reflect radiantly
> Your seductive moon,
> How sweet that divine moment,
> When the gentle breeze,
> Rocked my cradle,
> And descended to ask of me my first smile.[7]

José María de Heredia (1803–39) conjured up patria by way of the fragrances in the air, landscapes and products of the land, undulating fields of sugarcane (*cañaverales*), and majestic groves of royal palms (*palmares*). In "Placeres de la melancolía," he summoned the "sound of music / Of the sonorous palms and banana plants," and added: "Anxiously I seek in the distant breeze / The sound of its streams and its palms." In "Himno del desterrado," Heredia evoked Cuba nostalgically as "the sweet of land of light and beauty," while in "A Elpino" he contemplated patria as "lovely coasts," a "tranquil sea at midday," and "beautiful sky." In "¡Volver a Cuba!" expatriate poet Miguel Teurbe Tolón (1820–57) used English verse by Letitia Elizabeth Landon as epigram: "He thought of his home, of his own fair land / And the warm tear rush'd to his eye." Teurbe Tolón yearned for "a single ray of your warm sun," "to breath the perfume of your flowers," to hear the "celestial hymns that rise out of your forests and rivers," to behold "the splendid sky."[8]

The nineteenth-century meditation on patria was richly metaphoric and deeply cognitive. It acquired meaning around an emerging social stock of values as a way to inform belief systems, shape canons of self-represen-tation, and convey norms of conduct. The process lacked symmetry and order, of course, and must be presumed to have been incremental, over long stretches of time, implicating men and women of all social classes, black and white, at different times and in different ways. The possibility of a people bound together as a separate nationality was product of a deep-ening self-awareness of shared similarities as a source of community and from which the logic of "Cuban" obtained plausibility. Its principal expres-sion implied a reflexive knowledge through which to register cognizance of Cuban as an affinity of a like people linked together through shared ex-periences and common ground. In the end, it served as a moral framework to apprehend reality, consciousness of self as a function of awareness of nation.

The narrative of patria alluded frequently to criollos as "sons" and "daughters," a way to transform patria into an all-encompassing paradigm of kinship. The polity of patria assumed form as membership in a "family." That it functioned principally in the realm of metaphor should not, of course, obscure the power of its appeal. Vast numbers of men and women invested themselves deeply in a personal relationship to patria. Poet Belén de Miranda experienced exile with a deep sense of personal loss, in a way plausible only to one who had imagined herself as a "daughter" of Cuba. She recalled the "memorable and horrible day I found myself obliged to abandon my patria," likening herself to "an orphan, with my heart torn."[9]

The larger meaning of kinship as a means of self-representation had to do with the canons of conduct by which "good" sons and daughters were bound to the patria, central to which was the norm of duty. Values previously located in private spheres insinuated themselves into public realms and informed the terms by which Cubans invested themselves in the transcendental category of patria as a binding source of belonging. The power of metaphor in this instance was its capacity to elicit identifi-cation with patria through an appeal to emotions associated with family ties. Patria early obtained powerful emotional basis as a source of social cohesion through which to prescribe behavioral modes that appropriated duty and sacrifice as norms of nationality. All that was necessary to pre-vail in the struggle against Spain, provisional president Carlos Manuel de Céspedes insisted in 1871, was "the effort and the unshakeable determi-nation to triumph or to die as good and loyal sons of Cuba (buenos y leales hijos de Cuba)." "I will always be disposed to shed my blood for the patria," General Emilio Núñez affirmed, "to fight like a soldier and to die like a son of Cuba (*morir como hijo de Cuba*)." It was in this context that separatist Miguel Ramos, writing from Jamaica in 1878, could speak of a compatriot as "one of those good sons of Cuba (*uno de los buenos hijos de Cuba*)," adding: "I am desperate to return to the beaches of Cuba . . . and I am disposed to go out and fulfill the duty of a good son."[10]

Cubans propounded their claim to the island principally on the basis of nativity, as an affinity with place expressed as attachment to and affection for the land, sometimes in the form of homeland (*suelo natal*), often as homestead (*terreno*), occasionally through land as metaphor for country (*tierra*), and always as attachment to the land accompanied by a deep sense of territoriality. This was to imagine place as source of belongingness, conceived as a relationship of binding reciprocities: the island properly belonging to its inhabitants by virtue of birthplace and homeland, that is, people and place belonging to each other. "[We] have the right to present to the world," insisted the weekly *La Libertad* in 1869, "a new nationality that will sustain at all cost a true patriotism of those born in Cuba; it is the right of being the legitimate owners of the wealth that belongs to us."[11]

Attachment to place, with all its cultural and existential implications, assumed meaning through the experience of daily life, as source of passion and site of emotions, in the ways that people developed links to their origins and arrived at an understanding of how they became who they were. Place as repository of memories and associations gave meaning to being. These bonds reached deeply into domains of popular consciousness, whereby people could not imagine themselves without those attachments through which awareness of self had been formed. This was belonging as an essential facet of being, a way to give temporal meaning and spatial form to assumptions of antecedents and anticipation of descendants.[12] To be denied or otherwise deprived of patria was to be dispossessed of place of formation, to be without those relationships from which the earliest meanings of existence were derived.

This was to apprehend patria in deeply personal terms: as place of birth and setting of childhood, of family and forebears, as place of kin and community to which one was bound through memories and modalities of everyday life. Luis de Radillo proclaimed patria as "the cradle of my surname and that of my entire family." The weekly *El Independiente* provided poignant rendering of the personal meaning of patria: "The patria reminds us of our cradle, of our innocence, of the first maternal tenderness, of the first prayers that were raised to heaven from the pureness of our souls, of the first love that touched our heart."[13]

This was patria as burial ground, as place of one's past in the most personal of ways, often memorialized across the island by cemeteries filled with statuary and monuments of sacred intent.[14] Land assumed one more meaning, consecrated by the presence of the remains of forebears, as site to which personal history was inexorably connected. In "Adios a Cuba," poet Rosa Marrero y Caro evoked Cuba as the site of "the lonely tomb of my father." Poet Luisa Pérez de Zambrana proclaimed her love for patria by way of allusions to "the house in which we were born, with sweet images of infancy; with the school in which the teacher gave life to our intelligence; with the church where our aging grandmother clasped our hands together and taught us how to pray; with the cemetery where the remains of our forebears rest. We are in the company of friends of our childhood, members of the family, the youth with whom we shared our dreams of the future. . . . Everything lives within our lives." Poet Belén de Miranda experienced exile—that is, loss of patria—with deep personal anguish: "[M]y soul filled with bitterness and pain, I left my beloved corner, where I left behind my youth, my golden memories, my cheerful expectations, and where the ashes of all those who I loved so dearly were laid to rest. . . . Goodbye Cuba! Goodbye my blue sky! Goodbye my sweet home!"[15] In "Despedida a Cuba," poet Pamela Fernández evoked similar sentiments:

> Cradle of my grandparents,
> Delight of my father,
> The Eden where the beauty
> of my mother first glowed,
> Farewell! Within your embrace
> remain my loves,
> my laughter and the flowers
> of my childhood.[16]

❧ For the vast numbers of men and women implicated in the premise of Cuban, the realization of nationality could not be imagined under any circumstance other than independence and sovereignty (*independentismo*), that is, a people apart in possession of a place of their own. The proposition of patria always contained within its configuration properties of subversive reach. It encouraged meditation on a collective condition and aroused longing for precisely the kinds of associations not easily accommodated within the framework of Spanish colonial structures. Patria provided motive for mobilization, serving at once as a means of empowerment and a source of solidarity, but mostly it offered Cubans the possibility of agency as protagonists in pursuit of a nation of their own: the one eventuality to which the Spanish presence in Cuba was dedicated to preventing.

It would be a mistake, however, to accept the pursuit of a political project as the totality of the Cuban purpose. Certainly independentista sentiment acted to fashion a dissident polity with the intent to define itself and its members in relationship to Spain and Spaniards. But it was more complicated. This was also a constituency organized around a particular version of Cuban, one deeply invested in the proposition that self-determination was the minimum condition of self-fulfillment. The plausibility of Cuban as a transcendental category of identity was contingent on possession of place, unmediated and unencumbered, a condition vital to the very sustenance of the logic of a separate nationality. The premise of Cuban was derived from the promise of patria, without which the proposition of nationality possessed neither reason nor rationale. General Calixto García spoke for three generations of independentistas when he insisted in 1878 that "our independence is the basis of our future well-being."[17]

Independentismo was only one of several competing representations by which the actualization of nationality was possible. Other political formulations of nation included *integrismo*, advocated by creoles who defended Spanish colonial administration as the best guarantee of political stability and social order. *Anexionismo* was advanced by creoles who believed Cuba's interests were best served through annexation to and eventual statehood within the United States. *Autonomismo* was supported principally by creoles who advocated home rule within a constitutional commonwealth arrangement that provided Cuba with political participation in the Spanish parliamentary system.[18]

Each of the foregoing visions of Cuban structured nationality around a different set of value systems and envisioned a different means to obtain fulfillment of collective selfhood; each exalted very different attributes of *lo cubano*, drawing upon very different moral imperatives through which to pursue very different political projects. The real and indeed often unappreciated achievement of the independentista polity was registered as the affirmation of a particular representation of Cuban, a version scripted with attributes that were to endure as the dominant expression of nationality deep into the twentieth century.

Independentismo challenged more than the assumptions of Spanish colonial rule. It also lay claim to the dominant formulations through which the meaning of Cuban was transacted, and as such was engaged in the process of forging the terms of a new national identity. The independentista polity acquired internal coherence around a number of beliefs and practices shared among its proponents and transacted as obligatory conditions of membership. The terms of self-representation were fixed in function of liberation, assembled as attributes of Cuban directly instrumental to the project of self-determination.

The independentista polity expanded as a populist coalition, organized around cross-racial alliances and multiclass solidarities, between men and women, sustained over the course of repeated armed mobilizations all through the second half of the nineteenth century. It organized around the proposition of nationality as source of virtue and value, with the promise of status and dignity, that is, self-determination as means of self-esteem, and possessed above all of the capacity to transport its adherents across new thresholds of political solidarities and social unity. As a summons to agency independentismo implied empowerment, as a means of mobilization it offered mobility, as a movement it promised membership. Access to Cuban was, accordingly, expressed as an all-inclusive set of moral understandings, propounded through a new ethical vernacular, and open to everyone who embraced the means and meanings of patria.

That independentismo gained ascendancy as the dominant representation of Cuban must be considered as a development of singular importance in the formation of the terms of nationality in nineteenth-century Cuba. It was out of the premise of the primacy of Cuban interests, derived from the proposition of Cuba as separate and sovereign, that the formulation of nationality entered the discursive realms of creole self-awareness. Thus it was that the concept of cubano took form, as a consciousness of self derived from a sense of place, as a deepening recognition of the need to relocate power within Cuba and reorder the purpose of power on behalf of things Cuban, as affirmation of the prerogative of Cuban in Cuba.

Cuban came to signify a particular set of dispositions, of attributes and attitudes, a way of being, all derived from the independentista purpose and proclaimed as the sum and substance of "real Cuban." Proponents of alternative versions of Cuban were vilified and accused of treason and cowardice. "There is now no reason for irresolution," affirmed the protagonist in Raimundo Cabrera's autobiographical novel, *Ideales* (1918); "the die is cast. Between Spain that always oppresses us and Cuba that rebels anew to remove its yoke, there can be no indecision: with our people to struggle and to die. Those who do not come with us will be [considered] in the future traitors and cowards."[19] Integrismo and anexionismo fell into disrepute early.[20] The autonomistas drew the most sustained independentista attack largely because home rule offered the most credible alternative to independence. Autonomistas "were not worthy of being called Cubans," the weekly *El Vigía* insisted, "because they refuse to sacrifice and openly and secretly serve the enemy," alluding ominously to the necessity "to cross the foreheads of these false sons (*hijos espurios*) of the patria with ashen marks for future action." Proclaimed *El Vigía* outright: "They are traitors." *El Cubano Libre* was categorical about the meaning of "Cuban":

> [Independentistas] are the only ones who can and should call themselves Cubans. [Autonomistas] are without consciousness of their duty and throw themselves at the feet of tyrants. . . . Although sons of Cuba, they repudiate their patria, and their patria rejects them as unworthy sons. Those who kneel before tyrants to receive alms obtained from the pillage of the patria cannot be Cuban. Those who live in defeat, hiding their shame and cowardice in the shadows do not form part of the Cuban people. Those who witness violence and pillage in silence, lacking the courage to raise their voice in protest, cannot be Cuban. That group of weak men, without faith and without hope, whose very pettiness makes them incapable of great aspirations, cannot be part of the Cuban people. The Cuban people are made up of those for whom the cry of 'Patria and Liberty' kindled their dreams and who abandoned their homes and families and committed themselves to armed struggle. He who did not see the tears of his beloved mother or his orphaned daughter, he who abandoned his adored wife and his caring sweetheart, he who gave up all his dreams and all his hopes, did so and sacrificed everything in the pursuit of the most beautiful dream and the most sacred of all ideals: the patria.[21]

Autonomists were "false Cubans," insisted Fermín Valdés-Domínguez, "politically small-minded, who do not know how to love the land (*amar a la tierra*) that has given them their name. . . , who out of fear choose to live in peace with Spaniards, repudiate the Revolution of 1868, and call themselves Autonomists. They are all simply traitors." The day of reckoning would come, Valdés-Domínguez vowed, for "those of us who fight for the independence of the Patria with weapons in our hands must some day punish them for the statements they make. We would be cowards if we forgive those who in such a traitorous manner have aligned themselves with the Spanish and before our very eyes use insults and lies as weapons against us." Indeed, during the Ten Years War (1868–78) the provisional government promulgated a sweeping exclusionary decree: "All who by word or print express ideas contrary to the independence of the country will lose the right of citizenship and will be considered as traitors."[22] Independentistas could envision future reconciliation with Spaniards, the weekly *Oriente* suggested, for their conduct was comprehensible; they had, in the end, acted in a manner congruent with the interests of their country: "But those autonomistas, born on the beautiful island of Cuba, owing everything to Cuba, intelligent and fully conscious of the consequences of their deeds, aligning themselves with the enemy of their patria, first condemning the revolution [for independence] and then, like a snake, betraying the patria: that has no justification whatsoever. Those men ought to be grateful that the extraordinarily generous and noble Cuban has not proclaimed the lynch law (*la ley de Linch*)."[23] Only those engaged in the armed struggle—"those who have embraced the principle of 'Independence or Death,'" Tomás Estrada Palma insisted—possessed the moral authority to speak as Cubans and to serve as "the representatives of the Cuban people, for they are the only ones who have the courage of their convictions, who endure danger and make the sacrifice of lives and interests on the altar of principles sustained face to face with the government of Spain." The independentista newspaper *La República* was categorical: "[The future of Cuba] will be determined only by those who are exposed to danger in the field of the insurrection, those who have shed their blood in combat after having been despoiled of what they owned, those who have sacrificed on the altar of the patria their family, their positions, and their possessions, those who by their own hand have reduced to ashes all their worldly belongings."[24]

✥ The emerging formulation of Cuban was driven and defined as much by means as ends, specifically by the conviction that the promise of nationality could not be realized in any form other than independence—"a free and sovereign Patria, a free and independent people," General Antonio Maceo insisted—and that independence could not be achieved by any means other than armed struggle.[25] Only through war—planned, purposeful, and protracted war—would Cubans succeed in obtaining control of the island from Spain. "Our ideal is independence," editorialized *El Porvenir* in 1890, "and to obtain it war has to be made inevitable. . . . We accept the [need for] revolution, with all its consequences and all its disasters." Bernabé Boza outlined the independentista purpose succinctly: "To make war on Spain, [a war] of blood and fire, until the absolute independence of the Patria is obtained." This was the task to which General Antonio Maceo

Antonio Maceo, ca. 1880s.
Courtesy of Archivo Nacional
de Cuba, Havana, Cuba.

dedicated his adult life. "My sole and exclusive aspiration," he wrote in
1886, "is our revolution for the independence of the Patria. To make war
on the government of Spain in Cuba has been, is, and will be my only goal.
I have no other hope. I have no other ambition." José Martí alluded variously to "the necessity of war," "the indispensable war," and "the inevitable
war," affirming: "War appears to be the only means with which to redeem
the patria." He insisted upon "the duty to prepare for war," for there was
"no other way to save our country except by war," and added: "The republic is our end, but war is our means."[26]

Cuban assumed meaning around specific hierarchies of values and
modes of conduct, arranged as a condition of inclusion, to be sure, but also
as a system of collective representation deeply inscribed with instrumental purpose. The dominant elements around which the norms of nationality were assembled—that is, the formulations by which Cuban was idealized—were shaped principally by those qualities necessary to sustain the
independentista project, whereupon they were affirmed as attributes intrinsic to being Cuban. "Real Cuban" implied dedication to a specific
course of action, central to which was the disposition to sacrifice and commitment to armed struggle. All "true Cubans" (*los verdaderos cubanos*),
Gustavo Pérez Abreu insisted, were obliged to answer the summons of
revolution, while Ramón Roa insisted that "the duty of every good Cuban"
(*todo bueno cubano*) was to join the battle for the patria. Poet Martina Pierra

de Poo was lyrical about the need "To offer at the holy altar [of patria] / If necessary / The supreme sacrifice of life," adding: "And if there were a soul indifferent / To the call of his idolized patria / He could not be Cuban."[27]

The process of self-determination was at the same time a means of self-definition, the occasion to enact the meaning of Cuban around those attributes necessary to consummate liberation. "To sacrifice!" exhorted the weekly *La Doctrina de Martí*, "so that our enemies may see in light of our determination to prevail that it is absurd to persist in the idea they can defeat us!" And more to the point: "To sacrifice!—for the people (*el pueblo*) who do not know how to sacrifice a false well-being . . . deserve to succumb under the feet of despicable and cruel despotism!"[28]

❧ Much of what developed as norms of nationality was assembled over the course of the nineteenth century in response to specific historical circumstances, as vast numbers of men and women fashioned their collective selves within their understanding of the needs of their time. The experience served to define the cognitive determinants and shape the behavioral conventions by which ideals of nationality entered the realms of popular consciousness. These elements were configured into narrative order from speeches heard and read; by way of manifestos, pronouncements, and proclamations; through heroic deeds and meanings assigned to heroic deeds; were disseminated by word of mouth; were transmitted through patriotic poems and song, as legend and lore, sometimes as fully-blown myths, from which larger morals were drawn, all directed to one overriding ideological end.[29] The result was a running narrative of a work in progress, the means by which to summon and sustain a people engaged in a process of self-definition and a cause of self-determination, at once binding and integrative, as source of inspiration and means of inclusion to bring together the multiple and often diverse elements of discontent with the colonial order of things into an expanding voluntary association around the emerging consensus of Cuban.

The project of liberation was conceived always as a popular uprising against colonial rule, as a call to arms of a people ill-matched and ill-equipped to engage in a vastly unequal struggle of civilians against soldiers, of machetes against Mausers, where the only advantage possessed by Cubans was the will to win and the willingness to die. And that was the point: the call to arms was a summons to die. "Goodbye forever," Ignacio Mora took leave of his wife Ana Betancourt to join the insurgency in

1868. "Few will emerge alive from this struggle so unequal that we are about to launch. As of today consider yourself a widow, and that way the notification of my death will be far less painful." General Enrique Collazo later acknowledged the overriding truth about Cuban prospects during the Ten Years War: "There was no hope of victory," he wrote, "it was necessary to die or incur dishonor. The majority opted for death." This was a truth also understood by Comandante Luis Rodolfo Miranda: "Those who went to war accepted death as a very natural sacrifice to a supreme ideal." Manuel Arbelo characterized the 1895 insurrection as "an explosion of an irrepressible rage, with suicide on the minds of many, in order to obtain the rights of liberty"; while Horacio Ferrer recalled the 1890s as a time when the "political situation was discussed in every household, and everyone agreed that to launch a new war against Spain, without the resources to sustain it, was madness, but a necessary madness to which we had been driven by our desperation." Segundo Corvisón "abandoned family, well-being, and interests," he wrote, "in search of death." Corvisón recalled his decision to commit himself "to the field of such an unequal struggle to die honorably," and added: "Our destiny was to die." And at another point: "I joined the revolution the way fanatical Christians sacrificed themselves: to die serenely for an Ideal." Poet Luis Victoriano Betancourt gave lyrical form to the same sentiment:

> And upon seeing the wound of Cuba
> I entrusted myself to fate
> Together with the suffering patria
> And I bid farewell to life
> And went in search of death.

In 1896, *El Cubano Libre* paid homage to the "glorious legacy from the *suicide generation*" (*la generación suicida*) of the Ten Years War, the generation that provided the inspiration that "finally produced the present powerful rebellion."[30]

The presentiment of death was not ill-founded. When the fighting ended in 1898, few survivors of the nearly thirty years of war could fully comprehend that they had lived through a population disaster of frightful proportions. The total number of Cubans who perished in the course of the nineteenth-century wars of independence is mostly a matter of conjecture and may never be fully known. But a striking consensus developed in later years, and it provides a chilling estimate of the magnitude of Cuban losses. Over the course of the three principal insurrections—the Ten Years War (1868–78), the Little War (1879–80), and the Independence War (1895–98)—and a score of ill-planned, short-lived uprisings before and in between, tens of thousands died on the battlefield; many hundreds of thousands more perished as a result of the conditions of war. One-third of all the generals in the Liberation Army perished in the Independence War.[31] A population of 1.8 million before 1895 had declined to less than 1.5 million in 1898, a net population loss approaching 20 percent. Soldiers and civilians, as active participants or passive parties to the conflict, were killed in action or executed by firing squads; they perished in prisons on the island and in penal colonies in Africa; men, women, and children, by the tens of thousands, died of disease, illness, and malnutrition. In 1899, Cuba had the highest proportion of widowed to married persons in the Western Hemisphere: 34.6 per hundred. There was one widow or widower for every three married persons. The proportion of widowed women was higher: 51.2 per hundred, or one widow for every two wives.[32]

The proposition of patria was at once self-evident and self-implicating. For all who passed under its sway—and the numbers were considerable[33]—patria was the defining issue of their times: what Raimundo Cabrera recalled many decades later as "the supreme ideal of our youthful dreams."[34] To be Cuban—to be a "real Cuban"—implied devotion to patria, dedication to duty, and disposition to die: to be among those "good and honorable Cubans (*buenos y honrados cubanos*)," José Calero explained, "who cherish their beloved patria and who are disposed to die for it gladly, with a smile on their face, with conviction and serenity." Sacrifice of self was conflated with salvation of nation, and only through the willingness to die could the promise of patria be fulfilled. It was necessary to contemplate death as the principal means through which to envision the possibility of success. "The revolution needs lives," exhorted Ramón Céspedes Fornaris from New York in 1871, "mass numbers of lives, it needs immense suffering in all forms, for the tree of liberty bears fruit only in those places where the tears of the good fertilize the soil." The message was the same from the fields of insurgent Cuba. "Victory comes only to those who know how to die," affirmed Comandante Luis Rodolfo Miranda. "Here men have come to offer everything to our patria, including our lives," wrote Fermín Valdés-Domínguez in his campaign diary. "We are disposed to die for the independence of Cuba. . . . That is why we will prevail! (*¡Por eso vencere-*

mos!)" General Pedro Díaz wrote to his wife from the field with the same message: "Here we are many and very disposed to struggle until Cuba is free or we are all dead."[35]

If the Cuban purpose was to have any prospect of success over the long run—and it was indeed over the long run that the Cuban purpose was conceived[36]—it was obliged to subsume those attributes necessary for the achievement of liberation into properties of nationality. Formulations of self-representation were transformed into elements of self-determination, and vice versa. The losses would be incalculable, the struggle perhaps interminable. "If not in the first war," Ricardo Buenamar vowed in 1896, "then in this one; and if not this one, then in the next one. What this [struggle] signifies has no end. The Spanish must leave." General Calixto García contemplated a war without end. "It has been nearly thirty years since I began to fight for my country," he wrote in 1897, "and I am certain that I will not see the end."[37] The moral and meaning of nationality were unambiguous. To do what had to be done to prevail, at whatever cost, for however long, as discharge and display of being Cuban.

Nationality was assembled around discursive formulations derived from the project of liberation, a way to fashion diverse elements of self-representation into an organizing whole, central to which was the disposition to die as affirmation of Cuban. This was devotion to an ideal and dedication to a task, and once rendered as duty of nationality it served to fix the moral hierarchies around which the consensus on the meaning of Cuban was forged. Many of the central premises of nationality were registered as a normative condition, organized into a redemptive narrative of nation in the form of behavioral codes and prescriptive conduct by which Cuban was enacted. To die for patria was to participate consciously in the making of heroic history, to enable the past to speak to the future, to define the standard of conduct by which the meaning and measure of Cuban attained binding obligation. The past was future. Devotion was transformed into duty, and duty was destiny.

The idea of heroic conduct served as a powerful means of popular mobilization, imbued with egalitarian properties available to all—whatever the color of one's skin, whatever one's social origins, whatever one's age. The heroic deed promised status and stature, to oneself, of course, but also to one's family and friends. In a social order where recognition and reward were associated principally with property and power, the heroic act implied the possibility of passage into the realm of the sublime, there to be accorded the highest acclaim and accolade. There was perhaps no more compelling enactment of Cuban than heroic death on behalf of patria.

The pursuit of patria was sustained by a combination of appeals both to self-interest and selfless impulse, but most of all through the invocation of sacrifice as the ethical imperative of being Cuban. Félix Varela was categorical: "He who does not know how to make sacrifices in behalf of the patria is not a patriot."[38] The most powerful means of socialization into nationality was transacted within the paradigm of sacrifice, as standard of duty in which all Cubans were implicated by virtue of nationality, and acquired firsthand by people immersed in the task of liberation. This was to propound nationality as source of social knowledge, fashioned as an ethical and moral system, to delineate those values that served to distinguish Cubans as a people distinct from all others. José Martí repeatedly invoked sacrifice as the central thematic element in the formulation of duty as condition of being Cuban. Nationality was "a brotherhood of sacrifice," Martí insisted. He wrote of "the necessity of sacrifice," understood always as the need "to rise, with nobility, at the time of sacrifice and die without fear as an offering to the patria."[39] Fermín Valdés-Domínguez filled his field diary with reflections on sacrifice, characterized as what "duty and my love of patria have imposed upon me." He wrote of the necessity "to do what duty requires us to do, to reach the goal that duty sets out for us and to triumph or die." And at another point: "It is necessary to have faith and hope in the holy ideals that oblige us to suffer so that we do not fail. . . . It is necessary to be Cuban above all else, to suffer and wait, the way we should all suffer and wait."[40] Years later Manuel Secades Japón remembered his decision to join the insurgency: "Hardly more than an adolescent, I felt the call of the Patria, summoning a holy war for the purpose of obtaining independence and liberty. Obedient to the impulses of a patriotic sentiment and fulfilling a duty that I believed to be ineluctable, I abandoned the tenderness of the home, the tranquility of the family, the joys of a social life, and the academic pursuits upon which my very future depended to commit myself to the struggle, to contribute with my efforts to the redemption of the enslaved Patria."[41] In order to realize collective well-being, *La Estrella de Cuba* insisted in 1870, "the patria demands of its sons sacrifices that cannot be defined or in any way limited: true patriotism demands full commitment and, if necessary, the complete sacrifice of life and treasure." Seven years later, the independentista weekly *La Verdad* reflected on the course of the Ten Years War:

José Martí, Key West, Florida, 1891.
Courtesy of Centro de Estudios
Martianos, Havana, Cuba.

We have not wearied nor can we weary. Nine years is a long period of time in the life of a man, but it is only an instant in the life of a people. . . . We do not live for ourselves, but for the patria. . . . It does not occur to us, hence, to measure the passage of time nor weigh our suffering. Why invoke the past? Ruin, tears, blood, and death—here, in a few words, is the history of our patria during the last nine years, a history that is written in the hearts of all Cubans and that we do not have to recall. . . . [We] have signed a covenant with destiny: redemption or death.[42]

Nationality in this instance was at once—and inexorably—contextual and contingent. It fashioned the terms of self-representation principally around those attitudes and attributes conspicuous for their efficacy in the realization of nation, not always by choice—often not even by design— but rather out of need, deployed as moral strategies of mobilization, and shaped into usable representational motifs, and thereupon subsumed into the larger cosmology of Cuban: to construct the heroic self as the idealized sense and essence of Cuban. Much in the way that the meaning of Cuban insinuated itself into the narratives of nationality was product of instrumental needs, fashioned as response to specific historical circumstances, means expressed as ends and ends exemplified as means, at one and the same time a summons to mobilization and source of social integration.

This is to view nationality arranged as an ethical system by which to fix the terms of inclusion: interlocking reciprocal ideals extolling the virtues of Cuban, to be sure, but also speaking to obligations to be assumed as a function of being Cuban. The idealization of nationality had to do with ends and referred to the future; the obligations of nationality addressed means and responded to the present. But most of all these were norms that implied sacrifice as duty internalized as a function of nationality, as assumptions so taken for granted that they ceased to be apprehended in any way other than a natural discharge of moral responsibility owed by virtue of membership. For Néstor Carbonell, "Cuban" signified "a virile people who faced death with a smile on their face." Years later Ramiro Cabrera reminisced about the war: "The singular valor with which Cubans died during the war was astonishing. It was almost as if they didn't care about life. . . . Many who perished were from most modest social classes, of very humble origins. I saw Cubans die always with the same bravery and the same smile." General Enrique Collazo later wrote that "sacrifice for the patria was so commonplace that no one saw these efforts as anything extraordinary; to die for the patria was something so accepted by everyone that survivors saw nothing noteworthy in the deed, for it was understood that such a fate would befall everyone, sooner or later. The choice was clear: dishonor by joining the enemy or to die honorably."[43]

The narrative of sacrifice emerged as the dominant discursive mode by which the duty of death insinuated itself into the conventions of Cuban. It was something that one did by virtue of doing what a Cuban was supposed to do. To be Cuban implied the obligation to transcend the wish to live as discharge of purpose of life. Colonel Avelino Sanjenís reflected on the death of a soldier in his command: "His death was an example for us. To die for Cuba was our duty." At the other end of the island, Fermín Valdés-Domínguez mourned the death of a close friend: "Today glory, like a loving mother, embraces his body, and with the blood of his wounds inscribes upon the land that contains his remains: 'This is how Cubans honor the Patria.'"[44]

The existential logic of nationality drew Cubans inexorably to death as an act of self-reflective consciousness. To the degree that Cubans invested selfhood into nationhood, it was difficult for many to imagine the former without the latter. Formulations of nationality reached deeply into the sources of self-representation and self-esteem. But these formulations were also conditioned by and contingent on the promise of patria. Death was the inevitable fate of a subjugated people, Cubans insisted; a people unable to actualize their existence as a sovereign polity faced the prospects of certain extinction. The summons to sacrifice served to affirm that life without patria was not worth living. Patria was a means of salvation—and life.

The discharge of duty as a Cuban thus assumed formulaic resonance: patria or death. Nothing could obstruct the "redemptive will that was condensed in the brilliant symbolism of two words," Captain Angel Rosende later wrote: "'Triumph or death.' We knew that these two words made it clear that there was nothing in between. Either a free and sovereign patria or despotism ruling over the blood-drenched fields of Cuba." Manuel Arbelo and José Hernández Guzmán phrased the choice as "Independence or death"; the weekly *El Vigía* proclaimed "*Cuba Libre* or death!"[45] "There is now no alternative to death or victory," Domingo Goicuría wrote to his daughter in 1870, "and it is that purpose to which all of us who have the heart of a Cuban (*el corazón cubano*) are dedicated." The insurgent provisional government proclaimed the Cuban purpose clearly: "In one way or another, we will be free. As dead men or as victors, we will succeed in ridding ourselves of the cursed yoke. The objective is to be free: we will achieve it or we will die in the struggle. And if fate were to turn against us, our resignation is such that we know how to die in these fields." Martí characterized the independence war in 1895 as "a conflict that can end only in victory or the grave (*la victoria o el sepulcro*)."[46]

The deed of death was rendered as an act of exemplary purpose, commemorated with didactic intent as source of inspiration. Death as example was at the heart of the independentista project, without which the efficacy of armed struggle as a means of liberation could not be sustained. "Would that the example of my sacrifice is followed by others," Domingo Goicuría wrote as he awaited execution in 1870. This was the point made by Eusebio Hernández, in slightly different terms: "If the Spanish capture us in the city and execute us, the Revolution will fail; but if death overtakes us in battle, the Revolution will be saved because the example is sublime, and there will be a thousand patriotic souls who will follow the example."[47]

Exemplary death served to deepen the intransigence central to the purpose of liberation, to situate each generation between ancestry, to whom a debt was owed, and posterity, to whom an obligation was due. The living were implicated in a covenant with the dead, an inescapable commitment consecrated in blood, by way of a legacy to which they were simultaneously recipient and custodian. They looked back upon the fallen dead to draw from their example the sense of purpose and spirit of sacrifice as moral sustenance for their times. "The blood of our fathers and our brothers. . . ," Carlos Manuel de Céspedes explained to correspondent James O'Kelly in early 1873, "forbids our ever accepting any conditions from the Spaniards. They must go away and leave us in peace, or continue the war until we are all dead or they have been exterminated." Segundo Corvisón lived with "the memory of glorious dead (*los muertos ilustres*) who perished on those fields [of battle] and who summon us to sacrifice with their example," noting that "[they] died to teach us that all of us, if it were necessary, should follow their example to defend liberty." This was the relationship that José Martí drew explicitly "from one generation to another," among a "people of sublime martyrs," insisting that "every Cuban who falls, assumes a place in our heart." The "[members of the] new generation," Martí exulted, "[are] disposed to fight for the patria and thus discharge their debt to those who died for them." And, warned Martí: "The dead [will] arise from their graves to demand an accounting of those who fail to meet their duty."[48]

The cumulative effect of sacrifice and death could not but ratify the Cuban purpose, to make the logic of duty to die or to prevail all the more compelling. To commemorate past sacrifice was to consecrate future sacrifice. To fail or otherwise falter in the pursuit of liberation was to signify that all who had previously perished, those revered for the sacrifice as martyrs, had died in vain, for nothing, to have been betrayed by the generations that followed. "To venerate the dead is a pious act," the weekly *Cuba* insisted in 1897; "but more than honor those who perished to provide us with patria and liberty, death will always be the inescapable duty of all who have not yet fulfilled an obligation so sacrosanct."[49] "We need to triumph and we will triumph," Manuel Arbelo wrote in his field journal in October 1897. "We cannot go backward when we are so close to fulfilling the ideals of three generations." He added: "We would be completely unworthy of any respect if after having plunged the country into a bloody war, one that has resulted in ruin and misery, in which the flower of Cuban youth has perished, that has brought so much sorrow and so much desolation into our homes, if we now retreat, to become once again supplicants, shamed, confused and humiliated, to endure again a yoke that signifies degradation and disgrace. Only with victory or death will we come out of the fields of *Cuba Libre*."[50]

To die for the patria implied both personal redemption and national salvation. The meaning of sacrifice was drawn to its logical conclusion. Death was commemorated as a deed of devotion and dedication, at once heroic and holy, where the dead really did not die at all. On the contrary, the act of dying for the patria was a means of eternal life—per the lyric of the Cuban national anthem, "La Bayamesa": "Do not fear a glorious death / For to die for the Patria is to live." Patria thus promised life after death, and more: it offered immortality, a way to transcend oblivion through posteriority. "Such heroism and such glory," poet Mercedes Matamoros eulogized Cubans who had perished in the service of patria. "[They] remain eternally in the memory of the patria / Although they may die, heroes always live." Similar were the thoughts of Segundo Corvisón as he prepared to join the insurgency, "to realize my most intimate desire, aspiring to be an immortal hero of the idealized Patria, for which I was prepared to die in the field of battle." The weekly *La Revolución Cubana* celebrated martyrdom in precisely the same terms: "Combatants die to live in the memory of the future of the patria." A popular nineteenth-century short story, "Chicho," drew this moral explicitly. "I die content," said the mortally wounded protagonist as he contemplated his death. "To live without purpose simply to live one's life is to die morally; to die to enable the patria to break the chains of tyranny is to live." *El Republicano* insisted that through "the blood generously shed by its martyrs, [the patria] will overcome the rule of oppression. . . . Those who perish for a cause so noble and sacred live eternally in the memory of the centuries and their names will be carried atop the wings of time into the unknown regions of the future, to the limits of eternity." Colonel Avelino Sanjenís derived consolation from "the many who died and went to heaven crowned with holy laurel wreaths and who upon ascension bequeathed us glory, honor, and a patria." These were men who "knew how to die," wrote essayist Rosario Sigarroa, in pursuit of "the resurrection of the patria, who were called upon to occupy their positions in combat." Men like Carlos Manuel de Céspedes and José Martí, Sigarroa insisted, were martyrs, "who kept the purest faith, the loftiest patriotism, the most sublime abnegation. Both soaked this land with their redemptive blood, . . . [and] both entered the kingdom of eternal shadow with the halo of immortality above their majestic faces."[51]

Allusions to faith and immortality and the frequent invocation of sacral imagery underscore the extent to which the narrative of nationality drew upon religious iconography as a medium of representation. The invocation of the spiritual as a function of the political allowed the realms of the secular to approach the thresholds of the sacrosanct. This was to raise sacrifice to the level of sacrament, a source of political revelation and means of personal redemption. Patria offered a means of immortality embedded in the continuity of community. Death on behalf of patria was conceived as a means of transubstantiation, entrée to the larger domain of the nation that was itself immortal. Martí celebrated the "sublime transfiguration" of those who "bled and died" on behalf of the patria, who henceforth could not be looked upon with anything other than "reverence and tenderness."[52]

Patria was rendered variously as altar, as hallowed ground—"the patria is sacred," proclaimed Martí[53]—as site of worship, and as source of grace, at once transformative and transcendent, a means to transport ordinary men and women into heroic realms via commonplace deeds with the promise of an afterlife. To die was to become free, and more: to die was to enable others to become free. The image of altar served as metaphor for patria, to which all were summoned to discharge the duty of self-sacrifice. "Everything should be sacrificed at the altar of the patria," enjoined novelist Anselmo Suárez y Romero in 1839; and Emilia Casanova de Villaverde paid homage to Cubans who were "disposed to sacrifice themselves on the altar of the patria." In 1896 provisional president Salvador Cisneros Betancourt enjoined all men and women of good will "to join us and sing together with us the hymn of redemption that we raise in fervent veneration at the sacrosanct altar of the Patria."[54]

The war for independence assumed fully the proportions of a holy campaign. "My conscience is clear for having done all that I could do and having met my duty," Colonel Avelino Sanjenís wrote. "With the same faith as always, I continue the sacred work of actualizing Patria (*la obra santa de hacer Patria*)." "This struggle," affirmed Manuel Sanguily in 1876, "is thus a holy struggle; this war is thus a sacred war."[55] Domingo Goicuría made the point succinctly: "We have come into the world to be martyrs." Ignacio Mora was committed to the independentista cause as much as a condition of religious faith as a matter of political persuasion. "Am I perhaps in pursuit of an illusion in seeking to liberate Cuba?" he asked rhetorically. "I cannot decipher the meaning of this mystery, but it is a religion, and like all religions it must have its martyrs."[56]

❧ It was at this juncture that the function of exemplary death situated itself at one end of the spectrum of suicide, invested with noble intent and instrumental function, and entered the logic of Cuban with paradigmatic resonance. This was death as motif and modality, the mingling of sacrifice with suicide, fixed within the discursive structure of nationality as a celebrated act. It was a way to exemplify the deed of heroic intransigence and define the standard by which to fix the measure of Cuban.

Voluntary death affirmed decorum, an act of self-command as self-sacrifice by which duty as a Cuban was discharged. "Suicide in the Liberation Army," historian Francisco Pérez Guzmán has correctly suggested, "was never seen as something disgraceful—on the contrary. Suicide so as not to fall into the hands of the Spaniards was honorable."[57] Insurgent officers and soldiers often chose to die of wounds and illness rather than abandon the field. Others chose to fight to the death rather than surrender to Spanish forces. "When the Cuban soldier can no longer defend himself," *La Revolución de Cuba* exulted editorially in 1874, "he offers his bare chest to the cannon of the oppressor and perishes, proud to die for his patria and cursing Spain."[58]

Suicide in this instance was to die as an act of agency. To surrender represented a betrayal of conviction, to submit anew to Spain and be wholly at the mercy of the enemy: in a word, to experience powerlessness. Surrender implied dishonor and disgrace; it was to fall into the hands of vile men and suffer indignities unworthy of the cause to which Cubans were dedicated. To kill oneself was to thwart one's enemy. The ethical imperative of Cuban demanded death before dishonor. "It is preferable to die in the field of honor than live dishonorably under Spanish domination," Serafín Sánchez proclaimed. *El Republicano* eulogized the countless number of rural families (*pacíficos*) who abandoned their homes and fled into the woods, "preferring to die from hardship than fall captive to loathsome men," and concluded: "Death is preferable to dishonor. We would rather die a thousand times than live in dishonor." Comandante Luis Rodolfo Miranda was categorical: "We struggle for the independence of our beloved Cuba, and to the last man. We are all disposed to die before surrendering." Captain Gabino Venecia, wounded and surrounded on all sides, unsheathed his machete and charged into oncoming Spanish troops— "in the desperate resolution of sacrifice," wrote his biographer. Candelaria Figueredo also faced the choice of capture or death, with her only escape route reduced to a perilous flight by sea. She did not hesitate: "I wanted to leave by boat even if it meant drowning, for I would rather have been food for sharks than fall prisoner to the Spaniards." And on another occasion when encouraged to leave an insurgent field camp for shelter in the city, Figueredo responded: "I will commit suicide first."[59]

Others took their own lives rather than be taken alive. Colonel Avelino Sanjenís often contemplated capture by the Spanish and vowed that he would "never be taken alive," adding: "I would shoot at the Spanish and then kill myself." Provisional president Carlos Manuel de Céspedes

Calixto García, ca. 1890s, bearing the scar on his forehead from his attempted suicide in 1874. Courtesy of Archivo Nacional de Cuba, Havana, Cuba.

praised the *pacíficos* "who prefer death rather than surrender to the tyrants," a fate that Céspedes also contemplated for himself. "I do not know how I will die if I have the misfortune of falling prisoner," he remarked to his staff. "What I am certain of is that I pray that God gives me sufficient courage to die with the dignity with which a Cuban should die, although I do not think this will happen because my revolver has six bullets: five for the Spanish and one for me. They can take me dead—but as a prisoner, never!" In 1874, Céspedes died in battle, apparently true to his word, with an empty revolver gripped in his hand.[60] In the same year, General Calixto García Iñiguez unsuccessfully attempted suicide to avoid capture by the Spanish army. García eventually recovered from the self-inflicted gunshot wound to the head, but his unsuccessful suicide entered the annals of separatist lore as a gesture of heroic proportions. García was "lifted upon the wings of glory into sublimity," wrote Fernando Figueredo Socarrás, "[preferring] to kill himself rather than . . . endure the shame of falling into the clutches of the Spaniards." José Martí eulogized Calixto García as "the famous Cuban, the hero who preferred suicide to being captured"; while Fermín Valdés-Domínguez later described "the scar on [García's] forehead as the seal of his incontrovertible patriotism . . . and the most beautiful proof of the patriotism and valor of our men." The weekly *Oriente* celebrated García's failed suicide attempt in heroic terms: "Surrounded by soldiers, trapped, without hope of salvation, that virile soul . . . saw everything very dark, in a moment comparable only to those in which the heroes of antiquity killed themselves rather than fall into the power of the enemy, [and] in a moment of inspiration and lucidity, a bullet discharged by his own hand caused him to fall with equanimity, bathed in his own blood."[61] In 1896 Captain Francisco Gómez Toro refused to abandon the fallen Antonio Maceo and wrote a final note to his parents: "I die at my post, not wanting to abandon the body of General Maceo. I will remain with him. I am wounded in two places. Not wishing to fall prisoner to the enemy, I will kill myself. I do it with great satisfaction for the honor of Cuba." The suicide of Gómez Toro was similarly celebrated as an act of exemplary resonance. "He died in order not to fall in the hands of the enemy," Calixto García eulogized in 1896, "atop the body of that extraordinary man, Antonio Maceo. I too have sons in this war in which they are called upon to die and if they were to die I asked God to give them the courage to imitate Gómez Toro."[62]

Perhaps the most controversial instance of suicide involved José Martí, who was killed at Dos Ríos in May 1895 as he charged into a pitched battle atop a white horse. The matter of Martí's death has been the subject of lively debate for more than one hundred years.[63] Many have suggested that Martí deliberately placed himself in the line of fire in pursuit of martyrdom. His close friend and collaborator Fermín Valdés-Domínguez was certain that Martí "dream[ed] of suicide as the only means by which to prepare the way . . . and expedite the task of independence to which he had dedicated his life."[64] Biographer Joaquín Martínez Sáenz insisted that Martí believed that "the redemption of Cubans . . . needed his death more than his life. He gave the fullness of his martyrdom to the Patria." Gonzalo de Quesada y Miranda arrived at a similar conclusion:

> The death of Martí was no 'tragic mishap,' but was rather a deliberate sacrifice on his part, consistent with his most intimate feelings and with the full certainty that his death, far from weakening the revolution, would give it the supreme and necessary example with which to triumph, not immediately in a military sense but in its most important and transcendental aspect, which is to say its psychic facet, that of leaving his immortal imprint on the Cuban soul. . . . Any other end to his life is inconceivable and there is ample evidence that he understood this.[65]

Martí scholar Manuel Pedro González eschewed the use of the word "suicide" in his discussion of the death of Martí, judging the word to imply "the idea of escape, of flight from life or of mental disorder." Rather, González suggested, Martí's "death was voluntary, longed for, sought. . . . It was the act of a man who desires and seeks death and seizes the first opportunity that is presented to fulfill his wish."[66]

For much of his adult life, Martí was transfixed by death for the patria as destiny, a means of personal redemption and national salvation. He elevated sacrifice as duty to near mystical heights. "Some lament the necessary death," he affirmed. "I believe in it as a means of uplift and the triumph of life." Martí wrote of those "who dream to set foot once more on their own land" and "think only in the beauty of a mortal wound atop a horse, fighting for the country, and dying under a palm tree." And at another point: "I die content: death is of little concern for I have achieved the salvation [of the patria]. Oh, how sweet death is when one dies fighting bravely to defend the Patria." He wrote of the "greatness that renders sacrifice desirable and useful and confers everlasting majesty on those who were sacrificed," of the "heroism of death," and insisted that "death illuminates life with supernatural clarity." He reflected: "To die is nothing. To die is to live, to sow. He who dies, if he dies where he should, serves. In Cuba who lives more than [Carlos Manuel de] Céspedes, more than Ignacio Agramonte? Be worthy and you will live. Serve and you will live. Love and you will live. Take leave of yourself and you will live. Die well and you will rise up." Only days prior to joining the insurrection in Cuba, Martí wrote to his mother describing his as a "life that loves sacrifice" and alluded to his preparation for "the sacrifice of my life," adding: "The duty of a man is to be where he will be most useful." On the day before his death, Martí wrote to Manuel Mercado: "I am everyday in danger of giving my life as my duty."[67]

Whether Martí chose to die at Dos Ríos perhaps matters less than the fact that his death provided an enduring model for the enactment of death as duty. In fact, in the larger scheme of things, it does not matter if Martí's preoccupation with self-sacrifice for the patria sheds any light on the circumstances of his own death. Of far greater importance is the degree to which the formulations Martí fashioned as ethical imperatives corresponding to Cuban, central to which was death as duty, insinuated themselves into the larger narratives of nationality.[68] He was not some isolated thinker but a political writer deeply and constructively engaged in the debates of his time, whose particular genius was to distill the essences of the independentista discourse into a master narrative. Martí had a profound influence on the canons by which the meaning of Cuban entered the realms of national consciousness. His prodigious literary output, in the form of plays and poetry; essays, editorials, and correspondence; published speeches and manifestos, gained a vast reading public and thereupon served as the authorizing text for the evocation and experience of nationality. His preoccupation with death as means and modality of Cuban guaranteed that the proposition of self-immolation would inscribe itself deeply onto the discursive structures that transacted representations of nationality.

The death of Martí at Dos Ríos, whether by choice or by chance, served as exemplary inspiration, one to which Cubans then and thereafter would refer as the measure of duty required as a function of nationality. The Martí celebrated by his followers became the paradigm for all patriotic Cubans to imitate. If Martí could offer his life for the patria, who could do anything less? This was the moral that Ricardo Buenamar drew from Dos Ríos: "The sublime and legendary example of the great patriot [José Martí] who had exhorted the Cuban people to revolution, showed the way, and taught the Cuban people how to die." Avelino Sanjenís wrote with reverence about the meaning of the life and death of Martí. "We will soon consummate the sacred work of the Apostle of the Revolution," he wrote in 1897, "a work that will make him immortal, for the heart of every Cuban will contain an altar to the one who sacrificed himself to free us, who knew how to die . . . for the independence of the patria, leaving us his example that we here who are disposed to die know how to emulate." *El Cubano Libre* was categorical: "He died like Christ, to redeem us, and like Christ he bequeathed to us the example of his virtues and his martyrdom. His example must be followed."[69]

Cuban came to imply total commitment in pursuit of patria, as duty and dedication, and always as disposition to die as a deed of devotion. Anything less threatened to undermine the norms around which the pursuit of patria had been assembled and upon which the independentista polity depended for cohesion and purpose. "Everything for the patria (*todo por la patria*)," Cubans proclaimed, with nothing held back, nothing held in reserve. "The patriot is obliged to sacrifice everything for the patria," insisted the weekly *Cuba*, "and sacrifice it constantly." In Raimundo Cabrera's autobiographical novel, *Ideales* (1918), the protagonist Julian announces: "It is time for sacrifice in behalf of the independence of the patria, time to shed, if necessary, the last drop of our blood to obtain . . . our objective." For the liberation of the patria, General Manuel Piedra Martel recorded in his memoirs, "we were disposed to subordinate everything, to forget everything, including our absent and distant family, perhaps in hunger, without bread and without fire in the hearth, perhaps wandering in vagabondage or imprisoned by the enemy in his impotent rage."[70] "The patria before everything . . . ," proclaimed Antonio Maceo, "the glory of sacrificing everything." Similar were the sentiments of Fermín Valdés-Domínguez. "Everything, absolutely everything, has to be offered to the Patria," he exhorted. And at another point: "I should offer everything to the patria, and I offered everything to the Patria with the valor of a Cuban." He added: "[I] feel content dying in the fulfillment of my duties as a Cuban and as a man."[71]

Valdés-Domínguez contemplated death secure in his identity within an emerging paradigm of Cuban manhood, and thereby gave expression to a larger frame of reference in which the logic of sacrifice was transacted. The proposition of death as duty entered the narrative of nationality possessed of specific gender-differentiated attributes. The model fashioned duty as a function of manhood, specifically presenting men as warriors who received death stoically, and thereupon passed into martyrdom. It drew upon idealized norms of manliness, of sublime and noble sacrifice, expected of all men by virtue of being male. Codes of manhood—of "real men"—converged with norms of nationality—of "real Cubans"—to celebrate qualities of valor and virility, of honor and courage, but most of all to ratify the duty of sacrifice demanded of Cuban men. "There is no greater pleasure for the Cuban (*para el cubano*)," José López affirmed, "no greater feeling of pride, no greater sense of being a man, than when he considers that he has fulfilled his patriotic duty."[72] "To feel like men," Ramón Roa wrote during the Ten Years War, "to obey the impulses of conscience, to dream of the glory of becoming martyrs or heroes, . . . that is the height of sacrifice and abnegation."[73]

The pursuit of self-determination, rendered variously as affirmation of freedom and independence, operated easily enough in those domains where metaphors of manhood fused with the metaphysic of patria, where gender-driven canons of self-esteem insinuated themselves into duty-bound conventions of self-determination. The salvation of Cuba was conflated with the vindication of Cuban manhood. "I hope that he will vindicate himself," provisional president Carlos Manuel de Céspedes wrote of his brother-in-law, "and soon come to Cuba to triumph or die with his brothers as is the duty of a man of honor."[74] On this point Céspedes was categorical: "Desire is deed, especially for a virile people. [Let] all men resolve to put their lives on the line, if necessary, as respect due to the Patria. The time has long passed for half-hearted resolutions, of lip-service to conspiracy not backed up with action. . . . The time for heroic decision has arrived. The Patria asks for the assistance of all its sons. Those who do not present themselves, thereby deserting [the patria] in the supreme conflict, have no right to call themselves sons of Cuba."[75]

The paradigm of Cuban was not without means of coercion and compulsion, ways by which to exact compliance and conformity to those elements deemed essential to the Cuban purpose. They often took the form of subtle—and sometimes not so subtle—social pressure, ranging from censure to humiliation and including ostracism and exclusion, as ways to enforce the independentista consensus. Men who failed to meet the requirements of manhood on behalf of patria were not real men; they were effeminate, that is fainthearted and foppish, distracted and dependent, or simply cowards, upon whom was heaped scorn and contempt. General Manuel Piedra Martel denounced "the cowards, insolent emasculated men who were incapable of employing any weapon other than insults and lies." One conspirator in Havana during the Little War complained of the "prominent effeminized men" (los grandes afeminados) of Havana, "always terrified or affecting a shameful fear," failing to respond to the summons to arms. Colonel Eduardo Rosell y Malpica lamented "the character" of a comrade whom he denounced as being "of little use, for thinking like a woman (cerebro femenil) on political matters."[76] The coward represented both dereliction of duty as Cuban and default on the code of manhood, a disgrace, and more: in fact, he threatened the very norms from which the pursuit of patria derived moral subsidy. Failure to join the insurrection or in some other way provide moral and/or material support to the cause of Cuba Libre was tantamount to rendering aid and comfort to Spain, behavior unworthy of a Cuban, an act of treason and betrayal of the norms by which the dominant version of Cuban was forming. The coward could not be admitted into the community of Cuban; his conduct could not but visit shame on his family and discredit on his people. Always, the moral was clear: death was preferred to dishonor.

The terms of Cuban drew men into the independentista project as a function both of self-esteem and self-determination. But it was no less true—and no less important—that norms of nationality that assembled around the ideal of sacrifice also required the corroboration of expanded kinship networks, and especially the collaboration of women, who were expected to bear the loss of men with a resignation that was itself rendered as a condition of duty. Men and women together were drawn into reconciliation to death as a circumstance of destiny, inescapable and indeed indispensable for the realization of patria. The proposition of death among men and resignation to death among women served as mutually reinforcing discursive formulations through which normative renderings of Cuban worked to ratify commitment to specific forms of collective conduct. Provisional president Carlos Manuel de Céspedes differentiated the cost of patria through gender-specific attributes, an undertaking sustained by the blood of men and the tears of women. José Martí made a similar point in a slightly different way: "Great rights are not obtained by tears, but by blood."[77]

These were not categories invented by the emerging narratives of nationality, of course. On the contrary, to a greater or lesser extent they conformed generally to shared notions about those attributes with which gender-determined functions were most commonly associated. The designation of arms-bearing men as defenders of the homeland and child-bearing women as defenders of the home drew upon dichotomies deeply embedded in the conventions of received wisdom.

This is not to suggest that women did not participate on the front lines of the insurrection. Many did indeed risk their lives in the field and formed an important presence in the camps of the insurgent armies.[78] But the far more celebrated mode of participation of women, which is to say, the functions by which the formulations of Cuban most commonly socialized women into the domains of nationality, was in collateral roles as mothers and wives.

That these roles may have been conceived to lie principally within the domains of the domestic did not mean, of course, that women lived entirely within the confines of the private. No less than men, women were shaped by the circumstances of their times. "The Cuban woman is not insensible to the misfortune that has befallen her people . . . ," Aurora Coca de Granados affirmed in 1857, "and upon casting her fate with the suffering of her brothers she assumes a duty that will ennoble her."[79] Women also experienced love of patria and hatred of Spain; they reacted emotionally to the Cuban flag (*La Estrella Solitaria*) and the insurgent anthem ("La Bayamesa"); they wrote patriotic poems and composed *décimas* eulogizing the purpose of Cuban arms. Surviving correspondence, journals, and memoirs provide powerful testimony to their contribution to the moral environment in which the proposition of patria flourished and obtained enduring validation.[80] "The revolution of Cuba has prompted a moral revolution among us Cuban women," Emilia Casanova de Villaverde explained to General Federico Cavada in 1870, "and for my part I can say that I am capable of participation and much more." Casanova was categorical: "We

Emilia Casanova de Villaverde, ca. 1870. From Un Contemporáneo [Cirilo Villaverde], *Apuntes biográficos de Emilia Casanova de Villaverde* (New York, 1870).

are in revolution, and Cuban [women] can not remain indifferent in the face of the sublime effort that is being made to save the patria."[81]

Nationality implied more than affinity and affiliation with place and people. It also assumed social meaning through discharge of gender roles, especially as deployed in response to the specific needs of popular mobilization. Sacrifice was experienced and enacted in many forms, and its most remarkable feature was the degree to which its multiple facets were fashioned around interlocking and mutually reinforcing paradigms derived from gender-specific attributes. Men and women jointly sustained the logic through which death entered the norms of nationality, albeit in vastly different ways. Sacrifice by men necessarily implied sacrifice by women and could not have been transacted without the disposition of women to uphold the codes by which the determinants of duty were defined. Gendered concepts of duty situated men and women at different points along the spectrum of sacrifice, to be sure, but it is no less true that the assumptions derived from these dispositions were both reciprocal and binding.

The larger moral meaning of nationality was fashioned out of complex normative tensions, between competing attention and conflicting affections, between duty and love, between public responsibility and private obligations, with outcomes often difficult to reconcile within existing and otherwise all-encompassing gender conventions. Men often anguished over the conflicting demands between dedication to patria and devotion to family. "After the war," Fermín Valdés-Domínguez vowed to his wife,

"I will no longer owe myself to my Patria, I will then belong only to you. After having fulfilled my duty as Cuban, nothing and no one will ever again separate me from you."[82] Carlos Manuel de Céspedes despaired. "It has been twenty months since I last saw you," he wrote to his wife in 1872, and continued:

> During this eternity, how much pain I have endured! . . . Notwithstanding my fortitude and my firm resolve to die if I do not liberate my patria, a resolve that I believe you approve and should approve, I confess to you that I have suffered a grave anguish for which I have needed all my will power to overcome. There is no sacrifice comparable to that of living separated from you and the bonds of our love; but when I see so many Cubans indifferent to their patria or who turn their backs on [the patria] in order to be with their family, I am ashamed and I reaffirm my vow so that someday it can be said that Cuba has produced at least one man with dignity. I know you share these sentiments and that you do not hold me guilty for having left you alone, in exile, in charge of the family and without resources.[83]

"The resignation over our separation has been depleted," Ignacio Agramonte wrote to his wife in 1871, "and my hatred of the Spaniards increases. Separation has always brought us so much suffering! Cuba demands great sacrifices, but Cuba will be free at all costs. Adversity serves to make us more dedicated, more indomitable." José Hernández Guzmán agonized over the decision to abandon his family to join the insurgency. "I thought of my three small children, of my young and beautiful wife, in their helplessness upon my abandoning them," he recorded in his memoirs; "the struggle within me as love for the cause impelled me toward the field and my wild enthusiasm did not allow me to think of anything else, despite the influence my family exercised over me, with pleas and tears. This was one of the most painful days of my life." As he departed for war Hernández Guzmán continued to ponder: "Did I do right? Was I obliged to fulfill a sacred duty? I believed I was, even though I left behind a large family, abandoned, weeping children calling out for me and the home in darkness. They will die of hunger." Colonel Avelino Sanjenís also struggled between duty to patria and devotion to his wife and mother. "In those critical moments of my very existence," he wrote, "in which I owed myself only to my patria, I interrupted the course of my plans and my interests." It was impossible to "think about the future without having a patria," he wrote to his wife. "You, my mother, and my patria so confuse my ideas that I suffer and feel cruel despair. If I could only open my heart so that you could see the horrible struggle in which I am engaged over the three of you, without knowing which one has the greatest influence." Sanjenís enjoined his wife to "resign yourself to letting me leave, for awaiting me are the unforeseen fortunes of war." He sought to console his wife: "If I should become part of the countless numbers of the martyrs to duty, my last good-bye will be for my mother, my last breath will be for my patria, and the last memory that will emanate from my heart will be of you." The triumph of patria over family was thus complete. "Here," Sanjenís later wrote from the field, "there is no one who speaks of peace, nor is there anyone who remembers it, nor does anyone remember his home, or his sweetheart, or his wife, or his mother. We are preoccupied only with the patria."[84] In the poem "A mi madre," writer Luis Victoriano Betancourt, who served with distinction in the Liberation Army during the Ten Years War, addressed the ambivalence directly: "And meanwhile raged a conflict within me / Of my mother who I recalled / And my poor conscience was between duty and love." Resolving his ambivalence in categorical terms in favor of patria, Betancourt directed the final stanza to his mother:

> Nothing—nothing at all
> Can extinguish my love of patria;
> Because duty commands me
> Either free I will see you again
> Or free in Cuba to die.

Betancourt returned to this theme in "Simpatías del destino:"

> I know that my youth
> Was protected by your love,
> And I know that your virtue
> Was repaid with ingratitude
> For having left you abandoned.

And once again the moral was sharply drawn:

> Mother! Your name is so sacred,
> That to dry the tears from your eyes
> My life I would give!
> But I love Cuba so!
> Forgive me, mother of mine![85]

Women transacted meanings of sacrifice by way of complex negotiations through which to reconcile the moral contradictions and personal costs of nationality. The duty of Cuban demanded that women support men in the defense of the homeland, even if at the expense of the home, that love of fathers, husbands, and sons be subordinated to the needs of patria, precisely as the counterpart modality called upon men to subordinate love of mothers, wives, and children to the pursuit of patria. Manuel Arbelo secretly prepared to join the Liberation Army, telling no one of his plans—not even his wife. "Although I felt a powerful urge to discuss the matter with her," Arbelo recalled years later, "I was unable to engage in such a conversation due to the shame I felt simply thinking about the situation in which my wife would find herself as a result of my absence. She would be left without resources of any kind, with nothing to live on, in an uncaring society from which she could expect nothing." Arbelo continued:

But my wife took the lead. Understanding the source of my disquiet . . . that frustrated my desire to join the war, she faced the problem head on. One day she told me with a resolve of great serenity: 'If you wish to join the Revolution, don't hesitate on my account, for in comparison to the work for the independence of Cuba I have no significance.' I was left speechless, admiring the valor and the resignation in a frail woman who had no means of support in the world other than her husband. I said nothing, but at that moment, convinced that the time had arrived for every real Cuban (*cubano de corazón*) to face all sacrifices, whatever they may be, I decided to take leave the next day. . . . The following morning I awoke and dressed without making noise. I tip-toed through the room in which my wife slept restlessly, I gave her a sorrowful goodbye look, opened the door to the house and took to the street.[86]

Women gained entrée to and conferred moral vitality on nationality by ratifying the proposition of death as duty. Sacrifice insinuated itself deeply into the ideal of Cuban womanhood, per formulations of nationality, and acquired cultural meaning as resignation to the death of men in the service of patria and acceptance of the attending emotional loss and material impoverishment. Resignation was transacted as deployment of moral resources in the presentation of public demeanor, as exemplary carriage in the form of duty, an occasion to strike a pose of self-sacrifice and self-possession as heroic conduct, to bear sorrow as if to bear witness to those conventions by which death as duty was rendered as an ethical imperative of Cuban. Stoic bearing of grief was celebrated as sacrificial courage, proclaimed to be of no less valor and of no less importance to patria than battlefield courage. Women demonstrated exemplary valor, wrote Concepción Boloña at the end of the war, through "expressions of sublime abnegation and suffering borne with heroic resignation."[87]

The ideal of Cuban womanhood bearing sacrifice and suffering heroically, inscribed in canons of resignation, served to validate the death of men as duty, expand the consensual framework of nationality, and make women party to the formulations by which Cuban was fashioned. "When it involves matters of the patria," Francisco Aguilera exhorted his three daughters, "all sacrifices are small. You must provide example of a constant perseverance, of a heroic resignation, and pure virtue." Martí celebrated the archetypical "woman who prepared herself in exile during the years in which her husband would be bleeding for liberty [and] the widow who educated her three sons for war."[88] Provisional president Carlos Manuel de Céspedes praised criollas during the Ten Years War for their "sentiment [of sacrifice] and abnegation . . . , the purity of the love for their patria, the faith with which they commit themselves to the revolution, the valor and heroism with which they motivate their husbands and sons to war, remaining alone, and the tranquil acquiescence with which they suffer exposure, hunger, danger, illness, and all types of privation and pain." In writing to María Rojas about the death of her son, Céspedes added poignance to the idealized rendering of criolla virtue:

> I learned with gratification of the patriotic conduct you observed upon learning of the tragic event, reconciling yourself with remarkable resignation to the fate [your son] encountered, and encouraging your other sons to defend with even more ardor and enthusiasm—if that were possible—the liberty of Cuba. This heroic and noble deed serves to place you high among the mothers of history. It cannot but merit my praise and that of every good Cuban (todo buen cubano), for it reveals a magnificent and noble heart and a love for the liberty and independence of your country that is total and unwavering, even if it were necessary for you to sacrifice everything. . . . In these circumstances, I deeply commend the heroic conduct with which you have observed this difficult and tragic situation.[89]

The act of women bearing grief conferred meaning and purpose on the death of men, as a source of consolation and means of comfort, to be sure, as well as an occasion of commemoration as memorial. But it was also true that the difference between commemoration and celebration was often difficult to discern, which meant too that the act of grieving possessed the capacity to affirm the very logic of sacrifice as a function of Cuban. There could be no more powerful vindication of the ideal of sacrifice than through the conduct of mothers and wives who commemorated the death of sons and husbands as exemplary deeds in the service of patria, and who in the anguish of their bereavement lent the power of their moral authority to the validation of the higher purpose for which death was rendered. "Love and adoration of his patria, which is the greatest of all loves, led him to the [ultimate] sacrifice" wrote Ana Betancourt as she grieved the death of her husband. "Because all progress, because all great ideas, must be purchased with tears and nurtured with blood from the veins, the will of God must be honored. Let us pray for the Patria and its heroes." María Cabrales wrote of the death of her husband Antonio Maceo: "If it were possible that my suffering as beloved wife and my pain as patriotic Cuban could be mitigated it would be in the . . . exalted purpose of struggle without respite until achieving our absolute emancipation and sustenance at all cost of the unity of the Cuban people in the face of the common enemy." Commented one Spanish correspondent: "[Cuban women] have looked upon the bodies of their husbands and their sons with dry eyes, always firm and decisive, but with private supplication to heaven for the triumph of their men."[90]

These were the salient themes around which narratives of condolence were structured and the larger moral affirmed. "Your suffering and the heroic resignation with which you have borne your pain for the love of the patria are clear to me," Carlos Manuel de Céspedes consoled Manuela Cancino upon the death of her father. "There is, however, consolation for this grief: it is found in the . . . fulfillment of duty." Céspedes explained to Josefa Rodríguez de Peralta that her husband had perished "in service to his patria," adding: "This is a virtue that will survive him forever, and which should make his descendants proud. The patria, for its part, will be grateful and will be proud to include him among its distinguished sons (sus ilustres hijos)." To the mother of Ignacio Agramonte, Céspedes wrote: "Nothing can serve to console the pain of a mother. That her son no longer alive is reason for her to weep inconsolably forever. But, madam, you cannot be deprived the most justifiable pride. . . . For [heroic] men, always persecution and death, for their family an eternal coat of arms, for their patria the duty to build for them monuments of gratitude. This is the fate of those whose acts will be recorded on the pages of history." Rosalía García de Osuna lost two sons and was said to have "fulfilled her duty without hesitation and bore her grief like a mother and a Cuban." Josefa Pina was a "good wife," wrote the biographer of General Serafín Sánchez, "hard working, and when [Serafín Sánchez] was killed, she remained resigned, saddened, and a dedicated keeper of his memory."[91]

Consciousness of Cuban was fashioned under specific historical circumstances, not as immutable elements of national character, but rather as pragmatic formulations of national purpose, subject always to mediation of those overarching considerations by which people ordered their lives, often hardly cognizant at all of the forces to which their behaviors responded. Cubans through much of the nineteenth century were a people in continual dialogue with themselves, seeking to define duty and purpose in response to their times, within the context of gender conventions as they knew them, men and women speaking to each other and in the process setting into place normative systems from which the terms of nationality were fashioned. They drew their sense of purpose from the bonds of the common will that united them.

The project of liberation imposed demands on all who were implicated in its assumptions, a requirement that necessarily signaled modification of old conventions to meet new conditions. That these commitments were often enacted within the framework of established canons of gender matters less than the degree to which gender functions were deeply imbued with the purpose of nation. These issues were negotiated within complex realms of interpersonal relationships in which men and women made their expectations of each other known, per the standards that defined their world, sustaining one another, each looking for clues from each other as guide to comportment and carriage, seeking to fulfill the expectations held by each other, and in the process fashioning the solidarities by which nation came into being.

All through the nineteenth century, women gave voice and thereby added validation to Cuban mobilization. They addressed the issues of their times, inserted themselves consciously into history, and in the process defended and defined the duty required of both men and women. "The desire to serve the patria and contribute to its liberation is innate in me," explained Emilia Casanova de Villaverde in 1871. "Ever since I was a child. . . . I vowed to myself that I would consecrate my life to that sacred and noble objective. To this day I have done little else except to work and dream of the redemption of my patria . . . My love for the patria has always been greater than my love for anything else."[92] Sofía Estévez de Rodríguez, writing in 1897 as Spain prepared to grant Cuba autonomy, made her views known:

Cuban women, born under the weight of slavery, [are] accustomed to weeping all our lives under the despotic power that has always wrested from our arms those persons who we have loved with all our hearts and to take their lives on the gallows. We do not allow our spirits to weaken, our hearts will not falter. . . . It is too late for autonomy! We have never wanted autonomy, but perhaps at an earlier time, we would have accepted it by force because, in the end, it would have been something, like Sundays for the slave labor force on the sugar mills (*como los domingos para las dotaciones de los ingenios*) during the time of slavery. It is too late now. Too much innocent blood has been spilled; too many Cubans have been deported to African prisons; too many Cubans have been killed. The country has been devastated. *Most of all*, too many Cuban women have been brutally offended. Our husbands, our sons, our brothers, all Cubans with dignity, all men of honor, will continue to shed their blood. . . . These women — *above all* — are especially aggrieved by the outrages inflicted on many of our sisters: we spit in the face of the tyrant and his autonomy and [reject] any pact that could leave Cuba in any way tied to Spain.[93]

Women were indispensable in assembling the terms by which the conventions of Cuban were defined and deployed. They entered the realms of nationality conscious of the need to meet their responsibilities in the pursuit of patria, prepared to suffer personal loss and sacrifice material well-being, prepared to defer hopes for happiness and forgo the aspirations traditionally associated with family and home. "I was happy because he was good and loved me madly," Ana Betancourt recalled of the early years of her marriage to Ignacio Mora. "He made our home into a paradise. He shared with me not only all his material possessions but his knowledge. He and I became one in our ideas and sentiments." Everything changed when Mora joined the insurgency: "I was reduced to a pariah: without family, virtually alone in the world, but nevertheless I lived in peace with myself in the knowledge that my beloved was out there in the fields of my patria, watching over me in spirit, and whose name was for me a badge of honor."[94]

Gendered formulations of Cuban were arranged into highly complex moral hierarchies from which to fashion prescriptive conduct out of ascriptive codes, a process that served to implicate men and women alike in the validation of those formulations upon which the realization of patria depended. In no other way could the commitments that held men and women together in the pursuit of patria have been sustained. Emilia Casanova de Villaverde proclaimed her "devotion of all true Cubans (*los cubanos verdaderos*)" and insisted that "all Cuban women . . . know how to distinguish between the patriot of sincerity and stout-heart and the timid dilettante."[95]

The proposition of sacrifice expanded into an all-encompassing and self-implicating paradigm, as mothers and wives were called upon to motivate sons and husbands to serve patria even as they prepared themselves for the sacrifice of sons and husbands. "The patria depends on women," proclaimed the newspaper *Patria*. "If they fail, we perish; if they are loyal, we exist. The abnegation of women commits men to virtue."[96]

Men took cues from women, and to the degree that women's expectations served to inform or otherwise influence the constancy with which men gave themselves to duty, the impact of women on outcomes must be considered decisive. The ways that women acted to sustain those dispositions by which men transacted death as duty is, of course, a complex matter and difficult to ascertain with any precision. The evidence is scattered and anecdotal, but suggestive. Ana Betancourt appears to have fully assimilated the conventions of Cuban, to which she added her own moral authority. "Ignacio," she exhorted her husband with Spartan ardor as he prepared to leave for war, "return with your shield or atop your shield." There was no doubt in the mind of Julia Miranda de Morales where duty lay for her husband: "I, poor widow that I am, if I were again to be with my husband, as I once was, I would again believe that his obligation was to die for his country." It was a Spanish correspondent in Cuba who provided one of the most insightful commentaries on the contribution of women to the liberation project: "Women have made the insurrection in Cuba. If they were not the first to feel rage of offended dignity, they were the first to express it. The opinion that women form is irresistible among men. They spoke with clarity and with honesty, fearlessly: to us they spoke of [Spanish] abuses and to their men they spoke of rights and duties. . . . Like the women of Rome and Sparta, they pointed their men to the battlefields and told them, 'there is your place.'. . . When women think and act in this manner, men are invincible."[97]

Certainly José Martí was conscious of the ways that the expectations of women influenced the behavior of men when he purported to represent the preferences of women: "The woman loves the brave man; she despises the coward." With the founding of the Cuban Revolutionary Party (PRC), Martí exulted, men were now "filled with divine light of sacrifice," and added: "And the women were once again proud of their men." Carlos Manuel de Céspedes made a similar point: "With what profound contempt would a wife look upon her shirker husband, a mother view her cowardly son, the betrothed judge her weak fiancé. And with what pride would a woman in any of these three situations look upon her husband, her son, and her lover, covered with the powder of combat and crowned with the laurel of battle." If men saw women display their support of patria through "incontrovertible abnegation," the weekly *Patria* asked editorially, if they saw women "at their side, not simply with passive resignation with which they submit to the inevitable but with all the determination of active resolve, how then could men . . . not feel comforted in the selfless task to which they were summoned?" The *Diario Cubano* suggested that men "played a secondary role" in the insurrection, with "women as the will and men as the muscle." Colonel Eusebio Sáenz y Sáenz of the Spanish Guardia Civil similarly took note of the role of the wives of insurgents during the Ten Years War, observing that "they surpassed their husbands in [revolutionary] ideas . . . and exercised such superiority that the husbands obeyed them blindly."[98] Indeed, early in the Ten Years War, the Spanish army command in eastern Cuba mounted operations specifically against women. Announced a proclamation of April 1869: "Women who are not in their respective farms and dwellings, or in the homes of their parents, must relocate to camps in the towns of Jiguaní and Bayamo, where they will be cared for. Those who do not voluntarily obey this proclamation will be escorted [to Jiguaní and Bayamo] by force."[99]

Much of the moral sustenance with which men dedicated themselves to patria, including the willingness to die, was derived from intimacies exchanged with mothers and wives. Hovering over the narratives of liberation, at the time and thereafter, was a powerful sense of men disposed to die as a way to live up to the expectations of mothers and wives, a sense that husbands and sons who failed to meet their duty to die feared as much as anything else being subjected to revilement from mothers and wives. In ways perhaps all too imperfectly understood, the role of women in the formation of men's will to obtain deliverance of patria or die in the process cannot be overstated. Rodolfo Mederos had his mother very much in mind when he chose to die during the Ten Years War. Taken prisoner in battle, Mederos was offered an opportunity to avoid execution by claiming that he had surrendered. Mederos spurned the offer: "Never! My mother will be consoled when she learns that I have died like a Cuban. She would be shamed if she saw me enter Santiago as a surrendering coward." The

Lucía Iñiguez, n.d. Courtesy of Archivo Nacional de Cuba, Havana, Cuba.

solace that Domingo Goicuría offered his wife in his final letter prior to his execution was succinct: "Take consolation that your son like me has died without the stain of cowardice; no one could have done more for the Patria. To die for Cuba is a source of gratification. Believe me. I feel this deeply in my heart. I am not troubled in the slightest by the prospect of dying." Ignacio Tamayo wrote to his mother prior to his execution: "I die honorably and as a man of honor, and that should provide you with a measure of consolation."[100] It may be that Calixto García also had his mother in mind when he attempted suicide in 1874. Lucía Iñiguez had at first refused to believe that her son Calixto had been taken prisoner by Spaniards. "Calixto is my son," she insisted, "and for that reason he should not surrender." When told that he fell prisoner only after an unsuccessful suicide attempt, she responded: "Ah! Yes, that is my son Calixto! Death before surrender!"[101]

Sacrifice assumed multiple forms, of course, and for many women sacrifice was borne as resignation to the death of sons and husbands. Years later Ramiro Cabrera recalled his final days with his mother, as he prepared to depart to join the insurgency: "Not once did she ask me not to go to war. How sad she was. When alone she would pass the day crying. How great the suffering of a mother must be when she sees her only son join a war without quarter, one as terrible and sorrowful as ours, and she doesn't dare ask him to renounce his commitment, for however great her love, great too is the duty to struggle and die for the patria." Dominga

Moncada was imprisoned after spurning the Spanish governor general's request that she persuade her sons to abandon the ranks of the insurgent army. "Look, General," she retorted, "if I saw my sons coming down the road and I saw you approaching them from the other direction, I'd scream: 'Flee, my sons, for here comes the Spanish General!'" Spanish authorities urged Ana Betancourt to encourage her husband to surrender or face certain death in the field. "That is our destiny," she replied. Asked if she really loved her husband, Betancourt answered: "More than my very soul! But I prefer to be the widow of a man of honor than be the wife of a man in disrepute and without dignity." When her skeptical interlocutor suggested that surely she would have been delighted to see her husband return home, Betancourt responded unflinchingly: "I would rather find his body."[102]

The model of stoic bearing, of women discharging the duty of sacrifice as affirmation of being Cuban, assumed prominence in the larger narratives of nationality. Whether it described reality or sought to create reality was not always clear. But what was certain was that it suggested a standard of conduct that women were exhorted to uphold. "And our women?" asked Luis Quintero in 1875. "Could we ask for any greater abnegation?" Quintero continued:

> Are they not rivals of the daughters of Sparta? Have they not surpassed [Spartan women] in resignation and in suffering? . . . There is no task they have not performed, no misery they have not suffered, no sorrow that has not afflicted their heart. They have lost their dear brothers, their beloved husbands, their adored sons. Their sons! We who know how much a Cuban mother loves her son can appreciate the intensity of her sorrow. And yet, these women suffer their exile and their misery and their pain without the slightest complaint against the revolution, and they encourage and support the patriot who wishes to share with his brothers the horrors of war. The sons of such women cannot but know how to be free.[103]

"Raise the cry of war," poet Pedro Angel Castellón exhorted women, "to your son, to your father, to your husband, to show with your glorious example and passionate enthusiasm that you, too, like valiant men, know how to secure immortality."[104]

Men and women together fashioned mutually reinforcing bonds by which they held each other to the task of liberation. These formulations often operated as assumptions so thoroughly understood that they ceased to be apprehended at all. But it is also true that they induced a vast range of new behaviors consistent with the needs of liberation. This was a complicated process, by which people took in and acted out the larger social meanings of their times. The interior lives of vast numbers of men and women were shaped decisively by subjective experiences within a polity organized single-mindedly around a purpose to which everything was subordinated. When a group of criolla detainees were taunted by Spanish officials for having been abandoned by male relatives to join the insurgency, Candelaria Figueredo responded: "The men of my family do not dedicate themselves to the care of women; they assume their place in the army." Years later Ana Betancourt indicated that her refusal to urge Ignacio Mora to surrender was related less to the fear that he would actually accede to her appeal than to the concern that her request would "cause him sorrow in seeing my signature approving something that would diminish me in his eyes."[105]

The independentista project assigned new meanings to established gender-determined functions and in the process transformed the purpose for which men and women discharged socially ascribed roles. Exemplary motherhood was fashioned around those narratives that celebrated women who prepared their sons to serve patria, even if it meant—and especially if it meant—the loss of their sons' lives. The mother who lost a son was honored for the sacrifice discharged as duty to patria. It was often with pride that a mother acknowledged the loss of a son, for it ratified that she too had acquitted herself and raised her son correctly. "In the [Ten Years] war I lost all my possessions," recalled Clotilde Tamayo Cisneros. "But more than that, I lost seven beloved sons and grandsons; but if necessary I would do it again."[106] Mariana Grajales, whose husband and eleven sons participated in the wars for Cuban independence, acquired singular distinction in the iconography of patria. María Cabrales, the wife of Antonio Maceo, present in the Maceo household on the eve of the outbreak of the Ten Years War, would later recount how Mariana Grajales "entered her room and came out with a crucifix raised in her hand and said: 'Everyone on their knees, fathers and sons, before Christ, . . . and let us swear to liberate the Patria or die for it.'" Not long thereafter, upon learning that her eldest son had died in battle, Grajales is said to have summoned her youngest son and enjoined: "Stand tall so you can occupy the place of your brother." On another occasion in 1877, as her son José was nearing recovery from a battle injury, Grajales insisted: "You are already cured of your wound. Return to the front lines to fulfill your duty." Mariana lost her husband and nine of her eleven sons in the struggle for Cuban

Mariana Grajales, n.d. Courtesy of Archivo Nacional de Cuba, Havana, Cuba.

independence—and was reported to have expressed regret only that she did not have more sons to offer the patria.[107] "Go, fulfill your duty," Ana Josefa de Agüero Perdomo exhorted her husband, "so that the next time we embrace you will be a free man." At the burial of Guillermo Moncada, his mother gathered the family and proclaimed: "They have just buried Guillermo. He has died without seeing Cuba free, which was his dream. Now more than ever we must imitate him."[108] The annals of the Ten Years War tell of an insurgent soldier (*mambí*), José Caridad Vargas, accused of treason and sentenced by a Cuban court martial to death by firing squad. Days prior to the scheduled execution, his mother, accompanied by her two younger sons, appeared at the insurgent camp. Believing that she had come to plead for her son's life, the commander refused to see her, to which she responded: "No! I have not come here to request a pardon for my son. If he is guilty of treason, then the death sentence is just and may God forgive him. I have come here to tell you that I have these two other sons to add to the ranks of the Liberation Army and if it should come to pass that they too turn out to be traitors, I will not mourn the death of either one of them." Added the narrator of the story: "The [Military] Tribunal was amazed. Never had its members witnessed such display of valor and abnegation as in that woman, who placed her love for the independence of Cuba over the intense pain as a mother." No less celebrated was the account of a mother who had four sons serving in the Liberation Army and who entrusted her fifth and youngest son to an insurgent commander, affirming: "I bring to you my only remaining son, so that he may become one more defender of the Holy Cause. If he perishes, he would have died for his patria." Another story repeated often in the war narratives told of a dying woman leaving behind four sons, pleading with a priest during her final confession: "Father, so that I may die in peace, I commend to you my sons. Educate them in the hatred of Spain and the love of liberty; and if on this occasion fate renders our [war] effort a failure, that they can tomorrow offer their lives to redeem Cuba from the clutches of the tyrant."[109]

It is, of course, difficult to corroborate the veracity of these accounts. But it matters less if these stories were apocryphal than the degree to which they insinuated themselves deeply into the narratives of nationality, there to serve as the measure and model of motherhood in the service of patria. In an ode to *la madre cubana*, Néstor Carbonell celebrated the heroic mother who "shedding bitter tears in her eyes" understood that "there was no greater glory than to die fighting for the patria." José Martí repeatedly suggested that the highest purpose to which motherhood could be given was to instill in children love for the patria. He celebrated "the widowed mother who sees without tears her son depart for the wilderness in search of the grave of his father, to die to be worthy of his father, [and] provide with his body one more step toward the achievement of patria." Consuelo Alvarez eulogized Cuban mothers during the war: "I admire you, mother of mine, and the superior spirit and sublime resignation with which you have endured the sad fate that has befallen you."[110] The weekly *El Expedicionario* underscored the relationship between motherhood and nationhood:

> The Cuban mother, as a result of her particular way of being and feeling (*por su modo particular de ser y sentir*), above all other mothers generally speaking, perhaps sacrifices herself with the greatest abnegation. . . . Look at the glorious revolution and see the Cuban mother, through her spirit and often through her material support, encouraging her sons . . . so that they are not disheartened, so that they fight until victory or death, until they redeem the enslaved patria and that they may enjoy the holy liberty that they deserve and which the despicable metropolis seeks to prevent. The Cuban mother is the soul of the revolution of Cuba, for from the time she put her sons to sleep in the cradle and later taught them always to hate slavery and tyranny, [they] learned to love liberty and struggle to achieve it. Bless them![111]

Years later, the Cuban congress proclaimed Mariana Grajales "the Mother of the Patria," an act, one biographer wrote, that recognized the importance "of her life as an admirable example of the abnegation and sacrifice on the altar of the Patria." The biographer added: "The greatness of Mariana Grajales can be studied from two aspects: the deeds of her sons, whom she forged with her spirit and her blood, and through her own actions, which like a beacon illuminates the way for all generations."[112]

Motherhood was celebrated as the principal means by which to socialize children into the realms of nationality. The "moral education" of women, University of Havana professor of pedagogy María Corominas de Hernández later insisted, required "the development of patriotism as an inexhaustible source of effective power to love work and maternity for the good of the patria, offering [the patria] a vigorous, intelligent, and good generation." This view was shared by essayist Africa Fernández Iruela, who enjoined "mothers and sisters to encourage [sons and brothers] to support the struggle for Liberty, the way our grandparents encouraged their sons through word and deed during the glorious epoch of our Independence. It is not for nothing that we are a people among whom heroism has a throne and liberty a flag." Aurelia Castillo de González celebrated the "noble mission" discharged by women in the nineteenth century, who committed themselves to "preserving the sacred flame of the war of independence," and added: "Think that they swallowed their tears so as to not show weakness when their sons, fathers, brothers, husbands, and lovers were killed."[113]

⚜ Many of the dispositions by which the meaning of Cuban was transacted originated within the most intimate spheres of creole family life, by way of long-standing conventions and established customs, always in the process of adaptation during times of political conflict and cultural transformation. These were years during which concepts of duty and the meaning of loyalty were in transition, when a sense of private obligations assumed the form of public duty, and vice versa. The creole household was a highly politicized environment and served as one of the principal settings of national formation, a point of initiation and place of transmittal, where the proposition of patria entered realms of shared values as function of everyday family life.[114] Spanish colonial authorities long suspected the creole household as a site of subversion but could respond only with a deepening sense of foreboding. "[Creoles] wage an implacable campaign against us . . . within their domestic households," Spanish general Camilo Polavieja reported to Madrid in 1892. He elaborated on another occasion:

Affirmation of *Patria*, ca. 1898.
Courtesy of Biblioteca Nacional José Martí, Havana, Cuba.

Here there is only passion carried to the ultimate extreme on the part of those . . . who aspire to the ideals of independence. . . . These groups thrive on a . . . hatred of us. They do not reason. Every means that leads to emancipation from Spain appears to them to be legitimate, even moral. They wage a war without quarter against us, as much in the press as in public meetings, in private conversations within the innermost recesses of their families. They educate their children in hatred of Spain. . . . They see themselves as enslaved by us and hate us the way that a subjugated people hate their conquerors, the way that our grandparents hated the French invaders early this century.[115]

Consciousness of Cuban was itself fashioned within the intimacies of family life, the product of the very nurturing by which consciousness of selfhood was formed. The powerful moral authority of the family, with its complex codes of conduct and carriage, its established hierarchies of authority and reciprocity, served to a greater or lesser degree as source of solidarities by which independentista sentiment was forged. Indeed, the creole household must be considered as central to the process by which formulations of Cuban were assembled, the point at which the private dealings of kinship intersected with public doings of politics. Children were guided into the domains of nationality within the social conventions of family and household, on the occasions of family gatherings and reunions, during the times when different generations of the same family engaged each other, in the course of those personal and most private of conversations in which parents and grandparents sought to explain the world to their children, where the meaning and measure of Cuban passed as currency of childhood. "The example of the heroic unforgettable ten years of war," Fermín Valdés-Domínguez wrote in 1896, "was the lesson children learned and formed the holy cult of the Patria that parents transmitted to their children in their daily conversations. These lessons are the basis of the insurrection of today." Serafín Espinosa recalled growing up with "the accounts of the struggles of the war of 1868 told in the intimacy of the home by my father and my uncles who had participated in the war." These accounts made a lasting impression, Espinosa recalled, "for they lifted my spirits, and at a very early age the love of the land (amor a la tierra) took hold of my soul [and] has been with me ever since." Benito Aranguén recalled his childhood, when his parents recounted stories of the Ten Years War to him and his brother, which "influenced us in a decisive manner, fostering a firm love for our flag and a desire to see it flying over the beloved land in which we were born. From the time when we were very young we began to feel the necessity to contribute ... to the great project of obtaining Independence." Reminisced Aranguren: "That is how I became a mambí, that is how I began to discharge the duty that my father inculcated in me and that my stoic mother helped me realize."[116]

The accounts of the Ten Years War also had a decisive impact on Segundo Corvisón, who later wrote that stories he had heard as a child of the "fabulous war of ten years, of the heroic legends, had for us—the next generation of warriors—the effect . . . of awakening a love of danger and the desire for privation and suffering at the altar of liberty." Seven-year-old Rita Suárez del Villar was present when her "father's brothers and friends gathered . . . to conspire against the Spanish government." Years later she recalled vividly: "I listened to their conversations about the injustices committed against the poor patriots . . . and that experience affected me to the core of my being. Knowledge of the oppression in which my beloved Cuba lived produced in me great anguish. . . . This experience caused me to vow that as soon as I was old enough I would fight without rest until my beloved Patria became free and sovereign."[117]

That the household was so fully understood as the domain of the private, and per established gender conventions the place of the wife-mother, serves to underscore the central role women played in the formation of national consciousness. "The woman is the home," the women's club of Güinía de Miranda insisted in 1869, "and the home is patria." General Enrique Loynaz del Castillo remembered years later a childhood birthday present from his mother: "On one birthday she made me a small altar to the coat of arms of Cuba for my room . . . and adorned it with small Cuban flags. She gave direction to my life."[118] Colonel Horacio Ferrer recalled similar childhood experiences with his brother. "In the bosom of my family . . . ," Ferrer reminisced, "we would often exchange impressions about the subject of liberation." He added:

I was five years old and was very close to my mother. . . . She began to teach us, inculcating in us love of the truth and of study and of honor. And in talking about history she told us there was a man named Máximo Gómez, who fought for ten years [1868–78] to make Cuba independent. I also heard from her lips the very first mention of the names of Carlos Manuel de Céspedes and Ignacio Agramonte. She inculcated in us a love of the patria. . . . The seed of [my] love for Cuba, instilled in my spirit by my mother during my childhood, flourished during my adolescence. On one occasion my devoted mother, overcome with emotion but with total presence of mind, concluded one of those discussions by affirming: 'My sons have two mothers: the patria and me, and they should attend to the one that needs them the most!' On that day, for my brother and me, our fate was sealed."[119]

Children entered the domains of value ascription through birthdays, family gatherings, commemorative functions, even through their toys and games. In Key West and Tampa, émigré Cuban families celebrated patriotic holidays with picnics, at church services, and during baseball games. In the émigré communities of New York, children formed a ubiquitous presence at political events and patriotic rallies. They often appeared in public in patriotic attire: boys dressed as *mambises*; girls dressed to represent patria. Eva Adán recalled a patriotic function at which she dressed her son as a mambí and her daughter to represent Cuba wrapped in chains. Another observer described a meeting in New York in 1890: "Old folks, women, children, entire families, paid homage to the ideal [of the patria], demonstrating that with each passing day this ideal takes firmer hold in everyone's heart and seeks only a practical manner with which to reveal itself." The weekly *La Nueva República* reported on a youth dance (*baile infantil*) in Tampa organized by the Emilio Núñez Club, where "children paid patriotic tribute to the patria loved by everyone." Years later Flora Basulto de Montoya remembered the games of her childhood, including one in which children divided into "Cubans" and "Spaniards," each side led by children in assumed roles of commanders of the opposing forces, and thereupon proceeded to reenact the decisive battles won by the insurgent armies.[120] During the Ten Years War correspondent Grover Flint visited insurgent-held territory (*prefectura*) and observed Cuban children at play:

The children's games were all warlike. They played Spain and Cuba with sticks for guns, and carried on skirmishes in the underbrush. Sometimes it was a game . . . where one child hid a broom horse in the thicket and another played Spaniard and scouted about with a wooden machete to find and kill it. The first sound the babies mastered was 'Alto, quien va? Cuba,' and 'Pah, Pah,' 'Poom, poom, poom,'—for often sounds of shots came from the high-road, and the infants learned to distinguish between the bark of the Mauser and the slow detonation of the Remington.[121]

Studio photograph, Ybor City, Florida, ca. 1898.
Courtesy of University of South Florida Library, Tampa, Florida.

Son of Domingo Méndez Capote, ca. 1898. Courtesy of Biblioteca Nacional José Martí, Havana, Cuba.

Attachments and affinities to patria were thus forged during early childhood. Much had to do with the ways parents sought to prepare their children for their times, not necessarily as conscious acts of duty—although certainly they were conscious of the intent of their guidance—but rather because it seemed like the natural thing to do and especially because it was one more way to act out their own convictions. "I have seen children playing with their mothers," observed Ramón Céspedes Fornaris in 1871, "jumping up and down with joy, suddenly become angry. I have inquired into the cause of this behavior and have discovered it in the horror that their mothers experience at the approach of a Spaniard. There is something in a mother's look of love or look of contempt that immediately changes the mood of her children." José Martí celebrated the ways of criollo households, where the father "recounted to the children the glories of the past war and where the mother prepared them to fulfill their duty," where the "children are gathered around the piano as a choir and sing the music of war composed by the father—and the mother impatiently reacts if a single stanza is overlooked."[122] Ignacio Agramonte early suggested the destiny of his infant son as an insurgent (*mambisito*). "I think of nothing and dream of nothing but you and of our mambisito," Agramonte wrote to his wife from the field in 1868. And again several months later: "I am forming a cavalry squadron that will outfight the Spanish cavalry. Do you want me to reserve the position of first corporal for the mambisito?" And

To Die for the *Patria* | 117

not long thereafter: "How is *Don mambisito?*" Francisco Varona González learned of the death of several members of his immediate family, including his young son, and recorded in his campaign diary: "I will still persist in the liberty of the patria and I will have more sons who will also give their lives for [the patria] when it becomes necessary."[123]

The elegies that served to celebrate the independentista project were often addressed explicitly to parents in ways calculated to give patriotic purpose to the practice of child rearing. Aurelia Castillo de González gave voice to criolla mothers in "Canción de las Madres." When "Cuba asked for [our] sons . . . sadly we gave them," she wrote, and continued:

> When wounded, what agony!
> When killed, what anguish!
> How much pain if separated by the sea!
> When executed, rage!
> But all this rather than traitors.[124]

José Martí's narrator in "Versos Sencillos" exhorts his son to join him in the war for independence, but also contemplates the possibility of cowardice:

> Well, come, my virile son
> Together let us both go: If I should die
> Kiss me: If you. . . . I prefer
> To see you dead than to see you a coward.[125]

In "Paráfrasis de Ruckert," poet José Agustín Quintero denounced Spanish misrule in Cuba—"Fatigue and bitterness for you / Gold and the harvests for Spain"—and addressed his concluding comments to the criolla:

> Tell me woman, what do you rock in that cradle?
> A child! On him my eyes are fixed
> Ponder your fate, oh, you unfortunate mother
> Vigilant the sun and moon will find you
> For in the end you have provided the despot with another slave![126]

The criolla mother, of course, could not raise her son to live as a slave, and therein lay the moral. In the popular nineteenth-century *décima* "De la madre al hijo," the mother enjoins her son:

> Although I am your mother and love you
>   as son of the blood of my heart,

I prefer to see you dead in campaign
  than to see you slave.
Act like a warrior,
  for whom death does not frighten:
The dangers of war
  have been made for he who is a man.
And if you want to make a name for yourself
  go fight for your land.[127]

The use of slavery as metaphor for the Cuban condition under Spanish rule drew upon readily accessible meanings. The imagery of slavery has, of course, long served as a common discursive motif by which oppressed colonial people everywhere characterize their subjugation. In Cuba, however, the allusion to slavery was especially rich with metaphoric meaning and moral resonance, for it drew explicitly upon a condition with which virtually all Cubans were implicated. Spanish authorities used the prominence of people of color within insurgent ranks to disparage the liberation project;[128] Cuban insurgents invoked the imagery of slavery to discredit colonial rule.

Chattel bondage implied degradation, humiliation, exploitation—all conditions that were incompatible with the larger formulations of the norms of nationality. Luis Radillo alluded to Cuba as "the enslaved land," while Serafín Sánchez described the island as "the slave colony." *La Revista de Cuba Libre* attributed the outbreak of the insurrection in 1895 to "the Cuban people [being] weary of bearing the chains of the slave," as did Néstor Carbonell: "[Cubans] could no longer resign themselves to continue living the miserable life of the slave in their own country . . . ; they could no longer live on their knees in the silence of servitude." Antonio Maceo often invoked slavery as allegory of the Cuban condition, referring variously to "the enslaved patria," "the enslaved people of Cuba," and the need to wage war against those who "enslave the patria." Insisted Maceo, "Cuba wants to be free now; its men have convinced themselves that to be a slave is a condition of shameful cowardice." Calixto García drew the moral explicitly: "We will not sheathe our swords, nor will we rest our rifles until we reach the threshold of the palaces where the enemy forges our chains. Life as a slave is a despicable burden to bear."[129]

The comparison of colonial subjugation with the condition of chattel slavery also implied creole appropriation of the recourse to self-immolation as a model through which to enact the meaning of nationality: the choice of death as an expression of agency, as an option preferable to life under the ignominy of bondage. The self-immolation of the slave thus entered the realm of the heroic, thereupon transacted as model and metaphor of Cuban. "Onward Cubans!" *El Republicano* exhorted. "Life is not worth much, and much less life as slaves." Affirmed poet Mercedes Matamoros: "It is far preferable to die than to be a slave." One Liberation Army manifesto proclaimed that "the people prefer to die than to continue enslaved and oppressed, the people wish to perish rather than continue humiliated as slaves."[130] "The war blazes incessantly across our land," the weekly *Cuba* exhorted in 1897, "let our wealth disappear, let our towns perish, let our entire people be exterminated: we prefer everything to remaining slaves of Spain. Let the sea of the north join with the sea of the south and sweep the lovely island of Cuba off the face of the earth. This too we prefer."[131]

To invoke the self-immolation of the slave was to draw upon multiple meanings as a way to register the duty of nationality. It was through the exercise of the option of death as a function of choice, and hence the will to freedom as an act of agency, that the creole imagination contemplated death as affirmation of liberation. Acquiescence to the condition of slavery was to surrender claims to manhood. "He has lost his life gloriously like a man fulfilling his duty to the patria," Carlos Manuel de Céspedes wrote of the death of his brother. "Before we were slaves: today we have patria," he affirmed in 1871. "We are free. We are men!"[132]

The suicide of slaves acquired metaphoric resonance in the narratives of the patria, renderings that served to situate the proposition of death as duty at the heart of creole conduct. "Days of blood and sorrow await us," Federico Pérez Carbó predicted in 1890, "days when the Cuban will be tested and will know how to redeem his honor—or perish in the effort, shot or hacked to death, destroyed. But he will not carry around his neck the despicable collar [of slavery] nor bear the cowardly stigma of the submissive slave who, able to free himself by recourse to the last means of his will [through] suicide, chooses instead to accept with resignation his condition of servility and kisses the hand of the insolent master by whom he is whipped and humiliated." Fermín Valdés-Domínguez denounced Spaniards "who have written the laws that enslave the white son of Cuba and condemns him to another [type] of slavery even more ignominious than that of the black, given that—the prestige of his position notwithstanding—he is obliged to be servant and slave to the illiterate thieving bureaucrat." "Having been unable to accustom myself to bearing the heavy weight

Victoria de las Tunas, ca. 1900.
Courtesy of McKeldin Library, University of Maryland at College Park.

of the yoke of the slave . . . ," General Serafín Sánchez wrote to his father, "I broke with everything, resigning myself to endure all the sacrifices, all the sufferings, all the dangers, with no other objective than to obtain the well-being of my patria." Manuel Sanguily described Cuba "as a sugar mill (*ingenio*) and we Cubans are the slave labor force (*dotación*)"; while Gerardo Castellanos described Cuba in 1895 as a single armed community of runaway slaves: "*Cuba es un solo palenque.*"[133] For Rafael Serra, the choice was clear: "The vow to reduce ourselves to ashes rather than to remain Spanish is firm and sincere. There is far more virtue for us Cubans to remain reduced to few in numbers but free than to survive in great numbers as slaves."[134] Three times—in 1870, 1876, and again in 1897—Cubans destroyed the town of Las Tunas rather than surrender its control to Spanish forces. The order to burn Las Tunas in 1876 was given by General Vicente García, himself a native son, who included his family's house among the first burned. "Tunas," García proclaimed, "it is with a heavy heart that I set you ablaze, but I prefer to see you razed than to see you a slave." General Enrique Collazo eulogized the destruction of Las Tunas in 1897, insisting that "it was razed by its own inhabitants, as heroic proof of their resolution to prefer anything over the dishonor of slavery and proof that the war

Coat of Arms of Victoria de las Tunas: "Better Burned than Slave" (*Quemada antes que esclava*). Courtesy of Archivo Nacional de Cuba, Havana, Cuba.

could not end in any way other than the absolute independence of Cuba." Years later Ramiro Cabrera recalled Las Tunas: "In the final days of our occupation of Las Tunas we began to raze the town. It was very sad to see the houses destroyed. They were razed by opening holes in the walls and inserting wooden beams attached to several yoke of oxen, which were then made to pull the entire walls down. One by one we proceeded to demolish all the buildings so that the Spanish could not use them to advantage. We preferred to destroy the constructions than to allow enemy forces to occupy them again since we did not have the means to defend and preserve them."[135] To this day the coat of arms of Las Tunas bears the motto: "Better burned than slave." (*Quemada antes que esclava.*)

✺ The destruction of Las Tunas set in relief the range of choices by which the pursuit of patria shaped strategies of self-determination. Suicide and self-sacrifice assumed many forms and under certain circumstances served to convey multiple meanings through a single deed. The logic of sacrifice as self-immolation, in the end, was carried to its inexorable conclusion and implicated the very land from which sensibility of Cuban was derived, including, most especially, its productive capability—that is, the bounty of the land and the fields, the fauna and flora, the towns and villages, the farms and factories, the homes and households: all would be sacrificed in pursuit of independence. "Everything for Cuba" extended to and included Cuba itself: Cuba would be free or it would perish. "We are committed to the ruin of this beautiful country before humbling ourselves to the despotic Spanish government," proclaimed Agustín Ruiz in 1870, adding: "*Cuba Libre* even if it is in ashes is the ideal of all Cubans." Cuba, affirmed José García Montes during the war for independence in 1897, "has reached that terrible extreme of the celebrated dilemma of the Prince of Denmark: 'To be or not to be'—independence which is the former or annihilation which is the latter."[136] *El Cubano Libre* celebrated "the savage valor that characterizes the resolve of the Cuban people to prevail, even if it were atop a heap of rubble." Provisional president Salvador Cisneros Betancourt reiterated the Cuban intent to "purify the atmosphere with fire and leave nothing left standing from San Antonio to Maisí [i.e., from one end of the island to the other]. All this we prefer rather than to be ruled by Spain." Years later Colonel Avelino Sanjenís described the struggle for independence as the Cuban determination to remove "the yoke of slavery," a rebellion of "the enslaved people of Cuba disposed to disappear rather than to continue under the domination of Spain," and added: "The motto of 'Independence or Death' had been established in the hearts of all Cubans in arms. We had sworn to raise the our tri-colored flag, even if it was over the ruins of Cuba: a free people would be born upon the ashes of Cuba."[137] Cubans demanded independence, Manuel Sanguily proclaimed, and were prepared "to see our land transformed into an immense tomb, covered in ashes, bespattered with stains of blood." He continued:

> We have one unshakeable purpose: to fight [for independence], to fight without rest, to fight without pause, ... to fight until there are no more Cubans capable of clutching a rifle or until the last Cuban is buried under the rubble of the fires set by our indignation and ire. [To fight against] the adventurers who have the temerity to cross the ocean to oppose the indomitable will of a people whose martyrs and heroes have risen unanimously to cry: no more, Spain! No more pillage! No more outrages! ... We accept everything, we have accepted everything, we will [continue] to accept everything—death in battle, death on the gallows, death due to hunger and disease, exile, prison, assassination, ruin of our wealth, the devastation of our land—all the misery, all the torment: but all those calamities heaped on us are nothing in comparison with the affliction, the atrocity, and the shame of remaining a wretched vassal of the Spanish crown.[138]

"In the end," predicted Fermín Valdés-Domínguez, "[Spain] will not be able to defeat us—even if in the hour of our victory there is nothing left but a pile of rubble upon which to raise our avenging combat flag." Within months of the end of the Ten Years War, Nicolás Pérez called for a resumption of armed struggle: "It is necessary to die before humiliating our cause and, if necessary, to establish the Republic of Cuba atop our dead bodies. War is a cruel undertaking, but if the despots want extermination, blood, and fire, then let us give it to them. If it is necessary for the people of Cuba to perish among the flames, they will perish with pleasure. If it is necessary for the people of Cuba to burn, they will burn." Death and redemption early expanded to include destruction and resurrection of the island. "Cuba will rise again," predicted Nicolás Arnao, "bloodied, to be sure, a desert and atop piles of rubble and ruins, surrounded by the dead and filled with the wailing of mourning, but gloriously, indomitable, radiant as its sun: invincible, heroic, sublime." Writer Alfredo Vidal predicted in 1875 that one day Spanish soldiers would recount to their children that "we signed the independence of those men by the light of blazing fires."[139]

The line between an act of individual suicide as an alternative to surrender and the burning of a farm or a town to keep it out of Spanish hands was short and direct. José Martí called upon all Cubans to render homage to patria through "the burning of our cities with our own hands." Farmers often razed their own homes and fields rather than allow their property to pass under Spanish control. In his war memoirs Gustavo Pérez Abreu recalled instances of farmers burning their dwellings upon learning of the approach of Spanish forces, choosing "to wander in the wilderness like nomads and suffer the harshness of the elements, later to rebuild their farms with true stoic virtue." Pérez Abreu could gaze upon farms and plantations set ablaze in 1896 and recorded in his journal: "In less than an hour everything was a pasture of flame, burying miseries so that greatness could be born." Eva Adán de Rodríguez recalled her family estate with sadness—"the beloved home that we had in the country"—reduced to rubble: "Destroyed by a fire in 1870 and that fire was ordered by my father upon receiving word that a Spanish column approached to establish its field headquarters on our property. It would have been a strategic outpost for the [Spanish] forces and an immense danger for the insurgent army."[140]

The burning of Las Tunas was only one of many instances in which Cubans chose to destroy entire towns and villages rather than relinquish control to Spanish forces. "Independence or death!" Cubans proclaimed upon burning the town of Potrerillo in 1897, "and even if this bloody struggle lasts twenty more years, we will never yield. It is preferable to convert our bountiful island to smoldering cinders and ashes than to see it again in the hands of our oppressors." In the same year, insurgent General Vidal Ducasse burned the town of Bahía Honda. The town of Jicotea was razed, Colonel Simón Reyes explained, "to deny to the enemy anything that could serve as fortifications." Horacio Ferrer participated in the razing of Las Tunas in 1897 and years later explained that it had been "necessary to destroy it in order to prevent the Spanish from reestablishing their base in Las Tunas. The enemy had to be made to understand the extent to which Cubans were prepared to sacrifice." "Glorious men!" exulted Ferrer. "They were willing to make every type of sacrifice, giving everything—life, family, wealth—as an offering to the freedom of the patria." Aníbal Escalante Beaton was also present in Las Tunas in 1897 and explained that since Cubans "did not possess the necessary resources to retain control of [Las Tunas], the wise course of action was to destroy the town completely to prevent it from serving again as a [Spanish] center of supplies"—as "was almost always done in similar situations." Other towns similarly destroyed between 1868 and 1898 included Dátil, Sibanicú, Cascorro, San Andrés, Tiguabos, Jaruco, Güira de Melena, Sabanilla, Güinía de Miranda, Banes, and Candelaria.[141]

The two most celebrated instances involved the burning of the towns of Guáimaro and Bayamo. In April 1869, within days of the promulgation of the new Constitution of the Republic in Arms, an advancing Spanish army column forced the Cuban provisional government to evacuate Guáimaro. General Manuel de Quesada ordered the town burned so that "not a single home remained standing to quarter Spanish troops." More than 200 homes were destroyed. "I confess that my heart was heavy at the sight of the blinding blaze caused by the flames," José María Izaguirre later wrote, "at the sight of the poor women desperately grasping their children by the hand and carrying atop their heads a bundle of clothing, the only possessions they were able to salvage from that disaster. Within hours, the entire town, including its lovely church, was reduced to a mound of rubble." Ana Betancourt recalled the despair of Guáimaro during the "terrible night in which . . . all that one heard everywhere was that terrifying noise produced when doors, roofs, and windows are devoured by fire. The entire population was found in the streets and in the plaza in search of air; we found ourselves enveloped in a blanket of smoke that made breathing nearly impossible. I do not have words to describe what I suffered that night. . . . At 9 o'clock the next morning we left the city to which we had arrived with such joy and happiness, leaving behind only debris, ashes, and desolation."[142] "It is necessary to destroy in order to build," affirmed the weekly *La Libertad* one month later.[143]

The burning of Guáimaro passed into the lore of liberation. Nearly thirty years later, José Martí commemorated the town's destruction as a deed of heroic proportions:

The sacred town (*el pueblo sagrado*) was ordered burned to save it from the enemy, to create ruins where fortresses were expected to stand. Mothers did not cry, men did not waver. . . . With their very hands they set the holy city (*la santa ciudad*) ablaze, and when nightfall arrived, the sacrifice was reflected in the sky. It roared and blazed with rage [and] the billowing pure flames hissed. In the building where the Constitution was written, [the flames] were higher, more beautiful. Atop the wave of flames, in the church steeple, the hanging bell could be seen ablaze.[144]

Gustavo Pérez Abreu eulogized the residents of Guáimaro, who "would live with their dignity intact or die for the redemption of their land, the way Christ died to save the world. Guáimaro, so proud, knew how to endure the fire that destroyed its buildings so that they would not be fortified by the enemy. The clamor of its residents on the march and . . . its exalted war cry affirmed: 'To the wilderness, to live or to die.'"[145]

The 1869 burning of Bayamo, the largest city destroyed by Cuban hands, set in sharp relief the logic and lore of self-destruction as means of self-determination. A city of some 12,000 inhabitants, situated strategically in central eastern Cuba, Bayamo was seized by insurgent forces in October 1868 and evacuated in January 1869. Within twelve hours of the order to evacuate, insurgent forces in cooperation with local residents set the city ablaze, reducing most of the 3,000 public buildings and private dwellings to charred ruins. From a distance of several miles, Carlos Manuel de Céspedes gazed at the rising columns of smoke over the city and commented "Poor Bayamo!" and then exclaimed: "Long live the indomitable city!" Years later Candelaria Figueredo recounted the frightful sight of a red evening sky over Bayamo on the night of January 12, 1869: "'It looks like a great fire,' mamá said. And papá responded with a deep sigh: 'Indeed, it is a great fire; it is our beloved Bayamo.' And we all began to cry, but we all agreed that it was preferable to see it a blazing pasture land than in the possession of our enemies." Not long after, poet José Joaquín Palma celebrated the burning of Bayamo: "The duty of its sons and the cries of the Patria condemned it to fire rather than leave it as slave. And its lofty towers crashed rapidly to the ground in a sea of vivid flame and smoke, ashes, and tears. That city was Bayamo, whose illustrious heroism will give luster to its history and confer fame on Cuba." Bayamo passed

Bayamo, Calle de Comercio, view from Plaza de Armas after fire, 1870.
Courtesy of Archivo Nacional de Cuba, Havana, Cuba.

into folklore in the form of a popular verse: "You were burned by your children, no reason for sorrow / Better to die with honor / Than serve the oppressive tyrant."[146]

The burning of Bayamo quickly assumed near mythical proportions in the chronicles of liberation. "Bayamo should become sacred soil," Francisco Maceo insisted in 1873, "where the first sacrifice to the goddess of Liberty was consecrated, where the first temple was built, and where the priests of the new redemption were anointed." The burning of Bayamo, affirmed Francisco Sellén almost thirty years later, was "a magnificent manifestation of stoicism . . . , a consecration of Cuban patriotism." Tomás Estrada Palma depicted the scene as one "of dense columns of smoke rising upward darkening the vastness of space, by which to proclaim the irrevocable protest of the Cuban people against Spanish domination."[147]

The moral victory was registered in the knowledge that the destruction of the city and the dispersal of the population had been accomplished at the initiative of Cubans, that is, Cubans as agents of their own destruction rather than victims of Spanish retaliation, performing a deed of preemptive purpose, to deprive Spain the power of reprisal. Luis Lagomasino Alvarez recalled with pride that "the Spanish recaptured Bayamo, but they entered into ruins and desolation, into the still-smoldering rubble and immense emptiness, to find a dead city, [with] its inhabitants having fled into the forests and mountains." Years later, historian Antonio Miguel Alcover celebrated the burning of Bayamo as a momentous moral victory for Cubans: "[Spaniards] were denied the pleasure of discharging a single bullet against the people of Bayamo. Their desire [to exact revenge] was frustrated by the sight they beheld upon entering the city. The agents of despotism found only rubble and ashes. . . . Bayamo had surrendered to fire rather than allow itself to serve as the site of vengeful and outrageous abuse to which it would have been subject." This was also the way that writer José Ramón Betancourt memorialized the deed: "The sons of Bayamo . . . believed it to be far more dignified to commend their homes to the flames than to surrender them to the ferocity of their enemies, and they preferred to die in fight than accept their enslavement." Hardly five months had passed when J. M. Céspedes wrote to commemorate the burning of the city: "The men of Bayamo withdrew from their homes, taking with them their wives, their children, and their memories: they exchanged the comforts of material life to which they were accustomed for combat and struggle and for a war to the death with Spain, in forests and on the plains, in open fields and in the towns. . . . The revolutionary spirit found its origins in Bayamo."[148]

Sacrifice combined symbol and substance into a powerful logic of nationality. It served to consecrate the Cuban claim of nationhood even as it deepened a collective resolve to prevail, as much an exercise of dignity as an affirmation of an identity. It was a way to serve notice on Spain about the lengths to which Cubans were prepared to go and the price they were willing to pay in pursuit of patria. "The burning of Bayamo . . . ," Carlos Manuel de Céspedes explained days after the Cuban evacuation, "gave sufficient proof to convince Spain that there is no power that will crush our aspirations nor halt the march of a people who wish only to be free." Twenty-five years later, Diego Tamayo made a similar point: "It is necessary that Spain know that to achieve independence we are disposed to endure every type of disaster, accept the martyrdom of all, and die every kind of death."[149] The efficacy of suicide as preferable to slavery insinuated itself into the larger cosmology of Cuban. Affirmed Antonio Miguel Alcover in his homage to Bayamo:

> The people who opt for suicide rather than acquiesce to the illicit and the criminal rule of the despot . . . , whose only purpose is the exploitation and oppression of a people under the iron yoke of slavery, commit a sublime act. There is no more eloquent testimony to the abnegation

and the dignity of a people filled with love for the patria and hatred against the invader. . . . The horrible sights with which the burning of a town was offered to the oppressor cannot be viewed as anything other than a silent protest . . . raised to the Heavens from a people who choose to die in order not to be enslaved and so that the entire world learn of the desperation of a noble people who legitimately demands to be included within the world concert of civilized nations, free, independent, and sovereign over its destiny. To the ultimatum 'surrender or die,' the humble respond with moral rectitude: 'Take the ashes and secure your triumph over the rubble.'[150]

All through the nineteenth-century wars of liberation, the use of fire assumed near mystical properties as a means of purification and method of redemption, a way to purge the vices of the old order and to begin anew, cleansed of the iniquities of the past. The burning of Guáimaro and Bayamo, Comandante Luis Rodolfo Miranda exulted, "signified something very Cuban," representing "symbols of heroism . . . [that] constitute the cradle of national honor. . . . Both places have the magnificent significance of poetry and sacrifice. They were destroyed by the purifying fire (el incendio purificador) of our struggles for liberty." Fermín Valdés-Domínguez chronicled insurgent operations in the western plantation zones after 1895: "The war invades the Spanish zones. Fire purifies the zones where, to the shame of Spain, the crime of slavery raised those strongholds." Valdés-Domínguez spoke of the "redemptive flame" (candela redentora) and of fire as a means of purification. Years later, José Maceo Verdecia described the burning of Bayamo as "symbol of the purity, of the purifying fire—that is the living meaning of the sacrifice of Bayamo." Fire would consume the Spanish regime, Diego Vicente Tejera predicted in 1897: "The colony will be swept away, devoured by a hurricane of fire, and atop the purified ground (el suelo purificado) a republic will be raised."[151]

The norms of nationality were produced and continually reproduced in word and deed as a means of mobilization in defense of patria. New formulations were layered onto old foundations. In the early years of the twentieth-century republic, Cubans of all political persuasions would celebrate the burning of the cities as deeds of exemplary heroism and sacrifice. A consensus of remarkable endurance developed around the efficacy of self-immolation in defense of patria, as source of national pride and illustration of what it meant to be Cuban. The duty to sacrifice and to die became deeply embedded in the dominant formulations of nationality, where it acted to influence the character of national conduct. All through the twentieth century the models and motif of the nineteenth-century struggle for liberation were invoked as the standard by which Cuban was measured. Writer Francisco Figueras configured the meaning of Cuban into a notion of "morality," a condition shaped by the experience of the nineteenth century, where "to challenge death in battle was to be a hero. . . . To display disregard for danger and life was to be brave, and to be brave was to be honorable, and even to be wise." These elements reached deeply into the normative arrangements of nationality—into the very psychology of Cuban, Manuel Márquez Sterling suggested as early as 1906. After ten years of war, reflected Márquez Sterling, "everything was rubble, smoke, pain; and at every step a tomb was erected. In that revolution . . . [we] learned to die and kill; patriotism and self-esteem were defined along precise lines. And a sentiment of dignity took hold within the heart of the country."[152]

Life through Suicide

3

*With regard to self-inflicted deaths, we have been able to
observe an improvement concerning the evolution of this
social phenomenon, for while it is true that the number
of suicides that have taken place and been produced by
means of fire-arms, hanging and drowning have increased by twenty in comparison to those carried out in
the same way the previous year, those that have been
produced by other means, and especially by burning, are
less by 20 than those effected in that manner in 1909.
The difference of a total of 9 in favor of the present
report, while small, is encouraging when we considered
the progress made by this social evil.*

   Jorge LeRoy y Cassá, chief of statistics,
   Secretaría de Sanidad y Beneficencia (1911)

*It is sufficient simply to glance at any of the pages of
our daily newspapers to realize that among us suicide
possesses an endemic character.*

   Jorge Mañach, "Un pueblo suicida" (1931)

*Suicide as a social question . . . [relates] to those people
who lack resources and who lead a life filled with
privation, in an environment filled with the availability
of so many of the good things of life; they ruminate
about their failures, their lives become bitter, they
become demoralized and depressed.*

   El Mundo (February 1, 1950)

The felicity of living is only for some, not for everyone.

Suicide note of Joaquín Pedroso Mantilla

(May 31, 1931)

*I recall a tragic incident but not without its comic
element, close to where I lived in Vedado, . . . a girl set
herself ablaze but she had used so much gasoline that
when she lit herself on fire the entire block burned down.
Later nothing could be reconstructed there because of the
scarcity of building materials, and they subsequently
made it into a park.*

*Reinaldo Arenas, "Suicidio y rebeldía: Reinaldo
Arenas habla sobre el suicidio" (1983)*

❧ It is difficult to take measure of the phenomenon
of suicide as a facet of daily life during the second half of the nineteenth
century. The record of suicide among African slaves and Chinese contract
laborers has been preserved, more or less. But little is known about suicide among whites and free people of color.[1] Official records relating to
suicide in the colony are scarce and scattered. Aggregate totals often came
at the expense of particulars and rarely included any information other
than the jurisdiction in which suicides were recorded. The total number
of suicides in the course of the nineteenth century, on plantations and
in cities, among slaves and free people of color, among Chinese contract
workers and whites, among men and women, is all but impossible to ascertain. Data for some specific years was recorded. During 1858 and 1859,
with a population of almost 1.4 million inhabitants and a total number of
suicides of 404 and 420, respectively, the average annual rate of suicide
in Cuba approached 30 per 100,000, declining slightly to nearly 25 per
100,000 in 1862 (see Table 3.1). The analysis of suicide in the census data
for the year 1862 recorded a total of 346 suicides, including 173 Chinese
workers, 130 African slaves, and 43 whites.[2]

Statistical information made available at the end of the nineteenth century provided an aggregate overview of the rates of suicide during the

Table 3.1. Suicide in Cuba, by Jurisdiction, 1858–1859, 1862

Jurisdiction	1858	1859	1862
Western Department			
Bejucal	10	6	11
Cárdenas	38	29	36
Colón	52	45	45
Guanabacoa	16	14	5
Guanajay	32	27	14
Güines	26	38	17
Havana	38	50	40
Jaruco	9	6	6
Matanzas	26	34	30
Pinar del Río	8	10	13
San Antonio	11	10	4
San Cristobal	5	7	10
Subtotal	271	276	231
Eastern Department			
Baracoa	—	—	1
Bayamo	4	9	—
Cienfuegos	24	22	13
Santiago de Cuba	17	15	17
Guantánamo	3	5	2
Holguín	3	2	9
Manzanillo	2	4	4
Puerto Príncipe	11	15	11
Remedios	16	10	12
Sagua la Grande	22	27	28
Sancti-Spíritus	3	8	7
Trinidad	9	5	5
Villa Clara	19	22	6
Subtotal	133	144	115
Total	404	420	346

Sources: Havana, Audiencia, *Discurso que, en la solemne apertura del tribunal leyó el día 3 de enero de 1859, en la Real Audiencia Pretorial de La Habana, su regente el Excmo. e Illmo. Sr. D. Francisco González* (Havana, 1859); Havana, Audiencia, *Discurso que, en la solemne apertura del tribunal leyó el día 2 de enero de 1860, en la Real Audiencia Pretorial de La Habana, su regente el Excmo. e Illmo. Sr. D. Francisco González* (Havana, 1860); Cuba, Capitanía General, *Noticias estadísticas de la Isla de Cuba en 1862* (Havana, 1864).

Table 3.2. Suicide in Cuba, 1854–1867

Year	Number of Suicides	Year	Number of Suicides
1854	281	1861	405
1855	—	1862	346
1856	308	1863	318
1857	424	1864	—
1858	404	1865	298
1859	420	1866	262
1860	326	1867	363

Source: "La criminalidad en Cuba," *El Curioso Americano* 3 (September 15, 1899): 52–53.

middle years of the nineteenth century (see Table 3.2). No information was provided concerning the composition or locations of suicide.

During the closing decades of the nineteenth century, medical authorities in Havana appear to have taken note of developing patterns of suicide in the capital as a matter of general mortality trends. During the 1880s and 1890s, the *Crónica Médico-Quirúrgica* recorded an average 3 suicides per month in Havana.[3] One 1887 study of mortality in the capital recorded a total of 36 suicides, including 33 whites (31 men and 2 women) and 3 black men. The methods used by white men included guns (23), hanging (7), and jumping into the path of an oncoming train. Hanging, leaping from a building, and drowning accounted for the suicide of the 3 black men. The 2 women poisoned themselves. Of the 175 autopsies performed in Havana in 1890, 31 identified suicide as the cause of death; victims included 30 whites (28 men and 2 women) and 1 black male. Methods of suicide included principally firearms, hanging, poison, and drowning. Another demographic profile of Havana two years later reported a total of 39 suicides, including 35 whites (31 men and 4 women) and 4 blacks (all men). In 1894, a reported 52 *habaneros* committed suicide, including 48 whites and 4 blacks. For the preceding seven years, an average of 35 *habaneros* killed themselves annually.[4]

In one early analysis of patterns of suicide in Havana between 1878 and 1885, physician Tomás Plasencia expressed alarm over the rate of suicide and warned of the "rising rates [of suicide], which, if continued, will assume fully the character of an epidemic." For the eight years under study, Plasencia recorded a total of 279 cases of suicide among men and women,

Table 3.3. Suicide in Havana, 1878–1885

Method	White Male	White Female	Colored Male	Colored Female
Poison	10	12	2	1
Hanging	9	2	13	
Drowning	11	1	8	2
Firearms	99	3	8	
Edge instruments	10	1	2	
Leaping	2	1	1	
Other	27	3	11	3
Total[a]	168	22	43	9

Source: Tomás L. Plasencia, "Notas relativas al suicidio en la circunscripción de La Habana," Anales de la Real Academia de Ciencias Médicas, Físicas y Naturales de La Habana 22 (1885): 409–29.

[a] Plasencia was unable to ascertain information on 37 additional cases of suicide.

habaneros of all ages, white people and people of color, including categories of mestizos and asiáticos (see Table 3.3). Men accounted for nearly 90 percent of the recorded suicides (211 out of 242), with males killing themselves at a 4:1 ratio to females. White men accounted for almost 70 percent of all suicides (168 out of 242).[5]

The effort to develop systematic tabulations of suicide began with the inauguration of the republic in 1902.[6] The chronicle of suicidal death in Cuba is a sobering record indeed. Between 1902 and 1959 more than 30,000 Cubans killed themselves. It is likely that the actual number of deaths by suicide was far greater. The circumstances of suicide in communities of the provincial interior were often recorded haphazardly, if at all. Untold numbers died of unknown causes.[7] At the same time, well-to-do families possessed the means to protect their privacy and thereby conceal the act of suicide from the outside world. For households of nominally Roman Catholic affiliation, death by suicide was associated with sin and shame, a deed to be disguised or denied altogether, a death to be passed off as an accident or as a mishap of one kind or another.[8]

The presumption of underreported cases of suicide must thus inform all discussions of the circumstances of suicidal behavior and serves to set in relief the magnitude of the phenomenon of suicide in Cuba. In fact, the rate at which Cubans killed themselves must be considered as nothing

Table 3.4. Worldwide Suicide Rates (per 100,000 inhabitants)

	1901–1905	1920–1925	1945–1949
Denmark	22.7	14.0	17.7
Germany	22.2	22.1	28.4
France	21.7	18.8	18.7
Cuba	14.9[a]	16.2[b]	18.2[c]
Japan	13.2	19.6	13.8
Australia	12.5	11.1	10.6
Belgium	12.4	13.3	18.3
United States	10.2	10.2	14.3
England	10.1	9.9	11.3
Italy	6.3	8.5	5.9
Spain	2.2	5.6	6.1

Sources: W. S. Woytinsky and E. S. Woytinsky, eds., *World Population and Production* (New York, 1953), p. 226.

[a] Jorge LeRoy y Cassá, "Quo Tendimus? Estudio médico legal sobre el suicidio en Cuba durante el quinquenio de 1902–1906," *Anales de la Academia de Ciencias Médicas, Físicas y Naturales de La Habana* 44 (May 1907): 38–63.

[b] República de Cuba, Secretaría de Sanidad y Beneficencia, *Boletín Oficial* (1920–25).

[c] República de Cuba, Ministerio de Salubridad y Asistencia Social, *Boletín Oficial* (1942–59).

less than extraordinary. For much of the twentieth century, suicide ranked among the principal causes of mortality among Cuban adults. In 1924, for example, suicide was the sixth leading cause of death on the island, preceded by tuberculosis, bronco-pneumonia, heart diseases, cancer, and typhoid. A study of mortality in Havana in 1947 as determined by burials at Colón Cemetery identified suicide as twelfth on a list of 124 causes.[9]

The data published by government departments of health (Secretaría de Sanidad y Beneficencia and its successor Ministerio de Salubridad y Asistencia Social), generally considered as conservative official statistics, placed the rate of suicide in Cuba among the highest in the world (see Table 3.4). The information published by the Comisión Nacional de Estadística y Reformas Económicas between 1926 and 1931, on the other hand, recorded higher national rates of suicide. Indeed, the two agencies provided very different sets of data for the years 1926–29. While the Secretaría de Sanidad y Beneficencia calculated the rate of Cuban suicide at 16 per 100,000, the Comisión Nacional de Estadística y Reformas Económicas

Table 3.5. Suicide in Latin America, 1948–1958 (per 100,000 inhabitants)

Cuba	16.0[a]	Dominican Republic	3.0
Chile	4.9	Honduras	2.9
El Salvador	4.9	Bolivia	2.5
Argentina	4.5[b]	Nicaragua	1.6
Costa Rica	3.2	Peru	1.4
Guatemala	3.2	Colombia	1.3
Panama	3.1	Mexico	1.0

Source: United Nations, Statistical Office of the United Nations, Department of Economic Affairs, *Demographic Year . . . 1952–1964* (New York, 1952–65).

[a] República de Cuba, Ministerio de Salubridad y Asistencia Social, *Boletín Oficial* (1950–58).

[b] Argentina, Secretaria del Consejo Nacional de Desarrollo, Instituto Nacional de Estadística y Censos, *Hechos demográficos en la República Argentina, 1961–1966*, 2 vols. (Buenos Aires, 1967).

arrived at a rate approaching 26 per 100,000. According to the data collected by the Comisión Nacional, Cuba had the highest suicide rate in the world.[10]

What is not in doubt, however, is that both sets of statistics on mortality established Cuba as possessing the highest suicide rate in Latin America. The second highest suicide rate was registered by Chile and El Salvador at 4.9 per 100,000. Mexico, at the other extreme, recorded an average 1.0 suicide per 100,000 people (see Table 3.5). Employing a different formulation to tabulate mortality rates during the early 1930s, Domingo Espino, the President of the Comisión Nacional de Estadística y Reformas Económicas, calculated the rate of suicide in Spain at 67.8 for every one million inhabitants, in Mexico at 13.6 suicides per every one million, in Chile at 89.8, and in Uruguay at 122.7. In Cuba, the suicide rate was more than 253 per one million inhabitants.[11]

The rate of suicidal deaths in Cuba increased steadily all through the first half of the twentieth century, from 14.9 per 100,000 during the early years of the republic to 16 per 100,000 during the 1920s, reaching 18 per 100,000 by the late 1940s. Suicide rates declined during the early 1950s to 14.5 per 100,000 but turned upward again and surpassed 16 per 100,000 during the late 1950s. The data published by the Comisión Nacional de Estadística y Reformas Económicas between 1926 and 1931 recorded a far higher national rate of suicide, reaching what the Comisión Nacional characterized in 1930 as an "alarming increase" of 28 per 100,000 in 1929 and surpassing 31 per 100,000 in 1931. By the mid-1950s, an estimated 6 people a day—every day—attempted to kill themselves.[12]

⚘ The aggregate data on suicide in Cuba during the first half of the twentieth century (Table 3.6) suggests a number of discernible patterns. Men killed themselves at nearly a 2:1 ratio over women, a ratio generally higher than in many other countries.[13] Whites committed suicide at a ratio of 3.5:1 to people of color, numbers generally consistent with the composition of the population as recorded in the national censuses between 1899 and 1953.[14]

The methods of suicide employed similarly suggest a number of patterns, central to which were the striking age- and gender-differentiated ways by which men and women killed themselves (see Table 3.7). Suicide was often a deed for which elaborate plans were developed, sometimes with thought given to the preparation of death as a symbolic gesture, on other occasions planned for dramatic impact. The ways that men and women chose to end their lives conformed to a larger logic and serve to provide insight into the ways they lived their lives. Methods of self-destruction were typically a function of gender-determined attributes that shaped conduct through a lifetime and that acted to define behaviors, including ways to die, as acceptable or not acceptable.[15]

Men and women tended to commit suicide by the means most commonly available, usually employing something with which they were readily familiar as a facet of everyday life. For women this generally meant products found in the ordinary stock of household provisions, and most often involved the use of a wide range of poisons. Suicide by poison occurred among women at nearly a 2:1 ratio to men. The poisons of choice varied across the island. Women in Havana and other large provincial cities, for example, tended to use household medicines, cleaning fluids, corrosive acids, disinfectants, and pest poisons, including lye, hydrochloric acid, formic acid, Lysol, iodine, laudanum, arsenic, and rodent poison. Women in rural Pinar del Río, on the other hand, the principal region of tobacco cultivation, ingested insecticides (*sales de cobre*) commonly used to control tobacco beetles. Women in the ranching zones of Camagüey used *rompe roca*, a poison used to spray cattle against ticks. Turpentine was the local poison of choice in the mining community of Matahambre.

Women often swallowed anything that would do them harm as a means to kill themselves, including bleach, laundry detergents, and liquid shoe polish (*tinta rápida*). Often it was a matter of economy: what was avail-

Table 3.6. Suicide in Cuba, by Race and Gender, 1902–1959

| Year | White | | Colored | | Total |
	Male	Female	Male	Female	
1902	100	29	34	16	179[a]
1903	101	51	39	17	208[a]
1904	104	52	37	21	214[a]
1905	129	56	43	23	251[a]
1906	127	55	50	35	267[a]
1907	—	—	—	—	274[b]
1908	183	102	41	50	376
1909	185	93	43	48	369
1910	160	99	53	48	360
1911	183	100	38	60	381
1912	207	92	58	49	406
1913	235	95	44	59	433
1914	259	115	59	63	496
1915	238	104	66	43	451
1916	204	80	67	48	399
1917	203	103	60	34	400
1918	220	115	38	44	417
1919	189	110	48	48	395
1920	187	98	48	42	375
1921	300	90	63	36	489
1922	267	90	46	36	439
1923	212	132	59	42	445
1924	245	106	57	46	454
1925	280	147	56	46	529
1926	292	156	67	50	565[c]
1927	—	—	—	—	584[c]
1928	307	119	81	32	539[c]
1929	356	130	82	38	606[c]
1930	264	141	51	57	513[c]
1931	260	66	51	42	419[c]
1932	337	127	53	58	575[c]
1933	328	159	107	40	634
1934	239	152	62	58	511
1935	298	221	72	78	669
1936	275	160	71	42	548

Table 3.6. Continued

Year	White		Colored		Total
	Male	Female	Male	Female	
1937	303	187	63	59	612
1938	288	167	61	53	569
1939	344	208	82	52	686
1940	358	249	67	66	740
1941	—	—	—	—	—
1942	—	—	—	—	—
1943	297	151	65	34	547
1944	272	161	73	46	552
1945	307	195	70	65	637
1946	—	—	—	—	844[d]
1947	—	—	—	—	919[d]
1948	393	270	102	83	848
1949	416	271	106	91	884
1950	455	243	94	62	854[d]
1951	440	261	78	70	849
1952	430	240	93	70	833
1953	377	201	114	69	761
1954	—	—	—	—	—
1955	—	—	—	—	—
1956	—	—	—	—	—
1957	—	—	—	—	858[e]
1958	—	—	—	—	938[e]
1959	—	—	—	—	1,066[e]
Total	12,154	6,349	2,912	2,269	29,067[f]

Sources: Unless otherwise indicated, data derived from República de Cuba, Secretaría de Sanidad y Beneficencia, *Boletín Oficial* (1909–41); and República de Cuba, Ministerio de Salubridad y Asistencia Social, *Boletín Oficial* (1942–59).

Note: In addition to the care ordinarily required in the use of census data, a further caution must be added in the analysis of racial categories. Classifications of "white" and "colored" must be used with care, as they are often the result of impressionistic and wholly arbitrary determinations. These categories were employed by census enumerators between 1899 and 1953 and are used for the purpose of including the official classifications.

Table 3.6. Continued

[a] Jorge LeRoy y Cassá, "Quo Tendimus? Estudio médico legal sobre el suicidio en Cuba durante el quinquenio de 1902–1906," *Anales de la Academia de Ciencias Médicas, Físicas y Naturales de La Habana* 44 (May 1907): 38–63.

[b] Cuba, *Anuario estadístico de la República de Cuba 1914* (Havana, 1915).

[c] The Comisión Nacional de Estadística y Reformas Económicas provides very different statistics for these years, including 1926: 885 suicides; 1927: 838 suicides; 1928: 898 suicides; 1929: 1,017 suicides; 1930: 1,136 suicides; 1931: 1,217 suicides; 1932: 1,004 suicides. See República de Cuba, Comisión Nacional de Estadística y Reformas Económicas, *Estadísticas. . . . 1929–1932* (Havana, 1929–1932).

[d] República de Cuba, Oficina Nacional de los Censos Demográfico y Electoral, *Censos de población, viviendas y electoral. Enero 28 de 1953* (Havana, 1953), p. 320.

[e] C. Paul Roberts, ed., *Cuba 1968: Supplement to the Statistical Abstract of Latin America* (Los Angeles, 1970), pp. 48–49.

[f] Includes aggregate total for years 1907, 1927, 1946–47, 1950, and 1957–59, for which racial and gender information was unavailable.

able and what was cheap. Paulina Delgado and María García Facuente attempted to kill themselves by ingesting the phosphorus tips of matches.[16] In fact, matches were used frequently during the early twentieth century, noted one commentator in 1919, as "the cheapest means of suicide because no stamp tax had yet been put upon matches and a box of them was given away with every five-cent pack of cigarettes."[17] Carbolic acid (phenol), used chiefly as a disinfectant, was another popular poison, and the substance used by Altagracia Travieso, Florentina Romagosa, and Paulina Monsenos Troya to kill themselves.[18] Julia Castro, María Magdalena Valdivia, and Leonor Martínez Morales used strychnine.[19] Matilde Pita García and Evangelina Adrino Calzadilla used potassium permanganate.[20] Amelia Fernández, Adriana Candiani Valdés, and Eufemia Iglesias Valdés killed themselves by taking bichloride of mercury.[21] Cristina Queses, Matilde Barrero, and Catalina Días Alfaro attempted to kill themselves by swallowing kerosene. Benita Santa tried by drinking ink.[22] Other methods of attempted suicide were perhaps less common but far more grim. María González ingested ground glass in an effort to commit suicide. Paulina González attempted to kill herself by swallowing sewing needles and open safety pins.[23]

The conventional wisdom suggests that women who chose to die by their own hand were averse to methods of death involving physical disfigurement. "Suicide!" responds Elena to the threat of the woman with whose husband she is having an affair in the play *Screens*, by Dolores Prida.

Table 3.7. Suicide in Cuba, by Method, Age, and Gender, 1910–1949

Method	Age	Male	Female	Total
Poison	10–19	152	815	967
	20–39	656	1,259	1,915
	40–59	358	257	615
	60+	149	57	206
	Total	1,315	2,388	3,703
Hanging	10–19	287	225	512
	20–39	1,816	574	2,390
	40–59	2,098	317	2,415
	60+	1,547	145	1,692
	Total	5,748	1,261	7,009
Drowning	10–19	42	25	67
	20–39	179	66	245
	40–59	189	34	223
	60+	98	21	119
	Total	508	146	654
Firearms	10–19	256	174	430
	20–39	1,863	326	2,189
	40–59	667	39	706
	60+	232	11	243
	Total	3,018	550	3,568

"Taking your life is a cowardly act and in extreme bad taste. But if you insist, I recommend sleeping pills. It's a less dramatic suicide, but so much more hygienic."[24] Women who killed themselves by way of poison often used suicide notes to appeal to authorities to spare them of an autopsy, typically identifying the type of poison used as a way to obviate the need for a medical inquest. Aída Corona asked judicial authorities to forego a postmortem, volunteering the information that she had used eighty-eight barbiturate pills to kill herself.[25]

Male dispositions toward violence found logical expression in the preference of suicidal men toward that most potent symbol of manhood: the gun. Men used firearms at nearly a 5.5:1 ratio over women and usually shot themselves in the head; when women used firearms, they were more likely to shoot themselves in the heart.[26] Men hanged themselves at a

Table 3.7. Continued

Method	Age	Male	Female	Total
Edge instruments	10–19	23	11	34
	20–39	263	38	301
	40–59	209	27	236
	60+	75	5	80
	Total	570	81	651
Leaping	10–19	11	12	23
	20–39	103	42	145
	40–59	88	21	109
	60+	54	107	161
	Total	256	182	438
Other	10–19	48	765	813
	20–39	162	835	997
	40–59	107	200	307
	60+	47	74	121
	Total	364	1,874	2,238
Total		11,779	6,482	18,261

Sources: República de Cuba, Secretaría de Sanidad y Beneficencia, *Boletín Oficial* (1909–41); and República de Cuba, Ministerio de Salubridad y Asistencia Social, *Boletín Oficial* (1942–59).

Note: Does not include the years 1927, 1941–42, and 1946–47.

rate of more than 4.5:1 over women. Death by firearms and hanging accounted for nearly 75 percent of all male suicides. Men also used cutting and piercing instruments — typically razors and knives — to kill themselves at a rate of more than 7:1 over women, usually stabbing themselves or cutting their throats. When women employed a razor or knife, they usually attempted suicide by slashing their wrists. Men were more likely than women — at a ratio of 3.5:1 — to drown themselves, usually by walking into the sea; or by plunging to their deaths from bridges, off docks, or from the decks of ferries; or by jumping into deep wells used for drawing fresh water for household and farming purposes. Men leaped to their deaths from heights at a rate of more than 3:1 over women, usually from tall buildings and bridges; while women who leaped to their deaths from heights often jumped from church towers. Leaping from heights was predomi-

Table 3.8. Changing Methods of Suicide, 1908–1949 (percentage of total)

Method	1908–1918	1919–1929	1930–1938	1939–1949
Poison	18.7	17.4	21.0	23.2
Hanging	31.3	40.2	40.0	37.0
Drowning	4.0	3.1	3.3	4.0
Firearms	26.2	21.6	16.2	13.0
Edge instruments	4.1	3.6	1.5	2.3
Leaping	0.5	1.8	1.5	2.3
Other	15.0	12.2	14.0	18.2

Source: República de Cuba, Secretaría de Sanidad y Beneficencia, *Boletín Oficial* (1909–41); and República de Cuba, Ministerio de Salubridad y Asistencia Social, *Boletín Oficial* (1942–59).

nantly an urban phenomenon, most often recorded in the city of Havana. Every case of suicide recorded by jumping in 1916 and 1917 and again in 1921 and 1922, for example, occurred in Havana.[27] More than 80 percent of all suicides by jumping took place in the capital. Indeed, instances of suicide by leaping from buildings increased in direct relationship to the expansion of high-rise buildings in Havana. The rate increased dramatically after the 1910s, during the building boom in Havana, in the years that the construction of hotels, office buildings, and government structures transformed the city's skyline.

While methods of suicide remained generally constant through the first half of the twentieth century, several patterns suggest changing practices over the years (see Table 3.8). Between 50 and 60 percent of all suicides were achieved by poisoning or hanging. At the same time, however, the use of poison increased throughout the first half of the twentieth century, while death by firearms as a percentage of the total decreased from 26.2 percent in 1908–18 to 13 percent during 1939–49. Leaping to death also increased, as did the suicides registered in "other suicides" (*otros suicidios*).

In fact, suicide in Cuba became increasingly easier to commit, in a sense, all through the early decades of the twentieth century. The increase in suicide by poison, for example, reflects the greater availability of lethal substances in households across the island, principally in the form of disinfectants and cleaning agents, as well as the greater accessibility to tranquilizers, stimulants, depressants, and analgesics. Progress came to Cuba in the form of gas stoves, skyscrapers and bridges, trolley cars and passenger trains, all of which facilitated the act of suicide. This is not to suggest that individuals determined to kill themselves would not have found other means to achieve their purpose, but rather to note that means of suicide were within the easy reach of almost everyone and that even a suicidal whim could be acted upon immediately.

✻❧ Perhaps the most striking classification employed by Sanidad y Beneficencia appeared as the category of otros suicidios, generally understood as miscellaneous incidents of suicide. What made this category particularly noteworthy was that it recorded a remarkably high number of self-inflicted deaths by women, making for a conspicuous deviation from the otherwise predominant male-to-female ratio of suicides. In the category of otros suicidios female suicides outnumbered male deaths by a striking ratio of more than 5:1. Indeed, only in the category of suicide by poison did the number of suicides by women exceed the rate in otros suicidios. Taken together, poison and otros suicidios accounted for more than 65 percent of all female suicides (see Table 3.7).

The category of otros suicidios included instances of self-inflicted death by means often as varied as they were uncommon. Instances in which men and women hurled themselves into the way of oncoming trains or threw themselves under approaching trolley cars or buses, often recorded as *aplastamiento*, were reported frequently in the daily press. The introduction of gas stoves in increasing numbers of urban households increased the number of suicides reported by the inhalation of gas. Suicide among health care workers often involved injected overdoses of morphine.

The largest single method of death in the category of otros suicidios, however, and one employed principally by women, was burning (*quemaduras*), that is, women soaking their clothing with alcohol, or kerosene, or some other flammable liquid and thereupon setting themselves ablaze. It is impossible to ascertain with precision the number of deaths by burning included within the category of otros suicidios, for neither Sanidad y Beneficencia nor Salubridad y Asistencia Social identified quemaduras as a discrete method of suicide within its tabulation of mortality data. Public health agencies in Cuba employed the classification system of suicide adopted in 1893 by the International Institute of Statistics. That burning as a means of self-inflicted death was not considered a statistically significant method of suicide in the world at large meant that it would be subsumed in the category of "other."

In fact, burning was not a method of suicide used with any frequency in Cuba during the nineteenth century. Death by burning—rendered variously as *darse candela* and *darse fuego*—appears to have been a method that gained currency among women only in the twentieth century. The study of suicide in the city of Havana between 1878 and 1885 completed by physician Tomás Plasencia does not record a single instance of death by fire.[28] Similarly, a review of the Havana press through the decade of the 1890s yields only one published account of an attempted suicide by burning, a case in 1895 involving Tomasa Corrales in the town of Remates (Vuelta Abajo) in 1895.[29] Beginning in 1901, however, the Havana press began to report with increasing frequency accounts of suicide by fire across the island, mostly among women. In April 1901, twenty-two-year-old Cresencia Calderón—described as a "woman of the black race" (*una mujer de la raza negra*)—set herself on fire. In June 1902, eighteen-year-old Amelia Rodríguez Castaneda soaked her clothing with kerosene and set herself ablaze after her husband abandoned her. In December 1903, José de la Encarnación Marrero burned himself to death. One month later, twenty-year-old Esperanza Cabello Blanco attempted to kill herself through fire. In March 1904, Ana Cuervo Pazau used alcohol in an attempt to burn herself to death. One month later, sixteen-year-old María de Jesús Rivero killed herself by fire (*por el fuego*).[30] In the following six months, another three deaths by fire were reported. By mid-1904, reports of suicide by fire appeared weekly. After 1905 news accounts of suicide attempts por el fuego across the island appeared almost daily. A study of suicide in Havana in 1912 prepared by forensic physician Antonio Barreras recorded a total of nineteen cases of completed and attempted suicides as a result of quemaduras, sixteen of which were by women. By 1912, suicide by fire had developed into a commonplace occurrence. "This barbaric form of suicide is very common in Havana," reported Barreras, adding: "This type of suicide was very much used in Havana in 1912 by women."[31] By the late 1920s, the frequency of suicide by fire was sufficient to warrant the marketing of an over-the-counter medicine to promote the healing of burn wounds.

The high rate of suicide by burning in Cuba notwithstanding, Sanidad y Beneficencia rarely deviated from the format employed by the international classification system and continued to include quemaduras in the miscellaneous category of otros suicidios. Occasionally, however, the explanatory narrative accompanying annual statistical reports provided suggestive insight into the specific content of otros suicidios. The statistics for suicide in the city of Havana in 1918, for example, reported a total of 94 deaths, 23 of which were designated as otros suicidios and identified specifically in the text as "por el fuego." One study of suicide completed under

SUICIDAS

Nada adelantaréis con rociaros de alcohol y pretender morir abrasados si algún familiar inmediatamente os cubre las quemaduras con el maravilloso cicatrizante "ARNAO". Os salvará y evitará los horribles dolores. INFALIBLE Quemaduras. Heridas y Ulceras por rebeldes y antiguas que sean. Pídalo Sarrá. Johnson. Americana y Boticas. Rápida cicatrización.

Advertisement for medication directed to survivors of suicide attempts by fire, promoting the healing of burn wounds. From *Diario de la Marina*, August 12, 1929.

the auspices of the Cuban Academy of Medical Sciences examined cases of self-inflicted death between 1902 and 1906 involving a total of 1,119 suicides; the category of otros suicidios included 67 deaths, 50 of which were identified specifically as por el fuego: 44 by women, 6 by men.[32]

The most detailed analysis of suicide por el fuego was provided by the Comisión Nacional de Estadística y Reformas Económicas, whose careful evaluation of mortality in Cuba between the late 1920s and early 1930s provided annually detailed tabulations of the principal methods of suicide across the island. During the four years from 1926 to 1929, the Comisión Nacional recorded a total of 3,638 cases of suicide. The classification format employed by the Comisión Nacional included suicide as a result of quemadura as a separate category. The Comisión Nacional identified 766 deaths by burning, that is, more than 20 percent of the total number of all suicides. Between 1926 and 1929, burning was the second most common method of suicide in Cuba, preceded only by hanging (829) and followed by firearms (765), poison (521), and drowning (364). This percentage remained generally constant through the years that followed. According to the information published by the Comisión Nacional de Estadística y Reformas Económicas, quemaduras accounted for nearly 25 percent of all suicides in 1930 (281 out of 1,135), 22 percent in 1931 (268 out of 1,217), and 18 percent in 1932 (182 out of 1,002).[33]

The data published by the Comisión Nacional set the gender distinctions in sharp relief. Nearly 95 percent of all suicides by burning in 1930 (265 out of 281) were committed by women, at a female-to-male ratio of nearly 17:1. In the following year, the total of 268 quemaduras consisted of 246 women and 22 men. In 1932, of the 182 cases of death by fire, 173 were women and 9 were men.[34]

Provincial variations were also striking. During the years 1926–29, death by fire was the single most common method by which Cubans — mostly women — in Matanzas province took their own lives, accounting for nearly 44 percent of all suicides (183 out of 419), followed by Las Villas, where death by fire represented more than 25 percent of all suicides (192 out of 759).[35] Quemaduras were least common in Camagüey, accounting for less than 12 percent of all suicides in the province (40 out of 342). Of the 142 suicides recorded in Matanzas in 1930, fully 40 percent (58) were the result of fire, 57 of which were committed by women. In Las Villas, all 58 suicides by burning in 1930 (almost 30 percent of the provincial total) were by women.[36]

Striking too were the ages of the women who took their lives por el fuego. Almost all were young women, many of them adolescents. Fifteen-year-old Elsa Quintana García and seventeen-year-old Caridad Arencibia, both of Matanzas, burned themselves to death. Other adolescents included María Mercedes Gutiérrez, (eighteen years old), Natividad Fortún (seventeen years old), Modesta Trejo González (seventeen years old), Clotilde Domínguez Madán (seventeen years old), among many others.[37]

✴✴ Age appears as a salient differential element in the pattern of suicide among men and women (see Table 3.9). Indeed, the striking age difference at which men and women were most vulnerable to suicide underscores the way that gender-determined conventions shaped the coping mechanisms by which life was experienced — and ended. More than 80 percent of all suicides among women were registered between the ages of ten and thirty-nine. Men killed themselves in nearly equal numbers between the age ranges of ten to thirty-nine and forty and older. What is especially striking, however, is the reverse rates of suicide between young females of the ten-

Table 3.9. Suicide in Cuba: Age and Gender Distribution, 1951–1953

Age	1951	1952	1953	Total
5–14 years old				
Male	10	8	5	23
Female	15	10	11	36
15–24 years old				
Male	99	94	81	274
Female	168	129	115	412
25–44 years old				
Male	170	149	163	482
Female	89	110	82	281
45–64 years old				
Male	144	173	147	464
Female	40	43	44	127
65+ years old				
Male	95	99	92	286
Female	19	18	21	58
Subtotal				
Male				1,529
Female				914
Total	849	833	761	2,443

Source: República de Cuba, Ministerio de Salubridad y Asistencia Social, *Boletín Oficial* (1955–59).

to-nineteen cohort and older males above sixty years of age. Young women and older men appeared most susceptible to ending their own lives.

In general, suicide was mainly an act of the young. Between 1910 and 1949, men and women together between the ages of ten and thirty-nine accounted for more than 60 percent of all deaths by suicide, notwithstanding the fact that through the various census periods they made up an ever-smaller proportion of the total population. Between 1951 and 1953 the age cohort of fifteen to forty-four years old made up approximately 40 percent of the total population but accounted for nearly 60 percent of the total number of suicides (Table 3.9).[38]

Discernible patterns between 1910 and 1949 suggest tendencies of suicide within specific age cohorts. More than 70 percent of all suicides in the ten-to-nineteen age group (2,027 out of 2,848) were committed by females, whereas nearly 85 percent of all Cubans who killed themselves at the age of forty or older were males (5,918 out of 7,136). To put this in slightly different terms, nearly 32 percent of all suicides by women were committed within the youngest cohort of the ten-to-nineteen age group (2,027 out of 6,385); this age cohort accounted for barely 7 percent of total male suicides (821 out of 11,781). The male-to-female rate of suicide approached closest parity in the twenty-to-thirty-nine age group, accounting for almost 50 percent of all suicides by women (3,140 out of 6,385) and nearly 43 percent of all suicides by men (5,042 out of 11,781). Indeed, this was the age group in which both men and women most commonly killed themselves. After the ages of twenty to thirty-nine, the differences between men and women once more diverged sharply. In the age cohort of forty to fifty-nine, the percentage of female suicides dropped to 14 percent of the total number of suicides by women (895 out of 6,385); while the number of men who killed themselves in this age group accounted for nearly 32 percent of the total (3,716 out of 11,781). The group of sixty years and older accounted for nearly 19 percent of all male suicides (2,202 out of 11,779) and 5 percent of all female suicides (323 out of 6,385).

Similarly, the ratio of suicide of two men for every one woman varied markedly within specific age categories. Within the age cohort of ten to nineteen, the rate was reversed, with women killing themselves at a ratio of nearly 2.5:1 over men. Within the age group of twenty to thirty-nine, men overtook women with a 1.6:1 ratio. The disparity widened dramatically to a male-to-female ratio of more than 4:1 among Cubans within the forty-to-fifty-nine cohort and increased again to nearly 7:1 among those aged sixty and older.

Variations within each age cohort were no less striking. Between 1908 and 1910, for example, males between the ages of ten and nineteen were killing themselves at an average rate of 7.1 per 100,000 — that is, an average of 15 annually out of the total population of 210,000 males between the ages of ten and nineteen. At the same time, females in the same age cohort were killing themselves at a rate of 18.3 per 100,000. At the other end of the life cycle, women within the population cohort of sixty years of age and older were killing themselves at the rate of 13 per 100,000, while men were taking their lives at an annual rate of 77 per 100,000. By the early 1930s, the number of women killing themselves in the over-sixty age group had declined to 7.4 per 100,000, while for men it had increased to more than 86 per 100,000.[39]

The patterns of death by suicide for both men and women were themselves a function of the patterns of life, patterns largely shaped by the formulations of gender by which adulthood was experienced. Women in the young age cohort were engaged in the development of personal relationships with men, a matter of urgency per the conventions by which they were conducted into adult status. It was to the calling of wife, mother, and homemaker that vast numbers of women prepared themselves and into which they invested vast amounts of moral energy and emotional commitment. Suicide by women often responded to a disruption or some other difficulty within the realm of personal attachments, often involving a husband or lover, occasionally parents, sometimes children.

Clearly men and women experienced aging and the attending changes of life in very different ways.[40] Women appear to have adapted to old age with greater success than men, often with fewer disruptions to the daily routines of a lifetime and with less dislocation to the site and setting of the workplace. That many women were homemakers for much of their adult lives meant that the onset of old age did not necessarily signal a sharp break with the ways that everyday life had been experienced. Women effectively never "retired," and hence did not suffer a loss or diminution of those attributes from which they had to a lesser or greater degree obtained a sense of place and purpose.

Women also appear to have adapted to loss of spouse much more successfully than men. Far more independent and self-sufficient in the household, women who suffered the loss of male companionship, especially in retirement years, did not necessarily face insurmountable adjustments. Older women often relied upon support networks of kin and neighbors developed over the course of a lifetime, networks that were rarely available to men. Less engaged in the world of wage labor outside the home, women experienced fewer adjustments associated with the onset of retirement and old age.[41] Women also appear to have been socialized to anticipate widowhood as a condition of old age, and hence adapted to the loss of spouse as a change of life with far less trauma than men. Longevity did not come as a surprise to Cuban women. The 1953 census recorded nearly a 3:1 ratio of widows to widowers (140,516 to 46,856). Rates were higher in the cities. In Havana the widow-to-widower ratio was more than 4:1 (55,182 to 13,411).[42]

Old age for men, on the other hand, was frequently accompanied by withdrawal from participation in the wider world of work, experienced as an abrupt halt to an activity that had served as an overriding facet of adulthood. Retirement often signified confinement to domestic spheres and separation from work as the place of both source and means of self-esteem and self-worth. This was not experienced solely—or even principally—as a loss of livelihood, although certainly the reduction of income was not without far-reaching implications. At least as important, however, was the loss of purpose and diminution of status, previously invested in the role of provider, so central a facet to male identity and from which meaning in the lives of men had been derived and defined.

Men were especially susceptible to despair and demoralization attending the onset of afflictions and chronic infirmities associated with aging. Many found themselves in vastly transformed circumstances, physically weak, economically unproductive, dependent and defenseless, and increasingly perceived themselves as a burden to their families. Advancing age and chronic infirmities, the decline of physical vigor generally, further contributed to diminished capacity to command continued acquiescence to the exercise of patriarchy. "He's old and without work," Ana comments as she prepares to ignore her aging husband's wishes in Virgilio Piñera's play *Aire Frío*. "He's accustomed to being in charge. For thirty years he's the one who has given orders in this house, and now he thinks he can continue to hold the whip over us."[43]

Physical afflictions often induced brooding introspection, a deepening awareness of helplessness and dependence. Many men dreaded helplessness more than death. "I forgave him everything . . . ," María del Carmen Boza reflected on her father's suicide. "I understood his fears: that his illness—real, whether created by body or mind, and causing perverse pain—would impoverish my mother, exhaust her. . . . He left this world while he could still contribute to it, before his body humiliated his sense of himself. Pain and illness and old age grind us into the dust of death—or worse, if we let them, into a helpless, stinking mockery of life."[44]

Among men who lost the companionship of spouse, advancing age often signaled the disruption of life in almost every way that mattered most. The loss of a partner often coincided with withdrawal from workplace association, thereby deepening a sense of isolation and loneliness. Virgil Suárez recalled his grandfather with poignance and tenderness in his poem "In the House of White Light":

When my grandmother left the house
    to live with my aunts, my grandfather,
who spent so much time in the sugarcane
    fields, returned daily to the emptiness
of the clapboard house he built

with his own hands, and he sat in the dark
to eat beans he cooked right in the can.
    There in the half-light he thought of all he had lost,
including family, country, land; sometimes
    he slept upright on that same chair,
only stirred awake by the restlessness
    of his horse. One night during a lightning
storm, my grandfather stripped naked
    and walked out into the field around
the house saying '*Que me parta un rayo,*'
    May lightning strike me, and he stood
with his arms out. . . .[45]

Many men had become accustomed to and dependent upon female companions who provided all domestic needs, from shopping to cooking, from household maintenance to health care, women who typically met virtually all their daily emotional and personal needs. María de los Reyes Castillo recalled the household order of things during her marriage: "[My husband] was a very fussy eater. I had to wake up much earlier than him, because his breakfast consisted of white rice, fried eggs, and Sansón wine. In addition to that, when I awoke him I put his socks on, laid out his underwear and pants in such a manner that when he got out of bed all he had to do was to slip his feet into his shoes and pull up his underpants and trousers and button them up."[46]

Men who experienced old age alone often faced insurmountable hardships, driven to despair by infirmities and diminished economic means, without prospects of a tolerable existence, to the point where death seemed preferable. The verse of Roger de Lauria's poem "Ya estoy viejo y cansado" (1920) suggested the poignance and pathos of male aging:

    I am already old and tired; sadness crushes me
and the sorrow of never smiling disheartens me;
happiness was for me like an ungrateful girlfriend
that when I loved her the most, was when she made me suffer more.

    And today that I am in presence among the ruins of my wild
      dreams
that remain fixed within my bosom, like a spine, the pain,
its tenderness and its longing to see flowers of love
bloom within me are in vain.

It is too late. . . .

I have been transformed from an epicurean to a stoic, resigned,
and upon feeling that in my soul agony begins to take hold
I desire only the moment of rest and peace.[47]

The suicidal death rate among older men was striking and suggests in
palpable terms the hardships of male aging. Seventy-four-year-old widower Manuel Rojas Campos committed suicide by ingesting strychnine,
giving as reason the inability "to confront a difficult economic situation
and the loss of sight." Sixty-year-old Francisco Díaz Delgado, also a widower, attempted to kill himself first by swallowing phosphorous and then,
fearful that he would fail to die, slashed his throat with a barber's razor. "I
put an end to my days," he explained in his suicide note, "for being poor,
sick, and tired of life (*por estar pobre, enfermo y cansado de la vida*)." Teodosio González ended his life at the grave site of his recently deceased wife.
"Teodosio adored his wife," commented the daily *La Caricatura*, "and ever
since her death he lived in a state of profound melancholia."[48]

❦ Methods of suicide were also influenced by age (see Table 3.10). Male
suicide by hanging was distributed more or less evenly among the age
groups of twenty to thirty-nine (31.5 percent), forty to fifty-nine (36.5 percent), and sixty and over (27 percent). Hanging was the preferred method
of self-destruction among men sixty years of age and older, accounting
for more than 70 percent of all male suicide within that age cohort (1,547
out of 2,202). On the other hand, suicide through firearms was the preferred way of death of young males between the ages of ten to nineteen
and twenty to thirty-nine, accounting for 36 percent of all suicides in these
two age cohorts (2,121 out of 5,863). Men most likely to use poison as the
method of suicide were between the ages of twenty and thirty-nine, accounting for nearly 50 percent of the total male deaths by poison (656 out
of 1,315).

Patterns of suicide during the first half of the twentieth century appear
to have persisted into the early 1950s. The Secretaría de Sanidad y Beneficencia was reorganized into the Ministerio de Salubridad y Asistencia Social during the early 1940s, resulting in the adoption of a new statistical
format to tabulate national rates of suicide, in which the classification of
methods was eliminated and the age-cohort groupings reconfigured (see
Table 3.9). Men continued to kill themselves at a higher rate than women
(1.7:1). More than 60 percent of the total suicides in the age groups five

Table 3.10. Suicide in Cuba, by Age, Gender, and Method, 1910–1949

Age/Gender	Poison	Hanging	Drowning	Firearms	Edge Instruments	Leaping	Other	Total
10–19 years old								
Male	148	218	25	174	11	12	47	805
Female	803	282	42	252	23	11	747	1,990
20–39 years old								
Male	642	1,772	179	1,839	36	42	160	4,959
Female	1,239	554	66	323	261	106	818	3,078
40–59 years old								
Male	355	2,069	191	666	208	88	105	3,682
Female	254	310	33	39	26	21	197	880
60+ years old								
Male	146	1,527	96	226	75	47	46	2,163
Female	57	139	20	11	5	7	75	314
Total	3,644	6,871	652	3,530	645	334	2,195	17,871

Sources: República de Cuba, Secretaría de Sanidad y Beneficencia, *Boletín Oficial* (1909–41); and its successor, República de Cuba, Ministerio de Salubridad y Asistencia Social, *Boletín Oficial* (1942–59).

Note: Does not include the years 1927, 1941, and 1942.

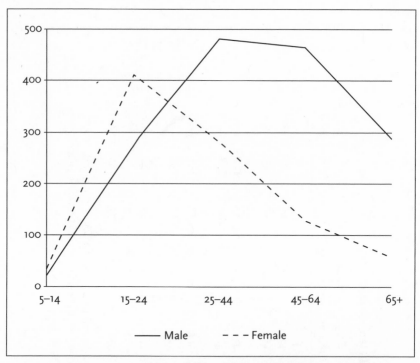

Figure 3.1. Age Patterns of Male-Female Suicide, 1951–1953. *Source*: República de Cuba, Ministerio de Salubridad y Asistencia Social, *Boletín Oficial* (1955–59).

to fourteen and fifteen to twenty-four (448 out of 745) were committed by women, while more than 72 percent of the number of suicides over the age of twenty-five (1,232 out of 1,698) were men. Nearly half of all male suicides were committed by men aged forty-five and older. Suicide continued to be the recourse of young women. The number of women who killed themselves before the age of twenty-five accounted for nearly 50 percent of the total number of female suicides (448 out of 914).

The evidence suggests that suicidal behavior often followed cycles, frequently across generations, often repeating itself within families. These are not circumstances to which public health agencies appeared to have given much attention, and hence it is all but impossible to develop family histories as a context to explore patterns of suicide. "Suicide is contagious," Margarita Engle reports learning from her grandmother. "[She] once told me about a time when it passed through our family like a virus, claiming so many men that the women wore mourning for twenty years. First an uncle killed himself, then his brother followed. Soon a son of the first man who committed suicide, then another brother. The women wore nothing but black and white for two decades, five years for each life, a small penance for such devastation, my grandmother said."[49] Occasionally news accounts made reference to a family member who had previously committed suicide. Manuel Morales killed himself about a year after his father had taken his own life. Twenty-two-year-old Dionela Scull Blanco burned herself to death shortly after her father killed himself the same way. María Luisa Castañeda also burned herself to death two weeks after her daughter committed suicide through fire. César Geli Castañeda, a member of the family that owned Los Reyes Magos toy store in Havana, was the second in the family to kill himself within several months. Rafael Zayas Bazán committed suicide within months of the self-inflicted deaths of his mother and brother.[50] In the short story "Pavo real y muerto grande" by Miguel de Marcos, set in the economic crisis of the early 1920s, the protagonist Juan Antonio Medina broods: "I am ruined. At 35 years of age, I am as poor as a rat . . . I have lost everything. My houses in Vedado have been foreclosed. The companies that bore my name are bankrupt. The rash of suicides that inevitably followed all great economic calamities have started. . . . Suicide tempts me. By the same token, I can not betray my family tree. My grandfather, Antonio María Medina, killed himself on his land in Ciego de Avila in the face of ruin. . . . My father, José Enrique Medina, with the knowledge that he had stomach cancer—that too is a type of ruin—also killed himself. They are the ones who point the way."[51]

Sites selected for suicide appeared to have varied little among men and women. It is difficult to know what to make of the places people chose to kill themselves. Information regarding sites of suicide was made available principally through press accounts and suggests that most men and women took their own lives in the privacy of their own homes, sometimes in hotel rooms, often in the homes of relatives. Many ended their lives in cemeteries, often killing themselves at the burial site of a relative or close friend. Celia Fernández Hermo chose the grave of her recently deceased daughter as the place to end her life through a self-inflicted gunshot wound. Nilda Vera Amador killed herself on sixth anniversary of the death of her mother at her grave site. Lieutenant Colonel Antonio Arredondo Zayas of the Liberation Army killed himself at the tomb of General Máximo Gómez, on whose staff he had served during the war for independence.[52]

Suicide in public places was undertaken by men and women who leaped to their deaths from heights, or by people who threw themselves in the way of an oncoming train or trolley. Suicides por el fuego in particular had as their intrinsic and indeed often defining characteristic death as an act of public display. Occasionally, however, death by burning was undertaken in the home, often with disastrous consequences. Only the quick action of neighbors prevented the apartment house in which Maria Vigil burned herself from being entirely destroyed. When Zoila Guanche Rodríguez burned herself to death in the family home in Santa Clara, the entire house was destroyed by fire.[53] The frequency of suicides in public places during the 1950s raised concern for the safety of the public at large. Essayist Mario Guiral Moreno was dismayed by the "ever increasing number of individuals, who, prematurely wearied of suffering the adversities produced by life, . . . resort to suicide as the easy way to avoid all types of responsibilities." But Guiral Moreno was dismayed even more by acts of suicide that placed innocent bystanders in harm's way:

> It is unseemly and in no way justifiable that instead of committing suicide in some private place, and through means that do not endanger the lives of others who simply happen to be present, these acts are consummated in public places, in the form of shootings, for example, at locations where people congregate and are hence exposed to the danger of stray bullets. Nor is the act of leaping from a tall building onto a public street, imperiling the life and security of passers-by, acceptable. Even more reprehensible is the act of stepping in the way of an on-coming motor vehicle, which has recently become very much in vogue, to be dragged to death by the driver, with grave consequences to innocent parties. . . . It would be desirable, hence, that those disposed to kill themselves refrain from imperiling the lives of other citizens and that in resorting to such extreme measures they be the only ones hurt.[54]

❧ The relationship between marital status and suicidal death is not altogether clear, for the data is sparse and only suggestive. The most complete information on marital status appeared in a study published under the auspices of the Cuban Academy of Medical Sciences in 1907. Of the 1,119 cases of suicide recorded between 1902 and 1906, nearly 62 percent (692) of the total consisted of unmarried men and women; nearly 8 percent (85) were widowed. Married persons made up 23 percent of the total (262); the balance (80) were classified as unknown and preadolescent. Nor was information on age and gender provided.[55] A later study of suicide in the city of Havana in 1912 identified 67 percent of suicides and attempted suicides as unmarried men and women (174 out of 258), followed by married (72) and widowed (12) men and women.[56]

The most useful information concerning occupation and suicide was also contained in the 1907 study (see Table 3.11). Self-inflicted deaths among working-class men, including workers in agriculture, industry, and transportation as well as day laborers, accounted for almost 55 percent of the total number of male suicides. Agricultural workers accounted for the single largest percentage, making up nearly 30 percent of all male suicides. Middle-class males—principally merchants, government employees, members of the liberal professions, rentiers—accounted for more than 17 percent of the total number of male suicides (132 out of 764).

The occupational data also provides suggestive information on the marital status of women who committed suicide. More than 56 percent of the total number of women who took their own lives (199 out of 355) were identified as homemakers (*amas de casa*). Almost all committed suicide through poison or por el fuego. After male agricultural workers, amas de casa made up the largest single category of suicide in Cuba. In the study of suicide in Havana in 1912, almost half of all suicides and suicide attempts (126 out of 258) were committed by amas de casa, 94 of which were by poison and 14 by fire.[57]

Social class appears to have had some bearing on methods of suicide. Middle-class men in the 1907 study appeared to have favored firearms as a means of suicide. More than 63 percent of middle-class male suicides (85 out of 134) involved firearms. Hanging was the method of choice for working-class men—workers in agriculture, industry, transportation as well as day laborers—and accounted for nearly 50 percent of all worker suicides (200 out of 412), followed by 110 instances of suicide by firearms (27 percent) and 41 cases of drowning (10 percent).

❀ Discernible differences appear also within racial categories (see Tables 3.12 and 3.13). White and nonwhite males killed themselves generally in the same proportions by the same means, approximately 75 percent and 72 percent respectively by hanging and firearms. On the other hand, the data suggests that the rate of suicide among men of color over the age of forty, accounting for more than 40 percent of the total number of self-inflicted deaths (910 out of 2,230), was lower than the corresponding white cohort (approximately 52 percent, or 5,008 out of 9,545).

Table 3.11. Suicide and Occupation, 1902–1906

Occupations	Poison Male	Poison Female	Hanging Male	Hanging Female	Drowning Male	Drowning Female	Firearms Male	Firearms Female	Edge Instruments Male	Edge Instruments Female	Leaping Male	Leaping Female	Other Male	Other Female	Subtotals Male	Subtotals Female	Total
Agriculture																	
Farmers			5				5								10		10
Workers	15		126	2	21		43		12				9		226	2	228
Other			1						1						2		2
Industry																	
Cigar makers	3	1	4		1		10		2						20	1	21
Carpenters	5		8				7		2				1		23		23
Shoemakers	1		3				2								6		6
Barbers	1		2				2		1						6		6
Mechanics			1				3		1				1		6		6
Bakers			1				3								4		4
Bricklayers	1		4												5		5
Other	2	3	4		1		15		1		1			3	24	6	30
Transportation																	
Merchant marines			2		2										4		4
Longshoremen					1										1		1
Teamsters					1		1								2		2
Mercantile	8		18		3		51		2				1		83		83
Government	1		3				16		2		1		1		24		24
Armed forces																	
Artillery corps							2								2		2
Rural guard					1		1								2		2
Police							6								6		6

Category	Male	Female	Total
Liberal professions			
Attorneys	2		2
Dentists	1		1
Pharmacists	1		1
Other	7	1	8
Property owning			
Rentiers	12	1	13
Hacendados	2		2
General			
Clerks	15	1	16
Day laborers	86	3	89
Domestic			
Homemakers	4	199	203
Cooks	7		7
Other	2		2
Nonproductive			
Students	8		8
Prisoners	3	1	4
Mendicants	3		3
Prostitutes		13	13
Unknown	154	127	281
Total	763	355	1,118

Source: Jorge LeRoy y Cassá, "Quo Tendimus? Estudio médico legal sobre el suicidio en Cuba durante el quinquenio de 1902–1906," Anales de la Academia de Ciencias Médicas, Físicas y Naturales de La Habana 44 (May 1907): 38–63.

Table 3.12. Suicide in Cuba, by Method, Age, and Gender: Colored, 1910–1949

Method	Age	Male	Female	Total
Poison	10–19	36	187	223
	20–39	141	250	391
	40–59	62	35	97
	60+	13	11	24
	Total	252	483	735
Hanging	10–19	70	63	133
	20–39	456	118	574
	40–59	331	56	387
	60+	293	28	321
	Total	1,150	265	1,415
Drowning	10–19	16	10	26
	20–39	50	12	62
	40–59	24	9	33
	60+	17	6	23
	Total	107	37	144
Firearms	10–19	41	31	72
	20–39	345	48	393
	40–59	67	7	74
	60+	10	3	13
	Total	463	89	552

Some of the most noteworthy disparities in rates and methods of suicide were registered among women. Whereas the use of poison was identified in 41 percent of all suicides of white women (1,905 out of 4,591), it accounted for less than 27 percent among women of color (483 out of 1,791). Hanging and firearms were similarly used with greater frequency by white women (22 percent and 10 percent respectively) than women of color (15 percent and 5 percent).

Perhaps the most dramatic difference was registered among women in the category of otros suicidios, most of which were completed by way of burning. Of the 44 women who killed themselves por el fuego between 1902 and 1906, 27 were identified as women of color.[58] Between 1910 and 1949, fire accounted for 22 percent of suicides (994 out of 4,591) among

Table 3.12. Continued

Method	Age	Male	Female	Total
Edge instruments	10–19	7	5	12
	20–39	58	10	68
	40–59	38	8	46
	60+	7	2	9
	Total	110	25	135
Leaping	10–19	4	1	5
	20–39	17	6	23
	40–59	8	1	9
	60+	7	3	10
	Total	36	11	47
Other	10–19	16	393	409
	20–39	63	387	450
	40–59	23	79	102
	60+	10	22	32
	Total	112	881	993
Total		2,230	1,791	4,021

Sources: República de Cuba, Secretaría de Sanidad y Beneficencia, *Boletín Oficial* (1909–41); and its successor República de Cuba, Ministerio de Salubridad y Asistencia Social, *Boletín Oficial* (1942–59).

Note: Does not include the years 1927, 1941–42, and 1946–47.

white women, while among women of color it made up nearly 50 percent of all suicides (881 out of 1,791). Women of color appear to have used fire as a means of suicide with far greater frequency than white women.

Significant too were the configurations of female suicide rates. Young women of color between ten and nineteen years of age accounted for nearly 40 percent of the total number of female self-inflicted deaths (691 out of 1,791), while among white females, this age cohort represented less than 30 percent of the total (1,337 out of 4,594). On the other hand, slightly more than 50 percent of men of color killed themselves between the ages of twenty and thirty-nine (1,130 out of 2,230), whereas for white men this age cohort accounted for 41 percent of the total (3,912 out of 9,549).

It is difficult, of course, to discern clear meaning out of this body of

Table 3.13. Suicide in Cuba, by Method, Age, and Gender: White, 1910–1949

Method	Age	Male	Female	Total
Poison	10–19	116	628	744
	29–39	515	1,009	1,524
	40–59	296	222	518
	60+	136	46	182
	Total	1,063	1,905	2,968
Hanging	10–19	217	162	379
	20–39	1,360	456	1,816
	40–59	1,767	261	2,028
	60+	1,254	117	1,371
	Total	4,598	996	5,594
Drowning	10–19	26	15	41
	20–39	129	54	183
	40–59	167	24	191
	60+	80	15	95
	Total	402	108	510
Firearms	10–19	215	143	358
	20–39	1,518	278	1,796
	40–59	600	32	632
	60+	222	8	230
	Total	2,555	461	3,016

data. Young females of color appear to have experienced youth as a more precarious life stage than white women. Men of color between the ages of twenty and thirty-nine, a time of family formation and peak wage-earning possibilities, appeared to have experienced life very differently from their white male counterparts. Also noteworthy were the sex disparities between whites and nonwhites (see Table 3.14). The data available for the years between 1910 and 1949 indicates that white men killed themselves at a 2:1 ratio to white women. The ratio within the population of color, on the other hand, approached near parity at 1.2 males for every 1 female. In the age cohort of ten to nineteen, on the other hand, women of color killed themselves at nearly a 4:1 ratio to men; while among whites the female-to-male ratio was approximately 2:1. The greatest male-to-female disparities are found within the cohorts of forty to fifty-nine and sixty and older.

Table 3.13. Continued

Method	Age	Male	Female	Total
Edge instruments	10–19	16	6	22
	20–39	205	28	233
	40–59	171	19	190
	60+	68	3	71
	Total	460	56	516
Leaping	10–19	7	11	18
	20–39	86	36	122
	40–59	80	20	100
	60+	47	7	54
	Total	220	74	294
Other	10–19	32	372	404
	20–39	99	448	547
	40–59	84	121	205
	60+	36	53	89
	Total	251	994	1,245
Total		9,549	4,594	14,143

Sources: República de Cuba, Secretaría de Sanidad y Beneficencia, *Boletín Oficial* (1909–41); and its successor República de Cuba, Ministerio de Salubridad y Asistencia Social, *Boletín Oficial* (1942–59).

Note: Does not include the years 1927, 1941–42, and 1946–47.

❧ Information on unsuccessful suicide attempts is incomplete and available principally in the form of news stories. Instances of failed suicide were reported frequently in the daily press, but public health agencies did not ordinarily maintain records of unsuccessful suicide attempts. One systematic effort to examine failed attempts at suicide was completed in 1912, based on mortality data for the city of Havana during the years between 1903 and 1912. The study recorded a rate of slightly more than two unsuccessful attempts for every completed suicide. In 1912, for example, a total of 82 suicides were completed and another 176 attempts were unsuccessful.[59] This pattern remained more or less constant for the years 1906–11, during which 710 suicides were completed and another 1,343 unsuccessful attempts made (see Table 3.15).

While the number of men who committed suicide surpassed women

Table 3.14. White and Colored Age Cohorts,
Male-to-Female Ratios, 1910–1949

Age	White	Colored
10–19	1:2	1:3.6
20–39	1.7:1	1.2:1
40–59	4.5:1	2.8:1
60+	7.4:1	4.7:1

Sources: República de Cuba, Secretaría de Sanidad y Beneficencia, *Boletín Oficial* (1909–41); and its successor República de Cuba, Ministerio de Salubridad y Asistencia Social, *Boletín Oficial* (1942–59).

Note: Does not include the years 1927, 1941–42, and 1946–47.

at a 2:1 ratio, the instances of women who made unsuccessful attempts at suicide greatly outnumbered men. The study of suicide in Havana in 1912 indicated that nearly 70 percent of all unsuccessful suicide attempts (118 out of 176) were by women. During the early 1950s, an estimated 1,200 women attempted unsuccessfully to kill themselves, a rate of three to four times higher than the number of women who succeeded. This was in part related to women's employment of less immediately lethal means, including poison and the slashing of the wrist, which required more time to result in death and thereby allowed greater opportunity for intervention. Of the 118 failed suicide attempts by women in Havana in 1912, 101 were attempted by use of poison. Even the use of fire as a means of suicide allowed for the opportunity of life-saving intervention. "The woman who sets herself on fire," quips Carucha in the play *Los excéntricos de la noche*, by Nicolás Dorr, "always goes running into the street, and since here nobody minds their own business, they immediately throw a blanket around you and prevent you from completing the act." The methods most often used by men, on the other hand, principally firearms and hanging, provided far more efficient means of death.[60]

✻ The voices of the men and women who took their own lives were expressed most vividly through their suicide notes. Most notes were written in the final moments of life, usually with a specific audience in mind, as a final attempt at self-expression, often to provide instructions for others to follow. The clinical research on suicide suggests that notes provide a generally accurate rendering of motive.[61] Notes directed to local magistrates charged with the task of a judicial inquest tended to be introspective and

Table 3.15. Unsuccessful and Completed Suicides: Havana, 1903–1912

Year	Unsuccessful	Completed
1903	115	58
1904	112	69
1905	122	57
1906	117	67
1907	105	50
1908	125	83
1909	147	93
1910	136	78
1911	188	73
1912	176	82
Total	1,343	710

Source: Antonio Barreras, "Estudios médico-legales: El suicidio en La Habana en el año de 1912," *Revista Médica Cubana* 21 (June 1912): 315–41.

intimate musings on the circumstances of the decision to die. María del Carmen Boza later reflected on her efforts to recover her father's suicide note from the possession of the police: "Without seeing it, his handwriting could not speak to us, could not tell us through the shape of letters and lines on paper what my father suffered during his last moments of unbearable consciousness—or what he meant us to know. Without it, his last message to my mother was as vapor before the leaden evidence that contradicted it."[62]

Suicide notes often sought to assuage the grief of surviving loved ones and asked for absolution and forgiveness. At times they sought to exculpate others who could be implicated as cause of the suicide.[63] "No one is responsible for my death," José Luis Valdés explained in his letter. "I take my life because I wish to, and nothing more. I forgive all my enemies."[64] A note could also serve as the means of final retribution, in which the cause of suicide was attributed to another person. "For your love, Asunción," was the purpose to which Antonio de Liz attributed his hanging; "you are responsible for what has happened to me." Jorge Navarro Pereira explained in his suicide note that "the cause of my death is Cuca, for her refusal to love me."[65] Suicide notes written by women tended to address in explicit terms general emotional conditions, including despair and despondency, personal disappointment, and often a sense of hopelessness. Younger women often addressed specifically relationships with men as a circumstance in the decision to end their lives and alluded to personal con-cern.[66] Men tended to address matters related to the difficulties associated with economic matters, usually in despair for having failed to meet their responsibilities as providers.

✥ Provincial variations of suicide rates remained more or less constant through much of the twentieth century, with Havana province—includ-ing the city of Havana—accounting for the largest percentage of all sui-cides in Cuba. Of the 1,119 cases of suicide reported between 1902 and 1906, nearly 41 percent (457) occurred in the province of Havana, followed by Las Villas (195), Oriente (166), Matanzas (151), Pinar del Río (101), and Camagüey (49). Of the 3,638 suicides reported by the Comisión Nacional de Estadística y Reformas Económicas between 1926 and 1929, Havana province accounted for approximately 30 percent (1,095), followed by Las Villas (759), Oriente (688), Matanzas (419), Camagüey (342), and Pinar del Río (335). Similarly, for the three years during 1930–32, the Comisión Nacional reported a total of 3,356 suicides on the island; Havana made up for nearly 30 percent (978) of the total, followed by Oriente (734), Las Villas (694), Matanzas (346), Camagüey (303), and Pinar del Río (301).[67]

The rates of suicidal death were registered disproportionally higher in the cities than in the countryside, although it must be presumed that the instances of underreported suicides in rural Cuba contributed to this dis-parity. The city of Havana, containing nearly 15 percent of the total popula-tion in 1907, accounted for 27 percent of the total number of self-inflicted deaths between 1902 and 1906 (302 out of 1,119). The recorded suicides in the capital were not only high as a percentage of the total, but they were extraordinarily high on a per capita basis. Where the national suicide rate in 1929 was more than 16 per 100,000, for example, the rate in Havana surpassed 46 per 100,000.[68]

Disproportionally high suicide rates were also recorded in the cities of Cienfuegos, Matanzas, Camagüey, and Santiago de Cuba.[69] The data pub-lished by the Comisión Nacional for the years between 1926 and 1929 also indicated that almost 32 percent of the total number of suicides (1,154 out of 3,638) were recorded in cities with a population of 25,000 or more, including Havana, Santiago de Cuba, Camagüey, Matanzas, Cienfuegos, Marianao, Cárdenas, Las Villas, and Sancti-Spíritus. Havana accounted for nearly 60 percent of urban suicides (676 out of 1,154), followed by San-tiago de Cuba, Camagüey, Matanzas, Las Villas, and Cárdenas. Overall, Havana accounted for approximately 20 percent of the total number of

Table 3.16. Provincial Rates of Suicide, 1926–1930 (per 100,000 inhabitants)

Province	1926	1927	1928	1929	1930
Pinar del Río	22.1	26.3	33.7	28.8	33.9
Havana	24.7	28.9	27.0	34.4	33.2
Matanzas	28.2	26.5	28.5	36.9	39.5
Las Villas	22.6	24.3	25.8	27.4	25.8
Camagüey	27.3	33.3	32.3	38.9	35.0
Oriente	28.2	15.9	17.9	17.9	28.3

Source: República de Cuba, Comisión Nacional de Estadística y Reformas Económicas, *Estadísticas 1930* (Havana, 1931).

suicides in the republic during the years 1926–29, a figure that would remain generally constant for much of the twentieth century.[70] On the basis of suicides per 100,000 inhabitants, the data tabulated by the Comisión Nacional between 1926 and 1930 situated the province of Camagüey at the high end of national suicide rates and Las Villas and Oriente provinces at the low end (see Table 3.16).

Patterns of differentiation in methods of suicide are also discernible among the provinces. The Comisión Nacional data for the years between 1926 and 1929 revealed that the single most preferred method of suicide in Pinar del Río was the ingestion of poison (37 percent of the total, 124 out of 335). In Havana, hanging accounted for the largest portion of suicide (21 percent, 233 out of 1,095). Por el fuego was the preferred method in Matanzas (44 percent, 183 out of 419), and in Las Villas it was hanging (nearly 26 percent, 196 out of 759) and por el fuego (25 percent, 192 out of 759). *Camagüeyanos* appear to have preferred firearms (27 percent) and hanging (26 percent, 91 and 89 respectively out of 342). In Oriente, firearms and drowning accounted for more than 45 percent of all suicides (167 and 148 respectively out of 688).[71]

✴⟟✶ The rate of suicide appears also to have corresponded to the seasonal cycles of sugar production. The Academia de Ciencias Médicas noted that fully 45 percent of all suicides between 1902 and 1906 (504 out of 1,119) were committed during the months after the harvest, with suicides peaking in the months of August (118) and July (110). Suicide rates dropped in February (77), December (86), and January (90).[72] Sanidad y Beneficencia similarly recorded a marked increase of suicides during the months of economic idleness (*tiempo muerto*). Nearly 46 percent of all suicides be-

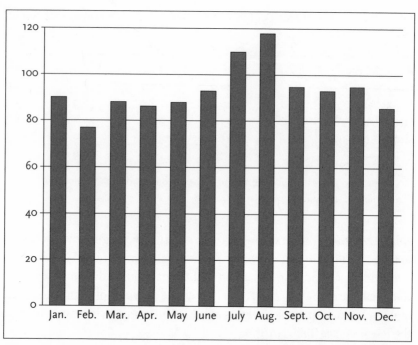

Figure 3.2. Seasonality of Suicide, 1902–1906. *Source*: Jorge LeRoy y Cassá, "Quo Tendimus? Estudio médico legal sobre el suicidio en Cuba durante el quinquenio de 1902–1906," *Anales de la Academia de Ciencias Médicas, Físicas y Naturales de La Habana* 44 (May 1907): 38–63.

tween 1911 and 1913 (560 out of 1,218) were committed during tiempo muerto, with peak months of May (121), July (121), and August (113). The forensic physician of the city of Havana, Antonio Barreras, similarly reported that the rate of suicide in Havana reached monthly peaks after the harvest, during the months between March and September.[73]

Tiempo muerto was more than an economic cycle. It also coincided with a time of year: with the stifling heat of the summer months, with languor and listlessness assuming the form of a generalized state of idleness. It undoubtedly falls far more within the realm of environmental history to determine the links between climate on one hand and the development of moral systems and psychological dispositions on the other. That there is a relationship, however, cannot be doubted.

The summer months were a time of pestilence and epidemics, of fatigue and fevers that announced the onset of disease and illness. The oppressive relentlessness of the heat of summer, unyielding and unbearable, referred to commonly in the late nineteenth century as *el bochorno colo-*

nial, was aptly described in a memorable line by nineteenth-century writer Anselmo Suárez y Romero in the novel *Francisco* (1875) as "that time of year when the sun begins to suffocate the inhabitants of Cuba with heat."[74] An asphyxiating stillness descended over much of the island; the environment of tropical torpor and a disinclination to exertion at a time that coincided with diminished employment enhanced summer susceptibility to suicide. Suicide often took on the epidemic appearance of illness, a development associated with the changing of the seasons, not dissimilar to the increase of yellow fever and malaria during the summer months.

Cubans of means fled the island during the summer months, seeking respite in Europe and the northeastern United States. Everyone else remained. Nineteenth-century geographer Esteban Pichardo wrote of "the summer sun beating down on the stagnant waters accumulating in the swamps, cesspools, and coastal marshes and the decaying plant and animal life that poison the atmosphere with those deleterious miasmas that contribute so much to epidemic fevers." The stillness of the air "is asphyxiating; one desperately strains to find air to breathe ...; the temperature is infernal." Disease-bearing mosquitoes, flies, cockroaches, and gnats multiplied prodigiously during the summer months. Wrote Pichardo:

> During the evening calm ... plagues of mosquitos and gnats fill the air, principally in the low-lying coastal areas, there to torment the population that lives constantly in motion trying to kill them. ... That combination of heat and humidity leads to the reproduction and decay of animal and plant life and accelerates life and death. That lassitude that the body experiences acts to resist work, it induces sleep, inactivity, and indolence; it encourages use of the hammock, the rocking chair, and the swing.[75]

Physician Ramón Pina y Peñuela described the summer as a time of "listlessness, prostration, insensibility, and indifference" and a season of "languor, indolence, apathy and weariness." Physician Julio LeRiverend reflected at length on what he identified as the "special pathology" of Cuba, with particular attention to the summer months. "Under these climactic conditions," LeRiverend observed, "the inhabitants generally experience notable changes in their moral faculties. They become irascible, jealous, and distrustful; they have little interest in any kind of work, either physical or intellectual. ... Everything causes them to tire and become fatigued. This is the season of the year when scores are settled, and suicides, homicides, and abortions increase."[76]

The circumstances of summer affected behaviors, if only as ways to cope, and induced among many a state associated with despair. The medical journal *La Higiene* warned of the perils attending "eight months of asphyxiating heat," creating "weather conditions that conspire against health and life," observing: "Our inclinations change with the weather, our character suffers notable variations, our spirit, in a word, is susceptible to all the influences of atmospheric changes." *La Higiene* counseled urban dwellers "to dedicate Sundays to the open air, to go out into the countryside or take excursions in shady and well-ventilated areas." Francisco Figueras identified climate—"regulator par excellence of customs"—as source of national vices, precisely due to the idleness occasioned by the summer and "the forms of entertainment improvised to kill time, from which developed creole indolence."[77]

Personal correspondence, diaries, and memoirs of nineteenth-century summers often evoked images of conditions approaching prostration. "The heat in the month of July was asphyxiating," Flora Basulto recalled of her childhood. Manuel del Monte endured the Cuban summer in quiet despair. "We have another kind of life here," he wrote his brother in Europe. "Even now, as I write you, the sun is above me, boiling my nerves and afflicting me with lassitude. It forces me to forget all pleasure and experience only unpleasant sensations. I crave water, rest, and quiet. So you see, this is another life. It is to live within the Tropics."[78] Mercedes Santa Cruz (Countess of Merlin) was nearly incapacitated during a July visit to Havana:

> The heat is excessive and the wind blows as if it originates from an oven. All work is impossible, and for my part I feel a vague anxiety caused by the struggle going on between the activity in my head and the weakness of my limbs. The active European customs, the resources that it offers to the civilization of the Old World, fail me completely here. There are occasions that I feel a kind of indignation for having degenerated to my Indian ancestors for *dolce far niente* is not sufficient for my well-being. . . . The sun—an implacable sun—perpetually imposes itself. . . . The implacable mosquitos test my patience. My arms and hands are in a deplorable state. If I cover them to write, I suffocate, I burn up, I die; if I leave them [exposed] to the mercy of these infernal enemies, it appears that they want to devour them.[79]

Downward economic cycles combined with the onset of sweltering seasonal change and took a toll on collective mood and morale. But seasonal change implied more than a time of unemployment and unbearable weather. It also involved time as a social phenomenon, conferring on the notion of "dead season" an important sociological dimension. This was social time, set against daily life in response to patterns of inescapable cultural demands. Responses took many forms. Suicide was one.

✻ An overview of suicide in Cuba during the first half of the twentieth century sets in relief a number of striking patterns. It was in the circumstances of life as lived, from day to day and year to year, that the data assumes salience. Perhaps among the most compelling aspects of suicidal behavior are found in the multiple levels at which gender acted to delineate the practice of self-destruction. Both men and women through the years of their youth and into the advancing years of old age experienced life very differently from one another and indeed chose to end their lives through very different means. Much has to do with the ways that Cubans developed expectations of achievements and learned to discharge obligations, of course, and that men and women learned to aspire to very different means of self-fulfillment at different phases of their lives must be considered as a factor of central relevance to the practice of suicide in Cuba.

Patterns of class and race are suggestive but less clear. That male agricultural workers killed themselves at a higher rate, and often during tiempo muerto, the peak period of idleness and unemployment, appears as a fixed facet of suicide in Cuba. Certainly, despair over joblessness is an obvious issue. But it is more complicated, and has also to do with the way that males learned to discharge the responsibilities of men, the way they were conducted into adulthood and its accompanying responsibilities in an environment of socioeconomic transformation.

A Way of Life, a Way of Death

4

Since 1924–25, the Cuban economy has been both unstable and undynamic. It has been barely holding its own in long-term trends of real income per capita. It has been characterized by large amounts of unemployment, under-employment, and general insecurity for independent producers and commercial people as well as for wage earners. Modern psychology has found that feelings of insecurity may affect human behavior—whether in individuals or groups—in a powerful way. They often lead to attitudes and actions which are not reasonable nor rational.

    International Bank for Reconstruction and
    Development, Report on Cuba *(1951)*

In Cuba . . . the opportunities for employment are insufficient. Unemployment, under-employment, and low wages constitute grave ills and are factors in the social demoralization, economic weakness, and political instability of the nation. This situation is extraordinarily sensitive to any national or international development and extends itself into the tranquility of the household and the well-being of youth. The fear of misery, produced by insufficient income, and the lack of confidence in the future encourage a search for a violent resolution of problems.

    Gustavo Gutiérrez, El empleo, el sub-empleo y el
    desempleo en Cuba *(1958)*

*The North Americans seized control of this island [after
1898]. . . . We gave them sugar, cigars, and whores for
their tourists, and they gave us everything else, including
razors that were of the highest quality. Peasants in Cuba,
when dispossessed of their lands and lacking the means
to feed their parasitic-infected children, slashed their
wrists with North American razors.*

   René Vázquez Díaz, La era imaginaria *(1987)*

*All you could do was hope that someday things would
change. But the years passed, years, . . . and nothing
changed.*

   Lázaro Benedí Rodríguez, in Oscar Lewis,
   Ruth M. Lewis, and Susan M. Rigdon, Four
   Women. Living the Revolution: An Oral History
   of Contemporary Cuba *(1977)*

*Today we again read the same news of everyday: men
again assaulting women. What cowardice! . . . We must
face up to this problem. This murder of women at the
hands of their exploiters cannot be allowed to continue in
the very bosom of Cuban society.*

   La Lucha *(February 17, 1929)*

✂ The republic for which so many had sacrificed so
much for so long was established amid devastation and ruin. Nearly four
decades of war had visited unimaginable suffering and incalculable losses
on the people of Cuba. Many tens of thousands of men, women, and
children had perished; a large proportion of survivors were maimed, or-
phaned, or traumatized. Where towns and villages once stood there remained only scattered piles of stone rubble and charred wood. Agriculture
was in ruins. What were previously lush farming zones were now scenes
of scorched earth and singed brush. Vast areas of the most productive regions of the island had been reduced to barren fields. Many thousands of

small farms, coffee *fincas*, tobacco *vegas*, cattle ranches, and sugar estates had perished. Fully two-thirds of Cuba's wealth had disappeared during the war of 1895–98.[1]

Slowly life returned to normal. Families were reunited and households reconstituted. People returned to the land, and the land returned to production. There was perhaps no more powerful indication of the optimism with which Cubans contemplated the future than the spectacular increase of fertility rates. Between the census years of 1899 and 1907, the population under five years of age increased from nearly 9 percent of the total (130,878 out of 1.5 million) to almost 20 percent (342,652 out of 2 million).[2] The postwar "baby boom" was to be the defining demographic circumstance of the new republic.

Peace did not favor everyone, however. Behind the promise of recovery were gathering signs of ominous portent. Revival after 1898 came principally in the form of a heavily capitalized economy dedicated to the production of a single export product, driven by vast infusion of North American capital, stimulated by privileged access to North American markets. These developments had their antecedents in the nineteenth century, of course. But what was different after 1898 was the speed and scope of capital inputs, made all the more preponderant in an economic environment of ruin and devastation. Sugar production soared, more than doubling from 1 million tons in 1903 to 2.6 millions tons in 1915 and doubling again to 5.2 million tons in 1925. Recovery of land idle during the war proceeded apace, increasing threefold from 848,000 acres in 1907 to 2.2 million acres in 1919; by the mid-1930s, an estimated 8.3 million acres of land were planted with sugarcane. Within decades of the establishment of the republic nearly 60 percent of the total land under cultivation had been allocated to sugar production.[3]

The salient facet of postwar economic revival was the degree to which the expansion of sugar implicated everything else, and more: the degree to which it acted to subordinate everything else. The imperative of sugar subjected virtually all facets of production to the larger logic of an export economy. Sugar fixed the function of tertiary sectors around export needs, thereby further integrating the disparate elements of economic development into the service of commodity production. By midcentury, sugar products accounted for 90 percent of Cuban export values. The production of sugar, traveler Harry Franck commented tersely in 1920, "is swamping all other industries in the island, nay, even its scenery, beneath endless seas of cane."[4]

An export economy of this magnitude could not but have arranged the attributes of the labor market in ways that were decisive and defining. The well-being of many tens of thousands of households across the island was subject to the chronic structural tensions to which the export economy was inherently susceptible, registered most dramatically as seasonal employment at low wages for three or four months of the year. An estimated 550,000 laborers were engaged in the field and factory work associated with the annual *zafra* (sugar harvest). The livelihood of another 250,000 Cubans, working class and middle class alike, employed principally in retail, transportation, and service, was similarly subject to the vagaries of seasonal production.[5]

But the worst was always what happened after the zafra, during the other eight or nine months of the year, the time of tiempo muerto—the "dead season"—when hundreds of thousands Cubans without work and wages succumbed to conditions approaching indigence. "Nine months of hunger" was the way writer Carlos Forment described tiempo muerto. Erna Fergusson could hardly contain her astonishment at conditions during her visit to the island in the mid-1940s. "As the grinding season is so short . . . ," she commented, "the crying human problem is what is to happen to all those people during the dead season. Under slavery they were at least fed."[6]

Hard times developed into a chronic condition, with the only variation being that in some years it was better, in other years it was worse. It was rarely good. "I recall those years in which the harvest was 60 days," José Angel remembered years later, "and lacking other work to do, hunger, misery, desolation and misfortune entered our homes. This was repeated every year like an implacable specter."[7]

Elements of this economy had existed in the nineteenth century and, in fact, were discernible as early as the 1880s. What was different about the early decades of the twentieth century was largely a matter of degree. But it is also true that the difference in degree was sufficiently great to make for a difference in kind. What was especially noteworthy about economic development in postwar Cuba was the speed with which the economy recovered, and the suddenness with which it faltered. Cuba plunged headlong into sugar production to the exclusion of almost everything else, and in the process forged a structural dependency upon a commodity that within the space of two decades lost the capacity to sustain continued economic development. This was an economy that had reached the limits of growth by the early 1920s, unable thereafter either to generate full employment for an expanding population or provide adequate wages for the population employed. Stagnation emerged as the salient condition of the Cuban economy. "Cuba's present standard of living . . . ," observed the International Bank for Reconstruction and Development in 1951, "depends mainly on an industry which stopped growing many years ago." Sugar production, the Economic Commission for Latin America of the United Nations concluded in 1954, was "inadequate either to act as a dynamic element in the economy or to promote a sustained expansion in the gross product." Cuban economist Alberto León Riva agreed. "The sugar industry," León Riva wrote in 1954, "which is the principal driving force of economic activity of the country, no longer offers any possibility of expanding its payroll. . . . The prosperity of sugar ended a long time ago."[8] Between 25,000 and 40,000 young men and women annually were entering the wage-labor force in an economy capable of generating only 7,000 new jobs a year. "How many of them will pass on to enlarge the long columns of the unemployed that make up the majority of our work-age men?" Leví Marrero asked in 1955. An estimated 665,000 Cubans, more than 30 percent of the labor force—about the percentage of unemployment in the United States during the worst years of the depression—were without full-time work, every year. "A third of the workers of the nation," wrote J. Merle Davis in 1942, "are thrown out of productive employment for a period of from two-thirds to three-fourths of the year, and, with their families, they sink into a subsistence economy with most serious physical, social and moral consequences to themselves." By the early 1950s, fully one-third of the total population, principally families of agricultural wage-workers—an estimated 350,000 workers and 2.1 million dependents—received between 5 and 10 percent of total national income.[9]

No less important, and indeed of far-reaching implications, was the fact that these developments coincided with the coming of age of the single largest population cohort in Cuban history. The "baby boom" generation was entering the labor market at about the time that the imperatives of commodity export had fixed the structural characteristics of the national economy. The post-1898 fertility rates had produced a generation that even under the best of circumstances, by virtue of its numbers, would have experienced employment hardship. In fact, this generation came of age during the worst of times, at precisely the moment the Cuban economy passed into a state of stagnation, at a time of declining sugar prices, diminishing employment, and decreasing wages.[10] In the census year of 1919, the number of Cubans between the ages of ten and twenty accounted for nearly 30 percent of the total population (833,000 out of 2.9 million). By the end of the 1920s, as the economy plunged headlong into the calamity of the worldwide depression, nearly one million Cubans had recently entered the labor force, many with newly established families of their own. In 1931, in the throes of the depression, almost 30 percent of the total population (1.1 million out of 3.9 million) was made up of dependent children nine years of age and younger.[11]

✻✻ Chronic unemployment and low wages are the hallmark features of commodity export economies almost everywhere, of course, and in this regard conditions in Cuba were not dissimilar to patterns of export-driven economies generally. What made Cuba different, however, and indeed what made the circumstances of tiempo muerto especially dire, was the absence of an adequate subsistence base, that is, something to which people could return to and live off during the long months of unemployment. "The advantage enjoyed by many tropical export economies but denied in good part to Cuba," explained economist Christopher Wallich in 1950, "[is] the presence of a subsistence sector in the economy, into which unemployed labor can retire during depressions."[12] What was also different in Cuba was the degree to which sugar subsumed into its purpose almost everything else, summoning into existence a vast wage-labor force whose well-being depended upon low-wage seasonal employment, in an international market of unstable commodity prices, in a local economic environment in which monetary transactions for the purchase of foreign imports developed as the principal means of meeting almost all needs of daily life.

Increased production for export signified decreased production for consumption and necessarily increased Cuban dependence upon food imports (see Table 4.1). The patterns of Cuban imports were striking. Between the census years of 1907 and 1919, the Cuban population increased approximately 40 percent, from 2 million to 2.8 million inhabitants. During the same period, however, imports of basic staples of the Cuban diet increased in exponential fashion: rice imports increased by more than 900 percent; barley, preserved vegetables, and cheese increased by more than 600 percent; imports of codfish, the staple of the nineteenth-century slave diet, increased by more than 900 percent. "Cuba imports from 75 to 80 per cent of its food supply," reported one trade publication as early as 1918, "principally from the United States, the concentration of island agriculture upon the sugar industry having caused the home production of food-

Table 4.1. Cuban Imports of U.S. Foodstuffs:
Average Quantity and Value, 1904–1909, 1915–1918

	1904–1909	1915–1918
Barley		
Lbs.	1,323	11,246
Value	$24,000	$449,000
Corn		
Lbs.	105,489	127,269
Value	$1,213,000	$2,563,000
Wheat flour		
Barrels	759	875
Value	$3,345,000	$6,699,000
Rice		
Lbs.	7,423	74,620
Value	$149,000	$3,830,000
Beans		
Kilos	3,946	13,111
Value	$345,000	$2,322,000
Potatoes		
Kilos	19,024	57,004
Value	$550,000	$2,771,000
Onions		
Kilos	848	4,360
Value	$50,000	$289,000
Dried fruits		
Lbs.	581	1,243
Value	$34,000	$120,000
Preserved vegetables		
Kilos	226	1,780
Value	$20,000	$201,000
Preserved meat products		
Kilos	1,257	1,326
Value	$266,000	$405,000
Condensed milk		
Lbs.	11,351	28,819
Value	$718,000	$2,707,000
Cheese		
Lbs.	215	1,653
Value	$40,000	$404,000
Codfish		
Lbs.	811	8,342
Value	$35,000	$918,000

Source: United States Tariff Commission, The Effects of the Cuban Reciprocity Treaty of 1902 (Washington, 1929).

stuffs to be neglected." Basic necessities, foodstuffs as well as consumer durables and nondurables alike, increasingly reached Cuban households by way of retail transactions and in the form of foreign imports—mostly U.S. products—usually at inflated prices. "Even the lower classes consume a substantial amount of imported goods," observed economist Wallich, "such as rice, lard, and beans—to mention only a few basic necessities." By midcentury the International Bank for Reconstruction and Development could affirm outright that "the average ratio of Cuban imports to national income appears to be among the highest in the world." The value of foreign foodstuffs more than doubled from $47 million in 1912 to $96 million in 1927 and increased again to $163 million by 1948. "The small Cuban population," one observer commented as early as 1916, "cannot produce $300 or $400 worth of sugar per capita and at the same time produce its own food."[13]

The salient features of the export economy were fixed early. Increasing numbers of men and women of all social classes participated in the economy as consumers and customers, as much by need as by choice, drawn into the conventions of a material culture with few counterparts outside the economies of industrialized nations and deeply implicated in the assumptions by which the market promised fulfillment and well-being. The expansion of wage labor as the principal mechanism for the distribution of income served to draw tens of thousands of households into the inexorable logic of the market environment. Increasingly, too, an ever-larger array of Cuban material needs, including many of the most fundamental household necessities, could be met only by way of retail exchanges, through cash and/or credit transactions.

Postwar Cuba developed within an all-encompassing paradigm of consumption, dominated by value-added norms associated with foreign imports and sustained by monetary transactions associated with the market economy. The same paradigm, however, also arrived accompanied with real costs and served to place households across the island under relentless cost-of-living pressures. "The cost of living is unusually high," reported the U.S. minister in Cuba as early as 1902. "Owing to high duties and the fact that almost everything of domestic use, excepting fruit and vegetables, is imported, the prices are dear."[14] The "heavy reliance upon imported goods," commented Wallich decades later, "is true of the lower as well as the upper income groups, because imported goods are not luxuries but necessities." The impact upon the cost of living was decisive. Observed Wallich: "Cuba was a 'dollar country,' heavily dependent upon American-made consumer goods, and hence her prices were in many respects similar to American prices."[15] "The Cuban people," economist Antonio Riccordi warned in 1948, "and especially the popular classes, can not live off what they earn, simply because everything becomes daily more expensive. Cuba is largely an importer country and almost everything that it needs and consumes must come from abroad for which we must pay whatever is demanded."[16]

The stability and indeed the very solvency of households across the island depended increasingly on adequate wages to satisfy daily needs for vital goods and services. "Despite its dependence on field crops," observed anthropologist Wyatt MacGaffey, "Cuba has not been (in the twentieth century) an agrarian society. . . . The Cuban countryman, therefore, is not typically a farmer and in fact he has rejected opportunities to become one. He works for a wage, or to produce a cash crop; from the proceeds he buys his foodstuffs and other needs." Sociologist Lowry Nelson recognized the plight of Cuban households specifically as a problem of consumption, noting in 1950 that "there were thousands of families in rural Cuba who could not afford to purchase at inflated prices the clothing and food articles in the stores." Visiting Cuba during the late 1940s, W. Adolphe Roberts reported that the cost of living "crushes the Cuban lower middle class, which has little share in sugar bonanzas. The ordinary clerk in a government job makes about seventy or eighty dollars a month, and . . . food for even the smallest family cannot be bought for less than fifty dollars a month."[17]

Simply put, vast numbers could not earn sufficient money to buy what they needed. Armando Cárdenas recalled the plight of agricultural workers in stark terms: "Our main problem was that we didn't earn enough to buy our food." Years later Gabriel Capote Pacheco remembered his childhood, and what he remembered most was the family without work, without wages, and without the wherewithal to buy food: "Many's the day we went hungry and had to scrounge a bit of food. The stores were full then — everywhere you looked there was plenty of everything — but you had to have money." This is also what María de los Reyes Castillo remembered. "During the 1950s in Cuba there was no lack of anything," she reminisced. "The shops were full of all the things that one could need. What was missing was the money to buy them. The jobs that were available paid low wages, that could not make ends meet. Those without many skills, which was the vast majority, were paid miserably if they found work." Julia de la Osa y Sierra had similar memories: "Before there used to be many things, but there was no money because there was no work and nothing to buy anything with."[18]

The pursuit of the goods and services upon which Cuban well-being depended developed increasingly into an abiding preoccupation, as wages seemed always inadequate for the necessities of everyday life. "The earnings of the Cuban family are not only small but also unstable," observed sociologist Mercedes García in 1938. She continued:

> This instability is the product of the economic organization of Cuba: the cultivation of sugar. It is from this reality that the average living standard is not only low but also unstable, for the ups and downs of this industry play havoc on the ability to make a living. This not only affects the rural family, but the entire population of Cuba, given that everyone is affected by this national industry. . . . This signifies a frightful period of time called 'tiempo muerto,' a time of unemployment, of paralysis, and of anxiety. . . . The economic life of the typical Cuban family is thus characterized by a short period of abundance during the harvest, followed by a long time of scarcity. Everything unfolds around the sugar industry, whose fluctuations are like the beating of the national heart. . . . Like a sword of Damocles, the fluctuations of sugar continue to threaten the stability of life of Cuba.[19]

Many hundreds of thousands of Cubans found the matter of making a living an endeavor of all-consuming proportions. They were engaged in a relentless pursuit of livelihood in an environment of depressed wages, diminishing employment, and rising costs of living. Lowry Nelson wrote of the "many Cubans living in poverty or on its margins," adding: "The struggle for mere survival is for many the chief preoccupation." Uncertainty and insecurity cast a dark shadow over households across the island. Cubans lived with the knowledge that joblessness could come to almost anyone at any time, without warning, and always with devastating consequences. They lived with an ever-present fear, tormented by anxieties that seemed never to let up or ease off. "The thing that really infuriated me," one sugar mill worker recalled years later, "was job insecurity; we were always beset by fear of being laid-off."[20] The 1935 short story "La leontina de oro," by Alfonso de Granados, depicted with poignance living life under the specter of fear through the experience of protagonist Juan de Dios Hernández. "Without land, without a house, without money—even his wife had died about a year earlier—: now, what course to take?" the narrator ponders. The account continues: "Whom to ask for work? He prepared himself for useless wandering. He drifted from town to town in filthy appearance unable to find work anywhere. At night time he slept wherever he found himself, the same in the middle of a sugar cane field as on the porch of some *bohío*. For the first time in his life he experienced fear. But fear not of a bandit, or death, or darkness, but fear of hunger, of the misery that with each passing day made him its prisoner, fear of his fate that from a distance seemed as if it were mocking him."[21] Commented *Bohemia* magazine editorially in 1938:

> The lack of work, the absence of opportunity, the futility of seeking day after day a job—any job—without finding anything. And to know that like you, in Havana, there are thousands and thousands. . . . And in the provinces? We know that people are dying of hunger. There is hunger, there is misery, there are hundreds of thousands of evictions. In Mazorra [insane asylum] there is no room for the insane (*no caben los locos*). In La Esperanza [sanatorium] there is no room for victims of tuberculosis. In the hospitals there are no beds for the poor. The ill die at the very doors of the hospitals. There is no work. There is no money. There is no peace in the homes. There is no hope in the certainty of tomorrow.[22]

Families moved about from place to place, from the countryside into the cities, often from town to town, in search of a way out of a penurious existence. They moved from temporary job to temporary job, carrying with them the sum total of their material possessions under their arms and on their backs, in search of a place to put down and earn a living. "The roads of Cuba," one day laborer recalled of the early 1920s, "were filled with workers moving from one place to another with their knapsacks on their back. We moved about like blind ants." By the early 1950s, commented one observer, this movement of people assumed fully the proportions of an "exodus" from the countryside to the cities. "We were so poor that there were days we didn't eat . . . ," Armando Cárdenas remembered years later. "Our problem was that we had no land to work and no way of making a living. Things were so bad for us that my folks migrated from place to place in search of a way to better their situation. . . . We kept wandering over highways and byways for almost a year trying to find a place to make a living. . . . But we had nothing. It was desperation that drove my folks on, looking for somebody to give them a piece of land."[23]

Increasing numbers of men and women, sometimes entire families, migrated to towns and cities in search of work, only to discover conditions materially worse than those from which they had sought to escape. It was in the realm of public health concerns that the deepening distress of Cuban households was most forcefully expressed. A large portion of the population of Havana, admonished the medical journal *La Higiene* as early as 1906, "uses the sum total of its daily earnings to live from one day to the next, without having any way whatsoever to save a single penny to confront the eventualities of the future," adding:

> The lives of these workers who have constituted their families are enormously difficult, for it is only with great hardship that their earnings meet the needs of maintaining the household. This is the result not only of the meager wages they earn but also due to the high cost of living. The price of housing in Havana is exorbitant. . . . The cost of food required to nourish the family is very expensive. And clothing? And medical attention and medicines? Misery reigns in our capital city. Most of these misfortunate souls . . . are at risk of dying of hunger, or their diet is of such poor quality that it could be said that they are in a permanent condition of enfeeblement.[24]

Indeed, the rising cost of living had far-reaching and potentially calamitous public health consequences. "The high cost of living," warned the *Revista de Medicina y Cirugía* in 1910, "is one of the most serious problems that the people of Cuba must confront in order to provide for their development and well-being. . . . The volume of imports is far greater than in most civilized nations in the world and falls upon Cubans with a truly oppressive weight. . . . In our large cities, and particularly in Havana, life is extraordinarily expensive." And to the point: "The high cost of living has decisive [epidemiological] implications which must be considered as a factor in mortality rates."[25] Attention should be given, insisted the *Revista de Medicina y Cirugía* on another occasion, "to the practical and positive ways that the State could lend assistance to families that live in indigence," and continued:

> Funds should be made available that provide aid to the households of the poor; laws should be enacted to reduce the cost of living for the needy so as to place within their reach access to a material well-being and good health. . . . This will contribute to the reduction of the number of illnesses, for when they afflict the heads of households, that is, those who through their daily labor are responsible for bringing in the necessary resources for the subsistence of the family, and thus make it

impossible for them to work, misery descends upon the entire family, with all its succession of hardship, adversity, and hunger. . . . It is necessary first and foremost to reduce the cost of living for the worker. At the present time in Cuba, the worker must struggle often without success against many obstacles. The question of subsistence, that is, the acquisition of articles of primary necessity, is increasingly transforming itself into a frightful problem (*un problema pavoroso*) that in any other country with even fewer problems than we have would have certainly provoked serious conflicts difficult to resolve. The high cost of those articles of primary necessity constitutes a serious threat to the well-being of workers, one that authorities and institutions who represent the interests of the people have not addressed.[26]

Many tens of thousands of families eked out a living by way of a hand-to-mouth existence, getting by as best they could. Men and women, and children too, took to the streets to beg for a living. Years later Nicolás Salazar Fernández remembered when his father lost his job, "and from then on he began to beg alms." Salazar Fernández continued: "What else could he do with no job and four children to support? It wasn't that he wanted to beg, but there was no other way out. . . . So that people would take pity and give them something to eat, he'd take [my brothers] from house to house, knock on the door, and say, 'I came to see if you could help me with a bit of food or something.' Then they'd drop the food in an empty can he carried, give him a shirt or a pair of pants or 20 or 30 centavos."[27]

Few visitors to Cuba failed to take note of the ubiquity of beggars and panhandlers in the cities, women and children, mostly, sometimes entire families, with hands outstretched imploring passersby for alms. Irene Wright noticed without sympathy: "To walk the streets of Havana is to court horror. Disease and deformity, in hideous variety. . . . To me the beggars, — the wry-limbed men, and especially the blear-eyed women — are by no means the most offensive among what one encounters. In the parks and on the promenades one passes, too often, male humans whose condition certainly warrants their removal from public thoroughfares. . . . If these things venture into public, one shudders to imagine what more exists hidden in the poverty and uncleanliness of the unlighted, unventilated cells in tenements." Anthropologist Pelayo Casanova was scandalized by the growing presence of beggars in Havana during the 1920s. He classified them into three categories. The first consisted of "the handicapped beggars, the crippled, the sick, the paralyzed, the blind, that is, all those who find themselves in a real and unquestionable incapacity to work." The second group was made up of "occasional beggars, that is those workers without jobs, furloughed public employees, and all those finding themselves willing and capable of making a living but who are unable to find work." The third category consisted of "professional beggars, those individuals who make a living through begging, who although fully capable of working chose instead to 'work' by simulating illnesses and needs and who prey upon the compassion of the passers-by." Complained Casanova: "Every day that passes the number of beggars who invade our thoroughfares and the central public places increases. . . . Nothing is more important than finding a solution to this problem."[28] One traveler reported similar conditions in eastern Cuba: "The villages are coming under the siege of the cane fields. What shall we eat? In Santiago de Cuba, during the early hours of the evening and on a central street, a young woman in miserable condition approached me, and extending her hand explained: 'Alms, for God's sake, neither my children nor I have eaten today.' There is hunger in the city, there is hunger in the countryside. Every day there are fewer farm plots (sitios), every day fewer fincas, every day fewer haciendas."[29] Writer Jesús Masdeu described desperate conditions: "The result is a horde of unemployed that expands across the entire national territory, the expulsion of peasant families from the land, massive importation of foodstuffs that long ago ceased to be produced in Cuba, neighborhoods (barrios) of indigents, tuberculosis, and the . . . strangulation of the economy of the nation."[30] In 1957 the weekly Bohemia provided a sobering description of conditions in the provinces:

> In Ciego de Avila, garbage strewn on the streets, fruit peddlers, mendicants, children selling lottery tickets, old ladies begging, itinerant vendors. In Florida, garbage strewn in the streets, fruit peddlers, lottery ticket vendors, children begging. In Guáimaro, in Victoria de las Tunas, in Santa Clara, in all the interior of Cuba: garbage in the streets, children soliciting, old ladies begging for alms, peddlers selling bread and pan sugar. In short: MISERY. Misery in capital letters that cannot be hidden although it is disguised. . . . A misery that some day, when it decides to rebel, will sweep all of us aside the way a hurricane sweeps across the abandoned countryside.[31]

Uncertainty and insecurity filled households across the island, circumstances of destitution and despair transmuted fully into permanent facets of the Cuban condition. Many hundreds of thousands of workers and millions of their dependents lived more or less permanently at the edge of indigence, and with no place to go. Vast numbers struggled to get by, many working at two or three jobs to make ends meet, from one day to the next. Reported the U.S. labor attaché in 1955: "The cost of living and the standard of living are so high in Cuba, [that] . . . many Cubans try to hold down two jobs at the same time."[32]

Memories of penury lasted a lifetime. "My father worked so hard," Pilar López Gonzales recalled years later, "he had to go without sleep a lot of the time. Once he had four jobs at the same time: he was a bus driver, a photographer, he sold jewelry, and he worked for Public Works. Even I could see how, to please mamá, he tried hard to find work, but it seemed like the minute he felt secure in a job, he'd get laid off. Then we had nothing, not even enough for food. And sometimes when papá did have a job, he didn't get paid because the boss claimed there was no money in the cash box." Miguel Valencia recalled the strategies of workers at one sugar foundry as tiempo muerto approached who, entitled to a total of three days of sick pay, "deliberately caused injury to themselves in an 'accident,'" adding: "In their desperation they were fully capable of injuring themselves to obtain extra days of wages to take a few pesos more to the house to feed hungry children."[33]

Adversity during normal times became calamity during hard times. The onset of the depression during the late 1920s, for example, caused the value of sugar exports to plunge by 80 percent. Producers struggled to remain solvent by reducing production and lowering wages. The length of the zafra was shortened to a sixty-two day harvest — that is, a total of two months of employment for hundreds of thousands of workers. Never before had Cuba experienced all at once a zafra so short, prices so low, and a harvest so small as in 1932–33. Commerce came to a standstill. Business failures reached record proportions. Plants and factories closed. Workers were laid off, and unemployment soared. Salaries and wages for workers with jobs were slashed. Wages for urban workers decreased by 50 percent. The wages of agricultural workers fell by 75 percent. In some sugar zones, wages fell as low as twenty cents for a twelve-hour work day. On one large estate, workers received ten cents a day: five cents in cash and five cents in credit at the company store. In some districts, laborers received only food and board for their work. "Wages paid . . . in 1932," one wage survey indicated, "are reported to have been the lowest since the days of slavery."[34]

Homelessness increased, as tens of thousands of families unable to pay their rent were evicted from their homes. Accounts of evictions filled

Havana newspapers all through the early 1930s. "Some 120 tenants who were behind in their rent were thrown out of their homes last week," reported the *Havana Post* in August 1932.[35] Between 1931 and 1932, the number of evictions rose from 75,198 to 86,998. Three years later, writer Antonio Penichet despaired over the "tragedy of the Cuban home," where one could "visit municipal courts and behold the anguished faces and see with one's own eyes the mountains of legal briefs filed against tenants who have been unable to pay the rent of their houses and apartments." Added Penichet: "The Cuban people have placed the home at the center of their activities and ideals. To cast their furniture into the street is an emotional experience and appears to us as something inconceivable."[36]

🌿 The reach of the export economy extended deeply into the realms of private recesses, those places where meanings of self-reliance and self-worth were acted out and actualized. It was not only that the expansion of the export economy consigned tens of thousands of households to a state of lived incoherence as more or less a permanent condition. It was also that market forces wrought havoc on those assumptions upon which vast numbers of men and women had made deeply personal decisions in their lives, the way they proceeded to plan for the roles of husband and wife, to assemble households as wage earners and homemakers, to assume responsibilities as fathers and mothers. These arrangements may not always have served the best interests of men and women equally, of course, but they did provide the stability by which the culture had conducted a people through watershed transitions of the previous century. They served as source of collective self-worth and assigned value to the ideals that many Cubans used to pursue fulfillment in their lives. Deeply inscribed with complex codes of duty and responsibility, they were transmitted as conventional wisdom and received as self-evident truths, fashioned as prescriptive roles and accepted as ascriptive status: in sum, they formed the moral order in which people learned to assume their place and pursue purpose in the society at large. They provided the basis used to sustain self-respect and command the respect of others. Men and women took their rights and responsibilities seriously, for these were the ways to give purpose to the activities that defined daily life.

What was particularly noteworthy about the transformations wrought by market forces was the ways that the imperative of the export economy so fully rearranged the terms by which ordinary men and women were obliged to negotiate their encounter with the world about them, in the complex interplay between the private and the public, and more: how the changing material circumstances of everyday life affected the capacity of increasing numbers of Cubans to meet the expectations with which they had been prepared to assume multiple roles associated with adulthood. These were at the heart of the formulations deployed to engage reality and set into place the normative markers from which almost everyone—men and women, black and white, young and old, working class and middle class alike—obtained cues regarding what they could reasonably expect out of life and around which the terms of selfhood were arranged. The process served to inform the ways that Cubans experienced the world at large, and especially to assemble the frame of reference to take measure of the circumstances of everyday life. Passage to adulthood implied the development of expectations of the future, shaped by those hopes to which one could plausibly aspire, of what was within the realm of possibility and within reach. Most men and women learned to live their lives within the parameters of the plausible, accepted as received wisdom of the natural order of things. Implicit within this scheme of things, however, certainly as an ideal, was the expectation that compliance with culturally scripted codes of conduct, such as they were, promised the possibility of fulfillment. Most accepted the rules as they found them and acted accordingly to sustain those arrangements from which they learned to expect well-being.

What was especially insidious about the disarray occasioned by market forces in the early republic was the extent to which adversity assumed chronic form, and inevitably the degree to which the structural shifts in the material basis of daily life acted to overturn the moral order that vast numbers of men and women had learned to make their way through the world. Tens of thousands of households foundered between precarious well-being and permanent poverty as the inescapable condition of their times. Many descended into desperate and enduring poverty. Despair under these circumstances implied not only a deepening hopelessness about the prospects for change but also the growing awareness that life was not possible without such change.

The malaise of the export economy was reproduced within virtually every social relationship in Cuba, in different forms and with different consequences, to be sure, but almost always in ways that affected the commonplace conduct of day-to-day life. For vast numbers of Cubans, life assumed the form of a relentless struggle for livelihood from year to year, every year. "The Cuban workers and their leaders are prey to the anxieties which result from the instabilities, the stagnation, and the chronic unemployment of the Cuban economy," reported the International Bank for Reconstruction and Development in 1951. "They see all about them the fearsome consequences to workers and their families from loss of jobs. . . . The insecurities, which result from chronic unemployment and from the instabilities and seasonal fluctuations of the Cuban economy, continue to keep the Cuban worker in a state of anxiety."[37]

Cuban commentators agreed. "Young men and women [are] spiritually overwhelmed by the reality they contemplate," wrote columnist Armando Soto in 1955. "Their greatest wretchedness is the lack of confidence in themselves, expressed in feelings of inferiority and insecurity." Analyst Ernesto Ardura struck a similar note: "Whoever lends an ear to public opinion, can appreciate the state of uncertainty and confusion in which the Cuban people live. There is something of a sensation of shipwreck. That psychological state of desperation can be observed in all social classes: among workers, industrialists, and merchants, in the suffering middle class. The common psychological denominator of the national moment is lassitude and profound disillusionment. . . . There is no enthusiasm, there are no great plans with an eye to the future, for the future is a huge cloud and offers security to no one." Columnist Jorge Martí warned that economic development was lagging far behind population growth, "and the result is flight or aggression." Continued Martí: "Some escape physically by emigrating or psychologically through neurosis. Many struggle and are sufficiently strong to survive, without violating legal norms and moral standards, with anonymous heroism; but others seek to break the cycle through violence." Rubén Ortiz-Lamadrid wrote of the "chronic unemployment that demoralizes a large part of the citizenry, not only during tiempo muerto but during 365 days of the year . . . and the near endemic lack of work that an alarming portion of the body social suffers, circumstances . . . that have assumed a permanent condition." Writer José Lezama Lima despaired privately. "We are now in the chaos resulting from the disintegration, confusion, and inferiority of Cuban life of the last thirty years," he confided to his diary in 1957. "On one hand, fear, bewilderment, confusion. On the other, desperation."[38]

❧ Market forces acted upon Cuban households with withering effects, not all at once, of course, but over time, and with debilitating impact on the normative determinants of daily life, that is, upon the very sources from which vast numbers of men and women had learned to assume their place and purpose in their society.[39] Market-borne change affected men and women in virtually all facets of their lives, and perhaps nowhere more directly than in the practice of the conjugal conventions that served to delineate form and function within the domain of Cuban private spaces.

The power of market forces to disrupt the premises and practices of everyday life registered its greatest impact within the intimate spaces of household. Chronic unemployment and relentless cost-of-living pressures subjected families across the island to tensions on a scale never before experienced and, of course, for which many were ill-prepared to respond with the cultural assets most readily at their disposal. Market forces insinuated themselves into virtually every aspect of family life, there to eviscerate the normative content of household arrangements and over time undermine those generally shared assumptions about the natural order of things around which day-to-day life was organized.

These were troubled times, as people attempted to sort through the disruptions of their lives, often unmindful of the sources of the transformations they were experiencing but still persisting in their determination to make sense of their world and pursue purpose in their lives. Men and women across the island succumbed to implacable circumstances of scarcity and subsistence even as they struggled to sustain their assumed roles in life, as husbands and wives, as wage-earners and homemakers, as fathers and mothers—and finding it increasingly difficult to do so. It was not only that the absence of adequate work and the lack of sufficient income were playing havoc with time-honored canons and conventions. It was, more broadly, that life itself was very difficult and its demands were relentless, and that things just never seemed to get better. Vast numbers toiled long and hard to get by on little, endlessly, as the permanent circumstance of their existence. They found themselves engaged in an all-consuming struggle just to get by—and barely making it.

The emerging export economy transformed in varying degrees the material basis and moral environment of households across the island and in the process acted to subvert the very paradigmatic sources of many of the most important social relationships in Cuba. Increasing numbers of men and women were rendered incapable of discharging those responsibilities and meeting those expectations with which they had been prepared to engage reality. The problem was that the conventions that had previously given meaning to their lives, the very modes and models used by people to prepare to live out their lives, did not correspond to life as actually lived.

Much in the patterns of household daily life corresponded to the logic of gender-determined reciprocities, principally as interconnected and complementary divisions of labor around which the order of domestic routines were organized and the tasks of household maintenance were assigned and accepted. But all was not well. Tensions were revealed precisely in the customs that gave structure and substance to gender relationships, and especially in family arrangements and child-rearing practices around which those relationships were produced and perpetuated. The household contained within its structures and consecrated through its functions a complex set of social relationships, enacted by internal allocation of resources, organized around prescribed gender codes, and sustained by the premise of patriarchy. Prevailing gender hierarchies obtained validation through usage, in the form of canons and conventions by which men and women completed their passage into the social world and arrived at an understanding of their places in their society. The process of household formation was rarely accomplished through negotiation or formal decision-making procedures. On the contrary, households evolved out of those suppositions embedded within received truths and conventional wisdom, from assumptions about the natural order of things and the expectations that men and women learned to have of themselves and of one another.

For men, it was paid labor in public realms as the means to uphold culturally defined responsibilities associated with manhood. Men worked for wages because they were men: that was what men were suppose to do by virtue of being male. Young males entered adulthood by way of cognitive structures of idealized manly conduct with which they proceeded to define themselves in the world at large. Work and wages were at the heart of the conventions of manliness, for upon the function of provider rested the premise of patriarchy and the proposition of male prerogative. The narrative voice in Luis Felipe Rodríguez's novel *La copa vacía* (1926) conveyed the conventional wisdom: "You should be a model husband. But do not allow the woman to impose her will on you, because the house in which the woman is in charge, everything will go wrong. . . . You should work hard and with dedication so that nothing is lacking in the kitchen, because if something is wanting the woman will take note and when the woman notices the shortage of food and beverage, well, that's the end of the kitchen and the conjugal edifice collapses." The protagonist of José Soler Puig's novel *El derrumbe* (1964) muses on the responsibility associated with manhood: "To become a man. . . . How much work . . . To be a man is very difficult. You must assert yourself, turn hard, move through life without contemplation, to live among beasts and like a beast."[40]

The meaning of manhood was understood to implicate men in responsibilities for the well-being of the household, the maintenance of the family, and the protection of women. "The ideal of the man," writer Dolores Larrúa de Quintana affirmed, "lies in the graceful discharge of the duties that society has imposed upon him, prevailing with firmness over all the difficulties that he may find in his path.... The father of the family dreams of the prosperity of the household that he has formed. All are morally sustained with faith in the success of his ideal, ... directed as if with a compass to guide the acts of our existence, the dreams that have us dedicate the best years of our lives in pursuit of the vision of happiness." Article 44 of the Civil Code fixed the basis of male authority over women, predicated explicitly on the duty of the husband "to protect the woman," in exchange for which the woman was expected "to obey the husband."[41] Fathers and mothers "have profoundly grave and important rights and duties toward each other . . . ," explained jurist Manuel de Jesús Ponce, "upon which depends the well-being of the family, the peace of the household, its development, and its progress. . . . [The woman's] first duty is to obey her husband. . . . She is the faithful companion of the husband, to assist him to help with the tasks of life. . . . The husband should defend, protect, and represent his wife. . . . If this model and conduct should regrettably not be met, his authority will decline, his power will weaken, and the dissolution of the family cannot be far behind."[42] "Men and women are different," wrote jurist Ricardo Alemán, defending the logic that ratified male authority within the household.

Each have their qualities and special inclinations and develop in different environments. . . . Domestic discipline is absolutely necessary in the shared household and this discipline cannot be entrusted to both marriage partners, for life between them would become impossible. From this fact emerges the necessity to assign responsibility to one or the other, and there is nothing more natural [than] to entrust this to the man, who is usually stronger, more energetic, the one who is most accustomed to the struggle to make a living and possessing the greatest familiarity with the world at large.[43]

Women were assigned place and purpose within domestic realms of unpaid labor, principally as wife, homemaker, and mother—that is, those functions associated with the maintenance of the home and family and meeting the needs of men engaged to meeting the needs of the household. It was within the domestic domain of family, in the context of home and household, that women were expected to derive self-esteem, achieve self-actualization, and find self-satisfaction. "I had a husband, a house, and I felt secure," was the way that María de los Reyes Castillo remembered her life upon marriage.[44]

The prescribed deportment of women as wives was fashioned around a culturally structured demeanor that emphasized passivity and acquiescence and enjoined subordination to husbands as protectors/providers. "Juan is the one who gives the orders in our family," said Mercedes Milián, explaining her understanding of the rightful order of things, "and that's the way it should be, since he is the man. . . . It isn't that he is dictatorial—far from it—but he wears the pants. He decides if we'll buy something or if something has to be fixed." Milián continued:

> Like mamá, I live exclusively for my family. I try above all to be a good wife and a good mother. A good wife looks after her husband and children, takes care of everything about the house, keeps the house clean and everything neat and orderly. She gives her husband dinner when he gets home, takes care of him when sick, and does the same for her children. Juan is a good husband, too. He's concerned about his home and his children and is close to them. And he brings home the money we need, instead of spending it with his friends or drinking it up.[45]

Cristina Saralegui learned at an early age about the proper order of things when she asked why her brother did not help set the table: "My mother, with that conspiratorial wisdom passed from generation to generation to perpetuate women's subservience replied, 'Because all of us have to justify our existence by working. Men work outside the house and bring money home. We women work in the house and take care of the men. We do the dishes and cook and do all the household chores.'" Sara Rojas explained the household order: "A husband was head of the house from the very first. He gave the orders and his wife obeyed. That was her duty. A man who didn't rule his own home was respected even less than a woman. It's up to the man to lay down the law in his own home. . . . A man must rule everything! If not, he's called a good-for-nothing."[46]

❧ This was a culture in the throes of transition, a condition Cubans experienced as circumstances of disruption and disarray, transferred from public spaces into private spheres, passed from material difficulty to moral disarray, thereupon transmuted into sources of stress and tension in the most private and intimate domains of daily life. Conditions of penury had so profoundly transformed the normative terms of public and private life as to leave vast numbers to cope with ways and means ill-suited to new times, and little immediately to take their place.[47]

It is in this larger context that the measure of the social overhead of the export economy in the republic must be taken. These were developments not dissimilar to circumstances described by Emile Durkheim in his formulation of anomie, that is, norms and values from which people had previously obtained direction and purpose passing into desuetude, and resulting in an increased susceptibility to suicide. Anomie was associated with rapid economic change and the erosion of long-standing norms as the disparity between aspiration and achievement widened and eventually reached the point where received norms appeared to lose the capacity to mediate the circumstances of new realities. Durkheim alluded to the larger implications of modernity as a source of emotional despair and social disarray, thereafter signaling a qualitative shift in the character of suicide as a product of an emerging normative uncertainty. This was to view suicidal behavior in relationship to readjustments occasioned by the changing paradigms of daily life associated with disruption of social norms.[48]

These were bewildering times in Cuba, with bewilderment experienced principally in the most personal and private of realms, rarely discernible from the outside except in those instances where it was registered in public domains as "deviant behavior," usually as alcoholism, crime, domestic violence, homicide, or suicide.[49] Certainly trained observers discerned the signs of troubled times. As early as 1912, forensic physician Antonio Barreras admitted to being puzzled by the high rate of suicide among middle-aged men in Havana, at "an age when there should be the lowest rate of suicide, for it is at this time in life that men have generally assumed the responsibility for the family [and] have the duty to protect it." Physician Jorge LeRoy y Cassá of the Secretaría de Sanidad y Beneficencia despaired over rising rates of suicide, evidence, he insisted, of a "state of social decomposition" and "a new illness that afflicts our people." In 1918 the *Diario de la Marina* reflected on the frequency with which news stories of suicide appeared on its pages, and took particular note of the young age at which so many Cubans were killing themselves. "None of these suicide victims had yet reached the age of exhaustion, weariness, and disappointment. Is our life of such insignificance and little value that it is necessary to destroy it the first time we experience physical pain?"[50]

During the early 1920s, at about the time the first republican-born generation was reaching adulthood, Fernando Ortiz was writing about the "economic and agrarian transformations that have converted the independent farmer into a wage laborer," and he despaired: "Cuban society is disintegrating." The country was "plunging headlong into barbarity," Ortiz warned, as he detailed the rising levels of criminality on the island, the increase in assaults, homicides, and robbery, and the rise in prostitution. But it was suicide that troubled Ortiz most, "statistics that serve as a disconsolate index of our deplorable condition of demoralization." Comparing the rate of suicide in Cuba with the United States, Ortiz concluded: "The inhabitants of Cuba have eight times the desire to kill themselves violently than their neighbors to the North." *La Lucha* bemoaned the "state of moral decomposition that reigned in Havana" and evoked the specter of an epidemic: "Our people are threatened by the menace of suicide. Everyone is in a state of sorrow, and the sensible among us live in dread of falling victim to such a terrible illness." Writer Carlos Trelles could hardly contain his dismay over the "frightful manner in which the number of suicides have increased on the Island." At about the same time, writer Raimundo Cabrera warned of "a frightful crisis (*una pavorosa crisis*)" that "has undermined the foundations of our cultural institutions, with grave and imminent danger for all the institutions of the Republic." Nothing could save Cuba, Cabrera insisted, "if the nation, engaged in unconscious suicide, lacks the desire to arouse itself with all the energy of its being."[51] Antonio Penichet wrote of the "terrible psychological effects" of the 1930s, adding: "To learn of a single suicide used to shock us. We might have found it comprehensible upon learning that it was the result of romantic passion. But for an individual in Cuba to kill himself as a result of the misery in which he lived was once beyond the admissible. It was a deed that never occurred, or if it did it was a shocking exception. Today suicide among the youth of both sexes . . . constitutes an endemic whose high rate shocks us."[52]

✥ That the export economy could not accommodate the needs of ever-increasing numbers of households served to set into relief the ways that the faith that Cubans had invested in traditional values and ways, especially in those assumptions that played so central a part in defining gender roles, conjugal relationships, and household management, could no longer obtain either corroboration or credibility in the experience of life as lived. The usefulness of time-honored truths and received wisdom revealed itself as increasingly inadequate to the needs of daily life in an all-encompassing market environment. It was within the ever-widening gap between the moral ideal and the material reality that social tensions stirred and deepened.

Changes of such fundamental character could not have occurred without producing varying degrees of distress and disorientation in households across the island. The signs of troubled times in Cuba revealed themselves in the experience of everyday life, in those multiple ways that normative systems often begin to accommodate to changing material circumstances, altering in the process the conventions to which people had previously subscribed as source of conduct. Chronic conditions of instability and insecurity acted to topple many of the signposts from which vast numbers of men and women had obtained their bearings and contributed to an environment of deepening normlessness.

Cubans worked at adjusting to changing times and uncertain circumstances, adaptive responses that increasingly included suicide as a means with which to cope. It was not that poverty and penury were themselves directly the source of suicidal behavior. Certainly hard times made life difficult, but hardship alone does not provide an adequate explanation of the recourse to suicide. Rather, it was within circumstances of transition, of change experienced on a daily basis, of the ever-widening discrepancy and deepening dissonance between received wisdom and acquired knowledge, that bewilderment seized hold of popular sensibilities. Men and women searched for a way to articulate the confusion they experienced in the face of changes taking place in their relationship with the wider society. Resorting to suicide was a function of the adaptive responses by which they sought relief and resolution.

Vast numbers of men strived mightily, against daunting odds, to meet their obligations only to fail, again and again. Alfredo Barrera Lordi recalled his efforts to fulfill his responsibilities to his wife and child in order "not [to] let myself down in my own estimation" and to maintain "my self-respect as a man." Francisco García remembered the hard times of tiempo muerto and the inability to find work, made all the more difficult by his desire "to improve my economic situation in order to get married." Soon after his marriage García had a new concern. "That year was doubly difficult for my wife became pregnant," he recalled. "I had no work and it was urgent for me to find a way by whatever means to increase my earnings. Since I was expecting a child, all efforts to find work had to be increased and produce results." The larger implications of the birth of his daughter were clear: "I was now a father and that doubled my responsibilities."[53]

The inability of men to find secure employment with adequate wages had far-reaching consequences. "In an infinite number of households," Roberto de Acevedo observed in 1939, "the resources provided by the man do not meet even the most urgent needs."[54] Men despaired as diminished prospects of livelihood eroded those norms by which self-worth had inscribed themselves on the construction of manhood, persuaded that they had failed in the discharge of those functions they had learned as central to their place and purpose in the world at large. Chronic unemployment acted to diminish self-esteem and increase self-doubt, and as a continual source of stress it shattered emotional stability and psychological well-being. The inability of men to perform the roles that had conducted them into the norms of manhood also implied a default on the reciprocities that sustained hierarchies of authority and eroded the conventions central to patriarchy. Unemployment diminished the credibility of the male claim as provider and breadwinner, making the performance of traditional male roles difficult to discharge, almost always at the cost of self-respect and self-worth.

Men strove mightily to act out the roles and discharge the responsibilities for which they had been prepared as the natural and indeed the obligatory order of things—and failed. They worked hard, played by the rules, did everything they were supposed to do, and still could not stave off discouragement and despair. Many men could not live with disappointment and diminished self-respect as a permanent condition of their daily lives, could not bear up under continued failure in the performance of those tasks so central to their prescribed purpose in life. Some men abandoned their wives and families as a response to a sense of failure. Others took to drinking. Still others committed suicide. "I have killed myself because I am tired of suffering," Miguel Robles explained in his suicide note. Manuel Guerra committed suicide by hanging himself, *La Lucha* reported, as "a result of the miserable state in which he and his wife were compelled to live." In Havana, Ricardo Rufín killed himself, leaving behind his wife and six children, for reasons, the press reported, having to do with "economic problems"; while in the town of Punta Brava, Leonicio Gómez Carrera hanged himself "for not having employment."[55] Driven to despair as a result of months of unemployment, thirty-year-old Adalio Valdés hanged himself, leaving a wife and six small children. Unemployed worker Tomás Ponce shot himself rather than face eviction from his Havana apartment. Miguel Dávalos Martínez attempted suicide, explained the *Diario de la Marina*, "due to his precarious economic situation and his inability to support his wife and six children."[56] José Arostegui slashed his throat, a deed he explained in his suicide note as a response to "being dragged along a grief-stricken life, without any more resources to live on." In Los Palacios, Severino Rodríguez killed himself as a result "of the state of misery" in which he found himself, leaving behind a wife and four young children. Unemployed bricklayer Antonio Fragosa burned himself to death, reported *Diario de la Marina*, "after realizing the futility of his efforts to engage in an honorable way to make a living."[57]

Nineteen-year-old Manuel Morales was planning to wed and had started to save money for married life when he was released from his job as mason. Unwilling to marry without work to support his wife properly, Morales delayed the marriage. Weeks turned into months, months stretched out endlessly, and despair deepened. *La Lucha* reported the outcome: "Manuel killed himself as a result of his inability to marry his fiancee, whom he deeply loved. Upon finding himself in a desperate situation as a result of his inability to find work, this young man, who was always hard-working and responsible in all facets of his life, determined to kill himself."[58]

Unemployed thirty-seven-year-old Marcelino Fuentes, with a three-year-old son suffering from bronchitis and a wife pregnant with their second child, ended his life through poison—"the result of inescapable misery that he was experiencing . . . and the lack of resources," commented *La Lucha*. "I will kill myself if I don't find work," Jaime Albertines vowed to his bride of only a few weeks as he departed home in search of employment. He was never heard from again. Vicente Santamaría of Pinar del Río killed himself, explaining in a suicide note to his daughter his desire "to end my life because it is no longer possible to continue to bear the weight of suffering owing to the scarcity of resources and the inability to care [for you]."[59] The suicide of Jesús Carrillo, explained judicial authorities, was due to his "desperation over the inability to find work and for the lack of economic means to bear the expenses of his household" (*sufragar los gastos de su hogar*). Carrillo was survived by his wife and five-year-old son.[60]

For vast numbers of men who experienced life as a struggle for subsistence, who lived day to day just getting by, an illness or an accident was often catastrophic. To fall ill without economic resources was as unthinkable as it was unendurable. "Suffering from tuberculosis," Julián Acosta Rodríguez wrote, explaining his decision to die, "and with no money, I have decided to shake off [my] mortal shackles." Truck-driver Eulogio Borges Oliva, apparently on the verge of losing his job, explained that he decided to kill himself because he was "ill and in a dreadful economic situation."[61] Carlos Hernández Ortiz slashed his wrists during a long illness but survived when his mother found him bleeding to death. "I was not getting better," Hernández Ortiz later said of his decision to commit suicide. "I lost all hope. Believing I was a lost cause, I decided to take appropriate action: to kill myself. That way, I would bring to an end my agony and the suffering of my poor mother."[62] Ezquiel Fundora Fernández was rescued after having leaped off a bridge into the Almendares river. He was distraught for having been saved. "They should have let me die," Fundora Fernández protested, "I cannot endure any longer the illness that has transformed me into a useless man. . . . I worked as a mason for many years but the dust exacerbated my sickness, forcing me to leave the occupation. I subsequently dedicated myself to garden work, but the asthma only worsened and finally made it impossible for me to do any kind of work. My economic situation became worse with each passing day and while everyone was celebrating the holidays at the end of the year, in my home I had nothing—nothing."[63]

Rates of suicide soared during hard economic times. The recurring downward cycles of the Cuban economy were most dramatically registered in the marked increase of suicidal deaths. That people killed themselves during hard times was not, of course, unique to Cuba. Rather, what was noteworthy about Cuba was the frequency with which people experienced hard times, setting further into relief the instability of the export economy. Suicide rates increased by more than 30 percent in the aftermath of the collapse of sugar prices in 1920, from 375 in 1920 to 489 in 1921. "Suicides were frequent," Carlos Franqui recalled of his childhood in the region around Sagua la Grande during the early 1920s; "men hanged themselves from trees, women poured alcohol over their bodies and set themselves on fire." Novelist Miguel de Marcos characterized the early 1920s as a time of "a rash of suicides in an environment of impoverishment," assuming fully the proportions of "a festival of suicides" (una comparsa de suicidas).[64]

Men of property and means were among the most prominent Cubans to commit suicide during the economic crisis of 1920–21. Wealthy financier Belarmino Alvarez, described by La Lucha as a man of "social prominence . . . and member of a distinguished family," shot himself to death. Merchants across the island killed themselves in the face of bankruptcy and ruin. In Palmira, Manuel Villar Barca, described as a "wealthy merchant and a person of great prestige," drowned himself. Merchant José Palomo of Artemisa shot himself. In Batabanó merchant Juan Vila Pérez hanged himself. Tobacco merchant Manuel González Suárez killed himself after

LA LUCHA
DIARIO DE LA TARDE

El acaudalado hombre de negocios Sr. Jose Lopez Rodriguez se suicidó esta mañana

Para poner fin a su vida se ahorcó con una sabana

Las preocupaciones derivadas de la crisis financiera y su estado de salud influyeron en la fatal resolución. La noticia produce en la Habana impresión enorme. Detalles del suceso.

Headline: "Wealthy businessman Mr. José López Rodríguez Committed Suicide this Morning." From *La Lucha*, March 28, 1921.

the loss of his warehouse business. *Colono* José Hernández of Alquízar hanged himself, leaving behind his wife and nine children.[65]

Perhaps the most sensational suicide of 1921 was that of industrialist José "Pote" López Rodríguez, one of the wealthiest men in Cuba. "The name of Pote had reached celebrity status from one end of the Republic to the other," eulogized *La Lucha*. Pote's death served to underscore how the accomplishments of a lifetime by a man of "demonstrable intelligence, sagacity, and entrepreneurial spirit" could so quickly be destroyed. His suicide added to the deepening uncertainty of the times. The narrator in Miguel de Marcos's novel *Papaíto Mayarí* reacts to the suicide of Pote: "One morning the news was horrifying upon learning that Pote, the millionaire Pote, who upon realization of his ruin, committed suicide—even though he still had millions of dollars. But in that fury of madness and fear that swept everything aside, he hanged himself from a tower in his palace. If that king of businessmen acted in that fashion, what could the others do?"[66]

Suicide reached epidemic proportions during the depression of the late 1920s and early 1930s. Newspapers filled weekly with hundreds of accounts of attempted and completed suicides. Official statistics provided two different sets of data for the years 1928–32. The Secretaría de Sanidad y Beneficencia recorded a total of 2,652 suicides. The data published by the Comisión Nacional de Estadística y Reformas Económicas for 1928–32 recorded almost twice that number, a total of 5,272 suicides, that is, a staggering rate of 26.6 per 100,000. According to the Comisión Nacional, more Cubans died in 1931 by suicide (1,217) than of natural causes (802).[67] "The wave of suicides through the island shows little sign of abatement,"

Caricature from *La Política Cómica*, depicting the collapse of the Banco Nacional de Cuba and the suicide of José "Pote" López in 1921. From Julio LeRiverend, *La república. Dependencia y revolución* (Havana, 1969).

reported the *Havana Post* in 1930. "Not surprisingly . . . ," Havana physician Jorge LeRoy y Cassá of the Secretaría de Sanidad y Beneficencia commented tersely in 1930, "suicide in all forms has increased [in Havana] by 51 over the year before as a result of the economic situation that the country confronts."[68]

Communities across the island, in provincial capitals as well as small interior towns, reported sharp and sustained increases in the number of suicidal deaths. "Everyday the press provides us with news of suicides resulting from misery," wrote Antonio Penichet as late as 1938.[69] For the first half of 1930, an average of 5 people a week committed suicide in the town of Banes (pop. 13,500). Officials in the town of San Nicolás (pop. 5,000) reported a total of 6 suicides in the first two months of 1930. "It can be said that a veritable wave of suicide has invaded this community," one observer reported from Alquízar. "The proportion of suicides that have been registered in recent weeks," commented an official in San Juan de las Yeras, "especially by way of fire, is truly alarming." Reports from Santa Clara and Camagüey described an epidemic of suicide by hangings, characterized by local observers as a "contagious mania." Authorities in Palma Soriano reported the "frightful increase in the frequency of [suicide] in our municipality."[70] Newspaper correspondents across the island filed sobering reports: "suicide fever has gripped Quemado de Güines"; "the high number of [suicides] has brought much grief to the peaceful town of Victoria de la Tunas"; "a rash of suicides in Sagua de Tánamo"; "the number of hangings that have occurred in [Santiago de Cuba] is alarming"; "an outbreak of suicide in Camagüey"; "the tragic act of suicides continues in the province of Villaclara."[71] The suicide of one working-class adolescent in Havana served to give representation to circumstances across the island in 1932. Reported the monthly *Azúcar*:

> For an adolescent of this class there was no work, and every man and woman in the city knew it. Thousands of families in Cuba find themselves face to face with an identical situation and God knows how many fathers of those families have given thought to a similar solution. The death of this youngster, in sum, lifted, if only for an instant, the veil that conceals the complete and fundamental condition of Cuba today. . . . A specter hangs over Cuba. It is a condition that, in normal times, would have aroused international sympathy and the editorials of the press in all parts of the civilized world.[72]

Men of means, including merchants, retailers, planters, and professionals, suffered irrecoverable losses and plunged into ruin. Hundreds killed themselves. In Güines, merchant Luciano Hernández Brito shot himself due "to the poor state of his business." Contractor Antonio Bolaños Arbelo in Ciego de Avila committed suicide as a result of "business reversals." In Rodas, merchant Alejandro Suárez Martínez hanged himself in response to "the despair over the misery in which [he] found himself." Cecilio Llarena Marañon, a respected merchant in Puerto Padre, killed himself as a result of the inability "to resign himself to the disastrous economic conditions that had brought him to the brink of ruin." Celestino López Díaz, owner of El Brasil café in Marianao, and César Gili Castañeda, owner of Los Reyes Magos toy store in Havana, killed themselves in response to failing businesses. Seventy-four-year-old businessman Antonio Vigo of Jovellanos committed suicide owing "to the decline of his business to the point of ruin and his refusal to spend his old age in a condition of misery." Planter Fermín de Armas killed himself in the face of impending bankruptcy.[73]

🌿 Much was related to the ways that the inequities of the market were reproduced as inequities of the household, and specifically the ways that oppression experienced in public realms affected oppression perpetrated in private spheres. The stability of the household depended on work and wages, as site of socialization, as source of both material sustenance and moral subsidy, from which men and women were incorporated into assigned functions of the household regimen: husband as wage-earner and father, wife as homemaker and mother. What men and women shared in common was a tradition of behavior shaped by culture, a knowledge of the ideal of who they should be and what they should do, and the disposition more or less to meet the expectations that they held of themselves and of each other. What they also shared in common was a deepening realization that something was awry, that it was becoming increasingly difficult to reach the ideal, but worse still, that the ideal once reached—and often at great sacrifice—seemed no longer capable of meeting the expectations that had sustained their faith.

Parents often experienced inadequacy in the most poignant and deeply personal ways, registered in those multiple activities that made up routine patterns of daily life. It was not only that urgent needs could not be met. It was also that parents were often unable to provide for the small joys and everyday delights associated with family life, the stuff of happy childhoods and enduring memories. Much of what otherwise passed elsewhere and at other times for commonplace observances could not be sustained, and precisely because they were generally understood as commonplace, their absence weighed heavily on family providers. Many parents were unable to celebrate children's birthdays, unable to provide their children with gifts on Christmas or *Los Reyes Magos* (Three Kings Day). Humberto Arenal's short story "En lo alto de un hilo" captures the pathos of a father coping with his son's disappointment. "You know," explains the father, "that things are very bad, that I now only work three days a week.

And this year the [Three] Kings are very poor, and that's why this morning they did not bring you anything. Your mother has a peso that I was able to earn for you and your sister." Years later María de los Reyes Castillo recalled the holidays with pained memories: "There was a time when I suffered a great deal on the Three Kings Day. It was so sad for the poor to get their children to believe in the Magi and not be able, even after the children had been so good and had behaved so well, to reward them with the things they had asked for in their letters. It was very sad to see their illusions destroyed.... I couldn't help but to cry when I saw their sad little faces, so disappointed because what they received did not in any way resemble what they had asked for."[74]

The inability of men to meet their responsibilities also hampered the capacity of women to meet their obligations within those assigned realms of division of labor. Anthropologist Mirta de la Torre Mulhare described the prevailing ideal: "[The man] holds complete economic supremacy.... His wife depends on him for any purchase she may wish to make."[75] In fact, to a greater or lesser extent women depended on men to enable them to fulfill the roles of mother, homemaker, and wife. Without adequate male wages, however, women were often beset with difficulties in meeting everyday requirements of purchasing cookware and commodities, securing adequate food supplies, obtaining clothing for children, and meeting all the other responsibilities associated with the maintenance of the household.

The pressure to maintain the economic solvency of households forced increasing numbers of women into the wage-labor force, often reluctantly, and almost always out of necessity in response to hard times, a way to arrest and perhaps reverse descent into penury. "Women have no alternative but to work . . . ," affirmed Mariblanca Sabas Alomá as early as 1930, "for the salary of a man is rarely sufficient to provide for all the necessities of the family." Ana María Borrero agreed. "Thousands of Cuban households," Borrero wrote, "are maintained by women. In those situations where the father, or brother, or husband, have not been able to find work, women have taken whatever jobs are available and have proceeded to make themselves indispensable as a result of their employment."[76]

That husbands may have acquiesced to the logic of wage-earning wives did not, of course, mean they were reconciled to the loss of self-esteem often associated with working spouses. Wage-earning wives often deepened the sense of male inadequacy, registered as diminution of self-esteem due to the inability to perform the role of provider. Certainly within the conventions of middle-class propriety, working wives/mothers signified the failure of husbands/fathers to meet culturally prescribed responsibilities as head of household. "Family life," wrote Renée Méndez Capote of middle-class domesticity, "until well into the twentieth century, was nothing more than the continuation of colonial life in all its aspects. . . . There was the head of the family, a man, upon whom rested the full weight of economic and moral support; an obedient wife, who acquiesced silently to all the decisions made by the husband. . . . The deep-seated belief that women should not go out into the street to work still prevailed . . . and that the man who allowed his female relatives to work was a dishonorable man."[77]

Working wives also threatened the established order of gender hierarchies. Women were attending the university and obtaining employment in public and private positions, observed writer W. Fernández Flórez in 1927, adding: "[They are], in every possible way, like a man." Almost twenty years later columnist Gervasio Ruiz made a similar observation: "The modern woman is 'all man.'" Ruiz wondered if "women who abandon the home, their traditional center of operations, to assume responsibilities . . . previously the exclusive [obligation] of the man, lost some of their essential characteristics." Asked Ruiz: "Are women happy or do they feel alienated in that new function by which they are converted into 'the man of the house?'"[78]

To suggest that women were "like a man" was to invert gender hierarchies, implying parity with men and, at the same time, challenging attributes of manhood. Writer Mariblanca Sabas Alomá observed astutely that the inferiority of women was very much related to perceptions of weakness and helplessness, "for the very word 'woman' has come to serve as symbol and synthesis of all forms of cowardice, of all types of misfortunes." Added Sabas Alomá: "When one wants to level the maximum insult against a man, he is told: 'You're acting like a woman.'" In the novel El derrumbe (1964), by José Soler Puig, a father humiliates his son who is afraid of thunderstorms: "You're afraid of thunder!? What absurdity! . . . You coward! Aren't you ashamed of yourself? You're thirteen years old! . . . A man already. And afraid of thunder. . . . You have become a little woman."[79]

In ways with far-reaching implications, and not all immediately apparent, the changes wrought by market forces acted to subvert the normative order of patriarchy within the household. The circumstances that impeded the ability of men to discharge their ascribed roles and meet assigned responsibilities as protector and provider and that at the same time often obliged women to enter the wage-labor force could not but affect power relationships within the household. The prerogative of manhood could be plausibly sustained only insofar as the duty of men was adequately discharged. Without work and adequate wages to maintain the household, without the material means to meet culturally prescribed functions of provider and from which the prerogative of the male obtained legitimacy, the internal logic of the household regimen, especially the norms that served to institutionalize hierarchies of patriarchy, was revealing itself increasingly ill-suited to the changing circumstances of daily life. The male claim to authority over the household was deeply invested in the discharge of the role of provider, responsibilities that men were finding difficult to meet. Tensions deepened as men struggled to retain positions of privilege and meet the responsibilities required of those positions.

Patriarchal distinctions between the private domain as the proper place of women and the public realm as the obligatory place of men became increasingly difficult to sustain, which meant too that the redistribution of responsibility for maintenance of the household was often accompanied by a reallocation of authority. Circumstances that rendered the ideal of male as provider difficult to actualize also acted to diminish the authority of men within the household. At the same time, it reduced the necessity of women to acquiesce to the normatively derived exercise of male authority, and increasingly contributed to volatile household environments.[80] "[A] man's authority within the family," Douglas Butterworth wrote of working-class households in Las Yaguas, "was frequently limited by his earning power. Women were thus relatively independent and often earned their own money." Anthropologist Mirta de la Torre Mulhare similarly observed that "the economic supremacy of the male may be challenged by a wife who works, and since she contributes to the family budget, may demand an equal share of responsibility in making financial decisions." One woman wrote of the "inferiority complex" that her husband had developed about her working, recounting that "he often accuses me of boasting to everyone that I maintain the household and that I dominate him. Things have gotten so bad that often weeks go by without our speaking to each other, and when we do speak it is only to quarrel. Recently our arguments have ended with him threatening to kill me." Indeed, it was not uncommon for men to reconcile themselves to lower standards of living as a strategy to retain control over women. "I've always been against women working," affirmed Lázaro Benedí Rodríguez. "I demand a lot in the way of housekeeping, and a woman who is holding an outside job can't tend her own house as she should. . . . Not only that, I was afraid if my wife worked outside, another man might fall in love with her. . . . Anyway, as soon as things settled down, María and I decided to live on what little I earned."[81]

❧ Women in Cuba shared with men common adversities. But it is also true that they experienced adversity at the hands of men. Little is known about the extent of domestic violence in Cuba during these years, but the anecdotal evidence is suggestive, and it suggests patterns of far-reaching proportions. Alcohol abuse, of course, made everything else worse, and alcoholism was often one of the more insidious responses to chronic unemployment. Reinaldo Arenas recalled times of unemployment and "my grandfather's drinking sprees, after which he would come home and beat [my grandmother] up."[82] Years later Gracia Rivera Herrera recalled the effects of unemployment on her father: "The business began to flounder and . . . [e]ventually he lost everything. . . . Times were hard for us then. Papá couldn't pay the rent so we were dispossessed. That happened more than once. There was no end to the degradation we suffered. . . . Rather than admitting he was unable to support his family, he looked for a way out, an escape, and started the drinking that took away everything we had." Rivera Herrera's father also recalled these years: "There I was, out of a job and broke. [My wife] Digna didn't complain. She was always contented with what we had, little or much. She was a good wife that way. But I felt frustrated and angry and I began to drink. I'd lose my temper and want to take it out on Digna. Many times I controlled myself and held back the blows. I used to hang out at a gambling joint and sleep in the poolroom, because I was boiling inside and knew I'd get rough with my wife if I saw her."[83]

Demoralization led easily to despair and often found tragic release within those private domains of self-destructive behaviors and abusive conduct. Men who faltered in the discharge of the prescribed role of provider also risked forfeiture of the rationale to exercise the prerogative of patriarchy, central to which was male dominance over women as means and measure of manhood. The use of physical force often served as a way to assert waning authority over women. "I sometimes wonder," Gracia Rivera Herrera remembered of her childhood, "whether papá's cruelty and his intolerance of normal childhood behavior weren't simply a desperate attempt to assert his authority."[84] Work and wages were central to both role and status, and impairment to the former could not but act to diminish the latter. The investment of male selfhood into productive wage labor as means of self-actualization, central to meeting gender-determined responsibilities and exercising culturally authorized rights, was essential to validate the normative assumptions that sanctioned the demands men could make of others, including and especially women.[85]

It would be unduly facile, of course, to attribute household violence entirely to the dislocation and disarray associated with an export economy. Violence in the household was far more complex and must be understood as a function of factors both immediate and proximate.[86] Male control over women was exercised as an entitlement associated with manhood, a means of self-worth from which men often obtained respect of self and others. The prerogative of maleness was sustained within those realms of the commonly understood natural order of things, as simply one element in an otherwise complex network of reciprocities by which men and women learned to assume their places in the world in relationship to each other, always with the presumption of women subordinate to the will of men as an immutable attribute of gender hierarchies. These assumptions passed as moral capital transmitted from one generation to the next, a matter of received wisdom to live by. "Gustavito," Gustavo Pérez Firmat was enjoined by his father on the eve of his marriage, "if you don't keep women in their place, they will walk all over you." Many years later Pilar López Gonzales recalled growing up in her grandparents' home: "[Grandfather] was an old-fashioned dictator with a terrible temper who ruled his home with an iron hand right up to his last breath. Only *his* orders were carried out and *his* whims were sacred. . . . *Mima* Bella was so meek it never occurred to her she could contradict [him]. If he said something was green, it was green for her, even if it was plainly yellow. . . . When I'd ask her why she let her husband push her around, she'd answer, 'When one marries, that's the way it must be. What would life be like if a wife refused to obey her husband?'"[87]

There was a brooding, dark underside to facets of private life in Cuba, where the exercise of the prerogative of patriarchy admitted the use of force or the threat of force as a means of male authority. The sources of household violence reached deeply into the structure of the family and were within the bounds of sanctioned conduct through which male authority was sustained. "[Ana] really deserved a good beating because she did not understand me," was the explanation Antonio Valdés Puig offered to the police upon his arrest for assaulting his wife.[88] Gracia Rivera Herrera had vivid memories of her childhood, and especially of her father. "Papá was difficult . . . and always self-indulgent," she recalled. "He wanted mamá to do everything for him, and she did. . . . His siestas were sacred, so no one made a sound. We couldn't clear the table or wash the dishes; not even a fly dared to buzz! When papá woke up ahead of time, poor mamá. She bore the brunt of his anger. He'd leave the house in a rage, and come home at night still angry." Rivera Herrera continued:

> He had a lot of peculiarities. He would eat only cold food. At home we cooked once for the whole day. . . . That's the way papá wanted it; the rest of us had to force it down, like it or not. Papá wanted the house spic and span all the time but he wasn't one to help out, not even when he was out of work. . . . Papá was the one who messed up the house. He smoked continually and never once did I see him drop the ashes anywhere but on the floor. Nor did he ever wipe his shoes before coming in out of the rain. One day, Aura had just finished scrubbing the floor and asked him in the most polite way, '*Pipo*, please wait until the floor is dry.' 'Nobody gives me orders!' papá roared, and he went out to the yard and deliberately muddied his shoes, walked back into the house, and scraped the mud off onto the floor. He had this explosive nature, and when he was drunk we were all scared of him. The slightest thing would make him fly into a drunken rage and beat us until we screamed 'Enough!'[89]

The household functioned as a domain of unchallenged male authority, contained and concealed entirely as a private sphere, and hence commonly understood as being beyond the jurisdiction of those governmental agencies otherwise charged with responsibility for public well-being. This arrangement allowed for the use of physical force, verbal abuse, and emotional intimidation designed to exact submission and subservience, all more or less acknowledged as the prerogative of men and apprehended generally as a means appropriate to the exercise of authority over women. Its most extreme form was contained in the penal code of the nineteenth century—not revoked until 1930—whereupon a husband could kill his wife for adultery without facing charges of homicide.[90]

That domestic violence was consigned to the domain of the private did not mean, of course, that it was beyond the reach of the public gaze. On the contrary, accounts of violence appeared frequently in full public view, in daily newspapers and weekly magazines, and more commonly as the stuff of rumors and gossip in those neighborhoods and communities where almost nothing could be kept secret. Accounts of assault and battery, news reports of family homicides and murder-suicides, filled the pages of newspapers across the island and developed fully into a stock-in-trade genre of the Cuban press. Neighbors and law enforcement authorities rarely intervened in matters of domestic violence, and usually only after fatal consequences. The murder of Delia González in 1958 was a tragedy long in the making. "Don't kill me!" Carmen González recalled her neighbor Delia González scream on the night of her murder. The account of the death of Delia continued: "[Carmen] understood what was happening. She knew that in the apartment below the same shameful scene was being repeated once more: that Eduardo Morfa was beating his wife. She and the other neighbors were already accustomed to hearing the screams of poor Delia, imploring, pleading. But this time the screams were more intense, more desperate." Delia died that evening of her injuries.[91]

It is all but impossible to determine the prevalence of violence in Cuban households. The search for clues often leads nowhere, but occasionally insight is obtained from the most unlikely sources. It is perhaps not unreasonable to infer the possibility of widespread conjugal violence from the realization that the theme of violence against women had insinuated itself into those everyday forms of verse and rhymes recited by children. Related one verse:

> My husband is in bed
> I am against the headboard
> with a rosary in hand
> praying to God that he die.

> (Mi marido está en la cama
> y yo a su cabecera
> con un rosario en la mano
> pidiendo a Dios que se muera.)

Another verse was even more explicit:

> My husband died
> and the Devil carried him off;
> there he will be paying for
> the beatings that he gave me.

> (Mi marido se murió
> y el Diablo se lo llevó;
> allí estará pagando
> las patadas que me dio.)[92]

Neither is it possible to ascertain fully the class determinants or racial correlates, nor to assess differences that may have existed between households in rural zones and families in urban centers, nor even to discern patterns of increase or decrease over any span of time. It must be presumed that differences in race and class meant that men and women experienced stress, tension, and frustration in different ways, although the immediate impact or long-term consequences of these differences are not readily apparent.[93] It is, in the end, possible only to suggest that violence was not an uncommon condition of Cuban conjugal relationships, reported both in the countryside and in the cities, inside households of black and white Cubans, probably with greater frequency within working-class and lower middle-class households than among middle-class families, a practice that by its very commonplace occurrence assumed the appearance of "normal" and to which the public sentiment seems to have more or less accommodated. That marital violence was most commonly associated with working-class households, moreover, made domestic violence easy to dismiss as idiosyncratic behavior peculiar to the poor and ignorant without bearing on anything else.[94]

This is not to suggest that domestic violence was unknown in the households of the well to do, but rather to note that reported incidents of battery among middle-class women were lower than those of working-class households. In fact, working-class men possessed fewer means with which to exercise control over women than their middle-class counterparts, and hence were more disposed to deploy violence in the exercise of power. Middle-class men had available a wider array of means of coercion, including money and political influence, and hence had commensurately less need to resort to force as a means of control.[95] Men of the middle class often availed themselves of the legal system to enforce their power over women. Prosecution of adultery, for example, deemed criminal behavior for women under the penal code, appears to have been limited almost entirely to white women of the middle class. Of the nineteen women serving prison terms for adultery in the women's prison in Guanabacoa between 1909 and 1927, eighteen were white and apparently middle class.[96] It is also true that middle-class families possessed far greater means with which to protect their privacy and thereby prevent incidents of household violence from reaching public attention. Middle-class women, moreover, possessed greater access to social and economic resources, and hence the means with which to resolve domestic conflict or extricate themselves from abusive relationships.

Many women endured abuse in the hope that it was a temporary condition that would eventually pass or the belief that it was a condition of their own making that they could work to unmake. "I have thought many times of running away with my son and leaving [my husband] to lead whatever life he wants," one woman acknowledged, "but my mother urges me to stay, insisting that these difficult times will pass." Another woman wrote of abuse and neglect in her failing six-year marriage: "He has started going out at night and coming home at all hours of the morning. . . . He has been very cold toward me and openly abusive, without caring in the slightest for the hurt that he's inflicting on me. But still, I would never have wanted to lose him, for I believed that things would one day change. I was stunned when he announced he was leaving me, three months pregnant with our third child. I pleaded with him to stay, promising to do whatever he wanted me to do, but he ignored my pleas and tears, ranting that he was fed up with me and the problems of the house." Another woman suffering abuse and neglect from her husband commented: "One puts up with mistreatment for the sake of the children in the hope that things will change. But they get worse with each passing day. I am tired of putting up with these conditions. I don't know what to do. I don't want to break up the household but I am so desperate that at times I have the urge to pick up a gun put two bullets [into my husband] and then kill myself, and that would be that."[97]

Marriage often turned into an inescapable trap for women. Indeed, the imagery of imprisonment was not an uncommon metaphor invoked by women to characterize marriage. "'Do this, do that!' I'd always had somebody giving me orders and never had been free to say or do what I wanted," Inocencia Acosta Felipe recalled. She continued: "It turned out that after I married and had my own home, I was more a prisoner than ever. I couldn't even hang a picture where I wanted. It had to go where Reinaldo said. I had everything in the house so pretty, but it all annoyed him, even the china closet where I kept the glass wedding gifts. It bothered him so much we sold it. The curtains annoyed him, the flowers annoyed him, and little by little everything was replaced by what *he* liked. It was humiliating to have to always bend to his will."[98] Another woman captured the bleakness of her marriage: "These routines, with me giving in all the time, day after day, endlessly, are destroying my life. I am profoundly sad all the time, disillusioned; nothing interests me. . . . Perhaps I have asked too much of life. . . . I am suffocated in the house. It feels like a prison. I often go outside to avoid going crazy." In the novel *Sonata interrumpida* (1943), Ofelia Rodríguez Acosta speaks through the newly married protagonist Mónica.

"You see," Mónica explains to her husband, "I, the rebel, the indomitable one, have by my own actions and free will ended up in slavery. I had envisioned myself playing all roles except that of housewife. I believed that I carried in myself an adventurer's spirit and now it seems that I have nothing but a domestic spirit."[99]

Infidelity developed into an ever-larger source of marital infelicity for women. Whether in the form of the *querida*, a mistress more or less tacitly accommodated within the conjugal order of things and often understood to possess acknowledged rights and claims, or the presumed propriety of unlimited access to extramarital affairs, male prerogative often subjected women to varying degrees of abuse and abandonment. These were practices deeply established in the conventions of manhood, which were not without class dimensions, of course, as acceptable, whether or not they could be enacted. But it is also true that however much women may have acquiesced to the practice of male infidelities, it was nevertheless often a source of profoundly personal anguish and humiliation. "Is it possible for a home to be happy with a man who rarely takes meals at home and almost never sleeps at home?" asked one wife, married twenty years, with four children. "Our married life is so impoverished and so dissolute that at times I wish that he would leave altogether, for it so depresses me to know that this is the result of his enjoying life with another woman. This is not a home. The woman is effectively transformed into an instrument, and the desperation that the woman feels for being so degraded by her husband is often sufficient to embitter her very character, and as result the children are the ones who suffer the unhappiness of their mother."[100]

Many women experienced marriage as a condition of enduring hardship, bearing primary responsibility for dependent children, often separated and secluded from friends and family.[101] Male authority expanded into the interior lives of women as a means of discipline, a way to control movement and mobility, and most of all to control female sexuality. This often implied spatial confinement and social isolation of women, including diminished access to associations outside the home, and inevitably limitations on the ability of women to act independently. "Reinaldo is the kind of person you have to say yes to in everything . . . ," Inocencia Acosta Felipe remembered of her husband. "[He] was a bitter jealous man. It annoyed him when the neighbors or even children were nice to me. He didn't like to share me with my family or friends: he wanted me to spend all my time on him." Digna Deveau remembered her mother's experience: "My father was a very jealous man. He didn't like visitors in the house and didn't want my mother to go out or anything like that. She used to cry all the time"; and her own marriage: "I finally had to leave Vicente because his jealousy got to be too much. He was always after me, telling me not to go to the grocery and giving some boy a few cents to do the shopping for me. He wanted me to buy water for a nickel so I wouldn't have to go to the public water tap. He also got upset whenever he saw me using makeup."[102] "I have known only the duties and none of rights of the household," wrote one woman after twelve years of marriage. "I have endured great scarcities, bad treatment, and foul language, for my husband did not let go me out, not even to see my mother unless he accompanied me and this he would only do once a month. . . . This is how I have passed the last three years, silently, and only I know the truth." Wrote another woman: "[My husband] is very jealous and he doesn't even allow me to breathe. He does not let me go out. I can't even go to the front door."[103]

Jealousy was a common cause of gender violence in Cuba, sometimes of women against men, but more frequently of men against women. Accounts of men killing women out of fits of jealous rage were virtually a news staple of the daily press. "Rare is the day," protested Leonor Martínez de Cervera, "when the press does not report the cowardly killing of a woman. Sometimes it is the scorned man who, filled with rage and not love, kills because his pride was injured as a result of rejection by a woman. On other occasions it is a husband who cleanses with blood the dishonor which, according to him, his wife has inflicted upon him. . . . But in either case, men commit these repugnant crimes always confident that society and the laws are disposed to relieve them from any punishment for their acts." In Bayamo, Silverio López Mendoza beat Hilda Castillo to death with a chair and thereupon surrendered to local authorities. "The killer was driven to act by jealousy," the police reported. In an act of jealous rage, Leocadio Quinta shot Obdulia González to death in Güira de Melena.[104] The internal dialogue in Arístides Fernández Vázquez' short story "Caminaban sin prisa por la acera" offers the brooding ruminations preliminary to a planned murder-suicide:

From that fatal day forward there was no peace in my soul. I could not love her more, or leave her, to separate myself from her side to suffer less. Impossible! I suffered when I was close, I suffered when I was far, I suffered all the time. . . . I experienced the horror of my situation without being able to remedy it. I reached the conclusion that I was abnormal. But something big and powerful buffeted my will and soul, like a hurricane beating down upon a weak leaf. . . . Nights of insomnia. . . . No, no, I couldn't love her and at the same time I wanted her more than anything else. Monstrous jealousy—stupid jealousy—tormented me. . . . Three days ago I told her: 'The thought that your eyes have noticed another man makes my life a hell; nevertheless, I love you, I love you madly. Listen: only death can make me happy'—I seized her by her arms and holding her tightly asked—'Do you want to die with me? If you love me, you would not let me leave alone.' She cried, buried her face in my chest, and murmured a barely audible 'Yes.' In my madness I brought her to an abyss, but I am not sorry. The demon of jealousy has made me hard and cruel. It's a horrible crime, I know, but it is necessary—very necessary. For me to die and leave her alive . . . to love again. No! No! The years will pass and happiness will again return to her life. Time erases everything. I would become something blurry in her memory. Simply to think that she could be happy intensifies my own suffering. I am sure that she would love again, she being so sweet, so affectionate. No! She must die with me. I need her to die with me.[105]

In a cultural setting in which male domination of women was so central an attribute of manliness, where the exercise of authority over women was registered in the form of possession, rejection by women often struck at the very source of male self-esteem. Indeed, an affront to the decorum of manhood was perhaps never experienced as acutely as when women acted to challenge the assumptions of power from which the norms of male-female relationships were drawn. The loss of control over women signified a diminution of power in what was otherwise perceived as a domain of uncontested male authority. This occurred most frequently when women sought to end or otherwise extricate themselves from relationships with men, and especially abusive relationships, an act that often set the stage for the use of deadly force as the ultimate method of asserting control.

Love was a dangerous undertaking for women. When men ended love affairs or dissolved marriages, women often killed themselves. When women ended relationships, they were often killed by men. It was on those occasions when men faced the prospect of loss of control and imminent change of those arrangements of which they were the principal beneficiary that the level of violence frequently escalated, the occasion, too, at which the likelihood of murder of women increased. "Following a fiery love affair which lasted two years," reported one Havana newspaper, "María Alvarez claims that her sweetheart became so jealous of her that he said that if she ever stepped out on him he would break her neck."[106] Sara Rojas recalled her fears as she prepared to end her marriage: "I was afraid to leave him because he'd threatened to cut my head off if I did." Rojas's worst fears almost came to pass when her husband threatened her with a machete. She recounted:

'Either you come back to me or I'll chop your head off!' he threatened. 'You may chop me into a hundred pieces,' says I, 'but I'll still say no, and I'll keep on saying no until the last handful of earth is dropped on my grave.'. . . . He moved his machete at me but I wasn't afraid of it or of anything else in the world. I don't know what was protecting me, but I felt no fear at all, alone as I was. I managed to calm him down. At about 2:00 in the morning he cleared out and has never bothered me. If I'd gotten scared and backed down, I'd still be with him, going through a thousand troubles.[107]

All through her three years of marriage, Perla Marina García had been subjected to beatings, verbal abuse, and death threats. When she decided to seek a divorce, her husband shot her to death. Tomasa Cisneros ended her relationship with Francisco Rodríguez, and when she rejected his pleas for reconciliation, he stabbed her to death.[108] A woman named Ilona discussed her pregnancy with writer Jose Yglesias: "[My husband] Mella wants me to have the child. He wants it because it would definitely chain me to the house, and there is so much work for me already that I do not know how I would survive." She continued:

And I do not want to give up, I do not want to break up this marriage. He says if I leave him, he will kill me. . . . I am not allowed to go out of the house—only when I go next door to the school to teach—except with women friends. . . . I have never gone swimming because I am not allowed to wear a bathing suit. Other men would be looking at me! I do not just teach at the school, I do all the work in the house. I clean house, wash clothes, cook, take care of the baby. . . . If I cross him in anything, he beats me or he treats me so badly that I prefer to do what he says. I have no one with me—just my son and he is too young—and I must have affection. I cannot bear to live in a house with an angry man who does not speak to me because I did some little thing he did not like. So I do not fight back.[109]

Incidents of murder-suicide, mostly men killing women and then themselves, occurred with frightfully commonplace frequency. The purport of these acts was rarely ambiguous: if a man could not possess the woman of his desire, then no other man could have her either. Gilda Enríquez Amaro in San Antonio de los Baños was beaten to death by ex-boyfriend Daniel Alfonso when he learned that she had become engaged to marry another man. Alfonso thereupon killed himself. In 1955, in Guáimaro, Luis Tercas surrendered himself to local police after having beaten Sara Bazán to death. They had lived together for six years, Tercas explained, when Bazán ended the relationship. "Driven crazy by the love he professed for her," explained the Havana daily *El Mundo*, "he determined to kill her before she became the lover of another man." Cristobalina Hernández Bravo was stabbed repeatedly and almost died upon breaking her engagement to Oscar González Blanco. "Blinded by jealousy and desperation" was the way that *El Mundo* described Ricardo Bacallao Díaz when he murdered Lourdes Eliza Vázquez upon learning that she was ending their relationship.[110] Concepción Fernández Pérez was shot to death by Carlos Tellería de la Vega, who immediately turned the gun on himself. In Camagüey, Lázaro Musoviche, described by the *Havana Post* as a "maddened suitor," already having been rejected once by sixteen-year-old Carmen Pérez—"whom he loved with a hopeless passion"—proposed marriage again, and "spurned afresh by the girl, he shot and killed her and then ended his own life with a second bullet."[111] In Marianao, Eldemiro Junco mortally wounded Severina Acuña with a butcher knife after she had indicated her intention to leave him. "At last I have killed, her," Junco was reported to have yelled on the street, whereupon he proceeded to kill himself.[112] Alfonso Ramos killed his wife of one month for "misbehavior," he explained in his suicide note, and then proceeded to kill himself because he "loved her so much and could not stand to live without her." Distressed by divorce proceedings initiated by his wife, Luis Verier Vergarda shot her and thereupon turned the gun onto himself and committed suicide.[113] Clara Moreda's short story "El preso" (1926) provides a variation of this pattern when Rodrigo, unable to persuade Carmelina to marry him, threatens suicide. "What would I do in this world, Carmelina, without you?" Rodrigo asks. "Is there no hope?" Carmelina answers, "None," to which Rodrigo responds: "Then you are the one responsible for my death." Unable to bear the guilt of Rodrigo's suicide but unwilling to marry him, Carmelina resolves her dilemma by joining a convent. Comments the narrator: "[Rodrigo] derived some consolation. Carmelina would not be his, but neither would she belong to anyone else. She was going to a convent and he would be content to be with her in heaven."[114]

The larger logic connecting the destruction of towns and cities that could not be held during the nineteenth-century wars for independence and the murder of women that could not be possessed in the twentieth century is not altogether clear, but that there is one cannot be doubted.

🔆 Vast numbers of women endured unhappy domestic circumstances in quiet despair, as a matter of fact and an unremarkable if inescapable condition of daily life, but especially as the fate to which women were consigned by virtue of being women. Many endured to satisfy the needs of others, usually children, often at the expense of their own happiness and well-being. "A woman will endure almost any measure of hardship, pain, and discomfort for the sake of preserving the happiness of her man and her children," observed anthropologist Mirta de la Torre Mulhare.[115] "I've been married for 18 years," wrote one woman,

> and from the third day of marriage I knew I would not be happy. My husband asked me for a towel and for not having handed it to him quickly enough, he threw it at my face. These acts of violence have been repeated a thousand times since then. He stays out every night until 3 or 4 in the morning. Tears and pleas have failed to induce him to change. He says he acts this way because he is not disposed to let himself be dominated by a woman. I thought he would change, but he hasn't. We have nine children. . . . Every day he tells me that he is tired of us and that he is going to leave forever. I know he has other women, but at this point I don't protest any more, for after so many years of fighting all I have is grief and misery. . . . I am in despair for the uncertain future of my children.[116]

For many women recourse to divorce was unthinkable. Middle-class proprieties, including the stigma of social scandal and religious proscription, acted as powerful deterrents to divorce. Oscar and Ruth Lewis described the situation of Inocencia Acosta: "She fantasized about leaving him but could find no moral support to do it. Unable to ignore the prevailing negative attitudes toward divorce and with no acceptable means of becoming self-supporting, Inocencia reluctantly tolerated marriage for the next 25 years." The protagonist Marianela in Lesbia Soravilla's novel *Cuando libertan los esclavos* (1936) finds herself helpless in a marriage to an abusive husband. "I could have returned home," Marianela explains, "but the fear of scandal stopped me. Although it may not be apparent, I am the only daughter of Hugo Cantero, of the Cantero family so well known in

Villaclara. . . . All my relatives were people very proud of their good name and with a very narrow view of life. I felt myself very alone."[117] Through the life of Berenice de Sola, another protagonist in *Cuando libertan los esclavos*, Soravilla offered poignant insight into the grief often visited upon women in abusive relationships. "She inflated his virtues, minimized his defects," the narrator recounts. "She made herself appear insignificant so that he could stand out as important. In the end, her exaggerated happiness deceived everyone." But it was only a matter of time before Berenice became a victim of the very lie she lived. How could she thereafter confess to a life of terror and torment? The beatings continued:

> If they argued he beat her. She then decided not to argue. But he continued to beat her, now because she appeared indifferent to his ideas. . . . Patience had its limits, and she decided to threaten to leave him, never to return. . . . But without realizing it, they began to argue again. It was hell. But what to do? If she were to leave the house, the law would hold her responsible as the spouse who abandoned the home. If she screamed when he beat her so that there would be witnesses . . . it would be so humiliating, so embarrassing to let people really know what was going on. After all, he was the father of her son. To return to live with her family would have been the best solution, but there a divorced women was viewed with scorn. Everyone believed that Orlandito was a model husband. She would be suspect and anyway the boy would be the loser in this solution. . . . [But she did] return to her home town and told no one of the true reasons behind the unexpected breakup. To the inquiries of the curious, she responded simply: 'It had to happen, we were not getting along.' People were surprised—'But Orlandito is a saint!' She smiled inwardly at these comments. No one would have believed her if she had confessed the truth. 'A man so good capable of beating his wife?' And among themselves: 'To what magnitude of desperation must she have driven him to provoke such a thing.' No—better just to keep quiet.[118]

Women with children confronted obstacles of other kinds. Many had no place to go, no place to live, no means of support. The transformation of the Cuban family during the early decades of the republic had far-reaching implications. Between 1899 and 1919, post-1898 fertility rates registered most notably in the expansion of the size of the average family, from 4.8 to 5.7 members. Never before—and never since—had Cuban families included as many dependent children as they did during the first half of the twentieth century.[119] A mother of five children, without the resources to maintain an independent household, was not likely to abandon a marriage, however wretched the circumstances of her own life. In 1932, María Gutiérrez reported her husband missing. She acknowledged that he was "a little off in his mind," but hastened to add: "It is better to have a husband who is a bit off than no husband at all."[120] Reminisced Inocencia Acosta:

> I believe men are superior to women—that is, they are more intelligent and stronger—but that doesn't give them the right to do what they do. It's not that a woman is inferior, but she's weaker and easier to impress; there are times when she simply has to depend on a man. Women fall in love, have children, and have twenty difficulties men don't have, and no matter how intelligent a woman is, she feels more protected if she has a man. And yet, no matter how much I needed my husband and how hard I tried to please him, there's no moment I can think of and say, 'Yes, he made me happy then.'[121]

"I can go live with my parents," one woman—mother of two children—pondered, "but I am very afraid of divorce. No one in my family has ever been divorced. I would be the first and I fear for the future of my children, for they may suffer a great deal. [My husband] has threatened to take the children if I leave. I feel as if I'm going to go crazy. At times I think of killing myself as the best way out and I would stop being such a nuisance."[122] "I live like a slave in my house," recounted one woman. "[My husband's] drunken sprees make my life miserable. My home is hell. I have left several times, leaving my children, but I returned because of them and because I had no place to go." Wrote another woman: "The terrible ways in which I am treated fill me with pain and disillusionment. There are moments that I think about all possible remedies, including killing myself, but I am too much of a coward to abbreviate the life that God has given me."[123] In Miguel de Carrión's novel, *La esfinge* (1919), the protagonist Amada lives in an unhappy marriage—"in truth," she says, "I suffer horribly [and] my heart bleeds"—with no escape. "Her spirit was crushed," observes the narrator, and adds: "[They] lived according to very strict dogmas, under very strict principles, and could not contemplate the repudiation of the sacrament of marriage. That a woman did not marry well could be regretted; but once having received the conjugal blessing, her destiny was inextricably tied to her spouse. That is why Amada did not even dare to think of taking issue with her circumstances, which would have in any case provoked a scandal in her house." Amada's rebellion set her on a course of suicide as means of liberation.[124]

Women unable to extricate themselves from unhappy households were among the most susceptible to suicide. The cause of suicide of twenty-one-year-old Paulina Delgado could not be verified, reported *La Discusión*. However, continued the news story, "according to what we hear, the husband mistreated her very badly and truly disagreeable scenes between them were repeated often. The day before her death, on one of these occasions, he beat her." Felipa Martínez Sepol committed suicide only days after neighbors had summoned police to protect her from a beating from her husband. Clotilde Cabrera killed herself after repeated beatings by her husband. Walda Regal and María Magdalena Valdivia were among the many women who in their suicide notes attributed the decision to die to mistreatment by their husbands. Josefa Gordon Vallé attempted unsuccessfully to poison herself to death, reported the *Diario de la Marina*, "because of the mistreatment she had received from her husband . . . who had threatened to kill her." The reason for Julia Casat Ferrer's attempt to kill herself, she explained, was due "to the mistreatment and threats that she received daily from her husband."[125] Writer Pablo Medina recalled the woes that marriage visited on his grandmother—"Juana María had a terrible time of it"—and remembered the frequency with which his grandfather "came home without his paycheck, having lost it at the races, other times smelling of women and liquor. . . . It fell on Juana María to scrounge for money among her family in order to pay rent, the grocer, the children's school. At times she was forced to pawn jewelry and furniture." Medina remembered: "And every time this happened, my grandmother told me between puffs of her cigarette, she wanted to die." An expression of an unhappy marriage is offered in the short story "Alguien tiene que llorar," by Marilyn Bobes, when Maritza inveighs against the husband of a friend: "It's better to commit suicide than to be married to a guy like that." In the novel *El pájaro: pincel y tinta china* (1998), by Ena Lucía Portela, the protagonist Camila is subjected to repeated beatings by her husband. "He wasn't going to kill her," comments the narrator, "because he needed a woman in the house, a wife, in the same way that a pawn is needed in chess in order to protect the more important pieces." Camila gains control over her life when she determines to end it: "We all have to die someday anyway. Everyone dies. There is nothing more certain or obligatory. Better then to rejoice in the possibility available to the patient in order . . . to avoid pain and darkness."[126]

The prospect of abandonment, of living life without the men around whom norms of fulfillment had been fashioned, and thereupon bearing full responsibility for the maintenance of a household and support of children, was no less terrifying and no less infrequently a source of suicide. Women living alone, many abandoned by men, with primary responsibility for children, were often unable to bear for long the crushing weight of poverty. Many succumbed to indigence. Default of the role of care provider, a purpose so deeply inscribed as obligatory female function, must be seen as a frightful psychological circumstance, capable at once of shattering self-identity and negating purpose in life. Women living alone with children were particularly susceptible to suicide. "I was left without work, living in misery everyday, and without the basic necessities of life," said one thirty-nine-year-old woman, recounting her life raising two sons ages ten and two when she was abandoned by her husband. "I had help from no one. . . . I have lived a hard life: from work to my house, everyday, and movies on Sunday. . . . I do not know happiness. I have dedicated my youth to raising my sons. Without illusions, without affection and ever more fearful of spending my old age alone. I ask God for the strength to permit me to continue to fulfill my responsibilities, but there are days that I don't have even the will to get up and go to work."[127]

Accounts of women with young children killing themselves filled the daily press. They were often rendered as the most tragic of the tragic, those human interest stories that served easily enough to implicate everyone in the failures of the existing moral order and social system. Caridad Báez Márquez, the mother of two small children, poisoned herself after her husband abandoned her, saying that she was "tired of living in misery." Twenty-one-year-old Tomasa Acosta Hernández, left to care for two young children after separation from her husband, attempted suicide as a result "of the terrible economic situation in which we find ourselves."[128] Before killing herself, Georgina Campos had lived in terror of her husband, an alcoholic who routinely beat her. When her husband abandoned her, however, she plunged immediately into indigence, and was forced "to wander through the neighborhoods of Havana . . . , at times sleeping in doorways and under trees."[129] Sofía Rosenda Avila explained her suicide in a note: "The family is experiencing very difficult circumstances. The children are without shoes. They have no clothing. Hunger besets us relentlessly." The demands of life overwhelmed thirty-seven-year-old Laudelina Cruz Fuente, a single mother of an adolescent daughter, who attempted to killed herself, explained her daughter, because "for a long time she has coped with a terrible economic situation due to the fact that her earnings at her modest employment are not sufficient to cover even the most urgent expenses and she has not been able to find better employment despite all her efforts." Antonia Miranda poisoned herself "for not having the means to support her children"; while Antonia Romero de García burned herself to death "out of despair over her poverty and the impossibility of giving her four small children food."[130] In 1926, after twenty years of marriage, Jacinta Bayo Mazón killed herself when her husband abandoned her and their two sons for another woman, explaining in her suicide note she could "not live with the sadness and sense of abandonment caused by [her husband's] departure."[131] In 1955 Aída Corona committed suicide and in a letter directed to judicial authorities explained:

> Your Honor: I implore you not to have an autopsy performed on me. I have ingested 88 pills of the barbiturate seconal. I have decided to take this measure because I find myself without employment, and although I am weary of seeking work, I only find expectations and one cannot live off expectations or make anyone happy. My parents and my only brother are dead. I divorced my husband of twelve years and I have become tired of struggling alone. Sometimes I receive assistance from my poor maternal grandmother. But she depends on her sons and is already 92 years old. I can no longer continue to be a burden to her. Please arrange my burial in the most convenient manner. If in life I have not had a family, I cannot have one after death.[132]

In one day in 1932 in San Juan de las Yeras, two women burned themselves to death: Dominga Pérez Cuéllar in the morning and Josefa Aguila Díaz in the evening. "Neighbors are alarmed," reported one observer, "over the repetition of suicides. It is occurring among peasant women, mostly mothers, who prefer to die in the face of the misery that their children are experiencing."[133] María García Facuente was an eighteen-year-old mother of a ten-month-old baby when she was abandoned by her husband. Lacking all resources and without any means of support, she descended into indigence, facing imminent homelessness. She chose to poison herself "rather than," she explained, "having to resort to prostitution to end the misery that has befallen me." Reinaldo Arenas wrote poignantly about his twenty-year-old unwed mother, disgraced as a "fallen woman," without prospects of marriage, at times overwhelmed by a brooding sense of melancholia and "a great sense of frustration." Arenas recalled his childhood: "One night, when I was already in bed, my mother asked me a question that at the time disturbed me greatly. She wanted to know if I would feel really sad if she died. I hugged her and started to cry. I think she cried too, and told me to forget she had ever asked. I realized later, or perhaps even then, that my mother was contemplating suicide but had refrained because of me."[134]

Mothers disposed to commit suicide who despaired at the prospects of leaving their children motherless often resolved the dilemma by killing their children before killing themselves. Infanticide-suicide was not uncommon. Of the seventy-one homicides registered in Havana in July 1920, a total of twenty-three were of children of less than one year. In twenty-one instances, the child was strangled to death by the mother. These developments, *La Lucha* pronounced, "give evidence of the advanced state of moral decomposition in which the city of Havana finds itself." By the mid-1950s, nearly 20 percent of all inmates in the national prison for women were serving sentences for infanticide. Cases of infanticide accounted for nearly half the women convicted of homicide and assault.[135]

Instances of infanticide-suicide were almost always associated with circumstances of adversity and indigence. In the town of Los Arabes, Josefa Porteles administered liquid shoe polish (*tinta rápida*) to her one-year-old son and thereupon proceeded to set herself on fire, a response, authorities learned, to "despair due to her terrible economic situation and finding herself completely abandoned." In one incident in Managua characterized by the daily *La Caricatura* as a "drama of misery," twenty-five-year-old Rosario Horta Marrero, in despair at the prospects of her three children "dying of hunger," proceeded to kill them—four years, three years, and six months of age—and thereupon hanged herself. Juana Cabrera explained her decision to commit suicide as a result of "finding myself demoralized, defenseless, and defeated"; she explained her decision to kill her twelve-year-old daughter as a way "to spare her of the disillusionment and scorn of life that I have experienced." Consuelo Navarro plunged into a well holding her two children, two and three years of age. In Camagüey, Esther Oramas Arias poisoned her three sons—ages three, six, and eight—and then proceeded to kill herself. After her husband had abandoned her, Oramas Arias found employment as a servant earning $18 monthly, with which she struggled unsuccessfully to make ends meet. She determined to kill her children and herself after her husband refused to pay child support. "I am killing my children," she wrote in her suicide note, "because [my husband] José Agustín has left them without support and I do not want them to experience the suffering that I have experienced ever since I was a child." In the city of Guantánamo, Isabel Galán soaked her clothing with alcohol and, clutching her infant daughter, set herself ablaze.[136] Dolores Batista chose Mother's Day 1952 to kill her two young children and end her own life, except that she survived. The day began with nothing to eat in the house. "I had to go out into the streets to find food for my children," she later recounted, "but returned with nothing. My children would be indigents, poor wretches always hungry and suffering, or they would soon die of hunger. They were dying of hunger!" That evening, Batista lay down with her children, poured alcohol over the two boys and herself, and set them all on fire.[137]

✲✿ The rhythm of the export economy affected collective morale in many ways, and nowhere perhaps with greater impact than in those cultural realms in which men and women obtain validation of place and purpose. The long months of tiempo muerto, of chronic joblessness, every year, had debilitating effects on household arrangements across the island, and inevitably on the circumstances of family life and the purpose to which time was put. Month after month of idleness and inactivity, without work, often with nothing to do, shaped the character of daily life in communities across the island. The pace of life slowed down, and in some instances halted altogether, as the effects of idleness transformed the meaning of time. Tiempo muerto was a time of struggle to make ends meet, to hold out, but it was no less a struggle to resist disappointment and demoralization. Life in Cuba often approached overbearing conditions of monotony and melancholia, as vast numbers of people experienced time stretching endlessly into a prolonged state of idleness, where idle hours and idle hands combined to sap the morale of workers and their families across the island. Men gathered as idle men often do at canteens and bars, in the parks and plazas, given to drinking as a way to pass the time away, waiting for something to happen that usually did not happen, waiting for better times that mostly never came.

The condition of boredom (aburrimiento) assumed fully the proportions of a national malaise and must be viewed as an affliction embedded deeply in those hierarchies of subjective meanings through which daily life was experienced. Political scientist Judith Shklar wrote generally of melancholia as induced "by social change that [people] cannot control in any way," adding: "Work, as we all know, is one of the great cures for melancholy and boredom. . . . It is also the source of social standing and respect. And unemployment can come swiftly to both blue-collar workers and middle-class people. Many give up looking for new employment too quickly as they become despondent." Philosopher Jennifer Radden reflected on melancholia and pointed to the association between boredom and "the state of idleness." The promise of work as remedy to melancholia, Radden affirmed, implied more than a job, however, adding: "It is meaningful work, and work outside of a system of domination and oppression to which we must look if work is to be a palliative against melancholy."[138]

Aburrimiento in this instance implied conditions of debilitation and demoralization, of weariness and hopelessness, circumstances that philosopher Seán Desmond Healy aptly described in his treatise on boredom as "the loss of a sense of personal meaning, whether in relation to a particular experience or encounter, or to an entire life-situation." The sources of boredom, Healy suggested, "seem to extend out into the entire culture," adding: "Man, in being bored, is betraying something of the nature of *the* situation, not just *his* situation," perceived as a condition in which certainty has deserted the culture and creating the sense that "the bottom has fallen out of the world."[139] Essayist Marcelo Pogolotti identified boredom in Cuba as "a cultural problem," one that could be remedied only through a "change of values."[140]

It was within the interminable idleness so very much associated with the patterns of the export economy that boredom insinuated itself into Cuban sensibilities, and this too assumed a place of prominence as a malady that acted continually to deplete collective moral resolve. Sociologist Wolf Lepenies wrote persuasively of the temporal dimensions of boredom, with direct implications for the Cuban condition. "When we are bored," Lepenies observed, "time grows long—it cannot be filled or used up; and finally, time is 'killed' when we notice that it seems endless. . . . Boredom appears to be eternal monotony, always the same, gaping void."[141]

Aburrido—to be bored—wrote lexicographer Juan Dihigo in 1928, was a "term very much used in Cuban speech and very much ours. It represents the idea of lethargy, of a person who is tired, without energy. . . . It does not appear in the Spanish-American lexicons. (*No aparece en los léxicos hispanoamericanos.*)" Esteban Rodríguez Herrera used the word *aburrido* in his lexicon to denote a condition of weariness and offered as example "*vida aburrida.*"[142]

Cubans were conscious of the condition of boredom to which they were subject. They discerned that things were not right but sensed too that neither remedy nor relief was attainable. As early as 1885, physician Tomás Plasencia wrote of a prevailing condition of "alienation in which there is boredom of life (*aburrimiento de la vida*) . . . associated with melancholia." Essayist Mario Muñoz Bustamante brooded over what he characterized in 1905 as "the Cuban affliction": "Cuba is not as happy a country as is commonly believed. Cuba is a bored and sad country. (*Cuba es un país aburrido y triste.*) The Cuban . . . is driven by tedium, he is bored and lethargic. . . . Ours is a forlorn society." Years later Reinaldo Arenas recalled "dying of boredom" in Holguín. Cristina Saralegui remembered Cuba as a "small island" where "everything was cyclical and seasonal—to avoid boredom." Writer José Baró Pujol hailed the inauguration of commercial radio broadcasting during the 1920s for its promise to raise morale across the island: "It is precisely there that radio can provide the greatest services and benefits to those who in their distance from the large population centers stagnate in their unproductive boredom."[143] Film director Vicente Revuelta associated his adolescent passion for motion pictures with his desire to escape boredom. "When I emerged from the movie theater it was like entering into boredom," he remembered. "In those times, as a result of having gone to the movies so often, I wanted to go to New York, for I believed that people there truly lived a different life. I lived in an impoverished environment, where nothing happened." Writing from Guantánamo in 1912, Regino Boti despaired: "I am at the point of mental exhaustion as a result of the monotony and isolation."[144]

Dispositions to die developed out of the moral context of daily life, within those patterns through which men and women negotiated their encounter with the requirements of perseverance. Vast numbers of men and women fixed their purpose in life within received conventions of well-being, which were becoming increasingly difficult to meet and maintain. Essayist Jorge Mañach reflected on the malaise of boredom as a condition to which Cubans were particularly susceptible. "People in Cuba are killing themselves out of boredom with life," Mañach commented in 1931, "that is, out of boredom with life in Cuba." He continued:

What is it about life in Cuba these past years that produces such tragic boredom? Boredom is that state of being into which we fall when circumstances do not permit the fulfillment of our most intimate desires, do not allow us to exercise our special aptitude, do not permit us to attend to our most pressing needs. Boredom is the spiritual repercussion of a great variety of external causes that range from the concrete condition of poverty to the most subtle forms of unmet needs. Total poverty, absolute misery, often produces suicidal desperation. But what leads to 'boredom with life' is relative poverty . . . : of the employee whose salary has been reduced twice; the professional who has had to let the maid go; the professor who has been left without a salary but still faces the obligation to 'dress decently;' the day laborer, the peasant, who is unable to put a roof over his house.[145]

Boredom developed into a circumstance of day-to-day existence and its most insidious impact was registered within the most deeply personal realms as a dispirited state of being, eventually as a weariness with life. This was manifested as being tired of living, where to be bored with life was to be bored to death. Many gave out and gave up. They wearied of life, worn down by living: overtaken by the weariness of getting through the day, every day. Segundo Corvisón made the point succinctly: "When in the struggle for existence the resources most essential to prolong life can no longer be found, then, ah, then we should resign ourselves to our fate and die." For the protagonist Agustín in Loló de la Torriente's novel *Caballeros de la marea roja* (1984), relates the narrator, "death no longer tormented him, suicide no longer intimidated him. He considered it a legitimate act, with permission from heaven, when there was no longer any reason to live for."[146] In the play *Los excéntricos de la noche*, by Nicolás Dorr, Carucha explains her decision to commit suicide. "Do you know when one wants to die?" she asks, and answers: "When life becomes a burden, an unbearable burden, and you feel that you can't endure, when you find no one to share your life, no one for support. It is then that we gather all the strength that remains to us, the little strength that we still have left, to take flight, just for that purpose, and to call out desperately a name, there's always a name. But there is no response, only silence, a crushing silence. It is then that we take our lives, although I don't know what life. Perhaps what we take is death."[147]

For many the demands of life simply overwhelmed their moral resolve and material resources: to wake up every day to resume the struggle for survival of the previous day, with diminishing expectations of short-term relief and dwindling hopes for long-term remedies. Cubans spoke often of being tired of life, just plain exhausted by the all-consuming effort required simply to eke out a meager existence. Writer José María López Valdizón described the circumstances of his protagonist Crispín with poignance in the short story "Las ánimas": "He was tired of working, and that was the truth. In the farm it is necessary to work much to earn little. And slowly one wastes away without fully knowing it. Then come the illnesses:

malaria and dysentery, and then you fall off a tree trying to cut down a fruit." Columnist Luis Rolando Cabrera brooded about conditions in the mid-1950s. "Nearly a million Cubans . . . wake up every day," he wrote, "not to work but to ask themselves, despondently, if that will be another day in which they do not find employment."[148]

Weariness of living and boredom with life (*aburrida de la vida*) were among the most frequent reasons given for committing suicide. Twenty-four-year-old Anastasio Fonseca Mena committed suicide by hanging, explaining in his suicide note: "I take leave of this world because I am tired." José Guerra Fernández attempted to stab himself to death as a result, he wrote in his suicide note, of "being bored with life and tired of working without earning sufficient [wages] for my maintenance [and] convinced that my misery will have no end." Antonio Arteaga hanged himself in his Havana apartment because, his wife explained, he was "bored with life as a result of being without work." In his suicide note, Arteaga explained that he had "been without work for some time and having little hope of again obtaining the work so necessary to maintain [himself] and his wife [he] intended to commit suicide." Francisco González Bosque decided to kill himself because he was "bored with this world and due to [his] economic situation."[149] In the short story "La navaja de afeitar," by Rolando Arteaga, the protagonist finds himself "slowly sinking, overtaken by darkness. Everything was slowly losing its significance. . . . Many afternoons he caressed the razor, marveling that such an ordinary and insignificant object possessed the capacity to spare him from continued painful and boring experiences of life." In the song "Chacumbele" (1941), Machito and His Afro-Cubans tell the story of Chacumbele:

> Bored with living
> Already tired of suffering
> Only yesterday he killed himself
>
> (Aburrido de vivir
> Ya cansado de sufrir
> Ayer mismo se mató)[150]

The circumstances of boredom as weariness with life appear to have afflicted women in very specific ways. In her 1935 essay "Aburrimiento," writer Leonor Barraqué warned of the "malaise of boredom that seems to befall women more than men." She exhorted women to resist the perils of facing each new day "with the withered brow of boredom" and to fill their lives "with activities that will defeat the phantasma of boredom."[151] Elena Burke recorded a haunting ode to boredom that addressed the despair of daily life:

Bored—I awoke this morning,
　Making the very bed where last night I was bored.
Bored—without pain, without pleasure: I traveled over the same
　route,
　From my house to the office.
Bored—with all that has happened, with all the people I have met,
　With the envy and with the lies.
Bored—with the piano-bar, with the people,
　Of not finding excitement to enliven this day.
Bored—with the house and with the kitchen,
　With work and with the neighbor, with even my very husband.
Bored—I look at myself as I bathe. The years have passed me by,
　So much—so much—that I have missed.
Bored—I went to bed again,
　To awake tomorrow, surely to be bored . . .[152]

In Ana María Simo's short story "Igual es igual a muerte," protagonist María Rosa is driven to take her own life by unchanging sameness. Relates the narrator: "She was very tired inside. . . . Everything always the same. The store windows, the cinema, the radio announcer, the town, the people and even she herself. . . . The same, the same, the same. She was defeated. The same, she muttered. She stepped onto the chair. The same, always the same. She stepped off the chair. She swung from the rope."[153] In "Cansada de vivir," poet Carmen Cordero addressed the weariness of life:

I am tired of living. I wish
　to close my eyes and sleep profoundly,
　unfold my soul against the blue sky.

I am tired of living. I would sleep
　the slumber of the dead in their graves
　so that not even rose petals
　would disturb my austere stillness.

I am tired of living. And I feel
　the anxiety of watching each
　moment race by like a spinning wheel.

Today, as this fierce anxiety torments me so,
   how much innocent sanctity I would give
   for a moment of extravagance—all my life![154]

"What does it matter," Isabel Carrasco Tomasetti asked in her 1926 essay "El dolor de vivir," "when monotony has imposed upon the heart its dark and heavy crape. What significance can tomorrow have for the heart heavy with thinking, waiting, loving? What is everything if not an immense disillusionment, a horrible monotony: day after day, week after week, month after month, stretching into years. . . . Why struggle? Why live?" In the essay "Melancolía," Carrasco Tomasetti described her "fear of an uncertain future" and of her "horribly monotonous gray days."[155] In Miguel Cofiño's short story "Magda, el mar, el aire," the protagonist broods constantly about suicide. She comments: "I have thought about killing myself for a long time. . . . It's an obsession. I do not believe happiness is possible." Ofelia Rodríguez Acosta alluded to "even elegant, beautiful women, with that air of weariness and boredom." And in the poem "Inquietudes," Rosario Sansores asked:

Why struggle against destiny
If its inexorable will
Buffets you along the way
And reveals to you its cruelty?[156]

These were themes that poet Graziella Garbalosa addressed often. "If life so saddens me / If the world is bitter and hard," she asked in "Escepticismo," "Why then dream of love / Why take flowers / To the tombs of the dead." In the poem "Neurosis" Garbalosa affirms outright: "I feel the weary sadness of life," a theme to which she returns in "Cansancio":

Life pains me so much
and its weight is so heavy,
that the soul so fully cold
finds it far too long!

The mind is asleep
in a dream of pain,
and lost thoughts
wander among the mists of horror.

Life pains me so much,
that Death beckons me
to its embrace!

And it appears that I
can seek it out without fear
of losing my way . . .[157]

The protagonist in Lesbia Soravilla's novel *El dolor de vivir* (n.d.) endures chronic boredom. Observes the narrator: "She was already bored with life in Havana. It turned out to be too small a city, too small-town for her adventuresome desires. She always saw the same people on the same streets. . . . Everything was so monotonous. She was bored in Havana the way she was bored in her home town." In the play *Mediodía cantante*, by Nicolás Dorr, Graciela addresses herself to her husband: "What am I to you? Tell me, I want to know. The cook, the dishwasher, the slave. I am so bored (*Estoy tan aburrida*) . . . I am so bored from being the maid."[158] In Zoé Valdés's novel *Café nostalgia* (1997), the protagonist Ana laments her condition to a friend:

> Look! I want to end my life for obvious reasons. . . . I am fed up with everything around me, and I don't know why. Because I am bored, I have the urge to fuck, and of course I end up pregnant. . . . I don't know what's happening. I feel vile. Why do you think I have the need to go to bed with every guy I meet. I don't understand it. . . . The fact is that I am bored at school, bored at home, bored at parties. The only time I am not bored is when I meet a guy, but after we go to bed I'm bored again. Aren't you weary of the fact that everywhere you go in this fucking country, bam! you come up against the ocean. There is no way out. We are surrounded by water.[159]

Boredom and monotony were experienced as particularly onerous afflictions in the circumstances of women's daily lives in the countryside. Households in rural Cuba tended to confine women on *colonias* and *cafetales*, on small *fincas* and *vegas*, on the *ranchos* and *ingenios*. Women often found themselves isolated within households as dependent homemakers, without social connections, devoted exclusively to household duties and child-rearing responsibilities. Frederick Ober wrote of the "monotony of country life in Cuba"; while Pablo Medina remembered the "isolation and loneliness of life in the country" in which his grandmother lived, of the colonias "far away from each other and social visits . . . at best occasional. While their husbands worked ten or twelve hours a day, six days a week, the women were deprived of contact with women other than domestic help." Ofelia Fernández wrote of Luisa Suárez, born in "a town like any other town of Cuba," who confronted dreary prospects: "Upon reaching 14 years of age, every day of her life had been the same. Of lucid intelligence and a spirit eminently restless, Luisa could not submit herself to that monotony. Her mother had aged prematurely as a result of so much housework and raising so many children. . . . Girls in the countryside married too young and aged too quickly." In Samuel Feijóo's novel *Juan Quintín en Pueblo Mocho* (1964), the protagonist Teresa lives a life filled with loneliness: "She was alone for long hours, almost all day. . . . From the distance she could see the mountain purple with dry vegetation . . . where the land seemed to disappear from slope to slope. . . . She worked singing hour after hour. But at times she was reduced to silence, tired, saddened by a distant pain. She wanted to see her father. . . . She wanted a friend, to have a conversation at least once. And then she laughed and thought: 'How crazy I am: this is my world, here in the mountain, next to [my husband] Juan.'"[160] Physician Julio LeRiverend described the circumstances of nineteenth-century criollas in a generally overdrawn diagnosis but one not without suggestive insight. Many women, LeRiverend observed, "are victim to a nervous temperament that increases . . . as a result of the inactivity to which they submit themselves after the birth of their first child, whereupon they become imprisoned. They are subject to a host of nervous illnesses, including hypochondria and hysteria. . . . These illnesses are found in the wealthy and well-to-do classes, for among the peasants and workers these illnesses are unknown."[161]

It is impossible to ascertain with precision the larger meaning of psychiatric diagnoses used to characterize "deviant behavior" among women in the early republic, for the categories employed and the conduct observed today have only limited clinical usefulness. But precisely because diagnostic categories were themselves implicated in the social circumstances they purported to describe, the patterns of insanity of female resident patients at the Hospital de Dementes de Cuba are suggestive. In 1913 the diagnosis of *melancolía* was made for 194 patients, while *locura histérica* accounted for another 167 patients. Both diagnostic categories accounted for almost one-third of all resident patients (361 out of 1,146). In 1925, *melancolía* was the diagnosis for 385 patients and accounted for 30 percent of patients (385 out of 1,274 patients), while *locura histérica* accounted for another 100 patients. In 1926 public health agencies revised diagnostic categories, adding *estado maniacio-depresivo*, in which more than half the female patients (720 out of 1,371) were classified, followed by *psicosis constitucional* (267) and *histeria* (98).[162] Indeed, "hysteria" appeared as the cause often attributed to suicide by women. Twenty-one-year-old Dolores Calvo attempted to poison herself, reported *La Caricatura*, as a result of her "suffering from hystericism (*histerismo*)," while twenty-three-year-old Josefina Llorens attempted to slash her throat due to "an accident of hystericism."[163]

The frequency with which women attributed *aburrida de la vida* as reason for suicide is astonishing. Paulina de Armas, Teresa Martínez, Blanca Satoya Otero, Rosa Peña Rodríguez, Adela Valdés Martínez, and Evangelista Rodríguez Betancourt were among the vast numbers of young women who gave their reason for wishing to kill themselves as being "bored with living."[164] *Cansada de la vida*—tired of life—was the reason that Carmen Alfonso López gave for killing herself. Amalia Fernández attempted unsuccessfully to kill herself, giving later as her reason "being bored in the world." Sixteen-year-old Mercedes Morey Ravelo shot herself to death, leaving a note pinned to her blouse: "Enough of life. Although I am young, I take my life because I know what the world has to offer. Good-bye forever."[165] María Rosell Rodríguez gave her desire to die as being "tired of living owing to many misfortunes"; and nineteen-year-old Juana Amaro Mazorra attempted to kill herself as a result of being "bored with living." Twenty-one-year-old María López Martínez explained in her suicide note: "I do this because I am tired of the world and I no longer love life."[166] On an isolated *finca* in Cobre, Angela García killed herself through fire, explaining that she "was bored with the life [she] led." Eustaquia Benítez Griñán, living with her parents on a *colonia* in Morón, burned herself to death, explaining she was "tired of life." In Manicaragua, fourteen-year-old Hilda Mejías burned herself to death "out of boredom." Ofelia Gómez of Consolación del Sur found herself "bored of life and no longer able to endure the heavy burden of the horrible misery under which I exist." She proceeded to end her life by setting herself on fire.[167]

An Ambience of Suicide

5

Life is a vast altar, and we are its offerings.
  Eugenio Hernandez, "El sacrificio" (1961)

— "What does it mean to be a Cuban woman?"
— "I really don't know; a destiny like any other. . . .
perhaps a special way of dreaming and failing."
  René Vázquez Díaz, La Isla de Cundeamor (1995)

The act whereby a man voluntarily ends his life for the
purpose of extricating himself from the unbearable
weight of his pain, setbacks, and misery is unfortunately
common in all countries. This ought to suggest to the
philosophical observer . . . the reason why it is a grave
error to look upon the [individual who commits] suicide
as a leaf that detaches itself from the tree without refer-
ring to the tree itself.
  Revista Científica de la Academia de Ciencias
  Médicas, Físicas y Naturales de La Habana (1908)

In the political history of Cuba, suicide plays a role of
transcendental importance in that it alters the evolution
of the Cuban people at the most decisive moments.
  Herminio Portell Vilá, "Tesis sobre el suicidio en la
  historia política de Cuba" (1959)

Death is a punishment for some, for others it is a gift,
and for many it is a favor.
  Iván Acosta, Un cubiche en la luna (1989)

*In keeping with the adage "New year, new life," 19
people [in Havana] have attempted to commit suicide
in the last twenty-four hours. Eight of them succeeded.
A police official commented that evidently it was a
matter of seeking a "new life," although not in this
world.*

El Mundo *(January 6, 1954)*

❧ The deed of suicide originated from those cognitive processes shaped in the ordinary course of daily life, from disappointments in personal affairs to frustrations associated with making a living, with the setbacks and mishaps to which vast numbers of Cubans were routinely subject. In the end, it bears repeating, only a small number of men and women ended their lives by choice. In fact, the overwhelming majority of Cubans found other ways to mediate hardship and make their way through life: not always salutary ways, to be sure, for when they took the form of alcoholism, or drug abuse, or domestic violence it involved behaviors no less destructive. The ways that people pursued self-destruction did not always result in sudden death. It may have taken years to consummate the desire to die.

What made suicide among Cubans remarkable as a facet of the national condition was set in relief in comparison with rates of suicide elsewhere. It is in this context that the disposition to die in Cuba—that is, the apparent propensity of Cubans to kill themselves with greater frequency and at higher numbers than almost all other people in the world—assumes noteworthy salience. The readiness with which Cubans availed themselves of the option of suicidal death as a response to afflictions large and small, in turn, was itself a function of the normative systems mediating the activities of everyday life. Suicide could be readily undertaken because it was easily imaginable, and that it was so easily contemplated suggests the degree to which it had entered those reflexive realms in which people intuitively devised ways to cope with life. Suicide under these circumstances was integrated into specific patterns of personal meanings, principally as a disposition shaped under commonly shared conditions from one generation to the next. But it was also true that the disposition to suicide was fashioned by cultural forms embedded in a social context. Cubans may have had more than ample reasons for wishing to commit suicide, and that so many did indeed act to end their lives speaks to dispositions that obtained validation in the larger condition of Cuban.

Some people who took their own lives suffered from a variety of infirmities, including emotional disorders and mental illness, that impaired their sense of reality; they might put an end to their lives without assigning meaning to the act or grasping the finality of its outcome. The conventional wisdom has long maintained that persons who committed suicide were insane and hence were not responsible for their own deaths. The evidence is scattered but abundant. Instances of men and women identified as suffering mental disorders who killed themselves were not uncommon.[1]

But the evidence does not permit a syllogism to be inferred from the deed of suicide under these circumstances. Not all—and the data suggests that not even most—of the men and women who chose to end to their lives were victims of mental illness. Indeed, to assume that there was something fundamentally "wrong" with the people who committed suicide is to negate the social reality in which they struggled to live their lives. The possibility of suicide as a rational act entered popular explanatory narratives early, as a deed possessed of an internal logic of its own, generally perceived as practical and plausible. As far as can be determined, most Cubans who chose to die had a firm grasp of their reality. They apprehended the deed of suicide as an act of individual volition, a deliberate self-inflicted death as an entirely reasonable and fully rational response to circumstances of affliction. The intent was to die. Suicide made sense, for death was the obvious solution to a condition when the problem was life itself. This is to construct a social meaning of suicide that implies above all consciousness of the deed and cognizance of intent as well as the capacity to summon awareness of purpose and anticipation of outcome. Under these circumstances, the desire to die must be seen as a disposition shaped by cultural models, usually in a manner consistent with commonly shared values. The act of suicide represented a gesture of self-affirmation, often a means of agency, and the measure of death under these circumstances can not fail but to include an assessment of life.

❧ Much had to do with prevailing belief systems, those canons that served as sources of coherence of kinship and community. The larger significance of religion as a factor in the phenomenon of suicide in Cuba is not consistently clear. Catholic condemnation of suicide was predicated on the proposition that life originated from God and that only God could separate the soul from the body. Suicide was tantamount to the usurpation of the authority of God by preempting divine power over life. "It is an error to believe that 'I am the master of my life and I can choose to do with it whatever I wish,'" insisted the weekly *Habana Católica*. "In fact, only God has legitimate and absolute claim over us. . . . Hence, we do not have the right to take our own life but [have] the duty to preserve it. We are merely usufructuaries (*usufructuarios*), not proprietors. . . . And if you intend to destroy that which is not yours, you are an outlaw."[2] Philosopher José Gálvez was unequivocal: "Under no circumstances of life can man exercise his impiety to the point of such barbaric extreme of killing himself." Suicide was a heinous crime, Gálvez insisted, and in its essence purported "to deny the existence of God and the immortality of the soul." He continued:

> If prior to arriving into the World man did not exist, and if upon open-ing his eyes he recognizes that he is not the creator of himself, he must realize that he is not the owner of what he has not created and conse-quently cannot dispose of that which is not his. . . . God in his infinite greatness . . . also gave man the power to reason. See how the suicide repays the goodness of the Creator: without knowing if his life has met God's designs, he dares to end it; without knowing if God calls him to his bosom, he dares to appear in his presence failing in the duties of his existence. . . . But there is more: the suicide must not only give an ac-count of his action to God, but he must also justify his action to society at large. From the time we enter the World we find ourselves bound by indestructible bonds to that congregation of brothers that is called society and to which we consign part of our free will. . . . Society can and should demand the suicide to account for a life that does not belong to him. Yes, the life of every man belongs to society: from the time we are born we contract an obligation to society that can be paid only with our living our lives. If we kill ourselves, how can we repay that debt?[3]

To commit suicide was to lose hope and abandon faith in God. No amount of privation, no length of suffering, justified death by suicide. "One commits suicide to escape other woes mistakenly judged to be worse than suicide," insisted theologian-philosopher Félix Varela. "That is, a per-son takes his own life because he does not have the courage to endure those other woes. Far from demonstrating valor, [suicide] is confirmation of pusillanimity." Writer Antonio Angulo y Heredia also used this argu-ment to condemn suicide. "If the heavy hand of misfortune falls upon our brow," he exhorted, "we must raise our eyes to heaven, asking Providence for the strength to endure our sorrow, to provide us with an example of holy resignation. . . . Even those weighed down with years, in the throes of pain, who see their suffering prolonged day after day: with the knowledge that their illness is fatal, do not have the right to accelerate their death. No: society demands the days, the hours, [and] the seconds that remain of their existence, because their example can be still useful to all those around them."[4] Catholic lay writer Alvaro de la Iglesia insisted that "poverty is a virtue," adding: "In order to endure the onerous weight of poverty, God has placed within our reach the virtues of patience, of acceptance, of resignation. By developing these virtues, which serve as a source of consolation, all struggles, all privation, all pain can be endured. . . . Even in the most humble household, in the most impoverished home, happiness can be found if there is love, if there is patience, if there is acquiescence to the will of God, who subjects us to these tribulations in order to allow us to demonstrate our faith."[5] Philosopher José de la Luz y Caballero was unequivocal: "What right does a man have to destroy that which is not his? That which may serve another purpose at a later time? Nonsense! . . . It is necessary to accept life under any conditions as a duty." For Luz y Caballero the meaning of suicide was indisputable: "Suicide. . . proves neither valor nor cowardice, it is a true disease, like fever. Like all illnesses it has many causes. Only the strongest religious and philosophical ideas can serve to overcome the tendency to suicide."[6] The only exculpation—and hence exoneration—of suicide was as a deed attributable to mental illness, behavior that was associated with insanity or the result of incoherence, in which case the demented person was viewed as victim and absolved of responsibility for the act of self-destruction.

It is not clear that Catholic doctrinal prohibitions against suicide had more than limited popular reach. In fact, Catholicism exercised only a tenuous hold over the lives of most Cubans. "*Habaneros* should be Catholics," traveler Nicolás Tanco Armero wrote of residents of Havana as early as 1861, "but many are indifferent to matters of religion."[7] José Antonio Saco brooded over what he perceived to be the relationship between rising suicide rates and declining religiosity. Saco was among the first to contemplate the sociological implications of suicide in Cuba, focusing upon a total of 346 suicides recorded in the census of 1862, including 173 Chinese workers, 130 African slaves, and 43 whites. Saco was not troubled by suicide among the Chinese, behavior he attributed to their "corrupt and perverse" nature. Nor was he concerned about suicide by Africans, a practice he ascribed to "ignorance." The 43 suicides by whites, however, drove

Saco to despair. "Certainly this figure is the lowest [of the three]," he conceded, "but note is taken of the fact that it involves our race. We must painfully recognize that we have gone a long way down this fatal path." Saco continued:

> I remember in my youth that suicide among whites was something of a phenomenon in Cuba. In those times, religious beliefs were far more prevalent and profound. Man was not totally fixated on his life on earth. During his tribulations he turned his eyes upward to heaven, and without succumbing to desperation he derived comfort from the idea of finding in another world the happiness that eluded him here among mortals. I will not deny that in those times superstition was far more prevalent than today. But I prefer this bane far more to impiety, for superstition rests on a base that presupposes a belief, and this belief acts to curb man and serves as a guarantee of the social order.[8]

More than twenty years later, physician Tomás Plasencia concluded that the capacity of the Catholic church to deter suicide in Havana appeared to have diminished markedly. Whereas previously the "denial of a religious burial to suicides . . . served to neutralize the pernicious influence of suicide to which this society was subject, the frequency with which people are currently perishing has increased in comparison with previous years." Warned Plasencia: "I see ahead many days of mourning for this society, a society that previously viewed suicide as something rare and with a certain amount of shock and pain. Today, in truth, its frequency makes suicide pass for something ordinary and commonplace."[9] In 1918, the *Diario de la Marina* attributed the rising rates of suicide to declining religiosity:

> All the parental love and sacrifice, all the philanthropic institutions, all the laws of man, and all the educational facilities are not sufficient when the will to live is not reinforced by religious beliefs. If there is no life other than the here and now, if the soul dies with the flesh, why then persist in a miserable existence oppressed by hunger, why suffer the torment and anguish of unrequited love, why endure cruel physical pain? . . . Souls not comforted by faith tremble . . . , they retreat in cowardice at the first sign of adversity and hardship. The oft-proclaimed triumphs of civilization, the marvelous advances of science, and the accumulated riches are not sufficient . . . to prevent a suicide. What is needed is prayer, a glance toward heaven to provide relief to the weight of life.[10]

Catholicism seemed to be of diminishing importance among increasing numbers of Cubans. Indeed, Cubans appeared more susceptible to the rationalist propositions that informed Masonic tenets and the materialist doctrines of communism than to religious precepts of the Catholic church. Then, too, Protestant evangelical denominations and *santería* offered alternative possibilities for meeting spiritual needs. Writing in the mid-1940s for the Catholic Association for International Peace, Richard Pattee lamented "the infiltration and flowering of secularism in Cuba," by which he meant principally Freemasonry and communism:

> Masonry took for itself much of the credit for the severance of the ties with Spain and by the same logic attributed to the Church a systematic antagonism to that independence. This particular conception of the history of Cuba has prevailed down to present time. . . . The Catholic Church is fully aware of . . . the infiltration of Communism. It must always be borne in mind that Communism in Cuba thrives because of the extraordinary maladjustments in the economic and social order; the absence of sufficient forces to express concern for the plight of the lowly and the humble; the fact that thousands of *guajiros* or peasants, live a hand to mouth existence in the rural areas with little hope of betterment for themselves and their families. In the urban centers, the problem of the proletariat has become acute. Workers . . . are bound to feel the impact of Communism if no other agency or doctrine is presented to them. . . . The work of Catholic organizations . . . is singularly opportune.[11]

Catholicism occupied an increasingly anomalous place in the lives of many Cubans. The Catholic Church was administered largely by Spanish clergy, ministering mostly to the needs of urban, white, upper middle-class congregations.[12] A survey in rural Cuba by the Agrupación Católica Universitaria in 1957 indicated that almost 55 percent of the population had never seen a priest and only 8 percent had personal contact with a priest. Of those who identified themselves as Catholic, nearly 90 percent never attended mass. Less than 5 percent attended church three times or more a year.[13] Only 16 percent of all marriages were officiated by the church, with the balance as civil ceremonies (39 percent) and consensual unions (45 percent).[14] Anthropologists Wyatt MacGaffey and Clifford R. Barnett wrote of the "Church's poor following," concluding that active Catholics made up a total of 10 percent of the population. "Churches continued to be found almost exclusively in urban areas," they wrote, and added: "Church congregations were made up largely of women from the middle class. The general male attitude was that religion was women's business and that the woman of the house was sufficient representative for the whole family." Sociologist Mercedes García similarly noted that the Cuban family was only nominally Catholic, because "in truth, religion as such was practiced almost exclusively by women in the cities; men due to fickleness or irreligiousness show a complete indifference."[15]

But it was not only that the Catholicism occupied a place of only nominal importance in the lives of most Cubans. At least as important was the fact that 41 percent of the Cubans surveyed in 1957 claimed to have no religion at all.[16] "There is no religious life at all," J. Merle Davis wrote of rural Cuba in 1942, adding: "The typical Cuban can hardly be called religious. Although the population is nominally Roman Catholic, the Church has small influence except among the women." Catholic lay philosopher Leslie Dewart wrote of the "profound alienation between the people and the clergy, (hence between the people and the sacraments and the liturgy)," noting that "indifference to the institutions of religion is the norm among Cubans." Added Dewart: "The Church and the clergy became figures . . . to be ridiculed." Historian Charles Chapman was succinct: "In Cuba the church seems to have lost its grip."[17]

Widespread religious detachment had far-reaching implications. What was particularly striking about the many hundreds of suicide notes published or summarized in the national press through the first half of the twentieth century was the infrequency with which reference to God and sin appeared. Only in rare instances did the men and women preparing to kill themselves ask for forgiveness from God or absolution for their sin. They were far more likely to ask for the forgiveness of loved ones.

Sociologist Emile Durkheim alluded to the power of religion, and especially Catholicism,—"Catholicism reduces the tendency to suicide," he insisted—to serve as a source of social integration and, through an all-encompassing body of moral and theological doctrine, to sustain normative proscriptions against suicide. Certainly for Catholics to kill themselves was to commit a mortal sin and thereby damn the soul to eternal perdition. But more was involved. Wrote Durkheim:

Religion has a prophylactic effect upon suicide. It is not . . . because it condemns it more unhesitatingly than secular morality, nor because the idea of God gives its precepts exceptional authority which subdues the will, nor because the prospect of a future life and the terrible punishment there awaiting the guilty gives its proscriptions a greater sanction than that of human laws. . . . If religion protects man against the desire for self-destruction, it is not that it preaches the respect for his own person to him with arguments *sui generis*; but because it is a society. What constitutes this society is the existence of a certain number of beliefs and practices common to all the faithful, traditional and thus obligatory. The more numerous and strong these collective states of mind are, the stronger the integration of the religious community, and also the greater its preservative value. The details of dogmas and rites are secondary. The essential thing is that they be capable of supporting a sufficiently intense collective life.[18]

❧ Insight into the disposition to suicide must be sought in the larger Cuban condition, to discern in the practice of self-destruction a socially defined and culturally validated pattern of behavior. The decision to die in this instance obtained social meaning within a context of cognitive process, as choice: that is, suicide not as an aberrant act or an irrational deed without awareness of outcome but, on the contrary, behavior as enactment of culturally approved conduct. As early as 1865, philosopher Diego de Fuentes at the University of Havana pondered the larger meaning of suicide and contemplated circumstances in which the decision to end one's life possessed historical logic. "It is an undeniable fact that in the lives of nations there are epochs of decadence in which the basest passions of people are released," he reflected, and continued:

> The notion of duty, the sentiment of justice, the love of liberty, all disappear: men scorn honor; women reject virtue. There is nothing to indicate the existence of the sentiment of morality. Treason and denunciation prevail. Slavery is sanctified; despotism dominates. Can those who act to end their lives under these calamitous circumstances be responsible for their deed? . . . Honorable citizens commit suicide, which is one thousand times far more preferable than the shame of submitting to tyranny. . . . To insist that suicide is committed only by the insane is to claim the impossible, it is to insult history and in the end to appear ridiculous. . . . Suicide is in its essence a personal and voluntary act, the clearest and conclusive manifestation of human liberty, the most forceful affirmation of man's superiority over his very nature.[19]

The function of culture in this instance is a matter of enormous complexity, either as a product of life as experienced or a means through which to experience life. The relationship was dialectical, of course, as the culture accommodated the phenomenon of suicide as an adaptive mechanism to destigmatize the deed even as it served as sanction for suicide, as frame of reference for social conduct and repository of social knowledge.

The larger significance lies in those circumstances from which suicide derived normative validation, from that body of generally shared meanings that served to sustain social consensus and model behavior, and more: from the system of received representations through which a people communicate to themselves collective attitudes toward life. Accommodation to suicidal death was central to this process. Suicide occupied a place of prominence in the public sphere, precisely at those conjunctures where convention and conduct combined to shape the sensibility of Cuban. In the end, suicide could obtain—and retain—cultural legitimacy only to the degree that it continued to discharge a socially useful function.

This is not to suggest, of course, that the act of suicide assumed the form of prescriptive imperative. It did not. But neither was it subject to proscriptive injunction. Suicide entered the realm of Cuban awareness as behavior that was at once culturally recognizable and socially acceptable, and the recurrence of self-inflicted death on such a scale could not but contribute to the circumstances that served further to enhance the efficacy of the deed.[20]

What matters too is an understanding of the multiple levels at which the normative coordinates of daily life acted in more or less coherent fashion to delineate sanction for self-destruction. The idea of suicide assumed a near pervasive presence in those domains of quotidian normality; the deed assumed such utter commonplace familiarity that it all but ceased to elicit anything more than passing acknowledgment. "Suicide as a newsworthy event in Cuba has become boring," *Carteles* could write in 1954. "With the possible exception of some spectacular occurrence, it lacks news interest."[21] Indeed, so prevalent a place had suicide come to occupy within realms of the commonplace that it could appear to be an ailment, like a headache or a common cold, for which existed a medication remedy.[22] In 1925, *Bohemia* magazine advertised Schering pills as a sure means to cure the afflictions contributing to suicide. One 1929 Bayer aspirin advertisement promised to relieve young women of "the desire to die." The Athaus medical practice in Havana pledged "results, not words" in its new regimen of "eminently humanitarian electric treatment for all nervous disorders" that contributed to suicide. In 1928, a number of local community organizations in Matanzas joined together to establish the Anti-Suicide

League (*la Liga Contra el Suicidio*) "to combat the alarming increase of suicides that is devastating a large part of our youth." The league announced its plans to use the press, public meetings, and active propaganda to "demonstrate the horrible consequences of suicide to society," adding: "It is important to emphasize the social responsibilities and sacred obligations contracted with the Patria [and] the circumstances in which the individual has had the good fortune to enter the world, to struggle and suffer valiantly, to prevail, in a word, and not succumb, over the shameful shortcomings found in society."[23] The Salvation Army in Cuba had another response. Reported the *Havana Post* in 1925:

> The Salvation Army recently made a statement regarding suicides. It was said that 'a $1 bill, a warm meal and the promise of a job will change the mind of almost any would-be suicide and tend to make him a valuable and optimistic citizen.' To some of us they come every day 'looking for a job.' If we could only look beneath the surface and know the pain and disappointment caused by our inability to give what they seek, we would surely do what we could for them. Perhaps it is some one who is thinking of committing suicide owing to his inability to find work who stands before us.[24]

❧ Suicide assumed fully the form of a culturally patterned practice, comprehensible within the context of the larger social environment, where life as lived was experienced in a combination of hopes and fears, joy and heartbreak, advances and setbacks, entwined always with the need to make vital decisions. Death by suicide appeared in the spaces of everyday life, where people engaged in the most commonplace and ordinary routines were subject to signals and suggestions by which the social meaning of life and death insinuated itself into all-inclusive modes of representation. The moral frequently found ratification in those aesthetic expressions by which conventions relevant to the conduct of the activities of day-to-day life came to be apprehended. These promptings were embedded within virtually all facets of institutional arrangements around which life was experienced, from conventions of family interaction to folkways, from popular culture to public morality, as both art imitating life and life simulating art. In the aggregate, these circumstances must be seen as the environment in which suicide was transformed from the unthinkable to the unremarkable.

Whatever else the commonplace invocation of self-inflicted death may

"Suicide is a crime, a manifestation of physical and mental weakness. Hence, take care of your health, cleanse your body, by taking Schering Pills, the most effective general antiseptic for internal and urinary systems. [It is a] powerful prophylactic against influences, angina, typhus, and all intestinal and biliary infections." From *Bohemia* 16 (December 27, 1925).

Advertisement for Bayer aspirin, with an endorsement from Señorita María Teresa Torrá: "I happened upon 15-year-old girls with desires to die. I thereupon, confidentially, suggested that they take CAFIASPIRINA and they all found [in Bayer] a sure relief for their afflictions." From *Bohemia* 21 (September 8, 1929).

A testimonial endorsement of a new electric shock treatment to cure the cause of suicide: "Many of us who have taken other types of electric treatment without success today enjoy perfect health due to this new method. This new advance of medical science is destined to relieve many victims of the pain and suffering that until now have been cruel and incurable and will reduce the frequent suicides among those who are tormented and tired of life." From *Bohemia* 8 (January 14, 1917).

have produced, it also served to make the proposition of suicide familiar, a readily available option within the reach of all as an acceptable response to a range of afflictions, large and small. In the process, it could not but have acted to diminish or otherwise dispel doubts about the propriety of suicide. This was an environment generally conducive to the contemplation of suicide as an appropriate solution to adversity, one that obtained if not popular approval then certainly public acquiescence as a normative circumstance. Indeed, the validation of the practice of suicide—through dominant cultural forms, in art and through literature, lodged within idiomatic formulations of conventional wisdom—served as the context in which ratification of the proposition of death by suicide gained currency.[25]

The practice of suicide entered realms of Cuban popular awareness through multiple mediums, each with discrete meaning, each embedded within a specific requirement of canons of comportment and codes of self-esteem. Suicide was the deed due for disgrace, understood as acknowledgment of and atonement for an act of dishonor. The culturally structured meaning implied less the possibility of recovering honor than repenting for dishonor, a way to discharge self-shame through self-destruction. The moral was enacted in the deed as obligatory gesture for unworthy behavior. But it is also true that notions of honor and shame were to a greater or lesser extent shaped within class-determined and gender-driven normative boundaries. Under other circumstances meaning implied deterrence and social control, pointing to suicide as prescriptive conduct for transgression of shared norms. Death by suicide was a common way out of a variety of deeds of dishonor. This consideration, for example, sets the model that drives a strike-breaker in Antonio Penichet's novel *La vida de un pernicioso* (1919) to take his own life. In this instance, male suicide served as atonement and punishment for having failed to live up to the code of the brotherhood of class. Reads the suicide note:

> I kill myself because it is impossible that I should live after having committed such a foul deed, of betraying my *compañeros* and the ideals that I have always supported. To be a strike-breaker, that is, to serve the interests of the bosses, to enable them to become slave drivers and craven exploiters, is an unspeakable deed. That is why I, who was a strike-breaker for a day—only for one day—consider myself an abject human being in this world. If I had courage to break a strike, then I also have the courage to commit suicide. I die, hence, like a man, repentant for

what I have done, but satisfied that I have applied to myself the punishment that my wrongdoing deserves.[26]

The failure to discharge duty demanded by class solidarity was compensated by upholding duty to gender, to have "the courage to commit suicide . . . like a man."

Suicide was possessed of multiple gender protocols in, for example, the distinct ways that men and women brought an end to their lives, generally apprehended as methods of death "properly" pertaining to the different ways that men and women lived their lives. The diversity of ways that men and women killed themselves entered popular consciousness as gender-fixed attributes of the act of suicide. Men killed themselves in certain ways by virtue of being men. In Pedro Juan Gutiérrez's novel *Dirty Havana Trilogy* (1998), in the chapter "Suicide of a Faggot," an unsympathetic nurse attending a failed suicide explains: "It was a suicide attempt, drug cocktail, sedatives and tranquilizer. And he injected air into his veins, too. His stomach and intestines were pumped, and now he's in critical condition, with a generalized infection. . . . That's how fags kill themselves. They want to do it but they don't have the. . . . Real men shoot themselves, hang themselves, or jump off a building." The gender and class connotations implicit in each method of suicide were set in relief in the short story "Mario in the Heaven's Gate," by Juan Francisco Pulido Martínez: "[Mario] had thought long about the best way to kill himself. He thought about an overdose of pills, but rejected pills for being too effeminate a way to commit suicide. He thought of a gun, but guns were too expensive and to steal one was a very bad idea because he was never any good at stealing anything. Hanging was the most practical method, although he believed that hanging was the method preferred by people of low culture and little intelligence."[27] The narrator in Marilyn Bobes's short story "Alguien tiene que llorar" (2001) reflects on the suicide of Maritza:

> They found her drowned. Like a character in a serial soap opera: an overturned glass and a half-empty bottle of rum on the tiled bathroom floor, a short distance away from the hand that hung over the edge of the bath tub. What remained of the pills in the mortar, still there atop the sink, and the wrinkled wrappers in the trash basket of the bathroom. At the wake, a man whose face seemed familiar said that it did not seem like the suicide of a woman. Except for the pills. It seemed too rational, anticipating the deep sleep from the barbiturates, sliding downward until her back rested on the bottom and water irreversibly filled her lungs.[28]

The gender and age disparities of suicide rates set in relief the differences in the ways that men and women experienced life, and especially the ways that normative systems acted to differentiate the sources of disappointment to which men and women were most susceptible. Women were obliged to live their lives within conventions very different from those of men, enjoined to uphold morality codes and family honor deeply invested in female sexuality. They were conducted into domains of social knowledge by way of models of virtue and norms of *una mujer decente*. That young women appeared particularly susceptible to suicide must be seen as an indication of the power of normative systems to exact penance from women who failed to live up to gender-driven ideals of womanhood. The standard for the decent woman had to do with sexuality, specifically with matters of virginity, illegitimacy, and marital fidelity, rendered in such characterizations as "a fallen woman" and "a dishonorable woman." These were codes imposed most rigorously on young women, complicated further by considerations of social class, where matters of disgrace and scandal could implicate family honor. The dishonorable deed of premarital sex also jeopardized marriage prospects. "The woman must know how to act virtuously at all cost," insisted one reader of *Carteles* identified as "a lady of the Havana high-life," "for as a rule men only marry virtuous women. . . . A woman who submits to dishonor could hardly be expected to perform as an honest wife and virtuous mother."[29] "To the single woman: Be a virgin! We do not care what desire in bloom is repressed," Mariblanca Sabas Alomá scorned the conventions designed to control the behavior of women. "To the married woman: Be faithful! We do not care at what humiliation, of how much suffering, of how many tears. Single or married, you are the repository of family honor. You suffer? It doesn't matter. That's why you were born a woman." In the short story "La pecadora," by Guillermo de Sanz, the protagonist, Julia, confides her infidelity to her best friend. The author has the friend respond: "You are not worthy of being a woman, for you are not loyal. . . . You are not a woman, you are a tramp."[30]

Received conventions acted in varying degrees to shape the private lives of young women. Norms of honor and dignity held women in their thrall as fully as men. "There are things worth more than life itself: honor, dignity, reputation," explained Margot García Maldonado. "Everyone dies — thousands of people die daily — and what remains among their loved ones is desolation and emptiness offset only by warm memories of the deceased. But 'moral death,' of one feeling buried in life, defamed and slandered, exposed to malicious gossip from the mouth of the insatiable monster that is public opinion, is worse—much worse!—than physical death, because one cannot aspire even to the hope of people forgetting and forgiving."[31]

It is impossible to ascertain, of course, the extent to which transgressions, including premarital sex, pregnancy, and illegitimacy, were factors in the high rate of suicide among young women. But that they were factors cannot be doubted. Seduction and betrayal in particular often had devastating effects. Shame and dishonor were often powerful factors in the suicidal behavior of women. On the matter of shame, historian Norbert Elias has correctly observed: "The individual's behaviour has brought him into conflict with the part of himself that represents . . . social opinion. It is a conflict within his own personality; he himself recognizes himself as inferior. He fears the loss of the love or respect of other, to which he attaches or has attached values. Their attitude has precipitated an attitude within him that he automatically adopts toward himself."[32] Adolescent Carmen Iglesias ran away from home, never to be heard from again, leaving behind a suicide note indicating that she had "sinned and now it can no longer be concealed," concluding: "I have given all, and it is useless to repent. I choose to die, rather than to listen to the world decry my dishonor."[33] During a prolonged courtship period, Rosinda recounted to Mirta de la Torre Mulhare, she acquiesced to her boyfriend's demands for sex, only to learn shortly thereafter that he was preparing to marry someone else. Rosinda remembered:

> I confronted him . . . and he did not deny it. He said I could not possibly expect him to marry me now since, after all I had done with him, he could not trust me as his wife. I wanted to kill him and kill myself. I became like a crazy woman. . . . He hit me and quieted me down but after that he refused to answer any of my calls at work or at home. I pursued him shamelessly but it was no use. . . . After what had happened I felt dirty and bad. I didn't think I could find a respectable man to marry me and my hope was to find a man to keep me well.[34]

Disgrace was not confined to an individual but often visited dishonor upon the entire family. Women were obliged to be mindful in ways that men were not of family reputation and were imbued at an early age with an understanding of the ways that personal conduct implicated family honor.[35] The narrative form in which women ordered a memoir of the personal almost always invoked family affiliation as the point of departure.

"I live in a small town," wrote one woman. "My family is generally well-known and highly respected. We are not fabulously wealthy, but we are well-off as a result of the high position of my father who owns a number of cattle ranches." "I belong to a decent family," wrote another unmarried young women twenty years of age upon learning she was pregnant, "with an honorable and decorous surname. We have always tried to follow the example of honor that our father has given us. . . . My life has become like a movie reel that I play in my mind over and over again: how my life was before and how much I have come to hate my life and what I have done to destroy my life. . . . In these moments of my disgrace what I want most of all is to die, for my heart is destroyed and I am without even the capacity to cry. I am in a state of desperation." María de los Reyes Castillo recounted the story of illegitimacy in her mother's life: "To avoid scandal, [the family] threw my mother, along with her baby boy, out of the house. There was no compassion. On the contrary, they accused my mother of being shameless and brazen. . . . Her life was sheer misery."[36]

The power of cultural canons to exact compliance to gender canons was often most forcefully suggested on those occasions where atonement for misconduct was registered through self-destruction as an act of self-punishment.[37] "Oh! If he doesn't honor his solemn word [to marry her]!" observes the narrator in Carlos Loveira's novel *La última lección* (1924). "The complete collapse of those supreme dreams, and the shame, and the pain, and the desperation of blighted hopes; all that tremendous moral disaster will overwhelm the strength of the poor girl. After that, prostitution. Or perhaps suicide." Nineteen-year-old Victoria González Llana attempted to kill herself, reported *La Lucha*, because "two months ago her boyfriend had seduced her and she felt herself betrayed because he refused to fulfill his promise of matrimony." Sixteen-year-old Juana Martínez set herself on fire, *Diario de la Marina* reported, "for having been seduced by Ramón Valero."[38]

It is in this context that the use of fire as a way by which women often killed themselves suggests social meaning. Much has to do with the place of fire in the sensibility of Cuban. Fire dwelled in the Cuban realms of awareness as a method of cleansing and renewal. "Fire cleans everything," poet María Elena Cruz Varela affirmed. "It purifies."[39]

Transgression of norms associated with idealized womanhood, including virginity, purity, and fidelity, appears to have often driven women to seek atonement by way of fire. "Women who kill themselves as a result of sexual reasons or romantic problems," one commentator suggested, "resort to fire with much greater frequency than women who kill themselves for other reasons." Fire in this instance was "a desperate erotic gesture."[40] The method of suicide implied self-inflicted pain as much as self-induced death. "Whereas in other forms of suicide," commented physician Jorge LeRoy y Cassá, "including hanging, drowning, poison, and fire arms, life is extinguished in short order and without great suffering, in the case of suicide by fire, dying is a prolonged process and is accompanied by great pain."[41]

The performance of suicide by fire was typically undertaken as a dramatic street event. Whereas suicide by most other means implied a private act, burning was a decidedly public event, undertaken in the presence of an audience, and almost always the subject of sensational press coverage. Reported the *Havana Post* in 1932:

> The spectacle of a human torch held spellbound hundreds of persons on the moon lit Malecón last night as 18-year-old Juliana Aballi Valdivieso dramatically obliterated the fires of misprized love in her heart in the more material flames of ignited alcohol. . . . Finding life no longer bearable, [she] decided to end her existence. And her plans for oblivion did not ignore the element of drama. Having previously selected her stage, a spot on the Malecón between Gervasio and Escobar, she repaired to the place at the time when the evening's throng of promenaders was the greatest. Before hundreds of spectators oblivious to the tragedy about to unfold before their eyes, she poured a bottle of alcohol over her clothing and struck a lighted match to it. Almost immediately her body was wrapped in a sheet of flame. Spellbound by the spectacle, the fire had consumed most of her clothing before those around her could rouse themselves to attempt her rescue. There is little chance for her recovery.[42]

Esperanza Rivero Prida committed suicide by fire after having sex with Ismael Consuegra, who after having promised marriage abandoned her.[43] The protagonist Tere in the novel *La situación* (1963), by Lisandro Otero— who had "learned from the nuns that everything having to do with sex was a sin"—experienced "disgust with the impurity of her body, a deepening and uncontrollable repugnance, for which she passed many hours in church praying." Tere finally ended her suffering by putting a match to her alcohol-soaked dress.[44] Ricardo Pau-Llosa's poem "Mulata" speaks powerfully to the deed of death by fire:

The shadow inside the flame will be human
for a while longer. Alcohol's bouquet is awash
in the incense of flesh, silk, and bone.
Only Buddhist monks and Cuban mulatas die like this.
Jilted and pregnant, it's either the whorehouse
or death by fire. By any means, but fire
is the preferred way because it cleanses . . .[45]

Women who survived a suicide attempt by burning appear to have expected to resume their lives with a sense of having survived a process of
purification. Survivors experienced renewal, observed one nurse in the
burn unit of Calixto García Hospital in Havana, and "now want to live more
than ever before and begin a new life."[46]

✿ Life experienced as struggle—*en la lucha*, as Cubans would say—
life known as a sequence of adversities alternating with setbacks always
held out the possibility of escape. Knowledge of suicide as an option both
readily accessible and generally acceptable, as a means to resolve the problems of life, gained early popular currency. Simply the capacity to imagine
the possibility of suicide could provide a source of comfort, a way to make
it through difficult circumstances by deriving consolation in the knowledge that, in the end, one always possessed as a last resort the means to
bring one's woes to an end. "I still have something that you can never take
away from me," affirms the protagonist in Humberto Rodríguez Tomeu's
short story "La musa." "I still have the power to die whenever I want to." In
the novel *Estrella Molina* (1946), writer Marcelo Pogolotti speaks through
his protagonist: "Well, if things really get so bad as a result of scientific
methods of repression, one can always resort to suicide." In the short story
"El suicida," writer Víctor Muñoz evoked the concept of "Platonic suicide,"
as the protagonist walks the city streets "contemplating the sweet peace-
fulness of death, no more problems, no more work, no more disquiet."
This was a way to get through life: "Death, what a pleasant prospect! How
delightful to think about it, and afterwards continue living until it finally
pleases one to put an end to the functioning of the human machine."[47]

The prominence of the option of suicide within the sensibility of Cuban, in its multiple aesthetic forms and social conventions, accurately reflected the range of cultural accommodations to the efficacy of suicidal
conduct. Indeed, the facility and the frequency with which the idea of sui-

cide entered the realms of the Cuban imagination as a plausible response to setbacks of consequence and insignificance alike served to confirm the power of normative determinants to shape dispositions to die.

The threshold at which individuals contemplated the act of suicide differed for everyone, of course. But what is striking is how often and indeed often how quickly Cubans arrived at that threshold. Ready recourse to suicide served as a literary staple. In Humberto Arenal's novel *The Sun Beats Down* (1959), the protagonist, Luis, has long contemplated the circumstances under which he would end his life: "The thought of going blind had always produced deep anxiety within him. From boyhood he had thought that if he were ever to lose his eye-sight he would commit suicide." In Virgilio Piñera's play *Aire frío* (1962), set in 1950, the character of Luz Marina recoils in horror at the prospects of living again through hard economic times similar to the 1930s, when she survived on a diet of flour and sweet potato: "Not me! At 15 years of age one can eat flour, but at 40. . . . Twenty capsules of [the barbiturate] seconal, you lay yourself down to sleep and no more stories to tell. . . . I propose that we buy a barrel of seconal. They say that one leaves with sweet dreams. Sweet dreams, darling." In the short story "Insomnia," Virgilio Piñera presents suicide as a response to sleeplessness: "The man goes to bed early. He can't fall asleep. He tosses and turns in bed, as might be expected. He gets tangled in the sheets. He lights a cigarette. He reads a little. He turns out the light again. . . . He does all that, but is still unable to fall asleep. . . . At six in the morning, he loads a revolver and blows his brains out. The man is dead, but hasn't been able to get to sleep. Insomnia is a very persistent thing."[48] In the short story "El chaleco del loco," by Pita Rodríguez, the protagonist kills himself as a result of his inability to button his vest. The autobiography on novelist Antón Arrufat's web page begins: "I was born in Santiago de Cuba on August 14, 1935, under the sign of Leo, obstinate and willful people, disposed to suicide when their projects failed." Journalist Iván Colás Costa recalled contemplating suicide in response to an unpleasant horoscope: "'Capricorn: Expect conflict from friends and acquaintances. It is imperative to exercise caution in all relationships. . . . Envious people will seek to damage your reputation and discredit you. The week promises to be adverse and you will have to struggle on many fronts. . . . You may be betrayed or deceived.' After having read my horoscope in this issue of *Bohemia* [magazine], the only thing left for me to do was to shoot myself."[49] In the short story "El juez de los divorcios," by M. Alvarez Marrón, a husband explaining to the judge his reason for seeking a divorce affirms: "[My wife] has me so fed-up,

Bisílabos Domésticos

TETÉ | PAPÁ
MAMÁ | FIFÍ
BEBÉ | PUM-PÚN

Cinco causas y una solución.

"Domestic Disyllables." Caption: "Five causes and one solution." From *Carteles* 9 (May 16, 1926).

so tired, and so bored that the very thought of living with her for another two weeks is sufficient for me to hang myself from a lamp post."[50]

Fact was at least as striking as fiction. Newspapers and magazines filled with accounts of men and women who seemingly killed themselves at the slightest provocation, often impulsively, sometimes impetuously. "Fans in the United States . . . must take a back seat to Cubans in baseball enthusiasm," reported *Collier's* magazine in 1951. "One fan threatened to kill himself if his team lost—and did!"[51] Nineteen-year-old Lidia López Arocha attempted suicide after losing her hearing. Guadencio Moreno Peno and Dulce María Conteras killed themselves in response to toothaches. Family servant Mercedes Malerio González committed suicide after being reprimanded by her employer. Sixteen-year-old Clara Torres attempted suicide because her family refused her permission to see a fireworks display. Digna Malina Hernández swallowed iodine after an argument with her younger sister; and Amelia Fernández Rico attempted suicide after an argument with a neighbor. Zoila Corral Azcuy attempted suicide due to her inability to nurse her baby.[52] In 1926 caricaturist Conrado Massaguer published a drawing in the magazine *Carteles* that provided a lighthearted solution for men facing five daily domestic woes: suicide as a way out of the aggravations of everyday life.

That the suggestion of suicide could be lighthearted should not obscure the reach of the proposition of suicidal death as solution. Humor often served as a powerful medium for the message. Suicide entered realms of popular self-representation with such commonplace occurrence as to render self-destruction an utterly familiar facet of the Cuban condition, and nowhere with more frequency that in Cuban domains of humor. The Cuban *choteo*—and the verb form *chotear*—combined a pose of irreverence with rejection of solemnity: a proclivity, essayist Mario Guiral Moreno wrote, "to mock and make light of all facets of life, even the most serious," adding: "The Cuban never misses the opportunity to seize upon the ridiculous side of everything that happens."[53] The choteo engaged those otherwise grave circumstances of life, the mishaps and the misfortune, from a stance of self-protective scorn. "Choteo is a type of mysterious assuagement emanating from popular consciousness," wrote essayist Antonio Gómez in 1902, "taking the form of mocking poetic expression [and] a sardonic scoffing of pain. . . . Everything is included within its scope." To laugh at something, especially something somber, writer Jorge Mañach explained, constituted a social gesture of protest against the solemnity of life, a way to scoff at the sacred: the combination of hubris and humor as defense of humanity. "Nothing is taken seriously," one Cuban explained to anthropologist Mirta de la Torre Mulhare, "not even death."[54] Perhaps nowhere was the proposition of suicide disassociated from the gravity of the gesture and with greater irreverence than in vignettes and anecdotes and in a variety of artistic forms, principally cartoons, caricature, and comic strips. "The visual data . . . ," wrote Fred Cutter in his study of art and suicide, "documents the transition of historical expectation into contemporary notions held by society in general and by the victims in particular."[55]

The theme of suicide expanded into Cuban realms of awareness by way of humor, through wit and whimsy, presented often with irony and cynicism, something to make light of and joke about. It is possible to contemplate an even higher rate of suicide without the resort to humor as a coping mechanism. "Perhaps the best defense against suicide," D. J. Enright has suggested, "is a strong sense of humour, of irony, and hence the ability not to take oneself dead seriously."[56] In the short story "Mi suicidio por amor," by Antonio Abalos, the protagonists, María and Antonio, agree to a suicide pact. As María lies dying she pleads, "Antonio, don't fail to die with me." Antonio recounts: "I was about to shoot myself when I realized that I had not paid up my annual subscription to the magazine *Muñecos*, and logically I postponed my suicide. Later, I just couldn't bring myself to commit suicide. Now, María's ghost comes to haunt me every night. She's really pissed off at me. Yesterday she threw an ashtray at my head and made an obscene gesture." In the short story "Un suicidio," by Juan de Dios Mohedano, Raquel prepares her suicide after her husband leaves town. The narrator relates: "The gun makes too much noise. The knife might fail. Leap from the window? No, that wouldn't work given the fact that she lives on the first floor. Poison? No. Poison results in terrible stomach pains and it's too slow. The only way that remained was open to full-blast the stove gas burners. Raquel turned them on without hesitation." When several days later the husband returns home to find his wife's body, continues the narrator, "he began to weep inconsolably. His friend, moved by his despair, sought to comfort him. He responded: 'If it were only a matter of the death of my wife, I would have already gotten over it. But what is most grievous, what really hurts me and drives me to despair, is the gas bill I will have to pay this month." In the whimsical ode "La prórroga de un suicidio," Manuel Pinos tells the story of Juan Antonio Loza, "who for a long time has been preparing to kill himself but always finds one reason or other to postpone the date of his suicide." On one occasion the suicide was planned for Sunday morning in response to unrequited love. "After that Sunday, I met him on the street.—'What? You didn't kill yourself?' I asked.—'No, I couldn't on Sunday like I wanted to. I had to postpone it for another day because I realized that I had to take my clothes to the laundry. You can't kill yourself leaving behind dirty underwear.'" The story continues with a new date for the suicide selected and postponed again, always for a trivial reason, and ends with the narrator exhorting his friend: "Look, enough is enough! You cannot continue to live a lie. You must fulfill your pledge. I will resolve your problem easily enough. Either you take your proclaimed last breath on Saturday at 4 p.m. exactly or I will shoot you the next time we meet."[57] In the satirical essay "Hay que reformar el suicidio," B. Jiménez Perdomo proclaimed that "we are supremely bored with the common ways of suicide, with the shootings, the poisonings, with the slitting of throats, with the hangings, and the jumping from heights. No, you would-be suicides, this state of affairs cannot continue. . . . You must find new ways to kill yourselves. I may be upsetting the established social order by suggesting in this article new methods of suicide . . . but I insist it is necessary to change the old system." Jiménez Perdomo continued:

Some days ago my friend Maximino Pérez informed me of his intention to kill himself, to which I responded—'I'm sorry, how terrible your situation must be.'—'I cannot stand my mother-in-law,' he explained in despair.—'What are you going to do?' I asked.—'Poison myself,' he answered soberly.—'Enough of that usual poisoning!' I replied indignantly.—'No, you're mistaken,' Pérez assured me. 'I'm going to bite my mother-in-law.' Two days later I received news of the death of my friend and the request to attend his funeral. When I arrived, sure enough, his mother-in-law had a bandage on her arm. I understood then that Pérez was a suicide worthy of my friendship and deserving of this chronicle, which signifies a eulogy: To an excellent friend and a no less excellent suicide.[58]

Cartoons depicting suicide appeared with remarkable frequency in all the principal newspapers and magazines, never with a hint of censure or an indication of disapproval. Not all cartoons were of Cuban origins. Some were from foreign sources, with the accompanying captions published in translation. But it was the frequency of their publication that spoke to the Cuban condition. It is difficult to identify another culture in which the subject of suicide was presented as often with greater levity or more light-heartedness than in Cuba. The cartoons portrayed male suicide, mostly by way of hanging, firearms, and drowning. Suicide notes were often prominently depicted. What is striking is that the humor is derived entirely from the circumstances of men killing themselves. Suicide by women appears not to have been a laughing matter.

This was choteo in full stride. Some cartoons derived their humor from the incongruous and the absurd; others mocked the human afflictions that led to the decision to die. Some invoked suicide as humor to address a larger social circumstance of death as an option preferable to other alternatives. They were at once product of and contributed to the clichés of daily life, especially as they related to matters of courtship and marriage. Many spoke to the clever ingenuity associated with preparation for suicide, of the creative energy deployed by people determined to kill themselves by whatever means most readily at their disposal. The popularity of the cartoons suggests one more way that the circumstances of suicide assumed a presence as a factor of ordinary and commonplace standing in the course of daily life. If historian John Johnson is only partially correct in his observation that cartoons offer "invaluable clues to the mood and mores and underlying attitudes of the society that produced and accepted them," the significance of the theme of suicide in Cuban cartoons cannot be exaggerated.[59]

❧ The efficacy of suicide obtained further endorsement in the multiple realms of public transactions, in the popular articulation of metaphor and allegory, in those usages of commonly shared figures of speech

Passerby: What are you doing up there?
Pole sitter: I'm going to hang myself.
Passerby: Why don't you put the rope around your neck?
Pole sitter: I already had it on my neck, but I couldn't breathe.
From *Bohemia* 19 (September 25, 1927).

Reporter: "Hurry up if you want to make the afternoon edition."
From *Carteles* 10 (November 6, 1927).

—"You're going to kill yourself? Are you crazy?"
—"It's just that I'm so bored."
—"Well, if you're going to kill yourself, do it in a way that you'll find entertaining."
From *Bohemia* 20 (April 22, 1928).

"The suicide, or the man who does everything backwards." From *Bohemia* 21 (June 2, 1929).

"The magician commits suicide." From *Bohemia* 24 (December 18, 1932).

—"Is the train that passes here late?"
—"It is a half-hour late. But if you're in a hurry, another train is scheduled to pass on the other tracks within 5 minutes."
From *Bohemia* 30 (April 3, 1938).

"And my parents said I would never reach a high position in life!" From *Bohemia* 30 (July 23, 1938).

"You rang, sir?" From *Carteles* 28 (November 3, 1946).

"Please! People are watching!" From *Bohemia* 40 (May 31, 1948).

"You wretch! Do you want to kill me?" From *Bohemia* 45 (May 24, 1953).

'Suicide." From *Bohemia* 45 (April 12, 1953).

"What was this knot supposed to remind me to do?" From *Bohemia* 45 (June 19, 1953).

"Suicide." From *Bohemia* 45 (June 21, 1953).

"Final preparations." From *Bohemia* 45 (August 9, 1953).

"Wait. . . . Wait my darling! It appears that I will be free this afternoon." From *Bohemia* 45 (August 2, 1953).

"It's clear: you don't know what else to do to spoil my vacation." From *Bohemia* 45 (September 6, 1953).

"What time is high tide?" From *Bohemia* 45 (October 18, 1953).

"Everything is aligned, sir." From *Carteles* 36 (January 17, 1954).

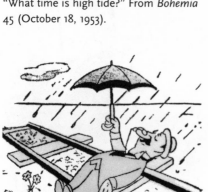

"The suicide of the rheumatic." From *Bohemia* 45 (November 8, 1953).

"Now you'll see whether or not I'm capable of killing myself." From *Carteles* 35 (May 2, 1954).

"Don't be so stupid! Let me show you how to make that knot." From *Bohemia* 46 (May 16, 1954).

"My God, Vicente! The mirror that mamá just gave me as a gift!" From *Bohemia* 47 (April 10, 1955).

"If the answer is NO—simply pull the string." From *Bohemia* 46 (October 3, 1954).

"Suicide." From *Carteles*, 36 (July 24, 1955).

"I wanted to commit suicide, but I didn't have any bullets." From *Bohemia* 47 (August 7, 1955).

"Careful with the vase!" From *Carteles* 36 (September 11, 1955).

"Photo souvenir." From *Carteles* 36 (October 2, 1955).

"Ernesto! You're going to wake up the baby!" From *Carteles* 36 (October 10, 1955).

"Complaint." From *Carteles* 37 (April 8, 1956).

"Have you forgotten that we have guests coming over this evening?" From *Carteles* 37 (March 25, 1957).

"When are you going to give up that vile habit of dropping the ashes on the floor?" From *Carteles* 37 (April 28, 1957).

"Suicide." From *Carteles* 37 (October 7, 1956).

HUMORISMO CRIOLLO

"Silent Tragedy." From *Bohemia* 49 (May 5, 1957).

"The fakir commits suicide." From *Bohemia* 50 (April 6, 1958).

— "Me, because she left me."
— "And me, because she returned."
From *Carteles* 37 (June 2, 1957).

"Determination." From *Bohemia* 50 (April 20, 1958).

"Suicide." From *Bohemia* 50 (July 20, 1958).

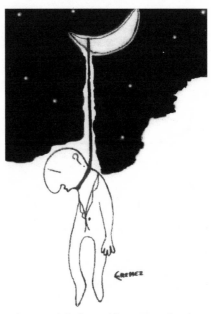

"The poet kills himself." From *Bohemia* 50 (December 14, 1958).

"Eleven thousand four hundred fifty-six. . . . Eleven thousand four hundred fifty-seven. . . . Eleven thousand four hundred fifty-eight. . . ." From *Carteles* 39 (September 21, 1958).

"Dramatic mendicant." From *Bohemia* 52 (January 17, 1960).

"El Hombre Siniestro (Prohías)." From *Bohemia* 51 (February 1, 1959).

"Hanging Prohibited." From *Bohemia* 52 (June 26, 1960).

"Love and Philosophy, or the suicide changes his mind." From *Bohemia* 25 (March 26, 1933).

and frames of reference that served to reveal deeper truths, in the ways that idiomatic constructs and vernacular forms of communication transmitted dispositions that bind a people together as a culture. Many of the assumptions of everyday life, and especially the degree to which those assumptions served to convey the logic of collective conduct, revealed themselves through commonplace usage, as adages and aphorism, as maxims, proverbs, and cliches.

Suicide assumed paradigmatic form through the frequent use of metaphorical constructs to represent self-destruction as consequence of imprudent decisions. Indeed, the metaphors were themselves powerful cognitive instruments that contributed to a larger cultural context and social environment. The decision by nineteenth-century pianist Ignacio Cervantes to remain in Cuba, for example, rather than live abroad and pursue a career in the great concert halls of Europe, was characterized by several of his biographers as "artistic suicide." José Martí evoked the notion of suicide as allegory to convey the consequences of undesirable government policies. If Spain acquiesced to Cuban independence, Martí predicted in 1873, "it would guarantee its existence, the same way that if it did not it would be committing suicide." And Martí on another occasion: "A people commit suicide the day that they entrust their subsistence to a single product." The daily *La Lucha* in 1891 argued that enacting a proposed political measure was "truly to commit suicide."[60]

Almost every aspect of daily life seemed to evoke similitude with suicide. Or perhaps it was the other way around: evoking suicide was a means with which to make sense of daily life. The possibility of suicide dwelled in the foreground of Cuban awareness. As social language it assumed epistemological form as argument, reasonable and plausible, possessed of a logic that was not easily undone. *La Habana Elegante* could affirm that "for the poet who lacks a thorough linguistic and cultural knowledge of the new setting, voluntary emigration is suicide." After a series of fatalities in bus accidents during the late 1920s, *La Lucha* warned: "To travel by bus is synonymous with suicide." Increased automobile traffic had transformed the Malecón into a congested highway, commentator Eladio Secades complained in 1953, and any attempt to cross was an "undertaking of suicide." For M. Millares Vázquez, the decline of public civility in Cuba was leading society "toward suicide." In a 1911 essay entitled "Un suicidio original," writer Enrique Barbarrosa uses the image of a woman running desperately through the streets of Havana, reaching El Morro, ascending the lighthouse, and leaping to her death. "Who was that woman in tatters that killed herself, who plunged into the ocean?—It was national decency (*La vergüenza nacional*)." In the short story "Suicidio," by María Teresa C.M., the protagonist, Clarita Marzo—described as "a delicate romantic woman, ultra-sensitive, filled with dreams"—announces her intention to commit suicide after having abandoned hope of fulfilling "the divine hopes in my soul." In this instance, the "suicide" is registered as a marriage announcement in the newspaper: "Miss Clarita Marzo, in the presence of a justice of the peace, was married to the popular heavy-weight boxer John Bill, known in the sports world as 'The Beast from the West.'"[61]

Debates of public policy and political discourse often employed the idea of suicide as allegory. Editorials ranged from a critique of employment law (*Una ley buena que se torna suicida*), to a budget debate (*Técnica presupuestal suicida*), to a lamentation of sugar export policy (*La tragedia del azúcar, o un pueblo que quiere suicidarse*).[62] *La Lucha* warned in 1921 that "without a rectification in all aspects of Cuban public life . . . the inevitable alternative would be national suicide."[63] In 1936, as a struggle for power between Colonel Fulgencio Batista and President Miguel Mariano Gómez threatened a political crisis, *Bohemia* warned that the deepening "intrigue is suicide." Columnist Diego Boada criticized a proposed taxation project in 1951, warning that a "government that unjustly attacks earnings is committing suicide." In 1957, writing about the failures of the Ortodoxo Party, columnist Otto Meruelo affirmed that partisan disputes had "taken the Ortodoxos to their ideological suicide."[64] Luis Aguilar León wrote of "the suicide of the Right in Latin America" and the necessity "to change suicide tactics." "The Cuban bourgeoisie has committed suicide four times," writer Jesús Díaz pronounced in his essay on the watershed years of 1825, 1866, 1895, and 1959. In the novel *En el año del enero* (1963), set in the year 1959, José Soler Puig speaks through his protagonist, Felipe Montemayor, reflecting on the need for some kind of reconciliation with the United States—"Anything else would be suicide." To have launched the Bay of Pigs invasion in 1961 without guarantee of U.S. assistance, writer María del Carmen Boza insisted, was tantamount to having embarked on a "suicidal mission." Delfín Rodríguez Silva, writing after twenty-five years of exile in the United States, looked back to January 1959, when Fidel Castro entered Havana, and affirmed: "For us it was like a collective suicide."[65] In 1961, Fidel Castro pondered the demise of imperialism as a function of suicide: "We have always said that we know that imperialism will disappear, that it is historically condemned to disappear, but we do not want

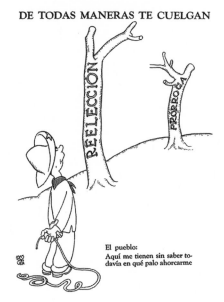

DE TODAS MANERAS TE CUELGAN

El pueblo:
Aquí me tienen sin saber todavía en qué palo ahorcarme

"In either case, they hang you."
Caption: "The People (*el Pueblo*):
Here I am, without knowing from
which branch to hang myself."
From *Carteles* 11 (April 29, 1928).

it to commit suicide at our expense. . . . That is, [we do not want it to] commit suicide on the occasion of an attack against us." More than thirty years later, reflecting on the collapse of the Soviet Union, Castro observed: "I might say that communism destroyed itself, that it committed suicide in the USSR, and that it had no reason for committing suicide."[66]

Political caricature often made metaphoric use of suicide to convey the outcome of public policies and political arrangements. In one 1928 caricature depicting *el pueblo* (the people) confronting the determination of President Gerardo Machado to remain in office through either an extension of his term or reelection to a new term—the upper caption of which read: "In either case they hang you"—the outcome was represented as foregone suicide for *el pueblo*. In 1932, the Machado government enacted the *reajuste*, a cost-saving measure that reduced the salaries of all public employees—except members of the armed forces—by 10 percent. A political cartoon that year depicted a civil servant preparing to plunge to his death. In a 1943 caricature, a dismissed civil servant facing the prospect of a change of presidential administrations is shown about to kill himself. The larger issue depicted by both cartoons, of course, is men preparing to kill themselves in response to the loss of wages and employment.

Stories that passed into folk narratives often invoked suicide as solution. One story with multiple endings tells of a prostitute who placed her daughter in a Catholic orphanage. When the daughter reaches the age of

An Ambience of Suicide | 279

"After *Reajuste*."
— "Is that a swimming champion?"
— "*Chico*, I think he's a public
  employee."
From *Bohemia* 24 (December 11, 1932).

DESPUES DEL REAJUSTE
—¿Ese será un campeón de na-
tación?
—Chico, yo creo que es un
empleado público.

eighteen she seeks to discover the truth about her mother. In one version, the daughter kills herself upon learning that her mother was a prostitute. In another version, the mother commits suicide rather than reveal her past to her daughter. In a third version, the daughter is engaged to the son of the man who is also her father. The mother is forced to tell the daughter the truth, whereupon the daughter kills herself.[67]

Readily available clichés and proverbial formulations also served to facilitate assimilation of suicide as a commonplace facet of everyday life, rendered as an option preferable to any number of undesirable outcomes. Popular usage invoked suicide as metaphor, both as vocabulary and vernacular with which to give dramatic emphasis to dread of some real or imagined fate. One popular cliché, used almost entirely by women, was the vow to slash one's wrist (*me corto las venas*) rather than face some disagreeable or demeaning fate.[68] "It is preferable to commit suicide than to commit an act of dishonor," asserts another popular maxim. News of a suicide was often met with some variation of *El pobre, no le quedó otro remedio* ("The poor guy had no other choice"). The circumstance in which one's own miscalculation or mistake resulted in one's misfortune was characterized in the saying: *Como a Chacumbele, que él mismito se mató* ("Just like Chacumbele, that he himself killed himself").[69] The saying *Tener un chino atrás* ("To have a Chinese behind one") was to be cursed, to live under a shadow impelling one toward suicide. *Ahorcarse* ("to hang oneself") was

—"You're going to kill yourself just because you have been dismissed? Listen, old man, they can reinstate you."
—"Yes, but for them to reinstate me I'd have to vote for [Presidential candidate Carlos] Saladrigas." From *Bohemia* 35 (August 8, 1943).

to find oneself in a dreadful situation. One also *se ahorca*—usually referring to men—when getting married.[70]

❧ It was within the context of the family that many Cubans first experienced the emotional function and social meaning of suicide, and from which the discursive modes of self-destruction thereupon expanded into the realms of the ordinary and commonplace. The use of suicide as a means to negotiate interpersonal relationships found its earliest expressions within the intimacy of the household, at once a way of social control and cultural formation.

Awareness of the possibility of suicide was often first registered within the deeply emotional domains of primary family relationships. Indeed, the family served as one of the principal sites for the reproduction of cultural meanings by which the practice of suicide obtained normative validation, specifically where the plausibility of self-destruction was first experienced and the utility of suicide was transmitted.

It is thus possible to view the propensity to suicide as a learned disposition, acquired within the household as a function of socialization. The norms that validated the efficacy of suicide originated within the household and subsequently passed as the moral currency by which to negotiate leverage. Suicide acquired an instrumental function, a means to parlay or otherwise trade on one's life—in the absence of other forms of leverage—to obtain outcomes, and thereupon developed into learned behavior, taught and transmitted as a means of commonplace interaction. In this instance the threat of suicide was employed as a child-rearing practice, to induce compliance with parental wishes and, of course, in the end, even if unwittingly, an act of socialization. Amalia Simoni described to her husband the ways of their four-year-old son: "On those occasions that he engages in those mischievous behaviors so common to his age, the punishment that I have imposed is to refrain from kissing him for two or three hours, or to tell him that I am going to die if my boy does not obey me." Mónica Reyes Ramos recalled her mother's way of exacting obedience: "When we did anything she didn't like, she wept and ranted and said we were killing her. One of her favorite tragic outbursts was, 'My children don't love me!' Or else, 'I'm going to kill myself.'" Monica's sister Renée had similar memories: "She'd say she was going to die or kill herself . . . , that I should go away. . . . When she was carrying on I'd get very nervous and want to change all the things she talked about, so I'd say, 'Forgive me. I won't do it anymore. I love you.'"[71] Evelio Grillo wrote of growing up with four brothers and sisters and of "the rigid, extreme control [mother] exercised over us and the ways she maintained it, including . . . threatening to harm herself if we did not behave. 'I am going to hang myself from a telephone pole!' she would scream at us when we had driven her to distraction."[72]

The frequency with which parents actually acted out their threat of suicide is not known. It is perhaps sufficient to indicate that such cases were not unknown. Jacinto Navarro Guadalupe attempted to stab himself to death, the *Diario de la Marina* reported, as a result of the "disobedience of his daughter." Belarmino Ricardo attributed the decision to kill himself to "no longer being able to endure the misbehavior of my daughters, which has brought so much grief to my life."[73]

Patterns established early as the logic of the household regimen often persisted unchanged for decades thereafter. It is fully within the realm of the plausible that the use of the threat of suicide used to manipulate the behavior of young children could also serve to control the conduct of adult children. In Beatriz Rivera's novel *Playing with Light* (2000) Rebecca's mother is in a permanent condition of disgruntlement, unhappy with her lot and especially resentful at being ignored by her daughter. Suicide is never far from her mind. "If I had known that this was my lot in life," she muses, "I would have gladly killed myself." At another point Rebecca overhears her parents quarreling, and her mother exclaims: "I'm tired of life! I want to die! Your daughter treats me like dirt! She's an ungrateful shit! My biggest failure." And at another point, the mother complains to Rebecca: "I have nothing to live for. . . . I should have had more children, it's been three days since I last spoke to you and yesterday I got a hold of [your daughter] Nell and she told me she was too busy doing her homework to talk to me, is that what you teach her, to have absolutely no love for me?"[74]

The threat of suicide as a means of leverage could be reversed, of course, and just as easily used by children as a way to exact parental acquiescence to their demands. Propensities to suicide were registered as early as childhood, and indeed the suicidal tendencies among Cuban children were nothing short of astonishing. Sociologist Antonio Estévez Carrasco lamented what he characterized in 1925 as a "veritable and profound social epidemic," and took particular note of suicide among children: "The deplorable example [of suicide] finds easy converts and rare is the day that we do not read newspaper accounts of these lamentable acts. This past spring has been terrible: boys 13 years of age attempting to kill themselves on account of failing grades in school; pubescent girls attempting to cut off the flower of their existence as a result of romantic discord. . . . It seems that children emerge from the cradle believing that life has no value worthy of preserving. It is lamentable that there are children who, at precisely the most wonderful time of life, at that age when everything should be hopes and dreams, already believe that life is without value."[75]

Suicide of children necessarily calls attention to the most intimate realms of family life, to the character of adult-child relationships, to parenting and child-rearing practices. "The propensity to suicide among youngsters," columnist M. Millares Vázquez observed in 1956, "is a phenomenon of our times." He continued: "It occurs often, every day with increasing frequency, a youth otherwise well-to-do, in an economically comfortable position, possessing the resources to meet all necessities, comes up against some small setback or obstacle—and it is as if the whole world has collapsed all around him. . . . It is not the fault of the youth, of course, but of parenting."[76]

Other facets of child-rearing practices may have further contributed to the disposition among youngsters to die by suicide. Anthropologist Mirta de la Torre Mulhare described the process of socialization of children, observing that "the child is asked to be an adult in miniature, without the rights and privileges of an adult but with many of his obligations." Cuban children thus learned a variety of methods to negotiate parental authority —or subvert it altogether. De la Torre Mulhare writes of the romanticism, sentimentality, histrionics, and intensity that Cuban children often displayed at an early age, including threats to run away. "The Cuban child . . . ," she writes, "does not accept parental, especially maternal, domination without resistance. Not only does he threaten to run away, but he has frequent outbursts of violent temper—to be expected within a cultural milieu that encourages the expression of emotion."[77]

The circumstances that prompted children to wish to die were not uncommon and included resentment, or fear of punishment, or thwarted desire, or family conflict, among other factors. The threat of suicide, that is, the imposing of conditions for continued living, speaks in profound ways to strategies routinely employed to engage the circumstances of daily life, beginning in childhood. Living was made contingent and conditional upon demands being met. Virginia Schofield recounts the story of one Cuban boy who demanded money from his mother, threatening: "If you don't give me money, I will kill myself"—to which the mother responded with 25 cents and the suggestion: "Here, go buy yourself some rope."[78] Many years later writer María del Carmen Boza remembered a childhood moment:

> Once when I was seven or eight [my father] poured his wrath on me, calling me an ingrate and threatening to beat me, when I repeated what I had heard from adults, with a great sigh, 'I wish I were dead.' Yet one afternoon in our living room in Miami in my eleventh year or so, my father said to me, 'If it weren't for you and your mother I would have committed suicide a long time ago.' He did not say it as if he were grateful to us, but rather as if our existence presented a huge burden of responsibility that kept him from fulfilling his fondest wish.[79]

Children appeared especially susceptible to suicide in the aftermath of reprimand and punishment by parents. The patterns suggest the use of suicide as a way for children to punish their parents, to pursue revenge by inflicting grief on their parents. Ten-year-old Roberto Fernández Estrada reacted to a scolding by his father by attempting to stab himself to death. Fourteen-year-old Luis Varas Pérez and fifteen-year-old Juan Cagiga

González responded to scoldings by their mothers by poisoning themselves to death.[80]

Published news accounts suggest that adolescent girls—more than boys—showed greater propensities to suicide as response to family attempts to control their behavior. Thirteen-year-old Juana Nicot set herself on fire after a scolding by her parents for having disobeyed them. Fifteen-year-old Zoila Núñez Lavastida attempted to poison herself after having been reprimanded by her older brother for having left the house without permission. Sixteen-year-old María Teresa Alvarez killed herself after being scolded by her mother for having gone to a dance without permission. Felicia Campos Zamora, fifteen years old, attempted to poison herself after being reprimanded for having returned home late from a party.[81] Adolescent América Nuicel Mongor from San Antonio de los Baños attempted to kill herself because her family's decision to move into the countryside would have required separation from her boyfriend.[82] Fifteen-year-old Regia Leonor Morales explained in her suicide note that her decision to die was the result of being "weary of family members who embittered [my] life with the constant scolding."[83] Adolescent Aurora Novón explained her decision to burn herself to death as a result of the mistreatment she had received from her mother. Eighteen-year-old Amelia Casanova attempted suicide after an argument with her father. The reason given for fifteen-year-old Isabel Cordoví Maderos burning herself to death was "family conflicts." After being scolded by a neighbor, fourteen-year-old Francisca Hernández García set herself on fire.[84]

Pressure to perform well at school similarly took its toll. Adolescent Prudencio Pérez Megret in Guantánamo died of a self-inflicted gunshot wound after having failed two courses at the Instituto Provincial. Juan Pablo Lascaille shot himself after having been reprimanded by his parents for poor grades in school. Eleven-year-old José Avalos Toledo was so unhappy at school that he decided to kill himself rather than continue going.[85]

Adolescent boys and girls—the latter more often than the former—whose parents sought to thwart romantic relationships frequently threatened suicide as a way to obtain parental acquiescence. The threat of suicide often involved circumstances of cross-racial or interclass relationships, where the desire to marry was thwarted by parents, inspired by the young couple's idea that if they could not live together they would die together.[86] Alfredo Barrera recalled the experience of his adolescent sister Anita: "Papá still tried to persuade Anita to give up [her boyfriend] Echegarrúa, but she faced up to all of us and said if she couldn't marry him she'd kill herself." One nineteen-year-old described how "my parents and sisters turned against me and asked me what could I possibly be thinking by contemplating marriage with a man not of my same social class. . . . There are times that I think of killing myself."[87]

Nor were these idle threats. The impact of dashed romance often fell upon young women with particularly traumatic effect. Writer Ofelia Domínguez remembered the early twentieth century and "the extreme measures that were taken when parents were opposed to a daughter's relations," and added: "In the best of circumstances, the girl was prohibited from all communication with the boyfriend. If that failed to end the relationship, she was locked up. In some cases this had fatal results, provoking elopement and even suicide."[88] Fifteen-year-old Patrocina Raboso shot herself after her mother opposed her relationship with Manuel Casanova on account of their being too young. Prohibited by her parents from seeing her boyfriend—"who she loved dearly," commented *La Lucha*—nineteen-year-old Constancia Sueyras González attempted to poison herself. Fourteen-year-old Amparo Endreida attempted to kill herself when her mother insisted that she end her relationship with Aniceto Hernández. Nineteen-year-old Carmen Losada burned herself to death when her father objected to her boyfriend.[89]

Double suicides committed by lovers were not uncommon. The suicide pact was often precipitated by some specific circumstance, real or imagined, that threatened to bring a romantic relationship to an end, typically in the form of parental intervention. Parents exercised considerable authority over their children, especially daughters, in matters of courtship and marriage. Marriage without parental blessings was not, of course, impossible, but neither was it advisable. Parental disapproval could easily threaten a relationship. Juanita Batorre and Pedro García killed themselves when her father demanded that she end the relationship, insisting that García was "an impoverished young man, without initiative, without a future." In Manzanillo sixteen-year-old Rafaela Martínez and eighteen-year-old Wenceslao Castro committed suicide together—she by poison and he by firearm—in what *La Lucha* called *un drama de amor*.[90] Suicide under these circumstances often suggested a means of consummation of love. Lucila Betancourt, fifteen years old, and Carlos Varela, seventeen years old, despondent over their parents' opposition to their marriage, chose St. Valentine's Day in 1955 to poison themselves. "We choose to leave this world," they wrote in their suicide note, "because of all the malice it contains. Everyone is mean to each other. Our final request is that we be buried together. We ask for forgiveness from our families and God, and that He may take us unto His bosom." Through the act of suicide, reported *El Mundo*, fifteen-year-old Ernestina Espina and Raúl Arraldi "vowed to love each other in eternity, in view of the fact that they could not do so in this life because of opposition by her parents."[91]

❧ The power of the culture to invest social meaning in the act of suicide cannot be overstated. A culture so fully informed of the uses to which suicide could be put could not but also transmit the conventions with which suicide was received. Central to any understanding of the decision to die—and at the heart of the deed—was forehand knowledge of the social consequences of suicide, specifically the capacity to envision the probable response of others as a predictable—and indeed often desired—outcome. The suicide in Cuba, observed writer Luis Rolando Cabrera, "knows that his death will produce a reaction or a series of reactions from the people he has lived among and the mere thought of these reactions provides added incentive to commit suicide."[92]

The proposition of suicide, scripted as a cultural practice, necessarily derived its logic within the imagined response, which meant too that the desired effect could serve as well as cause. It provided an opportunity to strike back, a way to receive attention that surely a spectacular suicide would provide, but most of all suicide offered an effective mode of communication, often a way to punish or exact revenge, at times a means to displace aggression as an act of self-harm as a way to hurt others. In the play *El premio flaco*, by Héctor Quintero, protagonist Octavio berates his wife for making his life miserable: "You destroyed my life. That's why, when I realized my situation, I told myself: 'I am going to get even.' And that's exactly what I have done. . . . During all these years I have attempted to torture you with my fake suicides. Of course I never intended to kill myself! I did it simply to see you anguish, to see you weep and suffer. I did it to take revenge for what you have done to me."[93] In the play *Morir del cuento*, by Abelardo Estorino, Antonia reflects on the suicide of her husband: "The degenerate! How could we not have remained in wretched condition as a result of his suicide. I am convinced that he killed himself to punish us, so that we would know what it would be like to live without his presence."[94]

The act of suicide thus lent itself to multiple uses and often with the intent to manipulate the action of others. A recurring theme in fictional narratives of suicides—and to what degree in real life is impossible to ascertain—is the phenomenon of men using the threat to kill themselves as a method of seduction. In "El timo del suicidio" short-story writer Rosario Sansores tells the story of Pepito Ariel's effort to seduce Marietta. When he appears to reach for a revolver to kill himself, Marietta exclaims: "Don't kill yourself! I will give myself to you!" In the short story "Mi suicidio," by Herminio Pola, the protagonist recounts his strategy to threaten to kill himself as a way to "conquer the love" of Berta. Raimundo Gantes in his short story "Un suicidio" has the protagonist Félix attempt to win the affection of an uninterested Emelina by appearing to commit suicide: "While talking on the telephone, Félix neared the gun to the mouthpiece so she could hear the revolver discharge. He fired the gun twice in the air, tumbled to the floor to simulate the sound of a body falling to the floor, and let out an anguished cry of pain. He then lit up a cigar and waited for Emelina to rush over to his apartment."[95]

The promise of suicide, that is, the incentive to contemplate self-destruction, was often contained within the possibility of using one's life as a means of leverage, a way to offset disparities of power. Suicide entered the realm of empowerment in an environment where access to power was held by some and not by others, an environment in which power over one's own life became a means of self-mastery and a medium of exchange. Powerlessness assumed many forms, of course, but it was not necessarily a fixed condition. Certainly class differences implied power disparities. So too did structures of racial hierarchies and gender relations. Powerlessness was also associated with phases of the life cycle: a child in relationship to adults, for example, or an older person hobbled by the infirmities of age.

Women appear far more often than men to have used suicide as a means of manipulation. The propensity to suicidal behavior was established early and indeed acted upon the ways that men and women learned to negotiate interpersonal power relationships. Suicide developed into a culturally conditioned means to mediate the disadvantages of unequal power relationships, employed by women vis-à-vis men, for example, or children vis-à-vis parents, as a way to secure a measure of control. Indeed, instrumental use of suicide tended to reflect specific gender determinants by which men and women experienced life. While men may have completed suicide at a 2:1 ratio over women, the evidence suggests that women attempted suicide with far greater frequency than men. To put this in slightly different terms, men had a higher rate of successful suicide than women, attributable in part to the fact that the preferred methods of male suicide, usually involving firearms and hanging, were self-inflicted traumas with little opportunity for successful intervention. The principal methods used by women, on the other hand, including poison, the slashing of wrists, and even burning, allowed time for medical intervention and life-saving treatment. Anecdotal evidence also suggests that many unsuccessful attempts to die by women were, in fact, designed as nonfatal gestures.

Gender-specific values were frequently attributed to the very enactment of suicide, with successful suicide rendered as a male strength and failed suicide depicted as a female weakness.[96] Suicide was most often performed as a nonfatal act when it could serve to obtain a desired change, usually in realms of interpersonal relationships, and not typically as a response to conditions of indigence or illness, where the nonfatal gesture possessed little likelihood of ameliorating conditions. A suicide attempt meant to fail was often designed to control the behavior of others, as an act not for the purpose of dying but rather for living under different circumstances. The gesture of suicide thus represented the enactment of a mode of negotiation with sources in child-rearing practices and norms of socialization. Women as subordinates in dependent relationships had comparatively fewer means through which to exercise control over those matters of vital interests. Under these circumstances women used their last remaining asset—their very lives—to change those facets of their lives that mattered most—more than life itself. Concepción Casanovas Sierra asked to purchase bichloride of mercury in a Havana pharmacy. Noting her state of agitation, the pharmacist sold her instead antiseptic alkaline pills. Upon leaving the store, Casanovas swallowed the pills and moments thereafter began to call for help, whereupon she was taken to the hospital.[97] Ignacio Domínguez Olivares, reported the *Havana Post*, who no longer lived with his wife, did "not want to be responsible for her death, so he notified the police that his wife Lydia has threatened him with committing suicide unless he allow[ed] her to come back home to him."[98]

The practice of suicide in Cuba served to set in relief a number of fundamental truths about the character of gender hierarchies. The use of suicide for instrumental purpose either as unsuccessful attempt or as accomplished deed, to parlay life into a medium of exchange or commodity for barter, underscored the powerlessness of women in those spheres that mattered most in their lives. Cultural acceptance of the proposition of suicide acted to create the social environment necessary to validate the instrumental function of suicidal behavior. Women tended to kill themselves in circumstances generally consistent with gender constructs, acting out and within normative hierarchies of male domination and female subordination so central to the conventions with which men and women defined central facets of their relationship to one another. Women were far more likely to contemplate suicide over questions related to interpersonal relationships, mostly with men, those relationships in which they had invested considerable self-esteem and self-worth and which had assumed a place of central importance in their lives. Considerable emotional resources were deployed to sustain these relationships, and indeed the culture was given unabashedly to the celebration of romance as source of happiness.

But relationships with men implied more than the enactment of a script of romantic love. They had real and immediate implications in those spheres of psychological fulfillment, material security, and social status. Indeed, urgent personal matters bearing on emotional security and economic well-being were often contingent on relations with men.

Most women entered the realms of adult autonomy formed by expectations of finding in marriage the principal means of well-being and fulfillment, and specifically to obtain by way of relationships with men livelihood in the roles of wife, mother, and homemaker, always in conformity with the constraints of class conventions and racial hierarchies. One middle-class woman in a provincial city attributed her difficulty in finding a husband to the fact that she lived "among men of poor and humble origins. That's probably why none of them have dared to think of winning my heart." In the short story "Gato con guantes," by Flora Basulto de Montoya, the impoverished protagonist Rosalina is described as "too attractive for a poor man to dare to aspire to make her his wife and too poor for a rich man to think of taking her to the altar."[99]

For many women, marriage was a dedicated life career. "In the past," Ofelia Domínguez wrote early in the twentieth century, "the natural destiny of women, practically the only one, was marriage. . . . The fate of the single woman was very hazardous." Domínguez recounted commonplace idiomatic expressions used to describe the adversity that befell single women: "'Of course, for the poor woman does not have a man to rely upon!' 'If she only had a man to represent her interests!' 'She is taken advantage of because she does not have a man to defend her!'" Women in Cuba must marry, Irene Wright was told. "To remain single is truly a calamity."[100] In the short story "La recaída," by María Alvarez Ríos, set in the town of Trinidad, the protagonist Lucía begins to despair in the absence of an acceptable suitor. "Lucía was going on 28 years of age," the narrator comments, "and still the anticipated suitor had not appeared." The narrator notes: "Everyone knew that she wanted to get married, but in the town of Trinidad there was no one for her. . . . The scarcity of single men was so great that many young women made the mistake of marrying the first suitor who presented himself, whether they really liked him or not, in the face of the terrifying fear of not having another opportunity and being consigned to tend to the saints and raise nieces and nephews (*vestir santos y criar sobrinos*) [i.e., living in spinsterhood]." Broods the character of thirty-six-year-old China in Gloria Parrado's play *Bembeta y Santa Rita*: "I need a man to take care of me. I'm tired of life. I just can't go on. . . . I feel as tired as an old lady 80 years old."[101] The lament of one thirty-year-old woman was not uncommon among single women:

> I live thinking that with every passing day I am getting old; that my youth is slipping through my hands without my ability or the ability of any power, human or divine, to arrest the devastating march of time. . . . At present I live in complete spiritual and material solitude. . . . Life is very cruel to women. We have nothing of value other than our youth and when that is gone, what is left to us? To care for our nieces and nephews? To live in church attending to the saints? Lock ourselves up inside the four walls of the home to die of tedium and boredom? And when our parents die, what becomes of us single women, alone in the world, in a harsh, perverse, and hypocritical world? I don't even want to think about this because I think I would go insane.[102]

The extraordinary rate of suicide among young women was powerful indication of their susceptibility during those points in their lives at which they were ordinarily most absorbed with ordering their lives around critical relationships with men, and more: it suggests too the degree to which conflict-ridden interpersonal relationships, including romance gone bad, marital discord, infidelity, and abandonment, served as source of female self-destructive behavior. Embedded in the performance of suicide was an interior if often only intuitive understanding of the relative powerlessness of women in relationship with men.

Romantic suicide—to die for love—had multiple variations, but almost always involved a woman who killed herself. "That women in love kill themselves or attempt to kill themselves when they lose the object of their passion," journalist Gervasio Ruiz affirmed outright, "is no big deal. It happens all the time."[103] Almost daily, published press accounts reported women acting to kill themselves in the throes of heartache and hopelessness, as response to romance gone awry. Twenty-two-year-old Verania Nieto Carmenates from Camagüey attempted to poison herself, and fifteen-year-old Adela Alvarez Abreu from Matanzas shot herself, the press reported, as a result of "romantic discord" (*contrariedades amorosas*). In Hoyo Colorado, nineteen-year-old María Lara died after using kerosene to set herself on fire for "reasons of romance." In Bejucal, Sabina Castillo poisoned herself with iodine for "reasons of love." Paulina Monsenos Troya attempted to take her life upon learning that her lover Victoriano Martínez was leaving her.[104] In the short story "Suicida por amor," Olivastro de Rodas conveys the sentiments of a lovelorn women preparing to kill herself after having been abandoned by her fiancé: "It's impossible to forget him. The love he inspired in me is so profoundly rooted in my heart that only death can extinguish it."[105]

The model of female suicidal behavior found more-than-adequate validation in literary forms, of course, but also in musical idioms, and nowhere more prominently than in the lyric of the *bolero*. The bolero as ballad was loaded with the refrain of the desolation of love lost, often accompanied with a prescriptive remedy that elevated self-immolation to the level of sublime deed, at once as discharge of virtue and script of conduct, to enact culturally fashioned ways of being a woman. Dying for love entered those normative domains in which cues and codes combined to fashion the conventions of conduct.[106]

The power of the bolero lyric was contained in the moral. It ratified the relationship with men as a matter of urgency, central to being, without which life was not worth living. Life itself acquired explicitly instrumental function as a means with which to defend those interests that mattered most. The response assumed formulaic structure: to turn the pain of lost love, heartache, and despair inward, as a threat of suicide to recover lost love or as self-destructive behavior to obtain relief. The bolero lyric suggested prescriptive responses to male-female relations gone awry, a way for women to respond to rejection, infidelity, and abandonment. "I cannot live if you are not by my side," Celia Cruz pleads in "Desvelo de amor," adding: "I cannot resolve my life without you."[107] Olga Guillot's lament in "Historia de una amor" offered the paradigmatic formulation:

You are no longer by my side, my love,
In my heart there is only loneliness.
. . .

You were always the reason for my being,
To love you was for me my religion.

. . .

[Your love] was what gave light to my life,
Later extinguishing it.
Oh, what a dark life,
Without your love I cannot live.

Xiomara Alfaro and Rosita Fornes pleaded in "Noche de ronda": "Tell him that I love him / Tell him that I will die from waiting / Tell him to return to me." Olga Guillot ruminates in "Me muero, me muero:" "To love you this morning, I will die." In "Adoro," Olga Guillot sings: "I would die to have you by my side," while in "Amor ciego" Guadalupe Victoria Yoli (La Lupe) pleads:

No, no—do not leave me alone
For I would die if I am not with you
Do not abandon me
For I would die if you were to leave me.

In the bolero "Como estoy sufriendo," María Ochoa laments:

Without you the hours are much longer
Without you my life is a desert
Without you I cannot live
Come quickly to me
For my heart will die for you.[108]

Celia Cruz, Celina González, Omara Portuondo, and Olga Guillot were only some of the vocalists who recorded the lament of "Lagrimas negras":

I suffer the immense hurt of your wanderings
And I feel the profound pain of your departure
And I cry without you knowing
That my weeping contains black tears
You want to leave me
I don't want to suffer
I will stay with you, my beloved
Even if it causes me to die.[109]

The lyric of "Si a tú lado no estoy" proclaims, "Without your love, I cannot live / I will die / If I cannot be by your side, my love"; in "Es al amanecer," the lyric vows: "If you do not return, I will perish / Have mercy and please return"; and María Teresa Vera sings in "Ven a verme" that "If you leave me / It will be the cause of my death." In "Moriré de amor," the lyric pleads:

I can no longer stand this torture
I can no longer bear this shame and pain
Your absence has filled me with anguish
And if you do not return soon
I will die of love.[110]

In the play Los excéntricos de la noche, by Nicolás Dorr, Carucha's lament over lost love takes the form of a bolero:

I would like to cut my veins slowly (abrir lentamente mis venas)
To see all my blood at your feet
In order to demonstrate to you that no greater love have I
and thereupon to die.[111]

It would be unduly facile, of course, to attribute suicidal behavior among women to the prompting of the lyric of the bolero. The decision to die was far more complex. What can be affirmed, however, is that the bolero formed part of a larger moral environment, possessed of the capacity to suggest self-destructive behavior as a culturally appropriate response to loss and longing, one more instance of life imitating art. That most of these boleros were written by men, moreover, raises issues of other kinds, suggesting—indeed, reinforcing—the means by which male centrality to female being was obtained.

It is important to underscore, lastly, that many of these boleros were also recorded by male vocalists, including Fernando Alvarez, Roberto Faz, Orlando Vallejo, Beny Moré, Vicentico Valdés, Roberto Ledesma, and Trio Matamoros, among many others. But it is also true that men abandoned by women did not typically kill themselves. They were more likely to kill women. Most men did not die lovelorn. On the contrary, male suicide for love was commonly perceived as an unmanly act. Male bolerista Moncho Usera was once asked in an interview if he had ever contemplated suicide "for love" (por amor). He responded: "No. One can become obsessed by a person, but if it gets to the point of suicide, then the person must be sick."[112] As Pachito Alonso affirms in the lyrics of "No esperes eso de mi": "That I would kill myself for you, that I would destroy myself for you— don't expect that of me. . . . I have too much self-respect to give you that pleasure."[113]

The idea of suicide occupied a special place in the realms of popular awareness, embedded deeply in the commonplace conventions of the time, over time and changing with the times, conveyed as a subject of aesthetic production and a motif of literary output, in fiction and poetry, in mass media and popular music. It appeared as a recurring theme of film and theater and as the stock in trade of a genre of Cuban journalism that thrived on the sensational and sordid. It bears repeating again that life and art acted upon each other in constant interplay, with life providing inspiration for the thematic of suicide and art ratifying the efficacy of suicide as a means of coping with life. The culture accommodated suicide within the realms of tolerable conduct, where it was apprehended as acceptable and appropriate. Drawn to its logical conclusion, the option of suicide insinuated itself into the popular imagination as one of the available responses to the circumstances of life. The point here is to underscore the degree to which consciousness of suicide acquired salience in the stock of social knowledge, in the form of daily news, to be sure, but also through the medium of aesthetic production, in art forms that routinely engaged the transgression between context and content, between the real and the imagined, to such an extent that the distinction between both could easily lose meaning.

Suicide loomed large in Cuban literary production. It was a theme rich with creative possibilities, from the heroic to the humiliated, for love and for love lost, as a means of relief and a method of revenge. Suicide found widespread appeal among Cuban intellectuals who could easily romanticize the decision to die as a noble and sublime act, worthy of acceptance and approval, proper to emulate and celebrate. It lent itself as a thematic device to probe the shadowy interiors of the Cuban unconscious, a means through which the unspeakable often obtained voice and validation.

To what degree the Cuban reading public was susceptible to the larger meaning of this literature and, more specifically, to what extent this literature acted to shape attitudes and influence behaviors are, of course, matters of conjecture and impossible to ascertain with any precision. But what is certain is that the power of suggestion in the form of cues for conduct and source of moral sanction contributed to an environment in which the recourse to suicide was everywhere visible. Just how strong the power of suggestion may have been will never be known. It is sufficient here only to note the ubiquity of the suggestion.

The proposition of suicide assumed a presence in the popular imagination, by way of historical literature and a variety of literary genres. It flour-

Charleston Isleño

Caricatura de Abril Lamarque.

"The Island Charleston."
From *Carteles* 9 (June 6, 1926).

ished in folklore and legend.[114] Images of suicide served as space fillers in newspapers and magazines. Illustrations of suicidal death accompanied short stories published in popular serial publications. The prominence of the subject of suicide as a literary theme, both in fiction and nonfiction alike, in addition to the prominence accorded to suicide in the daily press, contributed to an environment in which the practice of self-destruction functioned with such commonplace normality as to nullify the sense of extraordinariness and with such frequency as to negate the capacity to summon revulsion against the deed. The act of suicide assumed the form of an utterly ordinary occurrence, usually passing without reprehension and certainly without reproach. The power of the narrative of suicide was embedded in its capacity to frame the way that Cubans could take measure of the act of self-destruction and, at the same time, serve as an inducement to suicide.

The susceptibility to suicide as a disposition insinuated itself into multiple realms of Cuban awareness, through art and literature, through mass media, as a circumstance of the political culture: in sum, as an attribute of the very conditions in which nationality was transacted. Suicide served as one of the principal story elements of the Cuban novel, as literature and

Illustration accompanying short story by Eduardo Zamacois, "Momentos del camino." From *Bohemia* 13 (May 21, 1922).

Illustration accompanying short story by Arturo Ramírez, "Un hombre vulgar." From *Carteles* 23 (November 17, 1935).

life braided upon one another through themes of self-destruction. Fiction spoke to the conventions of the time and served to reflect and reinforce attitudes that gave purpose to conduct. This was the cultural context and aesthetic ambience that charged suicide with profound meaning. Literary representations often celebrated suicide as an act of courageous resolution, a way to vindicate honor and affirm love. The subject of suicide was the dominant story line of Tomás Justiz y del Valle's novel *El suicida* (1912), climaxing in the final and elaborately developed plan by which the protagonist, Julio, kills himself: "The image of Linda suddenly appeared before his eyes. 'For you Linda, my last kiss; for you my last breath.' He lifted the gun to cock the trigger. Suddenly a strange force held him back. The face of Doña Julia appeared behind the image of Linda. 'Mother!' 'Mother!' he exclaimed in a passionate outburst. 'For you my last thought.' He raised the gun to the height of his chest and shot himself in the heart. His body collapsed heavily, his hands futilely sought some kind of support and his body turned as it fell. He slipped down the hill, as the grass turned red and he drowned in his own blood."[115] Novelist Reinaldo Arenas, who later would himself die at his own hand, often employed the theme of suicide in his fiction. The novel *Otra vez el mar* (1982) ends with the protagonist committing suicide. In the novella *La vieja Rosa* (1966), Arenas depicts Rosa consumed by the fire of her suicide: "The flames continued to rise around Old Rosa, who went on crying in a measured and monotonous flow. There she was, her breath coming in hoarse rattles. . . . Old Rosa went on crying. . . . And so she remained, without protesting. . . . Then the flames rose up, stirred by the midnight breeze, and the tamarind tree shriveled, swept by a luminous explosion. Old Rosa could see the fire devouring her dress. . . . She could no longer stand."[116] In the novel *La era imaginaria* (1987) by René Vázquez Díaz, Félix's wife commits suicide, after which he permanently seals the room closed: "The door to the room was never opened again, not even to clean, and no one remembered if the room had furniture or if it was empty. There wasn't even the slight crack to allow the curious eye to peer inside. . . . And in the course of time, that inaccessible space was transformed into something surreal that dwelled in the spirit of everyone."[117] Other novels to accord prominence to the theme of suicide include José Antonio Ramos, *Almas rebeldes* (1906) and *Las impurezas de la realidad* (1929); Francisco Torres, *Amor y ruta* (1921); Carlos Loveira, *La última lección* (1924); Luis Felipe Rodríguez, *La copa vacía* (1926); Justo González, *Cubagua. Historia de un pueblo* (1941); Teresa Casuso, *Los ausentes* (1944); Miguel de Marcos, *Papaíto Mayarí* (1947); and Lisandro Otero, *La situación* (1962).[118]

The theme of suicide assumed fully the form of a genre of the Cuban short story. In the short story "Suicidio," by Maria Teresa C.M., the narrator observes that seventeen-year-old Clarita would resort to suicide so she did not have "to deal with romantic dreams, or anxiety, or tenderness, or fantasies, or love of the fine arts or the moon." In Armando Leyva's short story "Un suicida," the protagonist falls in love with a female mannequin in a department store window display. When the display is changed and the disassembled mannequin relegated to a corner of the showroom floor, the protagonist is overcome with despair at the sight of the "dismemberment" and proceeds to hurl himself before an oncoming trolley car. Another short story by Armando Leyva, "Cómo muere un buey . . .," tells the story of an ox that commits suicide by settling upon railroad tracks to await the oncoming train. In "El suicidio de la muñeca" writer Antonio Casas Bricio tells a story with multiple morals, revolving around the "beautiful, blond-haired, blue-eyed doll" who enjoys an idyllic existence in a department store display window, basking in the friendship of other dolls, marionettes, and toy soldiers. One day she is purchased:

> She felt herself being transported far away from her world. She knew very well that she was heading for a wealthy and well-appointed home, perhaps into the fickle hands of some little girl who was accustomed to unusual and expensive toys, and surely she would be quickly ignored if not destroyed in her hands. Toys do not like rich children. They are easily distracted, they are easily bored with their toys, which are quickly relegated and forgotten in some corner, where the lovely toys pass their time in tearful remembrance of their happy days in the department store. . . . She would have preferred to end up in the hands of a poor girl. She knew that poor children loved their toys very much, precisely because they owned so few.

The morning following the arrival of the doll, the family awakes to find her head shattered. Observes the narrator: "The truth is that the beautiful blonde doll had committed suicide." In Luis Rodríguez Embil's short story "Por qué se suicidió Juan Enríquez," the protagonist kills himself when he learns that a young woman he has admired from afar is engaged. Observes the narrator: "In the bewilderment of the rude blow he concluded that there was nothing left for him to do in this world, for he had just lost forever that which represented for him everything that was beautiful."[119] The theme of suicide is a recurring presence in the writing of Lino Novás Calvo. In "La luna de los ñáñigos," a black woman kills herself for the unrequited love of a white man. In "La abuela Reina y el sobrino Delfín," Teresita—"our lovely little cousin with green eyes"—perishes in the rising flames of a "fire that she herself started." The account of Silvia in "El milagro" concludes: "She had acted on her threat: she had leaped to her death from a high floor of the building." The protagonist in "El secreto de Narciso Campana" identifies with the misfortunes of fictional characters: "The idea of suicide haunted him, but since he was still young and possessed of a strong imagination he was able to keep his thoughts at bay. With regard to religious faith: he had none."[120]

Suicide is a salient theme in the work of other *cuentistas*. One character in Mirta Yáñez's short story "No somos nada" hangs himself in a closet. In "El perro del suicida," by J. B. Morales, Buche the dog gives up the ghost after his master kills himself. Suicide was also a recurring theme in the short stories of Alfonso Hernández Catá, almost always in the form of a brooding internal dialogue. In "Los muertos" the protagonist reflects: "I thought of killing myself and, you see, I have not done it. God gave me cowardice at the moment I contemplated dying and the courage to continue living. . . . I later summoned the courage to kill myself another way. So much valor is needed for one form of suicide or another, but this time I had the courage."[121] Other short stories on the theme of suicide included Jesús López, "De un suicida"; Vicente Menéndez Roque, "Mi amigo, el suicida"; Rosario Sansores, "El timo del suicidio"; A. Arroyo Ruz, "El misterio del cuarto de la bella suicida"; Julio Laurent Pagés, "De los suicidas"; Trinidad de Zequeira, "El suicidio"; Rafael González, "Un suicida"; Juan Nicolás Padrón Barquín, "Los suicidas"; Mario del Caspio, "Los candidatos al suicidio"; Alfonso Hernández Catá, "Parábola de los suicidas"; José Sanz, "Mi amigo el suicidio"; Francisco Casado, "Suicidio original"; Gerardo del Valle, "Páginas halladas en el bolsillo de un suicida"; Paco Romero, "La ceiba de los suicidas."[122]

The efficacy of suicide developed into one of the dominant narrative elements of twentieth-century fiction dealing with slavery. The larger metaphoric purport was unambiguous. The short story "El esclavo" (1928), by José Morales, sets the moral in sharp relief. "The punishing whip of the overseer had cruelly lacerated his dark skin," says the narrator, "but slowly the desire for liberty had filled his soul. . . . Like [other slaves] he had endured brutal treatment with the stoicism of a martyr, but he felt in his heart the rebelliousness of his free spirit." The slave Miguel runs away only to be hunted down, and to avoid capture he determines to plunge to his death from a cliff overlooking a river: "The unfortunate slave saw only a cruel choice of death or life, but a life of bitterness, filled with infliction of pain upon his flesh and spirit. And in the face of this frightful dilemma he chose the most expeditious means of his complete liberation. The deep dark blue waters of the river served as the soft posthumous bed for his long suffering body, the body of the slave . . . who sought in the holy grasp of death liberty from his enslavement."[123] In the short story "El cimarrón" (1930), by M. Siré Valenciano, runaway slave Apolonio "rather than surrender to the overseer and his 'justice,' prefers to commit suicide by swallowing his tongue."[124] César Leante develops a similar story element in the novel *Los guerrilleros negros* (1975). The *cimarrón* leader Coba is hunted down, and he too chooses to plunge to his death. The narrator recounts:

> He no longer believed that dead blacks returned to Africa, that they were reborn free in the native land. But he preferred death a thousand times more than to fall into the hands of his pursuers. They would not touch him, they would not mock him, they would never again clamp on him the chains of the slave. He had experienced freedom, he had experienced freedom intensely and could never again live without it. Neither would he give them the satisfaction of parading him on the streets of Baracoa, with his arms tied and a rope around his neck, as if he were some mountain beast they had captured. He would not allow them to torment his soul or torture his body through the application of the garrote, which was the certain fate they had awaiting for him. No one would offend his dignity as a man. Let their bestiality be satisfied, if they wished, by mutilating his body, because never would he belong to them alive.[125]

Also widely published in Cuba were short stories dealing with suicide written abroad and translated for publication in local magazines and periodicals. These included Cartier de Lancy, "Un suicidio misterioso"; Suzy Mathis, "El suicidio de Nina"; Al Bromley, "El suicidio perfecto"; H. J. Magog, "Suicidio"; Andrés Uccellini, "Yo suicida"; Garnett Kettering, "Crimen o suicidio"; Antoine de Courson, "Un suicidio"; Germain Survil, "Suicidio"; Leonard Merrick, "Los suicidas de la Rue sombre"; Victor Maxwell, "Un suicidio misterioso"; G. T. Fleming Roberts, "La casa de los suicidios"; Etienne Gril, "El suicidio de Berta de Arson"; Manuel Komroff, "El hari-kiri del barón Kura"; and William E. Hayes, "La carta del suicida."[126]

Poetry served as another popular literary form through which to contemplate the theme of suicide. In his poem "La prórroga de un suicidio," Manuel Pino recounts the agony of a friend contemplating suicide as a response to spurned love. The seven-stanza *décima* "El suicida" recounts in lighthearted fashion the tale of a would-be suicide contemplating all the possible ways to kill himself; finding none of the methods exactly to his liking, he decides to abandon the idea. In Virgilio Piñera's poem "Invitación al suicidio," the narrator is visited by a spectral presence: "I have come"—he tells him—"to invite you to your suicide / To bring an end to the rhythm of your despicable life."[127] In the poem "¡Me suicido!" E. A. Carrasco Mojena affirms:

I am tired of life or *bored*
(It's that this word is more sonorous,)
I am eager to kill myself without delay:
I have conceived of this idea with utter resolve.

In Fayad Jamis's poem "El ahorcado del Café Bonaparte," the narrator comments: "If I had not hanged myself / I would have died of that strange illness / that afflicts those who do not eat."[128] Other poems to engage the theme of suicide include Ernesto León G., "El suicida"; Manuel Pichardo, "El suicida"; Bonifacio Byrne, "De un suicida"; Esteban Foncueva, "De un suicida"; José Antonio Calcaño, "El suicida"; and Sigifredo Alvarez Conesa, "El puente del ahorcado."[129]

The print media, especially daily newspapers and weekly magazines, also contributed to an environment in which suicide was a staple of popular conversation as shared news and the stuff of "current events." Newspapers were filled almost daily with articles on suicides of all types, in and out of Cuba. This trend developed fully into *la crónica roja*: a news genre that thrived on sensational reporting of violence, especially homicides, street crime, domestic violence, and suicides.[130] Commented one observer: "We open the newspaper and on page one, two, five, and eight, some correspondent is reporting in endless succession three or four instances of suicide, sometimes fortunately about attempts that failed."[131]

It is impossible to determine, of course, if the frequency with which accounts of self-inflicted death appeared in newspapers and magazines responded to popular fascination with suicide or created public interest in suicide. It was perhaps both. What is certain, however, is that newspapers and magazines disseminated knowledge of suicide to a vast audience and, in the process, served as one of the principal ways from which people came to learn about suicide, to ponder its methods, its merits, its meaning. Accounts of suicide allowed the reader to contemplate the motives that drove others to their deaths, to try on the solution others had chosen as a possible resolution of one's own adversity. The publication of suicide notes or summaries of their contents, moreover, could not but call attention to the conditions that drove others to end their lives. It is not difficult to understand, under the circumstances, how the idea of suicide as a solution to the ordinary afflictions of modern life passed into domains of popular awareness.

The presentation of news of suicides generally adhered to standard format, and included name, sex, age, and race. Racial designations included *blanco/a, pardo/a, mestizo/a, moreno/a, asiatico/a*, and, variously,

A sampling of suicide news in the daily press. From *Carteles* 35 (August 1, 1954).

de la raza de color and *de la raza negra*. Social hierarchies were often conveyed through allusions to such markers as residence, occupation, and family. The account of the suicide of Juan Velásquez in Santa Clara identified him as "belonging to a distinguished family of this society"; Edith Ledón Martínez was described as a "member of a distinguished family [in Sagua la Grande]"; María Marques Salgado "was from a good family."[132] Unidentified suicides were typically described in terms of sex, race, and attire. The body of one suicide found in Puentes Grandes, for example, was reported as being that of "a white male decently dressed (*un individuo blanco decentemente vestido*)."[133]

Press coverage of suicide was not limited to deaths in Cuba and included the republication of stories dealing with suicide outside the island. News accounts of death by suicide almost everywhere in the world filled the Cuban press, and of course the more prominent the suicide or the more unusual the method, the greater the attention it received. Stories in-

El distinguido caballero José Pérez se dispone a leer la prensa diaria después del desayuno y si se lo consienten los gritos de los vendedores y el repiqueteo de las campanas.

¡Primera noticia espeluznante!: "Un hombre, furioso de celos. porque su mujer parece que "caminaba" como química. se ahorcó de la rama de un árbol y después ahorcó a la ingrata."

¡Otra! Y esta viene de París: "Un aviador, después de bailar el tango con la mismísima Luna (Colombina en persona) cayó a tierra, o aterrizó, mejor dicho, o, mejor dicho todavía: aterrorizó a todos los paseantes del Bosque"

¡Diablos! Esta si es grave!: "Con el mal tiempo reinante en estos días, se hundió un vapor que venía de Canarias, llegando a tierra solo un isleño baratillero y doscientos ratones atacados de bubónica".

¡Caracoles! ¡Cómo está México!: "Pancho Villa ha fusilado a otro inglés". ¡Y aquí dejamos a los malditos "ingleses" que campeen por sus respetos!

¡Quiquiribú! No sigo leyendo. Esto sí que no puedo soportarlo: "Se suprimirá la Lotería en la Cámara". ¿Qué hago yo si me quitan mi "botella"?

"Reading the Daily Press." The reader begins the day with a news account of a murder-suicide and ends the day with a planned suicide in response to news of a congressional suppression of the lottery system. From *Letras* 10 (March 29, 1914).

cluded accounts of socialite suicides in the United States and of royalty in Europe, suicides in Hollywood, and suicides of prominent foreign political leaders. Many feature articles published in foreign newspapers and periodical literature were translated into Spanish and republished in Cuba. Other articles were written by Cubans giving accounts of suicide by foreigners.[134] Newspapers and magazines published accounts of suicide abroad, with datelines from Berlin, Buenos Aires, Paris, and Chicago. Alejo Carpentier wrote from Paris about the "epidemic of suicides in Europe." Carpentier described the suicide of French artist Jules Pascin in 1930 in unabashedly celebratory terms: "Your death is terribly beautiful. It was in reality necessary to possess a great spirit to do what you did." José Juan Tablada wrote from New York about "the wave of suicide" in 1929. François de Cisneros in Monte Carlo reported on casino gambling and suicide. Félix Pita Rodríguez wrote about "the most spectacular suicide in history" after a visitor to the Nuremberg zoo killed himself by leaping into the lions' den.[135] La Lucha published one account of a suicide-murder in Madrid in which a mother killed her two children and proceeded to take her own life. Another news story with the headline "Two Lovers Commit Suicide" carried a dateline from Belgrade. One account described a "suicide completed in a sensational manner" in Austria that involved the use of forty kilos of dynamite and resulted in the destruction of homes and stores within a half-mile radius. Diario de la Marina published a feature story on "Suicide in Japan."[136] A news story titled "Crime and Suicide of a Multimillionaire" originated in London; other accounts included "The Sausage King in Budapest Commits Suicide" and "A Romantic Hungarian Husband Commits Suicide Outside Her Window." A magazine story by Mauricio Laporte entitled "El club de los suicidas" reported on a series of suicides in Germany. A published excerpt of a biography of nineteenth-century Spanish writer Mariano José de Larra ("Fígaro") selected material dealing with Larra's final days before his suicide.[137] General interest articles on the theme of suicide, its history, and its significance—mostly from abroad—were the stock in trade of the Cuban print media and included treatises on such diverse topics as the secret impulses of suicide, suicide as illness, and the possibility of animals acting to commit suicide, as well as a guide to the methods and varieties of suicide.[138]

Novels, short stories, poems, magazine feature articles, and press accounts dealing with suicide served to expand the public for the performance of suicide and, in the process, could not but conduct members of this audience into those realms where proposition of suicide assumed the appearance of plausible. Clifford Geertz was entirely correct to suggest that cultures transmit models of reality and models for reality, ways through which patterns of behavior assume meaning by shaping themselves to reality and shaping reality to themselves, as both models of what people believe and models for believing it.[139] The multiple narratives of suicide possessed the capacity to fashion easily enough the circumstances that spoke to the conditions of vast numbers of Cubans and to do so within an instrumental framework celebrated as remedy. "To disappear!" mused the protagonist in Georgina Cruz Salazar's short story, "Suicidio." "What a beautiful word, what a lovely idea. To disappear. A deed of towering scorn for the most valued precept of humanity. To die voluntarily. To die with an ironic smile on the lips and a profound disdain in the heart. To feel oneself admired by those who remain alive. Admired and envied by the multitude of the slaves to destiny, who entered this world without consent and who submissively await for the occasion—also without their consent—to announce their departure on the voyage without return."[140]

The fame and notoriety of men and women who contemplated or completed suicide in public forums, whether as fiction or fact, always suggested the possibility of redemption and recognition. Therein lay incentive and inspiration for others who confronted comparable disappointment and dashed hopes. The narrative of suicide always conveyed a moral—indeed, it had no other purpose than to transmit a moral—and often it was something akin to an authorizing text in which the circumstances of self-destruction were rendered as a compelling and often inexorable logic to which reasonable men and women were obliged to submit. Literary representations of self-destruction served to disseminate the very idea of suicide, to suggest the circumstances where suicide was possessed of purpose and propriety. In the short story "El suicidio de Morgan," by Jesús López, for example, the protagonist Juan Morgan prepares diligently to succeed in life: he studies hard and works tirelessly. Comments the narrator: "It could be said that Juan Morgan possessed profound knowledge, but those [coworkers] who knew nothing were always being promoted over Juan Morgan." This was a cautionary tale that could not but have resonated among many readers. The narrator continued:

> Waiting, always waiting, for his luck to change and that justice would be done. At 50 years of age, the unhappy Juan Morgan began to despair. Why was he born? Why so much effort to learn? Why be honorable and responsible? He had no answers to his questions. . . . His hair turned

gray and white, his faced furrowed with wrinkles, his heart filled with bitterness and despair, and his hands trembled for the lack of an adequate diet. It was becoming too late for new dreams as Juan Morgan's future became bleaker with each passing day and the value of living dissipated with ever increasing speed in the face of every new disappointment. Juan Morgan tied a rope around his neck and hanged himself from a beam in his dark and cold apartment. He was very hungry but could not bring himself to ask for charity.[141]

In César Leante's short story "El punto de partida," the protagonist, struggling writer Carlos Morales, despairs over his failed career. One evening he observes a beggar in downtown Havana and comments to a friend: "See that man? No one pays him any attention now. No one cares if he is cold or if he dies of hunger. But if tomorrow he were to be murdered or killed in a strange way, dismembered for example, the entire apparatus of the police force would be mobilized in his behalf. They would spend three times as much money to investigate his death as this poor man would need for the rest of his life." Morales is subsequently found dead in his apartment, presumed a suicide by hanging until the police take note of the absence of the chair or table that he would have needed to mount in order to kill himself. The death is proclaimed a homicide, and Morales is classified as a murder victim. Suddenly, all his unpublished works are in high demand. The friend observes:

> While he was alive no one ever paid attention to him or his work. With recurring futility he sent articles and stories to the editorial offices of magazines and newspapers. With recurring futility he offered his plays to the local theater. But now that he was dead and that his death had been something of a sensation, this same sensation reached his work. One of the great magazines publishes his stories and everything that he had written saw the light of day in one or another publication. The theater then discovered that in those works that it had previously rejected existed talent, originality, and innovation. . . . The reviews could not have been more praiseworthy of the 'deceased playwright.'

The story ends with the reader learning that Morales had indeed committed suicide, and at his request the friend had proceeded to move the chair away from under the body and remove all evidence of suicide. "My friend's wish had been met. He had chosen the dramatic way of suicide because all other ways [to success] were closed to him."[142] The disposition to suicide as a state of being was further conveyed in the form of diary entries in the short story "Páginas de un diario," by Rafael María Rubio:

> I have determined to kill myself. Nothing will deter me from acting on my firm resolution. . . . Why do I wish to kill myself? For no reason and for every reason. I find the world unbearable. And especially these past few days when so many unpleasant things have happened to me. . . . Everything bothers me. Everything conspires to make me angry. . . . Everything makes me weary, mortifies me, irritates me. I detest with all my heart politicians, peddlers, and women without teeth. I'm tired of my neighbors. . . . It's 7:30 in the evening, and I again ask myself: why do I want to kill myself? . . . I confess that I am not driven by the overwhelming tragic force associated with the usual suicides. But there are so many things that bewilder me. . . . Are they insignificant? Perhaps. But they are so many that I find myself unhappy. Does happiness exist? Yes. It does exist. But I am not happy. I am convinced that happiness is a quick rest that grief takes in order to continue with renewed vigor on its fatal mission. My grief is interminable.[143]

Embedded in the narratives of death by suicide, whether in the form of relief and redemption or pathos and tragedy, was a deeper moral, a message that offered at once motive and meaning. How a narrative of suicide may have been read fifty years ago—and more: how it may have affected behavior—may never be knowable. But the narrative served to convey knowledge of suicide variously as a mode of representation, or as a method of fulfillment, or as a means of manipulation, and in the process contributed the circumstances of environment. The act of suicide was often presented as a way to obtain through death what was unobtainable in life, whether in the form of relief, as in the case of the despair of Juan Morgan, or in the pursuit of success, as in the example of frustrated writer Carlos Morales. In a slightly whimsical essay "Prohibido suicidarse en Nueva York," columnist Mario Parajón celebrated the benefits of suicide. He discouraged his readers from committing suicide in New York, where the deed would be greeted with general indifference. Instead, he suggested, "select a village, a town along side a creek":

> If you choose to kill yourself in Holguín (or in San José de las Lajas, or in Bauta, or in Cienfuegos) you are guaranteed 48 hours of fame. Within minutes of passing into the condition of the dead, a large group of neighbors gather to speak well of you. . . . The following day, the

entire town is talking about you. Legends circulate about your past. A guitar player will compose a *décima* about you. Women will insist that you died for love. Men will talk about your worldliness. In the barbershop your name will be mentioned fifty times, while local parishioners will speculate on the motive that impelled you to take such action. In sum: for the mere cost of two bullets to the forehead you will achieve passing glory for two days. If you were to write Quijote you wouldn't receive this much time.[144]

Literary production repeatedly ratified the propriety of suicide as a plausible response to the afflictions of daily life. Without the bit of mystery surrounding his friend's death, "The [suicide] would not have had any significance," says the narrator of Leante's "El punto de partida," "for the misery in which he lived would have been sufficient to drive anyone to suicide." In the short story "Suicidio," by Enrique C. Henríquez, the protagonist contemplates suicide as a result of being "overwhelmed by the feeling that his own life was useless."[145] In the poem "El suicida," Nicolás Martínez Suárez rebukes those who condemned the suicide:

Why vilify him, when he is martyr
of a cruel fate to which he was born?
Why vilify him? Do you know
the tragic immensity of his pain?
Do you know the turmoil that troubles
his ailing heart and wounded soul?
Ah! Do not be so cruel toward the suicide. . . .
Temper the severity of your judgment![146]

Nicolás Guillén mocked the proscription of suicide in his poem "La amarga ironía":

They say that to kill yourself is a sin;
that life must be accepted as it is.
The optimist view is the following precept:
"Struggle to prevail."

Do not curse your life. Suffer silently;
Your heart aches? Find a doctor;
cure yourself!

If you are hungry think about what you have eaten;
— Fill your stomach with illusions!

But do not kill yourself, do not protest,
for God will punish you.

Humiliate yourself, degrade yourself, beg.
Life must be accepted as it is;
And when in the mud, say from the mud:
"Struggle to prevail. . . ."[147]

Fictional works occasionally offered usable instructions for suicide. In the short story "El suicidio," by Jesús Vega, the protagonist recounts: "The best way [to commit suicide] is in a bathtub filled with hot water. You submerge yourself in the tub, and with a razor cut your veins, and since your skin is reacting to the hot water you do not feel the cuts. All you feel is the sensation of weariness while the blood flows out of your body . . . , a weariness that obliges you to close your eyes and descend into a void while the warm water evaporates, precisely the way your life evaporates in that lethargic sleep, in that dream from which you will not return."[148]

Newspaper stories similarly conveyed value systems and ratified the moral hierarchies so very much at the heart of suicidal behavior. This is not to suggest, of course, that newspaper accounts of suicide alone provided explicit models or acted as direct encouragement to suicidal behavior. But they did offer representations that served to reflect and reinforce the normative determinants by which meanings of suicide entered domains of public awareness and popular acceptance. Accounts of famous deaths, for example, often sensationalized by the press, could not but suggest the possibility of suicide as a fashionable act. Press accounts not only "reported" the news of suicide, they also proceeded to corroborate and disseminate social meanings associated with suicide.[149]

The deed of suicide implied an act of communication, possessed of meaning, performed often with a specific audience in mind, what one commentator characterized as "theatrical representation."[150] In one more fashion, the act of suicide was performed before a larger public audience. Suicide notes meant as private communications, directed to a close family member or a judicial authority, invariably fell into the possession of medico-legal authorities, who thereupon made the notes or their contents available to the press. Private suicide notes thus passed immediately into the public domain. To what degree men and women contemplating suicide understood the public dimension of self-destruction is not clear. Certainly the suicide note provided the means for people to shape the larger meanings of their death, to be disseminated by newspapers, and that this was very much the protocol of suicide in Cuba certainly must have been known by many who prepared to end their lives.

In "reporting" the news, the press could not but convey the cultural paradigms by which the performance of suicide was enacted. Newspapers inflected accounts of suicide differently and conveyed the larger social circumstances in which men and women chose to end their lives. Deference to social standing, for example, was properly observed. The suicide of Cubans of status was reported respectfully, often sympathetically, usually as a tragedy befalling a family that deserved better. "News" in this instance was public eulogy in the national press. Suicidal behavior within the middle class was often attributed to overwhelming circumstances, with the act of suicide represented as a reasonable way to transcend an undeserved fate. The account of the suicide of Havana financier Ramón Depons by *La Lucha* commented on his "affable character, an honorable man who led an exemplary life of honor. He leaves his grieving widow with three children, to whom we send our sentiments of condolences and implore God to grant them holy resignation to sustain them through his lamentable misfortune." In another account of suicide, *La Lucha* described businessman Belarmino Alvarez as "a decent person, esteemed by all, and of considerable social standing," noting that "he adopted such extreme measures without his family knowing his intentions" and "rushed to the hospital with hopes of saving his life but the best medical efforts were thwarted." Concluded *La Lucha*: "We send his family members our deepest condolences." The *Diario de la Marina* account of the suicide of Rodolfo González Capiro lamented the circumstances surrounding the death, noting that the "deceased belonged to an old and distinguished family of Cienfuegos; he was an honorable man and distinguished himself by his honesty."[151]

Accounts of men and women who took their own lives as a result of poverty, on the other hand, were rarely as sympathetic, and indeed often carried the implication of cowardice or madness. The suicide of sixty-three-year-old cigar worker José de la Peña in response, he explained in his suicide note, to hard times and loneliness, was characterized by the *Diario de la Marina* as "an act of a madman."[152] The suicide of the aged and ill was often represented as plausible and entirely appropriate to the circumstances. Suicides over blighted love affairs were frequently depicted in romantic terms, highly sentimentalized and indeed often celebrated. Reported *La Lucha* on a double suicide in 1928: "One of those events from the romantic era, from those times when Love inspired sublime heroism, occurred in Holguín. Two young people sealed their love with death."[153] Suicide in solidarity with the death of a loved one was frequently reported with tenderness and sympathy, and especially as an act associated with middle-class sentimentality. *La Discusión* reported the suicide of León Broch Sains after the death of his wife María Luisa:

> He loved her deeply. From the moment of her death he lost all possibility of happiness. He was indifferent to life. He was alone in the world. María Luisa had departed from the happy household leaving behind her loving husband overwhelmed with sadness. Nothing could console him, not even the presence of his loving children—themselves enduring reminders of his short-lived love. . . . This state of affairs could not continue. León suffered deeply. Catastrophe neared. Why continue with life if the reason for living it was no longer with him? That is how our friend understood his situation. Yesterday, on the occasion of María Luisa's birthday, León visited her resting place . . . and there in the vault he put an end to his unhappy days with a bullet from his revolver. It was over.[154]

Death by suicide may have become an ordinary occurrence, but rarely was the suicide of the well-to-do treated as anything less than an extraordinary event. That Cubans of means, men and women of property and privilege, with every reason to live, killed themselves could not but produce consternation and bewilderment, for it suggested a darker and indeed inexplicable force to which, then, everyone might be vulnerable. The suicide of Agustín Canellas Martí, a member of a prominent local family in Cienfuegos, "has deeply disturbed this community," reported *Diario de la Marina*.[155] The act of suicide among the well-to-do was often represented as a desperate deed of a victim of circumstances and usually observed as a means to transcend adversity. In *Papaíto Mayarí* (1947), novelist Miguel de Marcos represents the suicide of ruined businessman Tin Boruga as: "Another suicide. . . . Another victim of the economic crisis." In Francisco Torres's novel of the economic crisis of 1920–21, *Amor y ruta* (1921), the protagonist, Carlos, kills himself after the loss of his business. Explains the narrator: "It was not the death of a defeated man or of a coward, but rather a sensible and lucid act, of a hero arriving at an apotheosis." *La Lucha* characterized the suicide of José "Pote" López Rodríguez in 1921 as "censurable from the moral point of view," but added "in this case it has an extraordinary significance and an indisputable value," noting: "José López Rodríguez acquitted himself with honor. And as a businessman, now undoubtedly embittered, perhaps deceived, he acquits himself intuitively with the only thing that remained to him: his life." In Miguel Barnet's *Canción de Rachel* (1969), the well-to-do Eusebio falls in love with Rachel, a cabaret performer, much to the dismay of his family. Unable to win family approval for marriage, he slits his throat. Eusebio is portrayed as a victim of Rachel's designs. Recalls Rachel: "Nobody sympathized with me. On the contrary, they held me responsible."[156]

The narratives of suicide served to represent and reinforce the gender codes associated with self-destruction. Women and men who commit suicide over love, physician Benjamín de Céspedes insisted, betrayed their sex. "If a woman kills herself [for love]," Céspedes indicated, "she proceeds to expunge from the feminine character the most highly valued qualities of her sex, which are resignation, piety, and modesty, and in turn fosters the development of those violent instincts associated with men." On the other hand, the man who kills himself for love, out of jealousy or for having been deceived or rejected, Céspedes suggested, "declines to fight, or take revenge, which are qualities of virility and his character is effeminized and enervated (*se afemina y enerva*) . . . to the point of experiencing disorientation in the manner similar to any hysterical woman or romantic young girl (*cualquier histérica o mozuela romántica*)." Concluded Céspedes: "Animals are endowed with a philosophy far more practical and expedient: when the female rebuffs the male, he does not kill himself but seeks another female and eventually finds one."[157]

On those occasions that men did attempt to kill themselves after having been rejected by women, an act associated in the popular imagination with female behavior, the recourse to suicide was scoffed at as foolishness. Francisco Ariza Royero was described in one news story as a "romantic fool" (*romántico bobo*) for having attempted to kill himself after Enriqueta Olavarrí ended their relationship.[158] When Ageda Alcázar ended her relationship with eighteen-year-old Angel Rivero, Angel attempted unsuccessfully to kill himself with poison. The news story published in the daily *La Caricatura* chided Angel: "Young man, realize that this world is a *fandango* [i.e., a dance]. Don't take love so seriously." One journalist expressed surprise to learn that Evelio González plunged to his death after his wife expressed her desire for separation: "Anyone else would have thought of murder, of killing his beloved."[159]

The degree to which—or even if—news reports served to stimulate suicide is not altogether clear. *La Lucha* took note of the increasing numbers of "thwarted suicides" and concluded editorially:

Women for whatever reason determine to put an end to their existence . . . and are saved by having their stomachs pumped. . . . Men regularly decide to seek hydrotherapy and jump into the ocean. . . . But there is always some bystander disposed to save their lives. . . . Everyday the newspapers continue to provide us with these hair-raising accounts that provide the weak-spirited with incentive and who, in the face of the most trivial setback, turn their attention to suicide. Through this means, they seek to undo whatever ills have befallen them and have their name appear on the front page of the newspapers, even though they are not around to see it.[160]

Columnist Andrés Valdespino was convinced that published press accounts of suicide served to "influence the decision of others who faced similar problems," and urged "as a preventive measure against suicide that the excessive publicity frequently given to cases of suicide be avoided."[161]

The conventional wisdom has long insisted that the number of people who killed themselves increased in the immediate aftermath of published accounts of suicide. Suicide often seemed to develop in trends, typically in response to cases of well-publicized suicides at home and abroad, as acts of imitation in which both the deed and the method served as a model for others.[162] Havana physician Jorge LeRoy y Cassá of the Secretaría de Sanidad y Beneficencia was convinced that newspapers contributed to the creation of an environment conducive to suicide, a condition he likened to a "moral contagion":

These germs operate in an infinite number of ways, but the most efficient way is through contagion: a suggestive contagion that is established by way of the spoken word and words in print, through conversation, through the scenes on the streets and within the home, by way of the theater, in books and the press—and especially through the press, which penetrates the palace of the rich just as easily as it reaches the shack of the poor, carrying within its columns at one and the same time the message of civilization and death. . . . Newspapers not only describe with rich details the crimes that daily disturb the social peace, but also publish photographs of victims, conceding to them an element of grandeur that in reality they do not possess. Newspapers are one of the principal sources of the moral contagion and as a result one of the direct causes of suicide.[163]

LeRoy y Cassá was also convinced that the "principal cause of suicide by burning (*por el fuego*) was the result of contagion, for as a general rule when the newspapers provide an account of one case others follow in a very short period of time."[164] Physician Tomás Coronado protested the romanticized rendering of one Havana news account of a suicide by fire of a young woman: "Not long ago I read a newspaper account . . . describing in detail the suicide of a young woman by fire. I counted 39 adulatory adjectives in the first two paragraphs describing the act of suicide. It proceeded to portray the protagonist as imbued with divine properties, comparing her to [a painting of] a Virgin of [Bartolomé Esteban] Murillo, with her arms folded across her chest and her large eyes turned upward to Heaven, within clouds of incense and a halo of sweet and ecstatic martyrdom."[165] Investigating the rising rates of suicide among women during the late 1940s and early 1950s, journalist Marta Vignier reported learning from the medical staff at Calixto García Hospital in Havana that "when a sensational suicide occurs, in which the woman is famous, or when a suicide receives a great deal of publicity, even if the victim is unknown, the instances of suicide multiply, with many replicating to the most minute detail the publicized suicide."[166]

The possibility of imitation must be considered as an important factor in the patterns of suicidal behavior. Whether an account of a death by suicide was transmitted by newspapers or word of mouth perhaps matters less than the presentation of an act as model. Observers across the island often reported suicides occurring in sudden succession through similar methods. When seventeen-year-old Amparo Fiallo of San Nicolás killed herself by fire in November 1931 she became the third young women in almost as many weeks to have burned herself to death. In Bolondrón, María Sánchez Amador, Salomé Berrier, and Ramona Modesta González killed themselves within days of each other by way of fire.[167]

The self-inflicted deaths of prominent Cubans also appears to have further contributed to the larger environment of suicide. Musicians, writers, and artists were among the most prominent suicides. Musician Fernando Collazo took his life in 1939. Television and screen star Eduardo Casado killed himself in 1954. A number of well-known writers also killed themselves. Esteban Borrero Echeverría passed the last ten years of his life in unrelieved anguish over the death of his daughter Juana—"the love of my loves"—in 1896. Ten years later, only months after the death of his wife, Borrero Echeverría hanged himself in a hotel in San Antonio de los Baños.[168] The much publicized case of the planned suicide—or perhaps the publicity stunt—of actor Miguel Lamas riveted the attention of the Havana public in 1920. A popular entertainer at the Payret Theater, Lamas prepared a suicide note affirming boredom with life as the reason for killing himself. "To live for what?" he asked. "In death I will find peace." In a manner appropriate to his flair for the dramatic, Lamas chose a novel way of death. Reported *Bohemia*: "He did not resort to those common methods of suicide such as the gun, or poison, or fire, or the noose, or the ocean. No, sir! There is nothing common about Lamas. He wanted to kill himself using the most modern means: aviation." Lamas rented an airplane and circled the Payret Theater, planning then to fly over Colón Cemetery, where he was going to plunge to his death directly into a grave site he had already prepared for himself. He apparently changed his mind, claiming that "the pure air in the high elevations over Havana cured him of his malady."[169] The theatrics of suicide thus entered the realms of popular awareness by way of one more highly publicized incident.

The suicide of prominent public personalities was the stuff of sensational headlines. Public figures killed themselves with astonishing frequency. Benjamín Guerra, a founder and later treasurer of the Cuban Revolutionary Party, took his own life in 1900. Autonomist leader Ramón Pérez Trujillo killed himself in the same year. In 1901, prominent separatist leaders Manuel Villanova Fernández and Miguel Betancourt Guerra killed themselves. Two years later, María Luz Noriega, one of the heroines of the liberation war, committed suicide. In 1919, one-time governor and senator from Camagüey province and former president of the Conservative Party Manuel Ramón Silva shot himself to death. Several years later, in protest against President Gerardo Machado's destruction of the judiciary system, president of the Supreme Court José Luis Vidaurreta killed himself. In 1934, Roberto Méndez Peñate, secretary of justice in the government of Carlos Mendieta, committed suicide.[170]

Times of political tumult were especially noteworthy for the marked increase in the rate of suicides. In the days and weeks following the fall of the government of Gerardo Machado on August 12, 1933, scores of *machadista* officials, especially personnel of the army, police, and *porra* (paramilitary death squad) took their own lives. These were days of mob wrath, as an aroused citizenry set out to hunt down officials associated with eight years of repression under Machado. Many officials implicated in government misdeeds chose suicide. The much hated chief of police Antonio Benito Ainciart took his own life rather than fall captive to a pursuing mob. But popular wrath was not appeased with Ainciart's suicide. His body was mutilated and dragged through Havana streets. A day after his burial, a mob disinterred the body and continued to mutilate the corpse, whereupon it was hanged from a telephone pole, dosed with gasoline, and set ablaze. Other suicides of prominent machadistas included police officer Domingo Jordán Hernández and porristas Carlos Souto, Domingo Chapiro Tapia, and Juan Sampol. Conservative Party Senator and prominent machadista Wilfredo Fernández killed himself in 1934.[171]

The suicide of political leaders developed into an enduring facet of public life. One of the more dramatic suicides occurred in May 1947, when Manuel Fernández Supervielle, the mayor of Havana and former president of the Inter-American Bar Association, killed himself as a result of his inability to fulfill his campaign pledge to provide the capital with adequate water supplies. Only days before taking his life, Fernández Supervielle had spoken publicly of his disappointment and anguish over his failure to make good his campaign promises. It was preferable, he reflected, "to die well rather than live in disrepute." He elaborated in his suicide note: "Owing to the insurmountable obstacles that prevent me from complying with my promise to the people of Havana, and facing the idea of failure, a thing which I cannot bear, I make this determination. As a man with a conscience, I prefer suicide."[172]

The death of Fernández Supervielle sets in sharp relief the complex codes at work in the cultural accommodations to the gesture of suicide. Suicide in this instance served as a means to enact male values, an affirmation of virtue and valor embodied in the decision to die as a noble deed, where conventions of duty and death intersected and thereupon assumed the function of a moral imperative. This was an act deserving of admiration and indeed worthy of emulation, an honorable deed of reason and resolution, not a gesture of emotional impulse. Suicide was rendered as discharge of duty, an example of a man living up to the highest ethical standards, and hence model behavior. Circumstances thus minimized personal responsibility for the act. Suicide was transformed into the inexorable and inescapable imperative of honor.

Reactions to the death of Fernández Supervielle provide compelling insight into the ways that the cultural script acted to inscribe the efficacy of suicide in domains of popular awareness. Almost all *habaneros* applauded the gesture and indeed almost immediately efforts commenced to raise funds to erect a statue in honor of the deceased mayor. "This man," President Ramón Grau San Martín affirmed in his eulogy, "died struggling, wishing to keep his promise to this city to which he was so dedicated and despaired for having failed to provide the water he had promised." Rubén de León, president of the House of Representatives, included Fernández Supervielle among those "men of honor [who] make the ultimate sacrifice when facing obstacles to meeting their duty." Representative Manuel Bisbé proclaimed the gesture "as a great lesson for the future," and added: "He could not solve the problem of water and he took his life. Responsibility for his death falls on those who for reasons of vanity and special interest obstructed his ability to find a solution to this problem. His resolve demonstrates that there are still men in Cuba who prefer honor to life. I would say that he has been the most valiant of our public men." The weekly magazine *Carteles* praised Fernández Supervielle as a "true hero of public dignity, who took his own life for having failed to fulfill his promise to the people of Havana," adding: "The memory of this mayor of Havana should be perpetuated as an example of the public official who backed his commitment with the highest human value: his life. When we confront officials who are fraudulent, corrupt, irresponsible, unscrupulous, and unprincipled, the gesture of Mayor Fernández Supervielle should serve as a lesson that points the way to civic dignity and stimulates in those who want to follow his example the generous desire to serve the holy interests of the citizenry with honor."[173] An editorial in the Havana daily *El Mundo* celebrated the suicide as an "exemplary sacrifice" and "a great act, of noble and austere heroism . . . when realized on the altar of national interest." *El Mundo* continued:

> And more: the act with its magnificent moral quality has resonated within the great affection of the Cuban people. [It is] a marvelous invocation to duty that will keep us from the abyss of irresponsibility and immoral conduct known as politics. . . . We cannot allow the death of this Cuban for honor and duty to be in vain. It will not be. Proof of this is found in the echo, as a vast wave, that has aroused popular spirit. The people have understood the full symbolism of his death. . . . This was a necessary dramatic act which Cuban people understand as an expression of the mayor's manly protest against corruption. Now, with the

Bust of Mayor Manuel Fernández Supervielle, Havana, Cuba. Photograph by Fidel Requeijo.

completion of this final act of heroic sincerity . . . the name of Fernández Supervielle lives in the heart of all. In face of widespread corruption, he has had to die to leave us with the meaning of his life.[174]

"There was much speculation about Fernández Supervielle's suicide," commented journalist Elio Constantín, "but one fact stood above everything else: a man of honor had died. And for honor." Within one year of the suicide, Fernández Supervielle's death found further validation in popular fiction. In the novel *Los desorientados* (1948), by F. L. Fesser Ferrer, the mayor of Havana kills himself and the protagonist, Aristarco, observes: "He was a man of impeccable decency. Life became too painful for him. . . . With a heightened sense of valor he pledged to deliver water to the people of Havana and as a result of deceptions all about him . . . , the poor guy was disconsolate. I imagine that rather than fail, he decided to kill himself."[175] The moral of Fernández Supervielle's suicide was self-evident, insisted Senator Eddy Chibás: "A good man preferred death to life without honor."[176]

Four years later Eddy Chibás was himself dead, the result of a self-inflicted gunshot wound. The suicide of Chibás must be considered as perhaps the most prominent political suicide in twentieth-century Cuba, although it is far from certain that Chibás actually intended to take his own life. Given to theatrics and staged melodramatics, Chibás shot himself in the stomach during a live radio broadcast in August 1951, an act of suicide many believed was designed to arouse public opinion and mobilize popular support. However, the instances of male suicides involving self-inflicted gunshot wounds to the stomach were rare indeed. Almost without exception, men who used firearms intending to end their lives shot themselves in the temple or the roof of the mouth. Chibás appears to have been a poor marksman.[177]

Suicide thus established itself in the repertoire of scripted conduct as a political act. In 1956, the distinguished octogenarian veteran of the Liberation Army Colonel Cosme de la Torriente organized a "civic dialogue" designed as a forum to negotiate a peaceful political settlement between the government of Fulgencio Batista and representatives of the opposition. The negotiations—what historian Hugh Thomas characterized as "the last hope for Cuban middle-class democracy"[178]—ended in dismal failure, with Batista subsequently ridiculing the civic dialogue and publicly humiliating de la Torriente. The story is told that days after the suspension of the negotiations, a young Haydée Santamaría arranged to meet de la Torriente to offer a proposal: "Look, Dr. de la Torriente, you are a veteran, you are a patriot, but you have failed in the dialogue with the dictatorship. You are already in the final years of your life, but you can still lend a great service to Cuba, a service that will be properly appreciated by history. Look, Dr. de la Torriente, why don't you commit suicide. Suicide is a political weapon."[179] Nearly twenty-five years later, Haydée Santamaría would die by her own hand.

Patria o Muerte

LIVING AND DYING THE REVOLUTION

6

The Cuban Revolution cannot be understood without a consideration of one of its integral—almost essential—elements: suicide.

  Guillermo Cabrera Infante, "Entre la historia y la nada. Notas sobre una ideología del suicidio" (1983)

Cubans! Once again there is a tyrant. . . . Once again there is oppression in the patria. But someday there will be freedom. I invite Cubans of courage: it is time for sacrifice and struggle! To lose our lives is nothing. To live in chains is to live in ignominy. . . . To die for the patria is to live!

  Fidel Castro (March 1952)

If it were you in this struggle, I would prefer a thousand times that you perish rather than becoming a cowardly deserter or traitor. If I were to die for this cause, you must feel proud of me. But if in cowardice I were to betray it, you would have to be ashamed of being my son. . . . I want my three sons to grow up to be brave and honorable men who know how to demand their rights, even if it were to cost them their lives, so that they never have to live like slaves in their patria.

  Sergio González López, letter to his oldest son (July 30, 1957)

I saw an interesting thing happen today. A rebel was being arrested by the military police. And rather than be taken alive, he exploded a grenade he had hidden in his jacket. He killed himself and took a captain of the command with him. . . . It occurred to me the soldiers are paid to fight, the rebels aren't. They can win.

Michael Corleone (Al Pacino), Godfather II (1974)

We are disposed to go out and face the enemy, with the National Anthem, with the blessing of the patriotic hymn, with the cry 'To battle,' with the conviction that 'To die for the patria is to live.'

Daura Olema, Maestra voluntaria (1962)

✿ The nineteenth-century project of liberation inscribed itself deeply into the dominant configurations of nationality. Its representation assumed multiple forms, imbued with ideological purpose, rendered as legend and lore, preserved in popular memory and passed on as learned history, celebrated in song, story, and verse, but most of all honored as legacy to live up to and make good upon. The experience forged the virtues around which the attributes of nationality were assembled, as ideals, to be sure, but as ideals so central to the terms of self-representation as to make them the standard by which the character of Cuban was measured.

Only at a distance of one hundred years does the experience of liberation reveal its hold on the Cuban national imagination. It served to fix the moral determinants of collective self-expression and thereupon stipulated prescriptive purpose within the normative hierarchies of nationality, of what Cubans could expect of themselves by virtue of being Cuban. Nationality in this instance must be seen as an outcome, on one hand, a historically determined condition bearing discernible traces of the circumstances of its formation and, on the other hand, the embodiment of ideals that all were enjoined to honor.

Legacy was celebrated in the construction of monuments and statues and consecrated in tombs and mausoleums, as "public works of historical

¡VIVA CUBA LIBRE!

El pueblo libre de Alquízar, dispuesto á seguir la política de perdón y de olvido que se viene recomendando por ser la que más conviene y la que más se adapta con el espíritu levantado y con los sentimientos nobles y generosos del elemento cubano, acordó, en manifestación pública que tuvo efecto el día 4 del corriente, cambiar los antiguos nombres de las calles de Alquízar, esos nombres que tantos horrores y tan funestas épocas le hacen recordar, por los nombres de los heróicos defensores de nuestra independencia, en la siguiente forma:

NOMBRES ANTIGUOS	NOMBRES MODERNOS
Paseo Escalada y calle de Purcia.	Paseo Martí.
Calle Real.	Antonio Maceo.
Calle de San Agustín.	Máximo Gómez.
Calle de la Iglesia.	Pedro Díaz.
Paseo Jauma.	Paseo Rius Rivera.
Calle de Alonso.	Juan Bruno Zayas.
Calle de Rincón.	Mayía Rodríguez.
Calle de Concha.	Aranguren.
Balaguer.	López Coloma.
Santa Rosa,	27 de Noviembre.
Muñoz.	Serafín Sánchez.
Concepción.	Zenea.
Cañedo.	Panchito Gómez.
Platería.	Rafael Castillo.
Paloma.	Flor Crombet.
Almacén Viejo.	Barnet.
Badiola.	Cuesta.
Vives.	Nodarse.
San José.	Isidro Acea.
Soria.	T. C. Celestino.
Soledad.	T. C. Villa.
Barrio de Chafarinas.	Barrio de los Mártires.

Patria y Libertad.—Alquízar, Diciembre ..... de 1898.

Imprenta Obispo 35.—Habana.

Announcement of street name changes in the town of Alquízar, Havana province, December 1898. Copy in author's possession.

utility," wrote historian Miguel Varona Guerrero, "in remembrance and honor of our heroes and martyrs of freedom and independence."[1] Memory was received and thereupon transmitted from person to person, from one community to another, from one generation to the next. Across the island, the names of towns, schools, parks, and streets were changed to honor the memory of martyrs of the patria.[2] Among the towns to change their names included Recreo (Máximo Gómez), Hato Nuevo (José Martí), Corral Falso (Pedro Betancourt), Lagunillas (Domingo Méndez Capote), Cuevitas (Ignacio Agramonte), and Cimarrones (Carlos Rojas). Monuments, markers, and memorials in honor of the martyrs of liberation were raised almost everywhere. Statues of José Martí multiplied prodigiously across the island, most notably in the central parks of Havana, Cienfuegos, and Matanzas; busts of Martí appeared in Palma Soriano, Pinar del Río, Bayamo, and Santiago de Cuba, among many other towns and cities. In 1922, the Cuban congress required every municipality of the island to dedicate a statue, bust, plaque, or memorial to Martí. Municipalities were exhorted to name at least one street after Martí. A bust of Martí was placed in every public school of the republic.[3] "Since the war ended," observed Frederick Ober during his travels across the island in 1904, "the Cubans have nearly impoverished themselves erecting marble memorials and monuments of other sorts, to their brothers slain by Spaniards."[4]

The remembered past celebrated those facets of the Cuban experience possessed of instrumental value in the sustenance of the nation. To be Cuban implied an obligation to remember, endlessly, what had made the nation possible and what would be necessary for the nation to endure. The moral of the past was fashioned as historical knowledge, learned at home and taught at school, given sensory embodiment in the form of the national anthem, "La Bayamesa," the flag, "La Estrella Solitaria," and the choice of the Tocoloro as the national bird, selected for its reputation for dying in captivity. Domains of selfhood and nationhood closed in upon one another, acting upon each other, that is, nationality as something to surrender to as frame of reference and source of self-esteem. Elements of identity formation developed in function of national ideals, so that to be Cuban implied comportment based upon attributes associated with the formation of nation. Children were conducted into domains of nationality implicated in those dispositions around which self-awareness of being Cuban was fashioned. "Look at the sea breeze as it gently caresses the star of my flag, your flag, our flag," exults the narrative voice in Luis Ricardo Alonso's novel *El palacio y la furia* (1976). "The blue and white, the triangle of red blood, the ideal and the reality. What made us cry as school children when we listened to the national anthem: 'To die for the patria is to live.'"[5] Historian Juan Leiseca explained the purpose of his textbook *Historia de Cuba* (1925): "I wrote it inspired with the sole purpose of offering Cuban children one more means by which to enrich their minds and spirit. . . . I wish to put in [their] hands a weapon for struggle (*un arma para la lucha*), but not a weapon that serves only to advance historical awareness, but one that, reaching deeply into the heart of the child, invigorates his capacity to admire the greatness of the patria and arouses in him the desire toward emulation and the awareness of the purest nationalism."[6] Writing in 1940 about the norms of nationality in the formation of adolescents in the early republic, sociologist Ciro Espinos assigned particular importance to the commemoration of sacrifice:

> The integral ideal of Cubanness (*cubanía*) central to the formative period of adolescence originates from the patriotic past. Because many Cubans heroically sacrificed their lives to obtain liberty for their contemporaries and for later generations; because the greatest Cubans of the past, the most intelligent, the bravest, Cubans of wealth and social standing, immolated themselves as martyrs in the redemption of the enslaved patria; because many Cubans of modest backgrounds, workers, peasants, artisans, young and old, all of the most humble social origins, also immolated themselves anonymously with unparalleled heroism on the altar of redemptive ideals of the patria, . . . later generations [now] possess and enjoy a free patria.[7]

Legacy was honored in annual commemorative observances: October 10 for the "Grito de Yara" and the Ten Years War; February 24 for the "Grito de Baire" and the War for Independence. Commemorative dates of the death of martyrs of the patria filled the Cuban calendar, occasions to honor the dead as a way to implicate the living in the duty of nationality: February 27 for the death of Carlos Manuel de Céspedes, May 11 for Ignacio Agramonte, May 19 for the death of José Martí, December 6 for Antonio Maceo. In provincial towns and cities across the island, communities honored the martyred *hijos predilectos*, such favorite sons as Calixto García in Holguín, Serafín Sánchez in Sancti-Spíritus, Pedro Díaz in Yaguajay, Francisco Carrillo in Remedios, Eusebio Hernández in Colón, Francisco Leyte Vidal in Mayarí, and Emilio Núñez in Sagua la Grande, among many others.

The burning of Bayamo was celebrated as heroic self-abnegation rising to the level of metaphor as obligatory conduct that all Cubans were exhorted to emulate. In 1928, Tomás Felipe Surós Pérez characterized the burning of Bayamo as "the most glorious act in our history. . . . By delivering the city to fire . . . so that the representatives of the tyranny found only ruins and desolation instead of the opulent city, [Cubans] demonstrated the most valued form of heroism." Juan Leiseca wrote that when the Spanish "arrived to the noble city, the ruins and the ashes spoke with sublime silent eloquence of the determination of the patriots and [demonstrated] what a people are capable of doing when they vow a war to the death against their oppressors." In the ode "¡Bayamo heroica!" poet Oscar Ugarte celebrated the "sacred and beautiful city, how heroic and how strong / It did not even fear fire." Luis Santana eulogized the burning of Bayamo as "an immortal gesture"; while José Maceo Verdecia rendered the deed as "a noble gesture of a people who prefer annihilation, who choose definitive dispersal into the wilderness and death itself, rather than to fall again under the whip of their oppressors."[8] Essayist Miguel Coyula remembered his childhood, his fascination with the accounts of the Ten Years War and "with the magnificent 'Grito de Yara,' with the great Carlos Manuel de Céspedes . . . , with the haughtiness of Ignacio Agramonte, with the Spartan valor of Calixto García, who—in peril of falling prisoner—placed the barrel of his revolver under his chin and pulled the trigger, preferring death to surrender." Continued Coyula: "But nothing produced as great an effect on my childhood imagination as the burning of Bayamo. The image of a people that transformed its homes into a gigantic torch and subordinated everything to the great task obtaining freedom fascinated me. From that point on Bayamo lived in my imagination in the realm of legend and the people of Bayamo acquired the prestige of giants." Writing of her travels through Cuba in 1946, Erna Fergusson recorded her first impression of Bayamo— "a forlorn little town, dusty, run-down, spiritless"—and told of her conversations with the local residents, for whom Bayamo "was the proud city of long ago." Recounted Fergusson: "Abandoning the city, Céspedes called upon all loyal freedom-loving Cubans to destroy [Bayamo] and leave the Spaniards only the shell. . . . The city burned. But its sacrifice had roused all of Oriente. . . . Suddenly, seeing through the eyes and the patriotism [of residents], I saw Bayamo truly. Not a dusty little town, too noisy and not clean enough. Now it was a symbol, a shrine, the city courageous. . . . Bayamo, however it looks to the unknowing, is Cuba's shrine to the two forces that made her independence possible: sacrifice and the spirit of human freedom."[9]

The influence of José Martí in Cuban imagination cannot be exaggerated. By the early twentieth century, Martí had developed into the principal authorizing figure of a version of nationality in which the standard of devotion was measured through the discharge of sacrifice. That he had elevated sacrifice of self—in word and deed—as the means of actualization of Cuban had far-reaching implications. Martí entered realms of multiple meanings, as metaphor and model, and always as the standard to live up to, which usually implied the example to die by. So deeply had Martí invested the norms of Cuban with the proposition of death as an act of devotion as to make self-sacrifice the obligatory duty of nationality.

✴✴ Contained within nineteenth-century formulations of nationality was also the expectation of patria as a means of Cuban betterment, that is, nation as source of fulfillment and well-being, always with the promise of a better life as reason to die. Much had to do with the egalitarian vision contained within the project of liberation, from populist impulses that evoked social justice, racial equality, and economic opportunity as the purpose to which the republic was to be dedicated. Aspiration to nationhood had to do with making life better for all Cubans. That was the point: the creation of a nation entrusted with the defense of Cuban interests as the reason for being. Three generations of Cubans over nearly four decades had sacrificed much in the struggle to make Cuba for Cubans. They had pursued *Cuba Libre* purposefully, and paid dearly for their pursuit. They accepted with equanimity the necessity of self-abnegation as the means of self-determination and with equal serenity contemplated sacrifice and self-immolation as the necessary price of nationhood. Cubans had entered into a covenant, as they understood the nature of their commitment, a social contract in which they devoted themselves to the realization of a republic charged with responsibility for their well-being. "The Republic," observes the narrator in Arturo Montori's novel *El tormento de vivir* (1923), "affectionate and paternal, was obliged to care for its children, the Cubans, who had suffered so much to create it." And more:

Especially the poor, the émigré workers who took bread from the mouths of their loved ones to raise money for the Revolution, the peasants who abandoned their families to all sorts of horrors and misery to join the insurgent ranks, and all . . . who endured humiliation and were prepared to take whatever risk required for the cause of liberty. They would now be, surely, the pampered children, the favored ones of the new situation, in which their needs would be met with affectionate solicitude, against the abuses of the strong, merchants, bourgeois, planters, owners of enterprises, all the new owners of the wealth, mostly foreigners.[10]

The establishment of the republic in 1902 was greeted with a combination of ceremony and celebration, and much was made of the transition from colony to republic. But it was not entirely clear that the notion of transition accurately reflected the Cuban social reality. Just how much was new was difficult to ascertain. Some things had changed, of course, but much had not. And therein lay the problem, for much of what had not changed was precisely what Cubans had set out to change in 1895.

Racial iniquity persisted. Hopes for the all-inclusive republic—in Martí's words, "with all, and for the good of all"[11]—remained unrealized. Armed intervention by the United States in 1898, followed by military occupation and the subsequent imposition of the Platt Amendment, thwarted Cuban aspirations for self-determination and sovereignty. "Those who raised the first cry of liberty for Cuba," General Agustín Cebreco protested in 1900, "confided in the expectation that upon their death others would continue with the work of liberation." He continued: "This task has not ended. Cuba is separated from Spanish domination, but has not been emancipated from foreign tutelage. It is necessary to die before allowing the betrayal of the vow given to the oppressed patria. In order to be a good Cuban (*para ser buen cubano*), it is not sufficient to have participated in the battle field. It is necessary to cooperate in everything that serves to obtain absolute independence. . . . Liberty should be our first religion."[12]

In the months and years that followed, disappointed Cubans could not but take stock of the meager results their sacrifice had wrought, wandering about the island asking, "What have we gained by this war?"[13] Captain Carlos Muecke wrote poignantly of the condition of his compatriots, whose "property whether in town or in the country has been destroyed and they must begin anew. . . . [They] have sacrificed all—[their] houses, even their clothes are gone . . . without money they cannot rebuild their houses, restock their farms, refit their offices, or go to work."[14] Not a few contemplated a cruel denouement indeed: perhaps they had created a future in which there was no place for them. "Where do I start?" a dispirited soldier asks himself in Salvador Quesada Torres's partly autobiographical short story "El silencio" (1923). "I have suffered much, a great deal, so much that were I to describe my suffering in detail it would result in a sorrow-ful book. . . . It is the story of humble men like us who liberated Cuba and today have nothing to eat. In my own land . . . I find myself with-out protection or assistance."[15] José de la Paz, who had served the cause of liberation in Key West, committed suicide two years after the found-ing of the republic, due, disclosed a friend, "to desperation as a result of his state of misery and poverty." The suicide note of a former soldier in 1900 expresses the pathos of the Cuban condition with poignant clarity: "My name is Manuel Valdés. I am a soldier of the Liberation Army and belong to the Third Corps. Since I do not have resources, or position, or employment, and I am convinced that independence will not be achieved any time soon, I choose to kill myself."[16]

✠ A sense of unfinished purpose settled over the diverse constituen-cies of Cuba Libre, registered variously as disappointment and disillusion-ment, but mostly as discontent. The failure to redress those grievances that had served to mobilize vast numbers of men and women to dramatic action and heroic sacrifice in the nineteenth century, and more, the fail-ure to actualize the aspirations of three generations of Cubans, created a yawning moral void in the civic realms of the republic. In the years that followed, thoughtful observers arrived at an understanding of the charac-ter of the malaise that had settled over the constituencies of Cuba Libre. "Lucky indeed were the Cubans who had the good fortune to die during the military campaign, who perished with the dream of patriotic aspirations still fresh in their heart," mused historian Emilio Roig de Leuchsenring in 1939. "Unlike their surviving comrades-in-arms, they were spared the heart-ache of having to witness the failure of the Republic." Luis Aguilar León described a "generalized pessimism . . . emanating from the natural disillusionment of the frustrated dream." Essayist Waldo Medina attrib-uted the sources of Cuban angst to the dashed hopes of liberation. "Every-thing has been a failure, frustration, a loss of confidence in the national destiny, an erosion of the sentiment of nation and nationality," Medina wrote in the early 1950s. "The redemptive revolutions of 1868 and 1895 were subverted, the genuine ideals of the old liberators were betrayed. The last war organized by Martí was won, but for others, not for Cubans, who continued to live without land, without bread, without peace. Bread and peace that signified justice and democracy." Medina described the lives of veterans of the war, who endured "the mediated peace of the first foreign intervention—a national humiliation . . . and [source of] the great Cuban frustration." The "valiant defenders of the . . . patria meditated in silence with the shame of knowing that they were vanquished even though they were the victors: without land and without resources. . . . Poverty was transformed into the sole virtue of many of the men of the war."[17]

What remained pending, hence, and what persisted into the early decades of the twentieth century, was a social compact yet to be honored. The aspirations of the nineteenth century persisted as hopes unfulfilled and goals unmet, but most of all as ideals that retained the capacity to summon Cuban mobilization, ideals that would not go away and indeed could not be made to go away without repudiating the purpose for which so many had sacrificed so much. This too was the legacy of liberation, understood as an unfinished project to whose fulfillment subsequent generations were committed as duty of being Cuban. Writing two decades after the establishment of the republic, historian Ramiro Guerra reflected: "The disillusionment is great, the sorrow of the national masses is sincere, while a wave of cynicism subdues and almost extinguishes the enthusiasm of the early days. But the Nation does not lose faith in the patriotic ideals."[18]

The aspirations of the nineteenth century persisted deep into the twentieth century and indeed developed into the principal source of oppositional discourse in the early republic, the frame of reference from which Cuban mobilizations during the first half of the twentieth century derived purpose and program. The diverse constituencies of *Cuba Libre* reconstituted themselves around parties and programs dedicated to actualizing the ideals that had guided the nineteenth-century liberation project. The organization of the Partido Independiente de Color in 1907 to protest persisting racial discrimination, for example, and the subsequent armed protest of 1912, responded to the unfulfilled promises of the independentista project. Historian Alejandro de la Fuente was correct to note that while the republic failed to make racial equality a reality, "the idea itself was so strong as to impose its acceptance on all quarters of Cuban society."[19] Ten years later, the ideals of liberation served to galvanize the Veterans and Patriots Movement in opposition to the government of Alfredo Zayas.[20] Members of the Directorio Estudiantil Universitario (DEU) of the University of Havana in 1927 identified themselves as "the sons and daughters of that handful of heroes, that small group of titans, who scaled the summit of Immortality and Glory in the legendary [battles of] Peralejo, Las Guásimas, [and] Mal Tiempo." It was now the turn of students to join "the struggle for an Ideal and for a *Patria Libre*." Students claimed inspiration from "the pages of the glorious History of Cuba and the many magnificent examples of abnegation, of sacrifice, of patriotism, and of virtue . . . that have given form to the sentiment of Nationality." The DEU vowed to fulfill the historic mission of those Cubans "who with Spartan valor immolated the noble lives of [their] beloved children in the sacrifice for the Patria Redeemed." Julio Antonio Mella, founder of the Cuban Communist Party, identified the struggle against the government of Gerardo Machado (1925–33) as a continuation of the nineteenth-century struggle for liberation. "The cry of six generations of Cubans," Mella exhorted in 1928, "from the time of [Joaquín] Agüero [1816–51] through our times has been '*Cuba Libre.*' What does it mean? A great desire for secure liberty: yesterday from the Spanish regime; today from *machadista* despotism and American imperialism."[21]

❦ The liberation project of the nineteenth century thus served as legacy to live up to and passed into the narratives of the republic as purpose to pursue. The armed struggles of the 1930s against Machado and during the 1950s against the government of Fulgencio Batista (1952–58) drew explicitly upon nineteenth-century formulations of sacrifice and self-immolation: the necessity to submit to death as duty and destiny as binding and inescapable.[22] It was within the cues and codes of nationality, in those domains of received canons of conduct, that the purpose of sacrifice was commemorated. The death of Martí, of course, set the example and for all time thereafter served as the standard by which to measure conduct as Cuban. "It was necessary to act the way Martí had taught us . . . ," Rebel Army captain José Cuza reflected in 1958, "to stand up on our feet, preferring to die standing than to live on our knees. The people will never forget its martyrs and now more than ever before they will not be considered as dead, for to die for the Patria is to live."[23]

The larger meaning of sacrifice was mediated within those symbolic realms through which the culture conveyed approval and conferred honor, acted out in behavior modeled on heroic deeds associated with the nineteenth-century project of liberation. The duty of self-offering was transmitted as historically conditioned representations and registered as an attribute of Cuban. "All doors for peaceful struggle being closed to the people," Fidel Castro affirmed in 1955,

there is no solution other than that of [the revolutions] of 1868 and 1895. . . . We are Cubans, and to be Cuban implies a duty: not to fulfill this duty is a crime, it is treason. We live proud of the history of our patria;

we learned it in school and we have grown up hearing of freedom, of justice, and of rights. We were taught early to venerate the glorious examples of our heros and martyrs. Céspedes, Agramonte, Maceo, Gómez and Martí were the first names inscribed in our minds. We were taught that [Maceo] had said that liberty is not begged for, but rather conquered through the edge of the machete. . . . We were taught that October 10 [1868] and February 24 [1895] are glorious dates . . . on which Cubans rebelled against the yoke of infamous tyranny. We were taught to . . . sing an anthem every afternoon, the verses of which say that "To live in chains is to live in shame and dishonor" and that "To die for the patria is to live."[24]

In a "Manifesto to the Cuban People" in 1955, Castro again affirmed:

The Cuban revolutionary movement is today organized and prepared for its great task of redemption and justice. . . . The streets and parks of our cities and towns bear the names and display with pride the statues of Maceo, Martí, Máximo Gómez, Calixto García, Céspedes, Agramonte, Flor Crombet, Bartolomé Masó, and other illustrious heroes who knew how to rebel. In school our glorious history is taught, and the dates of October 10 and February 24 are venerated with devotion. These were not dates of submission or of resigned and cowardly acceptance of existing despotism. . . . In adopting again the line of sacrifice we assume before history responsibility for our acts.[25]

The willingness to die in a manner befitting a Cuban, acquiting oneself per prescribed conduct, was consecrated through the exemplary lives and deaths of Cubans in the past. To do less implied dereliction of duty and dishonor to the ideal of Cuban. Good Cubans were expected to die for their patria. So many great ones had. Fidel Castro alluded often to the suicide of Eduardo Chibás, "from whom [those who perished at Moncada] learned to die when the patria is in need of heroic immolation to lift the faith of the people . . . in the inevitable realization of their historic destiny."[26] Comments the narrator in Luis Ricardo Alonso's novel of the attack on the Presidential Palace in 1957, *El palacio y la furia*: "Many were ashamed that they had escaped with their lives. Perhaps it was the influence of religion, of so many years hearing talk of the glory of martyrdom. And for those who did not believe in God, twelve years in school hearing talk of the martyrs of the patria: Martí, Maceo, hundreds of others. Since everyone was going to die, we use to say in school, it was preferable to die like the great heroes. There wasn't a single boy who wanted to die in bed."[27]

The act of death in discharge of duty was possessed of an internal logic, derived from the realms of self-knowledge as a Cuban, in function of those ideals perceived necessary to sustain the ideal of patria. Its principal instrumental value was as exemplary deed to mobilize others to action and thereby forge solidarities in service of the ideals of liberation. Leví Marrero wrote of the power of heroic sensibilities during the 1930s in his autobiographical novel *La generación asesinada* (1934). The narrative voice explains the clandestine activities of the protagonist: "He now gave his convictions expression in the sequence of daily deeds. The deaths aroused in their aftermath the dormant courage of youth, and no reprisal, even the most savage acts, could discourage the vital determination that aroused an entire generation, whose members did not go beyond the age of 25."[28]

The example of self-immolation, transacted as display of devotion and demonstration of duty to die, as symbolic protest, lay in its capacity to draw others into its purpose. "In a revolution . . . ," affirms the protagonist in José Soler Puig's novel *Bertillón 166* (1960), "the dead serve as a banner . . . to stir the living by way of a call to arms."[29] Sacrifice of self obtained moral vindication within the normative determinants of nationality as an affirmation of the dignity of Cuban. "Our deed will set an example for the people of Cuba," Fidel Castro assured his followers on the eve of the attack on Moncada barracks in 1953, "and from the people will arise other young men and women disposed to die for Cuba, to pick up our banner and move forward. The people of Oriente [province] and across the island will support us. . . . As in 1868 and 1895, here in Oriente, we make the first cry of 'Liberty or Death!'"[30] The burial of student leader Rubén Batista Rubio, killed by the police in 1953, provided an occasion to invoke the exemplary value of sacrifice. "The tomb is not an end but a means, as the Apostle [José Martí] said," student leader Enrique Huertas Pozo affirmed in a graveside eulogy. "Cubans! The death of leaders provides the example: Rubén will be the Spiritual Leader of the Cuban Revolution because he has given us the example of dying for the cause of Cuban liberty." José Joaquín Peláez, president of the University Student Federation (FEU), added: "For us Rubén will never die. The causes that never die . . . are the ones for which we die, and the cause of the University youth will never die."[31]

Sacrifice embodied meanings deeply inscribed in the narratives of nationality. This was propaganda of the dead, so fully historically conditioned that its meaning was at once self-evident and self-explanatory. "The duty to sacrifice one's self for the patria," insisted Fidel Castro, "is incumbent on everyone, not just a few."[32] The moral of sacrifice was enacted with didactic intent, to arouse popular indignation: to end one's life for the purpose of arousing others to action, to discharge the duty of Cuban, to be sure, but also to serve as example for others to follow in exponential numbers. "One hero dies and hundreds of combatants come forth," Faure Chomón of the Directorio Revolucionario proclaimed after the attack against the Presidential Palace in 1957. "It would be said," the narrative voice in Bernardo Callejas's short story "Para aprender a manejar la pistola" observes, "that the Movimiento [Revolucionario 26-7] and the Directorio had inexhaustible reserves . . . , that for each *compañero* who disappeared, for each face that dissolved in the bitterness of the struggle, five new ones emerged: all young, filled with vitality and, paradoxically, proclaiming their desire to die." The protagonist, Luis, in *El sol a plomo* (1959), by Humberto Arenal, comments tersely: "Here there is always someone disposed to die."[33]

It is impossible, of course, to determine the number of Cubans motivated to participate in or otherwise support armed resistance as a response to the sacrifice of others. But it is clear that if death registered any meaning at all, if it were not to be for nothing, if the lives of those who perished had value and virtue, the cause for which they died similarly acquired value and virtue. Inocencia Acosta Felipe remembered the death of a close friend at Moncada, and it was at that moment, she recalled, "when I really became a sympathizer of the Twenty-Sixth of July Movement, a *patria o muerte* revolutionary." She added: "Mario's death woke me up. I said to myself, 'If he died for this cause it must be something very good, therefore I too am willing to die for it.'. . . After Mario's death I pledged to do everything I could [for] the Revolution."[34] The death of student Rubén Batista Rubio in 1953, José Luis Llovio-Menéndez wrote years later, "sent shock waves throughout Cuba." Participation in the student demonstration, Llovio-Menéndez remembered, "had a galvanizing effect on me. . . . Moreover—and for the first time in my life—I felt, among us young boys of such different social, religious, and ethnic backgrounds, a Cuban solidarity. I was one of them. . . . My sense of right and wrong had been transformed into a political awakening. A naive act became the first step to my becoming a revolutionary." This was similar to the experience of Monica Ramos Reyes, who recalled the death of a family friend at the hands of the Batista police: "I was only a child when he died but I was deeply shocked and grieved. Through his death I lived the political moment intensely and reacted with hatred toward Batista and all his followers."[35]

Self-immolation served to discredit iniquitous rule through the enactment of the claim of a superior morality conveyed in the willingness to die. In Raúl González de Cascorro's play *El mejor fruto*, set in the year 1958, Rolando is told: "You will achieve nothing. You will be crushed. You cannot defeat them. They are stronger. They have all the force." Rolando responds: "But we have something far greater than more force: we fight for an ideal. To be free." In conversation with his mother Rolando explains the logic of sacrifice and sets the moral dimension of self-immolation in relief. "Far better to die than live under such indignity," he explains. "There is no solution," the mother responds, "why then this futile sacrifice? Why?" And Rolando answers: "To awaken conscience! It is necessary to demand. It is necessary to scream truth to the deaf, to all who are indifferent."[36] Teresa Casuso depicted the disposition to die during the 1930s with poignance in her autobiographical novel *Los ausentes* (1944). "There was constant discussion of the revolutionary expedition that was to deliver supplies and infuse a new spirit into [the struggle for] freedom," the narrator comments, and adds:

> The youth returned to the epic theme and to the casual mention of death, although they treated it almost like a sport, without giving it any serious thought or fear. They spoke of the possibility of dying and the suicide that could result from that expedition as if it were the most natural thing in the world. 'But if you know that it is futile, that the conditions in Cuba are not ready to respond to expeditions or uprisings, why don't you refuse to go?' I asked anxiously. 'What do you want us to do?'—responded Leopoldo. 'We have received word from Mexico and Miami that everything is already prepared. It is our only solution, the last card to play. And if they depart, even if it is suicide, we have to commit suicide with them. There is no other way.'[37]

To die, in the end, was to do something, as compared to doing nothing, to act out indignation, to die because there was nothing else to do, no other way to register resistance. This is what Haydée Santamaría recalled of the 1950s: "Death, imposing itself on us as a necessity."[38] In *El palacio y la furia*, novelist Luis Ricardo Alonso depicts the decision to die in the attack on the Presidential Palace "as an instrumental suicide. To be resolved to commit suicide but to do so as if to live and sacrifice everything. To give up life and to continue living. To release an immense current of energy." On the eve of the attack of the palace in 1957, José Antonio Echeverría drafted a farewell note in presentiment of his own death. "I try simply to fulfill my duty," he wrote. "If we fail, let our blood point the way to liberty."[39]

Suicide was registered as resistance and as a fate to which some simply must submit. This was a destiny inscribed within cognitive realms of nationality. It loomed large during the struggles against Machado and Batista. "We fight precisely to end this [intolerable] situation," affirms the protagonist in Leví Marrero's novel *La generación asesinada*. "To demonstrate how suicidal youth with a love for life can save a nation. . . . None of us surrender ourselves to death without understanding what it signifies." "Eternal and glorious life to those who die fighting for a better life!" exclaims protagonist Onelio Capote in Leonel López-Nussa's short story "Una caída suave, una sonrisa," and adds: "Am I going to die? I don't want to, but neither does it concern me. I will simply fulfill my duty." Novelist Roberto de Acevedo described the young men and women who perished during the 1930s as belonging to a "race of martyrs."[40] José Soler Puig characterized the resistance to Batista during the 1950s in similar terms. "Batista cannot cope with them," comments the protagonist in *Bertillón 166*. "They have the Sierra and thousands of young people who allow themselves to be killed, who commit suicide." The narrator reflects: "What will become of all those youths who, demanding liberty, throw themselves into the struggle against Batista with no weapon other than their blood? Good people, valuable people. Perhaps the only good people left in Cuba. The demand for liberty was driving them crazy and suicidal. The desire for liberty made everything else—misery, racial discrimination, class conflict—seem to lack importance. Liberty, liberty, and nothing but liberty. The desire for liberty was their obsession; to obtain it, their blood, by oceans."[41] "These victories," novelist Francisco Chao Hermida affirms through his protagonist in *Un obrero de vanguardia* (1972), "always have a price: martyrs," and adds: "Blood, vital for human beings, was also vital for revolution, and the former nurtures it to be spilled for the latter."[42]

Sacrifice of self, that is, death deliberately chosen, was celebrated as exemplary conduct and praiseworthy suicide and deemed indispensable to the success of armed resistance during the 1930s and 1950s. In the struggle against Machado during the 1930s, *New York Times* correspondent Ruby Hart Phillips wrote of the "action squads" of the ABC Revolutionary Society, made up of 150 youth "who were willing to sacrifice their lives." During the guerrilla war in 1958, Column 8 "Ciro Redondo," commanded by Ernesto Che Guevara, operated with a special "suicide platoon" led by Captain Roberto Rodríguez ("el Vaquerito"). Made up of 100 volunteers, the suicide platoon conducted special military operations in which high casualties were always incurred. Rodríguez perished in December 1958 during the battle of Santa Clara. "[Vaquerito] flirted with death a thousand and one times during the struggle for liberty," Guevara later wrote. "The 'Suicide Platoon' was a model of revolutionary morale, to which only select volunteers were chosen. Yet every time a man was killed—and this occurred in every battle—upon the designation of a replacement, those rejected displayed deep and often tearful disappointment. It was odd to see brave and noble veterans revealing their youthfulness through tears for not receiving the honor to have been chosen to occupy the front line of combat and death."[43]

Suicide was also a fate contemplated by members of the Civic Resistance. The men and women of the urban underground lived daily with an abiding fear of being captured alive and subsequently subjected to torture, including beatings, dismemberment, and rape. "In the Sierra [Maestra] . . . you could say: 'Well, if I'm killed, at least I'll die fighting,'" Vilma Espín explained the difference between guerrilla warfare in the mountains and clandestine operations in the cities. "In the city, you always felt like a hunted animal: cornered, quite simply, with no way of saving your life. In the city death comes after prison, torture, all those things. It's very hard."[44] In Julio Travieso's novel of the Havana underground *Para matar el lobo* (1981), the protagonist, Irene, is captured by the police and prepares for her death at the hands of torturers: "Life for the sake of living was worth nothing, and she would have preferred to have been killed on the street. . . . But alone, deprived of everything, naked in that sinister prison, in that black well. All that was left to her was her dignity. Better than her own death, her dignity would be her tribute to her fallen comrades. 'Anyone can die but not all know how,' she told herself. 'Dignity is all that remains to the crushed.'"[45]

Many in the urban underground carried in their possession cyanide pills or some other form of poison they were prepared to ingest if captured.[46] "If I fall prisoner again," Carlos Franqui vowed in 1958, "I will kill myself before enduring torture."[47] Journalist Sergio Carbó reported in 1958 of the large number of "youths who commit suicide out of fear of being captured alive by the police." In early 1958, Clemente Orlando Nodarse Verde, the 26 July Movement leader in Pinar del Río, was detained by the police and committed suicide during his interrogation. "My son had vowed to commit suicide before falling prisoner again," his father explained. "He had suffered too much during previous detentions."[48] The narrator in *Para matar el lobo* recounts the fate of one imprisoned member of the urban resistance: "The *compañero* went irremediably insane. He had to be committed to Mazorra [insane asylum]. Of course, after what they did to him it was to be expected. Before his very eyes they raped his daughter and his wife. . . . The daughter was thirteen years old. She soon thereafter committed suicide. Imagine, she was about to give birth."[49]

❧ Among the meanings around which the Cuban revolution was configured after January 1, 1959, none were as dominant as those that drew upon the purpose of the nineteenth-century mobilizations. Emphasis was given to national redemption in the name of self-determination and sovereignty, for which so much had been sacrificed, with the understanding that more sacrifice would be required. As early as 1956, in its "Manifesto-Program," the 26 July Movement claimed continuity with the nineteenth-century liberation project, insisting that armed struggle was "at least as justified today as it was in 1868 and 1895, perhaps more so. In reality, we are resuming the unfinished revolution of Martí." It continued: "Cuba fully possesses the geographical, historical, political, economic, and sociological justifications to constitute itself as a sovereign and independent nation. This is the first and basic affirmation of our struggle. Without it, the historical progress of the Cuban people in the last one hundred years would be totally devoid of sense."[50]

At stake in this formulation was the survival of patria, after which nothing remained and for which, hence, no sacrifice was too great, no struggle too long. The proposition of patria was conflated with the project of revolution, and by 1960 both became interchangeable and virtually indistinguishable from one another. The cry *Libertad o muerte* of 1958 was replaced by *Patria o muerte* in 1960, to which was added one year later *Socialismo o muerte*.[51] "The concept of '*Patria*' is no different from the concept of '*Revolución*'," Raúl Castro insisted in 1960. He continued:

After [the explosion of the French freighter] *La Coubre* . . . Fidel proclaimed '*Patria o muerte*' [and] before anything else, that has the fundamental significance to signify that the Cuban people have the resolve and the determination to defend their Patria, to defend the Revolution. '*Patria o muerte*' has nothing to do with a fatalist significance nor does this imply that everyone here is going to die, although everyone is disposed to die, if it becomes necessary. . . . The people today unanimously adopt the watchword '*Patria o muerte*' because 'Patria' means, in this instance, all the revolutionary laws, all the benefits that these times have brought to the people, including the glorious sacrifices that in the future will be beneficial for our children, for our grandchildren, for all our future generations.[52]

Sacrifice was celebrated as legacy of liberation, but also as duty consecrated by those who perished in the struggle against Batista. Just like the end of the war for independence, the triumph of revolution announced the change of names of thousands of public places, institutes, schools, and parks to honor the martyrs of the armed struggle against the Batista government, including the Manuel Fajardo Hospital, the Heroes of Yaguajay High School, the Gustavo Izquierdo Library, the René Fraga Park, the Julio Reyes Cairo Teaching Institute, Julio Pino Machado Secondary School, and the Fructoso Rodríguez Orthopedic Hospital, among others. The names of almost all the sugar mills were changed, and most bore the names of Cubans who perished in the insurrection: Orlando Nodarse, Esteban Hernández, José Antonio Echeverría, Obdulio Morales, Abel Santamaría, Braulio Coroneaux, Hermanos Ameijeiras, Pepito Tey, "El Vaquerito," Ciro Redondo, and Frank País.

The past assumed a new meaning in the service of old paradigms. The teaching of history after 1959 gave renewed emphasis to sacrifice as a condition of being Cuban. Heroic comportment of the past served as a model of conduct for all time, informed with the moral of debt owed to previous generations and duty required to future generations. "It is necessary," insisted a teaching manual for eighth grade history, "that students be taught by the instructor to become aware of the objective relationships that exist between new conditions and the circumstances of the past."[53] Fourth grade history lessons stressed the importance of students learning "that the transformations that have been produced in the lives of the Cuban people . . . are the results of many years of struggle to achieve independence, liberty, and happiness, for which many people gave their lives." The lesson plan for the Ten Years War—"a war of great sacrifices in which the Cuban people gave repeated examples of patriotism and valor"—emphasized the importance of the "great efforts and exemplary sacrifices" as a means to "contribute to the patriotic and moral education of the students." The lesson plan dedicated to José Martí emphasized the importance of students learning "how even a young Martí sacrificed for his oppressed patria." The enduring lesson of the nineteenth-century wars of liberation, stressed one eleventh grade history reader, "was in the example of valor and sacrifice . . . which should be imitated at all times and all places."[54]

The burning of Bayamo was remembered with renewed reverence. The moral was unambiguous. Historian Onoria Céspedes Argote character-ized the burning of Bayamo as "one of the most glorious pages of the his-tory of the patria: . . . a declaration to the world of the Cuban decision to secure its independence at any price, even if it were necessary to resort to the supreme sacrifices that such determination necessitated."[55] "The city does not exist: not a single house remains standing to live in," was the re-frain in José Miguel Garófalo's ode to Bayamo in 1968. He continued: "The city does not exist: not a single man to take prisoner. . . . The city does not exist: smoking rubble and empty streets. . . . The [Spanish] order to take the city cannot be obeyed: the city does not exist. . . . Bayamo, poor city— long live Bayamo, invincible city." Historians Eduardo Torres Cuevas and Oscar Loyola Vega characterized the burning of Bayamo as an "epic gesture [and a] demonstration of noteworthy energy and patriotic decisiveness"; while Rafael Acosta de Arriba celebrated "the heroic burning of Bayamo." Wrote poet Rafael Alcides Pérez in 1988: "And afterwards, we the people of Bayamo eternally continue singing the [national anthem] 'La Bayamesa' with the same air of testimony and the same spirit of suicide that we so beautifully sang on the morning of the Fire." The commemoration of the burning of Guáimaro invoked the obvious moral: "The patriotic act . . . demonstrated the decision of Cubans to sacrifice themselves as much as necessary in order to obtain liberty."[56]

The exhortation of *Patria o muerte* was not a sentiment invented by the leaders of the revolution, of course, but, rather, served to convey the very sentiments by which they themselves had been formed. Duty to die was the legacy of liberation, duly consecrated as a virtue of being Cuban. "We know how to fulfill our duty . . . ," Fidel Castro affirmed in 1960, "be-cause we Cubans have learned to face death serenely, without flinching. . . . The people of Cuba, its workers, its peasants, its students, its women, its young and old, even its children, will not waver in taking their positions with tranquility, without hesitation, without even blinking an eye, the day that any foreign force dares to land on our beaches. . . . This is a people pre-pared to defend itself. This is a people with the capacity to march against the mushroom cloud of nuclear bombs."[57] The centennial celebration of the Ten Years War in 1968 provided Castro with the occasion to reflect on the relevance of the nineteenth-century wars of liberation to the Cuban conflict with the United States: "As of that moment [1868], for the first time, the concept and awareness of nationality began to take form and for the first time the term of 'Cuban' was used to designate those who rose up with arms to fight against the Spanish colonial power." And to the point:

> The study of the history of our country will not only enlighten our consciousness and our thinking, but it will also help us find an inexhaustible supply of heroism, of the spirit of sacrifice, of the will to struggle and fight. What those combatants did, almost unarmed, should always be an inspiration for the revolutionaries of today, always a reason to have confidence in our people, in their strength, their capacity to struggle, their destiny. It should give our country the assurance that nothing or nobody in this world can defeat us. . . . And that this revolution cannot be defeated by anything, because this people, who have fought for 100 years for its destiny, is capable of fighting for another 100 years for the same destiny. This people that was capable of sacrificing its life (inmolarse) more than once, would be capable to die as many times as it were necessary.[58]

Reference to the Ten Years War was invoked with an unambiguous moral. "It is well-known," Castro exhorted in 1968, "that few people in the world were capable or had the capacity to undertake sacrifices so great, so incredibly difficult, as the sacrifices the Cuban people endured in the course of ten years of struggle. And to ignore those sacrifices is a crime against justice, it is a crime against culture, it is a crime for any revolutionary."[59]

The imperative of sacrifice reached deeply into discursive formulations of the revolution. The disposition to die was reaffirmed as an attribute of Cuban. "The heroic phase of the armed struggle must be continued during the no less heroic stage of construction of daily life under new circumstances," affirmed writer Pedro de Oraá in 1974. He continued: "All will achieve their full potential and meaning, which is within a collective origin. In this way everyone will achieve the possibility of heroism, central to which is the necessity of sacrifice. . . . To the [proposition of] sacrifice as immolation vital to bring the patria into existence and to protect it thereafter and forever is added the [idea of] sacrifice as an on-going example to construct the patria and develop its wealth. This concept of sacrifice unites us. . . . The supreme act of sacrifice fulfills us."[60]

The evocative power of the revolution resided in its capacity to render the experience of sacrifice as a historically conditioned attribute of Cuban.

The formulation of duty as an imperative of the revolution obtained endorsement precisely because it had historic antecedents as a prescriptive demand of nationality, understood as a legacy to uphold and heritage to honor. The dominant metaphors of an ideological system, Clifford Geertz has correctly suggested, and their capacity to mediate meanings, must be understood not for any objective reality they may serve to reveal but for their capacity to communicate social relationships and convey representations of purpose for the audience to which they are directed.[61] As Cuba pressed deeper into the realms of radical change, as opposition mounted at home and abroad, the duty of sacrifice developed into a dominant injunction of the revolutionary process. "It is necessary to save Cuba," army auditor Luis Pérez Perdomo exhorted militia trainees as early as 1959. "The Apostle [José Martí] said that liberty exacts a dear price, and that it is necessary either to live without it or purchase it for whatever it costs. And the price of liberty is the sacrifice of the best among us." He continued:

> When the Patria bleeds, it is necessary to heal the wound with blood. A nation that does not have martyrs, does not have liberty. . . . Liberty is forged through sacrifice, through martyrdom. A people are free only when the price of liberty is paid with lives. A people cannot be enslaved when the way to sacrifice is emblazoned with the names of Maceo, Martí, Agramonte, Céspedes, Guiteras . . . : all unforgettable. A people who offer men such as these were born for liberty. With these examples, with these names which are the banners and hymns of combat, you will advance into the battle field, where the fate of Cuba will be determined. . . . You are the representatives of a youth who wear sacrifice like a halo. . . . You cannot fail Cuba: you simply cannot fail in the face of the inexorable demands of the Patria. You must choose death before failure.[62]

Not since José Martí in the nineteenth century did the proposition of death as duty loom as large in the discursive domains of nationality as it did in the pronouncements of Fidel Castro. "That spirit of sacrifice of the people . . . ," Castro affirmed in 1959, "that disposition of the willingness to make every sacrifice necessary, [and] that conviction that the destiny of the Cuban people is achieved only through sacrifice—that is what sustains us: to count on a people disposed to make whatever sacrifices are necessary, . . . that the nation will defend itself until the last drop of blood, that Cuba will never allow itself to be defeated. . . . And we vow: Cuba will triumph or we will all die, for more than ever before we take onto ourselves the lyric of our National Anthem: 'To die for the Patria is to live.'"[63] "If we are disposed to die for the defense of our land," he exhorted one year later, "how can we not be disposed to sacrifice ourselves in the same way to defend our sovereignty; how can we not also be disposed to resist economic aggression." Cubans were disposed to defend themselves, Castro insisted, and "even the dead, our heroic dead, will rise to fight along side the Cuban people, to provide us sustenance and inspiration." "The truth . . . is sustained by an entire people who . . . have proclaimed '*Patria o muerte*,'" he insisted, "an affirmation that each of its sons is disposed to die for his patria." "What do we have to confront their power?" Castro asked on the occasion of the Bay of Pigs invasion. "Well, in the first place, . . . we do not fear them, and that is important, that of not fearing their power. . . . Second, [we have] the disposition to resist and face any type of attack, come what may. . . . There is only one position for us, and that is in the trenches. There is where we will await the enemy. There is where we will also await death, with tranquility." "Let there be no doubt," Castro insisted on another occasion, "that men here will die to defend their patria. . . . How naive [our enemies] are in not realizing that we here have cast our fate with the humble (*los humildes*) of our patria and that we will never again abandon that flag. We are all disposed to die for that flag; all the leaders of Cuba are disposed to die along side of that flag."[64]

The imagery recalled nineteenth-century dispositions to self-immolation rather than acquiescence to subjugation. On the occasion of the missile crisis of October 1962, Castro insisted that Cubans were disposed to face complete annihilation rather than permit the United States to violate national sovereignty through inspection of the island: "We believe in the right to defend liberty, sovereignty, and the dignity of this nation and we will exercise it resolutely up to the last man, woman, and child capable of holding arms in this territory." In 1975, Castro reaffirmed the duty of Cubans: "As of this moment I am saying that we will not yield to any demand, nor will we allow ourselves to be intimidated by any threat, or anything. We will always be here, ready as we have been these past 20 years, ready for anything, disposed to defend our country, disposed to defend the rights of our country, disposed to fight and disposed to die for our country. That is very clear, for that is the only thing that we can do."[65]

The summons to sacrifice assumed a new urgency during the 1990s, the years of the "Special Period," as the effects of the collapse of the Soviet bloc reverberated throughout Cuba and visited frightful hardships on Cubans across the island. "Liberty, dignity, equality, honor, [and] justice . . . ," Fidel Castro insisted in 1993, "are the values for which so many generations of Cubans have fought and for which so many Cubans have sacrificed themselves." He continued:

> We should know how to be their worthy descendants. These are the values that make us strong. These are the values that make us invincible. The patria must be defended. The nation must be defended. It has required much work and blood to keep [the United States] from swallowing us up. And now, without the socialist bloc, now when that empire has hegemony over the world, we must show it that there is a nation with sufficient decorum, with sufficient dignity, with sufficient spirit, with sufficient consciousness, and with sufficient revolutionary ideas [not] to be swallowed up, [not] to be made to surrender, [not] to be made to drop to its knees.[66]

All through the 1990s, in terms strikingly reminiscent of the imagery of the nineteenth century, Fidel Castro propounded on the importance of sacrifice as the means to prevail. "If we have to make thousands of sacrifices, we will make them . . . ," he exhorted in 1991. "If we are willing to make sacrifices for one, two, three or five years, we will make them, because we defend liberty, independence, the revolution, socialism, justice, [and] the future. . . . We will defend that hope which the nation, the revolution and socialism gives us, with our last drop of blood. We would rather die than be left without a nation. We would rather die than be left without the revolution and socialism, because the alternative is moral death, the most terrible of deaths."[67]

The duty of death was invoked repeatedly. "We know who our teachers were and we know who pointed the way. And none of those who showed us the way abandoned their position," Castro propounded in 1991.

> Céspedes never abandoned his position. Agramonte never abandoned his post. Neither did Máximo Gómez, nor Maceo nor Martí. Almost all of them died in that struggle for independence. . . . We do not proclaim 'Patria o Muerte' without the firmest conviction that together with our people, if it is necessary to die, we will all die. Imperialism will not find slaves among our revolutionary people. . . . Any sacrifice will be preferable to losing the country's independence, losing the revolution, losing socialism, which gave us complete dignity for the first time and gave us complete freedom for the first time.

In an address to the Federation of Secondary School Students Castro returned to this theme: "[The patria] did not lose hope when Martí fell at

Dos Ríos. Martí died knowing that he died for what we have today, for this that we are defending today. When Martí died at Dos Ríos, he knew that there would be men and women like you, willing to do what he did. When Maceo died at Punta Brava, he knew that he was dying for a people like this one, and that there would be men and women capable of dying as he did."[68] At the graveside eulogy of several Cubans killed in 1992, Castro exhorted that their deaths did not, "as Hemingway suggested in his novel *For Whom the Bells Toll*, diminish humanity. In this case, we do not feel diminished; we feel enriched, we feel stronger, we are inspired, by their example. They knew how to die. . . . [They] knew how to offer their lives to the Revolution and the Patria with valor. That is, they were disposed to give even their lives to defend the Revolution and the Patria. And what can we say at this moment of farewell? We should say, simply, that all of us feel capable of doing the same."[69] Addressing the Fourth Party Congress, Castro invoked the past as precedent and principle. "Each of us [is] willing to fight to the death," Castro exhorted. "What is life for us without the patria?" He continued:

We will always have present those who died in the fight against tyranny . . . and the many who died during our wars for independence. . . . The people of 1868 . . . and the people of 1895 and the Sierra Maestra never feared being put to a test, never feared making sacrifices. . . . The example of each will be multiplied, the heroism of each will be multiplied. If all the members of the party must die, then all the members of the party will die and we will not be weaker because of it. If all the members of the Union of Young Communists [UJC] must die, they will die, all the militants of the UJC will die. If to crush the revolution they have to kill all the people, the people would be willing to die in support of their leaders and their party. . . . Men may die, but ideals will never die, and here we are willing to shed our blood for our ideals. No worthy example, no just ideal has ever been defeated. Maceo, you were not defeated in 1868, nor in 1878. Maceo, you were not defeated the day you fell in Punta Brava. Martí, you were not defeated the day you fell in Dos Ríos. Because of you, your example and your death, today there are millions of Cubans willing to follow your example, willing to defend the ideals, and willing to die as you did to save freedom, to save justice, to save the honor and dignity of men. Without honor and dignity, there cannot be life, nor is life worth anything, nor do we want life. Without honor and dignity, life has no meaning, nor do we want life, not only ours, but even the life of those we love. Without honor, decorum, independence, and dignity, a country is nothing. The life of a country has no importance.[70]

To abandon the principles of the revolution, to compromise the principles of sovereignty and self-determination, was to give up on life altogether. And on this issue Fidel Castro was unambiguous. "We will not commit suicide with cowardly concessions and compromises," he insisted to the Sixth Congress of the Union of Young Communists (UJC). "Nor will we destroy ourselves or renounce our independence. We will not renounce our complete unity. We will not renounce hope. . . . To deprive us of what we have, they will have to exterminate us, if they can exterminate us."[71]

❧ The proposition of a socialist revolution did not draw everyone into its purpose, of course. Many Cubans lay beyond the appeal of its vision and approval of its means. Certainly the material condition of vast numbers of people improved immediately after 1959. But it is also true that the upward mobility of some came as a result of the downward mobility of others. Urban Reform reduced rents as much as 50 percent, at a corresponding loss of income to landlords and profits for investors. Real wages increased an average of 15 percent through a commensurate decrease in the earnings of employers. Entire sectors of the old economy became superfluous and disappeared, and with them vanished the jobs of thousands of Cubans. Insurance services, real estate agencies, mortgage brokers, advertising agencies, law firms, rent collectors, travel agencies, gambling casinos, and retail operations disappeared. The expropriation of North American property had immediate repercussions, as an estimated 150,000 Cuban employees, including attorneys, accountants, engineers, technicians, managers, clerks, and secretaries, suddenly found themselves under new management. The Revolutionary Offensive in the late 1960s culminated in the nationalization of all private property outside of agriculture, including an estimated total of 56,000 small businesses and enterprises.[72]

Many tens of thousands of Cubans, men and women of modest means and great wealth alike, from small vendors to large industrialists, dispossessed of property, denied a means of livelihood, often deprived of liberty, passed from discontent to dissent and eventually departed into exile. "The great emigration was simply because Cubans did not accept a real change in their life, their way of life . . . ," Fichu Menocal remarked to Lynn Geldof years later. "I think the people that left the island left because they loved their way of life better than their country. And they went to the States because there they would continue to live in the same way and they were not willing to do any sacrifice for their country."[73]

This was partly true, of course, but it was more complicated. The triumph of the Cuban revolution in 1959 announced one of the most far-reaching social transformations of the twentieth century. The speed and scope of change were breathtaking. Within the space of twenty-four months, the value system of a generation passed into desuetude, and worse: it fell into disrepute and disdain. What had previously been valued and virtuous was vilified; time-honored conventions of daily life, from child-rearing practices to modalities of public communication and language, canons of style and self-representation, no less than dress and demeanor, were disavowed and denounced. "The Revolution brought an abrupt change to my life," Irma de León recalled years later. "Everything that I had been taught and stood for changed." What Raquel Mendieta Costa later recalled most vividly "was amazement, amazement at a world that was radically changing, becoming the opposite of everything I had known up to that point. . . . The world was split into two irreconcilable halves: before and now. . . . Those were years of constantly dying and being born again, when everything that had up to then seemed familiar turned strange, unrecognizable."[74]

These were years of bewilderment: incomprehensible to some, inconceivable to others. The revolution had undermined the most basic assumptions by which vast numbers of people had come to understand the world and their place in it. An entire generation of middle-class Cubans had been cut adrift and displaced, without bearings, many late in their lives and at a loss for what to do next. They discerned things out of order and themselves out of place, without purpose, without prospects; they found themselves as outsiders in a place they had previously called home, strangers in their own land. In the play *Morir del cuento*, by Abelardo Estorino, Adela recalls the departure of her brother: "With the triumph of the Revolution, he decided to leave. No—'decided' nothing—he was obliged to leave. Because when one is accustomed to living one way and suddenly is told that he has to live another way. . . . Well, what was he going to do here!" In Juan Arcocha's novel *Los muertos andan solos* (1962), Esperanza despairs "as if the world was collapsing, without knowing what was coming next." Edmundo Desnoes gave first-person poignance to this experience in *Inconsolable Memories* (1967): "Reality seems to be slipping through my fingers. In the streets I hear things I no longer understand. . . . If I keep on being so isolated from everything that's going on around me, the day will come when I won't understand a thing." And at another point: "Cuba has been turned upside down; or downside up; it's possible." Broods the narrator: "I felt ready for suicide."[75]

Change was experienced directly and in deeply personal terms, as the values, habits, and motives with which many Cubans had defined themselves in the most basic and intimate facets of daily life no longer worked —or worse: worked against them. Vast numbers of people who had been formed under the old ways, those who had previously done the "right" things to make a place for themselves in Cuba, suddenly found that the rules had changed and, in fact, they no longer fit in. "I noticed that something fundamental had changed," comments Adriana in Freddy Artiles's play *Adriana en dos tiempos* (1972). "I did not fully understand what, but I sensed that it was something new and above all something different. Even the people seemed different. The outside world entered into the home and into one's self."[76] In Lisandro Otero's partly autobiographical novel *Arbol de la vida* (1990), the protagonist reflects on Cuba as he had previously known it: "And now all that was disappearing and the knowledge that the pillars of society as we knew them would cease to exist left me with a strange emptiness. . . . An unknown world opened before me, without the values that were familiar to me." He continues:

> I learned to live with insecurity. One woke up every morning with the impression that at the end of the day life would be over; no one could possibly know what complexities, what changes, reforms, and transfigurations would transpire in the course of a day. Everything was in transition: the earth could open and swallow us up in a flash and the Revolution go up in smoke and nothing would remain, not even a sentimental memory of our passing through this world. Millennia and seconds fused, permanence and ephemera began and ended in an eternal daily routine. Where was life and where was death?[77]

The revolution aspired to nothing less than the creation of a new consciousness of Cuban: "the New Man," imbued with selfless virtue motivated by social conscience. The project of the revolution demanded complete engagement—*vincularse*, as it was called—relentlessly and remorselessly, often ruthlessly: to demonstrate and participate, to join and volunteer—to act, in short, in display of solidarity and demonstration of support. The process was as pervasive as it was prepossessing, and at times it seemed as if nothing else mattered. "The Revolution just doesn't leave time to see family," Inocencia Acosta Felipe explained to Oscar Lewis, "except by chance at mass rallies, or here and there." Playwright Nicolás Dorr gave voice to the same sentiment through the complaint of Graciela in *Mediodía candente*: "This Revolution doesn't even allow time to keep up a household." In Héctor Quintero's play *Te sigo esperando*, Alcides comments: "It is a fact that the family has dispersed. And often all that remains are Sundays to get together for lunch. . . . The family has been reduced to one reunion on the weekend." Broods the protagonist, Menchu, in Uva de Aragón's novel, *Memoria del silencio* (2002): "Sometimes the Revolution transforms itself into a chattering witch who torments me. It is as if we did not have a private life, as if all the problems of the world, from the death of Ho Chi Minh to who should study in the university, invade my intimacy."[78]

The revolution transported Cubans deeply into the realms of social experimentation. It propounded an all-encompassing and self-implicating paradigm of engagement from which it was all but impossible to stay aloof —not at least without raising doubts about one's devotion to the new order of things. "There is no life outside the Revolution," Ernesto Che Guevara pronounced in 1965.[79] It was not simply, hence, that the revolution was intolerant of opposition. It was more complicated. The revolution was intolerant of indifference. Fidel Castro drew the dichotomy more starkly: "In a revolutionary process, there are no neutrals; there are only partisans of the revolution or enemies."[80] That insufficient enthusiasm for the revolution as a cause for suspicion, as a punishable failing, could indeed lead to discontent, dissent, and eventually opposition acquired a self-fulfilling logic. The combination of harassment, detention and interrogation, occupational displacement, and confiscation was cause enough to drive some Cubans, many of whom were guilty only of the desire to be left alone, into opposition.

By the end of the 1960s, the lives of countless tens of thousands of Cubans had been dramatically changed forever. Many had been dispossessed of property, their careers disrupted, and the order of daily life as previously lived thrown into permanent disarray. Thousands of others suspected of counterrevolutionary activity were detained and imprisoned. By the late 1960s, Fidel Castro disclosed to Lee Lockwood, an estimated 20,000 Cubans were in jail as political prisoners.[81]

The full dimensions of the psychological trauma and emotional stress to which many Cubans were subject during these years may never be known. Jorge Domínguez noted the marked increase of cases of psychiatric consultation during these years, indicating that admission to psychiatric facilities nearly doubled between 1964 and 1969, from 5,972 to

10,428. The rate of outpatient psychiatric consultation registered an astonishing fourfold increase, from 12,660 in 1964 to 53,250 in 1968.[82]

❧ If the conduct of life had changed, so too had the meaning of death. Insofar as the revolution laid claim to how life was to be lived—"no life outside the Revolution," in Guevara's words—it also implied claim to determine the circumstances under which life was to be ended. The revolution was proclaimed to have changed everything, including and especially giving Cubans a new reason for which to live and a new purpose for which to die. Emphasis on the larger collective ensemble as the basis for the society of the New Man implied renunciation of self-destruction for any purpose other than patria or pueblo.

The life of the dedicated revolutionary was to be held in sacred trust, possessed of value that transcended individual interests, and could not be ended in any fashion other than in function of a larger social purpose. The deed of suicide implied moral deficiency. The decision to die was to repudiate the obligation to others: suicide was an act, in short, tantamount to disavowal of revolutionary morality. The matter of suicide was rendered as a matter of consciousness, and revolutionary consciousness did not admit the possibility of suicide except in the service of the revolution or as an act of mental disorder. "Difficulties notwithstanding," affirmed Havana physician Antonio Clavero, "when there is consciousness . . . people do not think of killing themselves."[83] When, in 1964, minister of labor Augusto Martínez Sánchez shot himself upon learning of his impending removal from office, Prime Minister Fidel Castro and President Osvaldo Dorticós—who almost twenty years later would himself commit suicide—condemned suicide as a breach of revolutionary morality: "We are deeply sorry for this event. . . . According to fundamental revolutionary principles, we believe that this conduct is unjustifiable and improper for a revolutionary, and we are convinced that *compañero* Augusto Martínez Sánchez could not have been fully conscious when he engaged in such a deed, because every revolutionary knows that he does not have a right to deprive his cause of a life that does not belong to him, and which can only be legitimately sacrificed when facing the enemy."[84]

In July 1970, Comandante Eddy Suñol, a hero of the insurrectionary war and vice minister of the Ministry of the Interior, committed suicide. The official presentation of Suñol's suicide alluded to cumulative infirmities resulting from battle wounds and an automobile accident in 1960, which contributed to his despair, reported *Granma*, over his inability to "meet his obligations to the Revolution." Affirmed Raúl Castro at the graveside eulogy: "Thus the deepening conflict produced by his boundless enthusiasm to serve the Revolution in the face of physical limitations due his declining health . . . is what surely led him in a moment of depression, when he was no longer master of his acts, to end his life. . . . This is the reason why the Revolutionary Government and the leadership of Party, even in the face of an act of suicide, have decided to render the military honors that correspond to [Suñol], taking into consideration that it was the wounds he received while in the Rebel Army in heroic combat against the enemy that affected his health and led him to commit suicide. Although suicide has no justification whatsoever, this is an instance in which a *compañero* was afflicted with permanent wounds of war, and it was those wounds that contributed definitively to his death."[85]

Nearly ten years later, Haydée Santamaría, a celebrated heroine of Moncada and member of the Central Committee of the Cuban Communist Party and the Council of State, also committed suicide. José Luis Llovio-Menéndez, at the time a member of the Economic Department of the Central Committee of the Cuban Communist Party, recalled the reaction to the death of Haydée Santamaría: "Haydée's body did not lie in state at the foot of the José Martí monument in the Plaza de la Revolución. Rather she was perfunctorily buried, with few official expressions of respect befitting her revolutionary prestige, and no funeral oration from Fidel. . . . The state religion of Communism proscribes honor to suicides, no matter how exemplary their lives or heroic their careers. . . . As far as Fidel was concerned, Haydée Santamaría had betrayed the revolution."[86] Comandante Juan Almeida delivered the funeral oration:

In principle, we revolutionaries cannot accept the proposition of suicide. The life of the revolutionary belongs to his cause and to his people, and he should dedicate himself to the service of both with the last atom of energy and until the last second of his life. But we cannot so coldly judge *compañera* Haydée. Those of us who knew her understand that the wounds of Moncada never really healed. . . . Haydée was slowly succumbing to progressive deterioration of her health. In addition, some months ago, she was in an automobile accident that nearly took her life, which further aggravated her physical and psychological condition. Only these circumstances, that undoubtedly pushed her to the extreme of losing control of her faculties, can explain that a figure of such historical and revolutionary importance, with such high achievements in behalf of the Patria and socialism, whose fortitude was proven during the most difficult historic moments of our struggle, was able to consummate the tragic determination to take her own life.[87]

Ex-president Osvaldo Dorticós killed himself in June 1983, *Granma* explained, the result of "increasingly unbearable physical pain, related to a serious spinal affliction, to which was added in recent months the tragic loss of his *compañera* María Caridad Molina." Added *Granma*: "It appears that the physical pain and deep despair occasioned by the loss of his *compañera* proved to be greater than the iron will and extraordinary stoicism with which *compañero* Dorticós overcame adversity. He was no longer himself." At the graveside eulogy, José Machado Ventura, member of the Politburo, sought to explain the Dorticós suicide: "Upon his death, *compañero* Dorticós leaves us with the sorrow of a death produced by his own hand, a deed that was incompatible with the values and the revolutionary convictions he held dearly throughout his life. The agonizing physical pain and the deep depression to which he succumbed after the death of his *compañera* plunged him into a crisis of such magnitude that he was no longer in control of himself."[88]

❀ Suicide within the ranks of the political leadership was more than adequately replicated within the population at large. In fact, despite the moral prohibition of suicide after 1959, men and women in all age categories appear to have continued to kill themselves at a rate more or less comparable to prerevolutionary trends.

National patterns of suicide after 1959 do not lend themselves to easy analysis. Part of the difficulty has to do with the absence of systematic publication of mortality data of the type available before 1959. At the same time, press coverage of incidents of interpersonal violence, including assaults, homicides, and suicides, so very much the staple of prerevolutionary weekly magazines and daily newspapers—and important as sources of historical information—all but ceased after the early 1960s.

In the months and years immediately following the triumph of the revolution, during the period of political upheaval, arrests and trials of officials associated with the government of Fulgencio Batista, and abrupt social and economic transformations, the number of suicides increased markedly. The one notable exception occurred during the 1960s, during the years of mass mobilization, including the inauguration of the literacy campaign and the formation of the Committees for the Defense of the Revolution. A sense of exalted collective purpose seized hold of the popular imagination during these years. This was a time of mass demonstrations and rallies, a period of common hope and shared expectations, years of near euphoric optimism about the future. A sense of national solidarity took hold across the island, and the determination to prevail over obstacles and opposition enhanced the Cuban desire to live. "The truth is," journalist Mario Benedetti could write in 1968, "that in Cuba there is so much stimulating work that one has no time (and much less desire) to commit suicide."[89]

But socialism in Cuba was never easy. The revolution was indeed a relentless process of struggle and sacrifice, often on a heroic scale, against insuperable odds, in the face of chronic scarcities, shortages, and rationing, against internal mismanagement and external pressure. The effects on morale were often withering, as poignantly conveyed in Carlos Torres Pita's prize-winning 1971 play, *La definición*. "I am fed up with the promises of abundance every year that come to nothing," despairs María. "Fed up with eating the same thing day after day, or not eating at all. Fed up with the ration card, fed up with the lines even to use the public rest rooms. Fed up with the lack of bus service, of the CDR, of the speeches, of the meetings, of the news of the sugar harvest. . . . There is nothing."[90]

Beginning in the early 1970s, in the aftermath of the failure of the 10-million-ton sugar crop, through the following years of institutionalization and rectification, and into the Special Period of the 1990s, suicide rates turned upward and increased steadily (see Table 6.1). Men and women in socialist Cuba killed themselves for many of the same reasons that they had always killed themselves, in response to fear and frustration, as a solution to setbacks and suffering, as a means of agency. Suicide rates increased during the late 1980s and especially during the 1990s, years during which many Cubans experienced conditions as dire as the worst days of the Great Depression. "Things are very ugly this summer," despairs the protagonist Naty in the short story "Falsos profetas," by Nancy Alonso. "The cycle of blackouts are eight hours long. . . . There is practically no food and no transportation. Some months ago a neuropathy epidemic broke out and no one knows why. It's grim, it's Armageddon, the Apocalypse."[91]

The crisis of the Special Period had a debilitating impact on the conduct of everyday life across the island. It became impossible to go about normally in one's daily life, where so much of one's time and energy were expended in what otherwise and elsewhere were routine household errands and ordinary family chores, where days were filled with unrelieved hard-

Table 6.1. Number of Suicides, 1959–1999

Year	Male	Female	Total	Year	Male	Female	Total
1959	—	—	1,066	1980	—	—	2,070
1960	—	—	1,000	1981	—	—	2,117
1961	—	—	1,032	1982	—	—	2,279
1962	—	—	914	1983	—	—	2,163
1963	512	271	783	1984	—	—	2,098
1964	544	299	843	1985	—	—	2,183
1965	560	339	899	1986	—	—	—
1966	—	—	—	1987	—	—	—
1967	—	—	—	1988	—	—	—
1968	638	403	1,041	1989	—	—	—
1969	—	—	936	1990	—	—	2,163
1970	—	—	1,011	1991	—	—	2,296
1971	708	443	1,107	1992	1,334	966	2,300
1972	743	522	1,265	1993	1,410	964	2,374
1973	933	516	1,449	1994	1,442	837	2,279
1974	972	645	1,617	1995	1,410	813	2,223
1975	—	—	1,571	1996	—	—	—
1976	960	707	1,667	1997	—	—	—
1977	937	758	1,695	1998	—	—	2,056
1978	—	—	1,814	1999	—	—	2,051
1979	—	—	1,862				

Sources: World Health Organization, *World Health Statistic Annual* . . . 1962–1996 (Geneva, 1965–98); Cuba, Oficina Nacional de Estadísticas, *Anuario estadístico de Cuba* . . . 1972–1994 (Havana, 1973–95); Cuba, Centro de Estudios de Población y Desarrollo, Oficina Nacional de Estadísticas, *Anuario demográfico de Cuba* . . . 1998–2000 (Havana, 1999–2001); Latin American Center, University of California at Los Angeles, *Cuba 1968: Supplement to the Statistical Abstract of Latin America* (Los Angeles, 1970), pp. 48–49.

ship and adversity in pursuit of even the most minimum needs of daily life, day after day. "Life is very, very difficult," one émigré explained upon arriving in Florida in 1994. "I would say that it borders on the unbelievable. In Cuba, people practically live in constant search of daily survival, a survival that is based on a very lean, poor diet, with very difficult living conditions. Life in Cuba is barely livable—from any point of view."[92]

Idleness expanded across the island. Factory closings due to shortages of fuel and scarcity of raw materials meant that many tens of thousands of men and women remained without work, without something to do.

Boredom increased. Tedium brought on a particularly debilitating type of listlessness. Comments the protagonist in Pedro Juan Gutiérrez's *Dirty Havana Trilogy* (1998): "I had nothing to do that afternoon. In fact, it was the same every day. There was never anything to do." Remarks one character in Ana Menéndez's *Loving Che* (2003): "They have anesthetized us with boredom. Cuban days are the longest in all the world. Even work, such as it is, is boring."[93] Drug and alcohol abuse appears to have increased during the 1990s. Alcoholism, of course, made everything else worse and was identified as a contributing factor in the increase of suicide.[94] The level of domestic violence appears to have risen. One public health study completed in Camagüey reported that of a total of 310 women between the ages of fifteen and forty-nine interviewed, 226 told of having experienced acts of violence. Concluded one study of domestic violence in Havana: "The testimony of women interviewed demonstrates that acts of violence experienced at the hands of their spouses has produced serious harm to the mental health of women and their children."[95]

The purpose of the future and indeed the future of purpose weighed heavily on men and women across the island. "The future?" Doris asks incredulously in Rolando Díaz's film of the Special Period, *Si me comprendieras* (1998). "You can imagine. The future. I think about the future minute by minute. And with every passing minute, I become more fearful of the future. Because of the way things are . . ." One émigré explained his reason for leaving the island: "In Cuba there isn't a future of any kind. Always they talk about tomorrow, but if you don't have a present, you can't have a future." The possibility of the future was no longer certain. "Those years in Havana left me insecure and exhausted," Carlota Caulfield later recalled. "The word *future* lost all meaning."[96] In the short story "Mario in the Heaven's Gate," by Juan Francisco Pulido Martínez, the narrator describes the circumstances that impelled twenty-year-old Mario to prepare his suicide: "He was pained by everything around him. His world had been at one time beautiful . . . when he lived his life for his dreams, to struggle for his dreams. Ah, when he dreamed! But today . . . society demonstrated that dreams do not provide food." Sighs the protagonist, Lauri, in the novel *Memoria del silencio*, by Uva de Aragón: "The future that [the Revolution] promised has arrived and it is a frightful disaster."[97] One study of attempted suicides in Santiago de Cuba in 1993 attributed "demoralization" as the principal factor behind the suicidal impulse.[98]

Gazing into the future in hopes of seeing how or when or even if hard times would get easier usually drew a blank. "When hope is repeatedly frustrated year after year," observes the narrator in Daína Chaviano's 1998 novel *El hombre, la hembra y el hambre*, "people become skeptical and all possibilities of action are nullified. And with all that uncertainty weighing on one's shoulders there is no alternative to absolute inaction or escape to another world where the natural laws are more foreseeable. Any child, once warned of danger, would hasten to seek protection against this syndrome of social death; but not a disoriented people, who end up overtaken by the fire that they themselves had assisted starting. Or to say it in Cuban, a people that like Chacumbele killed themselves (*un pueblo que se mató él mismo como Chacumbele*)." In Héctor Quintero's play *Te sigo esperando*, set in the Special Period, Teté threatens suicide: "If you come near me I swear I'll light the match. You know better than anyone that I am capable of doing it. . . . The way I burned my doll when I was a little girl, when I still had expectations of my life ahead of me. You can imagine that today, when I have nothing left to live for, I can just as soon die as live."[99] In the short story "Develamiento de Matías," by Miguel R. Cañellas, the narrator describes the despair that drives the protagonist, José Manuel, to suicide: "He wanted to flee, to run away, to leave, but suddenly he had a moment of strange lucidity. He was filled with a new-found sense of peace. He went into the kitchen and mechanically, delighting in each gesture, he prepared another cup of tea." José Manuel poisons himself and thereupon proceeds to write a suicide note: "In the final moments of his life he fancied himself dying as martyr. An enigmatic smile came upon his face. 'I die for the Revolution,' was what he wrote."[100] The logic of suicide seemed self-evident. "Life has become difficult for us," affirmed one of the characters in the play *We Were Always Afraid*, by Leopoldo Hernández, "difficult and bitter to such an extent that I've come to desire death more and more with each passing day."[101]

🎋 Information on suicide between the 1960s and 1990s bearing on both age and gender is limited principally to material published for a total of thirteen years and suggests what may have—and what had not—changed after the triumph of the revolution (see Table 6.2). Facets of historic patterns appear to have generally persisted after 1959. The ratio of total male suicide (13,103) to female suicide (8,483) averaged 1.5:1, a pattern that remained more or less constant through the end of the twentieth century. The ratio of male to female varied from a high of 2.2:1 in 1965 to a low of 1.4:1 in 1972.[102] The susceptibility of women to suicide continued to be highest among the young. More than 32 percent of all female suicide

Table 6.2. Suicide in Cuba: Age and Gender Distribution, Select Years

Age/Gender	1963–1965/ 1968	1971–1974/ 1976–1977	1992–1995	Total
5–14 Years Old				
Male	12	33	10	55
Female	42	110	37	189
15–24 Years Old				
Male	337	609	596	1,542
Female	526	1,312	723	2,561
25–44 Years Old				
Male	631	1,620	1,749	4,000
Female	388	1,066	1,183	2,637
45–64 Years Old				
Male	705	1,709	1,503	3,917
Female	243	708	958	1,909
65+ Years Old				
Male	569	1,282	1,738	3,589
Female	113	395	679	1,187

Sources: World Health Organization, *World Health Statistic Annual . . . 1962–1996* (Geneva, 1965–98); Cuba, Oficina Nacional de Estadísticas, *Anuario estadístico de Cuba . . . 1972–1997* (Havana, 1973–98); Latin American Center, University of California at Los Angeles, *Cuba 1968: Supplement to the Statistical Abstract of Latin America* (Los Angeles, 1970), pp. 48–49.

(2,750 out of 8,483) occurred within the age cohort of five to twenty-four, an age group in which male suicide accounted for only 12 percent (1,597 out of 13,103). On the other hand, men aged forty-five and older accounted for nearly 60 percent of all male suicides (7,506 out of 13,103). One of the salient differences in post-1959 patterns was registered in the increase of suicide among women forty-five years and older, an age cohort that accounted for fully 36 percent of all female suicides (3,096 out of 8,483).

During the late 1960s, the national suicide rate reached 13.7 per 100,000. By the mid-1970s, the estimated rate of suicide had reached 17.6 per 100,000, as high as the late 1940s (see Table 6.3). In 1987, the rate of suicide reached 22.7 per 100,000, making it the sixth leading cause of death in Cuba. During the early years of the Special Period, the rate of suicide fluctuated between 20.2 and 21.8 per 100,000. Within the age cohort of fifteen to forty-nine, it was the second leading cause of death. In the province of Granma, including the cities of Bayamo and Manzanillo, the

Table 6.3. Suicide Rates in Cuba, 1970–2000 (per 100,000 inhabitants)

Year	Rate	Year	Rate
1970	11.8	1986	22.7
1971	13.3	1987	22.4
1972	14.3	1988	21.3
1973	16.1	1989	21.4
1974	17.7	1990	20.4
1975	17.3	1991	21.5
1976	17.6	1992	21.3
1977	17.6	1993	21.7
1978	18.9	1994	20.8
1979	19.3	1995	20.2
1980	21.4	1996	18.3
1981	21.7	1997	18.4
1982	23.2	1998	18.3
1983	21.9	1999	18.4
1984	21.1	2000	16.4
1985	21.8		

Sources: "Estadísticas de Salud de Cuba: Mortalidad por suicidio y lesiones autoinfligidas, 1970–2000," <http://www.dne.sld.cu>; Wilfredo Guibert Reyes, "Epidemiología de la conducta suicida," *Revista Cubana de Medicina General Integral* 18 (2002): 1–7.

rate of suicide reached 36.8, making it the third leading cause of death in the province, after cardiovascular disease and malignant tumors. A survey of 833 men and women over the age of fifteen in Bayamo between 1991 and 1992 determined that nearly 40 percent of the group was diagnosed with propensities to suicide. In Camagüey, suicide was the fourth principal cause of death, after cardiovascular disease, accidents, and malignant tumors.[103] By the late 1980s and early 1990s, medical and health authorities had arrived at the recognition that suicidal behavior constituted an urgent pubic health issue. In 1989, the Ministry of Public Health inaugurated a national campaign against suicide in an initiative known as the National Program for the Prevention and Control of Suicidal Conduct. By 2004, the Ministry of Public Health reported, the rate of suicide had fallen to 14.3 per 100,000.[104]

Suicide among the elderly increased markedly. Between 1989 to 1992, the rate of suicide increased from 46.3 to 54.4 per 100,000. In the following year, it increased again to 62.2, thereafter declining to 51.4 in 1995 and

47.9 in 1997.[105] The pattern of failed suicide attempts among the aged reveals a preponderance of women. In one study of failed suicides in Centro Habana between 1993 and 1997, a total of 16 out of 20 attempts of Cubans over sixty years of age were by women. The most frequent reasons given for attempting suicide included family conflict, physical disability, and despair.[106]

Suicide among the young also increased, and increased notably during the 1990s. Youth between seventeen and nineteen years of age, men and women alike, were particularly susceptible to suicide.[107] Suicide ranked as the third leading cause of death among youth, preceded by accidents and malignant tumors. The reasons most frequently attributed to adolescent suicide were family conflict and difficult socioeconomic conditions.[108]

Information on the rate of attempted suicide is fragmentary and only suggestive. The national ratio during the 1990s was 6 attempts to every 1 completed suicide.[109] The rate of unsuccessful attempts by women continued to outnumber failed attempts by men. In one study of adolescent mortality in 1999, the rate of attempted suicide for the female age cohort of ten to fourteen was 198 to every 1 completed suicide, while the corresponding male cohort registered 41 attempts to every 1 successful suicide. In the age cohort of fifteen to twenty-four, the ratio decreased to 52:1 among women and 8:1 for men. The pattern of suicide in the province of Sancti-Spíritus between 1995 and 1996 revealed that of a total 53 unsuccessful attempts, 37 were by women, and of the 15 completed suicides 9 were by men.[110] In the *municipio* of Palacios in Pinar del Río, of the total number of 79 attempted suicides between 1997 and 1998, almost 75 percent (58) were by women, 49 of whom were between twenty and thirty-nine years of age. In a detailed study of 243 attempted suicides in Santiago de Cuba between 1991 and 1996, almost 80 percent (191) were by women. Men and women between the ages of fifteen and twenty-nine accounted for almost 70 percent (169) of the total 243 attempts. More than 80 percent (197) attributed their desire to die to marital problems, family conflict, or troubled romantic relationships. The profile of the "typical" unsuccessful suicide attempt in Santa Clara during the early 1990s was a white woman between twenty-five and twenty-nine years of age, a housewife, having completed a secondary education.[111]

Suicide rates varied among provinces. The highest rates of suicide were recorded in Matanzas (24 per 100,000), followed by Havana (23.2) and Sancti-Spíritus (22.9). The lowest rate of suicide was recorded in Guantánamo (9.5 per 100,000).[112]

Table 6.4. Suicide in Havana (1996)

Age	Male	Female	Total
5–14	3	3	
15–24	9	9	18
25–49	61	41	102
50–59	18	15	33
60+	75	41	116
Total	163	109	272

Source: Acela Laferté Trebejo and Luisa Aleida Laferté Trabejo, "Comportamiento del suicidio en Ciudad de La Habana: Intervención de enfermería en la atención primaria de salud," *Revista Cubana de Enfermería*, 16 (2000): 78–87.

Suicide in the city of Havana provides insight into larger national patterns. The number of suicides increased from 282 in 1989 to 313 in 1990, and increased again to 336 two years later. It declined in subsequent years, falling to 272 in 1996 (see Table 6.4). Men killed themselves at a 1.5:1 ratio to women. What was particularly striking about the pattern of suicide in Havana was the apparent narrowing in the rate of men and women in the older age cohorts. More than half of all female suicides were among women fifty years and older. During the 1990s, more women appeared to be killing themselves at a later age than earlier in the twentieth century.

The material scarcity that settled generally over Cuba after 1959 influenced the methods of suicide. In the absence of readily available firearms, hanging developed into the method of choice among men. The scarcity of medicines, including aspirin and barbiturates, no less than the unavailability of previously common household poisons such as rodent poison, resulted in the increase of burning as a method of suicide among women.[113]

Local studies of suicide confirmed the persistence of distinctly gendered methods of self-destruction. Burning continued to be identified as a woman's way of death, and mostly used by young women. In the *municipios* of Puerto Padre and Jobabo in Las Tunas province, of the 57 cases of suicide by burning between February 1993 and February 1994, 50 were completed by women. Most deaths by suicide occurred outside hospitals, except in Las Tunas, where the high proportion of suicide attempts by fire, and subsequent treatment in hospitals, meant that more than half of all suicides were registered as deaths in hospitals.[114] Hanging was the preferred method among the 101 men who killed themselves in Matanzas between 1968 and 1974, while fire was the means of choice for the 82 women who committed suicide. Together, hanging and burning accounted for nearly 85 percent of all suicides in Matanzas between 1968 and 1974. In Cárdenas, more than 65 percent of all suicides in the year 2000 were by hanging and burning (30 out of 45). The study of suicide in Havana in 1996 indicated that hanging for men and burning for women were the principal methods of self-destruction, together accounting for more than 80 percent of all suicide deaths (219 out of 272).[115] Of the 15 suicides recorded in the province of Sancti-Spíritus during a twelve-month period between 1995 and 1996, 5 were by hanging and 5 were by burning. Of the 71 suicides reported in the *municipio* of Santo Domingo in Villa Clara province between 1995 and 1999, more than 75 percent of men (38 out of 49) chose to hang themselves, while more than one-third of the women (8 out of 22) died by burning.[116]

Cubans devised many ways to end their lives during these years. Suicide was often conceived as a long-term process for short-term gains. The Special Period coincided with the increase in reported cases of AIDS. The government responded with the establishment of sanitariums to quarantine patients within separate residential subdivisions to receive specialized medical attention, including housing facilities and enhanced diets. During the 1990s, an indeterminate number of young Cubans—as few as 30, perhaps as many as 200—mostly counterculture youth, *roqueros*, as they were known—deliberately injected themselves with infected blood with the intent of contracting AIDS. "I am injecting myself with AIDS blood," explains *roquero* Bobby in León Ichaso's film *Azúcar amarga* (1996), "with blood tainted with AIDS virus, because if I have to choose between 'Socialism or death,' I'll take death." Luis Enrique Delgado explained to Peter Katel of *Newsweek*: "We gave ourselves AIDS to liberate ourselves from society and those laws about obligatory work, and live in our own world."[117] One reason given for suicide through AIDS was to gain access to sanitariums, to receive better housing and improved diets. Relocation to sanitariums also offered disaffected youth a place of political refuge and protection from official harassment. "Sanitarium life," Katel noted, "offers far more comforts than most Cubans ever see: three full meals a day, air conditioning, no power outages . . . [and] the absence of police." Commented nineteen-year-old Juan Luis Pérez: "It was the only way to escape the police." "In any other country of the world," observed another youth, "this would be a problem of insanity; in Cuba it is a political problem."[118]

Suicide assumed multiple forms during the Special Period, and not all

LA ÚNICA SOLUCION

CARTELES

"The Only Solution." From *Carteles* 17 (June 7, 1931).

involved explicitly the intent to die. Some chose to risk death at sea rather than to endure life in Cuba. Flight by boat has deep historical antecedents, of course, but it was in the aftermath of the revolution, in the face of emigration restrictions in Cuba and the United States, that the number of rafters (*balseros*) increased markedly. By one calculation, an estimated 16,500 balseros reached the United States between 1959 and 1974. This number increased almost three-fold to 46,500 between 1989 and 1994 during the early years of the Special Period.[119]

These were often desperate crossings, what Holly Ackerman and Juan Clark describe in their study of balseros as "do-or-die" deeds, filled with risk and peril, and they inevitably resulted in loss of life that may have reached into the thousands.[120] "People began making rafts out of anything they could find," Julio J. Guerra Molina recalled of the exodus of 1994, "*¡Nos tiramos al mar!*" [We threw ourselves into the sea!][121] The act of crossing the Florida Straits aboard small boats, or on makeshift rafts, or on whatever other buoyant object was available, including inflated inner tubes, was possessed of discernible and often acknowledged elements of suicide. "To throw oneself into the sea" (*tirarse al mar*) was to pursue the possibility of a new future or die in the attempt. "Many people there have lost all faith," commented one balsero upon reaching Florida. "They presently see their lives without any future. They are depressed." The future was also very much on the mind of another émigré who reached the United States by raft. "The reason that many balseros, young people like me," he indicated, "decided to leave Cuba was that none of us felt that we had any kind of future. It was thus preferable to leave, even at the risk of dying at sea."[122] *Tirarse al mar* was to assert control over one's life, an act of agency, even if and especially if also a deed of self-destruction. "It was better to leave Cuba and go to [the] Guantánamo [Naval Station] . . . or die at sea," commented one balsero, "rather than continue dying little by little. Because it was more or less how I felt. I have a very restless disposition and the conditions were asphyxiating. For that reason, for me it was the same one way or the other." Another balsero explained his decision to leave in strikingly similar terms: "I no longer fit in Cuba. Conditions for me had become so unbearably difficult that I said, well, it's now or never: either I die or I am born again."[123]

Balseros did not throw themselves into the sea purposely with the intent of suicide, of course, but rather as an act undertaken after a rational calculation of costs and benefits, as a decision made with the conviction that life in the United States was better than life in Cuba, and that, in any case, death was better than life in Cuba. Many responded to the choice of *Patria o muerte* and *Socialismo o muerte* in favor of death. "They left without much chance of surviving," comments the narrator in Margarita Engle's novel *Skywriting* (1995), "and they knew it. They knew the risks, the one-in-three or one-in-four survival estimates." To take to the sea was to take control of one's life, even if at the risk of losing it. Many Cubans, comments the narrator in the Zoé Valdés novel *Te di la vida entera* (1996), "threw themselves into the ocean, to drown, or offered themselves up to the sharks, swimming in pursuit of a better world." María de los Angeles González Amaro characterized the flight of balseros as a "near mass suicide of young people, who threw themselves onto the ocean in pursuit of new horizons and found peace in the depths of the ocean."[124] For the narrator of Pedro Juan Gutiérrez's novel *Dirty Havana Trilogy*, the meaning of balseros was unambiguous: "People think they're brave because they paddle off to Miami on truck tires. But they aren't—they're kamikazes." Rubén Busquests recalled preparing to depart Cuba on a raft when two friends changed their minds at the last moment. "This is suicide," said one, to which Busquests replied: "No, no—in any event, I am dying by living here. I am killing myself by being in this country." Writer Reinaldo Arenas reflected at length on the perils of the sea, and understood too the need to confront the prospects of death as a means of a new life. "A desperate situation has only two alternatives," Arenas reflected in 1983, only three years after he himself had crossed the Florida Straits. "You either perish or you survive, and in either case you are free. It is the exact situation that presently confronts Cubans with regard to the sea: that sea will either swallow you up or you perish inside the island. Or you probably abandon the island and you are reborn abroad or you rebel and overthrow the system. But to cross the current of the Gulf [of Mexico] successfully is as improbable as it is to bring down the political system."[125]

❧ The specter of suicide is a haunting presence in much of the fiction of these years. In the lithographic poem "Oración para encontrar amor" (1986), illustrated with images of suicidal death, Zaida del Río invokes "three souls of suicides by hanging and three souls of suicide by burning" to assist her in finding true love.[126] The opening act of Nicolás Dorr's play *Los excéntricos de la noche* begins with Carucha preparing to hang herself, pronouncing to herself: "This noose will be the means of your freedom."[127] In Daína Chaviano's novel *El hombre, la hembra y el hambre*, suicidal behavior is rendered as a circumstance of daily life, as a means and metaphor, a solution to which almost everyone seems susceptible. "Perhaps he ended up committing suicide in some dark corner somewhere," the protagonist, Claudia, says of a friend she has not seen in many years. Concerning the whereabouts of another friend, Claudia concludes: "The guy probably committed suicide or left the country." At another point, the narrator recalls Claudia learning of the suicide of a high school acquaintance at an agricultural camp: "She had the misfortune of being the one to have discovered the body of a member of her brigade who had hanged herself in the bathroom." The Special Period takes its toll on Claudia, and she reflects: "I envy the bravery of those who decide to protest, who bear up under beatings, who do not allow themselves to be defeated. I dare only to resist. I envy those who prefer to take 100 pills and remain asleep like angels. To die. . . . To sleep. Maybe even to dream! . . . I continue to search for a way out of the chaos, to arrive to some promised land." For Claudia, the Malecón of Havana is a site of "love and farewells, of promises and suicide pacts." Claudia contemplates her choices: "To stay or leave? To whore (*putear*) or die of hunger? To be or not to be? The eternal dilemma." And in a poignant conversational exchange between two friends: "Ruben sighs. 'At times I try to convince myself that I am not so bad off. I think that the day I admit it, I will end up hanging myself. I have something of a suicidal tendency. Did you know that?' 'Here we all have suicidal tendencies,' responds Gilberto."[128] Alexis Díaz-Pimienta's poem, "Memorias del suicida," posits a susceptibility to suicide by virtue of being Cuban explicitly:

We all have a balcony or a window high-up
for when the day of suicide arrives,
to leap with dignity
without scandalizing others
without dishonoring those who have known how to do it.
All of us are suicides at some time.[129]

Suicide looms large in the Special Period novel *Dirty Havana Trilogy*, by Pedro Juan Gutiérrez. Again and again the protagonist comes upon suicide: "I peered into the woman's room. Her son was hanging there, with an electrical cord around his neck. He was naked, covered in stab marks, blood all over his body, a dried, dark blood." At another point: "The old man next door had killed himself." And again: "Before her father hanged himself, she had seen him hanging himself with a heavy rope in recurring dreams for ten years." And at another point in the novel: "Sometimes Clotilde wants to kill herself. She's thought about doing it with pills, dousing herself with alcohol and lighting a match, or hanging herself, but she doesn't dare. She's afraid. But she knows it's only a question of time until the fear passes. . . . Every day she gets drunk. Food doesn't interest her; only alcohol. Now it was dark, and she made up her mind." The short story "Una desconocida," by Jesús David Curbelo begins: "Without explanation, he shot himself through the roof of his mouth"; while José Miguel

Detail of Zaida del Río, "Oración para encontrar amor" (1986). Courtesy of Gladys Marel García Pérez.

Sánchez's short story "Círculos del dolor" ends: "They say it was a suicide, although she did not leave a note. She hanged herself, but nobody knows why." The protagonist in Magarita Engle's novel of the Special Period, *Skywriting*, observes from her hotel: "I found myself standing next to a window, looking down. There was no screen, no glass, just a gap in the wall, low enough for someone to step out of the building easily, and float or plummet eighteen stories to a patio where statues of mermaids were partially hidden by tropical foliage. A maid came ambling by, patting her stack of towels and washcloths. She noticed me leaning out of the dangerous window. 'We have a lot of suicides in Cuba,' she said, laughing at her own dark humor, 'so we try to make it easier for them.'"[130]

In another account of Havana during the Special Period, Margarita Engle is taken to a bedroom where a relative had only months earlier committed suicide. "Right here," explains her cousin, "is where my father killed himself. I knew he was going to do it because he told me. He was old and sick, and he was discouraged. He knew he wasn't getting better, nothing was getting better, and something in his spirit was already dead. The suffering was too much for him." Adds the cousin: "I have considered suicide myself, very profoundly." Engle dwells in the realm of suicide, re-

Detail of Zaida del Rio, "Oración para encontrar amor" (1986). Courtesy of Gladys Marel García Pérez.

calling her own past temptations to kill herself. She concludes that Fidel Castro is leading Cubans "into oblivion, into a collective suicide." At one point Engle describes seeing a *totí* bird fly through an open window and collide into a glass wall, an experience she renders as "witnessing the suicide attempt of a *totí* bird." Bitter irony fills Zoé Valdés's novel of the Special Period, *Café nostalgia* (1997): "What shit! One can't even hang oneself in this country! When the rope doesn't break, the ceiling lamp falls on top of your head."[131]

The theme of suicide insinuated itself as subtext in Cuban cinema. In the film *Adorables mentiras* (1992), Nancy (Mirta Ibarra) is shown preparing to take her own life three times: once, preparing to leap from the roof of an apartment building; the second time through an overdose of medication; and the third occasion by turning on the gas jets of the stove in her apartment. "I can no longer dream," laments Nancy after the second attempt. "I used to dream. Everything. I dreamed that I could have become something. . . . I thought that something good could happen to me. And waiting for it happen, time passed me by." In *Fresa y chocolate* (1993), the aging prostitute Nancy (Mirta Ibarra) is depicted making a fifth attempt on her life by slashing her wrist, inspiring an exasperated Diego (Jorge Perugorría) to comment: "If I were to commit suicide every time I had a problem . . ." At a later point, Diego chides Nancy—"What a great Revolution this is, where even whores are art critics!"—to which Nancy threatens: "Don't call me whore, otherwise I'll leap off the balcony. I'm no whore." In a later scene Nancy is shown preparing to hang herself in a sixth suicide attempt but changes her mind; she looks at herself in the mirror and comments, "Can't you think of something else?"

❧ Deepening Cuban discontent found outlet through emigration, principally to the United States. Between 1960 and 1970, nearly 250,000 Cubans arrived in the United States. By the end of 1980, in the aftermath of the Mariel emigration, approximately 500,000 Cubans had resettled in the United States. Emigration continued through the end of the twentieth century, by which time the estimated total number of Cubans in the United States had passed the one million mark.[132]

Emigration had far-reaching consequences on both sides of the Florida Straits. Countless thousands of families were shattered irrevocably. Families divided and dispersed, as some family members departed and others remained, often with bad blood and bitter feelings. Some who remained despaired and descended into unbearable sorrow. María de los Angeles Torres recalled: "A very close friend committed suicide when his father hung himself in despair after his daughter left through El Mariel [in 1980]." Writer José Lezama Lima despaired over the dispersal of his family. "With every day that passes," Lezama Lima wrote to his sisters in exile in 1962, "I notice that Mamá's anguish deepens, she is more melancholic. She cries frequently. Your departure is incomprehensible to her. . . . I don't think she can endure another year of your absence. . . . Life has become a labyrinth from which she cannot emerge; all she sees is the image of her departed daughters. . . . [She lives] year after year in solitude and suffering, and in the constant and terrible fear of dying distant from her daughters." And again two years later: "We have relied upon our spiritual reserves to endure the separation of the family. But what has happened? The reserves are depleted, we are exhausted. The incessant suffering is destroying us. My only joy is mother, but I see how much she suffers, how she despairs when she reminisces about the family. . . . The truth is that both of us are destroyed."[133]

Many who reached the United States experienced exile simultaneously as heartache to return and hardship to remain. Some Cubans used exile to organize armed resistance against the government of Fidel Castro. The summons to struggle and sacrifice, to die for the patria, reverberated anew, now from within the exile community in the United States. "To be Cuban is to live in the agony of the struggle," insisted exile poet Alfredo Leiseca.[134] Cubans in exile organized for war, first in Brigade 2506 for the Bay of Pigs invasion and subsequently in various paramilitary organizations and commando groups, including Alpha 66 and Omega 7. "In the memory of the great founders of the patria," wrote Captain Vicente Méndez of Alfa 66 on the occasion of the centennial celebration of the Ten Years War, "and of the martyrs and political prisoners of our time, I vow that I will fulfill my duty or perish in the necessary holy war. I am a descendant of a Cuban liberator of the nineteenth century. My call to arms is the same as the liberators: 'Liberty or Death.' For free and independent Cuba." Vowed Braulio de Gondomar in 1969: "Nothing and no one will be able to prevent the holy war that soon will be launched. No one will stop our sacrifice. We will obtain the future through our own efforts. Our blood will run like streams, but we will achieve our purpose with dignity. . . . That is the way we will obtain liberation."[135]

The narrative of sacrifice among Cubans in exile drew on familiar formulations: to die for the patria in the way exemplified by Carlos Manuel de Céspedes, Antonio Maceo, and José Martí. The lyric "To die for the Patria is to live" had resonance no less far-reaching in exile than it had on the island. "You have to understand . . . ," Manolo Llerena discussed the Bay of Pigs with José Llanes, "that we were talking about our homeland. José Martí and Antonio Maceo had suffered for it and died. It didn't matter that the odds were so long. . . . We had to go, no matter what the odds; we had to liberate Cuba at all costs." "Fortunate are those who die for the land ablaze / In a just war we never wanted," wrote exulted exile poet Pablo LeRiverend. Oscar Ruiz-Sierra Fernandez wrote from Puerto Rico: "No— to die matters not, for with death / You occupy a place of honor in our history."[136] Exhorted poet Beba del Mazo:

I ask of Cubans one favor,
That they not forget the patria of Martí,
That we unite all,
Like brothers,
To struggle for it,
Even die for it.[137]

Good Cubans, Juan Remos pronounced in 1967, "are those who sacrifice for the patria, the way they sacrificed in the past, the way they sacrifice in the present. . . . Those who have suffered and suffer today in the communist prisons of Cuba, those who risk their lives daily in the resistance and those who maintain themselves on a war footing in exile . . . by way of commando actions [who] proclaim to the world our protest and our courage."[138]

The history of Cuba written in exile also celebrated the traditional attributes of Cuban, if for different purpose. Emeterio Santovenia and Raúl Shelton pointed to the burning of Guáimaro as evidence of "the suffering and abnegation of the liberators that knew no limits and of a sacrifice that prevailed over the intentions of the enemy"; while Rafael Estenger proclaimed the burning of Bayamo as "heroic without any doubt." Rafael Guas Inclán wrote that "in their heroic desperation, the people of Bayamo had to make war with the torch in order to express to the world that they would not default in their momentous effort of liberation."[139] Ricardo Núñez García drew the moral explicitly in 1965:

[Bayamo] was a tragedy but it was also a lesson. Tragedy moves one to despair; a lesson is always beneficial. Bayamo serves to demonstrate that liberty deserves all necessary sacrifice, for without liberty there is neither well-being nor life worth living. . . . With Bayamo and Guáimaro, Cubans validated, as lesson and testimony that they revere today, that there is no material possession worth more than liberty. If today they have lost the liberty that they had once conquered, they will never weary until they have reconquered liberty. A people who have in their history two such dramatic episodes like the burning of Bayamo and Guáimaro, even if adversity torments and oppresses them, will never be resigned to tyranny. . . . Such sacrifice is the price of liberty. . . . And Cubans know—the real Cubans, who have not sold the patria to the Russians—that the second Constitution of Guáimaro will arise the same way that the heroic people of Guáimaro arose from the ashes.[140]

❧ While some Cubans plotted to return, many more prepared to remain in exile. They worked hard to adapt to new ways in the face of circumstances often no less daunting and no less demoralizing than those from which they had sought to escape. For many, expatriation developed into an endless wait for an expected return home, stretching from months into years, then into decades, in anticipation of a future that was never realized. "Unlike the immigrants," commented Gustavo Pérez Firmat, "we did not come to this country to start all over—we came to wait." Expectations of returning were raised, only to be dashed, again and again. For many time was running out and the future was slipping into the past. Eventually enough time passed so that the Cuba remembered had ceased to exist as anything more than a distant memory. "Every day," Pilar laments in Cristina García's *Dreaming in Cuban* (1992), "Cuba fades a little more inside me, my grandmother fades a little more inside me. And there's only my imagination where our history should be." Exclaims one character in Uva Clavijo's play *With All and For the Good of All*: "The Cuba you left, and you live constantly longing for, you're never going to return to, because it doesn't exist."[141] In *Miami en brumas* (2000), novelist Nicolás Abreu Felipe poignantly depicts the debilitating effects of waiting endlessly to return to Cuba. The narrator situates the protagonist, Máximo, in this environment:

The housing units in Hialeah are often depressing and horrible: the houses built one atop of the other in order to save space, all alike, in rows, the same color. With ownership of these houses many Cubans are happy, thinking that in this way they have obtained the necessary security to live in a country where they arrived years earlier with only a change of clothing. . . . They are growing old in the small cafés, proudly boasting of the sacrifices they have made to own the little they possess. They live in despair for the day that someone finally kills Fidel Castro so that Cuba could be free and they can return. Thousands have died without again ever seeing the land in which they were born. . . . Thousands still have the desire to retire to a small apartment in Old Havana. . . . The goal is to die under the sky that they previously abandoned and to rest in peace in Colón Cemetery. That's how they spend their lives. Máximo also lived in this world, in the world of return, certain that the years of exile were nothing more than a stage and that his life was in Cuba . . . and that to return was his only salvation, the only way to find himself again. As he often said: it is better to commit suicide than to die in this sandy ground.[142]

Exile could not but arouse powerful longings for home and induce melancholia and nostalgia for a place and time long past and growing longer, memories of friends and family growing dimmer, of fading remembrance of all those things that had made Cubans who they were. Many experienced exile as an inconsolable existence, one of heartache and sorrow. "[We] carr[ied] the pain of Cuba on our backs like a cross," Vivián de la Incera described her years of exile. "For me," Ada Manero Alvaré brooded, "leaving Cuba meant leaving behind my memories of infancy and youth; it meant leaving behind my friends; it meant leaving behind my entire world. Can you imagine, at sixty years of age I had to start my life all over again." One émigré identified simply as Ernesto remembered leaving Cuba: "You are leaving part of your body, your very being behind. You know that later, if you survive, you will wake up in a total strange, unknown world. It is as if you have to be born over again into a new life." For Jorge Luis Romeu exile was a "painful decision to leave our dead and our childhood friends behind to go to a totally different country with a completely different language." María de los Angeles Torres recalled the early years of her exile: "Everything had changed. My mother was chronically sad and worried constantly about the relatives she'd left behind. My father, in an effort to compensate, even started washing the dinner dishes. Everything that had held our family together . . . was left in the past."[143] Virgil Suárez remembered his father: "My father always spoke of what he had forgotten about Cuba":

> his homeland, how the specifics
> blurred, and he blamed this condition
> on the in-betweenness of spirit that occurs
> in immigrants, those who live in exile
> in the United States. . . .
> And when he stared out the bedroom
> window where he sat all day, he thought
> of the rivers, the valleys, the cane fields
> of his childhood, atop a horse he rode,
> straddled tight, over into the horizon,
> no longer a man afflicted with the idea
> of middle, no in-between, no refuge, absence.[144]

Life resumed, as best it could. The duty to discharge prescribed gender roles did not, of course, diminish in exile. On the contrary, the pressure on men to meet the responsibilities of provider and protector and on women to maintain the household weighed heavily on émigré families. For vast numbers of families the experience of exile signaled precipitous downward mobility. Careers were disrupted and professions lost, never to be resumed or recovered.[145] Many men who in their previous lives held prestigious positions and practiced respected professions, men with careers of distinctions as physicians, attorneys, and architects, as engineers and entrepreneurs, found themselves obliged in their new lives to wash dishes, wait on tables, and sweep floors, often with debilitating effect on morale and always with a brooding sense of diminished status and loss of self-esteem. "My father took his identity from his work," Gustavo Pérez Firmat remembered. "Take that away, and the damage done is incalculable." Families of comfortable means in Cuba often fell upon hard times in Miami. Cristina Saralegui recounted how "women of a certain position in Cuba" became "true women in exile." Recalled Saralegui: "You would have to have seen the leaders of Havana's Society washing underwear to survive, working as clerks in shoe stores, scrubbing dishes. The men scrambled just as hard to make their way. Lawyers, doctors, professionals from every field had to clean toilets in the hotels of Miami Beach, or pump gas, or sell produce in the markets. Our first years in the country that took us in were hard—in many cases humiliating." And at another point: "Doctors, lawyers, bankers, and teachers accepted jobs as elevator operators, dishwashers, waiters, janitors in Miami Beach's largest hotels."[146] In his *Los dioses ajenos* (1971), novelist Luis Ricardo Alonso describes the plight of Clotilde and Adela, a late-middle-age couple, who first emigrate to Miami. A former colonel in the Cuban army, Clotilde—"tired of living off *café con leche* in Miami"—obtains employment as a security guard in a Chicago department store:

> As long as the summer lasted, he was adapting very well. The manager of the store, a corpulent and extroverted American, treated him quite well. The employees called him 'Mr. Colonel.' But when the dark cold of winter arrived, Adela succumbed to a state of melancholic depression. The wind off the Great Lakes made his soul shiver. . . . He would wake up at night and, so as not to alarm Adela, go to the bathroom to cry. She knew, but said nothing. His therapy sessions were very expensive. Medical insurance did not cover the costs. . . . They returned to Florida . . . but neither Clotilde nor his wife could find employment. 'Too old,' they were told. Nor did they qualify for social assistance. The Cubans who returned to Miami 'were crazy,' said one local official. . . . But still they returned. In search of the sun and sky. To die, if there was nothing else to do.[147]

Conventional gender roles were difficult to maintain for both men and women. Old sources of status and self-esteem no less than old means of standing and self-sufficiency did not reproduce themselves easily. Men often could not find work; women were often obliged to work. "In order for the family to adjust economically," Elizabeth Meyer Rogg observed of Cubans in New Jersey, "most Cuban women work, a situation that places additional strain on the traditional Cuban male role of sole provider. The man feels that he has lost prestige and influence in the eyes of both his children and wife." Marta Elena Acosta Stone remembered "arguments between my parents" as "a weekly, if not daily, event," and added: "They fought over everything: finances, children, jealousies, my dad's work, religion. . . . I understand now that at the root of their conflicts was the Cuban past and its irretrievability. It was a past that offered models of strict gender roles, extended family, and a more stratified society with clear values, all of which life in this new country had eliminated or placed under doubt." Alicia Serrano Machirán Granto remembered language as the source of difficulty. "Due to his inability to speak English," she recalled, "my father was unable to find work in Niagara Falls. In addition to feeling culturally isolated, he felt emasculated, for he was unable to fulfill his traditional role as provider and 'man of the house.'"[148] Psychiatrist Ismael Damasu, with clinical experience in a Dade County mental health facility, reflected on the consequences of expatriation. "The dislocation of life in exile are many and very important in terms of self-concept," Damasu observed, and continued:

> The devaluation of things you know—how to speak the language, how to get from one place to another, who to call to get what action—is almost total. All these things have to be learned again from the start. Particularly when the individual comes to an environment where there are few others like him, the forced devaluation of knowledge is complicated by a decline in status, causing serious problems of self-image. Cuban lawyers and physicians who had to learn English to get a job selling shoes suffered a great onslaught upon their self-image. . . . [Women] are now not only homemakers, but also breadwinners. And very often, they are the only ones who speak English. The pressure of changed roles is intolerable for the men. The women sense this, so they assume a greater burden in the relationship. The traditional male-female roles are shattered. Yet the cultural expectations remain.[149]

Flor Fernández Barrios recalled her parents' "way[s] of escaping reality." Her father "sat in front of the television and cruised through the channels with a distant look on his face, too tired to talk or to listen to me talk about my day." Her mother found refuge in sewing: "Every evening after dinner, she sat in front of her sewing machine and lost herself in the quiet world of her creations."[150]

Cubans in the United States struggled mightily to adapt to the demands of daily life in exile. Suicide was a facet of this adaptation. "We had survived a history of revolutions, executions, and suicides," María del Carmen Boza reflected, "to enter into a state of eternal expectation. . . . It was a terrifying day, the one when we woke up alone and realized that we belonged nowhere." Journalist Ramiro Boza shot himself on May 19, 1989 — the date of Martí's death — in Miami. Reflected his daughter: "Of course, my father chose 19 May because of Martí's death. How could he not have, when he thought about him and, like him, about Cuba, Cuba, all the time like a mistress, an obsession apart from which there could not be a life? . . . He had chosen his time, as had Martí." Elena Maza recalled the death of her sister: "[Cecilia] went to a shopping center that had a drugstore where she usually got her prescriptions filled. At some point she doused herself with gasoline and then set herself on fire. . . . She just couldn't face her problems, so she decided not to deal with them anymore."[151]

Age-adjusted mortality rates of the Cuban-born population in the United States were uniformly lower in virtually every cause of death category except one: suicide. The Cuban tendency to suicide reproduced itself in exile. Certainly, the experience of expatriation must be seen as a factor of determining consequence. Sociologist Sergio Díaz-Briquets is undoubtedly correct to suggest that "the higher-than-average suicide rate among Cubans is consistent with the trauma of political emigration implicit in the forced, and in most cases, permanent separation from a familiar environment and loved ones. In many instances, emigration has involved downward social mobility and loss of status, conditions often associated with despondency and despair." No doubt, too, as Díaz-Briquets suggests, the "disproportionately high rates" of suicide of Cubans on the island and in exile were "due to a similar set of determinants that manifested themselves differently in the two nations, that is, the major changes in Cuba society both domestically and abroad, brought about by the Cuban Revolution."[152]

But it is also true that patterns of suicide in exile possessed long historical antecedents, and the circumstance of expatriation did little to vitiate the efficacy of self-destruction as a means of coping with life. Cubans in exile could not but draw upon the complex conventions embedded in *lo cubano*. It could hardly be otherwise. Suicide was among the methods

Table 6.5. Comparative Suicide Rates in the United States, 1978–1981 (per 100,000 inhabitants)

Gender	Cuban-Born	Mexican-Born	Puerto Rican-Born	White	Black
Male	26.3	11.7	24.2	21.7	12.7
Female	4.6	2.4	3.5	6.5	2.8
Total	14.6	7.2	12.9	13.7	7.3

Source: Sergio Díaz-Briquets, "Mortality Patterns of Cubans in the United States," in Ira Rosenwaike, ed., *Mortality of Hispanic Populations: Mexicans, Puerto Ricans, and Cubans in the United States and in the Home Countries* (Westport, Conn., 1991), p. 126.

Cubans in exile employed as a means of agency. "Immigrants reproduce in their adopted country," observed psychiatrist Lino Fernández, "the suicidal behavior from their country of origin, not in a fatally deterministic cultural fashion, but because of a psychological mechanism that will affect them no matter where they live. From a psychological perspective the individual's ability to challenge the future is founded in his personal history."[153] Between 1979 and 1981, the rate of suicide for Cuban-born residents was the highest among population groups in the United States, reaching 14.6 per 100,000 (see Table 6.5). The 5:1 male-to-female ratio of suicide among Cubans in Miami-Dade County during 1990–91 was the highest of all population groups. The rate of Cuban/Cuban-American male suicide in Dade County in 2002 reached 30.2 per 100,000, compared to 26.4 for whites and 12.6 for blacks.[154]

Among the prominent Cubans to have committed suicide in exile were Miguel Angel Quevedo, the former editor of *Bohemia* magazine, who killed himself in Venezuela in 1969. Former President Carlos Prío Socarrás shot himself in Miami in 1977. José Pérez San Román, leader of the invading Brigade 2506 at Playa Girón, committed suicide in 1989. Magaly Muguercia was correct to suggest that "a significant number of characters in Cuban drama and dance of the eighties committed suicide."[155] But not all artists killed themselves in Cuba. Many took their lives in exile. Calvert Casey killed himself in Rome in 1969, and Reinaldo Arenas committed suicide in New York in 1990. Artist Ana Mendieta leaped to her death from a New York apartment building in 1985.

Conditions for the elderly were particularly difficult, as the infirmities associated with aging were exacerbated by the circumstances of exile. Suicide rates among males sixty years and older between 1990 and 1993 were almost twice as high as all other cohort ethnic and racial populations. "After a short period of apparent adjustment," one study of elderly Cubans in the United States reported, "[they] began to experience feelings of futility and helplessness." The report described "a pervasive sense of hopelessness and quiet despair," with individuals describing themselves as useless and burdensome to their families. . . . [There] was the feeling that there was no role available for them, nothing that could be offered or given that would make life worthwhile. They felt out of step with the culture and their own families."[156]

The theme of suicide among émigrés informs much of the literary production in exile as a salient theme in Cuban/Cuban-American fiction. "Suicide is our one constant ideology; our muddy heart's single desire," broods the narrative voice in Ana Menéndez's novel *Loving Che*. In *Dreaming in Cuban* Cristina García employs suicide as remedy to disillusionment: "Celia steps into the ocean and imagines she's a soldier on a mission—for the moon, or the palms, or El Líder. The water rises quickly around her. It submerges her throat and her nose, her open eyes that do not perceive salt. Her hair floats loosely from her skull and waves above her in the tide. She breathes through her skin, she breathes through her wounds." García returns to the theme of suicide in her second novel, *The Agüero Sisters* (1997), as Reina and Constancia Agüero attempt to sort out murder and suicide in the family history. The presumed suicide of Blanca Mestre de Agüero was, in fact, a homicide, and Ignacio Agüero "put the twelve-gauge shotgun to her heart." García captures one character's brooding reflection on the decision to die: "When he died, Reina knew somehow that José Luis had chosen it. Death, she is certain, begins from within. It doesn't wait onstage like a retired general, eager for the podium but overcomes a body cell by cell. For a few people, this happens long before the accidents and wrinkles, long before the conjugation of regret."[157]

In the play *Un punto que se pierde en la distancia y en el tiempo*, by Yolanda Ortal-Miranda, Doña Isabel kills herself by slashing her wrist (*se abrió las venas*), after having explained: "I will not drag chains around; I will break them." In *The Killing of the Saints* (1991), novelist Alex Abella recounts the suicide attempt by Doris Dias, an inmate in a county prison: "Doris has tried to kill herself. A matron had found her in time and cut down the bed sheet that she had looped through the overhead window bars." In *Playing with Light* (2000), Beatriz Rivera explores the tensions in the transformation and transgression of traditional gender roles among Cuban-American women in Miami. Suicide is one outcome, with the death of Alma, who had one previous unsuccessful attempt. "She always wanted to be the center of attention," the narrator insists, "that was the reason she tried to commit suicide." In the end, she succeeds: "Alma checked into a Holiday Inn near the airport. . . . [She] took out the .22 caliber pistol she had brought in her handbag, she lay down on the Holiday Inn bed, put the gun to her temple, and shot herself. She didn't die right away."[158] Suicide is a specter in the lives of the Márquez Hernández family in Eduardo Machado's play *Broken Eggs*. Oscar asks Lizette: "Does [your husband] know about the suicides, how they drank till they explode . . . the violence we live with, the razor blades, the guns, the hangings, the one woman in our family who set herself on fire while her three kids watched?" Suicide is present in Eliseo Alberto's novel *Caracol Beach* (2000), in which a Cuban veteran of Angola who passes into exile in Florida is tormented by memories of combat and continually contemplates suicide.[159] The specter of suicide establishes its presence in the fiction of Roberto Fernández. "Her father couldn't stand her," comments one character in the novel *Raining Backwards* (1988), "that's why he set fire to himself." But it is in the story of Cuban-American adolescent Caridad ("Connie") Rodríguez y López, a story of seduction and betrayal, that suicide serves as the principal narrative theme of *Raining Backwards*, as Connie moves ineluctably to the contemplation of suicide as the result of her pregnancy. "Caridad, our only daughter . . . ," her mother rues, "she lost her virtue, if you know what I am telling you. She disgraced us. I asked myself many times: 'Who is going to take to the altar a virtueless woman?'" Connie prepares to kill herself. At the last moment she changes her mind, but she dies anyway: "She took the rope and made a rudimentary knot. Immediately, I knew she had never been a girl scout. She placed it around her neck, grabbed an old stool . . . to stand on. Once she made sure it could support her, she threw the rope over one of the branches and tested it."[160]

A romantic encounter in the novel *Fallen Angels Sing* (1991), by Omar Torres, is rendered with suicide in mind: "During her prolonged and persistent laughter, her round, full, red-lips created an abyss that was a invitation to a suicidal leap of pleasure." Suicide looms large in the fiction of Virgil Suárez, much of which is focused on the Cuban/Cuban-American condition in the United States. In the novel *Havana Thursdays* (1995) the narrator comments on Maura's drinking problem: "Drinking made the bad thoughts go away; thoughts of death and suicide. How many times had she not contemplated the absolute end? The various ways of leaving this life, this situation . . . this world—this harsh and intolerable reality."

Elsewhere in the novel, suicide is the subject of Gisell's internal dialogue. Explains the narrator:

> She needed to do something.
> Act.
> Maybe kill herself.
> She was an emotional retard.
> Something dramatic, yes.
> Slash her wrists.
> Watch the blood ooze out of her.[161]

Suicide and the Cuban condition in the United States are also addressed in the novel *The Greatest Performance* (1991), by Elías Miguel Muñoz, as the protagonist reflects: "I hated American music and if I didn't find some way of entertaining myself, of alleviating my Cuban depressions, I'd surely commit suicide, as cut and dried as that. Suicide."[162] Exile writer Nicolás Abreu Felippe begins his novel *Miami en brumas* with the protagonist, Máximo, in meditation on suicide in Miami:

> The solitude that revealed itself across the landscape affected him. He thought of suicide. That refreshing tranquility always made him think in the same way. He allowed himself to be carried away by the idea [of suicide] and he saw himself sinking in the ocean with an anchor tied to his foot and a shot to the head to excite the sharks. But everything remained in his imagination, for in the worst moment he was filled with thoughts of his family. Images of his son, his wife, his parents and the love surrounding these visions filled his thoughts and brought him back to reality—although, in the end, he understood that suicide was the ultimate and only hope. That's why perhaps he always carried a .38 caliber revolver in his boot.[163]

In the novel *Memoria del silencio*, by Uva de Aragón, the protagonist, Lauri, dreams of the death of her estranged husband as a suicide: "A shot. That sound—my God, how does one describe a sound?—startling, so brief, such a blow, so definitive. Nor can I forget his face, when I saw him for the last time through the glass door, the exact moment he raised the pistol to his temple and shot himself. . . . For him to come to the patio of my house to commit suicide represents a monumental egoism, the final mockery."[164]

Suicide also serves as a recurring theme in the short story written in exile. The protagonist José Pérez Prieto in Jesús Alvariño's story "El suicida" commits suicide after losing all hope of recovery from cancer: "He despaired. . . . The cancer has already sealed his fate. There was no cure. What to do? José Pérez Prieto decided to kill himself. He preferred to end his life because he could not bear up under his cancer. Why despair? He killed himself." The story ends with a newspaper account the day following the suicide that a Hungarian physician had found a cure for cancer and the final observation: "José Pérez Prieto died because he had cancer and he did not have faith." In the short story "Waters," Achy Obejas resorts to the imagery of suicide to describe the pose of Isabel lying atop the hood of a car: "Her body was spread out on the hood of her gray Lada, looking like someone who'd thrown herself down in an attempt at suicide." In "Abril es el mes más cruel," by Guillermo Cabrera Infante, the new bride plunges to her death from the seaside cliffs.[165] Other short stories engaging the theme of suicide include Enrique C. Henríquez, "Suicidio," and Oscar Gómez-Vidal, "El suicida."[166]

The poetry of Cubans living outside the island similarly dwells in the realm of self-destruction. Carolina Hospital lamented "Graciela's Suicide," and Rafael Campo wrote of "Suicidal Ideation."[167] The poetry of María Elena Cruz Varela often contemplates the possibility of suicide. In "Bajo el paso del fuego," for example, she writes:

And say to him also that on my bed
personal objects are committing suicide,
that I distill light through my wounds
and that I write this poem over the fire.

In "Arte poética de primera instancia," "A poet hangs himself, for example / when he cannot conform to his own design"; and in "El salto" she writes:

At midnight the jump.
Always the same jump in the same place.
Antinous is jumping. And we all jump with him.
Sweet, the suicides' vocation. To be devoured.[168]

"I know what suicide is," begins Carlos Alberto Montaner's poem "Le hablaré a la semilla"; while in "Paredón" Ricardo Pau-Llosa contemplates:

Staring down the mountainous wall
I imagine my ear against the suicidal
waves as if the sea itself were a shell
against my cheek.[169]

Virgil Suárez observes the possibility of suicide in "After the Accident":

> [The accident] took away any semblance
> of the man I knew, the man
> I know now acts defeated,
> *has* given up, contemplates
> the lives that could have been,
>
> speaks of suicide,
> of hurling himself from a second story
> but the apartment in Hialeah
> has bars on the windows,
> he knows this is not viable.[170]

Poet Felipe Lázaro broods in "El suicida borracho":

> To feel anxiety to stop life,
> of not continuing
> to say enough,
> good-bye,
> I'm leaving
> and leave.[171]

And in "El sueño suicida," Pablo LeRiverend speaks of going "in search of support / so that the sole truth lived does not collapse."[172]

Epilogue

*We can see now why it is that the suicidal drive appears
to be endowed with such an elemental force; it has such a
force because it springs from the most vital drive man
possesses, the instinct of self-preservation. . . . Here and
there within the frame of our civilization this old method
of self-assertion revives and re-enacts itself with the result
that the individual destroys himself.*

The American Journal of Psychiatry *(1936)*

*Suicidal conduct appears so threatening to the social
order exactly because it is so radical in its symbolic
meaning—because it affirms most directly the ultimate
value of individual freedom and dignity. Suicide offends
society because it is the most direct, uncompromising
expression of modern culture's core value of individual-
ism.*

*Realino Marra and Marco Orrù,
"Social Images of Suicide" (1991)*

*Suicide was an indirect accusation of the sociopolitical
and religious authorities themselves. It was proof of their
failure to provide justice and a decent life for the entire
population. . . . Suicide was an accusation directed at
society and its leaders because those who kill themselves
show a preference for nothingness or choose the risks of
the afterlife over a world that has become a living hell.*

Georges Minois, History of Suicide:
Voluntary Death in Western Culture *(1999)*

When a nation is born and grows, when it suffers
and is humiliated, when it cries and is provoked, and it
struggles, and it prevails or dies, it is said of that nation
that it has obtained in triumph or in death immortality.
Aurelio G. Silveira y Córdova, Cuba ante el espejo
de su pasado y el horoscopo de su porvenir *(1893)*

He who knows how to die always prevails.
José María de Heredia, "Himno del desterrado"
(1825)

Suicide entered the cosmology of Cuban from many sources. It implied the choice of death over life as an acceptable course of action. If life as experienced held no prospects, and if the future as expected had no promise, living had no purpose. Suicidal behavior was a way to cope, to impose one's will upon circumstances as an act of individual autonomy. Vast numbers of Cubans struggled to maintain their dignity even as they were pulled down by the undertow of despair and demoralization. Many replaced the will to endure with the desire to die. There was nothing left to do but seize control of one's life to end it.

There is perhaps no more useful way to engage the phenomenon of suicide in Cuba than through the acknowledgment of its familiarity as a frame of reference. Suicide dwelled in the domains of daily life, at every turn, in an imaginary context where awareness of its possibility and acquiescence to its admissibility contributed to its feasibility. To suggest that suicide in Cuba was ordinary is not exactly correct. It is more that it was not extraordinary.

Somewhere among the determinants that acted to bind the formation of personality to the fashioning of nationality, among the practices that contributed to making self-awareness a source of national identity, emerged the cognitive assets that men and women across the island employed to make sense of reality and meet the demands of daily life. Social purpose in life derived its bearings within the circumstances of life as lived, pursuits always in flux, to be sure, but at the same time pursuits commonly understood as proper and plausible. They provided a normative framework in which life practices acquired a measure of usable coherence within a moral order of prescribed canons and authorized comportment. In this sense, the idea of suicide served to transmit an acceptable form of cultural conduct; it entered individual realms of consciousness as a form of knowledge, conveying shared consensual values from which vast numbers of people derived their bearings in the living of their lives.

Suicide assumed multiple cultural manifestations, disseminated in both highbrow venues and lowbrow forms. Its representation provides markers possessed of the capacity to reveal meanings associated with the gesture of self-destruction, over time and at any given time, providing in the process insight into the way that cognitive engagement with the world at large acted to shape interior life. The place of suicide in Cuban aesthetics, for example, or as a subject of cartoons, must be seen at once as cause and effect of a deepening awareness of the efficacy of suicide, as a disposition validated in a larger moral environment.

The decision to die implied an attitudinal stance, to be sure, but one deeply conditioned within the normative determinants by which Cubans negotiated the experience of daily life. It filled Cuban imaginative spaces as shared cultural awareness. It obtained meaning in the context of a larger social consensus that fashioned the terms of approval and disapproval by which people took measure of their conduct, associated always with patterns of commonly recognized symbolic meaning, both as a private deed and a public act. To end one's life was often an exercise of agency, especially for men and women in moral circumstances and material conditions that prevented or otherwise precluded the exercise of individual autonomy.

The practice of suicide could assume the appearance of a wholly reasonable and rational response to adversity, a culturally plausible way to cope with life, to be exercised on those occasions when the gravity of life demanded that *something* be done—as compared to doing nothing—as an act of will, a way to obtain relief from an unbearable condition.[1] To seize control of one's life, to dispose of it as one saw fit, offered a means of resolution to the many afflictions that daily beset men and women across the island.

The disposition to die reached deeply into personal meditations on life, almost always with the understanding that, in the end, the exercise of control over one's life, that is, choosing whether to live or to die, offered the possibility of empowerment. The phenomenon of suicide offers a way to examine the confrontation between historical forces, on one hand, and human will and agency, on the other. However many ways the proposition of suicide entered the Cuban imagination, at the heart of what were often sober deliberations was the possibility of using life as a plausible means of autonomous action. Men and women learned early the different uses to which they could put their lives, which always included assigning specific value to their lives, as a function of self-dialogue and as communication with others. The larger historical significance of suicide in Cuba lies in its capacity to reveal the workings of normative systems and cultural constructions, to suggest the presence of internal tensions and moral contradictions associated with the most intimate experiences through which men and women engaged everyday life and determined the desire to continue to live at all.

Agency comes in many forms, of course, and it is far from certain that all people are disposed to act out agency in any form. But awareness of agency, that is, consciousness of choice and cognizance of consequences, have been at the heart of the Cuban meditation on self-destruction. Within the interior spheres of the personal and private, no less than in the external spaces of the collective and public, social knowledge of suicide enabled the enactment of autonomy often unavailable by any other means.

The efficacy of suicide was contained in the proposition of self-destruction as an act of self-determination, a means by which to claim possession of all that remained of one's humanity: life itself. The short-story collection *Cuentos sobre el clandestinaje* (1983), depicting the circumstances of imprisoned members of the urban resistance during the 1950s, conveys the pathos of prisoners, stripped naked, isolated in damp prison cells, subjected daily to unspeakable torture, and unable to exercise the only power of agency left to them: to end their lives.[2] This was life as a fate worse than death.

❧ Authorization of suicide was embedded in the very sources of national formation. Suicide assumed both resonance and rationality as a way for Cubans to incorporate themselves into their history. Per the dominant terms by which the duty of nationality entered realms of popular awareness, self-sacrifice was asked of all who aspired to meet the ideal of Cuban. There were times where the imperative of suicide took hold and gathered Cubans into its purpose, when self-immolation appeared as the only plausible response to historical circumstances. Vast numbers did indeed die for the patria. The proposition of suicide acquired national logic as a function of choices celebrated in the remembered past. "The Ten Years War," reflected Cuban historian Joel James Figarola in 1999, "inscribed, at once and permanently, a dimension of individual and collective political virtue that has guided the conduct of our society. The disposition to confront death . . . thus emerges as a salient aspect of the cultural personality of the Cuban."[3]

The very idea of patria developed as a proposition contingent upon and conditioned by the discharge of sacrifice as duty. Self-immolation was at the heart of the norms of nationality as fashioned by José Martí. Years ago poet Manuel Navarro Luna reflected on the meaning of Martí and what it meant to be a follower of Martí (*un martiano*). "It is not enough to have knowledge of the life of Martí, or his works, or his achievements," Navarro Luna insisted in 1938. He continued:

> Martí is not a type. Nor is he an archetype. Rather, simply put, he is a norm. A type can be studied. An archetype can be imitated. But norms have a single purpose: to be followed. . . . [This implies] a committed and joyful determination to die for others: a joy in the act of dying for others, which is the only noble way for us to live. . . . *Un martiano* must be capable of renouncing everything, including family—his wife, his son, his mother—to meet his principal duties. . . . He must also be prepared to abandon them for the over-riding duty that is the patria. Otherwise, he may be a good son, a model husband, and excellent father. But never an authentic *martiano*.[4]

In an essay published in 1999, historian Liudmarys Chaviano Martínez addressed the larger meaning of suicide in Martí's thinking: "Martí considered the [individual who committed] suicide not simply as someone voluntarily ending his life, but rather as one deliberately risking his life, especially on those occasions when the cause for which one risked one's life was the most just of all: that of liberating the patria."[5] As long as Martí continues to hold Cubans in his thrall, as long as Martí serves as the principal authorizing figure by which the meaning of Cuban is mediated and the comportment of Cuban is measured, the disposition to die will persist as a celebrated attribute of the character of Cuban.

The practice of suicide inscribed itself deeply in the repertoire of Cuban comportment. It dwelled in domains of metaphor and musing, as an act of valor and an expression of virtue in defense of dignity and decorum, both individual and collective. It assumed the status of heroic conduct, honored and hallowed as a norm of virtuous deportment. There seems always to have been occasion to acclaim suicide as a gesture in celebration of an ideal, or the exoneration of a purpose, or the condemnation of injustice. Indeed, the gesture of self-immolation has become so commonly associated with upholding the ideals of nationality as to pass easily enough for a virtue of Cuban. "The practice of suicide," writer Guillermo Cabrera Infante has insisted, "is the sole and, of course, definitive Cuban ideology: an ideology of the rebel—of permanent rebellion by way of perpetual suicide." Reinaldo Arenas arrived at a similar conclusion: "Suicide in the history of Cuba . . . is a constant that has manifested itself since the time of the Indians until our present time. . . . There is an attitude of desperation that leads to suicide: often an act of powerlessness but at the same time of rebellion. Suicide can be seen as an act of rebellion. I see in the [action of the] Indians and perhaps in the political suicides of Cuba an act of rebellion: in the absence of any other solution, I escape through suicide. . . . A liberation: it is what we can call flight." Writer Eliseo Alberto celebrated suicide as a facet of national character. "Each country has its own way of death," Alberto wrote, "for each country has its own way of life. . . . To kill oneself in Cuba is not to surrender. On the contrary: to kill oneself in Cuba is to triumph over oneself. Our way of Death has taught us that to wish it, to seek it, to find it in the barrel of a gun was an act of courage."[6]

The meaning of suicide assumed salience as social behavior within the realm of normative transactions. To choose to die was to enact a mode of communication appropriate to the social environment, at once a function of exchange and an act of engagement. The choice had at least as much to do with popular acquiescence to suicide as with the personal desire to die. But it is also clear that attempts to deter or otherwise discourage suicide through the logic of larger metaphysical systems, through theological formulations, for example—life belonged to God—or by way of ideological imperatives—that life belonged to the revolution—had little enduring effect on Cuban behavior. In fact, the culture was loaded with mixed messages. Cubans made the decision to die in response to deeply personal circumstances, sometimes under conditions of unbearable pain, often in the grip of despair and in a state of hopelessness, with the conviction that death was not simply the only solution but the best one. At that moment, life belonged to the person who lived it.

That death by suicide in Cuba assumed fully the form of cultural conduct, loaded with meaning, suggests that the deed possessed the means to transmit message even as it acted to validate means. It could mean many things, as both a private deed and a public event, and its intent was not always readily apparent. Suicide suggested different things to different people, of course. Once the act of suicide entered the public domain, the motives that served to determine the decision to die often mattered less than the meaning others assigned to the act. These were cognitive transactions by which suicide gained cultural currency and popular endorsement. Much had to do with the ways that men and women learned to become Cuban and thereupon live up to those canons consecrated as norms of national conduct. The practice of suicide was inscribed in the roles that Cubans learned to assume in the multiple spaces of private pursuits and public purpose, how men and women acted, reacted, and interacted as a function of shared familiarities and collective norms.

Suicidal death has come to imply a complex subjectivity, fashioned over time but very much a product of a time, developed within a context of a generally shared moral order. Despite the fact that the practice of suicide frequently cut so many lives short at an early age, and indeed has historically figured as one of the principal causes of mortality in Cuba, it was not until the late 1980s that suicidal behavior was identified as a public health issue. That an otherwise advanced health care system was for so long oblivious to the magnitude of self-destruction suggests the degree to which suicide by its very prevalence had been normalized as a condition of being Cuban.

It was in the context of acquiescence and accommodation that the proposition of suicide settled into Cuban awareness. To imagine suicide as an attribute of the Cuban condition is to locate the disposition to die within a cultural setting of received conventions reinforced in an environment of moral cues and ethical codes. To what degree second- and third-generation Cuban-Americans born and raised entirely in the United States will be implicated in the dispositions of their parents and grandparents remains to be seen.

The efficacy of suicide was a point of view with which Cubans early acquired familiarity, if not always firsthand then as a condition of the larger moral environment, transmitted through a variety of culturally determined modalities: in the form of humor in a cartoon, as intimated in the lyric of a song, as a gesture of dramatic purpose in a short story, as a deed celebrated in history. The circumstances under which death appeared as an appropriate response to life changed over time, to be sure, as did the methods employed. But what remained constant was the proposition of suicide as an appropriate response, thereby contributing to a larger moral setting that served to ratify the efficacy of death by suicide.

Life in the final years of the twentieth century and into the early years of the twentieth-first century has continued to weigh heavily on Cubans, as individuals and as families, as a people and a nation. Most men and women choose to persist as best they can; some determine to die. In both cases the decision implicates moral stamina and individual will, where and how people place their faith in the future. It often takes as much courage to live as it does to die. These are not unfamiliar historical conditions. But also familiar and no less historical is the determination of men and women in Cuba to live life under the circumstances of their choosing and to accept the choice of death as a means toward that end. It has been thus since Yumurí.

Notes

INTRODUCTION

1. Juan Pérez de la Riva, "La desaparición de la población indígena cubana," *Universidad de La Habana* 196–97 (1972): 79–84. See also Rafael Azcárate Rosell, *Historia de los indios de Cuba* (Havana, 1937), pp. 215–17; and Salvador Morales, *Conquista y colonización de Cuba. Siglo XVI* (Havana, 1984), pp. 21–25.

2. Jorge Castellanos, "Crónica de la rebeldía de los indios cubanos (1520–1550)," *Universidad de La Habana*, 136–41 (1958–59): 227–28.

3. Bartolomé de las Casas, *Historia de las Indias*, 3 vols. (1875; reprint, Madrid, 1957), 2:364.

4. Girolamo Benzoni, *History of the New World*, trans. W. H. Smith (London, 1857), pp. 77–78. Benzoni arrived to the region in 1541 and traveled extensively through Cuba, Santo Domingo, and Puerto Rico.

5. Legend tells that the name "Yumurí" is the corruption of "yo morí," the cry of Indians as they plunged to their deaths. See Samuel Feijóo, *Mitología cubana* (Havana, 1985), p. 23.

6. José Barreiro, "Indians in Cuba," *Cultural Survival Quarterly* 13 (1989): 56–60.

7. David Wood, "Suicide as Instrument and Expression," in M. Pabst Battin and David J. Mayo, eds., *Suicide: The Philosophical Issues* (New York, 1980), p. 150.

8. Víctor Zamora, *Escuela luminosa* (Havana, 1957), p. 5.

9. Leland E. Warren, "The Conscious Speakers: Sensibility and the Art of Conversation Considered," in Syndy McMillen Conger, ed., *Sensibility in Transformation: Creative Resistance to Sentiment from the Augustans to the Romantics* (Cranbury, N.J., 1990), p. 26; Stephen Cox, "Sensibility as Argument," ibid., p. 67. For G. J. Barker-Benfield, sensibility denotes "the material basis for consciousness" and is a word "synonymous with consciousness [and] with feeling." See G. J. Barker-Benfield, *The Culture of Sensibility* (Chicago, 1992), p. xvii. See also Chris Jones, *Radical Sensibility: Literature and Ideas in the 1790s* (London, 1993), pp. 20–58; and Janet Todd, *Sensibility: An Introduction* (London, 1986), pp. 6–9.

10. Lino Novás Calvo, "El pathos cubano," in José María Chacón y Calvo, ed., *Homenaje a Enrique José Varona en el cincuentenario de su primer curso de filosofía (1880–1930): Miscelánea de estudios literarios, históricos y filosóficos* (Havana, 1935), p. 212.

11. Abelardo Estorino, *La casa vieja*, in Abelardo Estorino and Andrés Lizarraga, *Teatro* (Havana, 1964), p. 108.

12. José Jorrín Bramosio, "El Suicida," *La Siempreviva* 1 (1838): 133–35.

13. Diego Tamayo, "Reflexiones sociológicas sobre las causas de mortalidad en La Habana," *Anales de la Real Academia de Ciencias Médicas, Físicas y Naturales de La Habana* 30 (1893): 44.

14. Manuel Márquez Sterling, *Alrededor de nuestra psicología* (Havana, 1906), pp. 197–98; Evelio Rodríguez Lendián, "El porvenir de Cuba," *Revista de la Facultad de*

Letras y Ciencias de la Universidad de La Habana 29 (July–December 1919): 173–74; Enrique Gay Calbó, "El cubano, avestruz del trópico: Tentativa exegética de la imprevisión tradicional cubana," *Universidad de La Habana* 17–18 (March–June 1938): 142.

15. Ramón Ferreira, *Teatro: Donde está la luz* (Miami, 1993), p. 25.

16. Miguel A. Garrido, "Fe en el porvenir," *El Mundo Ilustrado* 2 (May 14, 1905): 234. See also Un Cubano Práctico [Rafael Padró], *El porvenir de Cuba* (New York, 1898).

17. Eduardo González Velez, "Soledad," *La Lucha*, January 20, 1929, p. 11.

18. Quoted in Zoé Valdés, *Yocandra in the Paradise of Nada*, trans. Sabina Cienfuegos (New York, 1995), p. 1.

19. Héctor Quintero, *Contigo pan y cebolla*, in *Teatro* (Havana, 1983), p. 56.

20. Miguel Barnet, *Canción de Rachel* (1969; reprint, Havana, 1985), p. 48.

21. For one particularly sensational case of a murder made to appear as a suicide see Salvador Díaz Versón, *La muerte de Andrea Barrios* (Havana, 1937); Israel Castellanos, "El caso de Andrea Barrios desde el punto de vista de la ciencia," *Bohemia* 29 (March 28, 1937): 34, 58; and "El misterioso crimen de Andrea Barrios," *Carteles* 29 (April 4, 1937): 31. Other apparent homicides made to look like suicides are treated in Tomás L. Plasencia, "Notas relativas al suicidio en la circunscripción de La Habana," *Anales de la Real Academia de Ciencias Médicas, Físicas y Naturales de La Habana* 22 (1885): 411–12; Fidel de las Heras, "¿Crimen o suicidio en la muerte de Estrella Rivero?" *Carteles* 34 (June 21, 1953): 94–95; and Custodio Duquesne y Barcala, "El crimen de la 'suicida' que no disparó," *Bohemia* 46 (January 10, 1954): 21–24, 26, 112. Murder disguised as suicide is the theme of Loló de la Torriente's short story "Suicidio." See Loló de la Torriente, *Narraciones de Federica y otros cuentos* (Havana, 1988), pp. 12–14.

22. See Eloy G. Merino Brito, "El suicidio y el seguro de vida," *El Mundo*, February 3, 1957, p. A-9.

23. The "suicide" of prisoner Juan José de la Caridad Orama in Holguín, many believed, was in fact murder by the police. See *La Lucha*, July 10, 1926, p. 4. See also Reynaldo González, "Abelardo Noa se suicidió anoche," in *La fiesta de los tiburones*, 2 vols. (1926; reprint, Havana, 1978), 2:209–10.

24. República de Cuba, Sanidad y Beneficencia, *Boletín Oficial* 33 (January–June 1928): 450, 563; República de Cuba, Ministerio de Salubridad y Asistencia Social, *Boletín Oficial* 53 (January–June 1950): 72. See also Waldo Medina, "Se ha suicidado un niño," July 24, 1953, in *Cosas de ayer que sirven para hoy* (Havana, 1978), pp. 60–61.

25. See República de Cuba, Sanidad y Beneficencia, *Boletín Oficial*, 1930–1935 (Havana, 1931–36); República de Cuba, Comisión Nacional de Estadística y Reformas Económicas, *Estadísticas. . . . 1929–1932* (Havana, 1929–32).

CHAPTER ONE

1. Doria González Fernández, "Acerca del mercado cafetalero cubano durante la primera mitad del siglo XIX," *Revista de la Biblioteca Nacional 'José Martí'* 31 (3ra Epoca) (May–August 1989): 151–59; H. E. Friedlaender, *Historia económica de Cuba* (Havana, 1944), p. 211; Cuba, Capitanía General, *Cuadro estadístico de la Siempre Fiel Isla de Cuba, correspondiente al año 1827* (n.p.); "Resumen general de partidos, número de negros de la dotación de los ingenios . . . y de los cafetales que se hallan en

el Obispado de La Habana," 1832–33, Legajo 3772, No. Añ, Fondo Miscelánea de Expedientes, Archivo Nacional de Cuba, Havana, Cuba (hereinafter cited as ANC); "Ingenios y cafetales," 1832–33, 1834–35, Legajo 3772, No. Añ, Fondo Miscelánea de Expedientes, ANC; Susan Schroeder, *Cuba: A Handbook of Historical Statistics* (Boston, 1982), p. 246.

2. Leví Marrero, *Cuba: economía y sociedad*, 15 vols. (Madrid, 1972–88), 10:88, 93, 278; Alexander von Humboldt, *The Island of Cuba*, ed. John Thrasher (New York, 1846), p. 271; Manuel Moreno Fraginals, *El ingenio: complejo económico social cubano del azúcar*, 3 vols. (Havana, 1978), 1:137–48; José García de Arboleya, *Manual de la Isla de Cuba. Compendio de su historia, geografía, estadística y administración*, 2nd ed. (Havana, 1859), pp. 138–39; Schroeder, *Cuba*, p. 260. The information concerning the sugar mills in 1846 is found in Cuba, Capitanía General, *Cuadro estadístico de la Siempre Fiel Isla de Cuba, correspondiente al año de 1846* (Havana, 1847).

3. Ramón de la Sagra, *Historia económico-política y estadística de la Isla de Cuba, o sea de sus progresos en la población, la agricultura, el comercio y las rentas* (Havana, 1831), pp. 5–6; Humboldt, *Island of Cuba*, pp. 218–23; Cuba, Capitanía General, *Resumen del censo de población de la Isla de Cuba a fin del año de 1841* (Havana, 1842), p. 56.

4. Richard Robert Madden, *The Island of Cuba: Its Resources, Progress, and Prospects* (London, 1853), pp. 174–75.

5. Robert Baird, *Impressions and Experiences of the West Indies and North America in 1849*, 2 vols. (Edinburgh, 1850), 2:225; Humboldt, *Island of Cuba*, p. 271; Joseph John Gurney, *A Winter in the West Indies* (London, 1841), p. 209; Fredrika Bremer, *Homes of the New World*, trans. Mary Howitt, 2 vols. (New York, 1854), 2:333–34.

6. Baird, *Impressions and Experiences*, 2:180.

7. Richard Robert Madden, *Poems by a Slave in the Island of Cuba, Recently Liberated. . . . With the History of the Early Life of the Negro Poet, Written by Himself, to Which Are Prefixed Two Pieces Descriptive of Cuban Slavery and the Slave-Traffic*, ed. Edward J. Mullen (1840; reprint, Hamden, Conn., 1981), pp. 70–71.

8. Mary Gardner Lowell, *New Year in Cuba: Mary Gardner Lowell's Travel Diary, 1831–1832*, ed. Karen Robert (Boston, 2003), p. 89.

9. Madden, *Poems by a Slave*, pp. 83–84.

10. Esteban Montejo, *Biografía de un cimarrón*, ed. Miguel Barnet (Havana, 1966), p. 39.

11. Hady López Borges, "Estudio de la Vitamina B1 en algunos alimentos cubanos," Salubridad y Asistencia Social, *Boletín Oficial* 46 (July–December 1943): 140–44.

12. Manuel Vázquez y Torres, *El mayordomo de un ingenio* (Havana, 1837), p. 22. See also José Mauricio Quintero, *El mayoral de ingenio. Su historia* (Matanzas, 1875).

13. José Antonio Saco, "Carta sobre el cólera morbo asiático," 1833, in *Colección de papeles científicos, históricos, políticos y de otros ramos sobre la Isla de Cuba*, 3 vols. (1857; reprint, Havana, 1960–62), 2:260–97; J. A. Benjumeda, *Fiebre amarilla en la Habana* (Cádiz, 1870); Luis Perna, *Memoria histórica de la epidemia de viruelas en Cienfuegos* (Cienfuegos, 1888). Detailed analyses of mortality associated with disease are found in Angel José Cowley, *Ensayo estadístico-médico de la mortalidad de la diócesis de La Habana durante el año 1843* (Havana, 1845); Honorato Bernard de Chateusalins, *El vademecum de los hacendados cubanos, o guía práctica para curar la mayor parte de las enfermedades*

(Havana, 1854); María Dolores Pérez Murillo, *Aspectos demográficos y sociales de la Isla de Cuba en la primera mitad del siglo XIX* (Cádiz, 1988), pp. 82–105; and Alejandro de la Fuente, "Indice de morbilidad e incidencia de enfermedades entre los esclavos en La Habana, 1580–1699," *Revista Cubana de Salud Pública* 16 (January–March 1990): 101–17.

14. Sagra, *Historia económico-política y estadística*, p. 22; Baird, *Impressions and Experiences*, 2:181.

15. Physician Gregory Zilboorg described the phenomenon whereby the decision to die is made as a welcome release, where "young men and women lie down and die as any one lies down and sleeps," of "peaceful, voluntary deaths." See Gregory Zilboorg, "Suicide Among Civilized and Primitive Races," *American Journal of Psychiatry* 92 (May 1936): 1347–69.

16. Georges Daremberg, "La nostalgia; o el mal del país," *El Genio Científico* 2 (July 1874): 264–66.

17. George Howe, "The Last Slave-Ship," *Scribner's Magazine* 8 (July 1890): 123; Wilson quoted in W. O. Blake, *The History of Slavery and the Slave Trade* (Columbus, Ohio, 1860), pp. 135–36; Alexander Falconbridge, *An Account of the Slave Trade on the Coast of Africa* (1788; reprint, New York, 1973), pp. 23, 31–32; Blake, *The History of Slavery*, p. 129.

18. Francisco Barrera y Domingo, *Reflexiones histórico físico naturales médico quirúrgicas: prácticos y especulativos entretenimientos acerca de la vida, usos costumbres, alimentos, bestidos, color y enfermedes a que propenden los negros de Africa, venidos a las Américas* (1798; reprint, Havana, 1953), pp. 72, 145.

19. Gurney, *Winter in the West Indies*, p. 210; Madden, *The Island of Cuba*, pp. 160–61; Thomas Fowell Buxton, *The African Slave Trade and Its Remedy* (London, 1840), pp. 191–92.

20. "Defunciones por suicidio de negros esclavos, Yaguajay, 1853–1872" (unpublished manuscript, 1874). The author acknowledges with appreciation receipt of a copy of this document provided by Rosalba Díaz Quintana. Copy in author's possession.

21. See Orlando Patterson, *The Sociology of Slavery* (London, 1967), p. 146; "Expediente promovido sobre la averiguación del suicidio cometido por el negro Andrés," Legajo 149, No. 4, Fondo Intendencia General de Hacienda, ANC. "Many slaves commit suicide," observed one traveler in 1854, "—so many, that this is to be reckoned among the serious causes of their diminished numbers. . . . It is related that on one estate eight were found hanging in company, in one night." See "Cuba and Cubans," *North American Review* 79 (July 1854): 118–19.

22. Joseph Goodwin Jr., "Diary," Manuscript Department, New-York Historical Society, New York, N.Y.

23. See "Comunicación sobre el suicidio del esclavo Francisco Arará en el Río San Agustín," August 20–September 26, 1849, Legajo 23, No. 52-A, Fondo Esclavos, Archivo Histórico Provincial de Matanzas, Matanzas, Cuba (hereinafter cited as AHPM); "Comunicación sobre el suicidio del negro José Carabalí en el potrero de su amo, Ambrosio González de Chávez," August 6–September 29, 1843, ibid.; Pedro A. González to Capitán Juez, August 20, 1849, ibid.

24. "Expediente suicidio del negro José María Congo," June 1843, Legajo 2756,

No. V, Fondo de Miscelánea de Expedientes, ANC; "Expediente," Legajo 1413, No. 7455, Fondo Instituciones Judiciales Coloniales, Archivo Histórico Provincial de Pinar del Río, Pinar del Río, Cuba (hereinafter cited as AHPPR); Consul to Henry C. Hall, July 8, 1872, Despatches from U.S. Consuls in Havana, General Records of the Department of State, Record Group 86, National Archives, Washington, D.C. See also "Expediente suicidio del negro Anselmo Lucumí," July 1860, Legajo 2777, No. S, Fondo Miscelánea de Expedientes, ANC.

25. *Congressional Globe*, 35th Cong., 2nd sess., February 1859, p. 1080; María Poumier Taquechel, "El suicidio esclavo en Cuba en los años 1840," *Anuario de Estudios Americanos* 43 (1986): 73.

26. Gurney, *Winter in the West Indies*, p. 211; Bremer, *Homes of the New World*, 2:332; Audiencia de La Habana, "Testimonio del expediente instruido sobre las causas que influyen en el frecuente suicidio de los esclavos y medidas que son de adoptarse para evitarlos," 1845–52, Legajo 371, No. 14137, Fondo Gobierno Superior Civil, ANC. Writing in the early 1830s, Ramón de la Sagra estimated a 10–12 percent mortality rate among "recently arrived slaves" without specifying cause. See Sagra, *Historia económico-política y estadística*, p. 22.

27. Audiencia de La Habana, "Testimonio del expediente instruido."

28. Charles Augustus Murray, *Travels in North America During the Years 1834, 1835 and 1836*, 2 vols. (London, 1839), 2:175–76; José María de la Torre, *Compendio de geografía física, política, estadística y comparada de la Isla de Cuba* (Havana, 1854), p. 53. See also Manuel Moreno Fraginals, "Africa in Cuba: A Quantitative Analysis of the African Population in the Island of Cuba," in Vera Rubin and Arthur Tuden, eds., *Comparative Perspectives on Slavery in New World Plantation Societies* (New York, 1977), p. 191. For descriptions of the different African ethnic groups in Cuba see Fernando Ortiz, *Los negros esclavos* (1916; reprint, Havana, 1975), pp. 40–57; and Jesús Guanche, *Componentes étnicos de la nación cubana* (Havana, 1996), pp. 44–71. The overwhelming majority of recorded suicides during the early decades of the nineteenth century in the coffee and sugar growing zones of Pinar del Rio were attributed to the Lucumí. See the "Expedientes" in Legajo 1507, No. 7754; Legajo 225, No. 1372; and Legajo 1507, No. 7757, Fondo Instituciones Judiciales Coloniales, AHPPR.

29. Samuel Johnson, *The History of the Yorubas* (1921; reprint, Lagos, 1976), pp. 188–273; Robin Law, *The Oyo Empire, c. 1600–c. 1836: A West African Imperialism in the Era of the Atlantic Slave Trade* (Oxford, 1977), pp. 260–99; Robert S. Smith, *Kingdoms of the Yoruba*, 3rd ed. (Madison, 1988), pp. 61–75.

30. J. F. Ade Ajayi and Robert Smith, *Yoruba Warfare in the Nineteenth Century* (London, 1964), pp. 51–52.

31. F. Amaury Talbot, *The Peoples of Southern Nigeria* (London, 1926), p. 698.

32. "The Africans (as is well known)," wrote British planter Matthew Lewis in 1834, "generally believe, that there is a life beyond this world, and that they shall enjoy it by returning to their own country; and this idea [is] used frequently to induce them, soon after their landing in the colonies, to commit suicide." See Roger D. Abraham and John F. Szwed, eds., *After Africa: Extracts from British Travel Accounts and Journals of the Seventeenth, Eighteenth, and Nineteenth Centuries Concerning the Slaves, Their Manners, and Customs in the British West Indies* (New Havana, 1983), p. 341.

33. José de la Luz y Caballero, *Aforismos y apuntaciones*, ed. Roberto Agramonte (1847; reprint, Havana, 1945), p. 243; Bremer, *Homes of the New World*, 2:332; Abiel Abbot, *Letters Written in the Interior of Cuba* (Boston, 1829), p. 44.

34. Murray, *Travels in North America*, 2:261.

35. José Antonio Saco, "La estadística criminal de Cuba en 1862," *La América*, January 12, 1864, p. 5.

36. Anselmo Suárez y Romero, *Francisco* (1875; reprint, Havana, 1970), pp. 162–63. The novel was completed in 1839. "Francisco punishes his master," writes William Luis of Francisco's suicide. See William Luis, *Literary Bondage: Slavery in Cuban Narrative* (Austin, 1990), p. 48.

37. In Daniel Pratt Mannix and Malcolm Cowley, *Black Cargoes: A History of the Atlantic Slave Trade, 1518–1865* (New York, 1962), p. 118; in Blake, *The History of Slavery*, pp. 130, 132.

38. Henri Dumont, "Antropología y patología de los negros esclavos: Memoria inédita referente a Cuba," *Revista Bimestre Cubana* 10 (July–August 1915): 273. See also "El proceso contra Ildefonso Carabalí, esclavo de Don Diego Francisco de Unzaga, por intento de suicidio," September 11, 1807, in Gloria García Rodríguez, ed., *La esclavitud desde la esclavitud: La visión de los siervos* (Havana, 1996), pp. 102–4.

39. Richard Kimball, *Cuba and the Cubans* (New York, 1850), p. 154; Maturin M. Ballou, *History of Cuba; or, Notes of a Traveller in the Tropics* (Boston, 1854), p. 181.

40. Among the recorded instances of suicide by hanging from a guásima tree see "Expediente suicidio del negro Nicanor Lucumí," June 1843, Legajo 2736, No. Ap, Fondo Miscelánea de Expedientes, ANC; "Expediente suicidio del negro Tomás Lucumí," March 1843, Legajo 2756, No. V, ibid.

41. "Expediente suicidio del negro Nepomoceno Lucumí," 1844, Legajo 2780, No. Q, Fondo Miscelánea de Expedientes, ANC; Audiencia de La Habana, "Testimonio del expediente instruido." See also "Expediente suicidio del negro Pedro José Lucumí," March 1843, Legajo 2756, No. O, Fondo Miscelánea de Expedientes, ANC; and "Expediente suicidio del negro Ramón Carabalí," August 1844, Legajo 2779, No. LL, ibid.; "Expediente suicidio del negro Vicente," October 1828, Legajo 2775, No. I, ibid.; "Expediente suicidio de Crecencio," May 1848, Legajo 2735, No. AK, ibid.

42. Michael A. Gomez, *Exchanging Our Country Marks* (Chapel Hill, 1998), pp. 117–18; Montejo, *Biografía de un cimarrón*, p. 42.

43. M. Hurtado de Mendoza, "Leyenda mandinga," *Archivos del Folklore Cubano* 2 (May 1926): 174–75.

44. See "Expediente criminal por haberse encontrado ahorcado el esclavo Florencio Lucumí de D. Lucas Díaz," August 1844, Legajo 2779, No. B, Fondo Miscelánea de Expedientes, ANC; "Causa criminal por haberse encontrado ahogado al negro Leandro Lucumí," August 1844, Legajo 2735, No. I, ibid.; "Expediente criminal por el suicidio del negro Matías Lucumí," September 1844, Legajo 2780, No. Az, ibid.; "Expediente criminal por haberse encontrado ahorcado el negro Andrés Lucumí," December 1844, Legajo 2759, No. M, December 1844, ibid.; "Expediente promovido sobre la averiguación del suicidio cometido por el negro Andrés, esclavo de S.M. y destinado de serviente en el hospital Real de San Ambrosio," Legajo 149, No. 4, Fondo Intendencia General de Hacienda, ANC.

45. William Henry Hurlbert, *Gan-Eden; or, Picture of Cuba* (Boston, 1854), p. 199; "Expediente," Legajo 1507, No. 7770, Fondo Instituciones Judiciales Coloniales, AHPPR; Hurtado de Mendoza, "Leyenda mandinga," p. 175.

46. "Expediente suicidio del negro Luciano Lucumí," 1837, Legajo 2749, No. O, Fondo Miscelánea de Expedientes, ANC; "Expediente suicidio del negro Nicolás Carabalí," October 1843, Legajo 2723, No. Aa, ibid.; "Expediente suicidio del negro Damián Lucumí," January 1843, Legajo 2770, No. R, ibid. See also "Expediente suicidio de José Lucumí," July 1859, Legajo 2729, No. V, ibid.; and "Expediente suicidio del negro Joaquín Congo," January 1840, Legajo 2820, No. X, ibid.

47. A Physician, *Notes on Cuba* (Boston, 1844), pp. 255–56.

48. Pedro Calderón to Gobernador, April 2, 1842, Legajo 45, No. 67, Fondo Gobierno Provincial (Defunciones), AHPM. See also Gabino La Rosa Corzo, *Los palenques del oriente de Cuba: Resistencia y acoso* (Havana, 1988); José Luciano Franco, "Palenques del Frijol, Bumba y Maluala," *Universidad de La Habana* 160 (March–April 1963): 178.

49. "Suicidio por hambre," *La Habana* 1 (September 15, 1858): 74–75. See also the case of *cimarrón* Paulino Congo, in "Expediente suicidio del negro Paulino Congo," April 1859, Legajo 2725, No. Aa, Fondo Miscelánea de Expedientes, ANC; and "Expediente suicidio del negro Francisco criollo," July 1841, Legajo 2759, No. D, ibid.

50. Audiencia de La Habana, "Testimonio del expediente instruido." See also Teresa Díaz Canals, *Moral y sociedad: Una intelección de la moral en la primera mitad del siglo XIX cubano* (Havana, 2002), p. 97; Robert L. Paquette, *Sugar Is Made with Blood: The Conspiracy of La Escalera and the Conflict between Empires over Slavery in Cuba* (Middletown, Conn., 1988), p. 221; and Marrero, *Cuba*, 10:182.

51. "Expediente de la negra Basilia," April 1838, Legajo 2745, No. Y, Fondo Miscelánea de Expedientes, ANC; "Expediente de la Lucumí Carmen," Legajo 1507, No. 7756, Fondo Instituciones Judiciales Coloniales, AHPPR; "Expediente de la negra Eustaquia," July 1844, Legajo 2780, No. N, Fondo Miscelánea de Expedientes, ANC. See also "Expediente suicidio de la esclava Carmen, nación Lucumí," Legajo 2799, No. J, Fondo Miscelánea de Expedientes, ANC. Historian María del Carmen Barcia discusses the case of sixteen-year-old domestic slave Ciriaca, who attempted to kill herself by cutting her throat after being punished by her owner. See María del Carmen Barcia, *La otra familia: Parientes, redes y descendencia de los esclavos en Cuba* (Havana, 2003), p. 66.

52. Audiencia de La Habana, "Testimonio del expediente instruido." A slightly different version of this collection of documents is found as "Testimonio del expediente formado para averiguar las causas que influyen en el frecuente suicidios de los esclavos," Legajo 4655, No. 816, Ultramar, Archivo Histórico Nacional, Madrid, Spain (hereinafter cited as AHN); David Eltis, "The Nineteenth-Century Transatlantic Slave Trade: An Annual Time Series of Imports in the Americas Broken Down by Region," *Hispanic American Historical Review* 67 (February 1987): 122–23; Cuba, *Cuba, resumen del censo de población de la Isla de Cuba a fin del año de 1841* (Havana, 1842).

53. Rómulo Lachatañeré, "El sistema religioso de los lucumís y otras influencias africanas en Cuba," *Estudios Afrocubanos* 3 (1939): 54–56.

54. Audiencia de La Habana, "Testimonio del expediente instruido"; Bishop Francisco Fleix y Solans to Captain General José Gutiérrez de la Concha, June 9, 1850,

Legajo 1667, No. 34, Ultramar, AHN. One reason planters sought to obstruct official investigation in the operation of the estate had to do with the Cuban participation in the contraband slave trade. Noted the *fiscal*: "The number of slaves in the Western Department is actually higher than reported in the official census of 1842, because at the time of the enumeration slave owners concealed the actual number of slaves on their estates." See Audiencia de La Habana, "Testimonio del expediente instruido."

55. Ramón Piña y Peñuela, *Topografía médica de la isla de Cuba* (Havana, 1855), p. 107. See also Audiencia de La Habana, "Testimonio del expediente instruido."

56. Abbot, *Letters Written*, p. 44; Lowell, *New Year in Cuba*, p. 89. The public burning of cadavers in Cuba apparently failed to obtain the desired results. "Not even through these means," the intendant reported, "was it possible to prevent acts of imitation, . . . where taking advantage of the first distraction to the overseer they hanged themselves from the very same trees as their very *compañeros* had." See Audiencia de La Habana, "Testimonio del expediente instruido."

57. Pedro Pinazo, *Discurso pronunciado en el acto de apertura de la Real Audiencia Pretorial el día 2 de enero de este año* (Havana, 1849), p. 7; "Expediente del negro Salvador Gangá." October 1837, Legajo 2809, No. T, Fondo Miscelánea de Expedientes, ANC; Audiencia de La Habana, "Testimonio del expediente instruido"; José Giralt, "Conato de suicidio," *Revista de Jurisprudencia* 3 (1858): 94–95.

58. Bishop Francisco Fleix y Solans to Governor General, June 9, 1850, Legajo 1667, No. 34, Ultramar, AHN; Audiencia de La Habana, "Testimonio del expediente instruido."

59. Audiencia de La Habana, "Testimonio del expediente instruido." Emphasis in original.

60. These dispositions suggest what Michel de Certeau characterizes as a reconfiguration of the "calculus . . . of relations of force," most recognizable as "tactics . . . essentially determined by the *absence of power*." See Michel de Certeau, "On the Oppositional Practices of Everyday Life," *Social Text* 3 (Fall 1980): 3–43. Emphasis in original.

61. "El proceso contra Ildefonso Carabalí," p. 103.

62. See Mervyn D. W. Jeffreys, "Samsonic Suicides: or Suicides of Revenge among Africans," in Anthony Middens, ed., *The Sociology of Suicide*, (London, 1971), pp. 185–96. See also the two essays by Paul Bohannan, "Theories of Homicide and Suicide" and "Patterns of Murder and Suicide," in *African Homicide and Suicide* (Princeton, 1960), pp. 3–29, 230–66.

63. Barrera y Domingo, *Reflexiones histórico*, pp. 81–82.

64. See Juan Losada and Jorge Mayor, "Esclavitud y psicología: una investigación interdisciplinaria," *Revista de la Biblioteca Nacional José Martí* 22 (September–December 1980): 133–43.

65. Blake, *The History of Slavery*, p. 130; Barrera y Domingo, *Reflexiones histórico*, p. 74.

66. Cirilo Villaverde, *Cecilia Valdés, o la loma del angel* (1839; reprint, Havana, 1923), p. 291.

67. Leopoldo O'Donnell to Secretary of State and the Office of Gobernación, September 18, 1847, in Marrero, *Cuba*, 9:183; *Boletín de Colonización* 1 (April 30, 1873): 2.

68. Joseph J. Dimock, *Impressions of Cuba in the Nineteenth Century: The Travel Diary of Joseph J. Dimock*, ed. Louis A. Pérez Jr. (Wilmington, Del., 1998), p. 97; David Turnbull, *Travels in the West. Cuba; with Notices of Porto Rico, and the Slave Trade* (London, 1840), pp. 281–82.

69. Vázquez y Torres, *El mayordomo de un ingenio*, p. 20.

70. Chateusalins, *El vademecum de los hacendados cubanos*, p. v.

71. Audiencia de La Habana, "Testimonio del expediente instruido."

72. Leopoldo O'Donnell to Secretary of State, February 15, 1845, in Gwendolyn Midlo Hall, *Social Control in Slave Plantation Society* (Baltimore, 1971), p. 16.

73. José Gutiérrez de la Concha to Minister of War, July 2, 1851, in Carlos Sedano y Cruzat, *Cuba desde 1850 a 1875: Colección de informes, memorias, proyectos y antecedentes sobre el gobierno de la Isla de Cuba* (Madrid, 1873), pp. 136–37.

74. Audiencia de La Habana, "Testimonio del expediente instruido."

75. Ibid.

76. Moreno Fraginals, *El Ingenio*, 2:83–90; Poumier Taquechel, "El suicidio esclavo en Cuba," p. 73.

77. James J. O'Kelly, *The Mambi-Land, or Adventures of a Herald Correspondent in Cuba* (Philadelphia, 1874), p. 64; A Physician, *Notes on Cuba*, p. 256.

78. Dimock, *Impressions of Cuba*, pp. 96–97.

79. A. W. Reyes, "Estudio comparativo de los negros criollos y africanos," *Eco Científico de Las Villas* 1 (October 1, 1884): 87.

80. See "Expediente instruido contra D. Francisco Moresma por excitar a la dotación del ingenio Aguila a que abandone la finca," December 4–30, 1879, Legajo 20, No. 41, Fondo Esclavos, AHPM; "Comunicación al Gobernador de Matanzas sobre detención de la negra Mercedes, iniciadora de disturbios en el ingenio Rosa," Legajo 20, No. 50, ibid.; "Expediente sobre insubordinación de la dotación del ingenio Esperanza," April 17–July 1881, Legajo 20, No. 49, ibid.; "Comunicación sobre el descontento de la dotación del ingenio Santa Leocadia por la falta de raciones que deben dárseles," June 1875, Legajo 24, No. 89, ibid. For an excellent discussion of these developments generally see Rebecca J. Scott, *Slave Emancipation in Cuba* (Princeton, 1985), pp. 111–24.

81. "Slaves Refusing to Work on the Sugar Estates in Cuba," *New York Times*, April 3, 1866, p. 5.

82. Antonio L. Valverde, "La trata de chinos en Cuba," in *Estudios jurídicos e históricos* (Havana, 1918), pp. 23–44; Guillermo Tejeiro, *Historia ilustrada de la colonia china en Cuba* (Havana, 1947), pp. 8–14; Marshall K. Powers, "Chinese Coolie Migration to Cuba" (Ph.D. diss., University of Florida, Gainesville, 1953), pp. 106–23.

83. Ramón de la Sagra, *Cuba en 1860, o sea cuadro de sus adelantos en la población, la agricultura, el comercio y las rentas públicas. Suplemento a la primera parte de la historia política y natural de la Isla de Cuba* (Paris, 1863), pp. 42–43; "Inmigración de asiáticos en esta Isla," *Anales de la Real Junta de Fomento* 4 (1851): 183–98; "The Traffic in Coolies," *Hunt's Merchants' Magazine* 36 (1857): 570–73; Juan Pérez de la Riva, "Aspectos económicos del tráfico de culíes chinos a Cuba, 1853–1874," in *El barracón y otros ensayos* (Havana, 1975), pp. 255–81; Denise Helly, *Idéologie et ethnicité. Les chinois Macao à Cuba (1847–1886)* (Montreal, 1979); Mary Turner, "Chinese Contract

Labour in Cuba, 1847–1874," *Caribbean Studies* 14 (July 1974): 66–81; Evelyn Hu-Dehart, "Chinese Coolie Labour in Cuba in the Nineteenth Century: Free Labour or Neo-slavery?" *Slavery and Abolition* 14 (April 1993): 67–86; Duvon C. Corbitt, *A Study of the Chinese in Cuba, 1847–1947* (Wilmore, Ky., 1971), pp. 1–86; Cuba, Capitanía General, *Noticias estadísticas de la Isla de Cuba en 1862* (n.p.). In 1873, the *Boletín de Colonización* fixed the total number of resident Chinese workers in Cuba at 58,400. See *Boletín de Colonización* 1 (October 15, 1873): 2.

84. Henry B. Auchincloss, "The Chinese in Cuba," *Merchants' Magazine and Commercial Review* 52 (January–June 1865): 186, 188.

85. Francisco Diago, "Informe," October 17, 1851, in Antonio L. Valverde y Maruri, "Colonización e inmigraciones en Cuba," republished in Academia de la Historia, *Discursos leídos en la recepción pública del Doctor Antonio L. Valverde y Maruri, la noche del 28 de junio de 1923* (Havana, 1922), p. 53; Urbano Feijóo Sotomayor, "Informe," November 17, 1848, in Corbitt, *A Study of the Chinese in Cuba, 1847–1947*, p. 10.

86. *The Cuba Commission Report. A Hidden History of the Chinese in Cuba* (1876; reprint, Baltimore, 1993), p. 99; R. W. Gibbes, *Cuba for Invalids* (New York, 1860), pp. 158–59; O'Kelly, *The Mambi-Land*, pp. 66, 71. Similar estimates are found in Gonzalo de Quesada, *The Chinese and Cuban Independence* (Leipzig, 1925), p. 5.

87. Cuba, Capitanía General, *Noticias estadísticas*; Ortiz, *Los negros esclavos*, pp. 359–60; Juan Pérez de la Riva, *Los culíes chinos en Cuba* (Havana, 2000), p. 186.

88. "Discurso del Sr. Regente de la Real Audiencia Pretorial de la Apertura de Tribunales y Juzgados en el año que empieza de 1858," *Revista de Jurisprudencia* 3 (1858): 55.

89. "Expediente relativo a fallecimientos de asiáticos," March 13, 1857–July 29, 1879, Legajo 91, No. 9848, Fondo Negociado de Colonización, AHPM; Miguel Cosalis to Civil Governor, April 18, 1871, Legajo 45, No. 69, Fondo Gobierno Provincial (Difunciones), AHPM. See also "Expediente suicidio del asiático Lanchín," January 1851, Legajo 2822, No. T, Fondo Miscelánea de Expedientes, ANC.

90. *The Cuba Commission Report*, p. 48. The petition of Li Chao-ch'un was signed by 165 signatories.

91. Ibid., pp. 48–50.

92. Antonio Carlo Napoleone Gallenga, *The Pearl of the Antilles* (London, 1873), pp. 88, 127. Emphasis in original.

93. Auchincloss, "The Chinese in Cuba," pp. 188–89; Eliza McHatton Ripley, *From Flag to Flag* (New York, 1889), p. 178; Montejo, *Biografía de un cimarrón*, p. 42.

94. *The Cuba Commission Report*, p. 57.

95. Gibbes, *Cuba for Invalids*, pp. 91–92.

96. *The Cuba Commission Report*, pp. 100–103.

97. José Luis Alfonso (Conde de Montelo) to José Antonio Saco, November 26, 1866, Colección de Manuscritos, Fondo José Luis Alfonso, No. 32, Biblioteca Nacional 'José Martí,' Havana, Cuba.

98. See "Expediente criminal por el suicidio del asiático Simón del ingenio 'Estrella,'" December 17, 1867, Legajo 2746, No. M, Fondo Miscelánea de Expedientes, ANC; "Causa criminal por el suicidio del asiático Onofre," October 21, 1868, Legajo 2725, No. P, ibid. See also Powers, "Chinese Coolie Migration to Cuba," pp. 135–

37. For an account of autopsies performed on the bodies of Chinese suicides see Antonio Caro, *Del Instituto de Investigaciones Químicas de La Habana: Su origin y creación* (Havana, 1865), pp. 24–25.

99. Juan Pérez de la Riva, "Demografía de los culíes chinos en Cuba (1853–1874)," in *El barracón y otros ensayos*, p. 483; R. J. Levis, *Diary of a Spring Holiday in Cuba* (Philadelphia, 1872), pp. 88–89.

100. *The Cuba Commission Report*, pp. 100–103; José Pascual to Civil Governor, June 15, 1874, Legajo 45, Fondo Gobierno Provincial (Defunciones), AHPM.

101. *The Cuba Commission Report*, pp. 100–108. See also *El Pueblo*, February 15, 1872, p. 3.

102. *The Cuba Commission Report*, pp. 49–51.

103. Julia Ward Howe, *A Trip to Cuba* (Boston, 1860), pp. 219–20.

104. Félix Erenchun, *Anales de la Isla de Cuba. Diccionario administrativo, económico, estadístico y legislativo: 1856* (Havana, 1857), p. 784.

105. *The Cuba Commission Report*, pp. 51, 53–54. For accounts of Chinese murder of their tormentors see James C. Dorsey, "Identity, Rebellion, and Social Justice among Chinese Contract Workers in Nineteenth-Century Cuba," *Latin American Perspectives* 31 (May 2004): 18–47; and James Arthur Osberg, "The Chinese Bondage in Cuba: 1847–1931," (M.A. thesis, Southern Illinois University, 1967), pp. 58–60.

106. Levis, *Diary of a Spring Holiday*, pp. 88–89; O'Kelly, *The Mambi-Land*, p. 63; Manuel Villanueva, "La emigración de colonos chinos," *Revista Contemporánea* 7 (1876–77): 343–44.

107. Saco, "La estadística criminal," p. 5.

108. M. Huc, *The Chinese Empire. A Sequel to Recollections of a Journey Through Tartary and Thibet*, rev. ed. (London, 1860), p. 180; and Upendra Thakur, *The History of Suicide in India* (Delhi, 1963), p. 187.

109. Huc, *The Chinese Empire*, p. 182; Pérez de la Riva, *Los culíes chinos en Cuba*, p. 189.

110. Huc, *The Chinese Empire*, p. 181. Italics in original.

111. Saco, "La estadística criminal," p. 5.

112. See Ernest Alabaster, *Notes and Commentaries on Chinese Criminal Law* (1899; reprint, Taipei, 1968), pp. 303–45.

113. C. F. Gordon Cumming, *Wanderings in China*, 2 vols. (Edinburgh, 1886), 2:301. Cumming estimated a total of 160,000 opium suicides in China annually. Ibid.

CHAPTER TWO

1. For useful discussions on the formation of national identity see Sergio Aguirre, *Nacionalidad y nación en el siglo XIX cubano* (Havana, 1990); Rafael Duharte Jiménez, *Nacionalidad e historia* (Santiago de Cuba, 1991); Enrique Ubieta Gómez, *Ensayos de identidad* (Havana, 1993); Eduardo Torres-Cuevas, "En busca de la cubanidad," *Debates Americanos* I (January–June 1995): 2–17; Virgilio López Lemus, *Décima e identidad: siglos XVIII y XIX* (Havana, 1997); Sergio Valdés Bernal, *Lengua nacional e identidad cultural del cubano* (Havana, 1998).

2. The most representative *costumbrista* collections include Gaspar Betancourt Cisneros, *Escenas cotidianas* (Havana, 1950); Luis Victoriano Betancourt, *Artículos de cos-*

tumbres (Havana, 1929); Carlos Genaro Valdés, *Colección escojida de cantos cubanos* (Havana, 1890); Olallo Díaz González, *Tipos de La Habana: recopilación de artículos de costumbres populares* (Havana, 1895). For a general discussion of *costumbrista* literary forms see Instituto de Literatura y Lingüistica de la Academia de Ciencias de Cuba, *Diccionario de la literatura cubana*, 2 vols. (Havana, 1980), 1:239–41. On *décimas* see López Lemus, *Décima e identidad: siglos XVIII y XIX*, pp. 39–75. On music see El Vueltarribero, ed., *La lira criolla: guarachas, canciones, décimas* (Havana, 1895); Jorge Ibarra, "La música cubana: de lo folclórico y lo criollo a la nacional popular," in Radamés Giro, ed., *Panorama de la música popular cubana* (Santiago de Cali, 1996), p. 21; Zoila Lapique Becali, *Música colonial cubana* (Havana, 1979); Marta Esquenazi Pérez, "Música popular tradicional," in Centro de Investigación y Desarrollo de la Cultura Cubana Juan Marinello, *Cultura popular tradicional cubana* (Havana, 1999), pp. 161–74; Caridad B. Santos Gracia, "Danzas y bailes populares tradicionales," ibid., pp. 175–86.

3. José Antonio Saco evoked the idea of a *"nacionalidad cubana"* as the sum total of "our ancient origins, our language, our usages and customs and our traditions. All this makes up the actual *nacionalidad* that we call *cubana* because it has formed on and is rooted in an island called Cuba." Saco added: "All people who inhabit the same land, and have similar origins, similar language, common usages and customs—those people have a *nacionalidad*." See José Antonio Saco, *Colección de papeles científicos, históricos y de otros ramos sobre la isla de Cuba*, 3 vols. (Havana, 1960–63), 3:442–43, 445.

4. Jorge Mañach, "La pintura en Cuba desde sus orígenes hasta 1900," *Cuba Contemporánea* 36 (September 1924): 5–23; Guy Pérez Cisneros, *Características de la evolución de la pintura en Cuba* (Havana, 1959), pp. 43–91; Marta de Castro, *El arte en Cuba* (Miami, 1970), pp. 40–49; Narciso G. Menocal, "An Overriding Passion: The Quest for a National Identity in Painting," *Journal of Decorative and Propaganda Arts* 22 (1996): 187–96.

5. Poems on the countryside include: Manuel de Zequeira y Arango, "A la vida del campo"; Ramón Vélez Herrera, "Despedida del campo"; José Fornaris, "En el campo"; Manuel Cecilio Blanco, "La noche oscura en el campo"; Ignacio María de Acosta, "La vuelta al campo"; Carlos Rafael, "Una tarde en el campo"; and Julia Pérez Montes de Oca, "Al campo." On rivers see: Francisco Pobeda, "A Zaza"; José Fornaris, "Al Cauto"; Juan C. Napolés Fajardo, "El Cauto"; Miguel Teurbe Tolón, "La ribereña del San Juan"; José Victoriano Betancourt, "A las ninfas y genios del Almendares"; José Güell y Renté, "Al río Almendares"; Ambrosio Echemendía, "Al Damují"; and Antonio Vidaurreta, "Al Hanabanilla." Poems on trees include: Pedro Santacilia, "Bajo el mango"; José Jacinto Milanés, "Bajo el mango"; and Julia Pérez Montes de Oca, "A un árbol." For palm trees see: Francisco Pobeda, "A la palma"; Rafael María de Mendive, "La música de las palmas"; José Fornaris, "Las palmas"; María Josefa Murillo, "A una palma"; José Joaquín Betancourt, "Bajo las palmas"; and Mercedes Matamoros, "Las palmas." For agricultural products see: Manuel Justo de Rubalcava, "Las frutas de Cuba"; Manuel de Zequeira y Arango, "Oda a la piña"; Gabriel de la Concepción Valdés, "La flor de la piña"; and Juan C. Napolés Fajardo, "La papaya." These poems are found in Samuel Feijóo, ed., *Cantos a la naturaleza cubana del siglo XIX* (Havana, 1964); Rafael Estenger, ed., *Cien de las mejores poesías cubanas* (Havana, 1943); José Fornaris, *Poesías de José Fornaris* (Havana, 1888); Antonio González Curquejo, ed., *Florilegio de escritoras cubanas*,

3 vols. (Havana, 1910–19). In a series of "album" odes entitled "Cuadros de la naturaleza cubana" published between 1846 and 1858, novelist Anselmo Suárez Romero celebrated the cane fields, the palm trees, the seashore, the clouds, and the hills. See Anselmo Suárez Romero, *Colección de artículos* (1859; reprint Havana, 1963), pp. 291–330.

6. Francisco Iturrondo, "Rasgos descriptivos de la naturaleza cubano," in Feijóo, *Cantos a la naturaleza cubana*, p. 21; Juan Cristóbal Nápoles Fajardo, "Amor a Cuba" and "Galas de Cuba," in ibid., pp. 119, 120.

7. Carlota Robreño, "Mi vuelta a Cuba," in González Curquejo, *Florilegio de escritoras cubanas*, 3:197. See also José Fornaris, "Mi vuelta a Cuba," in *Poesías de José Fornaris*, pp. 45–50.

8. José María de Heredia, *Poesías completas*, ed. Emilio Roig de Leuchsenring, 2 vols. (Havana, 1940), 1:209; 2:74, 167; Miguel Teurbe Tolón, "¡Volver a Cuba!" in Feijóo, *Cantos a la naturaleza cubana*, pp. 142–44.

9. Belén de Miranda, "La flora cubana," 1886, in González Curquejo, *Florilegio de escritoras cubanas*, 3:30.

10. Carlos Manuel de Céspedes to Manuel Agramonte, March 24, 1871, in Fernando Portuondo del Prado and Hortensia Pichardo Viñals, eds., *Carlos Manuel de Céspedes: Escritos* (Havana, 1974), p. 152; Emilio Núñez to Carlos Roloff, May 17, 1879, in Rafael Rodríguez Altunaga, *El general Emilio Núñez* (Havana, 1958), p. 242; Miguel Ramos to Carlos Roloff, December 1, 1878, in Cuba, Archivo Nacional, *Documentos para servir a la historia de la Guerra Chiquita (Archivo Leandro Rodríguez)*, 3 vols. (Havana, 1949), 1:99.

11. *La Libertad*, August 1, 1869, p. 1.

12. "Finally the land on which we were born belongs to us / At last the beautiful Island belongs to us," poet Dulce María Borrero exulted with the independence of Cuba. See Dulce María Borrero, "Tierra propia," in González Curquejo, *Florilegio de escritoras cubanas*, 1:301.

13. Luis de Radillo y Rodríguez, *Autobiografía del cubano Luis de Radillo y Rodríguez, o episodios de su vida histórico-político-revolucionario* (Havana, 1899), p. 8; "A Cuba," *El Independiente*, October 18, 1890, p. 1.

14. See Domitila García de Coronado, *Cementerio de La Habana: Apuntes de su fundación* (Havana, 1888); Antonio de Gordon y de Acosta, *Datos históricos acerca de los cementerios de la ciudad de La Habana* (Havana, 1901); Eugenio Sánchez de Fuente y Peláez, *Cuba monumental, estuaria y epigráfica* (Havana, 1916).

15. Rosa Marrero y Caro, "Adios a Cuba," in *Poesías* (Havana, 1867), p. 59; Luisa Pérez de Zambrana, "Amor patrio," in González Curquejo, *Florilegio de escritoras cubanas*, 1:284–85; Belén de Miranda, "La flora cubana," 1886, in ibid., 3:30.

16. Pamela Fernández, "Despedida a Cuba," in Domitila García, ed., *Album poético-fotográfico de las escritoras cubanas*, 2nd ed. (Havana, 1872), p. 98.

17. Calixto García, "Manifiesto del Comité Revolucionario Cubano," October 1878, in Cuba, Archivo Nacional de Cuba, *Documentos para servir a la historia de la Guerra Chiquita*, 1:43.

18. For informative accounts of these political movements see María del Carmen Barcia Zequeira, *Elites y grupos de presión. Cuba 1868–1898* (Havana, 1998); Josef

Opatrny, *U.S. Expansionism and Cuban Annexationism in the 1850s* (Prague, 1990); and Mildred de la Torre, *El autonomismo en Cuba, 1878–1898* (Havana, 1997). In his 1944 essay, "El estilo en Cuba y su sentido histórico," Jorge Mañach provides a thoughtful analysis of the cultural representations of each political tendency. Reprinted in Jorge Mañach, *Ensayos*, ed. Jorge Luis Arcos (Havana, 1999), pp. 152–227.

19. Raimundo Cabrera, *Ideales* (1918; reprint, Havana, 1984), p. 345.

20. "To change masters," José Martí affirmed, "is not to be free." And on another occasion: "[Annexation] would be death for me and for our country." See José Martí to Gonzalo de Quesada, November 12, 1889, in José Martí, *Obras.completas*, ed. Jorge Quintana, 5 vols. (Caracas, 1964), 3:150; and José Martí to Serafín Bello, November 16, 1889, ibid., 1:392. The weekly *La Estrella Solitaria* similarly affirmed: "To succumb to annexation would be suicide. And we who love life . . . do not want to commit suicide." See "La anexión," *La Estrella Solitaria*, October 1, 1898, p. 2.

21. *El Vigía* 1 (September 25, 1897): 1; *El Vigía* 1 (December 4, 1897): 1; *El Vigía* 1 (October 16, 1897): 1–2; "El pueblo cubano," *El Cubano Libre*, September 10, 1896, p. 1.

22. Fermín Valdés-Domínguez, *Diario de soldado*, ed. Hiram Dupotey Fideaux, 4 vols. (Havana, 1972–74), 1:233, 330, 434; República de Cuba, Secretaria de Relaciones Exteriores, "Manifiesto," in *La Verdad*, September 23, 1876, p. 1.

23. *Oriente* 1 (July 14, 1899): 3.

24. Tomás Estrada Palma to José de Armas y Céspedes, September 3, 1895, in León Primelles, ed., *La revolución del 95 según la correspondencia de la delegación cubana en Nueva York*, 5 vols. (Havana, 1932–37), 1:281; *La República*, August 19, 1871, p. 1.

25. Antonio Maceo to Anselmo Valdés, June 6, 1884, in Antonio Maceo, *El pensamiento vivo de Maceo*, ed. José A. Portuondo (Havana, 1971), p. 76.

26. Enrique Trujillo, *Apuntes históricos* (New York, 1896), p. 123; Bernabé Boza, *Mi diario de la guerra*, 2 vols. (1924; reprint, Havana, 1974), 1:49; Antonio Maceo to José A. Rodríguez, November 1, 1886, in Gonzalo Cabrales Nicolarde, ed., *Epistolario de héroes: cartas y documentos históricos* (Havana, 1996), p. 146; José Martí, "La primera conferencia," June 18, 1892, in *Obras completas*, 1:635; José Martí, "La confirmación," April 23, 1892, in ibid., 1:311; José Martí, "¿Con que consejos, y promesas de autonomía?" April 10, 1893, in ibid., 1:403; José Martí, "La independencia de Cuba y la prensa de los Estados Unidos," August 27, 1892, in ibid., 1:663; José Martí, "Discurso," October 10, 1887, in ibid., 1:361; José Martí to Presidents, Revolutionary Clubs, Key West, June 9, 1892, in Luis Alpízar Leal, ed., *Documentos inéditos de José Martí a José D. Poyo* (Havana, 1994), pp. 28–31.

27. Gustavo Pérez Abreu, *En la guerra con Máximo Gómez* (Havana, 1952), pp. 40, 95; Ramón M. Roa, *A pie y descalzo de Trinidad a Cuba (Recuerdos de campaña)* (Havana, 1890), p. 28; Martina Pierra de Poo, "El Ateneo," in González Curquejo, *Florilegio de escritoras cubanas*, 2:14.

28. *La Doctrina de Martí*, June 30, 1897, p. 1.

29. For a useful discussion of the poetry during the Ten Years War see Otto Olivera, "La poesía de la Guerra de los Diez Años," *Revista Cubana* (New York) 1 (January–June 1968): 69–99.

30. Ana Betancourt, "Datos biográficos sobre Ignacio Mora," *Revista de la Biblioteca Nacional 'José Martí'* 10 (January–April 1968): 68; Enrique Collazo, *Cuba heroica*

(1912; reprint, Santiago de Cuba, 1980), p. 442; Luis Rodolfo Miranda, *Con Martí y con Calixto García (Recuerdos de un mambí del 95)* (Havana, 1943), p. 71; Manuel Arbelo, *Recuerdos de la última guerra por la independencia de Cuba. 1896–1898* (Havana, 1918), p. 41; Horacio Ferrer, *Con el rifle al hombro* (Havana, 1950), p. 15; Segundo Corvisón, *En la guerra y en la paz: episodios de la revolución por la independencia y consideraciones acerca de la República cordial* (Havana, 1939), pp. 13, 292–93; Luis Victoriano Betancourt, "A mi madre," in Serafín Sánchez Valdivia, ed., *Heroes humildes y los poetas de la guerra* (1911; reprint, Havana, 1981), p. 161; *El Cubano Libre*, February 24, 1896, p. 2 (italics in original). "Without arms, without resources, without the material elements necessary to triumph," the weekly *La Revolución de Cuba* affirmed, "the Cuban people plunged into a cruel and bloody war . . . because much sacrifice and many lives given up as offerings are the price that freedom demands. The Cuban people have not hesitated to meet the cost." See "Diez de octubre," *La Revolución de Cuba*, December 27, 1878, p. 2. See also M. Gutiérrez Najera, "Para entonces," *El Expedicionario* (Tampa), April 18, 1897, in the Juan and Nicolás Arnao Papers, Manuscript Division, Library of Congress, Washington, D.C.

31. Joel James Figarola, *La muerte en Cuba* (Havana, 1999), p. 44.

32. U.S. War Department, Office of the Director of Census of Cuba, *Informe sobre el censo de Cuba, 1899* (Washington, D.C., 1900), pp. 152–53. Census officials in 1899 estimated the loss of life at a minimum of 300,000. More recent demographic studies suggest the total may have been much closer to 400,000. For census figures see the English-language edition of the 1899 census: U.S. Department of War, Office of the Director of Census of Cuba, *Report on the Census of Cuba, 1899* (Washington, D.C., 1900), pp. 717–18. See also Juan Pérez de la Riva and Blanca Morejón Seijas, "Demografía histórica: la población de Cuba, la guerra de independencia y la inmigración del siglo XX," *Revista de la Biblioteca Nacional 'José Martí'* 13 (May–August 1971): 17–27.

33. "Creoles are divided into three groups," explained Spanish general Camilo Polavieja in an 1881 confidential memorandum to Madrid. "The smallest group is openly pro-Spanish and supports everything that guarantees our control. The next group in size is made up of good people, loyal and honorable, who desire union with Spain but who, because of their ideas, good will and ties of friendship and family, desire many important things that favor only the separatists, who are the third and the strongest group." A decade later Polavieja again reiterated: "The separatist tendency is an integral and principal characteristic of the nature of nearly all the creoles of the Island of Cuba, including the children of the resident *peninsulares*." See Camilo G. Polavieja to Ramón Blanco, April 19, 1881, in Camilo G. Polavieja, *Relación documentada de mi política en Cuba* (Madrid, 1898), pp. 62–63; Camilo G. Polavieja to Minister of Ultramar Antonio Maura, 1892, ibid., p. 175.

34. Raimundo Cabrera, *Desde mi sitio* (Havana, 1911), p. 77. Segundo Corvisón described himself as "obsessed by an ideal," and Ricardo Batrell Oviedo wrote of his heart "swollen with love for the sacrosanct Ideal and burning with faith for the reason of its Cause." See Corvisón, *En la guerra y en la paz*, p. 10; and Ricardo Batrell Oviedo, *Para la historia. Apuntes autobiográficos* (Havana, 1912), p. 80.

35. Ramón Céspedes Fornaris, "A los cubanos," *La República*, August 26, 1871, p. 2; Luis Rodolfo Miranda, *Reminiscencias cubanas de la guerra y de la paz* (Havana, 1941),

p. 173; Valdés-Domínguez, *Diario de soldado*, 1:100, 222; José Calero to Leandro Rodríguez, October 18, 1879, in Cuba, Archivo Nacional de Cuba, *Documentos para servir a la historia de la Guerra Chiquita*, 2:276; Pedro Díaz to Juana González, May 2, 1897, in *Cuba*, June 22, 1897, p. 2.

36. "The war for Cuba may be interminable," Antonio Maceo wrote in 1895. See Antonio Maceo to Joaquín Crespo, October 30, 1895, in Antonio Maceo, *Ideario cubano: Antonio Maceo*, ed. Emilio Roig de Leuchsenring (Havana, 1946), p. 83.

37. Ricardo Buenamar, *Episodios de la guerra de Cuba: Mi vida en la manigua* (México, 1898), pp. 314–15; Calixto García to Tomás Estrada Palma, August 15, 1897, *Boletín del Archivo Nacional* 33 (1936): 81.

38. Félix Varela, *Lecciones de filosofía*, 5th ed., 2 vols. (1841; reprint, Havana, 1961): 1:279.

39. José Martí to Ricardo Rodríguez Otero, May 16, 1886, in Martí, *Obras completas*, 1:411; José Martí, "Manifiesto de Montecristi: El Partido Revolucionario Cubano a Cuba," March 25, 1895, in ibid., 1:243; José Martí, "El Delegado en Nueva York," November 1, 1892, in ibid., 1:342–643; José Martí, "Fermín Valdés-Domínguez," November 28, 1893, in ibid., 1:41. A discussion of these themes is expertly developed in John M. Kirk, *José Martí: Mentor of the Cuban Nation* (Tampa, 1983), pp. 3–18; Paul Estrade, *José Martí: Los fundamentos de la democracia en Latinoamérica* (Madrid, 2000), pp. 359–69.

40. Valdés-Domínguez, *Diario del soldado*, 1:44, 50, 62, 145.

41. Manuel Secades Japón, "El derecho a la vida, o luchar en vano," *Bohemia* 18 (December 12, 1926): 9.

42. *La Estrella de Cuba*, April 16, 1870, p. 3; "¡Adelante!" *La Verdad*, October 6, 1877, p. 2.

43. Nestor L. Carbonell, "La patria está hecha," *Revista de Cuba Libre* 1 (February 19, 1898): 5; Ramiro Cabrera, *¡A sitio Herrera!* (Havana, 1922), p. 251; Collazo, *Cuba heroica*, p. 12.

44. Avelino Sanjenís, *Memorias de la revolución de 1895 por la independencia de Cuba* (Havana, 1913), p. 130; Valdés-Domínguez, *Diario del soldado*, 1:238.

45. Angel E. Rosende y de Zayas, *1895–1898: Conspirador y de soldado a capitán* (Havana, 1928), p. 39; Arbelo, *Recuerdos de la última guerra por la independencia de Cuba*, p. 202; José Hernández Guzmán, *Memorias tristes: Apuntes históricos* (Havana, 1934), p. 32; *El Vigía* 1 (November 1, 1897): 1. See also Fernando de Zayas, "Triunfo o exterminio," *El Expedicionario*, January 31, 1897, p. 2.

46. Domingo Goicuría to Amalia Goicuría, January 9, 1870, in "Cartas del mártir cubano Domingo Goicuría," ed. Miguel Angel Carbonell, *Islas* (July–December 1963), p. 56. See also Miguel Angel Carbonell, *Un héroe pintado por sí mismo* (Havana, 1939), p. 44; Consejo de Gobierno, Secretaria de Guerra, "Circular," January 9, 1898, in *El Cubano Libre*, February 5, 1898, p. 2; José Martí, "Manifiesto de Montecristi," March 25, 1895, in *Obras completas*, 1:241.

47. Domingo Goicuría to Antonio Goicuría, May 1, 1870, in "Cartas del mártir cubano Domingo Goicuría," p. 58; Eusebio Hernández to Antonio Maceo, September 27, 1885, in Cabrales Nicolarde, *Epistolario de héroes*, p. 242.

48. James J. O'Kelly, *The Mambi-Land, or Adventures of a 'Herald' Correspondent in Cuba* (Philadelphia, 1874), p. 246; Corvisón, *En la guerra y en la paz*, pp. 207, 303; José Martí, "A la raíz," August 26, 1893, in *Obras completas*, 1:668, 670; José Martí to Máximo Gómez, December 16, 1887, in ibid., 1:90.

49. *Cuba*, May 6, 1897, p. 2.

50. Arbelo, *Recuerdos de la última guerra por la independencia de Cuba*, p. 283.

51. Mercedes Matamoros, "Los héroes," in González Curquejo, *Florilegio de escritoras cubanas*, 2:105; Corvisón, *En la guerra y en la paz*, p. 20; *La Revolución Cubana*, October 17, 1874, p. 2; "'Chicho,' escenas de la guerra," *Revista de Cayo Hueso* 2 (March 13, 1898): 19; *El Republicano*, October 17, 1874, p. 3; Avelino Sanjenís, *Mis cartas: Memorias de la revolución de 1895 por la independencia de Cuba* (Sagua la Grande, 1900), p. 343; Rosario Sigarroa, "El mártir de San Lorenzo y el de Dos Ríos," in González Curquejo, *Florilegio de escritoras cubanas*, 3:422–23.

52. José Martí to Enrique Collazo, January 12, 1892, in Martí, *Obras completas*, 2:412–13.

53. José Martí, "El Partido Revolucionario a Cuba," May 27, 1893, in ibid., 1:336.

54. Anselmo Suárez y Romero to Domingo del Monte, October 21, 1839, in Academia de la Historia de Cuba, *Centón epistolario de Domingo del Monte*, ed. Domingo Figarola-Caneda, Joaquín Llaverías y Martínez, and Manuel Mesa Rodríguez, 6 vols. (Havana, 1923–53), 4:100; Asunción Adot de Miranda, August 17, 1870, in *Un Contemporáneo* [Cirilo Villaverde], *Apuntes biográficos de Emilia Casanova de Villaverde* (New York, 1874), p. 84; Salvador Cisneros Betancourt, "Manifiesto," July 13, 1896, in Cuba, Secretaria de Gobernación, *Documentos históricos* (Havana, 1912), p. 158. Writer Ismael Perdomo employed a similar metaphor: "We will enter the sacred temple of the *Patria* with our heads held high, with our conscience clean, and with the religion of honor in our bosoms." See Ismael Perdomo, "¡Adelante!" *Revista de Cuba Libre* I (February 19, 1898): 6.

55. Sanjenís, *Memorias de la revolución de 1895*, p. 270; Manuel Sanguily, "La guerra sagrada," April 10, 1876, in *Frente a la dominación española*, ed. Violeta Serrano (Havana, 1979), p. 56. Calixto García praised Miguel Aldama for his "love of Cuba and our Holy Cause [*Santa Causa*]." See Calixto García to Miguel Aldama, May 2, 1874, in José Miguel Abreu Cardet and Elia Sintes Gómez, eds., *Calixto García Iñiguez: Pensamiento y acción militar* (Havana, 1996), p. 62.

56. Trujillo, *Apuntes históricos*, pp. 49–50. "Cartas del mártir cubano Domingo Goicuría," p. 54; Betancourt, "Datos biográficos sobre Ignacio Mora," p. 68.

57. Francisco Pérez Guzmán, *La guerra en La Habana: Desde enero de 1896 hasta el combate de San Pedro* (Havana, 1974), p. 177.

58. "Cuba: 10 de octubre," *La Revolución de Cuba*, November 7, 1874, p. 2.

59. Serafín Sánchez to Carlos Roloff, May 29, 1879, in Cuba, Archivo Nacional de Cuba, *Documentos para servir a la historia de la Guerra Chiquita*, 2:89; *El Republicano*, January 22, 1870, p. 2; Miranda, *Reminiscencias cubanas*, p. 58; Juan Jerez Villarreal, *Gesta de bravos: poemas epicos en prosa. Episodios inéditos de la revolución de 1868* (Havana, 1926), p. 72; 110–25; Candelaria Figueredo de Portillo, *La Abanderada de 1868: Candelaria Figueredo (Hija de Perucho). Autobiografía* (Havana, 1929), pp. 21, 22.

For an account of the deaths in the Liberation Army see Alejandro del Pozo y Arjona, *Páginas de sangre, o el libro del cubano. Relación de los caudillos cubanos muertos en la actual campaña (1895–1898)* (Havana, 1898).

60. Sanjenís, *Memorias de la revolución de 1895*, pp. 139–40; Carlos Manuel de Céspedes to Ana de Quesada, August 7, 1872, in Carlos Manuel de Céspedes, *Cartas de Carlos Manuel de Céspedes a su esposa Ana de Quesada* (Havana, 1964), p. 124; José María Izaguirre, *Recuerdos de la guerra* (Havana, 1936), p. 54. See also Hortensia Pichardo, "La muerte de Céspedes," in *Facetas de nuestra historia*, ed. Ricardo Repilado (Santiago de Cuba, 1989), pp. 246–62. Commented Elio Constantín in 1951: "[Céspedes] is thus seen as the Father of his Country and its first great suicide." See Elio E. Constantín, "Los grandes suicidios de Cuba," *Carteles* 32 (August 26, 1951): 60. The gesture of suicide insinuated itself into the realms of popular awareness in unexpected ways. The case of Céspedes appears in Arnaldo Correa's novel *Spy's Fate* (2002), with the protagonist Carlos Manuel listening to a friend of his father reminisce about his naming at birth: "I was with your father . . . the day you were born, back in 1950. I asked him what he was going to name his first male child and he answered quickly, 'Carlos Manuel, just like Céspedes.' After a few drinks, celebrating your birth, I remarked, joking, 'That's quite a responsibility for such a small boy, bearing the name of the father of our country—a man who shot himself rather than be taken alive by the enemy.' Your father stared at me. 'That's exactly the way I want him to be,' he answered, his face very grave." Arnaldo Correa, *Spy's Fate* (New York, 2002), p. 8.

61. Fernando Figueredo Socarrás, *La revolución de Yara*, 2 vols. (1902; reprint, Havana, 1969), 1:167; José Martí, "Calixto García Iñiguez," January 16, 1894, in *Obras completas*, 1:596; Valdés-Domínguez, *Diario de soldado*, 1:318; "Calixto García Iñiguez," *Oriente* 1 (June 23, 1899): 4.

62. José Luciano Franco, *Antonio Maceo. Apuntes para una historia de su vida*, 3 vols. (Havana, 1975), 3:365; Calixto García Iñiguez to Bernarda del Toro, January 22, 1897, in Abreu Cardet and Sintes Gómez, *Calixto García Iñiguez*, p. 222.

63. For a discussion of this debate see Antonio Martínez Bello, "El 'suicidio' de Martí—su 'inadaptación," *Archivo José Martí* 4 (July–December 1948): 372–92; Antonio Martínez Bello, "El 'suicidio' de Martí," *Carteles* 29 (May 23, 1948): 14–17; Antonio Martínez Bello, "Cartas inéditas de Martí frente a la tesis del 'suicidio,'" *Revista de la Biblioteca Nacional* 6 (July–September 1955): 69–70; Marcelo Pogolotti, "¿Lirismo o suicidio?" *El Mundo*, December 14, 1954, p. A-6; Pedro Baeza Flores, "¿Quiso morir Martí en Dos Ríos?" *Bohemia* 48 (May 20, 1956): 32–33, 114–15; Richard Butler Gray, *José Martí, Cuban Patriot* (Gainesville, 1962), pp. 32–33; Enrique H. Moreno Plá, "Reflexiones sobre la muerte de Martí," *Anuario Martiano* 3 (1971): 201–23.

64. Valdés-Domínguez, *Diario de soldado*, 1:447.

65. Joaquín Martínez Sáenz, *Martí, el inadaptado sublime* (Havana, 1948), p. 119; Gonzalo de Quesada y Miranda, *Alrededor de la acción en Dos Ríos* (Havana, 1942), pp. 7–8. Another collaborator of Martí, Néstor Carbonell, arrived at a similar conclusion: "[Martí] believed it was necessary to die in order for his death to guarantee the existence of his *patria*." See Néstor L. Carbonell, "José Martí," *Cuba*, May 16, 1896, p. 2. In fact, this has been the principal significance given to Martí's death. "The sacrifice at Dos Ríos," Jorge Mañach wrote in his 1950 biography of Martí, "whipped the revo-

lution into raging flame, like a kernel of resin dropped into a brazier, and Cuba was pervaded, as with a fragrance, by an almost mystic heroism." See Jorge Mañach, *Martí, Apostle of Freedom*, trans. Coley Taylor (New York, 1950), p. 361.

66. Manuel Pedro González to José Antonio Portuondo, December 18, 1948, in Cira Romero and Marcia Castillo, eds., *Cuestiones privadas: Correspondencia a José Antonio Portuondo (1932–1986)* (Santiago de Cuba, 2002), p. 247.

67. José Martí, "Discurso conmemorativo," November 27, 1891, in *Obras completas*, 1:37; José Martí to Enrique Collazo, January 12, 1892, in ibid., 1:412–13; José Martí, "Abdala," in ibid., 4:623; José Martí, "Con todos y para el bien de todos," November 26, 1891, in ibid., 1:701; José Martí, "Manifiesto de Montecristi," March 25, 1895, in ibid., 1:243; José Martí, "Pobres y ricos," March 14, 1893, in ibid., 1:485; Cintio Vitier, *Ese sol del mundo moral* (Havana, 1975), p. 86; José Martí, "Carta a su madre," March 25, 1895, in *Obras completas*, 4:915; José Martí to Manuel Mercado, May 18, 1895, in ibid., 1:271.

68. For a thoughtful discussion of the place of death in the thinking of José Martí see Figarola, *La muerte en Cuba*, pp. 71–94.

69. Buenamar, *Episodios de la guerra de Cuba*, p. 9; "A la memoria de los mártires cubanos," *El Republicano*, October 17, 1874, p. 3; Avelino Sanjenís to Cloridano Betancourt, 1897, in Sanjenís, *Mis cartas*, p. 165; "19 de mayo," *El Cubano Libre*, May 19, 1897, p. 1. Writing two years after Martí's death, Arístides Agüero affirmed: "His example has so dignified the need for sacrifice that I am disposed to do everything for my country." See Arístides Agüero to Gonzalo de Quesada, March 5, 1897 in Gonzalo de Quesada, *Epistolario*, ed. Gonzalo de Quesada y Miranda, 2 vols. (Havana, 1948), 1:14.

70. *Cuba*, May 27, 1897, p. 2; Cabrera, *Ideales*, p. 345; Manuel Piedra Martel, *Campaña de Maceo en la última Guerra de Independencia* (Havana, 1946), pp. 89–90.

71. Antonio Maceo to María Cabrales, March 25, 1895, in Cabrales Nicolarde, *Epistolario de héroes*, p. 57; Valdés-Domínguez, *Diario del soldado*, 1:34, 65, 238.

72. José A. López, "Nuestro deber," *La Nueva República* 1 (July 3, 1897): 10.

73. Roa, *A pie y descalzo de Trinidad a Cuba*, p. 86. "He was a man, very much a manly man [*muy macho*]," Ramón Roa described a fallen comrade at another point, "and that is the way we should all be, for this war will not be won through frivolous methods." See Ramón Roa, *Con la pluma y el machete*, 3 vols. (Havana, 1950), 1:31. Eduardo Rosell y Malpica attributed Cuban military success to the "virility that defines our young men." See Eduardo Rosell y Malpica, *Diario del teniente coronel Eduardo Rosell y Malpica*, 2 vols. (Havana, 1950), 2:76.

74. Carlos Manuel de Céspedes to Ana de Quesada, February 21, 1871, Céspedes, *Cartas de Carlos Manuel de Céspedes*, pp. 31–32.

75. Carlos Manuel de Céspedes to the Junta Revolucionaria de La Habana, August 25, 1871, in Portuondo del Prado and Pichardo Viñals, *Carlos Manuel de Céspedes: Escritos*, p. 237.

76. Piedra Martel, *Campañas de Maceo en la última Guerra de Independencia*, p. 97; A. N. [*sic*] to Calixto García, May 30, 1879, in Cuba, Archivo Nacional de Cuba, *Documentos para servir a la historia de la Guerra Chiquita*, 2:92; Rosell y Malpica, *Diario del teniente coronel Eduardo Rosell y Malpica*, 1:148.

77. Carlos Manuel de Céspedes to Editor, *New York Sun*, December 15, 1870, in Portuondo del Prado and Pichardo Viñals, *Carlos Manuel de Céspedes: Escritos*, p. 79;

José Martí, "Lectura en la reunión en emigrados cubanos," January 24, 1880, in *Obras completas*, 1:693.

78. See Daniel Tabares, "La mujer en la guerra," *La Lucha*, May 20, 1916, p. 54; José A. Rodríguez García, *De la revolución y de las cubanas en la época revolucionaria* (Havana, 1930); Francisco J. Ponte Domínguez, "La mujer en la revolución cubana," *Revista Bimestre Cubana* 33 (March–April 1933): 277–300; Rosario Rexach, "Las mujeres del 68," *Revista Cubana* (New York) 1 (January–June 1968): 123–42; Armando O. Caballero, *La mujer en el 68* (Havana, 1978); Armando O. Caballero, *La mujer en el 95* (Havana, 1982), pp. 24–94; José Sánchez Guerra, *Mambisas guantanameras* (Guantánamo, 2000). For the role of women in espionage see Luis Alfonso García, *La inteligencia mambisa en Santa Clara* (Santa Clara, 1999), pp. 24–28, 37–41. On the participation of women in liberation projects in exile see Paul Estrada, "Les Clubs Feminins dans le Parti Revolutionaire Cubain (1892–1898)," in Claire Pallier, ed., *Femmes des Amériques: colloque international 18–19 avril 1985* (Toulouse, 1986), pp. 85–105; and Nancy A. Hewitt, *Southern Discomfort: Women's Activism in Tampa, Florida, 1880s–1920s* (Urbana, 2001), pp. 69–81.

79. Aurora Coca de Granados, "Por deber," *El Eco de Martí*, May 15, 1897, p. 4.

80. See Figueredo de Portillo, *La Abanderada de 1868*; Rita Suárez del Villar, *Mis memorias* ([Havana], n.d.); Flora Basulto de Montoya, *Una niña bajo tres banderas (Memorias)* (Havana, 1954); María Josefa Granados, *La otra María, o la niña de Artemisa*, ed. Ana Núñez Machín (Havana, 1975).

81. Emilia Casanova de Villaverde to Federico Cavada, October 4, 1870, in Un Contemporáneo [Cirilo Villaverde], *Apuntes biográficos de Emilia Casanova de Villaverde*, p. 99; Emilia Casanova de Villaverde to Asunción Adot de Miranda, August 17, 1870, ibid., p. 84.

82. Valdés-Domínguez, *Diario de soldado*, 1:378.

83. Carlos Manuel de Céspedes to Ana de Quesada, August 7, 1872, in Céspedes, *Cartas de Carlos Manuel de Céspedes*, p. 130. "[Francisco] Aguilera found himself in a difficult situation," wrote his biographer, "summoned at one and the same time by two conflicting sentiments: the *patria* and the family." See Eladio Aguilera y Rojas, *Francisco V. Aguilera y la revolución de 1868*, 2 vols. (Havana, 1909), 1:211.

84. Ignacio Agramonte to Amalia Simoni, January 12, 1871, in Ignacio Betancourt Agramonte, *Ignacio Agramonte y la revolución cubana* (Havana, 1926), p. 406; Hernández Guzmán, *Memorias tristes*, pp. 33–35; Sanjenís, *Mis cartas*, pp. 27, 37–38, 65, 213.

85. Betancourt, "A mi madre," in Sánchez Valdivia, *Heroes humildes*, pp. 161–63; Betancourt, "27 de diciembre," in *Artículos de costumbres*, pp. xxx–xxxi; Betancourt, "Simpatías del destino," in Sánchez Valdivia, *Heroes humildes*, p. 166.

86. Arbelo, *Recuerdos de la última guerra por la independencia de Cuba*, pp. 24–25.

87. Concepción Boloña, *La mujer en Cuba*, 2nd ed. (Havana, 1899), p. 21.

88. Francisco Vicente Aguilera to Caridad, Juan, and Anitica, September 14, 1871, in Francisco Vicente Aguilera, *Epistolario* (Havana, 1974), p. 48; José Martí, "Carácter," July 30, 1892, in *Obras completas*, 1:661. Indeed, widowhood as the result of loss of spouse during the wars for independence achieved commemorative status. See Juan Sierra Pando, "Viudas ilustres," *El Fígaro* 15 (March 26, 1899): 69.

89. Carlos Manuel de Céspedes to Miguel de Aldama, March 25, 1871, in Portuondo del Prado and Pichardo Viñals, *Carlos Manuel de Céspedes: Escritos*; Carlos Manuel de Céspedes to María Rojas, July 5, 1871, ibid., p. 184.

90. Ana Betancourt's notation is found in Ignacio Mora, "Diario de campaña de Ignacio Mora," in Nydia Sarabia, *Ana Betancourt Agramonte* (Havana, 1970), p. 187; María Cabrales Viuda de Maceo to Tomás Estrada Palma, January 20, 1897, in *Patria*, February 10, 1897, p. 2; Antonio Pirala, *Anales de la guerra de Cuba*, 3 vols. (Madrid, 1895–96), 1:355.

91. Carlos Manuel de Céspedes to Manuela Cancino, April 16, 1873, in Portuondo del Prado and Pichardo Viñals, *Carlos Manuel de Céspedes: Escritos*, p. 340; Carlos Manuel de Céspedes to Josefa Rodríguez de Peralta, December 27, 1872, in ibid., p. 433; Carlos Manuel de Céspedes to Filomena Loynaz de Agramonte, July 8, 1873, in ibid., p. 445; Juan Vilaró, "Una familia de heroes," *Revista de Cayo Hueso* 2 (June 12, 1898): 14; Gerardo Castellanos G., *Un paladín (Serafín Sánchez)* (Havana, 1926), p. 74. Writing about Elena González, the widow of José Maceo, María Julia de Lara Mena celebrated her "resigned stoicism," adding that the life of Elena provided a "message of support and hope for all [women] who suffer." See María Julia de Lara Mena, *La familia Maceo. Cartas a Elena. Conversaciones patrióticas al calor del hogar* (Havana, 1945), pp. 49, 50.

92. Emilia Casanova de Villaverde to Carlos Manuel de Céspedes, May 13, 1871, p. 147, in Un Contemporáneo, *Apuntes biográficos de Emilia Casanova de Villaverde*, p. 147.

93. Sofía Estévez de Rodríguez, "Las mujeres," *Cuba*, October 19, 1897, p. 2. Emphasis in original.

94. Betancourt, "Datos biográficos sobre Ignacio Mora," pp. 68, 88.

95. Emilia Casanova de Villaverde to Carlos Manuel de Céspedes, October 4, 1870, in Un Contemporáneo, *Apuntes biográficos de Emilia Casanova de Villaverde*, p. 97.

96. *Patria*, October 10, 1894, p. 2.

97. Betancourt, "Datos biográficos sobre Ignacio Mora," p. 78. The account of Julia Miranda de Morales is found in José Martí, "Un cubano en New Orleans," May 8, 1893, in *Obras completas*, 1:584; Pirala, *Anales de la guerra de Cuba*, 1:355.

98. José Martí, "La recepción en Filadelfia," August 20, 1892, in *Obras completas*, 1:319; José Martí, "La confirmación," April 23, 1892, in ibid., 1:311; Carlos Manuel de Céspedes, "Al pueblo cubano," February 7, 1870, *Boletín del Archivo Nacional* 53–54 (1956): 179–80; *Patria*, September 3, 1892, p. 2; "La muger cubana y la insurrección," *Diario Cubano*, June 24, 1870, p. 1; Eusebio Sáenz y Sáenz, *La siboneya, o episodios de la guerra de Cuba*, 3rd ed. (Madrid, 1891), p. 141.

99. Conde de Valmaseda, "Proclama," April 4, 1869, in Melchor Loret de Mola y León, *El 6 de enero de 1871. Episodios de la guerra de Cuba* (Puerto Príncipe, 1893), p. 104.

100. The account of Rodolfo Mederos is related in Collazo, *Cuba heroica*, p. 439; Domingo Goicuría to Carlota Goicuría, May 1, 1870, in "Cartas del mártir cubano Domingo Goicuría," p. 59; Ignacio Tamayo to Agustina Milanés Bazán, August 16, 1870, in José Maceo Verdecia, *Bayamo*, 2nd ed. (Havana, 1941), p. 209. A similar story appears in Izaguirre, *Recuerdos de la guerra*, pp. 47–48.

101. In Fernando Portuondo, *Historia de Cuba*, 6th ed. (Havana, 1965), p. 458. His-

torian Fernando Portuondo described the conduct of Lucía Iñiguez as "an episode that depicts the heroic character of Cuban women of the revolutionary era." Ibid. A slightly different version of this story appears in José Miró Argenter, *Cuba: Crónicas de la guerra. Las campañas de invasión y de Occidente, 1895–1896*, 3 vols. (Havana, 1945), 2:209. See also Nicolás Peña, "Lucía Iñiguez, madre y mujer ejemplar," *Bohemia* 60 (May 10, 1968): 7, 113.

102. Cabrera, *¡A sitio Herrera!*, p. 110. The account of Dominga Moncada is found in José Martí, "De Cabo Haitiano a Dos Ríos: Diario," 1895, in *Obras completas*, 1:288; and Abelardo Padrón Valdés, *Guillermón Moncada: Vida y hazañas de un general* (Havana, 1980), pp. 141–42; Betancourt, "Datos biográficos sobre Ignacio Mora," p. 77.

103. Luis Quintero, "Unión-Patriotismo," *El Pueblo*, October 13, 1875, p. 2.

104. In Juan J. Remos, *Colonia y protesta. (Vetas del proceso cubano en sus luchas por la independencia)* (Havana, 1956), p. 109.

105. Figueredo de Portillo, *La Abanderada de 1868*, p. 24; Betancourt, "Datos biográficos sobre Ignacio Mora," p. 78.

106. In José G. Mármol, *Donato Mármol: Mayor General en la revolución del separatismo cubano* (Miami, 1993), p. 240.

107. María Cabrales de Maceo to Francisco de Paula Coronado, May 6, 1897, in Antonio Maceo, *Papeles de Maceo*, ed. Emeterio Santovenia, 2 vols. (1947; reprint, Havana, 1998), 2:75; Lara Mena, *La familia Maceo*, p. 13; Nydia Sarabia, *Historia de una familia mambisa: Mariana Grajales* (Havana, 1975), p. 101. See also Aída Rodríguez, *Mariana Grajales, madre de la patria* (Havana, 1957). For an informative discussion on Mariana Grajales as exemplary mother see Jean Stubbs, "Social and Political Motherhood of Cuba: Mariana Grajales Cuello," in Verene Shepherd, Bridget Brereton, and Barbara Bailey, eds., *Engendering History: Caribbean Women in Historical Perspective* (New York, 1995), pp. 296–317.

108. Emeterio S. Santovenia, *Huellas de gloria. Frases históricas cubanas*, 2nd ed. (Havana, 1944), p. 31; in Padrón Valdés, *Guillermón Moncada*, p. 144.

109. Maceo Verdecia, *Bayamo*, p. 221; Boloña, *La mujer en Cuba*, p. 22; J. Rodríguez Acosta, "La mujer en la revolución," *La Revista de Cuba Libre* 1 (March 5, 1898): 3. This theme is explored in K. Lynn Stoner, "Militant Heroines and the Consecration of the Patriarchal State: The Glorification of Loyalty, Combat, and National Suicide in the Making of Cuban National Identity," *Cuban Studies* 34 (2003), pp. 73–75.

110. Néstor L. Carbonell, "¡La madre cubana... ! 1891," reprinted in *El Villaclareño*, September 29, 1901, p. 7; José Martí, "Carácter," July 30, 1892, in *Obras completas*, 1:661; José Martí, "Hora supreme," March 14, 1893, in ibid., 1:437–38; Consuelo Alvarez, "¡Madre mía!" *El Cubano Libre*, September 10, 1896, p. 3.

111. "La madre cubana ante la Revolución," *El Expedicionario*, January 2, 1897, p. 5.

112. Lara Mena, *La familia Maceo*, pp. 115, 121. See also Angel Augier, "Mariana Grajales, la madre ejemplar," *Mujeres Cubanas* 1 (July–September 1950): 3–4; Lázaro Torres Hernández, "Mariana Grajales, una madre sublime," *Bohemia* 64 (January 28, 1972): 100–104; Adys Cupull and Froilán González, *Mariana, raíz del alma cubana* (Havana, 1998); and Ana Baldomero Alvarez Ríos, *Mariana Grajales, heroína de la nación* (Havana, n.d.).

113. María Corominas de Hernández, "Estudio sobre la mentalidad de la Maguire,"

in González Curquejo, *Florilegio de escritoras cubanas*, 3:191; Africa Fernández Iruela, "La mujer cubana," ibid., 3:240; Aurelia Castillo de González, "Ignacio Agramonte en la vida privada," in *Escritos de Aurelia Castillo de González*, 6 vols. (Havana, 1913–18), 2:136–37; Ignacio Agramonte Lanes, *Patria y mujer*, ed. José Manuel Pérez Cabrera (Havana, 1942). "There is a task of nationalism that the woman must initiate in the home," insisted Hortensia Lamar. "[This is] to teach her sons to read in the magnificent missal of our heroes, telling them: 'This is the sacred book of the past; the future one is for you to make, with your father, with your brother. All of us who live in the present must fulfill [our duty] with our actions. We must be careful to be worthy of our dead who live in eternity.'" See Hortensia Lamar, "Protección y defensa del hogar cubano," *Revista Bimestre Cubano* 18 (May–June 1923): 211.

114. For a useful discussion of the nineteenth-century family see Ana Vera Estrada, ed., *Cuba: cuaderno sobre la familia (época colonial)* (Havana, 1997). See also Elda E. Cento Gómez, "Apuntes para la historia de la familia de Salvador Cisneros Betancourt," *Universidad de La Habana* 256 (Second Semester 2002): 66–76.

115. Camilo Polavieja to Minister of Ultramar Antonio Maura, 1892, in Camilo Polavieja, *Relación documentada de mi política en Cuba* (Madrid, 1898), p. 176; Camilo Polavieja to Antonio María Fabié, December 10, 1890, ibid., p. 115.

116. Valdés-Domínguez, *Diario de soldado*, 1:469; Serafín Espinosa y Ramos, *Al trote y sin estribos (Recuerdos de la Guerra de Independencia)* (Havana, 1946), p. 21; Benito Arangurén y Martínez, *Recuerdos* (Havana, 1934), pp. 23, 83, 87.

117. Corvisón, *En la guerra y en la paz*, pp. 103, 193; Rita Suárez de Villar, *Mis memorias* ([Havana], n.d.), p. 13.

118. Junta de Güinía de Miranda, "A las ciudadanas de Las Villas," 1869, in Pirala, *Anales de la guerra de Cuba*, 1:653; Enrique Loynaz del Castillo, *Memorias de la guerra*, 2nd ed. (Havana, 1989), p. 18.

119. Ferrer, *Con el rifle al hombro*, p. 15.

120. Eva Adán de Rodríguez, *Hojas de recuerdos* (Havana, 1935), p. 35; Trujillo, *Apuntes históricos*, p. 174; *La Nueva República* 1 (June 5, 1897): 6; Basulto de Montoya, *Una niña bajo tres banders*, pp. 103–9.

121. Grover Flint, *Marching with Gomez. A War Correspondent's Field Note-Book Kept During Four Months with the Cuban Army* (Boston, 1898), p. 85. See also José Miguel Trujillo, "La independencia y los niños," *Bohemia* 9 (November 24, 1918): 4.

122. Ramón Céspedes Fornaris, "Pensamientos: Palabras de una insurrecta," *La República*, September 30, 1871, p. 5; José Martí, "Oración de Tampa y Cayo Hueso," February 17, 1893, in *Obras completas*, 1:707–17. See also José Martí, *Antología familiar*, ed. Félix Lizaso (Havana, 1941).

123. Ignacio Agramonte to Amalia Simoni, December 1868, June 9, 1869, and February 6, 1870, in Eugenio Betancourt Agramonte, *Ignacio Agramonte y la revolución cubana* (Havana, 1928), pp. 383, 388, 393; Juan Ramírez Pellerano, ed., *Cartas a Amalia* (Havana, 1994), pp. 53–54; Francisco Varona González, "Diario de operaciones," in Víctor Manuel Marrero, ed., *Vicente García, leyenda y realidad* (Havana, 1992), p. 69.

124. Aurelia Castillo de González, "Canción de las Madres," in *Escritos de Aurelia Castillo de González*, 4:297–98.

125. José Martí, "Versos sencillos," in *Obras completas*, 4: 472.

126. José Agustín Quintero, "Paráfrasis de Ruckert," in Estenger, *Cien de las mejores poesías cubanas*, pp. 114–15.

127. "De la madre al hijo," in Jesús Orta Ruiz, *Décima y folclor* (Havana, 1980), p. 95. See also Samuel Feijóo, ed., *Cuarteta y décima* (Havana, 1980), p. 94.

128. Historian Ada Ferrer has noted that opponents of independence "manipulated racial images in an effort to question and ultimately defeat [the] nationalist insurrection." Observes Ferrer: "By emphasizing that the rebellion was multiracial, critics in fact stressed that it was at least in part a black rebellion. And claims about the black character of rebellion, originally made and continuously repeated by Spanish officials and detractors, then found their way into broader public perceptions of the independence movement. In these public representations, insurgency constantly verged on the brink of race war and savagery." See Ada Ferrer, *Insurgent Cuba: Race, Nation, and Revolution, 1868–1898* (Chapel Hill, 1999), p. 49. Writing early in the 1895 insurrection, Calixto García observed: "The [Spanish] government is following the same old tactics: it publishes the names of the insurgent leaders of color, but not the names of whites. We thus know that [Guillermo] Moncada and [Quintín] Banderas have revolted in Santiago, but we know nothing of the leaders of the forces in Baire and Manzanillo." See Calixto García to Gonzalo de Quesada, March 10, 1895, in Quesada, *Epistolario*, 1:171.

129. Radillo y Rodríguez, *Autobiografía del cubano Luis de Radillo y Rodríguez*, p. 81; Sánchez Valdivia, *Heroes humildes*, p. 39; "El tercer aniversario," *Revista de Cuba Libre* I (March 5, 1898): 6; Néstor L. Carbonell, *Resonancias del pasado* (Havana, 1916), p. 79; Antonio Maceo to José Martí, January 4, 1888, in Maceo, *El pensamiento vivo de Maceo*, p. 91; Antonio Maceo to Enrique Trujillo, August 22, 1894, in ibid., p. 94; Antonio Maceo to María Cabrales, [March 1895], in ibid., p. 101; Antonio Maceo to Carlos Varona, n.d., in Maceo, *Papeles de Maceo*, 1:123; Calixto García, "Al Ejército Cubano," 1880, in Emilio Bacardí y Moreau, *Crónicas de Santiago de Cuba*, 2nd ed., 10 vols. (Madrid, 1973), 6:349–50. See also Francisco Javier Cisneros, *La verdad histórica sobre sucesos de Cuba* (New York, 1871), p. 63.

130. *El Republicano*, January 8, 1869, p. 2; Mercedes Matamoros, "La muerte del esclavo," in González Curquejo, *Florilegio de escritoras cubanas*, 2:111 (See also Mercedes Matamoros, "El esclavo," *Cuba Literaria* 2 (July 21, 1905): 213); "Manifiesto al pueblo de Sierra Morena," December 25, 1898, in Sanjenís, *Mis cartas*, p. 400.

131. *Cuba*, February 4, 1897, p. 4.

132. Carlos Manuel de Céspedes to Joaquina de Céspedes, November 22, 1873, in Portuondo del Prado and Pichardo Viñals, *Carlos Manuel de Céspedes: Escritos*, p. 115; Carlos Manuel de Céspedes to Ana de Quesada, August 5, 1871, in Céspedes, *Cartas de Carlos Manuel de Céspedes*, p. 48.

133. Federico Pérez Carbó to Enrique Trujillo, April 29, 1890, in Trujillo, *Apuntes históricos*, p. 47; Valdés-Domínguez, *Diario de soldado*, 1:272; Serafín Sánchez to José Joaquín Sánchez, April 4, 1889, in Serafín Sánchez, *Apuntes biográficos del Mayor General Serafín Sánchez: Perfil libre*, ed. Berta Hernández (Havana, 1986), p. 52. On another occasion, Sánchez denounced the Autonomist Party, "at the head of which are found the defenders of the slave colony [*los prohombres de la colonia esclava*]." Serafín

Sánchez, "Diario," 1879–80, in Castellanos G., *Un paladín (Serafín Sánchez)*, p. 240; Manuel Sanguily, "Un insurrecto cubano en la corte," November 1888, in *Frente a la dominación española*, p. 112; Castellanos G., *Un paladín (Serafín Sánchez)*, p. 160.

134. Rafael Serra, "Ahora empieza la guerra," *La Doctrina de Martí*, December 30, 1896, p. 1.

135. Eugenio O. Rodríguez, *Tunas de ayer y de hoy* (Las Tunas, 1951), p. 4; Marrero, *Vicente García, leyenda y realidad*, p. 69; Collazo, *Cuba heroica*, p. 388; Cabrera, *¡A sitio Herrera!*, pp. 253–54. See also Miranda, *Con Martí y con Calixto García*, p. 51; and Víctor Marrero Zaldívar, *Las Tunas: Localidad, cultura e identidad* (Las Tunas, 2002), pp. 106–46.

136. Agustín Ruiz to Tomás Estrada Palma, January 16, 1870, *Boletín del Archivo Nacional* 53–54 (1956): 181; José M. García Montes, "Discurso del Señor José M. García Montes," November 5, 1897, in *Por la independencia* (New York, [1897]), p. 36.

137. *El Cubano Libre*, December 31, 1896, p. 1; Speech made by Salvador Cisneros Betancourt, in *El Cubano Libre*, April 15, 1897, p. 2; Sanjenís, *Memorias de la revolución de 1895*, p. 209; Sanjenís, *Mis cartas*, p. 19.

138. Manuel Sanguily, "Los exterminadores," April 1, 1875, in Sanguily, *Frente a la dominación española*, p. 39; Manuel Sanguily, "Discurso del Señor Manuel Sanguily," November 5, 1897, in *Por la independencia*, p. 45.

139. Valdés-Domínguez, *Diario de soldado*, 1:221; Nicolás Pérez to Antonio Maceo, December 12, 1878, in Maceo, *Papeles de Maceo*, 1:158; Nicolás Arnao, "Cuba, la ley de la fuerza y la justicia de su causa," *La Contienda* 1 (December 24, 1897): 2; Alfredo Vidal, "Cuba se quema," *El Pueblo*, November 24, 1875, p. 2.

140. José Martí, "Vindicación de Cuba," March 25, 1889, in *Obras completas*, 1:652; Pérez Abreu, *En la guerra con Máximo Gómez*, pp. 50, 196; Adán de Rodríguez, *Hojas de recuerdos*, p. 21. Adán de Rodríguez characterized the gesture as "a heroic and patriotic deed." Ibid.

141. Manuel Sueiras y Miralles, "De Cuba Libre," November 2, 1897, in *Revista de Cayo Hueso* 2 (January 23, 1898): 10–11. The burning of Bahía Honda is found in "Bahía Honda quemada," *La Doctrina de Martí*, April 15, 1895, p. 2. The account of the destruction of Jicotea is related in Boza, *Mi diario de la guerra*, 2:253–54; Ferrer, *Con el rifle al hombro*, pp. 90–91; Aníbal Escalante Beaton, *Calixto García: su campaña en el 95* (Havana 1976), p. 283. For Las Tunas see Cabrera, *¡A sitio Herrera!*, pp. 253–54. For San Andrés and Candelaria see Antonio Maceo, *Diario de campaña*, ed. Aisnara Perera Díaz (Havana, 2001). For Tiguabos see *La Revolución de Cuba*, March 30, 1872, p. 2. On Jaruco and Güira de Melena see Miró Argenter, *Cuba: Crónicas de la guerra*, 2:70–71; and Boza, *Mi diario de guerra*, 1:109. Sabanilla is discussed in Eduardo F. Lores y Llorens, *Relatos históricos de la guerra del 95* (Havana, 1955), p. 12. The burning of Güinía de Miranda is reported in *Guáimaro*, December 5, 1895, p. 3.

142. José María Izaguirre, "En Guáimaro," in *Asuntos cubanos: Colección de artículos y poesías* (New York, 1896), p. 34; Betancourt, "Datos biográficos sobre Ignacio Mora," p. 74.

143. *La Libertad*, May 12, 1869, p. 1.

144. José Martí, "El 10 de abril," April 10, 1892, in *Obras completas*, 1:537–38.

145. Pérez Abreu, *En la guerra con Máximo Gómez*, p. 365.

146. Hortensia Pichardo, "Bayamo: Rebelde y heroica," in *Facetas de nuestra historia*, p. 143; Figueredo de Portillo, *La Abanderada de 1868*, p. 18; José Joaquín Palma, "Al poeta Miguel G. Gutiérrez," in José Martí, *Los poetas de la guerra* (1893; reprint, Havana, 1968), p. 79; "La copla política en Cuba: 'La Bayamesa,'" *Archivos del Folklore Cubano* 3 (January–March 1928): 84. General Donato Mármol, a native of Bayamo and a participant in the burning of the town, wrote to his mother: "I have had the honor of setting your house on fire." See Mármol, *Donato Mármol*, p. 126.

147. Francisco Maceo, "Una página de mis apuntes," *La Revolución de Cuba*, April 5, 1873, p. 3; Francisco Sellén, "Bayamo," *Revista de Cayo Hueso* II (April 5, 1873), p. 2; Tomás Estrada Palma, "Bayamo," in Izaguirre, *Asuntos cubanos*, p. 19. For Spanish views of the burning of Guáimaro and Bayamo see Gil Gelpi y Ferro, *Album histórico de la guerra de Cuba* (Havana, 1870); and Dionisio Novel e Ibañez, *Memoria de los sucesos ocurridos en la insurrección que estalló en la ciudad de Bayamo in octubre de 1868* (Granada, 1872).

148. Luis Lagomasino Alvarez, *Reminiscencias patria* (Manzanillo, 1902), p. 14; Antonio Miguel Alcover, *Bayamo (su toma, posesión e incendio): 1868–1869* (Havana, 1902), p. 84; José Ramón Betancourt, *Las dos banderas. Apuntes históricos sobre la insurrección de Cuba* (Sevilla, 1872), p. 28; J. M. Céspedes, "Bayamo y los bayameses," *Diario Cubano*, May 5, 1870, p. 3.

149. Carlos Manuel de Céspedes to Hortensio Tamayo, January 19, 1869, in Francisco Javier Cisneros, *La verdad histórica sobre sucesos de Cuba* (New York, 1871), p. 47; Diego Tamayo, "Discurso del Señor Diego Tamayo," November 5, 1897, in *Por la independencia*, p. 29.

150. Alcover, *Bayamo*, p. 86.

151. Miranda, *Reminiscencias cubanas*, p. 172; Valdés-Domínguez, *Diario de soldado*, 1:124; Fermín Valdés-Domínguez to Gonzalo de Quesada, March 31, 1897, in Gonzalo de Quesada, *Archivo de Gonzalo de Quesada: Espistolario*, ed. Gonzalo de Quesada y Miranda, 2 vols. (Havana, 1948), 2:312; José Maceo Verdecia, *Bayamo*, 2nd ed. (Havana, 1941), p. 18. The 1897 speech by Diego Vicente Tejera was published as "La indolencia cubana," *Cuba Contemporánea* 28 (March 1922): 170.

152. Francisco Figueras, *Cuba y su evolución colonial* (1907; reprint, Havana, [1959?]), p. 182; Manuel Márquez Sterling, *Alrededor de nuestra psicología* (Havana, 1906), pp. 205–6.

CHAPTER THREE

1. Commenting on the paucity of adequate statistical information on matters of criminality and mortality in late-nineteenth-century Cuba, demographer José Jimeno Agius observed: "Notwithstanding the importance of this island . . . , statistics are very scarce. They are so few that they constitute little more than mere notices of numbers and classification of crimes (*delitos*) in the territory." See José Jimeno Agius, *La criminalidad en España y sus colonias. El suicidio en España y en el extranjero* (Madrid, 1886), pp. 129–30.

2. Cuba, Capitanía General, *Noticias estadísticas de la Isla de Cuba en 1862* (Havana, 1864), n.p.; Havana, Audiencia, *Discurso que, en la solemne apertura del tribunal leyó el día 3 de enero de 1859, en la Real Audiencia Pretorial de La Habana, su regente el Excmo. e*

Illmo. Sr. D. Francisco González (Havana, 1859); Havana, Audiencia, *Discurso que, en la solemne apertura del tribunal leyó el día 2 de enero de 1860, en la Real Audiencia Pretorial de La Habana, su regente el Excmo. e Illmo. Sr. D. Francisco González* (Havana, 1860). The total number of suicides recorded in 1871, during the Ten Years War, decreased to 286. See Havana, Audiencia, *Discurso pronunciado en la apertura del tribunal de la excelentísima Audiencia Pretorial por el Exmo. e Illmo. Sr. Don Joaquín Calurton, bajo su presidencia el 2 de enero de 1872* (Havana, 1872). See also Francisco Javier Bona, "El suicidio en la isla de Cuba," *La América*, November 27, 1866, p. 3.

3. See *La Discusión*, July 11, 1893, p. 2; and *La Discusión*, August 4, 1893, p. 2.

4. Francisco Obregón Mayol, "Medicina legal: estadística del Necrocomio de esta ciudad [La Habana] durante el año 1887," *Crónica Médico-Quirúrgica de La Habana* 14 (1888): 85–87; Francisco Obregón Mayol, "Medicina legal: estado referente a los sucesos del Necrocomio durante el año 1890," *Crónica Médico-Quirúrgica de La Habana* 17 (1891): 101–2; Francisco V. de la Guardia, "Estadística demográfico-sanitaria de La Habana-Año 1893," *Anales de la Real Academia de Ciencias Médicas, Físicas y Naturales de La Habana* 31 (1894): 194–240; "Demografía de la Habana durante el año de 1894," *Crónica Médico-Quirúrgica de La Habana* 21 (1895): 104; "La mortalidad en La Habana," *El Progreso Médico* 1 (1890): 298–300; Diego Tamayo, "Causas de mortalidad en La Habana: consideraciones sociológicas," *Revista de Ciencias Médicas* 8 (May 20, 1893): 110–14. See also Aquiles Solano, *¡Misterios. . .!! Episodio histórico de un suicida (Hojas arrancadas de la cartera de un reporter)* (Havana, 1886).

5. Tomás L. Plasencia, "Notas relativas al suicidio en la circunscripción de La Habana," *Anales de la Real Academia de Ciencias Médicas, Físicas y Naturales de La Habana* 22 (1885): 412–13. A slightly different version of this study appears as Tomás L. Plasencia, "El suicidio en la circunscripción de La Habana," *Revista General de Derecho* 5 (1887): 98–106.

6. See Antonio de Gordon y de Acosta, "Sobre el suicidio," *Revista Científica de la Academia de Ciencias Médicas, Físicas y Naturales de La Habana* 44 (April–May 1908): 825–29.

7. The data employed in this discussion is derived principally from the annual *Boletín Oficial* published by the República de Cuba, Secretaría de Sanidad y Beneficencia and Ministerio de Salubridad y Asistencia Social between 1909 and 1959. The *Boletín Oficial* consistently provided the most detailed statistical information on suicide in Cuba. However, it is also true that Sanidad y Beneficencia and Salubridad y Asistencia Social provided the most conservative tabulations. The evidence suggests that the *Boletín Oficial* routinely undercounted cases of suicide. Virtually all alternative sources of information for suicide rates report higher numbers than Sanidad y Beneficencia. In many instances, Sanidad y Beneficencia and Salubridad y Asistencia Social included acts of self-destruction in categories other than suicide. The Comisión Nacional de Estadística y Reformas Económicas, for example, provided very different numbers for the years during which it operated between the late 1920s and early 1930s. Whereas Sanidad y Beneficencia reported a total of 565 suicides in 1926, for example, the Comisión Nacional counted 885. The discrepancies persisted in the years that followed: 1927: 584/838; 1928: 539/898; 1929: 601/1,017; 1930: 513/1,008; 1931: 419/1,099; 1932: 575/860. The circumstances by which the instances of suicide

were underreported are not unique to Cuba. See Jack D. Douglas, *The Social Meaning of Suicide* (Princeton, 1967), pp. 233–46.

8. See the case of José Eugenio Rodríguez Mejía, who was said to have shot himself accidentally while examining his revolver. *Diario de la Marina,* October 21, 1918, p. 9.

9. Jorge LeRoy y Cassá, "Informe anual sanitario y demográfico de la República de Cuba, correspondiente al año 1924: Carta de remisión," April 24, 1929, in República de Cuba, Secretaría de Sanidad y Beneficencia, *Boletín Oficial* 34 (January–December 1929): 100; Cristobal de La Habana, "Muérete y verás," *Vanidades* 13 (August 15, 1944): 24–25; Carlos Muller, "De qué se muere en La Habana," *Carteles* 28 (November 9, 1947): 64–65.

10. República de Cuba, Secretaría de Sanidad y Beneficencia, *Boletín Oficial,* 1929–34 (Havana, 1930–35); República de Cuba, Comisión Nacional de Estadística y Reformas Económicas, *Estadísticas. Segundo Semestre de 1929* (Havana, 1930); República de Cuba, Comisión Nacional de Estadística y Reformas Económicas, *Estadísticas 1930* (Havana, 1931).

11. María Luisa Rodríguez-Sala de Gómezgil, *Suicidios y suicidias en la sociedad mexicana* (México, 1974); República de Cuba, Comisión Nacional de Estadística y Reformas Económicas, *Estadísticas, 1932* (Havana, 1933), p. 157.

12. República de Cuba, Comisión Nacional de Estadística y Reformas Económicas, *Estadísticas. Segundo Semestre de 1929* (Havana, 1930), p. 225; República de Cuba, Comisión Nacional de Estadística y Reformas Económicas, *Estadísticas 1930* (Havana, 1931); Rolando R. Pérez, "¿Por qué se matan?" *Carteles* 35 (May 8, 1955): 47.

13. One study of suicide in Cuba in 1954 indicated that the male-to-female ratio had increased to 3:1. See M. Velilla de Solórzano, "Los que se matan," *Carteles* 35 (August 1, 1954): 63. In the context of the rates of suicide in nearly twenty countries during the late 1950s, the World Health Organization identified the highest male-to-female ratios in Norway (4.1:1), Finland (3.3:1), and Sweden (2.9:1). At the low end were found Japan (1.4:1) and England (1.4:1). Cuba occupied the upper half of the male-to-female ratio. See World Health Organization, *Epidemiological and Vital Statistics* (1961) in Louis I. Dublin, *Suicide: A Sociological and Statistical Study* (New York, 1963), p. 25. For a general discussion of male-to-female ratios in other countries see David Lester, "An International Perspective on Female Suicide," in David Lester, ed., *Why Women Kill Themselves* (Springfield, Ill., 1988), pp. 17–19; and John L. McIntosh and Barbara L. Jewell, "Sex Difference Trends in Completed Suicides," *Suicide and Life-Threatening Behavior* 16 (Spring 1986): 16–27.

14. See United States War Department, *Informe sobre el censo de Cuba, 1899* (Washington, D.C., 1900); Cuba, Oficina del Censo, *Censo de la República de Cuba, 1907* (Washington, D.C., 1908); Cuba, Dirección General del Censo, *Censo de la República de Cuba, 1919* (Havana, 1919); Cuba, Dirección de Demografía del Comité Estatal de Estadística, *Memorias inéditas del censo de 1931* (Havana, 1978); Cuba, Dirección General del Censo, *Censo de 1943* (Havana, 1945); Cuba, Oficina Nacional de los Censos Demográficos y Electoral, *Censo de población, viviendas y electoral. Enero 28 de 1953* (Havana, 1955).

15. For a general discussion on gender-differentiated methods of suicide see Alan Marks and Thomas Abernathy, "Toward a Sociocultural Perspective on Means of Self-Destruction," *Suicide and Life-Threatening Behavior* 4 (Spring 1974): 3–17.

16. *La Discusión*, August 19, 1893, p. 2; p. A-12; *La Lucha*, March 25, 1902, p. 2.

17. "Archaic suicide," *Havana Post*, March 5, 1919, p. 4.

18. *La Caricatura*, April 13, 1902, p. 4; ibid., March 11, 1906, p. 4; *La Lucha*, May 6, 1910, p. 4.

19. *La Lucha*, April 5, 1902, p. 2; *Diario de la Marina*, June 15, 1916, pp. 1, 15; *El Mundo*, December 7, 1919, p. 14.

20. *La Lucha*, April 16, 1910, p. 4; ibid., July 28, 1926, p. 3.

21. *La Caricatura*, August 20, 1906, p. 4; *Diario de la Marina*, February 22, 1917, p. 8; ibid., April 7, 1917, p. 7.

22. *La Caricatura*, November 12, 1905, p. 4; ibid., December 10, 1905, p. 4; *Diario de la Marina*, December 11, 1916, p. 9; ibid., September 25, 1931, p. 16.

23. *Diario de la Marina*, March 5, 1932, p. 14; ibid., January 23, 1901, p. 4.

24. Dolores Prida, *Screens*, in Luis F. González-Cruz and Francesa M. Colecchia, eds., *Cuban Theater in the United States: A Critical Anthology* (Tempe, Ariz., 1992), p. 138.

25. *El Mundo*, April 9, 1955, p. 7.

26. For accounts of women shooting themselves in the heart see *La Lucha*, September 6, 1920, p. 2; *El Mundo*, October 20, 1953, p. A-10; ibid., October 20, 1953, p. A-10.

27. See República de Cuba, Secretaría de Sanidad y Beneficencia, *Boletín Oficial* 22 (July–December 1919); República de Cuba, Secretaría de Sanidad y Beneficencia, *Boletín Oficial* 31 (January–December 1926); República de Cuba, Secretaría de Sanidad y Beneficencia, *Boletín Oficial* 33 (January–December 1928).

28. Plasencia, "Notas relativas al suicidio," pp. 409–29.

29. See *La Lucha*, April 4, 1895, p. 2.

30. *Diario de la Marina*, April 1, 1901, p. 4; *La Caricatura*, June 29, 1902, p. 4; ibid., December 13, 1903, p. 4; *Diario de la Marina*, January 8, 1904, p. 4; ibid., January 18, 1904, p. 4; ibid., March 18, 1904, p. 4.

31. Antonio Barreras, "Estudios médico-legales: El suicidio en La Habana en el año de 1912," *Revista Médica Cubana* 21 (June 1912): 338, 340.

32. República de Cuba, Secretaría de Sanidad y Beneficencia, *Boletín Oficial* 22 (July–December 1919): 371, 403; Jorge LeRoy y Cassá, "Quo Tendimus? Estudio médico legal sobre el suicidio en Cuba durante el quinquenio de 1902–1906," *Anales de la Academia de Ciencias Médicas, Físicas y Naturales de La Habana* 44 (May 1907): 51–54.

33. República de Cuba, Comisión Nacional de Estadística y Reformas Económicas, *Estadísticas. . . . 1929–1932* (Havana, 1930–33).

34. Ibid.

35. Details of the numerous cases of suicide by fire among women can be found in Provincial Governor Juan Gronlier to Secretary of Government, July 20, 1929, Legajo 45, Fondo Gobierno Provincial (Defunciones), Archivo Histórico Provincial de Matanzas, Matanzas, Cuba (hereinafter cited as AHPM); Luis Pérez, Alcalde, Bolondrón, to Provincial Governor, September 17, 1929, ibid.; Juan Jiménez, Alcalde, San José Ramos, to Provincial Governor, March 3, 1928, ibid.; Sixto Sánchez, Alcalde, Manguito, to Provincial Governor, September 2, 1928, ibid.; Evasio Martínez, Alcalde, Limonar, to Provincial Governor, July 3, 1928, ibid.; Jefatura de Policía, Policía Espe-

cial, Matanzas, to Provincial Governor, December 11, 1934, ibid; Inspector José R. Hidalgo to Jefe, Policía Especial, Matanzas, February 11, 1946, Legajo 21, Expediente 858, Fondo Gobierno Provisional de Matanzas Neocolonial, ibid.

36. República de Cuba, Comisión Nacional de Estadística y Reformas Económicas, *Estadísticas. . . . 1929–1932* (Havana, 1929–1933); República de Cuba, Comisión Nacional de Estadística y Reformas Económicas, *Estadísticas 1930*, p. 153.

37. *El Mundo*, October 18, 1953, p. A-10; ibid., December 2, 1953, p. A-12; ibid., January 24, 1950, p. 20; ibid., January 3, 1954, p. D-3; *Havana Post*, March 25, 1932, p. 1; *La Lucha*, November 18, 1926, p. 1.

38. See República de Cuba, Secretaría de Sanidad y Beneficencia, *Boletín Oficial*, 1909–41, and its successor, República de Cuba, Ministerio de Salubridad y Asistencia Social, *Boletín Oficial*, 1942–59.

39. Cuba, Oficina del Censo, *Censo de la República de Cuba, 1919* (Havana, 1919); Cuba, Dirección de Demografía del Comité Estatal de Estadística, *Memorias inéditas del censo de 1931* (Havana, 1978).

40. For an informative general discussion of the susceptibility of the elderly to suicide see Judith M. Stillion and Eugene E. McDowell, *Suicide across the Life Span: Premature Exits*, 2nd ed. (Washington, D.C., 1996), pp. 169–96; and Jane L. Pearson and Yeates Conwell, eds., *Suicide and Aging: International Perspectives* (New York, 1996).

41. See Peter N. Stearns, "Old Women: Some Historical Observations," *Journal of Family History* 5 (Spring 1980): 44–57.

42. República de Cuba, Oficina Nacional de los Censos Demográfico y Electoral, *Censos de población, viviendas y electoral. Enero 28 de 1953* (Havana, 1953), pp. 83–85.

43. Virgilio Piñera, *Aire frío*, 1962, in Ana Cairo Ballester, ed., *Letras: Cultura en Cuba*, 7 vols. (Havana, 1989–92), 3:74.

44. María del Carmen Boza, *Scattering the Ashes* (Tempe, Ariz., 1998), p. 367.

45. Virgil Suárez, "In the House of White Light," in *Palm Crows* (Tucson, 2001), p. 65.

46. María de los Reyes Castillo, *Reyita, sencillamente*, ed. Daisy Rubiera Castillo (Havana, 1997), p. 133.

47. Roger de Lauria, "Ya estoy viejo y cansado," *Bohemia* 11 (February 1, 1920), p. 7.

48. *La Lucha*, March 21, 1902, p. 3; *La Caricatura*, July 30, 1905, p. 4.

49. Margarita M. Engle, *Singing to Cuba* (Houston, 1993), p. 56.

50. *La Lucha*, May 12, 1926, p. 2; *La Caricatura*, August 21, 1904, p. 4; *La Lucha*, June 30, 1902, p. 1; *Havana Post*, February 26, 1932, p. 1; *Diario de la Marina*, June 27, 1929, p. 13.

51. Miguel de Marcos, "Pavo real y muerto grande," in *Fábula de la vida apacible* (Havana, 1943), pp. 10–14.

52. *La Lucha*, May 4, 1926, p. 7; Luis Rolando Cabrera, "Hurgando en los raíces del suicidio," *Bohemia* 48 (July 28, 1956): 52; *Havana Post*, March 9, 1921, p. 1.

53. *Diario de la Marina*, November 18, 1931, p. 8; ibid., October 30, 1931, p. 8.

54. Mario Guiral Moreno, "Suicidios con imprudencia," *El Mundo*, December 5, 1956, p. A-6.

55. LeRoy y Cassá, "Quo Tendimus?" p. 47.

56. Barreras, "Estudios médico-legales," p. 323.

57. LeRoy y Cassá, "Quo Tendimus?" p. 47; Barreras, "Estudios médico-legales," pp. 324, 340–41.

58. LeRoy y Cassá, "Quo Tendimus?" p. 52; Jorge LeRoy y Cassá, "Suicidio por el fuego," *Revista de Medicina y Cirugía de La Habana* XII (June 10, 1907): 251.

59. Barreras, "Estudios médico-legales," pp. 318–19.

60. Ibid., pp. 322, 340–41; Marta Vignier, "Las suicidas: ¿Enfermas mentales o víctimas de la sociedad?" *Carteles* 37 (May 13, 1956): 16–18, 97; Nicolás Dorr, *Los excéntricos de la noche*, 1996, in *Teatro insólito* (Havana, 2001), pp. 40–41. For a general discussion of issues related to completed and attempted suicides see E. Stengel, "The Social Effects of Attempted Suicide," in Anthony Giddens, ed., *The Sociology of Suicide* (London, 1971), pp. 375–83; Calvin F. Schmid and Maurice D. Van Arsdol Jr., "Completed and Attempted Suicide: A Comparative Analysis," *American Sociological Review* 20 (June 1955): 273–83.

61. Antoon A. Leenaars, *Suicide Notes: Predictive Clues and Patterns* (New York, 1988), pp. 171–211; Edward Robb Ellis and George N. Allen, *Traitor Within: Our Suicide Problem* (New York, 1961), pp. 170–85.

62. Boza, *Scattering the Ashes*, p. 86.

63. See "Carta de suicida," *El Mundo Ilustrado* 6 (July 25, 1909): 604.

64. *La Lucha*, December 17, 1903, p. 3.

65. Ibid., September 15, 1910, p. 2; *Diario de la Marina*, May 4, 1920, p. 2.

66. For a general discussion of this phenomenon see Antoon A. Leenaars, "The Suicide Notes of Women," in Lester, *Why Women Kill Themselves*, pp. 53–71; and Jerry Jacobs, "A Phenomenological Study of Suicide Notes," in Giddens, *The Sociology of Suicide*, pp. 332–48.

67. LeRoy y Cassá, "Quo Tendimus?" pp. 38–63; República de Cuba, Comisión Nacional de Estadística y Reformas Económicas, *Estadísticas. . . . 1929–1932.*

68. República de Cuba, Sanidad y Beneficencia, *Boletín Oficial* 22 (January–December 1935): 69–72; Jorge LeRoy y Cassá, "Informe anual sanitario y demográfico del término municipal de La Habana correspondiente al año 1929: Carta de remisión," January 13, 1930, in República de Cuba, Secretaría de Sanidad y Beneficencia, *Boletín Oficial* 25 (January–June 1930): 8.

69. LeRoy y Cassá, "Quo Tendimus?" p. 44.

70. República de Cuba, Comisión Nacional de Estadística y Reformas Económicas, *Estadísticas. Segundo Semestre de 1929* (Havana, 1930), pp. 228–29.

71. República de Cuba, Comisión Nacional de Estadística y Reformas Económicas, *Estadísticas. Segundo Semestre de 1929* (Havana, 1930), pp. 227–228.

72. LeRoy y Cassá, "Quo Tendimus?" pp. 50–51.

73. República de Cuba, Secretaría de Sanidad y Beneficencia, *Boletín Oficial*, 1913–15; Barreras, "Estudios médico-legales," pp. 319–21. For a general discussion of the relationship between economic cycles and suicide see Daniel S. Hamermesh and Neal M. Soss, "An Economic Theory of Suicide," *Journal of Political Economy* 82 (January–February 1974): 83–98.

74. Anselmo Suárez y Romero, *Francisco* (1875; reprint, Havana, 1970), p. 51.

75. Esteban Pichardo, *Geografía de la Isla de Cuba* (Havana, 1854), pp. 248–54.

76. Ramón Pina y Peñuelo, *Topografía médica de la Isla de Cuba* (Havana, 1855),

p. 16; Julio J. LeRiverend, *Patología especial de la Isla de Cuba, o tratado práctico de las enfermedades observadas en dicha Isla durante un periódo de treinta años* (Havana, 1858), p. lxiii. See also Carlos Finlay, "Apología del clima de Cuba," *Gaceta Médica de La Habana* 1 (December 1, 1878): 1–3.

77. "El verano y el invierno," *La Higiene* 1 (September 27, 1891): 2–3; "Algunos consejos de verano," *La Higiene* 9 (June 10, 1904): 1226; Francisco Figueras, *Cuba y su evolución colonial* (1907; reprint, Havana, 1959), pp. 381–82. See Antonio de Gordon de Acosta, "Higiene colonial en Cuba," *Anales de la Real Academia de Ciencias Médicas, Físicas y Naturales de La Habana* 31 (1894): 440–70, 476–507; and Diego Vicente Tejera, "La indolencia cubana," *Cuba Contemporánea* 28 (March 1922): 169–77.

78. Flora Basulto de Montoya, *Una niña bajo tres banderas (Memorias)* (Havana, 1954), p. 31; Manuel del Monte to Domingo del Monte, July 15, 1845, in Academia de la Historia de Cuba, *Centón epistolario de Domingo del Monte*, ed. Domingo Figarola-Caneda, Joaquín Llaverías y Martínez, and Manuel I. Mesa Rodríguez, 6 vols. (Havana, 1923–53), 6:222.

79. Condesa de Merlin, *Viaje a La Habana* (Havana, 1974), pp. 99–100.

CHAPTER FOUR

1. José R. Alvarez Díaz et al., *A Study on Cuba* (Coral Gables, 1965), pp. 96–97; Francisco López Segrera, *Sociología de la colonia y neocolonia cubana, 1510–1959* (Havana, 1989), p. 73; George B. Rea, "The Destruction of Sugar Estates in Cuba," *Harper's Weekly* 41 (October 16, 1897): 10–34; Jorge Quintana, "Lo que costó a Cuba la guerra de 1895," *Bohemia* 52 (September 11, 1960): 4–6, 107–8; U.S. Tariff Commission, *Effects of the Cuban Reciprocity Treaty* (Washington, D.C., 1929), p. 167.

2. U.S. War Department, *Report of the Census of Cuba 1899* (Washington, D.C., 1900); Cuba, Oficina del Censo, *Censo de la República de Cuba, 1907* (Havana, 1908); Cuba, Dirección General del Censo, *Censo de la República de Cuba, 1919* (Havana, 1921).

3. Cuba, Oficina del Censo, *Censo de la República de Cuba, 1907*, p. 39; Cuba, Dirección General del Censo, *Censo de la República de Cuba, 1919*, p. 83; P. G. Minneman, "Cuban Agriculture," *Foreign Agriculture* 6 (February 1942): 49–50; Byron White, *Azúcar amargo. Un estudio de la economía cubana* (Havana, 1954), p. 36. See also Raúl Maestri, *El latifundismo en la economía cubana* (Havana, 1929), p. 57; Raymond Leslie Buell, et al., *The Problems of the New Cuba* (New York, 1935), pp. 294–95.

4. Harry A. Franck, *Roaming Through the West Indies* (New York, 1920), p. 70.

5. See Carmelo Mesa-Lago, *The Labor Force, Employment, Unemployment and Underemployment in Cuba, 1899–1970* (Beverly Hills, 1972), pp. 5–34.

6. Carlos E. Forment, "Tiempo muerto," *Bohemia* 30 (September 4, 1938): 4; Erna Fergusson, *Cuba* (New York, 1946), p. 242. For a moving first-person account of daily life in the times of *tiempo muerto* see Francisco García, *Tiempo muerto: Memorias de un trabajador azucarero* (Havana, 1969).

7. Ana Núñez Machín, ed., *Memoria amarga del azúcar* (Havana, 1981), p. 72.

8. International Bank for Reconstruction and Development, *Report on Cuba* (Baltimore, 1951), p. 7; United Nations, Secretariat of the Economic Commission for Latin

America, *Economic Survey of Latin America, 1953* (New York, 1954), p. 161; Alberto León Riva, "Coyuntura económica y desempleo," *El Mundo*, March 30, 1954, p. A-10.

9. Jorge Ibarra, *Cuba: 1898–1958. Estructura y procesos sociales* (Havana, 1995), pp. 176–78; Leví Marrero, "Graduación-¿Luego que?" *El Mundo*, June 22, 1955, p. A-6; International Bank for Reconstruction and Development, *Report on Cuba*, p. 66; Henry Christopher Wallich, *Monetary Problems of an Export Economy: The Cuban Experience, 1914–1947* (Cambridge, 1950), pp. 195–253; Melchor W. Gastón, Oscar A. Echeverría, and René F. de la Huerta, *Por que reforma agraria* (Havana, 1957), p. 7; Archibald R. M. Ritter, *The Economic Development of Revolutionary Cuba: Strategy and Performance* (New York, 1974), p. 32; J. Merle Davis, *The Cuban Church in a Sugar Economy* (New York, 1942), p. 33; Gustavo Gutiérrez, *El empleo, el sub-empleo y el desempleo en Cuba* (Havana, 1958), p. 20; Carlos M. Castañeda, "¡665,000 cubanos sin trabajo," *Bohemia* 50 (February 16, 1958): sup. 16, 82–83.

10. The work of Richard Easterlin makes a persuasive case for the adversity befalling a high-fertility cohort generation as it reaches adulthood and seeks employment in a job market inadequate for a population bulge. The accompanying economic stress, Easterlin suggests, "will lead to deferment of marriage and, for those already married, to the [avoidance of] childbearing" and an increase in alienation, homicide, and suicide. See Richard A. Easterlin, "Relative Economic Status and the American Fertility Swing," in Eleanor Bernert Sheldon, ed., *Family Economic Behavior: Problems and Prospects* (Philadelphia, 1973), pp. 170–223; and Richard A. Easterlin, "The Conflict Between Aspirations and Resources," *Population and Development Review* 2 (September–December 1976): 417–25.

11. Cuba, Dirección General del Censo, *Censo de la República de Cuba, 1919*, p. 418; Cuba, *Memorias inéditas del censo de 1931* (Havana, 1978), p. 200. Conditions for Cuban workers were exacerbated by the vast immigration of hundreds of thousands of Spaniards and tens of thousands of Haitian and Jamaican contract workers who arrived in Cuba all through the early decades of the twentieth century. For Spanish immigration see Jordi Maluquer de Motes, *Nación y inmigración: los españoles en Cuba (ss. XIX y XX)* (Barcelona, 1992). On Haitian and Jamaican workers see Juan Pérez de la Riva, "Cuba y la migración antillana, 1900–1931," in Juan Pérez de la Riva et al., *La república neocolonial*, 2 vols. (Havana, 1975–79), 2:1–75.

12. Wallich, *Monetary Problems of an Export Economy*, p. 17.

13. "Food Supply Problem in Cuba Causing Anxiety," *Facts About Sugar* 6 (January 12, 1918): 22; Wallich, *Monetary Problems of an Export Economy*, p. 201; International Bank for Reconstruction and Development, *Report on Cuba*, pp. 726, 743; Luis Marino Pérez, "La actual situación económica de Cuba," *Reforma Social* 6 (March 1916): 521–31.

14. Herbert G. Squiers to John Hay, August 16, 1902, Despatches from U.S. Ministers to Cuba, 1902–6, General Records of the Department of State, Record Group 59, National Archives, Washington, D.C. (hereinafter cited as DS/RG 59).

15. Wallich, *Monetary Problems of an Export Economy*, pp. 157–58, 233.

16. Antonio Riccardi, "¿Por qué encarece más cada día el costo de la vida en Cuba?" *Carteles* 29 (August 1, 1948): 46.

17. Wyatt MacGaffey, "Social Structure and Mobility in Cuba," *Anthropological Quarterly* 34 (January 1961), p. 97; Lowry Nelson, *Rural Cuba* (Minneapolis, 1950), p. 201; W. Adolphe Roberts, *Lands of the Inner Sea* (New York, 1948), p. 47. In one study of 113 Cuban families during the mid-1930s, sociologist Carle Zimmerman identified the percent food expenditures of "poor" families at 59.8 percent; "comfortable" families at 54.7 percent; "well-to-do" at 49.1 percent; and "wealthy" at 35.9 percent. See Carle C. Zimmerman, *Consumption and Standards of Living* (New York, 1936), pp. 117–34.

18. Oscar Lewis, Ruth M. Lewis, and Susan M. Rigdon, *Neighbors: Living the Revolution: An Oral History of Contemporary Cuba* (Urbana, 1978), p. 173; Oscar Lewis, Ruth M. Lewis, and Susan M. Rigdon, *Four Men. Living the Revolution: An Oral History of Contemporary Cuba* (Urbana, 1977), p. 453; María de los Reyes Castillo, *Reyita, sencillamente*, ed. Daisy Rubiera Castillo (Havana, 1997), p. 104; Antonio Núñez Jiménez, ed., *La abuela* (Havana, 1998), p. 32.

19. Mercedes García, "La familia cubana: Su tipo y medio de vida," *Revista Bimestre Cubana* 42 (November–December 1938): 292–93.

20. Nelson, *Rural Cuba*, p. 216; Noel Navarro, ed., *Marcial Ponce: De central en central* (Havana, 1977), p. 72.

21. Alfonso de Granados, "La leontina de oro," *Bohemia* 27 (December 1, 1935): 7, 71.

22. *Bohemia* 30 (July 24, 1938): 38.

23. Reynaldo González, ed., *La fiesta de los tiburones* (Havana, 2001), p. 202; Jesús Masdeu, "Efectos de la política capitalística en la economía rural de Cuba," *Bohemia* 44 (June 29, 1952): 74; Lewis, Lewis, and Rigdon, *Neighbors*, pp. 157–58.

24. "¿Hay miseria en La Habana?" *La Higiene* 11 (February 10, 1906): 77–78.

25. Horacio Ferrer, "Apuntes sobre la ración alimenticia del obrero cubano," *Revista de Medicina y Cirugía de La Habana* 15 (July 10, 1910): 420–24.

26. Juan B. Fuentes, "Como puede intervenir el estado en el auxilio de las familias pobres. El seguro del obrero," *Revista de Medicina y Cirugía de La Habana* 13 (April 25, 1908): 155–56.

27. Lewis, Lewis, and Rigdon, *Four Men*, pp. 330–31.

28. Irene A. Wright, *Cuba* (New York, 1910), p. 95; Pelayo Casanova, "La mendicidad en La Habana," *Revista de la Facultad de Letras y Ciencias de la Universidad de La Habana* 35 (January–June 1925), pp. 256, 258. See also Rodolfo Arango, "La mendicidad infantil," *Bohemia* 27 (January 20, 1935): 14; and Juan M. Chailloux Cardona, *Síntesis de la vivienda popular* (Havana, 1945), pp. 106–55.

29. Carlos Martí, *Films cubanos. Oriente y Occidente* (Barcelona, 1915), pp. 76–77.

30. Masdeu, "Efectos de la política capitalística," p. 90.

31. *Bohemia* 49 (April 14, 1957): 63.

32. Juan de Zengotita to Department of State, September 20, 1955, 837.061/9-2055, Confidential State Department Central Files, Cuba, Internal Affairs, 1955–58, DS/RG 59.

33. Oscar Lewis, Ruth M. Lewis, and Susan M. Rigdon, *Four Women. Living the Revolution: An Oral History of Contemporary Cuba* (Urbana, 1977), p. 242; Andrés D. García Suárez, ed., *Los fundidores relatan su historia* (Havana, 1975), p. 53.

34. Sergio Aguirre, *Eco de caminos* (Havana, 1974), p. 398; José Antonio Taboadela, *Cuestiones económicas cubanas de actualidad* (Havana, 1929), p. 54; Gustavo Gutiérrez y Sánchez, *El problema económico de Cuba. Sus causas, sus posibles soluciones* (Havana, 1931); Buell, *Problems of the New Cuba*, pp. 52–54; Gerardo G. Peraza, *Machado, crímenes y horrores de un régimen* (Havana, 1933), pp. 71–160; "General Survey of Wages in Cuba, 1931 and 1932," *Monthly Labor Review* 35 (December 1932): 1403–4.

35. *Havana Post*, August 23, 1932, p. 4.

36. Buell, *Problems of the New Cuba*, p. 54; Antonio Penichet, "Desahuicios y suicidios en Cuba," *Bohemia* 27 (February 17, 1935): 22, 49–50.

37. International Bank for Reconstruction and Development, *Report on Cuba*, pp. 358–59. See also "La tragedia del desempleo," *Carteles* 32 (October 16, 1938): 21.

38. Armando Soto, "Mensaje a la juventud cubana," *Bohemia* 47 (September 18, 1955): 3, 134; Ernesto Ardura, "Raíces de la crisis cubana," *El Mundo*, January 11, 1953, p. A-6; Jorge L. Martí, "Juventud sin horizontes," ibid., May 7, 1957, p. B-8; Rubén Ortiz-Lamadrid, "Desempleo y tiempo muerto," ibid., April 9, 1953, p. A-6; José Lezama Lima, *Diarios*, ed. Ciro Bianchi Ross (México, 1994), pp. 107–8.

39. For a general discussion of theories of status change as a factor in suicide see Jack D. Douglas, *The Social Meanings of Suicide* (Princeton, 1967), pp. 109–23.

40. Luis Felipe Rodríguez, *La copa vacía* (Havana, 1926), p. 145; José Soler Puig, *El derrumbe* (Santiago de Cuba, 1964), p. 75.

41. "Proyecto de Código Civil," *Revista General de Derecho* 1 (November 30, 1883): 54. See also Dolores Larrúa de Quintana, "¿Cuál debe ser el ideal o aspiración del la mujer cubana?" *Revista de la Asociación Femenina de Camagüey* 3 (February 1923): 5; Arturo Montori, "La inferioridad jurídica de la mujer," *Cuba Contemporánea* 29 (May 1922): 106–36; K. Lynn Stoner, *From the House to the Streets: The Cuban Woman's Movement for Legal Reform, 1898–1940* (Durham, 1991), p. 41.

42. Manuel de Jesús Ponce, "Nuestra Ley Civil como expresión del desenvolvimiento armónico de la familia en el matrimonio," *Revista Cubana* 9 (1889): 27–31.

43. Ricardo M. Alemán, *Capacidad de la mujer en el derecho civil* (Havana, 1917), p. 4.

44. de los Reyes Castillo, *Reyita, sencillamente*, p. 62.

45. Lewis, Lewis, and Rigdon, *Neighbors*, p. 242.

46. Cristina Saralegui, *Cristina! My Life as a Blonde* (New York, 1998), p. 66; Lewis, Lewis, and Rigdon, *Neighbors*, p. 268.

47. The relationship between women in the wage labor force and female suicide is suggested in John F. Newman, Kenneth R. Whittemore, and Helen G. Newman, "Women in the Labor Force and Suicide," *Social Problems* 21 (Fall 1973): 220–30.

48. Emile Durkheim, *Suicide. A Study in Sociology*, trans. John A. Spaulding and George Simpson (New York, 1951), pp. 254–58. See also Stjepan G. Mestrovic, *Durkheim and Postmodern Culture* (New York, 1992); and Elwin H. Powell, "Occupation, Status, and Suicide: Toward a Redefinition of Anomie," *American Sociological Review* 23 (April 1958): 131–41.

49. See Lucas Alvarez Cerice, "El alcoholismo como causa de enagención mental," *Revista Médica Cubana* 2 (June 15, 1903): 325–29.

50. Antonio Barreras, "Estudios médico-legales: El suicidio en La Habana en el año de 1912," *Revista Médica Cubana*, 21 (June 1912): 323; Jorge LeRoy y Cassá, "Suicidio

por el fuego," *Revista de Medicina y Cirugía de La Habana* XII (June 10, 1907): 250; *Diario de la Marina*, June 16, 1918, p. 3.

51. Fernando Ortiz, "La decadencia cubana," *Revista Bimestre Cubana* 19 (January–February 1924): 17–44; *La Lucha*, August 2, 1920, p. 1; ibid., December 4, 1926, p. 2; Carlos M. Trelles, "El progreso y el retroceso de la república de Cuba," *Revista Bimestre Cubana* 18 (September–October 1923): 359–60; Raimundo Cabrera, "Llamamiento a los cubanos," *Revista Bimestre Cubana* 18 (March 1923): 81, 83. An examination of these years is thoughtfully present in Jorge Ibarra's essay "La conducta patógena como manifestación de la sensibilidad republicana," in Jorge Ibarra, *Un análisis psicosocial del cubano: 1898–1925* (Havana, 1985), pp. 235–64.

52. Penichet, "Desahuicios y suicidios en Cuba," pp. 22, 49–50.

53. Lewis, Lewis, and Rigdon, *Four Men*, p. 219; García, *Tiempo muerto*, pp. 57, 65–66.

54. Roberto P. de Acevedo, "Mujeres de 1939," *Bohemia* 31 (January 15, 1939): 6–9.

55. *Diario de la Marina*, February 16, 1930, p. 11; *La Lucha*, May 4, 1910, p. 7; *El Mundo*, June 26, 1957, p. A-4, and June 27, 1957, p. A-13.

56. *Diario de la Marina*, October 24, 1928, p. 19; ibid., June 13, 1929, p. 30; ibid., May 6, 1930, p. 23.

57. *La Lucha*, June 9, 1902, p. 1; *Diario de la Marina*, June 4, 1917, p. 8.

58. *La Lucha*, August 8, 1932, p. 12.

59. Ibid., September 27, 1910, p. 2; *Havana Post*, August 6, 1932, p. 4; *La Lucha*, March 27, 1910, p. 2.

60. *El Mundo*, November 18, 1954, p. 9.

61. *Havana Post*, April 27, 1932, p. 1; *La Lucha*, March 18, 1920, p. 2.

62. Arturo Alfonso Roselló, "Hablando con Carlos Hernández Ortiz, un inventor inválido," *Carteles* 16 (August 17, 1930): 36–37.

63. *El Mundo*, January 6, 1950, p. 19. See also "Suicidios por miseria," in Manuel Linares, *Un libro más. Fragmentos de 1881 a 1906* (Havana, 1906), pp. 108–9.

64. Carlos Franqui, *Diary of the Cuban Revolution*, trans. Georgette Felix, et al. (New York, 1980), p. 29; Miguel de Marcos, *Papaíto Mayarí* (1947; reprint Havana, 1997), pp. 339, 356.

65. *La Lucha*, December 23, 1926, p. 10; *Diario de la Marina*, June 6, 1921, p. 21; ibid., July 27, 1921, p. 4; ibid., December 10, 1921, p. 3; ibid., August 26, 1921, p. 13; *Havana Post*, April 26, 1921, p. 3.

66. *La Lucha*, March 28, 1921, p. 1; Marcos, *Papaíto Mayarí*, p. 339.

67. See República de Cuba, Secretaría de Sanidad y Beneficencia, *Boletín Oficial, 1928–1932* (Havana, 1934–36); and República de Cuba, Comisión Nacional de Estadística y Reformas Económicas, *Estadísticas. . . . 1929–1932* (Havana, 1929–32); República de Cuba, Comisión Nacional de Estadística y Reformas Económicas, *Estadísticas, 1931* (Havana, 1931), p. 123.

68. *Havana Post*, April 23, 1930, p. 1; Jorge LeRoy y Cassá, "Informe anual sanitario y demográfico del término municipal de La Habana correspondiente al año 1929: Carta de remisión," January 13, 1930, in República de Cuba, Sanidad y Beneficencia, *Boletín Oficial* 35 (January–June 1930): 9.

69. Antonio Penichet, "El problema social en Cuba," *Bohemia* 30 (June 5, 1938): 87.

70. *Diario de la Marina,* June 13, 1930, p. 12; ibid., February 27, 1930, p. 21; ibid., April 2, 1930, p. 14; ibid., May 10, 1931, p. 5; ibid., August 20, 1929, p. 19.

71. Ibid., May 11, 1930, p. 16; ibid., April 28, 1930, p. 19; ibid., September 18, 1930, p. 14; ibid., September 2, 1930, p. 14; ibid., November 16, 1931, p. 12; ibid., May 14, 1931, p. 1. A similar headline appeared again in Villaclara one year later. See ibid., April 14, 1932, p. 3.

72. *Azúcar* 4 (1932), Recorte Abad, vol. 9, no. 5, Biblioteca Nacional José Martí, Havana, Cuba.

73. *Diario de la Marina,* May 13, 1930, p. 1; ibid., June 7, 1929, p. 13; ibid., August 27, 1930, p. 12; ibid., October 28, 1930, p. 12; ibid., May 7, 1928, p. 13; ibid., February 25, 1932, p. 10; ibid., September 5, 1928, p. 28; ibid., November 22, 1931, p. 12.

74. Humberto Arenal, "En lo alto de un hilo," in *La vuelta en redondo* (Havana, 1962), p. 24; de los Reyes Castillo, *Reyita, sencillamente,* p. 18.

75. Mirta de la Torre Mulhare, "Sexual Ideology in Pre-Castro Cuba: A Cultural Analysis," (Ph.D. diss., University of Pittsburgh, 1969), p. 248.

76. Mariblanca Sabas Alomá, *Femenismo* (Havana, 1930), p. 55; Ana María Borrero, "El marido de la maestra," *Carteles* 24 (November 3, 1935): 35.

77. Renée Méndez Capote, *Memorias de una cubanita que nació con el siglo* (Havana, 1964), pp. 146–47. The subject of women and the family in the early republic is examined in Ana Vera Estrada, "Mujer, familia y pobreza en la sociedad republicana," *La Universidad de La Habana* 256 (Second Semester 2002): 95–106.

78. W. Fernández Flórez, "La moda como consecuencia," *Bohemia* 19 (March 13, 1927): 28; Gervasio G. Ruiz, "Mujeres que trabajan," *Carteles* 36 (October 16, 1955), p. 6.

79. Sabas Alomá, *Femenismo,* p. 50; José Soler Puig, *El derrumbe* (Santiago de Cuba, 1964), p. 39.

80. The correlation suggested in scholarship on domestic violence between the emotional stress associated with hard economic times and the incidence of household violence has far-reaching implications for Cuba. For representative studies see Carol O'Donnell and Heather Saville, "Domestic Violence and Sex and Class Inequality," in Carol O'Donnell and Jan Craney, eds., *Family Violence in Australia* (Melbourne, 1982), pp. 52–66; and the essays in Dorothy Ayers Counts, Judith K. Brown, and Jacquelyn C. Campbell, eds., *To Have and to Hit: Cultural Perspectives on Wife Beating,* 2nd ed. (Urbana, 1999).

81. Douglas Butterworth, *The People of Buena Ventura: Relocation of Slum Dwellers in Postrevolutionary Cuba* (Urbana, 1980), p. 10; de la Torre Mulhare, "Sexual Ideology in Pre-Castro Cuba," pp. 123–24; "Esperanza" to Juan Giró Rodés, December 29, 1953, *El Mundo,* January 8, 1954, p. B-2; Lewis, Lewis, and Rigdon, *Four Men,* p. 29.

82. Reinaldo Arenas, *Before Night Fall,* trans. Delores M. Koch (New York, 1993), p. 4.

83. Lewis, Lewis, and Rigdon, *Four Women,* pp. 134–37.

84. Ibid., p. 149.

85. These issues are thoughtfully examined in Jack P. Gibbs and Walter T. Martin, "A Theory of Status Integration and Its Relationship to Suicide," *American Sociological Review* 23 (April 1958): 140–47.

86. See Iliana Artiles de León, "Violencia contra la mujer," in Iliana Artiles de León, ed., *Violencia y sexualidad* (Havana, 1998), pp. 84–100.

87. Gustavo Pérez Firmat, *Next Year in Cuba* (New York, 1995), p. 117; Lewis, Lewis, and Rigdon, *Four Women*, pp. 250–52.

88. *La Lucha*, May 29, 1932, p. 8; *Havana Post*, May 28, 1932, p. 1.

89. Lewis, Lewis, and Rigdon, *Four Women*, pp. 144–45.

90. Stoner, *From the House to the Streets*, pp. 148–55.

91. Luis Rolando Cabrera, "La muerte de Delia González," *Bohemia* 50 (May 18, 1958): 78–79.

92. María Alvarez Ríos, ed., *Folklore del niño cubano* (Havana, 1961), p. 151. For a brief discussion of domestic violence in nineteenth-century Cuba see Raquel Vinat de la Mata, "¿Reinas del hogar? Mujeres en las unidades familiares cubanas del siglo XIX," *Universidad de La Habana* 256 (Second Semester 2002): 77–94.

93. One study of patients in state-operated and private mental health facilities in Havana during the late 1930s identified a total of 3,449 residents, of which 2,211 were identified as *blancos*, 666 as *negros*, 487 as *mestizos*, and 85 as *amarillos*. See José Angel Bustamante, *Las enfermedades mentales en Cuba* (Havana, 1948), pp. 173–299.

94. See Sabas Alomá, *Femenismo*, pp. 74–75.

95. The scholarship on domestic violence points generally to circumstances in working-class and middle-class households. See Craig M. Allen and Murray A. Strauss, "Resources, Power, and Husband-Wife Violence," in Murray A. Strauss and Gerald T. Hotaling, eds., *The Social Causes of Husband-Wife Violence* (Minneapolis, 1980), pp. 188–208; Shawn D. Haley and Ellie Braun-Haley, *War on the Home Front: An Examination of Wife Abuse* (New York, 2000), pp. 26–37.

96. For brief biographical sketches and photographs of women convicted of adultery see Israel Castellanos, *La delincuencia femenina en Cuba*, 3 vols. (Havana, 1929), 3:15–100.

97. "Desesperada del Vedado" to Juan Giró Rodés, July 3, 1953, *El Mundo*, July 15, 1953, p. B-4; "Desorientada de Camagüey" to Juan Giró Rodés, September 9, 1953, ibid., October 16, 1953, p. B-2; "Una Víctima del Destino" to Juan Giró Rodés, November 28, 1953, ibid., December 8, 1953, p. B-4.

98. Lewis, Lewis, and Rigdon, *Four Women*, p. 358.

99. "Dagmara to Juan Giró Rodés," October 15, 1954, *El Mundo*, November 7, 1954, p. C-7; Ofelia Rodríguez Acosta, *Sonata interrumpida* (México, 1943), p. 111.

100. "Una Mujer que Piensa" to Juan Giró Rodés, n.d., *El Mundo*, June 2, 1955, p. B-6.

101. Women "gain less than men in marriage," Emile Durkheim suggested, adding that "in itself conjugal society is harmful to the woman and aggravates her tendency to suicide. . . . In general, the wife profits less from family life than the husband." See Durkheim, *Suicide. A Study in Sociology*, pp. 184, 188, 275. See also Kathryn K. Johnson, "Durkheim Revisited: 'Why Do Women Kill Themselves?'" *Suicide and Life-Threatening Behavior* 9 (Fall 1979): 145–53. Lenore Radloff indicates that the rate of depression for married women—both housewives and women in the wage-labor force—is higher as compared with married men. "Marriage is better for men," Radloff af-

firms. See Leonore Radloff, "Sex Differences in Depression: The Effects of Occupation and Marital Status," *Sex Roles* 1 (September 1975): 249–65.

102. Lewis, Lewis, and Rigdon, *Four Women*, pp. 357, 360; Lewis, Lewis, and Rigdon, *Four Men*, pp. 72, 74.

103. "Una Esperanzada del Vedado" to Juan Giró Rodés, January 25, 1955, *El Mundo*, February 2, 1955, p. B-5; "Una Guajira que Sufre" to Juan Giró Rodés, March 4, 1954, ibid., March 11, 1954, p. B-6.

104. Leonor Martínez de Cervera, "¿Hasta cuando?" *La Mujer* 1 (March 15, 1930): 9; *El Mundo*, April 12, 1955, p. F-3; *Diario de la Marina*, March 18, 1918, p. 1.

105. Arístides Fernández Vázquez, "Caminaban sin prisa por la acera," in *Cuentos* (Havana, 1959), pp. 92–93, 97–98.

106. *Havana Post*, July 3, 1932, p. 4; and July 25, 1932, p. 4.

107. Lewis, Lewis, and Rigdon, *Neighbors*, p. 277.

108. Luis Rolando Cabrera, "Abatió a balazos a la mujer que decía amar," *Bohemia* 50 (May 30, 1958): 74–75, 94; *La Caricatura*, June 12, 1904, p. 4.

109. Jose Yglesias, *In the Fist of the Revolution: Life in a Cuban Country Town* (New York, 1968), pp. 268–69.

110. *El Mundo*, March 8, 1955, p. A-8; ibid., October 27, 1953, p. A-1; *Havana Post*, April 25, 1932, p. 1.

111. *Carteles* 24 (October 27, 1935): 24; *Havana Post*, May 4, 1932, p. 1.

112. *Havana Post*, July 25, 1932, p. 4.

113. *Diario de la Marina*, December 24, 1917, pp. 1, 7; *El Mundo*, August 13, 1953, p. A-8.

114. Clara Moreda, "El preso," in *Al caer de la tarde* (Havana, 1926), p. 209.

115. de la Torre Mulhare, "Sexual Ideology in Pre-Castro Cuba," p. 150. Writer Pedro José Cohucelo provided a sober description of women in working-class households: "The woman finds no relief. . . . She lives with dark uncertainty and without hope. She has to wash the clothing of her husband and children, she has to cook, to sew, to iron, and so much more. . . . She is eternally sacrificing herself for her children." Pedro José Cohucelo, *Apostolado de amor. Por la mujer, por la patria, por la raza* (Havana, 1925), pp. 64–65.

116. "Mater Dolorosa" to Juan Girón Rodés, December 12, 1953, *El Mundo*, December 24, 1953, p. B-6.

117. Lewis, Lewis, and Rigdon, *Four Women*, p. xxxvi; Lesbia Soravilla, *Cuando libertan los esclavos* (Havana, 1936), pp. 26–27.

118. Soravilla, *Cuando libertan los esclavos*, pp. 53–54, 60–70.

119. U.S. War Department, *Report of the Census of Cuba 1899*; Cuba, Oficina del Censo, *Censo de la República de Cuba, 1907*; Cuba, Dirección General del Censo, *Censo de la República de Cuba, 1919*.

120. *Havana Post*, April 25, 1932, p. 1.

121. Lewis, Lewis, and Rigdon, *Four Women*, p. 360.

122. "Una Guajira que Sufre" to Juan Giró Rodés; "Confidencialmente," *El Mundo*, March 11, 1954, p. B-6.

123. "Una Arrepentida" to Juan Giró Rodés, January 27, 1954, *El Mundo*, Febru-

ary 4, 1954, p. B-4; "Una Mujer to Juan Giró Rodés," April 5, 1954, ibid., April 14, 1954, p. B-6.

124. Miguel de Carrión, *La esfinge* ([1919], 1961; reprint, Havana, 1976), pp. 300, 308–9. *La esfinge* was completed in 1919 but not published until 1961.

125. *La Discusión*, August 19, 1893, p. 2; *Diario de la Marina*, August 9, 1920, p. 9; *La Caricatura*, February 2, 1902, p. 4; *Diario de la Marina*, May 8, 1916, p. 8; ibid., June 15, 1916, pp. 1, 15; ibid., August 21, 1919, p. 9; ibid., August 10, 1932, p. 12.

126. Pablo Medina, *Exiled Memories: A Cuban Childhood* (Austin, 1990), pp. 68–69; Marilyn Bobes, "Alguien tiene que llorar," in *Alguien tiene que llorar otra vez* (Havana, 2001), p. 34; Ena Lucía Portela, *El pájaro: pincel y tinta china* (Havana, 1998), pp. 24–25, 59.

127. "Amargada" to Juan Giró Rodés, January 20, 1955, *El Mundo*, March 13, 1955, p. B-4.

128. *La Caricatura*, March 30, 1902, p. 4; *Diario de la Marina*, March 8, 1932, p. 2.

129. José Bernal, "La 'inquilina' del Parque Maceo," *La Lucha*, August 18, 1929, p. 18.

130. *El Mundo*, January 11, 1952, p. 9; ibid., January 21, 1950, p. 19; *La Caricatura*, May 14, 1905, p. 4; *Havana Post*, November 18, 1928, p. 6; *El Mundo*, January 21, 1950, p. 19; *La Caricatura*, May 14, 1905, p. 4; *Havana Post*, November 18, 1928, p. 6.

131. *La Lucha*, June 12, 1926, p. 6.

132. *El Mundo*, April 9, 1955, p. A-7.

133. *Diario de la Marina*, January 4, 1930, p. 3; ibid., February 18, 1932, p. 10.

134. *La Lucha*, March 25, 1902, p. 2; Arenas, *Before Night Falls*, pp. 2–3.

135. *La Lucha*, August 2, 1920, p. 1; Ena Fabregas, "Por qué delinque la mujer en Cuba?" *Vanidades* 35 (September 1, 1957): 18.

136. "El extraño suicidio del reparto Almendares," *Carteles* 22 (September 28, 1941): 24; *La Caricatura*, March 20, 1904, p. 1; *Carteles* 31 (March 11, 1950), p. 16; *Diario de la Marina*, October 24, 1904, p. 2; *El Mundo*, October 6, 1954, p. A-1; *Diario de la Marina*, October 9, 1931, p. 1.

137. Juan Amador Rodríguez, "Bosquejo y recuento del año policiaco," *Bohemia* 44 (December 21, 1952): 174–75.

138. Judith N. Shklar, "Foreword," in Wolf Lepenies, *Melancholy and Society*, trans. Jeremy Gaines and Doris Jones (Cambridge, Mass., 1992), p. xvi; Jennifer Radden, ed., *The Nature of Melancholy* (New York, 2000), pp. 17–18.

139. Seán Desmond Healy, *Boredom, Self, and Culture* (Rutherford, N.J., 1984), pp. 10, 60, 64, 67, 92. Italics in original.

140. Marcelo Pogolotti, "El aburrimiento," *El Mundo*, June 5, 1954, p. A-6.

141. Lepenies, *Melancholy and Society*, p. 87.

142. Juan M. Dihigo, *Léxico cubano*, 2 vols. (Havana, 1928), 1:21; Esteban Rodríguez Herrera, *Léxico mayor de Cuba*, 2 vols. (Havana, 1958), 1:15.

143. Tomás L. Plasencia, "Notas relativas al suicidio en la circunscripción de La Habana," *Anales de la Real Academia de Ciencias Médicas, Físicas y Naturales de La Habana* 22 (1885): 423; Mario Muñoz Bustamante, "La tristeza cubana," *El Mundo Ilustrado* 2 (September 24, 1905): 462; Arenas, *Before Night Fall*, p. 34; Saralegui, *Cristina!*, p. 24; José Baró Pujol, "Radio y electricidad," *La Lucha*, January 3, 1929, p. 5.

144. Vicente Revuelta, *El juego de mi vida: Vicente Revuelta en escena*, ed. Esther Suárez Durán (Havana, 2001), p. 36; Regino E. Boti to José M. Poveda, November 19, 1912, in Sergio Chaple, ed., *Epistolario Boti-Poveda*, (Havana, 1977), p. 186.

145. Jorge Mañach, "Un pueblo suicida" was originally published in 1931 and subsequently republished in Jorge Mañach, *Pasado vigente* (Havana, 1939), pp. 101–4. See also Eladio Secades, "Aburrirse de la vida," *Bohemia* 33 (December 16, 1951): 204.

146. Segundo Corvisón, *En la guerra y en la paz* (Havana, 1939), p. 350; Loló de la Torriente, *Caballeros de la marea roja* (Havana, 1984), pp. 119–20.

147. Nicolás Dorr, *Los excéntricos de la noche*, 1996, in *Teatro insólito* (Havana, 2001), p. 35.

148. José María López Valdizón, "Las ánimas," in *La vida rota* (Havana, 1960), p. 10; Luis Rolando Cabrera, "Está aumentando día a día la desocupación en el país," *El Mundo*, March 28, 1954, p. A-12.

149. *El Mundo*, February 1, 1950, p. 24; *La Lucha*, February 21, 1910, p. 4; ibid., May 2, 1910, pp. 5, 7; ibid., April 9, 1926, p. 2.

150. Rolando Arteaga, "La navaja de afeitar," *Carteles* 38 (February 17, 1957): 66; "Chacumbele" was written by Alejandro Mustalier. The Machito recording is found on the album "Machito and his Afro-Cubans—1941," re-released in CD format by Palladium Latin Jazz and Dance Records, PCD-116, 1989.

151. Leonor Barraqué, "Aburrimiento," *Carteles* 23 (September 29, 1935): 4.

152. Elena Burke, "Aburrida," from the album *Canta lo Sentimental* (Egrem, CD 0069, 1993).

153. Ana María Simo, "Igual es igual a muerte," in Antón Arrufat and Fausto Masó, eds., *Nuevos cuentistas cubanos* (Havana, 1961), pp. 245–47.

154. Carmen Cordero, "Cansada de vivir," *Bohemia* 27 (October 20, 1935): 20.

155. Isabel Carrasco Tomasetti, "El dolor de vivir," *Bohemia* 18 (August 22, 1926), p. 27; Isabel Carrasco Tomasetti, "Melancolía," *Revista de la Asociación Femenina de Camagüey* 3 (September 1923): 5.

156. Miguel Cofiño, "Magda, el mar, el aire," in *Un pedazo del mar y una ventana* (Havana, 1979), p. 55; Ofelia Rodríguez Acosta, *En la noche del mundo* (Havana, 1940), p. 55; Rosario Sansores, "Inquietudes," *Bohemia* 10 (October 12, 1919): 4.

157. The three poems—"Escepticismo," "Neurosis," and "Cansancio"—appear under the title of "De Graziella Garbalosa," in *Social* 5 (February 1920): 22.

158. Lesbia Soravilla, *El dolor de vivir* (Havana, n.d.), pp. 58–59; Nicolás Dorr, *Mediodía cantante*, in *Dramas de imaginación y urgencia* (Havana, 1987), pp. 330, 339.

159. Zoé Valdés, *Café nostalgia* (Barcelona, 1997), pp. 163–64.

160. Frederick A. Ober, *Our West Indian Neighbors* (New York, 1904), p. 116; Medina, *Exiled Memories*, p. 33; Ofelia Fernández de Hernández Corujo, "Recuerdos de ayer," *Vanidades* 13 (August 15, 1944): 13; Samuel Feijóo, *Juan Quinquín en Pueblo Mocho* (Havana, 1964), pp. 80–81.

161. Julio J. LeRiverend, *Patología especial de la Isla de Cuba, o tratado práctico de las enfermedades observadas en dicha Isla durante un periódo de treinta años* (Havana, 1858), pp. LXXV–LXXI. For a useful general discussion of the condition of women in late-nineteenth-century Cuba see de la Mata, "¿Reina del hogar?" pp. 77–94.

162. "Movimiento general de asiladas en el Hospital de Dementes de Cuba, según

la raza a que pertenecen y la enfermedad mental que padecen, durante el mes de diciembre del año . . . ," 1913–26, in Castellanos, *La delincuencia femenina en Cuba*, 2:n.p. See also Bustamante, *Las enfermedades mentales en Cuba*, pp. 126–70.

163. *La Caricatura*, May 7, 1905, p. 4; ibid., October 7, 1906, p. 4.

164. *La Lucha*, May 7, 1910, p. 2; *Diario de la Marina*, January 21, 1916, p. 9; ibid., January 24, 1916, p. 5; *La Lucha*, April 23, 1920, p. 2; ibid., April 30, 1920, p. 1; Inspector Serafín Robaina to Jefe, Policía Especial, Matanzas, January 8, 1945, Fondo Gobierno Provincial de Matanzas Neocolonial, Legajo 21, Expediente 858, Archivo Histórico Provincial de Matanzas, Matanzas, Cuba.

165. *Diario de la Marina*, April 6, 1920, p. 7; *La Lucha*, August 5, 1910, p. 4.

166. *La Lucha*, September 3, 1903, p. 1; ibid., July 19, 1926, p. 11; *Diario de la Marina*, January 18, 1904, p. 4.

167. *La Lucha*, October 5, 1926, p. 9; ibid., April 3, 1930, p. 10; *El Mundo*, April 15, 1954, p. A-10; *La Lucha*, April 28, 1929, p. 8.

CHAPTER FIVE

1. See Armando de Córdova y Quesada, *La locura en Cuba* (Havana, 1940), pp. 38–42, 133–38; Gustavo López, "Higiene general de la locura," *Crónica Médico-Quirúrgica de La Habana* 21 (1895): 591–607; Gustavo López, "La locura palúdica," *Revista Científica de la Academia de Ciencias Médicas, Físicas y Naturales de La Habana* 34 (1898): 65–74; Gustavo López, "Los locos en Cuba: Apuntes históricos," *Revista Científica de la Academia de Ciencias Médicas, Físicas y Naturales de La Habana* 36 (1899): 83–112; Antonio de Gordon y de Acosta, "Sobre el suicidio," *Revista Científica de la Academia de Ciencias Médicas, Físicas y Naturales de La Habana* 44 (1908): 826–29; Rafael Pérez Vento, "Crimen y locura," *Revista de Medicina y Cirugía* 15 (December 10, 1910): 727–36; José A. Malberti, "Los dementes de Cuba," *Boletín Oficial de la Secretaría de Sanidad y Beneficencia* 9 (January 1913): 147–60.

2. Luis Marrero, "El suicidio," *Habana Católica* 2 (February 10, 1895): 42–44; and *Habana Católica* 2 (February 17, 1895): 50–52.

3. José B. Gálvez, "El suicidio á los ojos del moralista," *Revista de La Habana* 5 (1856): 30–32, 68–70, 80–82.

4. Félix Varela, *Lecciones de filosofía*, 5th. ed., 2 vols. (1841; reprint, Havana, 1961): 1:263; Antonio Angulo y Heredia, "El suicidio," *Brisas de Cuba* 1 (1855), pp. 27–28. See also "Frecuencia en los suicidios," *Repertorio Médico-Habano* (2nd ser.) 1 (September 1, 1842): 53–55.

5. Alvaro de la Iglesia, *Hojas sueltas. Artículos de propaganda católica (Aprobado por la censura eclesiástica)* (Matanzas, 1893), pp. 37–38. For a general discussion of Catholicism and suicide see Franco Ferracuti, "Suicide in a Catholic Country," in Edwin S. Shneidman and Norman L. Farberow, eds., *Clues to Suicide* (New York, 1957), pp. 70–78.

6. José de la Luz y Caballero, *Aforismos y apuntaciones*, ed. Roberto Agramonte (1847; reprint, Havana, 1945), pp. 242–43.

7. Nicolás Tanco Armero, *Viaje de Nueva Granada a China y de China a Francia* (Paris, 1864), p. 52.

8. José Antonio Saco, "La estadística criminal de Cuba en 1862," *La América*, Janu-

ary 12, 1864, p. 5. Traveling between Havana and Matanzas as early as 1831–32, Mary Gardner Lowell was informed by one local resident that "the Catholic religion here . . . has lost much of its influence among the Spaniards." And at another point: "In fact there is a great falling off in observances of religion." See Mary Gardner Lowell, *New Year in Cuba: Mary Gardner Lowell's Travel Diary, 1831–1832*, ed. Karen Robert (Boston, 2003), pp. 52, 68.

9. Tomás L. Plasencia, "Notas relativas al suicidio en la circunscripción de La Habana," *Anales de la Real Academia de Ciencias Médicas, Físicas y Naturales de La Habana* 22 (1885): 412–13.

10. *Diario de la Marina*, June 16, 1918, p. 3. See also Benjamín de Céspedes, "Los suicidas por amor," *La Habana Elegante* 8 (February 9, 1890), p. 6.

11. Richard Pattee and the Inter-American Committee, *Catholic Life in the West Indies* (New York, 1946), pp. 18–19, 31.

12. Writing as early as 1899, José Antonio González Lanuza complained: "Cuba has been liberated from Spain in every regard. But from the ecclesiastical point of view, the extensive territory that is represented by the Dioceses of Havana continues to belong to Spain. It is truly a Spanish 'ecclesiastical province' in every regard. . . . Is it possible to believe that anything constructive is possible with a Bishop and a Spanish clergy who blessed [General Valeriano] Weyler and his soldiers and who publicly and solemnly beseeched God [during the war for independence] to deliver our destruction? No, these men cannot be anything other than a source of conflict." See José Antonio González Lanuza to Gonzalo de Quesada, August 20, 1899, in Gonzalo de Quesada, *Epistolario*, ed. Gonzalo de Quesada y Miranda, 2 vols. (Havana, 1948), 1:237–39. A survey in the mid-1940s reported that nearly 85 percent of all priests in Cuba (432 out of 514) were foreigners, mostly Spaniards. See Gustavo Amigó, "La Iglesia Católica en Cuba," *Revista Javeriana* 18 (September 1947): 171.

13. Oscar A. Echevarría Salvat, *La agricultura cubana, 1934–1966: Régimen social, productividad y nivel de vida del sector agrícola* (Miami, 1971), pp. 13–17.

14. Francisco Dorta-Duque, *Justificando una reforma agraria. Estudio analítico-descriptivo de las estructuras agrarias en Cuba* (Madrid, 1959), p. 48.

15. Wyatt MacGaffey and Clifford R. Barnett, *Twentieth-Century Cuba: The Background of the Castro Revolution* (Garden City, N.Y., 1962), pp. 236, 243; Mercedes García, "La familia cubana: Su tipo y medio de vida," *Revista Bimestre Cubana* 42 (November–December 1938): 289. See also Francisco Figueras, *Cuba y su evolución colonial* (1907; reprint, Havana, 1959), pp. 254–71.

16. Dorta-Duque, *Justificando una reforma agraria*, p. 48; Melchor W. Gastón, Oscar A. Echeverría, and René F. de la Huerta, *Por que reforma agraria* (Havana, [1957]), p. 36.

17. J. Merle Davis, *The Cuban Church in a Sugar Economy* (New York, 1942), pp. 32, 49; Echevarría Salvat, *La agricultura cubana, 1934–1966*, p. 14; Leslie Dewart, *Christianity and Revolution: The Lesson of Cuba* (New York, 1963), pp. 92, 94; Charles E. Chapman, *A History of the Cuban Republic* (New York, 1927), p. 604.

18. Emile Durkheim, *Suicide: A Study in Sociology*, trans. John A. Spaulding and George Simpson (New York, 1951), pp. 169–70, 354.

19. Diego A. de Fuentes, "Discurso leído en la Academia de Derecho de la Universidad," November 30, 1865, *La Idea* 1 (May 10, 1866): 279–80.

20. David Lester propounds a "critical mass theory," suggesting that "when the rate of people committing suicide in a society reaches a high level, then the behavior becomes increasingly common because, among other reasons, it is seen as socially more acceptable." See David Lester, *Why People Kill Themselves. A 1990s Summary of Research Findings on Suicidal Behavior*, 3rd ed. (Springfield, Ill., 1992), pp. 77–78.

21. M. Velilla de Solórzano, "Los que se matan," *Carteles* 37 (August 1, 1954), p. 62.

22. See Gerardo del Valle, "La enfermedad del suicidio," *Bohemia* 23 (November 15, 1931): 11–12.

23. *Heraldo de Cuba*, December 17, 1928, p. 6.

24. *Havana Post*, November 11, 1925, p. 3.

25. The linkage between suicide rates and cultural norms generally is explored in Barbara J. Snyder, "A Note on the Importance of Cultural Factors in Suicide Studies," *Suicide and Life-Threatening Behavior* 7 (Winter 1977): 230–35; Robert Agnew, "The Approval of Suicide: A Social Psychological Model," *Suicide and Life-Threatening Behavior* 28 (Summer 1998): 205–25.

26. Antonio Penichet, *La vida de un pernicioso* (Havana, 1919), p. 178.

27. Pedro Juan Gutiérrez, *Dirty Havana Trilogy*, trans. Natasha Wimmer (1998; reprint, New York, 2002), p. 36; Juan Francisco Pulido Martínez, "Mario in the Heaven's Gate," in *Mario in the Heaven's Gate y otros cuentos suicidas* (Pinar del Rio, 1999), p. 9.

28. Marilyn Bobes, "Alguien tiene que llorar," in *Alguien tiene que llorar otra vez* (Havana, 2001), p. 18.

29. This letter was published in the Mariblanca Sabas Alomá article, "¡Mátalo . . . ! ¡Salva tu honor!" *Carteles* 16 (March 2, 1930): 20, 32.

30. Mariblanca Sabas Alomá, *Femenismo* (Havana, 1930), p. 50; Guillermo de Sanz, "La pecadora," *Bohemia* 19 (July 17, 1927): 57.

31. Margot García Maldonado, "Margot García Maldonado relata a *Bohemia* las memorias de su vida," *Bohemia* 30 (July 3, 1938): 7, 55.

32. Norbert Elias, *Power and Civility: The Civilizing Process*, trans. Edmund Jephcott (New York, 1982), pp. 292–93.

33. *Havana Post*, June 27, 1932, p. 4.

34. Mirta de la Torre Mulhare, "Sexual Ideology in Pre-Castro Cuba: A Cultural Analysis," (Ph.D. diss., University of Pittsburgh, 1969), pp. 161–62.

35. This theme is examined for the nineteenth century in Verena Martínez-Alier, *Marriage Class and Colour in Nineteenth-Century Cuba*, 2nd ed. (Ann Arbor, 1989), pp. 103–19. In her ethnographic study of one Cuban family, Mirta de la Torre Mulhare noted: "Lola's virginity is a matter of family honor." See de la Torre Mulhare, "Sexual Ideology in Pre-Castro Cuba," p. 171.

36. "Rosa con Espinas" to Juan Giró Rodés, April 19, 1956, *El Mundo*, April 26, 1956, p. B-2; "Una Atormentada" to Juan Giró Rodés, July 10, 1955, ibid., July 23, 1955, p. B-4; María de los Reyes Castillo, *Reyita, sencillamente*, ed. Daisy Rubiera Castillo (Havana, 1997), p. 29.

37. Suicide as punishment is examined in Karl Menninger, "Expression and Punishment," in Edwin S. Shneidman, ed., *On the Nature of Suicide* (San Francisco, 1969), pp. 68–73.

38. Carlos Loveira, *La última lección* (Havana, 1924), p. 187; *La Lucha*, June 4, 1893, p. 2; *Diario de la Marina*, August 29, 1931, p. 3.

39. María Elena Cruz Varela, "Despedida del ángel," in *Balada de la sangre/Ballad of the Blood*, trans. Mairym Cruz-Bernal and Deborah Digges (Hopewell, N.J., 1996), p. 103.

40. Velilla de Solórzano, "Los que se matan," p. 63.

41. Jorge LeRoy y Cassá, "Suicidio por el fuego," *Revista de Medicina y Cirugía de La Habana* XII (June 10, 1907): 250. See also Antonio del Sol, *Ensayo histórico sobre las quemaduras en Cuba* (Havana, 1979), p. 37.

42. *Havana Post*, March 2, 1932, p. 1.

43. *La Lucha*, February 21, 1910, p. 4.

44. Lisandro Otero, *La situación* (Havana, 1963), pp. 78–79.

45. Ricardo Pau-Llosa, "Mulata," in *Cuba* (Pittsburgh, 1993), p. 61.

46. Juan Amador Rodríguez, "Porque se queman las mujeres," *Bohemia* 44 (June 1, 1952): 28–29, 112–13.

47. Humberto Rodríguez Tomeu, "La musa," in *El hoyo* (Havana, 1950), p. 144; Marcelo Pogolotti, *Estrella Molina* (Havana, 1946), p. 32; Víctor Muñoz, "El suicida," in *Junto al capitolio (Croquis de la vida americana)* (Havana, 1919), pp. 57–61.

48. Humberto Arenal, *The Sun Beats Down* (New York, 1959), p. 62; Virgilio Piñera, *Aire frío*, 1962, in Ana Cairo Ballester, ed., *Letras: Cultura en Cuba*, 7 vols. (Havana, 1989–92), 3:107; Virgilio Piñera, "Insomnia," in *Cold Tales*, trans. Mark Schafer (Hygiene, Colo., 1987), p. 115.

49. Pita Rodríguez, "El chaleco del loco," *Bohemia* 23 (September 20, 1931): 55, 66–67; "Premio Nacional de Literatura: Biografía," <http://www.cubaliteraria.com/anto narrufat/> (2000); Iván Colás Costa, *¡De película!* (Havana, 1991), pp. 48–49.

50. M. Alvarez Marrón, "El juez de los divorcios," in *Burla-burlando. Colección de artículos festivos y de costumbres* (Havana, 1920), p. 1.

51. See Tom Meany, "Play Ball, Amigos," *Collier's*, January 20, 1951, pp. 34–35.

52. *Diario de la Marina*, December 10, 1932, p. 4; ibid., May 15, 1918, p. 5; ibid., July 25, 1932, p. 11; *La Caricatura*, June 12, 1904, p. 4; *Diario de la Marina*, June 15, 1918, p. 2; ibid., February 25, 1904, p. 4; ibid., March 25, 1928, p. 4; ibid., October 22, 1929, p. 23; ibid., March 4, 1929, p. 11.

53. Mario Guiral Moreno, "Aspectos censurables del carácter cubano," *Cuba Contemporánea* 4 (February 1914): 125.

54. Antonio Gómez, "El choteo," in *Reflejos (Estudios literarios)* (Havana, 1902), pp. 115–18; Jorge Mañach, *Indagación del choteo* (Havana, 1936); de la Torre Mulhare, "Sexual Ideology in Pre-Castro Cuba," p. 83. See also Manuel Márquez Sterling, *Alrededor de nuestra psicología* (Havana, 1906), pp. 60–71.

55. Fred Cutter, *Art and the Wish to Die* (Chicago, 1983), p. 258.

56. D. J. Enright, "Where There's Life," *Times Literary Supplement*, May 18, 2001, p. 5.

57. Antonio Abalos, "Mi suicidio por amor," *La Lucha*, September 10, 1928, p. 3; Juan de Dios Mohedano, "Un suicidio," *Bohemia* 22 (May 24, 1930), p. 74; Manuel Pinos, "La prórroga de un suicidio," *Bohemia* 19 (September 4, 1927): 53.

58. B. Jiménez Perdomo, "Hay que reformar el suicidio," *Bohemia* 20 (January 8, 1928): 18.

59. John J. Johnson, *Latin America in Caricature* (Austin, 1980), p. 26.

60. On Ignacio Cervantes see Glenn Jenks, "Ignacio Cervantes: Piano Dancer," <http://www.stevenestrella.com> (August 27, 2002); José Martí, "Cuba y la primera república española," February 15, 1873, in José Martí, *Obras completas*, 5 vols. (Caracas, 1964), 1:48; José Martí, "El tratado comercial entre los Estados Unidos y México," March 1883, ibid., 3:308; *La Lucha*, January 24, 1891, p. 2.

61. Pablo Medina, "Un poeta cubano en Nueva York," *La Habana Elegante*, Segunda Epoca (August 2002), <http://www.habanaelegante.com> (August 2002); *La Lucha*, December 2, 1929, p. 1; Eladio Secades, "Mangas de camisa," *Bohemia* 45 (August 23, 1953): 55; M. Millares Vázquez, "Hacia el suicidio," *El Mundo*, November 10, 1955, p. A-6; Enrique Barbarrosa, *El proceso de la república* (Havana, 1911), p. 198; María Teresa C.M., "Suicidio," *Bohemia* 20 (July 1, 1928): 15.

62. "Una ley buena que se torna suicida," *Carteles* 29 (March 21, 1937): 19; "Técnica presupuestal suicida," *Carteles* 29 (August 20, 1937): 17; "La tragedia del azúcar, o un pueblo que quiere suicidarse," *Bohemia* 26 (March 25, 1934): 12–13.

63. Two versions of this editorial were published: "Rectificación o suicidio," *La Lucha*, April 20, 1921, p. 2; "Rectification or Suicide," *La Lucha* [English supplement], April 4, 1921, p. 1.

64. "Laborantismo suicida," *Bohemia* 28 (December 20, 1936): 35; Diego Boada y Boada, "Suicidio," *El Mundo*, November 1, 1951, p. 23; Otto Meruelo, "Pobreza mental y política," ibid., July 26, 1957, p. A-6.

65. Luis E. Aguilar León, *Cuba: Conciencia y revolución* (Miami, 1972), pp. 148, 185; Jesús Díaz, "Los suicidios de la burguesía cubana y el dilema del futuro," *Revista Encuentro de la Cultura Cubana* 23 (Winter, 2001–2): 86; José Soler Puig, *En el año de enero* (Havana, 1963), p. 185; María del Carmen Boza, *Scattering the Ashes* (Tempe, Ariz., 1998), p. 276; Delfín Rodríguez Silva, *Memorias de un periodista: Protagonistas y testigos* (New York, 1984), p. 181.

66. Fidel Castro, "El imperialismo yanqui sufre en América su primera gran derrota," April 23, 1961, in *El pensamiento de Fidel Castro*, 2 vols. (Havana, 1983), 1:170; "Exclusive Interview with Fidel Castro," Foreign Broadcast Information Service, published originally in *Clarín* (Buenos Aires), January 2, 1994, p. 28.

67. This folk account is conveyed in de la Torre Mulhare, "Sexual Ideology in Pre-Castro Cuba," p. 223.

68. In the play "La familia de Benjamín García" by Gerardo Fernández, Rosa threatens her parents: "I don't know why you brought me into this world. To suffer, nothing more. . . . Any day now I will get into the bath tub and slash my wrist (*me abro las venas*)." See Gerardo Fernández, "La familia de Benjamín García," in Rine Leal, ed., *Seis obras de teatro cubano* (Havana, 1989), p. 243.

69. The Chacumbele saying is of unknown origins. One of the earliest references to Chacumbele is found in the song "Chacumbele," written by Alejandro Mustalier, with the lyric: "Ay, Chacumbele, él mismito se mató / el negro se envenenó / él mismito se mató." For one recording of "Chacumbele" refer to the album "Machito and

his Afro-Cubans—1941," rereleased in CD format by Palladium Latin Jazz and Dance Records (PCD-116, 1989).

70. See Darío Espina Pérez, *Diccionario de cubanísimos* (Barcelona, 1972); José Sánchez-Boudy, *Diccionario de cubanísimos más usuales. (Come habla el cubano)* (Barcelona, 1978); Argelio Santiesteban, *El habla popular cubano de hoy* (Havana, 1982); Carlos Paz Pérez, *Diccionario cubano de términos populares y vulgares* (Havana, 1994).

71. Amalia Simoni to Ignacio Agramonte, April 30, 1873, in Ignacio Betancourt Agramonte, *Ignacio Agramonte y la revolución cubana* (Havana, 1926), p. 515; Oscar Lewis, Ruth M. Lewis, and Susan M. Rigdon, *Four Women. Living the Revolution: An Oral History of Contemporary Cuba* (Urbana, Ill., 1977), pp. 4–5, 17. For a general discussion of the relationship between childhood and the shaping of self-destructive impulses by parents see David Lester, *Suicide as a Learned Behavior* (Springfield, Ill., 1987), pp. 5–60; and Martin Gold, "Suicide, Homicide, and the Socialization of Aggression," *American Journal of Sociology* 63 (May 1958): 651–61.

72. Evelio Grillo, *Black Cuban, Black American: A Memoir* (Houston, 2000), p. 23.

73. *Diario de la Marina*, July 8, 1901, p. 4; *El Mundo*, August 4, 1953, p. A-10.

74. Beatriz Rivera, *Playing with Light* (Houston, 2000), pp. 3, 5, 99.

75. Antonio Estévez Carrasco, "Los suicidios," *Revista de la Asociación Femenina de Camagüey* 5 (December 1925): 6.

76. M. Millares Vázquez, "Los que van al suicidio," *El Mundo*, February 5, 1956, p. A-8.

77. de la Torre Mulhare, "Sexual Ideology in Pre-Castro Cuba," pp. 207, 210, 216–17, 223–25.

78. Discussion with Virginia Schofield, October 26, 2001, Washington, D.C.

79. Boza, *Scattering the Ashes*, p. 89.

80. *El Mundo*, July 8, 1955, p. A-9; *La Lucha*, September 15, 1910, p. 8; *Diario de la Marina*, February 14, 1916, p. 16. See also Waldo Medina, "Se ha suicidado un niño," *El Mundo*, July 24, 1953, p. A-6.

81. *Diario de la Marina*, November 22, 1929, p. 20; ibid., March 20, 1916, p. 6; *La Caricatura*, September 24, 1905, p. 4; *Diario de la Marina*, April 7, 1919, p. 16.

82. *La Lucha*, December 25, 1903, p. 2.

83. Ibid., October 27, 1920, p. 1.

84. Ibid., May 20, 1920, p. 2; *Diario de la Marina*, January 23, 1901, p. 4; ibid., September 8, 1931, p. 12; ibid., August 19, 1932, p. 3.

85. *La Lucha*, September 27, 1910, p. 2; *El Mundo*, March 16, 1958, p. A-11; *Diario de la Marina*, October 22, 1928, p. 3.

86. The general phenomenon of the double-suicide pact is examined in K. Ohara and D. Reynolds, "Love-Pact Suicide," *Omega* 1 (August 1970): 159–66. For discussion of the phenomenon in Cuba see Eladio Secades, "Suicidio por amor," *Bohemia* 49 (November 10, 1957): 24.

87. Oscar Lewis, Ruth M. Lewis, and Susan M. Rigdon, *Four Men. Living the Revolution: An Oral History of Contemporary Cuba* (Urbana, Ill., 1977), p. 187; "La Estudiante que Sufre en Silencio" to Juan Giró Rodés, September 1, 1954, *El Mundo*, September 4, 1954, p. B-6.

88. Ofelia Domínguez, *50 años de una vida* (Havana, 1971), p. 60.

89. *La Caricatura*, July 2, 1905, p. 4; *La Lucha*, August 14, 1895, p. 2; *La Caricatura*, September 6, 1903, p. 1; *Havana Post*, January 20, 1932, p. 1. See also Nicolás Rivero, "Suicidio de un niño de quince años," in *Actualidades (1903–1919)* (Havana, 1929), p. 181.

90. *La Lucha*, September 10, 1910, p. 2; ibid., March 21, 1902, p. 2.

91. "Cuando los padres se oponen," *Bohemia* 47 (February 27, 1955): 52; Rolando R. Pérez, "Un pacto suicida y un crimen que no es un crimen," *Carteles* 35 (February 27, 1955): 29–30; *El Mundo*, August 31, 1916, p. 1. See also Eloy C. Merino Brito, "Pacto suicida," *El Mundo*, May 30, 1956, p. A-9. For one sensational account see Enrique Gutiérrez and Generoso Funcasta, "'No me pesa morir porque me voy con Concha,'" *Carteles* 35 (October 3, 1954): 46–48.

92. Luis Rolando Cabrera, "Hurgando en los raíces del suicidio," *Bohemia* 48 (July 28, 1956): 52.

93. Héctor Quintero, *El premio flaco*, in *Teatro* (Havana, 1983), p. 152.

94. Abelardo Estorino, *Morir del cuento*, in Rine Leal, ed., *Seis obras de teatro cubano* (Havana, 1989), p. 97.

95. Rosario Sansores, "El timo del suicidio," *Bohemia* 20 (October 7, 1928): 13, 65; Herminio Pola, "Mi suicidio," *Bohemia* 21 (December 1, 1929): 74–75, 79; Raimundo Gantes, "Un suicidio," *Bohemia* 24 (July 3, 1932): 66, 71.

96. For a general examination of the gender dimensions of suicide see Raymond Jack, *Women and Attempted Suicide* (East Sussex, U.K., 1992); Silvia Sara Canetto and Isaac Sakinofsky, "The Gender Paradox in Suicide," *Suicide and Life-Threatening Behavior* 28 (Spring 1998): 1–23.

97. *Diario de la Marina*, July 26, 1916, p. 9.

98. *Havana Post*, March 14, 1932, p. 5.

99. Rosa con Espinas to Juan Giró Rodés, April 19, 1956, *El Mundo*, April 26, 1956, p. B-2; Flora Basulto de Montoya, "Gato con guantes," *Vanidades* 14 (October 1, 1944): 22, 42.

100. Domínguez, *50 años de una vida*, pp. 65, 67; Irene Wright, *Cuba* (New York, 1910), p. 101.

101. María Alvarez Ríos, "La recaída," *Vanidades* 15 (February 1, 1945): 22; Gloria Parrado, *Bembeta y Santa Rita*, in *Triptico* (Havana, 1984), pp. 72, 89.

102. Rosa con Espinas to Juan Giró Rodés, April 19, 1956, *El Mundo*, April 26, 1956, p. B-2.

103. Gervasio G. Ruiz, "Pagó su propio sepelio antes de intentar suicidarse," *Carteles* 30 (September 4, 1949): 45.

104. *El Mundo*, June 3, 1954, p. D-3; *La Lucha*, November 22, 1928, p. 12; ibid., August 10, 1910, p. 1; ibid., August 24, 1910, p. 1; ibid., May 6, 1910, p. 4.

105. Olivastro de Rodas, "Suicida por amor," *Minerva* 6 (April 1914): 14–15.

106. See Gladys Lara, "El modelo comunicativo del bolero," in Alicia Valdés Canter, ed., *Nosotros y el bolero* (Havana, 2000), pp. 199–202.

107. Celia Cruz, "Boleros" (Polydor, 314 521 210-2, 1993).

108. These recordings have been reissued in compact disc format and are found in Olga Guillot, "50 años" (Musart, CDN 610, 1991); Xiomara Alfaro, "Lo mejor de

Xiomara Alfaro: Grabado en La Habana, Cuba, 1956–1957" (Siboney/RCA Victor, CD 74321-177721-2, 1993); Rosita Fornes in "Ayer . . . Hoy / Yesterday . . . Today" (Panart/Rodven Records, CD 5171, 1994); María Ochoa y Corazón de Son, "Así quiero vivir" (Blue Jacket, CD 5039, 2000).

109. Celia Cruz, "Irresistible" (Orfeon/Sony 11391, 1995); Celina González, "Alborada guajira" (Egrem/CD 238, 1997); Omara Portuondo, "Dos gardenias" (Tumi/CD 105, n.d.); Olga Guillot, "Se me olvidó otra vez" (Sony/CDB 81138, 1993).

110. Candito Ruiz, "Si a tú lado no estoy" (Havana: Peer y Compañía, n.d.); José Sláter Badán, "Es al amanecer" (Havana: Peer y Compañía, n.d.); María Teresa Vera sings "Ven a verme" with the Sexteto Occidente, released originally on the Columbia label in 1926 and reissued in CD format as "Hot Music From Cuba, 1907–1936" (Harlequin, HQ CD 23, 1993); Leopoldo Ulloa, "Moriré de amor," in Helio Orovio, ed., *300 boleros de oro* (Havana, 1991), p. 196.

111. Nicolás Dorr, *Los excéntricos de la noche*, 1996, in *Teatro insólito* (Havana, 2001), p. 17.

112. Víctor Colomer, "'Moncho,' sus boleros: 'Los cantantes tenemos más oportunidad de ligar,'" <http://web.drac.com> (2002).

113. Pachito Alonso, "No esperes eso de mi," included in CD "Siempre en contacto con la música cubana" (Caribe Productions CD, 1998).

114. See, for example, "La mujer suicida," in Samuel Feijóo, ed., *Mitos y leyendas en Las Villas* (Havana, 1965), p. 250; and "El suicida," in Samuel Feijóo, *Mitología cubana* (Havana, 1985), p. 437.

115. Tomás Justiz y del Valle, *El suicida* (Havana, 1912), pp. 226–27.

116. Reinaldo Arenas, *Otra vez el mar* (Barcelona, 1982), pp. 415–18; Reinaldo Arenas, *Old Rosa*, trans. Ann Tashi Slater (New York, 1989), p. 43.

117. René Vázquez Díaz, *La era imaginaria* (Barcelona, 1987), p. 52.

118. José Antonio Ramos, *Almas rebeldes* (Barcelona, 1906) and *Las impurezas de la realidad* (Havana, 1929); Francisco Torres, *Armor y ruta* (Havana, 1921); Carlos Loveira, *La última lección* (Havana, 1924); Luis Felipe Rodríguez, *La copa vacía* (Madrid, 1926); Justo González, *Cubagua. Historia de un pueblo* (Havana, 1941); Teresa Casuso, *Los ausentes* (México, 1944); Miguel de Marcos, *Papaíto Mayarí* (Havana, 1947); and Lisandro Otero, *La situación* (Havana, 1962).

119. Maria Teresa C.M., "Suicidio," *Bohemia* 20 (July 1, 1928): 15; Armando Leyva, "Un suicida," in *Las horas silenciosas* (Santiago de Cuba, 1920), pp. 179–86; Armando Leyva, "Cómo muere un buey . . . ," in *Del ensueño y de la vida* (Gibara, 1910), pp. 32–36; Antonio Casas Bricio, "El suicidio de la muñeca," *Bohemia* 29 (August 14, 1927): 5, 63; Luis Rodríguez Embil, "Por qué se suicidió Juan Enríquez," in Salvador Bueno, ed., *Antología del cuento en Cuba (1902–1952)* (Havana, 1953), pp. 41–42.

120. Lino Novás Calvo, "La luna de los ñáñigos," *Revista de Occidente* 35 (January 1932), p. 87; Lino Novás Calvo, "La abuela Reina y el sobrino Delfín," "El milagro," and "El secreto de Narciso Campana" in *Maneras de contar* (New York, 1970), pp. 125, 237, 341. Other works by Novás Calvo in which the theme of suicide is treated include "'Aliado' y 'Alemanes,'" *Romance* 1 (October 22, 1940): 8, 14; and *No sé quién soy* (México, 1945).

121. Mirta Yáñez, "No somos nada," in *Narraciones desordenadas e incompletas* (Ha-

vana, 1997), p. 10; J. M. Morales, "El perro del suicida," in *Al pie del coco* (Havana, 1915), pp. 123–28; Alfonso Hernández Catá, "Los muertos," in *Los frutos ácidos* (Madrid, 1915), pp. 227–28.

122. Jesús J. López, "De un suicida," *El Mundo Ilustrado* 6 (February 28, 1909): 171; Vicente Menéndez Roque, "Mi amigo, el suicida," in *Otros días* (Havana, 1962), pp. 98–102; Rosario Sansores, "El timo del suicidio," *Bohemia* 20 (October 7, 1928): 13, 65; A. Arroyo Ruz, "El misterio del cuarto de la bella suicida," *Carteles* 26 (August 9, 1936): 55, 58; Julio Laurent Pagés, "De los suicidas," *El Mundo Ilustrado* 5 (August 30, 1908): 769; Trinidad de Zequeira, "El suicidio," in *Flores de ensueño: Novelas, artículos y poesías originales* (Havana, 1918), pp. 37–38; Rafael U. González, "Un suicida," *Bohemia* 14 (August 12, 1923): 5; Juan Nicolás Padrón Barquín, "Los suicidas," in *Crónica de la noche* (Havana, 1994), p. 59; Mario del Caspio, "Los candidatos al suicidio," *Bohemia* 9 (June 9, 1918): 9, 33; Alfonso Hernández Catá, "Parábola de los suicidas," *Social* 12 (September 1927): 14; José Sanz, "Mi amigo el suicida," *La Lucha*, July 14, 1929, p. 17; Francisco M. Casado, "Suicidio original," in *Pasatiempos* (Havana, 1913), pp. 65–67; Gerardo del Valle, "Páginas halladas en el bolsillo de un suicida," *Bohemia* 21 (April 28, 1929): 18–21; Paco Romero, "La ceiba de los suicidas," *La Lucha*, June 25, 1928, p. 3. Other short stories in which the theme of suicide was prominent include Angel E. Blanco, "El clown verde," *El Hogar* 14 (June 20, 1897): 8–9; Felipe Pichardo Moya, "Los viejos gavilanes," *Social* 11 (February 1926): 32–33, 58; Félix Solani, "Obsesión," *Bohemia* 11 (April 4, 1920): 9, 26; José A. Valdés León, "Incertidumbre," *Vanidades* 14 (September 15, 1944): 14; María Teresa Leyva, "La sequía," *Carteles* 28 (January 12, 1947): 11.

123. José M. Morales, "El esclavo," *Bohemia* 30 (June 12, 1928): 11.

124. M. Siré Valenciano, "El cimarrón," *Bohemia* 32 (February 16, 1930): 71.

125. César Leante, *Los guerrilleros negros* (Havana, 1975), pp. 310–11. For a discussion of the theme of suicide as a facet of the fictional literature on slavery see William Luis, *Literary Bondage: Slavery in Cuban Narrative* (Austin, 1990).

126. Cartier de Lancy, "Un suicidio misterioso," *Bohemia* 20 (March 18, 1928): 19, 21, 57–58; Suzy Mathis, "El suicidio de Nina," *Bohemia* 20 (October 14, 1928): 77, 79; Al Bromley, "El suicidio perfecto," *Bohemia* 22 (December 7, 1930): 40; H. J. Magog, "Suicidio," *Bohemia* 23 (January 11, 1931): 8, 60; Andrés Uccellini, "Yo suicida," *Bohemia* 23 (October 4, 1931): 6–7, 48; Garnett Kettering, "Crimen o suicidio," *Carteles* 18 (February 7, 1932): 48, 52; Antoine de Courson, "Un suicidio," *Bohemia* 24 (May 1, 1932): 4–5; Germain Survil, "Suicidio," *Bohemia* 27 (October 13, 1935): 7, 67; Leonard Merrick, "Los suicidas de la Rue sombre," *Carteles* 14 (August 25, 1929): 10–11, 64–65; Victor Maxwell, "Un suicidio misterioso," *Bohemia* 27 (November 10, 1935): 6–7, 59; G. T. Fleming Roberts, "La casa de los suicidios," *Carteles* 21 (June 9, 1941): 22–23; Etienne Gril, "El suicidio de Berta de Arson," *Bohemia* 25 (March 6, 1933): 8–9, 16; Manuel Komroff, "El hari-kiri del barón Kura," *Carteles* 32 (February 5, 1939): 70–73; William E. Hayes, "La carta del suicida," *Bohemia* 30 (January 22, 1938): 3–5, 56. See also "El Buda que evitó un suicidio," *Bohemia* 22 (August 17, 1930): 74–75, 79.

127. Manuel Pinos, "La prórroga de un suicidio," *Bohemia* 19 (September 4, 1927): 53; "El suicida," in Samuel Feijóo, ed., *Cuarteta y décima* (Havana, 1980), pp. 221–23; Virgilio Piñera, "Invitación al suicidio," 1935, *Letras Cubanas*, 15–16 (July–September

1990): 234–35; Fayad Jamis, "El ahorcado del Café Bonaparte," in Fayad Jamis, *La pérdida: Selección poética (1951–1973)*, 2nd ed., ed. Víctor Casaus (Havana, 1985), p. 62.

128. E. A. Carrasco Mojena, "¡Me suicidé!" in *Horizontes poéticos (Poesías)* (Havana, 1919), p. 19.

129. Ernesto León G., "El suicida," *El Palenque Literario* 4 (1883): 249; Manuel S. Pichardo, "El suicida," *El Fígaro* 4 (October 14, 1888): 2; Bonifacio Byrne, "De un suicida," *El Fígaro* 15 (April 2, 1899): 79; Esteban Foncueva, "De un suicida," in *Horas del olvido (Poesías)* (Havana, 1907), pp. 85–86; José Antonio Calcaño, "El suicida," *El Mundo* 1 (May 20, 1883): 203; Sigifredo Alvarez Conesa, "El puente del ahorcado," in *Matar el tiempo* (Havana, 1969), pp. 17–18.

130. See "Una bella joven se suicida para escaparse del poder del diablo," *La Lucha*, August 23, 1926, p. 12; "Misterioso suicidio en un buque de plata," ibid., March 16, 1926, p. 7. For a discussion of the popularity of this genre of journalism in Cuba see Manuel Márquez Sterling, *Alrededor de nuestra psicología* (Havana, 1906), pp. 31–38.

131. Velilla de Solórzano, "Los que se matan," p. 62.

132. *Diario de la Marina*, May 3, 1931, p. 1; ibid., May 12, 1931, p. 15.

133. Ibid., January 6, 1904, p. 2.

134. See Mary Lugo, "El suicidio de una figurante," *La Lucha*, March 7, 1926, p. 6; William A. Russell, "7 'estrellas' del teatro se suicidan en 7 meses," *Carteles* 17 (June 28, 1931): 16–17, 30; W. F. Morris, "Un suicidio extraordinario," *Bohemia* 26 (April 1, 1934): 16–17; 53; Gerard Deville, "Los grandes suicidas de la política," *Carteles* 35 (October 31, 1954): 60–61, 102; Cyril H. Hare, "El caso del suicidio del inglés americanizado," *Bohemia* 49 (June 2, 1957): 26–28, 119; M. Gregoire, "El suicidio del yerno de Churchill," *Carteles* 37 (October 27, 1957): 6, 88. Among Cubans reporting on prominent suicides in the United States see José Manuel Bada, "Los suicidios de Evelyn Nesbit," *Bohemia* 19 (January 2, 1927): 18; and Miguel de Marcos, "El suicidio de Charles Schwartz," *Bohemia* 22 (August 24, 1930): 19.

135. Alejo Carpentier, "El suicidio del rey de las cerillas suecas," *Carteles* 18 (May 1, 1932): 16, 52; Alejo Carpentier, "El suicidio de un gran artista," 1930, in *Crónicas*, 2 vols. (Havana, 1976), 2:444–45; José Juan Tablada, "Crónica de New York: La marea suicida," *Bohemia* 21 (March 17, 1929): 33, 57; François G. de Cisneros, "El principado del placer y de la muerte," *Social* 6 (April 1921): 39, 64; Félix Pita Rodríguez, "El suicidio más espectacular de la historia," *Bohemia* 46 (July 25, 1954): 64.

136. *La Lucha*, July 18, 1920, p. 3; ibid., July 29, 1926, p. 2; "Suicidio por explosión," *Bohemia* 29 (May 30, 1937): 6; *Diario de la Marina*, September 24, 1917, p. 6.

137. *La Lucha*, November 7, 1926, p. 7; ibid., September 15, 1926, p. 2; ibid., November 5, 1926, p. 1; Mauricio Laporte, "El club de los suicidas," *Bohemia* 23 (November 15, 1931): 31–32, 52; Carmen de Burgos, "El suicidio de Fígaro," *Social* 6 (January 1921): 62, 84.

138. Alicia Mulcahey, "Los secretos del impulso suicida," *Bohemia* 50 (July 20, 1958): 12–13, 146; Jean de Kerderland, "Una enfermedad que progresa: el suicidio," *Carteles* 37 (January 20, 1957): 14–15, 84; Henry S. Galus, "La horripilante manía de los suicidios," *Carteles* 35 (September 26, 1954), 16–17; Sarah Diamond, "¿Se suicidan los animales?" *Carteles* 18 (May 15, 1931): 14, 66; Mario de la Viña, "¿Piensa usted a suicidarse?" *Carteles* 35 (January 10, 1954): 28.

139. Clifford Geertz, "Religion as a Cultural System," in Michael Banton, ed., *Anthropological Approaches to the Study of Religion* (New York, 1966), pp. 7–8, 29.

140. Georgina Cruz Salazar, "Suicidio," *Vanidades* 13 (June 15, 1944): 28.

141. Jesús J. López, "El suicidio de Morgan," in *Cuentos perversos (El libro de los sarcasmos)* (Havana, 1925), pp. 265–67.

142. César Leante, "El punto de partida," *Carteles* 37 (February 3, 1957): 66–68.

143. Rafael María Rubio, "Páginas de un diario," *Bohemia* 24 (November 27, 1932): 11, 51.

144. Mario Parajón, "Prohibido suicidarse en Nueva York," *El Mundo*, July 22, 1955, p. A-6.

145. Leante, "El punto de partida," 66; Enrique C. Henríquez, "Suicidio," in *El esclavo y el reflejo* (Miami, 1977), p. 114.

146. Nicolás Martínez Suárez, "El suicida," *El Ramillete* 9 (June 28, 1885), p. 36.

147. Nicolás Guillén, "La amarga ironía," in *Obra poética*, 2 vols. (Havana, 1972–73), 1:21–22.

148. Jesús Vega, "El suicidio," in *Wunderbar, ¡Maravilloso!* (Havana, 1994), p. 52.

149. Suicide in Cuba could be praised in the United States under certain circumstances. In 1961 one UPI despatch from Sancti-Spíritus gave an account of sixteen-year-old Teresita Saavedra, who burned herself to death after interrogation by Cuban authorities. An act that might have otherwise elicited horror was instead set in the context of "stories of brave Cubans who chose death rather than knuckle under [communism]" and described as a deed that "illustrates the bold spirit which prevails among many anti-Castro Cubans." See *St. Petersburg Times*, March 30, 1961, p. 3.

150. Velilla de Solórzano, "Los que se matan," p. 102.

151. *La Lucha*, May 12, 1894, p. 2; ibid., December 23, 1926, p. 10; *Diario de la Marina*, July 26, 1931, p. 3.

152. *Diario de la Marina*, April 28, 1916, pp. 1, 8.

153. *La Lucha*, June 2, 1928, p. 1.

154. *La Discusión*, August 26, 1896, p. 3.

155. *Diario de la Marina*, November 8, 1931, p. 3.

156. Marcos, *Papaíto Mayarí*, p. 358; Francisco Torres, *Amor y ruta* (Havana, 1921), p. 176; *La Lucha*, March 28, 1921, p. 1; ibid., March 30, 1921, p. 22; Miguel Barnet, *Canción de Rachel* (1969; reprint, Havana, 1985), pp. 19–24.

157. Céspedes, "Los suicidas por amor," p. 6. The very act of suicide was often identified as feminine conduct. "Weak people possessing some culture are susceptible to suicide," commented one observer. "On the other hand, uncultured people of strong character are given to homicide. Thus the saying that homicide is a crime of men and the uncouth, while suicide is the act of women and cultured people." See Velilla de Solórzano, "Los que se matan," p. 103.

158. *La Caricatura*, February 15, 1903, p. 4.

159. The advice was based on the popular saying: "La vida es un fandango, que el que no la baila es un tonto." See *La Caricatura*, September 3, 1905, p. 4; Cabrera, "Hurgando en los raíces del suicidio," p. 84.

160. "Suicidios modernos," *La Lucha*, June 20, 1929, p. 3; Andrés Valdespino, "Prevención del suicidio," *El Mundo*, September 13, 1956, p. A-6.

161. Andrés Valdespino, "Prevención del suicidio," *El Mundo*, September 13, 1956, p. A-6.

162. "The type of publicity devoted to suicide," sociologist David Phillips has suggested, "indicates that a model is more likely to be imitated if he is prestigious and if his circumstances are thought to be similar to those of the imitator." The suicide of a prominent personality, or a person held generally in high public esteem, often precipitated a succession of imitation deaths. See David P. Phillips, "The Influence of Suggestion on Suicide: Substantive and Theoretical Implications of the Werther Effect," *American Sociological Review* 39 (June 1974): 352. The Centers for Disease Control warned of a "suicide contagion," described as "a process by which the exposure to the suicide or suicidal behavior of one or more persons influences others to commit or attempt suicide." See "Suicide Contagion and the Reporting of Suicide: Recommendations from a National Workshop," *Morbidity and Mortality Weekly Report* 43 (April 22, 1994), p. 2, <http://www.cdc.gov> (September 2004).

163. Jorge LeRoy y Cassá, "Quo Tendimus? Estudio médico legal sobre el suicidio en Cuba durante el quinquenio de 1902–1906," *Anales de la Academia de Ciencias Médicas, Físicas y Naturales de La Habana* 44 (May 1907): 61–62.

164. Ibid.," p. 54. See also Jorge LeRoy y Cassá, "Suicidio por el fuego," *Revista de Medicina y Cirugía de La Habana* 12 (June 10, 1907): 253. For useful general discussions of the relationship between suicide and newspaper accounts see Jerome A. Motto, "Suicide and Suggestibility—the Role of the Press," in Anthony Giddens, ed., *The Sociology of Suicide* (London, 1971), pp. 307–13; and A. Schmidtke and H. Hafner, "Public Attitudes Towards and Effects of the Mass Media on Suicidal and Deliberate Self-Harm Behavior," in René F. W. Diekstra, et al., eds., *Suicide and Its Prevention: The Role of Attitude and Imitation* (Leiden, 1989), pp. 313–30.

165. Tomás V. Coronado et al., "Informe emitido por la comisión nombrada para juzgar la memoria presentada en opción al Premio de Medicina Legal, fundado por el Dr. Antonio de Górdon, cuyo lema es ¿QUO TENDIMUS?" in Jorge LeRoy y Cassá, *Quo Tendimus? Estudio médico-legal sobre el suicidio en Cuba durante el quinquenio de 1902–1906* (Havana, 1907), p. 31. This *"informe"* appears as an appendix in the reprint version of LeRoy y Cassá's essay, which was first published in the *Anales de la Academia de Ciencias Médicas, Físicas y Naturales de La Habana* in May 1907.

166. Marta Vignier, "Las suicidas: ¿Enfermas mentales o víctimas de la sociedad?" *Carteles* 37 (May 13, 1956): 16.

167. *Diario de la Marina*, November 19, 1931, p. 12; ibid., February 2, 1932, p. 10.

168. "It was a shock so violent for me," Borrero Echeverría wrote in 1900 of the loss of Juana, "that I still have not recovered from its ravages." See Esteban Borrero Echeverría, "Autobiografía," *Revista de la Facultad de Letras y Ciencias de la Universidad de La Habana* 3 (July 1906): 59–71. At another point Borrero Echeverría wrote of a "pain so great that it was on the verge of killing me." See Esteban Borrero Echeverría to Nicolás Heredia, March 25, 1900, in Esteban Borrero Echeverría, *Narraciones*, ed. Manuel Cofiño (Havana, 1979), p. 179.

169. See "El suicidio frustrado de Miguel Lamas," *Bohemia* 11 (April 11, 1920): 12.

170. See Rafael Soto Paz, "Cubanos prominentes que se suicidaron," *Bohemia* 45 (March 15, 1953): 154, 159; "El extraño suicidio del coronel Méndez Peñate," *Carteles*

22 (April 15, 1934): 20; Julio E. Gaunaurd, "Los dos suicidas," *Bohemia* 26 (April 8, 1934): 32; "La gran tragedia de un caudillo," *Bohemia* 26 (April 8, 1934): 33, 36. Méndez Peñate attributed his decision to kill himself to the frustration he experienced in administering the Ministry of Justice. See Roberto Méndez Peñate, "¡La nota sensacional del momento! El testimonio político de Roberto Méndez Peñate," *Bohemia* 26 (May 20, 1934): 34–35.

171. Benjamín Olivero, "Como capturé a Wilfredo Fernández," *Bohemia* 26 (March 4, 1934): 32, 47; "Cartas póstumas de Wilfredo," *Bohemia* 26 (March 4, 1934): 33, 41. Years later, his nephew would write an ode, "Yo tuve un tío suicida." See Wilfredo Fernández, *El libro del Wilfredo: poesías completas* (Madrid, 1978), pp. 47–50.

172. *El Mundo*, May 6, 1947, pp. 1, 10. "Supervielle had been the butt of frequent public manifestations of displeasure over his failure to provide the promised water supply," reported the U.S. chargé d'affaires in Havana days after the suicide. "At a recent business luncheon, for instance, he had been resoundingly booed; when he appeared on the streets children jeered at him shouting '*agua, agua.*' In the moving picture houses, likewise, newsreel shots of him had evoked catcalls and shouts. All this, it now appears, had been more than the gentle Mayor's sensitive feelings could stand." See Albert F. Nufer to Secretary of State, May 9, 1947, 837.00/5-947, Confidential U.S. State Department Central File, Cuba, 1945–49: Internal Affairs, General Records of the Department of States, Record Group 59, National Archives, Washington, D.C.

173. *El Mundo*, May 6, p. 10; Osvaldo Valdés de la Paz, "Una frase del doctor Fernández Supervielle: 'Es preferible morir bien a vivir mal,'" *Carteles* 28 (May 18, 1947): 38–39; Ruby Hart Phillips, *Cuba, Island of Paradox* (New York, 1959), p. 239.

174. *El Mundo*, May 6, 1947, p. 12.

175. Elio E. Constantín, "Los grandes suicidios de Cuba," *Carteles* 32 (August 26, 1951): 61; F. L. Fesser Ferrer, *Los desorientados* (Havana, 1948), p. 256. See also Eduardo Ordóñez, *Suicidio histórico: Manuel Fernández Supervielle* (Havana, 1955).

176. *El Mundo*, May 6, 1947, p. 15.

177. For a brief discussion of the death of Chibás and the phenomenon of political suicide in Latin America generally see James Dunkerley, *Political Suicide in Latin America and Other Essays* (London, 1992), pp. 1–47. On Eddy Chibás see Luis Conte Agüero, *Eduardo Chibás. El Adalid de Cuba* (México, 1955); and Elena Alavez Martín, *Eduardo Chibás en la hora de la ortodoxia* (Havana, 1994).

178. Hugh Thomas, *Cuba, the Pursuit of Freedom* (New York, 1971), p. 874. See also Jorge Ibarra Guitart, *Sociedad de Amigos de la República: Historia de una mediación, 1952–1958* (Havana, 2003), pp. 106–71.

179. "La generación del Mariel," <http://wwww.eddosrios.org> (April 2002).

CHAPTER SIX
1. Miguel Varona Guerrero, *La guerra de independencia de Cuba, 1895–1898*, 3 vols. (Havana, 1946), 3:1792. See the ode "A la memoria de los mártires de la revolución cubana (1868–1878)," in Francisco Sellén, *Cantos de la Patria* (New York, 1900), pp. 8–10.

2. Historian Marial Iglesias Utset describes this process as "the decolonization of

names." See Marial Iglesias Utset, *Las metáforas del cambio en la vida cotidiana: Cuba 1898–1902* (Havana, 2002), pp. 150–73.

3. Richard Butler Gray, *José Martí, Cuban Patriot* (Gainesville, 1962), pp. 102–3; Antoni Kapcia, "Cuban Populism and the Birth of the Myth of Martí," in Christopher Abel and Nissa Torrents, eds., *José Martí: Revolutionary Democrat* (Durham, 1986), pp. 32–64.

4. Frederick A. Ober, *Our West Indian Neighbors* (New York, 1904), p. 27.

5. Luis Ricardo Alonso, *El palacio y la furia* (Barcelona, 1976), p. 9.

6. Juan M. Leiseca, *Historia de Cuba* (Havana, 1925), p. 1.

7. Ciro Espinos, "Ideario y república a través de la adolescencia," *Revista Cubana* 21 (January–December 1940): 103–4.

8. Tomás Felipe Surós Pérez, *El incendio de Bayamo y el heroísmo cubano* (Bayamo, 1928), pp. 21–22; Leiseca, *Historia de Cuba*, p. 224; Oscar Ugarte, "¡Bayamo heroica!" *Bohemia* 15 (October 5, 1924): 6; Luis Santana, *Historia de Cuba* (Trinidad, 1938), p. 160; José Maceo Verdecia, *Bayamo*, 2nd ed. (Havana, 1941), p. 18. See also Sotero Figueroa, "Bayamo," *Minerva* 3 (March 30, 1911): 2; Consuelo Alvarez, "Bayamo," *Letras* 9 (August 24, 1913): 318; and J. Jerez Villarreal, "El incendio de Bayamo," *Bohemia* 20 (January 22, 1928): 11, 62.

9. Miguel Coyula, "La gloriosa Bayamo," *Bohemia* 30 (October 23, 1938): 28; Erna Fergusson, *Cuba* (New York, 1946), pp. 47–49. See also Manuel Márquez Sterling, "Bayamo, la inmortal," *El Mundo Ilustrado* 1 (October 23, 1904): 11.

10. Arturo Montori, *El tormento de vivir* (Havana, 1923), pp. 20–21.

11. José Martí, "Con todos y para el bien de todos," November 26, 1891, in José Martí, *Obras completas*, ed. Jorge Quintana, 5 vols. (Caracas, 1964), 1:697–706.

12. Agustín Cebreco to Editor, *El Fígaro* 16 (October 28, 1900): 482.

13. See *La Lucha*, April 11, 1899, p 2; *La Discusión*, September 23, 1900, p. 1; "Confidential Report: Province of Santiago de Cuba," n.d., Records of the Post Office Department, Record Group 28, National Archives, Washington, D.C.

14. Captain Carlos Muecke to G. Creighton Webb, September 3, 1898, G. Creighton Webb Papers, Manuscript Department, New-York Historical Society, New York, N.Y.

15. Salvador Quesada Torres, "El silencio," in *El silencio* (Havana, 1923), pp. 18–19.

16. *El Pilareño* 19 (May 8, 1940): 8; *El Villaclareño*, August 19, 1900, p. 7.

17. Emilio Roig de Leuchsenring, "Heroísmo y martirio de nuestros mambises libertadores," *Carteles* 33 (September 3, 1939): 46; Luis Aguilar León, *Cuba: conciencia y revolución* (Miami, 1972), p. 159; Waldo Medina, "El tesoro de un pueblo," 1953, and "Recuento necesario," 1954, republished in Waldo Medina, *Cosas de ayer que sirven para hoy* (Havana, 1978), pp. 68, 112–13; Medina, "Eustaquio y Liborio," 1955, ibid., pp. 44–45.

18. Ramiro Guerra, "Difusión y afirmación del sentimiento nacional," *Social* 9 (November 1924): 22.

19. Alejandro de la Fuente, *A Nation for All: Race, Inequality, and Politics in Twentieth-Century Cuba* (Chapel Hill, 2001), p. 14. See also Rafael Fermoselle, *Política y color en Cuba: La guerrita de 1912* (Montevideo, 1974); Thomas T. Orum, "The Politics of Color: The Racial Dimension of Cuban Politics During the Early Republican Years,

1900–1922," (Ph.D. diss., New York University, 1975); Aline Helg, *Our Rightful Share: The Afro-Cuban Struggle for Equality, 1886–1912* (Chapel Hill, 1995); Silvio Castro Fernández, *La masacre de los Independientes de Color en 1912* (Havana, 2002).

20. See Ana Cairo, *El movimiento de Veteranos y Patriotas* (Havana, 1976).

21. Directorio Estudiantil Universitario, "Manifiesto contra la prórroga de poderes," 1927, in Olga Cabrera, ed., *Antonio Guiteras: Su pensamiento revolucionario* (Havana, 1974), pp. 60–69; Julio Antonio Mella, "El porque de nuestro nombre," May 1928, in Julio Antonio Mella, *Mella: Documentos y artículos* (Havana, 1975), p. 415.

22. For the opposition against the government of Machado see Lionel Soto, *La revolución del 33*, 3 vols. (Havana, 1977–78); Mirta Rosell, *Luchas obreras contra Machado* (Havana, 1973); Robert Whitney, *State and Revolution in Cuba: Mass Mobilization and Political Change, 1920–1940* (Chapel Hill, 2001), pp. 36–121.

23. José L. Cuza, "Combate del Centro Industrial de Moa," in Luis Pavón, ed., *Días de combate* (Havana, 1970), pp. 123–24.

24. Rodolfo Rodríguez Zaldívar, "Encuestas de *Bohemia*: Opiniones sobre el regreso de Prío," *Bohemia* 47 (July 10, 1955): 64.

25. Fidel Castro, "Manifiesto No. 1 del 26 de Julio al pueblo de Cuba," August 8, 1955, *Pensamiento Crítico* 21 (1968): 207–20.

26. Fidel Castro to Luis Conte Agüero, December 12, 1953, in Fidel Castro, *Cartas del presidio*, ed. Luis Conte Agüero (Havana, 1959), pp. 21–22.

27. Alonso, *El palacio y la furia*, pp. 235–36.

28. Leví Marrero, *La generación asesinada* (Havana, 1934), pp. 145–46.

29. José Soler Puig, *Bertillón 166* (Havana, 1960), pp. 98–99.

30. Fidel Castro, "Este movimiento triunfará," July 26, 1953, *Verde Olivo* 5 (July 26, 1964): 5. See also Jules Dubois, *Fidel Castro: Rebel-Liberator or Dictator?* (Indianapolis, 1959), p. 31.

31. "Ante la tumba de un mártir," *Bohemia* 40 (February 22, 1953): 59, 71.

32. Fidel Castro, "Manifiesto No. 2 del 26 de Julio al pueblo de Cuba," December 10, 1955, *Pensamiento Crítico* 21 (1968): 224.

33. Faure Chaumón, "El Directorio Revolucionario hace pública su posición ante de las declaraciones del Doctor Fidel Castro," *Bohemia* 50 (February 2, 1958): 85–87; Bernardo Callejas, "Para aprender a manejar la pistola," in *¿Que vas a cantar ahora?* (Havana, 1971), p. 43; Humberto Arenal, *El sol a plomo* (New York, 1959), p. 50.

34. Oscar Lewis, Ruth M. Lewis, and Susan M. Rigdon, *Four Women. Living the Revolution: An Oral History of Contemporary Cuba* (Urbana, Ill., 1977), p. 371.

35. José Luis Llovio-Menéndez, *Insider: My Hidden Life as a Revolutionary in Cuba*, trans. Edith Grossman (New York, 1988), pp. 52–53; Lewis, Lewis, and Rigdon, *Four Women*, p. 34.

36. Raúl González de Cascorro, *El mejor fruto*, in *Arboles sin raíces* (Havana, 1959), pp. 181–83.

37. Teresa Casuso, *Los ausentes* (México, 1944), p. 179.

38. In Carlos Franqui, *Cuba: el libro de los doce*, 2nd ed. (México, 1970), p. 61.

39. Alonso, *El palacio y la furia*, p. 153; José Antonio Echeverría, "Testamento político de José Antonio Echeverría," March 13, 1957, in Organización Nacional de Bibliotecas Ambulantes y Populares, *13 documentos de los insurrección* (Havana, 1959), p. 47.

See also "Si caemos, que nuestra sangre señale el camino de la libertad," *Bohemia* 67 (March 14, 1975): 4–7. In addition to the attacks against Moncada and the Presidential Palace, Nelson Valdés includes as acts of "implicit suicide" the following: the attack by Antonio Guiteras against the Batista military in 1934, the Organización Auténtica assault on the Goicuría barracks in 1956, and Josué País challenging the police to fight on the streets of Santiago de Cuba in 1957. See Nelson P. Valdés, "Cuban Political Culture: Between Death and Betrayal," in Sandor Halebsky and John M. Kirk, eds., *Cuba in Transition: Crisis and Transformation* (Boulder, 1992), pp. 207–28.

40. Marrero, *La generación asesinada*, p. 141; Leonel López-Nussa, "Una caída suave, una sonrisa," in *Tabaco* (Havana, 1963), p. 248; Roberto P. de Acevedo, *La ráfaga* (Havana, 1939), p. 97.

41. Soler Puig, *Bertillón 166*, pp. 28, 39.

42. Francisco Chao Hermida, *Un obrero de vanguardia* (Miami, 1972), pp. 15–16.

43. Ruby Hart Phillips, *Cuba, Island of Paradox* (New York, 1959), p. 47; Ernesto Che Guevara, "Una revolución que comienza," in *Obra revolucionaria*, 2nd ed., ed. Roberto Fernández Retamar (México, 1968), p. 274.

44. Vilma Espín, "Deborah," in Jane McManus, *From the Palm Tree: Voices of the Cuban Revolution* (Secaucus, N.J., 1983), p. 53.

45. Julio Travieso, *Para matar al lobo* (Havana, 1981), p. 173.

46. Interview with Gladys Marel García, December 20, 2002, Havana, Cuba. García participated in the urban resistance between 1957 and 1958 in Matanzas and Santa Clara.

47. Enrique Oltuski, *Gente del llano* (Havana, 2001), p. 114.

48. "En Cuba," *Bohemia* 49 (February 9, 1958): Sup. 8. See also "Orlando Nodarse Verde," *Bohemia* 59 (June 16, 1967): 108–9. Some of the most gripping accounts of the torture of members of the urban resistance by the Batista government appear in fictional form. See Humberto Arenal, *El sol a plomo* (New York, 1959); Travieso, *Para matar al lobo*; Julio Travieso, ed., *Cuentos sobre el clandestinaje* (Havana, 1983).

49. Travieso, *Para matar al lobo*, p. 95.

50. Movimiento 26 de Julio, "Manifiesto-Programa del Movimiento 26 de Julio," November 1956, in *Humanismo* 7 (November–December 1958): 12–13.

51. The exhortation of "Patria o muerte" was first used by Fidel Castro in the aftermath of the explosion of the French freighter *La Coubre* in March 1960. See Fidel Castro, "Frente al monstruoso crimen de *La Coubre*: ¡Patria o muerte!" March 5, 1960, in Fidel Castro, *El pensamiento de Fidel Castro*, 2 vols. (Havana, 1983), 1:34–44.

52. *Obra Revolucionaria* 2 (May 17, 1960): 5–6.

53. Regla María Albelo Ginnart et al., *Orientaciones metodológicas: Historia de Cuba (Octavo grado)* (Havana, 1986), p. 14.

54. Teresita Aguilera Vargas et al., *Orientaciones metodológicas: Relatos de historia de Cuba (Cuarto grado)* (Havana, 1978), pp. 156–57, 195; Regla María Albelo Ginnart et al., *Historia de Cuba* (Havana, 1985), pp. 30–31.

55. Onoria Céspedes Argote, "El incendio de la ciudad," in Angel Lago Vieito et al., *Bayamo: En el crisol de la nacionalidad cubana* (Bayamo, 1996), p. 91.

56. José Miguel Garófalo, "La ciudad no existe," *Cuba* 7 (October 1968): 25; Eduardo Torres Cuevas and Oscar Loyola Vega, *Historia de Cuba, 1492–1898: Formación*

y liberación de la nación (Havana, 2002), p. 241; Rafael Acosta de Arriba, *Los silencios quebrados de San Lorenzo* (Havana, 1999), p. 140; Rafael Alcides Pérez, "Idea de Bayamo," in *Y se mueren, y vuelven, y se mueren* (Havana, 1988), p. 127; Lucilo Tejera Díaz, "El 'pueblo sagrado' ardió por la Patria," *Camagüey: Tierra de leyendas y llanuras,* <http://www.camaguey.cu>, September 17, 2002.

57. Castro, "Frente al monstruoso crimen de *La Coubre,*" 1:42–43.

58. Fidel Castro, "Si las raíces y la historia de este país no se conocen, la cultura política de nuestras masas no estará suficiente desarrollada," *Granma,* October 11, 1968, pp. 4, 6.

59. Fidel Castro, "En el centenario del inicio de la lucha revolucionaria en nuestra patria," in Juan José Soto Valdespino, ed., *De La Demajagua a Playa Girón: 'Un encuentro del pueblo con su propio historia'* (Havana, 1978), pp. 67–68.

60. Pedro de Oraá, "La expresión y la acción revolucionaria (Apuntes)," *Unión* 18 (January 1974): 5–6.

61. Clifford Geertz, "Ideology as a Cultural System," in David E. Apter, ed., *Ideology and Discontent* (New York, 1964): 47–76.

62. Arnaldo Rivero, "La disciplina revolucionaria en la Sierra Maestra," *Humanismo* 7 (January–April 1959): 377–79.

63. Fidel Castro, "Quien intente apoderarse de Cuba solo encontrará el polvo de su suelo anegado en sangre," October 26, 1959, in Castro, *Pensamiento de Fidel Castro,* 1:28.

64. Fidel Castro, "Nuestras dos grandes tareas: Defender la revolución y hacerla avanzar," March 13, 1960, in ibid., 2:46–54; Fidel Castro, "Ante el zarpazo yanqui: Las nacionalización de las grandes empresas norteamericanas," August 6, 1960, in ibid., 2:111; *Obra Revolucionaria* 15 (April 26, 1961), pp. 35–36; Fidel Castro, "La revolución es irreversible," July 18, 1960, in Castro, *El pensamiento de Fidel Castro,* 2:433–34.

65. Fidel Castro to U Thant, Secretary General, United Nations, November 15, 1962, in *Revolución,* November 16, 1962, p. 1; *Granma,* October 1, 1979, p. 4.

66. *Granma,* February 15, 1993, p. 7.

67. Ibid., December 10, 1991, p. 5.

68. Ibid., December 18, 1991, p. 6; Ibid., December 10, 1991, p. 5.

69. Ibid., February 19, 1992, p. 3.

70. Fidel Castro, "Closing Speech: Proceedings of Fourth PCC Congress," October 14, 1991, Castro Speech Data Base, Latin American Network Information Center (LANIC), University of Texas, Austin, Texas, <http://lanic.utexas.edu> (February 2004).

71. *Granma,* April 7, 1992, p. 11.

72. These included 9,603 industrial enterprises in areas such as lumber, metal, textiles, tobacco, and printing; 17,212 food retailers such as grocery stores, butcher shops, fish stores, and vegetable stands; 11,299 bars, snack shops, and restaurants; 14,172 services such as laundry and dry cleaning businesses, auto repair shops, barber shops, and shoe repair shops; and 2,682 retail businesses such as hardware stores, drug stores, clothing shops, furniture stores, and cigarette counters. See *Granma* (International Edition), April 7, 1968, p. 3.

73. Lynn Geldof, *Cubans* (London, 1991), pp. 14, 18–19.

74. Terry Doran, Janet Satterfield, and Chris Stade, eds., *A Road Well Traveled: Three Generations of Cuban American Women* (Newton, Mass., 1988), p. 66; Raquel Mendieta Costa, "Only Fragments of Memory," in María de los Angeles Torres, *By Heart/De Memoria* (Philadelphia, 2003), pp. 134, 136.

75. Abelardo Estorino, *Morir del cuento*, in Rine Leal, ed., *Seis obras de teatro cubano* (Havana, 1989), p. 96; Juan Arcocha, *Los muertos andan solos* (Havana, 1962), p. 111; Edmundo Desnoes, *Inconsolable Memories* (New York, 1967), pp. 74–75, 120, 123.

76. Freddy Artiles, *Adriana en dos tiempos* (Havana, 1972), p. 150.

77. Lisandro Otero, *Arbol de la vida* (México, 1990), pp. 128–29.

78. Lewis, Lewis, and Rigdon, *Four Women*, p. 413; Nicolás Dorr, *Mediodía candente*, in *Dramas de imaginación y urgencia* (Havana, 1987), p. 331; Héctor Quintero, *Te sigo esperando/Antes de mí: el Sahara*, ed. Juan Antonio Hormigón (Madrid, 1998), p. 50; Uva de Aragón, *Memoria del silencio* (Miami, 2002), p. 141.

79. Ernesto Che Guevara, "El socialismo y el hombre en Cuba," March 1965, in Guevara, *Obra revolucionaria*, p. 638.

80. Lee Lockwood, *Castro's Cuba, Cuba's Fidel* (New York, 1969), p. 231.

81. Ibid., p. 230.

82. Jorge I. Domínguez, *Cuba: Order and Revolution* (Cambridge, Mass., 1978), pp. 504–5.

83. Fernando Peirone, Hugo Vázquez, and Fabián Vernetti, "Reportaje al Dr. Antonio Clavero Machado," *Revista Lote* 44 (2002): 4, <http://www.revistalote.com.ar> (December 2002).

84. *Revolución*, December 9, 1964, p. 1.

85. *Granma*, July 2, 1971, p. 1; ibid., July 3, 1971, p. 3.

86. Llovio-Menéndez, *Insider*, p. 412.

87. *Granma*, July 29, 1980, p. 1; and July 30, 1980, p. 1.

88. Ibid., June 24, 1983, p. 1; ibid., June 25, 1983, p. 3. Prominent personalities who committed suicide in the decades following the triumph of the revolution included Jorge Enrique Mendoza, formerly the editor of *Granma* and director of the Institute of History, and civic resistance leader Rodolfo de las Casas. Other *comandantes* of the old Rebel Army who subsequently killed themselves were Félix Peña and Alberto Mora. Artist Belkis Ayón, poet Raúl Hernández-Novas, essayist Teodoro Espinoza, and writer Miguel Collazo were other prominent Cubans who killed themselves during the 1980s and 1990s.

89. Mario Benedetti, *Cuaderno cubano* (Montevideo, 1971), p. 77.

90. Carlos Torres Pita, *La definición* (Havana, 1971), p. 23.

91. Nancy Alonso, "Falsos profetas," in Mirta Yáñez, ed., *Habaneras* (Tafalla [Navarre], 2000), p. 48.

92. Felicia Guerra and Tamara Alvarez-Detrell, eds., *Balseros: historia oral del éxodo cubano del '94* (Miami, 1997), p. 29.

93. Pedro Juan Gutiérrez, *Dirty Havana Trilogy*, trans. Natasha Wimmer (1998; reprint, New York, 2002), p. 259; Ana Menéndez, *Loving Che* (New York, 2003), pp. 187–88.

94. See Aimee Capote Betancourt and Keller Oliveira Lima, "Intento suicida y su relación con el abuso de alcohol," 2003, <http://bvs.sld.cu>; Jorge Alderguía y Yuri

Kormarov, "La determinación del estado de salud de la población. Principales factores," *Revista Cubana de Salud Pública* 16 (January–March 1990): 51–55; Tomás Rodríguez López, "El estrés y la habituación alcohólica," *Revista Cubana de Medicina General Integral* 14 (1998): 398–406.

95. Alexis Culay Pérez et al., "Mujer y violencia: ¿Un problema de salud comunitario?" *Revista Cubana de Medicina General Integral* 16 (2000): 450–60; Caridad Navarette Calderón, "Caracterización criminológica victimológica de mujeres comisoras de lesiones de Ciudad de La Habana" (Departamento de Investigaciones Jurídicas, Ministerio de Justicia, unpublished report, 2002), p. 10. Copy in author's possession.

96. Lorrin Philipson and Rafael Llerena, eds., *Freedom Flights* (New York, 1980), p. 146; Carlota Caulfield, "Even Names Have Their Exile: Collage of Memories," in Andrea O'Reilly Herrera, ed., *ReMembering Cuba: Legacy of a Diaspora* (Austin, 2001), p. 239.

97. Juan Francisco Pulido Martínez, "Mario in the Heaven's Gate," in *Mario in the Heaven's Gate y otros cuentos suicidas* (Pinar del Río, 1999), pp. 7–8; Aragón, *Memoria del silencio*, p. 194.

98. See Bárbara de la C. Santos Céspedes et al., "Tentativa de suicidio y apgar familiar modificado," *Revista Cubana de Medicina General Integral* 13 (1997): 325–29.

99. Daína Chaviano, *El hombre, la hembra y el hambre* (Barcelona, 1998), p. 259; Héctor Quintero, *Te sigo esperando/Antes de mí: el Sahara*, ed. Juan Antonio Hormigón (Madrid, 1998), p. 94.

100. Miguel R. Cañellas, "Develamiento de Matías," in Claribel Terré Morell, ed., *Perverso cubano* (Buenos Aires, 1999), pp. 188–89.

101. Leopoldo Hernández, *We Were Always Afraid*, in Luis F. González-Cruz and Francesca M. Colecchia, eds., *Cuban Theater in the United States: A Critical Anthology* (Tempe, Ariz., 1992), p. 20.

102. Luis Salas, *Social Control and Deviance in Cuba* (New York, 1979), p. 182.

103. Sergio Pérez Barrero and Francisco Reytor Sol, "El suicidio y su atención por el médico de la familia," *Revista Cubana de Medicina General Integral* 11 (October–December 1995): 3; Lidia Arlaes Nápoles et al., "Conducta suicida: Factores de riesgo asociados," *Revista Cubana de Medicina General Integral* 14 (1998): 1; World Health Organization, *World Health Statistic Annual . . . 1993–1995* (Geneva, 1995–98); Sergio Pérez Barrero et al., "Factores de riesgo suicida en adultos," *Revista Cubana de Medicina Integral General* 13 (1997): 7–11; Ileana Castañeda Abascal and Ricardo Pérez Cedrón, "Mortalidad según causas de muerte en la población de 15 a 59 años: Provincia Camagüey, 1980 a 1991," *Revista Cubana de Salud Pública* 24 (1998): 85–91. Between 1980 and 1991, suicide was the fourth leading cause of death in Cárdenas. In the province of Pinar del Río during the late 1990s it was ranked as the seventh leading cause of death. See Norma B. Trenzado et al., "Suicidio, cuarta causa de muerte en Cárdenas," *Revista Cubana de Higiene y Epidemiología* 39 (2001), 115–19; Sonia Catasús Cervera, *Cuba: Estudio de la incidencia de las diferentes causas de muerte en los niveles de mortalidad de su población* (Havana, 1982); Marcos A. Montano Díaz, Ana Carmen Valdés Vento, and Zoé Lam Hernández, "Mortalidad por suicidio en la provincia Pinar del Río en el año 2000," *Boletín de Medicina General Integral* (Pinar del Río) 6 (2002), <http://www.pri.sld.cu>.

104. *Granma Internacional* (digital edition), January 29, 2004, <http://www .granma.cu>.

105. Leocado Martínez Almanza et al., "The Elderly in Cuba: Main Demographic Trends, Morbidity and Mortality," *Medic Review* 2 (2000): 6, <http://www.medic.org> (December 2002). See also Nurys B. Armas Rojas et al., "Evaluación de algunos aspectos del Programa Nacional de Prevención de la Conducta Suicida. Municipio Playa, 1995," *Revista Cubana de Higiene y Epidemiología* 36 (1998): 108; and Leocadio Martínez Almanza et al., "Las personas de edad en Cuba. Principales tendencias demográficas y morbimortalidad," *Resumed* 12 (1999): 77–90.

106. Evis Devesa Colina et al., "El envejecimiento como problema," *Revista Cubana de Salud Pública* 19 (July–December 1993): 93–99; Wilfredo Guibert Reyes and Omar Trujillo Grás, "Intento suicida del anciano en un área de salud," *Revista Cubana de Medicina General Integral* 15 (1999): 509–15; Wilfredo Guibert Reyes and Liana Rosa Sánchez Cruz, "Ancianos con intento suicida en el municipio 10 de Octubre," *Revista Cubana de Higiene y Epidemiología* 39 (2001): 126–35.

107. Wilfredo Guibert Reyes and Ada P. Alonso Roldán, "Factores epidemiológicos y psicosociales que inciden en los intentos suicidas," *Revista Cubana de Medicina General Integral* 17 (2001): 155–63; Ariane Hernández Trujillo et al., "Influencia del medio familiar en un grupo de 5 a 19 años con riesgo suicida," *Revista Cubana de Medicina General Integral* 15 (1999): 372–77.

108. Adalgizar Martínez Jiménez et al., "Comportamiento de la conducta suicida infanto-juvenil," *Revista Cubana de Medicina General Integral* 14 (1998): 554–59; Estadísticas de Salud de Cuba, "Temas de estadística de salud: Panorama de salud de adolescentes y jóvenes cubanos," April 2003, <http://www.dne.sld.cu>.

109. Wilfredo Guibert Reyes, *El suicidio: Un tema complejo e íntimo* (Havana, 2002), p. 34; Wilfredo Guibert Reyes, "Epidemiología de la conducta suicida," *Revista Cubana de Medicina General Integral* 18 (2002): 1–7.

110. Miriam Aliño Santiago et al., "Indicadores de la situación de salud de la adolescencia en Cuba," *Al Día: Publicación de Salud de Cuba* (2002), <http://www.infomed .sld.cu>. See also Wilfredo Guibert Reyes and Niurka Torres Miranda, "Intento suicida y funcionamiento familiar," *Revista Cubana de Medicina General Integral* 17 (2001): 452–60; Ariane Hernández Trujillo et al., "Influencia del medio familiar en un grupo de 5 a 19 años con riesgo suicida," *Revista Cubana de Medicina General Integral* 15 (1999): 372–77; and Arlaes Nápoles et al., "Conducta suicida," p. 4.

111. Justa C. Hernández Montano, Dianelys Pérez Sánchez, and Leydiana Andarcio Camejo, "Características epidemiológicas de pacientes que realizaron intento suicida," *Revista de Medicina General Integral* (Pinar del Río) 5 (2001), <http://www.pri.sld .cu>. Maricela Charón Miranda, Eresmilda Vargas Fajardo, and Emilio Mesa Laurente, "Análisis comparativo de la conducta suicida en un área de salud," *Revista Cubana de Enfermería* 17 (2001): 51–55; Silvia González Arias et al., "Epidemiología del intento suicida en el municipio de Santa Clara," April 2003, <http://capitro.vcl.sld.cu>.

112. Wilfredo Guibert Reyes, "Epidemiología de la conducta suicida," 1–7.

113. Rochanah Wiessinger, "Cuba Report No. 1," November 1998, <http://www .rochanah.com>. In rural Cuba, pesticides persisted as a commonly used means of suicide. Between 1995 and 1997, an estimated 576 deaths were attributed to the in-

gestion of pesticides. See María Luisa González Valiente et al., "Mortalidad por intoxicaciones agudas causadas por plaguicidas," *Revista Cubana de Higiene y Epidemiología* 39 (2001): 136–43.

114. Iris Montes de Oca Campos et al., "Autoagresión por quemaduras," *Revista Cubana de Medicina General Integral* 12 (1996): 113–19; Alfredo Espinosa Brito et al., "Adultos fallecidos en 3 provincias cubanas (1981–1982). Algunos factores relacionados con el lugar donde ocurrió la muerte," *Revista Cubana de Salud Pública* 15 (October–December 1989): 245–58.

115. Luis Calzadilla Fierro and Narciso Calles Bajos, "Epidemiología del suicidio en la regional Matanzas: 1968–1974," *Revista del Hospital Psiquiátrico de La Habana* 18 (January–March 1977): 118–19; Trenzado et al., "Suicidio, cuarta causa de muerte en Cárdenas," p. 115; Acela Laferté Trebejo and Luisa Aleida Laferté Trabejo, "Comportamiento del suicidio en Ciudad de La Habana: Intervención de enfermería en la atención primaria de salud," *Revista Cubana de Enfermería* 16 (2000): 84.

116. Arlaes Nápoles et al., "Conducta suicida," p. 4; Maricela García Pérez et al., "Algunos aspectos epidemiológicos del suicidio en el municipio Santo Domingo," *Medicentro* 6 (2002): 1–6.

117. Peter Katel, "Choosing to Die," *Newsweek*, May 16, 1994, p. 42.

118. Ibid.; Carlos Bonfil, "Del suicidio como resistencia pasiva," September 26, 2002, <http://www.jornada.unam.mx>. See also Alan West, "Dystopia Latina: Writers and Other Tropical Disturbances," *Village Voice Literary Supplement*, May 1994, p. 33.

119. Holly Ackerman and Juan M. Clark, *The Cuban Balsero: Voyage of Uncertainty* (Miami, 1995), pp. 9–24.

120. Ibid., p. 4.

121. "Beyond Fear: An Interview with Julio J. Guerra Molina," in O'Reilly Herrera, *ReMembering Cuba*, p. 44.

122. Guerra and Alvarez-Detrell, *Balseros*, pp. 25, 30.

123. Ibid., pp. 15, 24.

124. Margarita Engle, *Skywriting* (New York, 1995), p. 32; Zoé Valdés, *Te di la vida entera* (Barcelona, 1996), p. 112; María de los Angeles González Amaro, "En busca del paraíso perdido," February 26, 2002, <http://www.elenamederos.org>.

125. Gutiérrez, *Dirty Havana Trilogy*, p. 222; "La pérdida: Rubén Busquests," BBC World Service, June 21, 2001, <http://www.news.bbc.co.uk>; Jesús J. Barquet, "Suicidio y rebeldía: Reinaldo Arenas habla sobre el suicidio," in Reinaldo Sánchez and Humberto López Cruz, eds., *Ideología y subversión: Otra vez Arenas* (Salamanca, 1999), p. 112.

126. Copy in author's possession. Among other poems engaging suicide during the Special Period see Heriberto Hernández Medina, "La ciudad de los puentes se suicida," in *Discurso en la montaña de los muerto* (Havana, 1994), pp. 26–28; and Juan Nicolás Padrón Barquín, "Los suicidas," in *Crónica de la noche* (Havana, 1994), p. 59.

127. Nicolás Dorr, *Los excéntricos de la noche*, 1996, in *Teatro insólito* (Havana, 2001), p. 7.

128. Chaviano, *El hombre, la hembra y el hambre*, pp. 32, 42, 62, 123, 155, 235, 285–86.

129. Alexis Díaz-Pimienta, "Memorias del suicida," in *Yo también pude ser Jacques Deguerre* (Valencia, 2001), p. 31.

130. Gutiérrez, *Dirty Havana Trilogy*, pp. 23, 138, 264, 374; Jesús David Curbelo, "Una desconocida," in Terré Morell, *Perverso cubano*, p. 123; José Miguel Sánchez, "Círculos del dolor," in ibid., p. 27; Engle, *Skywriting*, p. 27.

131. Margarita Engle, *Singing to Cuba* (Houston, 1993), pp. 42–43, 53–54, 80; Zoé Valdés, *Café nostalgia* (Barcelona, 1997), p. 163.

132. See Félix Roberto Masud-Piloto, *With Open Arms: Cuban Migration to the United States* (Totowa, N.J., 1988); Ernesto Rodríguez Chávez, *Emigración cubana actual* (Havana, 1997); Consuelo Martín and Guadalupe Pérez, *Familia, emigración y vida cotidiana en Cuba* (Havana, 1998); Hedelberto López Blanch, *Descorriendo mamparas: La emigración cubana en los Estados Unidos* (San Juan, P.R., 2001).

133. María de los Angeles Torres, "Beyond the Rupture: Reconciling with Our Enemies, Reconciling with Ourselves," *Michigan Quarterly Review* 33 (Summer 1994): 427; Margaret L. Paris, *Embracing America: A Cuban Exile Comes of Age* (Gainesville, Fla., 2002), p. 1; José Lezama Lima to Eloísa and Rosa Lezama Lima, April 9, 1962, in José Lezama Lima, *Cartas a Eloísa y otra correspondencia*, ed. José Triana (Madrid, 1998), p. 64; José Lezama Lima to Eloísa and Rosa Lezama Lima, May 10, 1964, in ibid., p. 78.

134. Alfredo P. Leiseca, "No digas que eres cubano," in Ana Rosa Núñez, ed., *Poesía en éxodo: El exilio cubano en su poesía, 1959–1969* (Miami, 1970), p. 356.

135. Vicente Méndez to Consejo Nacional de Veteranos, October 10, 1968, in Miguel L. Talleda, *Alpha 66 y su histórica tarea* (Miami, 1995), p. 64; Braulio de Gondomar, ed., *Cuba: esplendor, terror, liberación* (Miami, 1969), n.p.

136. José Llanes, *Cuban Americans: Masters of Survival* (Cambridge, Mass., 1982), pp. 65–66; Pablo LeRiverend, "Oración para los que saben morir," in Ana Rosa Núñez, ed., *Poesía en éxodo: El exilio cubano en su poesía, 1959–1969* (Miami, 1970), p. 89; Oscar Ruiz-Sierra Fernández, "A los mártires del castrismo," in ibid., p. 178.

137. Beba del Mazo, "Grito de dolor," in Núñez, *Poesía en éxodo*, p. 375.

138. Juan J. Remos, "Empeños por la liberación de Cuba," in Josefina Inclán, ed., *Cuba en el destierro de Juan J. Remos* (Miami, 1971), pp. 132–33.

139. Emeterio S. Santovenia and Raúl M. Shelton, *Cuba y su historia*, 4 vols. (Miami, 1965), 2:32; Rafael Estenger, *Sincera historia de Cuba (1492–1973)* (Miami, 1974), p. 186; Rafael Guas Inclán, "En defensa de la República," in Gondomar, *Cuba: esplendor, terror, liberación*, n.p. See also Nieves del Rosario Márquez, "Una bayamesa. Quema de Bayamo: 12 de enero de 1869," in *Una isla, la más bella* (Miami, 1981), p. 37.

140. Ricardo Núñez García, *La otra imagen de Cuba* (Miami, 1965), pp. 71–78.

141. Gustavo Pérez Firmat, *Next Year in Cuba* (New York, 1995), p. 121; Cristina García, *Dreaming in Cuban* (New York, 1992), p. 138; Uva A. Clavijo, *With All and For the Good of All*, in Rodolfo J. Cortina, ed., *Cuban America Theater* (Houston, 1991), p. 167.

142. Nicolás Abreu Felippe, *Miami en brumas* (Miami, 2000), pp. 53–54.

143. "The Thirteenth Suitcase: An Interview with Efraín J. Ferrer and Vivián de la Incera," in O'Reilly Herrera, *ReMembering Cuba*, p. 34; "One Mother's Testimonial:

An Interview with Ada Manero Alvaré," in ibid., p. 127; Philipson and Llerena, *Freedom Flights*, p. 103; Jorge Luis Romeu, "Political Exile," in ibid., p. 168; María de los Angeles Torres, *In the Land of Mirrors: Cuban Exile Politics in the United States* (Ann Arbor, 1999), p. 4.

144. Virgil Suárez, "Middle Ground, or *El camino del medio*," in *Palm Crows* (Tucson, Ariz., 2001), p. 82.

145. In her 1974 study of one Cuban community in New Jersey, Eleanor Meyer Rogg made note of "the enormous downward mobility that refugees formerly holding middle- and high-level occupations have experienced in the United States." See Eleanor Meyer Rogg, *The Assimilation of Cuban Exiles: The Role of Community and Class* (New York, 1974), p. 105. See also Manuel Carballo, "A Socio-Psychological Study of Acculturation/Assimilation: Cubans in New Orleans," (Ph.D. diss., Tulane University, 1970), pp. 215–81.

146. Pérez Firmat, *Next Year in Cuba*, p. 118; Cristina Saralegui, *Cristina! My Life as a Blonde* (New York, 1998), pp. 37, 55.

147. Luis Ricardo Alonso, *Los dioses ajenos* (Barcelona, 1971), p. 46.

148. Rogg, *The Assimilation of Cuban Exiles*, p. 76; Marta Elena Acosta Stone, "Understanding del Casal," in O'Reilly Herrera, *ReMembering Cuba*, p. 183; Alicia Serrano Machrián Granto, "Life al revés," in ibid., p. 119. See also David Williamson, "Adaptation to Socio-Cultural Change: Working-Class Cubans in New Orleans," *Caribbean Studies* 16 (October 1976–January 1977): 217–25; José Szapocznik et al., "Cuban Value Structure: Treatment Implications," *Journal of Consulting and Clinical Psychology* 46 (October 1978): 961–70.

149. Llanes, *Cuban Americans*, p. 108.

150. Flor Fernández Barrios, *Blessed by Thunder: Memoir of a Cuban Girlhood* (Seattle, 1999), pp. 207–8.

151. María del Carmen Boza, *Scattering the Ashes* (Tempe, Ariz., 1998), p. 40; ibid., p. 30; Paris, *Embracing America*, p. 159.

152. Sergio Díaz-Briquets, "Mortality Patterns of Cubans in the United States," in Ira Rosenwaike, ed., *Mortality of Hispanic Populations: Mexicans, Puerto Ricans, and Cubans in the United States and in the Home Countries* (Westport, Conn., 1991), pp. 125, 128.

153. In Maida Donate-Armada and Zoila Macías, *Suicide in Miami and Cuba* (Miami, 1998), p. 14.

154. Pedro Antonio Noguera, "Violence Prevention and the Latin Population," *In Motion Magazine* 22 (1996): 2–5, <http://www.inmotionmagazine.com> (August 2002); Donate-Armada and Macías, *Suicide in Miami and Cuba*, pp. 31–32; Ira Rosenwaike, "Mortality Differentials among Persons Born in Cuba, Mexico, and Puerto Rico Residing in the United States, 1979–1981," *American Journal of Public Health* 77 (May 1987): 603–6.

155. Magaly Muguercia, "The Body and Its Politics in Cuba of the Nineties," *Boundary 2* 29 (Fall 2002), p. 180.

156. Ramón A. Boza and Teresita Boza Fernández, "The Psychopathology and Prognosis of the Elderly Cuban Refugee," *Psychiatry On-Line* (2000), <http://www.priory.com> (August 2002).

157. Menéndez, *Loving Che*, p. 35; García, *Dreaming in Cuban*, p. 244; Cristina García, *The Agüero Sisters* (New York, 1997), pp. 70–71, 238.

158. Yolanda Ortal-Miranda, *Un punto que se pierde en la distancia y en el tiempo*, in *Balada sonámbula de los desterrados del sueño* (New York, 1991), p. 214; Alex Abella, *The Killing of the Saints* (New York, 1991), p. 188; Beatriz Rivera, *Playing with Light* (Houston, 2000), pp. 235, 236.

159. Eduardo Machado, "Broken Eggs," in M. Elizabeth Osborn, ed., *On New Ground: Contemporary Hispanic-American Plays* (New York, 1987), p. 180; Eliseo Alberto, *Caracol Beach*, trans. Edith Grossman (New York, 2000).

160. Roberto G. Fernández, *Raining Backwards* (Houston, 1988), pp. 76, 187, 190.

161. Omar Torres, *Fallen Angels Sing* (Houston, 1991), p. 19; Virgil Suárez, *Havana Thursdays* (Houston, 1995), pp. 28, 57.

162. Elías Miguel Muñoz, *The Greatest Performance* (Houston, 1991), p. 82.

163. Abreu Felippe, *Miami en brumas*, p. 7.

164. Aragón, *Memoria del silencio*, p. 183.

165. Jesús Alvariño, "El suicida," in *Otro libro* (Hialeah, 1978), p. 18; Achy Obejas, "Waters," in Naomi Holoch and Joan Nestle, eds., *The Vintage Book of International Lesbian Fiction* (New York, 1999), p. 258; Guillermo Cabrera Infante, "Abril es el mes más cruel," in *Así en la paz como en la guerra: Cuentos*, 2nd ed. (Montevideo, 1970), p. 171.

166. Enrique C. Henríquez, "Suicidio," in *El esclavo y el reflejo* (Miami, 1977), p. 113–16; Oscar Gómez-Vidal, "El suicida," in *Diez cuentos de ciudad amarga* (Madrid, 1975), pp. 58–60.

167. Carolina Hospital, "Graciela's Suicide," in Carolina Hospital, ed., *Cuban American Writers: Los atrevidos* (Princeton, 1988), p. 166; Rafael Campo, "Suicidal Ideation," in *Diva* (Durham, 1999), p. 11.

168. María Elena Cruz Varela, *Balada de la sangre/Ballad of the Blood*, trans. Mairym Cruz-Bernal and Deborah Digges (Hopewell, N.J., 1996), pp. 3, 5, 17.

169. Carlos Alberto Montaner, "Le hablaré a la semilla," in Núñez, *Poesía en éxodo*, p. 227; Ricardo Pau-Llosa, "Paredón," in *Cuba* (Pittsburgh, 1993), p. 59.

170. Virgil Suárez, "After the Accident," in *Spared Angola. Memories from a Cuban-American Childhood* (Houston, 1997), p. 133.

171. Felipe Lázaro, "El suicida borracho," in *Despedida del asombro* (Madrid, n.d.), p. 65.

172. Pablo LeRiverend, "El sueño suicida," in *Un aliento de poros* (Barcelona, 1977), p. 24.

EPILOGUE

1. For a useful discussion of this phenomenon generally see Michael J. Kral, "Suicide as Social Logic," *Suicide and Life-Threatening Behavior* 24 (Fall 1994): 245–55. The debate on suicide as a rational act is explored in James L. Werth Jr., ed., *Contemporary Perspectives on Rational Suicide* (Philadelphia, 1999).

2. Julio Travieso, ed., *Cuentos sobre el clandestinaje* (Havana, 1983).

3. Joel James Figarola, *La muerte en Cuba* (Havana, 1999), p. 47.

4. Manuel Navarro Luna, "Martianos y amartianos," *Bohemia* 30 (June 5, 1938): 115, 127, 146.

5. Liudmarys Chaviano Martínez, "Comentarios martianos acerca del suicidio: Algunas consideraciones," *Islas* 41 (April–June 1999): 76.

6. Guillermo Cabrera Infante, "Entre la historia y la nada. Notas sobre una ideología del suicidio," *Escandalar* 5 (January–June 1982): 83; Reinaldo Arenas, "Suicidio y rebeldía: Reinaldo Arenas habla sobre el suicidio," ed. Jesús J. Barquet, in Reinaldo Sánchez and Humberto López Cruz, eds., *Ideología y subversión: Otra vez Arenas* (Salamanca, 1999), pp. 112–13; Eliseo Alberto, *Informe contra mí mismo* (México, 1997), p. 55.

Index

H. Eugene and Lillian Youngs Lehman Series

Lamar Cecil, *Wilhelm II:*
   Prince and Emperor, 1859–1900 (1989).

Carolyn Merchant, *Ecological Revolutions:*
   Nature, Gender, and Science in New England (1989).

Gladys Engel Lang and Kurt Lang, *Etched in Memory:*
   The Building and Survival of Artistic Reputation (1990).

Howard Jones, *Union in Peril:*
   The Crisis over British Intervention in the Civil War (1992).

Robert L. Dorman, *Revolt of the Provinces:*
   The Regionalist Movement in America (1993).

Peter N. Stearns, *Meaning Over Memory:*
   Recasting the Teaching of Culture and History (1993).

Thomas Wolfe, *The Good Child's River,*
   edited with an introduction by Suzanne Stutman (1994).

Warren A. Nord, *Religion and American Education:*
   Rethinking a National Dilemma (1995).

David E. Whisnant, *Rascally Signs in Sacred Places:*
   The Politics of Culture in Nicaragua (1995).

Lamar Cecil, *Wilhelm II: Emperor and Exile, 1900–1941* (1996).

Jonathan Hartlyn, *The Struggle for Democratic Politics in*
   the Dominican Republic (1998).

Louis A. Pérez Jr., *On Becoming Cuban:*
   Identity, Nationality, and Culture (1999).

Yaakov Ariel, *Evangelizing the Chosen People:*
   Missions to the Jews in America, 1880–2000 (2000).

Philip F. Gura, *C. F. Martin and His Guitars, 1796–1873* (2003).

Louis A. Pérez Jr., *To Die in Cuba: Suicide and Society* (2005).